THE **ESSENTIAL HISTORY** OF **RANGERS**

FOREWORD BY ALLY McCOIST

STEPHEN HALLIDAY

The right of Stephen Halliday to be identified as the Author of the Work has been asserted by him in accordance with the Copyright, Designs and Patents Act 1988.

First published in 2002
by HEADLINE BOOK PUBLISHING
for WHSmith, Greenbridge Road, Swindon SN3 3LD

1 3 5 7 9 10 8 6 4 2

ISBN 0 7553 1145 0

Design by designsection, Frome, Somerset
Pictures on pages 7 and 8 courtesy of the Mitchell Library

The author would like to thank Ange Halliday for her invaluable and painstaking assistance with this book, the staff of the Mitchell Library for their help and courtesy with the research, and Chris and Craig Halliday for their motivation.

Printed and bound in Great Britain by Clays Ltd, St Ives PLC, Bungay, Suffolk

HEADLINE BOOK PUBLISHING
A division of Hodder Headline
338 Euston Road
London NW1 3BH

www.headline.co.uk
www.hodderheadline.com

Contents

Foreword
by Ally McCoist

As someone fortunate enough to spend 15 years of my life playing for Rangers, it is a genuine pleasure to pen a few words of introduction to this unique book on one of the most remarkable football clubs in the world.

Having grown up in East Kilbride as a Rangers supporter, I raised more than a few eyebrows when, on two occasions, I turned down the opportunity to sign on at Ibrox. Happily, my feeling that moves to St Johnstone and Sunderland were better for my career in those early stages were justified when John Greig eventually signed me for Rangers in 1983.

The pressure of playing for Rangers, with the massive expectation of the club's supporters, is as intense as anything in the game. The early days of my time at Ibrox were not all a bed of roses but, as in life, the bad times in football make you appreciate the good times all the more.

It was ultimately my good fortune to enjoy plenty of good times during one of Rangers' most successful eras. To be part of the squads which won nine championships in a row and to become the club's record goalscorer were achievements I could hardly dare dream about as a youngster.

As this book shows, the 130 years of Rangers' existence have been filled by the stuff of schoolboy dreams. At home and in Europe, the club have come a long way from the days of Moses McNeil and his brothers kicking a ball around for fun on Glasgow Green.

At Rangers, while success today and in the future is always the priority, the past is never far away. Meeting and talking to great players like Bob McPhail and Willie Thornton around the stadium was always such a joy for me. History is important to Rangers, it's what makes them such a special club, and you will find it all here. I believe there are many more chapters of success to be written about a club which will always be special to me. For now, just enjoy the story so far...

Chapter One: 1872-90
From Flesher's Haugh to Ibrox

As bright ideas from a 16-year-old go, Moses McNeil's has proved stunningly successful. When Moses, his older brother Peter, William McBeath and Peter Campbell decided to form a football club on Glasgow Green, it was the young man from Rhu in Dunbartonshire who came up with the name which would one day resonate throughout the game.

Rangers were an English rugby club Moses had read about and his suggestion that the Scottish teenagers appropriate the name for their exciting venture met with warm approval. So, sometime in May 1872, Rangers took the field for the first time at Flesher's Haugh on Glasgow Green. Details of the goalless draw against Callander are sketchy, but it was something of a family affair; Moses being joined in the maiden line-up by brothers Peter, William and Harry, the latter borrowed from Queen's Park.

The famous Hampden club, formed five years earlier, were at the vanguard of organized football's growing popularity in the country. Harry spent the prime years of his career with Queen's Park as one of the greats of his era. He was capped 10 times for Scotland at a time when international fixtures were infrequent, and lost only once in six appearances against England.

Such fame and ability were beyond the young men who represented Rangers in those formative years, but Harry was doubtless a huge inspiration to Moses and his team-mates.

The first two years of the club's existence are not well documented, although a number of friendly matches are known to have been undertaken with a significant level of success. Rangers were formally constituted in 1873 and Tom Vallance, a robust and able full back who would go on to win seven caps for Scotland, emerged as a leading light both on and off the pitch as a captain and administrator.

Rangers gained membership of the Scottish Football Association in time to take part in the Scottish Cup for the first time in season 1874-75. They were drawn at home to Oxford in the first round and held the match at the Queen's Park Recreation Ground on 10 October 1874. Rangers' first competitive fixture was a success and, appropriately enough, Moses McNeil was one of the scorers in their 2-0 win. The other goal came from David Gibb.

The Rangers line-up in that historic match read: John Yuil, Tom Vallance, Peter McNeil (captain), William McNeil, William McBeath, Moses McNeil, George Campbell, George Phillips, James Watson, David Gibb, John Campbell.

The club's first cup run was not to be a protracted affair. The second round paired them with Dumbarton, one of the most powerful and successful clubs of the Victorian era, and after a creditable goalless draw at Flesher's Haugh, Rangers travelled to Boghead where they lost the replay 1-0.

Growing Ambition

Rangers' by now growing ambition to join Queen's Park, Vale of Leven and others in the elite of Scottish football was hampered by the lack of a ground to call their own. Although Flesher's Haugh had initially suited Rangers, it was in a public park and not always easy to reserve on any specific date or time.

In the summer of 1875, Rangers believed they had found the solution at Burnbank just off Glasgow's Great Western Road. As it turned out they would play no more than a handful of fixtures on the ground, including two Scottish Cup ties. John Campbell claimed the first competitive hat-trick in the club's history as First Lanark were swamped 7-0 in the first round before once again making their exit, albeit controversially, in round two. Rangers had won the tie 1-0, but after successfully protesting to the SFA that Rangers had illegally kicked-off in both halves, Third Lanark won a replay 2-1.

The season also saw Queen's Park agree to play Rangers for the first time and although the young upstarts, as they were unquestionably viewed at the time, lost the friendly match 2-0 at Hampden, their performance won them many new admirers.

For season 1876-77 Rangers relocated to the south side of the city, not far from where the current Ibrox Stadium is situated. Clydesdale, then both a football and cricket club, had vacated the Kinning Park ground in favour of a switch to Titwood where the sound of leather on willow can still be heard.

The new venue appeared to suit Rangers who embarked on a tremendous Scottish Cup campaign that took them to their first major final. Queen's Park Juniors were beaten 4-1 at Kinning Park in the first round and Rangers were scarcely troubled as they went on to dismiss Towerhill, Mauchline and Lennox in subsequent ties, scoring 14 times without reply in the process.

Fortune favoured Rangers with a bye in the semi-finals and on 17 March 1877, they lined up at Hamilton Crescent in Glasgow to face Vale of Leven in the final. The Dunbartonshire side were hot favourites, having eliminated cup holders Queen's Park in the fifth round, but Rangers firmly announced their arrival as a serious force in Scottish football as they pushed Vale all the way in a remarkable three-game marathon.

After a 1-1 draw in the first match, a late McDougall own goal levelling the scores for Rangers after Paton's opener for Vale, the first replay at Hamilton Crescent on 7 April produced another stalemate. William Dunlop had given Rangers an early lead this time, which was cancelled out by Baird in the second half. Extra time brought controversy; Dunlop believed he had scored again, only for referee James Kerr to rule that the ball had not crossed the line.

Dr George McLeod, an eminent Glasgow physician of the time, verified claims that the ball had crossed the line before rebounding back into play off a spectator. But such reports were of little consolation to Rangers who had to steel themselves for the second replay at Hampden six days later.

In front of a 15,000 crowd, goals from Peter Campbell and William McNeil turned a 1-0 half-time deficit into a 2-1 advantage. Once again though, a tenacious performance wasn't quite enough for the underdogs. Rangers were unable to hold on to their lead as strikes from Baird and, in the dying minutes, Paton saw Vale of Leven claim a 3-2 triumph and the trophy.

Glasgow Green – the site of Rangers' first pitch.

Tom Vallance, Rangers' founding member and club captain for nine seasons.

Record Victory

The same opponents would end Rangers' Scottish Cup interest the following season with a painful 5-0 thrashing in a fourth round replay, the teams having drawn 0-0 at Kinning Park in the initial tie. At least the campaign was not without its highlights, as Rangers recorded what is still their record victory margin twice in little more than a month. Both Possilpark and Uddingston were dismantled to the tune of 13-0 in first and third round ties respectively.

Rangers had now established themselves as one of the country's leading football lights and boasted some of Scotland's best players in Tom Vallance, Peter Campbell and George Gillespie. In season 1878-79, they reached the Scottish Cup final for the second time, having recorded a first ever win over Queen's Park in a fourth round tie at Hampden.

A semi-final bye saw Rangers return to Hampden on 19 April 1879 where, almost inevitably, their opponents were a Vale of Leven side seeking to emulate Queen's Park's achievement of winning the Scottish Cup three years in a row. Yet again the contest was overshadowed by controversy. William Struthers, an ever-present and leading scoring in the campaign, fired Rangers in front and then appeared to have doubled their lead on the stroke of half-time.

Referee James Wallace from Beith saw it differently, ruling that Dunlop had been offside when he provided the cross for the subsequently disallowed goal. Rangers' sense of injustice was doubtless cooling as the final whistle neared and their first major trophy was within touching distance. However, Vale of Leven shattered those notions with a softly conceded equalizer two minutes from full-time.

The following week's replay at Hampden was, literally, a one-horse race. Rangers, having failed in a protest to the SFA over their disallowed goal, did not turn up and Vale of Leven were awarded the trophy. If Rangers' petulance is difficult to understand today, it clearly was of little concern to them at the time as they reportedly spent the day of the final at a race meeting.

First Silverware

Some consolation came their way on 20 May when the club claimed its first ever piece of silverware as they defeated Vale 2-1 at Hampden in the Glasgow Charity Cup final. Rangers though, had their sights set on bigger prizes.

They were to endure a lengthy wait before those ambitions were realized. The Scottish Cup adventure of 1879-80 was the briefest yet, Queen's Park dishing out a 5-1 thrashing in a first round replay at Hampden after a goalless draw at Kinning Park. As some of Rangers' leading early players departed the scene, including founder member Peter Campbell and the influential Hugh McIntyre, the club underwent a period of transition.

Scottish football as a whole was undergoing trying times as the rise of professionalism in English football, rife though not yet legal, lured many of the country's best players south of the border. The Scottish Cup continued to provide the only real competitive challenge for clubs like Rangers and they enjoyed a lively 1880-81 campaign, including an 11-0 fourth round thrashing of Clyde, before making a quarter-final exit at home to Dumbarton.

---

50 Greatest Players

MOSES McNEIL   **Winger**

Joined Rangers: February 1872 (founder member)

Debut: v Oxford, Scottish Cup, 10 October 1874

Appearances: 34   **Goals:** 9

Left Rangers: 1882 (retired)

Honours won with Rangers: 2 caps (Scotland)

Put quite simply, Rangers Football Club would not exist had it not been for Moses McLay McNeil. Born in Dunbartonshire on 29 October 1855, McNeil was a young student of 16 when he formed and named the club in February 1872. One of seven brothers, two of whom – Peter and William – also played for Rangers, while Harry was an outstanding midfielder with Queen's Park and Scotland, Moses is recalled as a muscular, committed winger not lacking in talent.

He was capped twice by Scotland, against Wales in 1876 and England four years later, becoming Rangers' first international player. McNeil played in the Scottish Cup finals of 1877 and 1879, but sadly a major domestic honour eluded him as Rangers lost out on both occasions to Vale of Leven. McNeil was a commercial traveller by trade and lived long enough to see his brainchild become Scottish football's dominant force. He died in 1938.

Rangers' 1877 Scottish Cup final team. Despite ultimate defeat, this match took the club to the forefront of Scottish football.

The men from Boghead were Rangers' nemesis in the tournament at the same stage the following year. David Hill, a Scottish international who was one of Rangers' most productive players at the time, saw an early goal count for little as the Sons stormed to a 5-1 victory. It merely emphasised the gulf which still stood between Rangers and Scottish football's major powers.

The departure of hugely popular captain Tom Vallance was an equally significant blow to the club and 1882-83 offered little in the way of encouragement, even if Rangers did perform creditably in losing 3-2 to holders Queen's Park in the second round of the Scottish Cup at Hampden.

Rangers enjoyed a more successful cup run in the following season, reaching the semi-finals, only to lose 3-0 in Alexandria to Vale of Leven. Behind the scenes, however, there was considerable discontent, much of it aimed at John Mackay, the club's match secretary and a controversial and often unpopular figure.

Tom Vallance, now back at the club as president, attempted to bring some stability to Rangers who clearly lacked proper direction and leadership off the field. The Scottish Cup dream, which had turned into something of an obsession, was shattered again in 1884-85, although there was no real disgrace in a 5-3 quarter-final defeat at eventual winners Renton.

Far less palatable was the first round elimination at the hands of Clyde n the following season. The campaign saw Rangers undertake an increased fixture list of over 40 friendly matches, only to produce wildly inconsistent performances. Included among the defeats was a 10-2 Kinning Park drubbing at the hands of Airdrie which remains the club's heaviest recorded loss.

For the 1886-87 season, Rangers widened their horizons by entering the English FA Cup, as Scottish clubs were permitted to do at the time. They had in fact been in the draw the previous year, only to refuse to play their first round tie against Rawtenstall in protest that the English club had professionals on their books.

Backing down from such moral high ground this time, Rangers embarked on a remarkable FA Cup run which nearly lead them to the final of the famous tournament. Charlie Heggie, a prolific striker who unfortunately left the club midway through the season, scored the only goal as Rangers stunned Everton in a first round tie at Goodison.

Subsequent victories over Church, Cowlairs and Lincoln City guided Rangers into the quarter-finals where, in what would be the last match played at Kinning Park, they crushed Old Westminsters 5-1. Aston Villa were Rangers' semi-final opponents at Nantwich Road in Crewe on 5 March 1887 and confidence was high that they could emulate Queen's Park who had reached the English FA Cup finals of 1884 and 1885.

Rangers, indeed, had recorded 7-1 and 4-1 victories over Villa in friendly matches in the not too distant past. When it mattered most, however, they were unable to contain the Birmingham side, with a poor performance from goalkeeper Willie Chalmers contributing to their 3-1 defeat. Villa went on to defeat West Bromwich Albion in the final. Though it was a close-run, no Scottish club would ever win the English FA Cup.

Their exploits in England's premier tournament at least compensated for another miserable performance in the Scottish Cup. Rangers were dismissed at the third round stage, their supporters in a 4000 crowd at Kinning Park not slow to voice their discontent at the impoverished display which saw them lose 2-0 to Cambuslang.

The Move to Ibrox

With the Kinning Park ground in increasingly poor condition, Rangers moved on in the summer of 1887 to a new piece of land at nearby Ibrox. Built by Fred Braby & Co, the new ground was situated where Edmiston House now stands beside the current stadium. However the opening was hardly an auspicious affair. Although the 1,200-seat grandstand was full and the standing terraces packed to reach the estimated 15,000 capacity, an 8-1 hammering administered by a brilliant Preston North

End side on 20 August 1887 ensured that it felt like anything but a gala occasion for Rangers.

The rest of the season, if not quite so traumatic, brought little cheer to the Ibrox side. They were knocked out of the Scottish Cup in the second round, losing 2-1 at Partick Thistle, and then lost 3-1 to Cambuslang in the final of the newly introduced Glasgow Cup. However, the most notable fixture of the campaign, although it most certainly would have not seemed the case to those involved at the time, took place on 28 May 1888.

Rangers agreed to travel across Glasgow to face a newly-formed club called Celtic who were staging their first ever fixture at their Parkhead ground. There was no hint of the deadly rivalry which would develop between them as Celtic won 5-2 in a match played in a spirit of genuine friendship.

The emergence of new local adversaries was the least of Rangers' concerns at the time and season 1888-89 proved a pivotal one for the club. It had not gone unnoticed that the reserve team, under the guidance of William Wilton, had been enjoying considerable success. Known as the Swifts, they possessed the kind of organization and consistency the first team so sadly lacked.

This was evident yet again in the Scottish Cup, Rangers losing 3-0 at home to Clyde in a desperately disappointing second round replay. The Ibrox club had become an easy target for the critics and it was clear a change of direction was required to prevent them becoming one of Scottish football's also-rans.

Wilton Appointed Match Secretary

Wilton emerged as the cure for Rangers' ills. He was appointed as the club's match secretary and if 1889-90 was far from a glorious season, it was one in which Wilton sowed the seeds of far happier and more successful times ahead. The club's record victory was equalled when Kelvinside Athletic were hammered 13-0 in the second round of the Scottish Cup, and Rangers were considered unfortunate to lose 3-2 in a replay against Vale of Leven at the next stage of the tournament.

Meanwhile, Scottish football was facing up to reality. Professionalism, resisted for so long by so many, was now inevitable and in March 1890 Rangers were among 12 clubs who met in Glasgow to discuss the formation of the Scottish League. The Ibrox side's deputation was headed by Wilton who enthusiastically supported the new concept of organized, competitive football.

Before the first Scottish League season began, Wilton made sure Rangers were prepared. Improvements were made to Ibrox, with the erection of a new stand, and several new players were headhunted, most notably John McPherson from Cowlairs. He would be one of the major celebrities of an exciting new era for Scottish football, one in which Rangers would play a leading role.

Chapter Two: 1890-1920
The Wilton Years

The Rangers team and directors line up in front of the pavilion at Ibrox before the 1895-96 season.

The bulk of the 4,000 fans who gathered at Ibrox on 16 August 1890 to witness the dawn of Scottish league football would have given the new competition an immediate thumbs-up. Rangers had begun their first championship campaign with an impressive 5-2 victory over Hearts. Two goals from Neil Kerr, signed earlier that year from Cowlairs, an own goal and further strikes from Hugh McCreadie and John McPherson earned Rangers their first two league points.

When McPherson, hinting at what a significant recruit he would become, scored four times in the 6-2 win at Cambuslang the following week, the signs were promising for William Wilton's side. A third straight win over Renton, then a major power in the game, increased confidence but that 4-1 success would later be expunged from the records when Renton were expelled from the league for playing an unauthorized friendly against St Bernard's.

In any case, Rangers were brought crashing to earth in their next two games. Willie Groves scored the only goal as, in the first-ever competitive Old Firm fixture, Celtic won a Scottish Cup first round tie at Parkhead and seven days later matters got worse as Rangers were crushed 5-1 by Dumbarton at Boghead.

Dumbarton established themselves as the early pacesetters in the championship, but a 13-match unbeaten run, kick-started by a spectacular 8-2 win over St Mirren in which McPherson scored five times, kept Rangers firmly in the hunt. They were two points behind Dumbarton with a game in hand when the sides met at Ibrox on 25 April 1891 and a 4-2 win appeared to give Rangers a firm advantage.

In their final fixture Dumbarton won 4-2 at St Mirren, while Rangers went down 2-1 to Celtic at Ibrox. The pressure was on. Only a win in their last match against Third Lanark would be good enough for Rangers. In front of a tense Ibrox crowd, a hat-trick from Alick McKenzie inspired the home side to a memorable 4-1 win and the two points they needed to draw level at the top of the table.

Remarkably, McKenzie's two previous first team appearances that season had been as goalkeeper, but his unexpected call-up to the forward line had kept Rangers in with a chance of winning the very first Scottish League title.

Either goal average or goal difference would have seen Dumbarton crowned as champions, but these factors were yet to be used to decide such issues. Instead, Cathkin Park was chosen to host a play-off between the teams. In front of 10,000 fans, Rangers seized a 2-0 half-time lead with goals from David Hislop and Hugh McCreadie and looked set to become Scotland's first champions. Dumbarton, though, were not prepared to be denied their own piece of history and hit back after the break to earn a 2-2 draw. There were no complaints when the Scottish League declared the clubs joint champions.

The Title Surrendered

Rangers never looked remotely capable of defending the title the following season. In losing three of their first four fixtures, including a 3-0 defeat against Celtic at Parkhead, it was clear the loss of key players such as Hislop and Donald Gow, both of whom had been lured to English football, had seriously weakened the Ibrox men.

An embarrassing 5-1 home defeat to Clyde in October ended any lingering thoughts of mounting a serious title challenge as Dumbarton, Celtic and Hearts opened up a sizeable gap at the top of the table. Even when Rangers did manage their best spell of the campaign, racking up six consecutive wins, they were soon given a reality check when crushed 6-0 by champions-elect Dumbarton at Boghead on 4 May 1892. Hugh McCreadie's goal in a 1-1 draw with Celtic at Ibrox three days later restored some pride; the Parkhead men ultimately lost out on the title by two points to Dumbarton.

Great Matches

SCOTTISH LEAGUE CHAMPIONSHIP PLAY-OFF　　Cathkin Park, 21 May 1891

Rangers 2　　　**Dumbarton 2**　　　　　　　　Attendance 10,000

Hislop　　　　　　Bell

H. McCreadie　　　J. Miller

The Scottish League could not have scripted a more dramatic finale to their inaugural championship. After 18 matches, Rangers and Dumbarton had finished level on points at the top of the table and a play-off match would take place at Third Lanark's Cathkin Park.

On a balmy Thursday evening, a near capacity crowd thronged to the ground on a public holiday in recognition of Queen Victoria's birthday. Dumbarton were boosted by the return from injury of their Scottish international forward John Bell, but it was the Ibrox side who made a whirlwind start. In the first minute, they opened the scoring when David Hislop forced the ball home from close range. With full back Donald Gow inspiring his team-mates from the back, Rangers were totally dominant and were unfortunate to have a goal disallowed for an infringement on the Dumbarton keeper. They did however double their advantage before half-time when Hugh McCreadie beat McLeod with a long-range shot.

Rangers continued to control matters in the second half and the championship appeared firmly within their grasp. The tide turned suddenly, however, when Dumbarton pulled a goal back just after the hour mark. Dangerman Bell, who had been effectively policed by Hodge until that point, beat Rangers' keeper David Reid with a well-placed effort. The pressure was now firmly on the Rangers goal and it was no surprise when John Miller equalized for the Boghead side. In the closing stages, Dumbarton were the likelier side and Rangers were relieved to hear the final whistle.

After consultation with both teams, it was decided not to have a period of extra-time. The League subsequently decided against a second play-off match and declared the clubs would share the honour of being the first ever champions of Scotland.

Rangers: Reid, Gow, Hodge, Marshall, A. McCreadie, Mitchell, Henderson, H. McCreadie, Kerr, McPherson, Hislop

Dumbarton: McLeod, Watson, A. Miller, McMillan, Boyle, Keir, Taylor, Galbraith, J. Miller, McNaught, Bell

Referee: J. Marshall (Third Lanark)

Three months earlier, Celtic had ended Rangers' Scottish Cup aspirations for the second successive season. In a remarkable semi-final at Parkhead, Rangers looked set for one of their most humiliating defeats when they trailed 5-0 early in the second half, but they at least reclaimed some credibility with goals from John Law, Jimmy Henderson and Neil Kerr making the final score 5-3.

Having limped to fifth place in the league, a massive 13 points behind Dumbarton, dramatic improvement was demanded of Rangers in 1892-93. The impetus was to be provided by the signing of full back Jock Drummond from Falkirk. Drummond did not disappoint, becoming one of the club's most committed and influential players and a driving force behind many successes.

He missed just one game in his debut season, a campaign which saw Rangers start brightly with four straight league wins followed by a 2-2 draw against Celtic at Ibrox. The title race gradually developed into a battle between the two and Rangers were well placed to become champions when they remained unbeaten after 15 of their 18 league fixtures. A 3-0 defeat against Dumbarton at Boghead, however, opened the door for Celtic who inflicted the same scoreline on Rangers at Parkhead a week later.

Rangers defeated Hearts 2-1 at Ibrox on 6 May 1893 in their final game to move a point clear at the top, but Celtic, needing a win from their last game to become champions for the first time, made no mistake three days later when they defeated Leith Athletic 3-1 at Parkhead.

At least Rangers could reflect on a season in which they had been more consistent and competitive throughout. The major blemish was a surprising 3-2 loss to St Bernard's in Edinburgh in the quarter-finals of the Scottish Cup in January, but the Ibrox club were compensated for that when they defeated Celtic 3-1 in the Glasgow Cup final at Cathkin Park in the following month. It was a competition that had come to enjoy a high profile in the Scottish game and Rangers savoured the moment, especially against opponents who had been so dominant against them.

Scottish Cup Finally Won

Such success would be eclipsed the following season as Rangers, at their 20th attempt, finally won the Scottish Cup. Although the SFA legalized professionalism at the start of that 1893-94 campaign, it would be some time before the league championship would take precedence over the Scottish Cup in any club's list of priorities.

This was the trophy they all wanted and Rangers were consumed by a desire to put their name on it. They certainly played like men possessed as they swept to the semi-finals beating Cowlairs, Leith Athletic and Clyde and scoring 15 goals without reply. There they were paired with cup holders Queen's Park. The famous amateur club still frowned upon the Scottish League, which they would not join for another six years, but were strongly fancied to defeat Rangers as they anticipated an 11th Scottish Cup triumph.

Great Matches

SCOTTISH CUP FINAL   **Hampden Park, 17 February 1894**

Rangers 3 **Celtic 1**   **Attendance 17,000**
H. McCreadie Maley
Barker
McPherson

Rangers had reached their first Scottish Cup final since 1879 by upsetting the odds in the semi-final against Queen's Park. They went into the final as firm underdogs once more against league champions Celtic who were already well on course to retain their title.

However, a 5-0 Old Firm league victory by the Ibrox men the previous September gave Rangers supporters hope of lifting the trophy on a dreary February afternoon.

In a goalless first half, Rangers came close to an early opener when McCreadie shot narrowly wide of the Celtic goal. The Parkhead men, however, were unfortunate not to snatch the lead just before the interval when a shot from Blessington struck the crossbar.

In the second half there was no doubt as to who merited victory. In a remarkable 13 minute period, Rangers scored three times to shatter Celtic. Hugh McCreadie broke the deadlock on 55 minutes, driving the ball beyond Cullen from 12 yards after being picked out by captain Davy Mitchell's right wing free-kick. Ten minutes later a marvellous solo effort from James Barker doubled Rangers' lead, as he weaved his way past several despairing challenges before lashing home a fierce shot from just inside the penalty area. Any lingering doubt about the outcome was dispelled after 68 minutes when John McPherson pounced on a defensive error to beat Cullen from close range.

Celtic were clearly a beaten side but refused to throw in the towel, pulling a goal back 15 minutes from time when Willie Maley converted a McMahon corner from a few yards out. It was but a consolation and the final whistle sparked joyous scenes among the Rangers players and supporters as they savoured the club's first Scottish Cup triumph.

Rangers: Haddow, Smith, Drummond, Marshall, A. McCreadie, Mitchell, Steel, H. McCreadie, Gray, McPherson, Barker

Celtic: Cullen, Reynolds, Doyle, Maley, Kelly, Curran, Blessington, Madden, Cassidy, McMahon, Campbell

Referee: J. Marshall (Third Lanark)

When Rangers needed a David Boyd goal to grab a 1-1 draw at Ibrox, Queen's Park were installed as even hotter favourites to reach the final. But in front of 16,000 fans, it was Rangers who dominated the Hampden replay with goals from Nicol Smith, McPherson and James Steel earning a 3-1 win.

Just seven days later Rangers were back at Hampden for the final against Celtic. As champions and league leaders, the Parkhead side came into the match as slight favourites, but Rangers had no need of an inferiority complex. Earlier in the season William Wilton's men had enjoyed one of their most satisfying victories with a 5-0 league success over Celtic at Ibrox and had also beaten their rivals by the only goal of the game in the semi-finals of the Glasgow Cup. The confidence that win brought Rangers was plain to see, as goals from McCreadie, Barker and McPherson delivered a memorable 3-1 triumph and brought the Scottish Cup to Ibrox for the first time.

Celtic's 3-2 win at Parkhead a week later provided a considerable measure of revenge as it saw them formally retain the league title. However, even a fourth-placed finish wasn't going to dilute the pleasure Rangers derived from winning the trophy they had been chasing so desperately for so long.

Disappointingly for the club's increasing supporter base, they failed to build on their Scottish Cup success in 1894-95. After a promising start which saw them win their first four league matches, Rangers were beaten 5-3 by Celtic at Parkhead in September and, even more significantly, went down 1-0 to Hearts at Ibrox the following month. The Edinburgh club went on to finish worthy champions, five points clear of Celtic and a further four ahead of a maddeningly inconsistent Rangers side which was able to win only one of their last six league games.

Having strived for so long to win the Scottish Cup, it was a bitter blow for Rangers when their defence of the trophy was ended at the first hurdle. Again, Hearts found Ibrox to their liking as they edged the first round tie 2-1. With defeats to Celtic in the finals of both the Glasgow and Charity Cups, it was a barren campaign all round, but it did at least provide Rangers with some optimism for the future in the shape of two new signings who made their first appearances.

Alec Smith, who would become one of the club's all-time greats and the first in a long tradition of brilliant outside lefts, was recruited from amateur football in his native Darvel, while Neil Gibson, snapped up from junior outfit Royal Albert, would emerge as one of the most complete half backs in British football.

The impact these two players would make at Rangers was not immediately apparent in a hugely forgettable 1895-96 season. A 4-0 loss at home to Third Lanark in their second league fixture was a warning of the unreliable form to follow and a 4-2 defeat at the hands of Celtic at Ibrox two games later suggested the championship would again be well beyond Rangers' reach. Surprisingly, Rangers were able to stay in the hunt until the closing weeks of the campaign when a 6-2 thrashing by Celtic at Parkhead quashed any delusions of a late charge for the title. Indeed, the loss of both Old Firm league fixtures proved crucial. Celtic won the championship by four points from Rangers. However, there was no doubting the Parkhead men's superiority that season as they also recorded a 6-1 win over Rangers in the semi-final of the Charity Cup.

The Ibrox men's biggest problem had been replacing goalkeeper David Haddow, who had left to join Motherwell in the summer of 1895. Astonishingly, no fewer than six men were tried between the sticks during the course of the season, and it was clear that none of them were of the standard required. John Bell, who had kept two of only three clean sheets recorded by Rangers that campaign, appeared to be the best prospect but, somewhat melodramatically, he walked out on the club in apparent self-disgust after Hibs won 3-2 at Ibrox in the quarter-finals of the Scottish Cup.

The signing of Matt Dickie from Renton solved the goalkeeping crisis in time for 1896-97 and he was one of many new faces introduced by Wilton in what proved to be a far happier season for the club. Peter Turnbull and Tom Hyslop quickly proved themselves to be shrewd acquisitions from Blackburn Rovers and Stoke City respectively, netting 10 goals each as Rangers comfortably finished as leading scorers in the league with 64 goals. Unfortunately prolific scoring was not enough to bring the championship back to Ibrox.

Despite beating Hearts 5-0 at Ibrox early in the 1896-97 campaign, it was the Tynecastle club who went on to capture the title by two points from city rivals Hibs, with Rangers a further point adrift in third place. If their league form wasn't quite good enough, Rangers were untouchable in cup competition. The Glasgow Cup was the first pot collected, Turnbull scoring both goals in the 2-1 final replay victory over Celtic at Cathkin Park in November. Then, in the Scottish Cup, Rangers scored 18 times and conceded just four goals as they swept past Partick Thistle, Hibs, Dundee and Morton to reach the final where their opponents at Hampden on 20 March 1897 were Dumbarton. The Boghead men were now far removed from the force that had dominated Scottish football less than 10 years before and shared the first league championship with Rangers.

Relegated the previous season, they had just finished bottom of the Second Division with a paltry six points from their 18 games. Even allowing for a benevolent draw, Dumbarton had confounded all expectation simply to reach the final. It was therefore no surprise when Rangers romped to a 5-1 victory in front of 15,000 spectators. James Miller, signed earlier in the season from Sunderland, scored twice with further goals from Hyslop, McPherson and Alec Smith bringing the Cup to Ibrox for the second time.

Rangers show off their three-cup haul in 1896-97.

Rangers completed an immensely satisfying season by adding the Charity Cup to their collection, following up a 4-1 defeat of Celtic in the semi-final at Hampden with a 6-1 thumping of Third Lanark in the final at the same venue a few days later.

Although Rangers were a free-scoring side at this time, curiously enough they lacked an out-and-out striker. That was rectified spectacularly by the arrival of Robert Cumming Hamilton from Queen's Park at the start of the 1897-98 season. Known to one and all as 'RC', he was a supreme poacher of goals and the first celebrity No.9 to play for Rangers.

Hamilton scored twice on his competitive debut for the club, a 4-2 win at St Bernard's which got the league campaign off to a flier, and proceeded to grab 26 goals in 22 games in his first season. It was not enough to bring the championship to Ibrox, however, a 4-0 home defeat to Celtic in September forced Rangers to play catch-up. They made a decent fist of it, winning nine games in a row after that Old Firm reverse, but were not helped by the abandonment after 70 minutes of the New Year's Day return fixture against Celtic at Parkhead because of a pitch invasion.

The score had been 1-1 at the time, with Rangers looking just as likely as their hosts to grab a winner. By the time the game was replayed at the end of the season, Celtic had already clinched the title and the goalless draw ensured a four point gap between the teams at the top of the table.

Rangers again found comfort in cup competition. Having beaten Celtic en route to retaining the Glasgow Cup, they proceeded to make a successful defence of the Scottish Cup. It took three matches to get past Third Lanark in a marathon semi-final and, as 12 months previously, Rangers found themselves facing Second Division opponents in the final.

Kilmarnock, however, would provide a far sterner test at Hampden. The Ayrshire club were on the verge of winning their championship and, having shocked Dundee in the semi-finals, were confident of upsetting the odds once more. While Rangers' keeper Dickie was seldom troubled

R.C. Hamilton brought a new dimension to Rangers' attack.

throughout the contest, there was some concern in the Ibrox ranks when half-time came and went with the scoreline still blank. James McAllan, a former Rangers keeper, was in excellent form for Killie, but Alec Smith finally made the breakthrough with a 59th-minute opener and, appropriately enough, Hamilton capped his wonderful debut season with the second and clinching goal.

A 100 Per Cent Record

Hamilton's arrival had provided Rangers with a focal point for their potent brand of attacking football and he was complemented superbly by inside forwards Miller and McPherson, as well as wingers Alec Smith and John Campbell, when the Ibrox men recorded a quite astonishing feat in 1898-99. The league championship was won outright for the first time in the club's history in scarcely credible fashion.

Rangers won all 18 of their league fixtures, a 100 per cent points tally which remains a world record to this day. Hamilton, from the moment he notched a hat-trick in the opening day 6-2 drubbing of Partick Thistle at Ibrox, was in irresistible form and he ended the season with 25 goals from 23 competitive appearances. When Celtic were swamped 4-0 at Parkhead in September to make it six straight league wins, it was apparent that Rangers were on course for a special season.

As the victories kept being racked up, the closest Rangers came to a blemish on their record was when, after trailing 3-2 at Easter Road, they fought back to snatch an unlikely 4-3 win courtesy of a last minute penalty kick converted by defender Bobby Neil. For most of the campaign, Rangers and their supporters were spared such tension as they won most of their games with something in hand.

The title was clinched with four games to spare when Dundee visited Ibrox on 17 December 1898 and were thumped 7-0. Almost inevitably, Hamilton grabbed the limelight with a hat-trick while Smith and McPherson both scored twice. Perhaps the Rangers supporters of the time failed to appreciate the magnitude of the team's achievement as only 3,000 of them were there to see the championship sealed.

Ten times that number were present for the visit of Celtic on 2 January 1899, however, as Rangers emphasised their superiority with a 4-1 win which featured Hamilton's third hat-trick of the season. Rangers finished 10 points clear of runners-up Hearts and a further two in front of third-placed Celtic.

The early finish to the league campaign – Rangers played their 18th and final fixture on 7 January – saw attention focus on the Scottish Cup in which the Ibrox side were seeking to emulate Vale of Leven and Queen's Park in winning the trophy three years in succession.

The Prestige of the Cup

A crowd of 20,000 at Ibrox for the first round tie against Hearts again underlined the Scottish Cup's still greater stature and prestige, compared to league football, in the public consciousness. Rangers won the match 4-1 and subsequent victories over Ayr Parkhouse, Clyde and St Mirren took them through to the final against Celtic at Hampden on 22 April.

Standing just one match short of winning every competitive fixture that season, Rangers finally succumbed to the law of averages. They were unable to justify their status as pre-match favourites against a determined Celtic side who avenged their defeat in the final of five years earlier. Second half goals from Sandy McMahon and Hodge earning a 2-0 win for Maley's team.

It had been a momentous season for Rangers in more ways than one. On 10 May 1899, the club became a limited company as they continued to keep pace with the professionalism sweeping across the game. William Wilton was handed the new title of manager and secretary, his influence at the club as wide-ranging and powerful as any of those who have succeeded him.

As Scottish football welcomed the dawn of the 20th century, Rangers were ready for the challenges it would bring on and off the pitch. While the perfect league form of the previous campaign was impossible to repeat, Rangers comfortably retained the championship in 1899-1900 by seven points from Celtic.

Boosted by the signing of the brilliant Scottish international half back Jacky Robertson from Southampton, Rangers won 12 and drew two of their first 14 league games. Hamilton, with 23 goals from 20 appearances, was once more a significant influence.

The turn of the year saw Rangers housed in a new Ibrox Stadium, on a site next to the now outdated first ground. Boasting a 4,500-seater grandstand, the second Ibrox had an estimated capacity of around 75,000, but this was never tested by a Rangers fixture. Tragically, the ground had inadequacies that would come to light in desperate fashion two years later.

50 Greatest Players

JOHN McPHERSON Inside forward

Joined Rangers: April 1890   **From:** Cowlairs

Debut: v Hearts, League, 16 August 1890

Appearances: 218   **Goals:** 121

Left Rangers: May 1902 (retired)

Honours won with Rangers: 5 league championships; 3 Scottish Cups

McPherson, born in Kilmarnock in 1868, started his career with his home town club and was already a firmly established international player when he joined Rangers from Cowlairs in 1890. Remarkably versatile – he played in every position from goalkeeper to outside left – it was at inside left that 'Kitey' was most effective, falling into the role by default in a Scottish international trial at Ibrox in 1888. His performance for the 'possibles' against the 'probables' that day earned him his Scotland call-up and he would go on to win nine caps, scoring five goals.

McPherson scored on his Rangers debut, grabbed four goals in a 6-2 win over Cambuslang the following week, then struck five times in an 8-2 mauling of St Mirren. It was an astonishing start to an amazing Ibrox career. When Rangers won the Scottish Cup for the first time in 1894, McPherson was one of the key performers. He scored six goals in six ties, including the third in the 3-1 defeat of Celtic in the final at Hampden.

After 12 hugely successful playing years with Rangers, in which McPherson enhanced his standing in the game considerably, he went on to play a pivotal role in the club's ascendancy. In 1907, five years after hanging up his boots, he became a director and remained on the Ibrox board until his death in 1926.

The only league defeat of the season, and Rangers' first in almost two years came on New Year's Day when they went down 3-2 to Celtic at Parkhead, but the title was already secure. Although Rangers defeated Celtic in the finals of both the Glasgow and Charity Cups that season, most notably by 5-1 in the latter competition, their city rivals once again proved their nemesis in the blue riband tournament, the Scottish Cup. After slamming in 22 goals to dispose of Morton, Maybole and Partick Thistle, Rangers lost out to Celtic in the semi-finals, going down heavily 4-0 in a Parkhead replay following a 2-2 draw at Ibrox.

When Rangers surrendered five points from their first nine league games of 1900-01, including defeats at main rivals Hibs and Celtic, it appeared as if the dominance of the previous two seasons was under serious threat. However, they responded in the style of true champions, winning their last 11 fixtures to retain their title by a convincing six points from Celtic who were beaten 2-1 at Ibrox in the crucial New Year's Day encounter.

50 Greatest Players

JOCK DRUMMOND Full back

Joined Rangers: March 1892   **From:** Falkirk

Debut: v Leith Athletic, League, 16 April 1892

Appearances: 223   **Goals:** 2

Left Rangers: May 1904   **For:** Falkirk

Honours won with Rangers: 4 league championships; 4 Scottish Cups

A menacing figure, Jock Drummond was one of the first in a long line of powerfully committed defenders who have captured the hearts and minds of Rangers followers throughout the club's history. Drummond had already won international recognition as a Falkirk player when Rangers signed him in 1892 and he went on to win 14 caps for Scotland, equalling the existing record for appearances. Curiously, Drummond wore a cloth cap while playing football, pulling the peak down over his eyes to add to his intimidating appearance.

A native of Clackmannanshire, he often adopted an agricultural approach to the game but he was not without skill. Possessed of a tremendous will to win, Drummond was uncompromising in his tussles with opposition forwards and very few got the better of him. Drummond was involved in Rangers' four successive championship triumphs from 1899 to 1902, was a member of the club's first Scottish Cup winning side and collected three further winner's medals in the tournament. He left Ibrox at the end of the disappointing 1903-04 season, rejoining Falkirk as a coach. He later became a director of the Brockville club and died in 1935 at the age of 65.

Finlay Speedie, an excellent inside forward signed two months earlier from Clydebank Juniors, scored the opener in that match. Another new recruit was Jamie Stark, a defender from the Glasgow Perthshire junior outfit, and both men would become outstanding players for the Rangers in the seasons ahead.

While the league was won for the third consecutive season, Rangers also notched up an unwanted hat-trick when their Scottish Cup involvement was yet again ended by Celtic, this time going down by the only goal in a first round tie at Parkhead.

A 4-2 defeat at Kilmarnock on the opening day of the 1901-02 season hinted at the difficulties Rangers would face winning their fourth title in a row. Despite winning their next five league games, two defeats and two draws in the next eight matches handed the initiative firmly to Celtic who built up a commanding lead going into the final stages of the campaign.

Unexpectedly, however, the Parkhead side began frittering away their advantage with some shock defeats. Suddenly the New Year's Day fixture at Parkhead became crucial. Victory for Celtic would have been enough to clinch the championship, but the faltering form of their rivals gave Rangers, with three more games remaining, fresh hope.

In one of the most explosive and controversial fixtures yet between the teams, Rangers ran out 4-2 winners with goals from Nicol Smith, John Campbell, Jacky Robertson and R.C. Hamilton. Celtic were incensed, believing three of the Rangers goals should have been disallowed. A subsequent protest, with Celtic manager Maley claiming his side were the victims of 'vile treatment' from the referee, cut no ice with the authorities and Rangers were now in position to hold onto the championship again. This they did, winning their three remaining fixtures against Queen's Park, St Mirren and Dundee to edge out a hugely frustrated Celtic by two points at the top of the table.

The Scottish Cup eluded Rangers again, although at least they had the novelty of being eliminated by someone other than Celtic. This time it was an excellent Hibs side, who would go on to defeat Celtic in the final, who beat Rangers 2-0 in a semi-final watched by 35,000 at Ibrox.

Tragedy at Ibrox

The whole season, however, was overshadowed by the first Ibrox Disaster on April 5 1902. Chosen by the SFA to stage the Scotland-England international match, the stadium dismally failed its first serious test since its construction just over two years earlier. With at least 75,000, the reputed capacity, packed into the ground, part of the west terracing suddenly collapsed with horrific consequences.

50 Greatest Players

NEIL GIBSON Wing half

Joined Rangers: November 1894   **From:** Royal Albert

Debut: v Dumbarton, League, 1 December 1894

Appearances: 192   **Goals:** 22

Left Rangers: May 1904   **For:** Partick Thistle

Honours won with Rangers: 4 league championships; 3 Scottish Cups

When William Wilton persuaded 21-year-old Neil Gibson to sign for Rangers in 1894, he secured the services of a precocious talent who would emerge as one of the greatest players seen anywhere in the Victorian era. Eulogies from opposition players and managers came Gibson's way as easily as his remarkable ball control and accuracy of passing. Steve Bloomer, the legendary England international star, labelled Gibson as the best player he had ever seen. It was a remarkable compliment, no doubt prompted by the sandy-haired Larkhall lad's outstanding performances for Scotland in their victories over England in 1896 and 1900.

Known as 'Neilly' by his team-mates and the Rangers followers, he was a fixture in Wilton's first team for the duration of his exemplary 10-year career at Ibrox. Although he had to wait three years for his first major honour with the club, the 1897 Scottish Cup final victory over Dumbarton, he soon made up for lost time as he added to his collection.

Gibson, who had honed his fabulous skills in Lanarkshire football with Larkhall Thistle, Larkhall Juniors and Royal Albert, won his final honour for Rangers in the 1903 Scottish Cup final, although he suffered the disappointment of missing the conclusive second replay against Hearts after playing in the first two drawn matches at Parkhead. He left Ibrox in 1904 for Partick Thistle, with whom he earned the last of his 14 caps for Scotland.

Twenty-six people plunged to their deaths through a gaping hole in the wooden structure and almost 600 were injured. Staggeringly, play was restarted after a stoppage of less than 20 minutes, but the 1-1 result was later scratched from the record books and the international replayed in Birmingham.

The tragedy dealt a shattering blow to Scottish football and to Rangers in particular. To raise funds for the victims, Everton and Sunderland came north to compete with Rangers and Celtic in a British League Cup tournament, won by the Parkhead men. And, while the human loss was paramount in everyone's minds, the cost of rebuilding meant that the Ibrox club also suffered financially.

Having lost one of their all-time greats when John McPherson announced his retirement, Rangers' prospects of winning a fifth successive championship were further diminished when they began the 1902-03 season with the whole of their first-team squad available for transfer. The drastic measure had been taken by manager Wilton and the club's directors as they sought ways to raise funds to cope with the rebuilding work necessary at Ibrox. In the event, there were no high profile departures from the club, but what was now an ageing side produced inconsistent form which was never likely to be good enough to hold onto the title.

Rangers lost three of their first five fixtures, including a 1-0 defeat at Easter Road to Hibs. The Edinburgh club, enjoying one of the best periods of their history, went on to win the championship for the first time by six points from Dundee, with Rangers back in third place.

The loss of the title was soothed by a successful Scottish Cup campaign. The quarter-final draw sent Rangers to Parkhead where goals from Alec Smith, John Walker and R.C. Hamilton earned a highly satisfying 3-0 win. Relations between the clubs were strained at the time, Rangers unhappy at Celtic's unwillingness to return the Exhibition Cup trophy to Ibrox. The cup, initially won by Rangers in September 1901 with a 3-1 win over Celtic, was then donated to the British League Cup tournament in aid of the Ibrox Disaster Fund in June 1902. Although Celtic defeated Rangers 3-2 in the final, the Ibrox club had believed the trophy would eventually be returned to them to keep in perpetuity. It remains at Parkhead to this day.

Rangers, then, derived great pleasure from winning the Scottish Cup at, of all places, Parkhead. Their opponents in the final were Hearts, who had

The shattered terrace at Ibrox after 26 people had lost their lives in the tragedy at the Scotland against England international match in April 1902.

finished one place below them in the league table, and it turned into an exhausting three-match marathon. Jamie Stark's goal was cancelled out by Bobby Walker on 11 April 1903, forcing a replay seven days later which ended 0-0 despite Rangers being reduced to 10 men for much of the second half because of an injury to John Walker. The second replay on 25 April saw Rangers finally overcome the determined Tynecastle side with goals either side of half-time from Mackie and Hamilton.

The club's fourth Scottish Cup triumph had been achieved despite the loss to injury of the inspirational Jock Drummond, who limped through the second replay, and Rangers' share of the £2,650 gate receipts accumulated over the three matches was welcome at such a financially testing time.

Despite the continuing prolific form of Hamilton, who managed 31 goals in 28 appearances, Rangers endured a barren 1903-04 season. Their first defeat of the campaign would prove the most telling as they went down 1-0 at Ibrox to Third Lanark, a fixture which was actually the Cathkin men's 'home' game. Thirds went on to win the championship for the only time in their history with Rangers five points adrift in fourth place.

The Ibrox men could have no complaints, dogged as they were by inconsistency which saw them drop points carelessly and unexpectedly at Port Glasgow and St Mirren. Rangers came through the toughest draw imaginable, ekeing out single goal victories over Hearts and Hibs, to reach the Scottish Cup final where they faced Celtic at Hampden on 16 April 1904.

With both league fixtures having been drawn that season, the teams were clearly evenly matched, but Rangers appeared to be cruising to a successful defence of the trophy when they took an early 2-0 lead thanks to a Finlay Speedie double. This, however, was to be remembered as the day Jimmy Quinn made history. The Celtic striker became the first man to score a hat-trick in a Scottish Cup final as the Parkhead side hit back to win 3-2 in front of a then record attendance of 64,472. The spiraling pulling power of Rangers and Celtic prompted *Scottish Sport*, an influential publication at the time, to label them as the 'Old Firm'. The moniker has stuck.

For the next few seasons, however, Rangers were forced into the role of junior partners as Celtic enjoyed their first real era of dominance in Scottish football. A great Rangers team was gradually breaking up and in the summer of 1904, two of its finest moved on when Neil Gibson joined Partick Thistle and Jock Drummond returned to Falkirk as a trainer.

John May, who would become a Scottish international, was recruited from Derby County to strengthen the defence, but Rangers were badly affected by the absence through injury of their captain Jamie Stark for much of the

50 Greatest Players

R.C. HAMILTON Forward

Joined Rangers: August 1897 **From:** Queen's Park

Debut: v St Bernard's, League, 4 September 1897

Left Rangers: 1906 **For:** Fulham

Rejoined Rangers: 1907 **From:** Fulham

Left Rangers: 1908 **For:** Morton

Appearances: 209 **Goals:** 184

Honours won with Rangers: 4 league championships; 2 Scottish Cups

One of the first Highlanders to gain prominence in a Rangers jersey, Elgin-born Robert Cumming Hamilton was a prince among predators long before the cult of the goalscorer started to dominate football.

'RC' joined the Ibrox club in 1897 from Queen's Park, having spent a year with the Amateurs, and his impact was stunning and immediate. He scored twice on his debut against St Bernard's and went on to claim 26 goals in 22 competitive appearances in his first season, including the clincher in the 2-0 Scottish Cup final win over Kilmarnock at Hampden.

Hamilton was, plain and simple, a goalscorer. He claimed 25 the following season, including a hat-trick in a 4-0 win over Celtic as Rangers won the league championship outright for the first time in their history, the historic campaign which saw them win all 18 matches.

His prolific scoring rate continued, as did the flow of winner's medals, until he left the club for the first time at the end of the disappointing 1905-06 season. Hamilton, who also served Fulham, Hearts, Morton and Dundee, returned to Ibrox for the 1907-08 campaign but was unable to repeat his former glories. He remains one of the greatest strikers ever to wear a Rangers jersey and only Ally McCoist has scored more goals for the club in Old Firm matches. A teacher by profession, Hamilton died in 1948 at the age of 71.

1904-05 season. Stark had become an increasingly influential figure at the club and it was hardly a coincidence that he was missing when Rangers dropped eight points in their first 13 league games, including home and away defeats against struggling St Mirren.

Stark's return initiated a revival, Rangers winning eight of their next nine matches to stay firmly involved in a two-horse race for the championship with Celtic. A 4-1 defeat at Ibrox in the Old Firm fixture on 18 February 1905 meant Rangers needed to win their last three games to tie on points at the top of the table with Celtic who had now completed their programme.

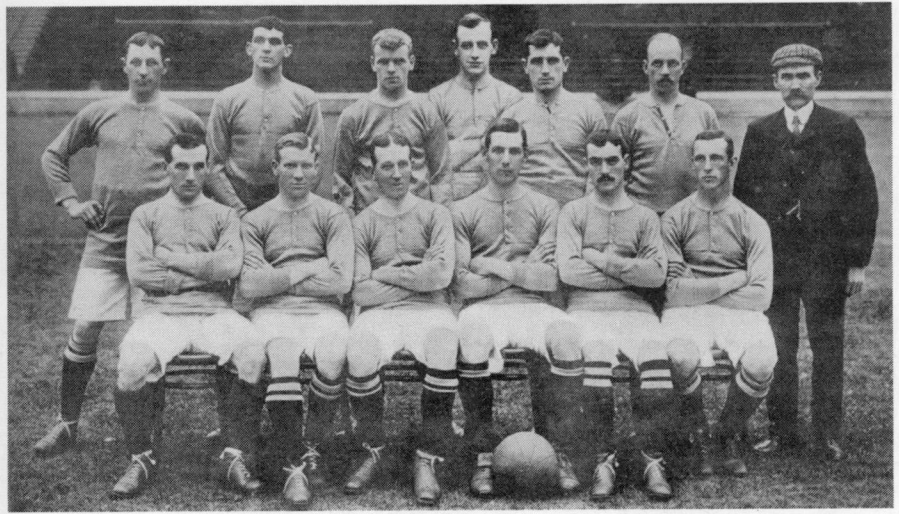

The re-built Rangers squad before the 1905-06 season. From left. Back row: Fraser, Sinclair, Craig, Speedie, Stark, May, Wilson (trainer). Front row: Dalrymple, Gray, McColl, Hamilton, Kyle, Smith.

Rangers did so fairly comfortably, forcing a championship play-off at Hampden Park on 6 May. The Scottish League were still to introduce goal average or goal difference to decide such matters and, unlike 14 years before when they played off against Dumbarton, Rangers were unfortunate in that they would have been champions on both counts.

Celtic won the play-off 2-1, Jacky Robertson's late goal mere consolation, and it would prove to be the first of six consecutive championship triumphs for the Parkhead men. Rangers had at least knocked their biggest rivals out of the Scottish Cup earlier in the season, Celtic conceding the semi-final tie at Parkhead after their fans invaded the pitch with Wilton's men leading 2-0 through goals from Speedie and Robertson. The final, however, provided huge disappointment for Rangers who could have no complaints about a 3 -1 replay defeat at the hands of Third Lanark at Hampden after a goalless draw in the first match.

A Sad Farewell

It was another season touched by tragedy for the club. The death in January 1905 of Nicol Smith at the age of 32 stunned Rangers and the wider Scottish football community. Arguably the greatest Scottish full back of his era, Smith died of enteric fever just a couple of weeks after his wife had lost her life to the same disease. Capped 12 times for Scotland, he served Rangers brilliantly for 12 years, winning four league championships and three Scottish Cups.

Another of the club's leading lights, Jacky Robertson, left in the summer of 1905 to become player-manager of Chelsea. Rangers followers looking for more positive signs for the future could at least reflect on the capture of goalkeeper Tom Sinclair from Morton, a decent successor to Matt Dickie who had left to join Clyde, and the imaginative signing of the famed Scottish international striker R.S. McColl from Newcastle United.

In truth, however, Rangers did not see McColl at his best and he was not especially prolific in his three seasons with the club. A more successful recruit was James Speirs, an intelligent inside forward snapped up from Maryhill Juniors at the start of the 1905-06 campaign. Rangers made a wretched start, losing 5-1 at Airdrie and going down 5-0 at home to Hearts in their first six league fixtures.

Though a 3-2 win over Celtic at Ibrox in October offered some hope of a revival, Rangers were simply far too inconsistent to mount a credible challenge. Their home form was quite dreadful, recording losses to Third Lanark, Morton and Airdrie as they finished fourth in the table, 12 points behind champions Celtic. Overall, it was a nightmare season for the Ibrox club, capped by their shock quarter-final exit from the Scottish Cup when they lost 1-0 at Port Glasgow who finished second bottom of the league.

Changes were made for 1906-07, Alex Newbigging arriving from Reading to take over the goalkeeping duties from Sinclair, while Finlay Speedie joined Newcastle United for £600. R.C. Hamilton also moved on, joining Fulham after nine goal-filled seasons. He was badly missed as Rangers toiled through another barren season. They were seldom in the title race after winning just two of their first six league games, eventually finishing in third place 10 points behind Celtic. The Parkhead men rubbed in their superiority by coming to Ibrox and winning 3-0 in the quarter-finals of the Scottish Cup.

The arrival of Scottish international forward George Livingston from Manchester City midway through the season hinted at greater ambition from the club, but there was a blow at the start of the 1907-08 campaign when captain Jamie Stark left to join Chelsea. Although R.C. Hamilton returned from Fulham, he was unable to recapture his former glories as Rangers again struggled to make the impact they had hoped for in the championship.

Back-to-back defeats at the hands of Airdrie and Queen's Park in November said everything about another feckless season. Rangers finished third in the table once more, albeit having halved the deficit between themselves and champions Celtic to five points. For the second successive year, they were knocked out of the Scottish Cup on their own ground by their Old Firm rivals, Celtic winning a second round tie 2-1.

If there was nothing tangible in the way of major honours to cheer Rangers and their supporters, the emergence of teenage midfielder Jimmy Gordon as a first-team regular was the most encouraging aspect of the season. The Saltcoats lad would go on to have an outstanding Ibrox career. Robert Gordon Campbell, known to everyone as 'RG' was another success, top scoring with 25 goals from 32 appearances. Remarkably, Campbell, a full back, had been signed from Celtic two seasons earlier for the princely sum of £350. The decision to move him to centre forward may have been borne of necessity, but it proved to be a good one.

With Billy McPherson, a nephew of Rangers legend John McPherson, signed from Liverpool at the start of the 1908-09 campaign, the brilliant former Scotland goalkeeper Harry Rennie snapped up from Hibs and international forward Alec Bennett pinched from Celtic, there was initially a much stronger title challenge from the Ibrox club. Crucially, however, they lost 3-1 to Celtic at Ibrox on New Year's Day, a defeat which seemed to knock the stuffing out of the team. They limped over the line in the championship race, winning only one of their last six fixtures as they finished in fourth place, five points behind the Parkhead men who took the title for a fifth consecutive year.

Scottish Cup Drama

The real drama of the season, however, centred on the Scottish Cup. Rangers emerged from a testing draw, which saw narrow victories over Dundee, Queen's Park and Falkirk, to reach the final against Celtic at Hampden on 10 April

Goalkeeper Harry Rennie was signed from Hibernian in 1908.

1909. In a marvellous contest, Jimmy Quinn fired the Parkhead men in front but Rangers hit back to lead 2-1 with goals from Tom Gilchrist and Bennett. It must have seemed an odd moment for Bennett, winner of the Scottish Cup as a Celtic player in the previous two seasons.

Sadly for Bennett and Rangers, his goal was not the winner as, 10 minutes from time, an uncharacteristic mistake from goalkeeper Rennie saw him help a Munro cross into his own net to hand Celtic an equalizer. The replay at Hampden seven days later saw Rangers hand Willie Reid, a centre forward just signed from Portsmouth, the most dramatic stage imaginable for his debut.

The day, however, would be remembered for all the wrong reasons. Rangers took an early lead through Jimmy Gordon and felt they had doubled it when Jamie Stark, back at Ibrox after little more than a season with Chelsea, had the ball in the net only for the goal to be controversially disallowed for an unspecified infringement.

Celtic, however, deserved their second half equalizer from Quinn and almost snatched victory when Peter Somers struck the crossbar late on. When the final whistle blew, several players lingered on the pitch as if unsure as to whether extra-time was to be played. There had been much press comment in the build-up to the replay on suggestions that Rangers and Celtic may contrive another drawn game in order to force another lucrative replay.

Gate receipts of almost £4,000 from the first two matches, watched by a combined attendance of 130,000, fuelled this speculation. When it became clear no extra period would take place, hundreds of spectators began to spill onto the pitch in protest. Events quickly got out of control; the police struggling to control the angry crowd who began setting the payboxes at the Somerville Road end of the stadium alight.

The worst riot Scottish football had witnessed lasted for over three hours and saw 130 people injured, six seriously. Directors of Rangers and Celtic issued a joint statement the following day which read: 'Although it was mooted during the week that extra-time might be played in the event of a draw, it was found that the cup rules prevented this. On account of the regrettable occurrences of yesterday, both clubs propose that the final tie be abandoned.' The SFA agreed, the trophy was withheld for the season and both halves of the Old Firm were fined £150.

Surprise Signings

Manager Wilton spread his net further afield for 1909-10 as Rangers sought to avoid a seventh successive season without one of the two major honours. Three Charity Cup successes since the 1903 Scottish Cup win were welcome but hardly adequate for a club of Rangers' standing in the game.

Wilton pulled off the surprise signings of goalkeeper Herbert Lock from Southampton and right winger Billy Hogg from Sunderland. Hogg was a full England international, the first ever signed by Rangers, while his compatriot Lock was only denied similar status by the brilliant Liverpool keeper Sam Hardy. Both would prove to be outstanding acquisitions by Wilton.

First, however, they would have to endure one more season of disappointment with their new team-mates as Rangers never recovered from a poor start in the league which saw them win only two of their first six

Billy Hogg's goals made him an Ibrox favourite.

matches. They eventually finished third, eight points behind Celtic who set a record of six successive championships which would stand for some time.

Fortunes were no better in the Scottish Cup, Rangers slipping to a 2-0 defeat against Clyde at Shawfield in the second round. It was an unhappy final season at the club for Jamie Stark, a brilliant captain and outstanding defender, who moved to Morton in the summer of 1910 along with wing half John May.

Stark's replacement, as Wilton continued reshaping the squad, was George Chapman from Blackburn Rovers who was immediately handed the captaincy. When an emerging Aberdeen side took the early initiative in the title race, Rangers appeared set for another frustrating campaign. A 5-1 home defeat at the hands of Morton in October, indeed, suggested the Ibrox men were no-hopers.

However, inspired by Hogg and centre forward Willie Reid, Rangers then reeled off five straight wins to get back in the hunt. From Christmas Eve until the end of the season, they were unbeaten and finished four points clear of runners-up Aberdeen. After nine long years Rangers were the champions again, with Reid's 41 goals in 36 games a major factor.

Ideas of a double were dashed by a familiar face in the quarter-finals of the Scottish Cup. Rangers lost 2-1 to Dundee at Dens Park with R.C. Hamilton, who had left Ibrox for a second and final time in 1908, one of the scorers for the Tayside club.

Rangers set out purposefully in defence of the championship and made a tremendous start to the 1911-12 season. With James Bowie, a wing half signed from Queen's Park midway through the previous campaign, emerging as a significant influence, they won 13 and drew one of their first 14 league fixtures to establish a healthy lead over a Celtic side desperate to reclaim the title. Jimmy Quinn's hat-trick gave Celtic a 3-0 win at Parkhead in the New Year's Day Old Firm game and hopes of a comeback, but Rangers recovered their earlier consistency to stay unbeaten for the rest of the season. They clinched the title with three games to spare, winning 1-0 at Raith Rovers on 23 March 1912.

Shawfield proved the graveyard for the club's Scottish Cup ambitions for the second time in three years. Clyde were leading 3-1 when a pitch invasion forced the second round match to be abandoned after 75 minutes. Rangers, who had looked well beaten, conceded the tie.

Rangers were disappointed to lose the services of Scotland right back George Law to Leeds City in the summer of 1912, but the squad was strengthened by the signing of Aston Villa's Jimmy Logan. Meanwhile, youngster James Paterson began to emerge as a potential successor to the evergreen Alec Smith who, at 36, was still providing sterling service on the left wing.

Losing five of their first 20 league games, including home and away reverses to Celtic, did nothing to encourage the belief Rangers could win a third successive title. However, after the 1-0 Old Firm defeat at Ibrox on New Year's Day, Rangers responded magnificently by winning 12 and drawing two of their last 14 fixtures to finish four points clear of their great rivals.

In the Scottish Cup, more frustration awaited Rangers who missed injured keeper Herbert Lock. His deputy, John Hempsey, was blamed by many for the 3-1 defeat at Falkirk in the third round. In fairness to Hempsey, it should be pointed out that he kept seven clean sheets in 11 matches in the championship run-in and that a fine Falkirk side went on to win the Scottish Cup.

Season 1913-14 saw many significant departures and arrivals for Rangers but no major silverware. The loss of the popular Billy Hogg to Dundee was a blow to the club's supporters and three defeats in the opening stages of the league campaign, including home losses to Hogg's new employers and Celtic, meant a fourth successive title was a long shot.

Wilton moved to strengthen the side, England international inside right Jimmy 'Tadger' Stewart snapped up from Newcastle United along with Scott Duncan, a right winger who compensated somewhat for the loss of Hogg. In November 1913, Wilton made one of his best ever signings when Tommy Cairns, a 23-year-old inside left, was recruited from St Johnstone. Although his impact was not immediate, Cairns would go on to become one of the club's all-time greats.

Rangers were never able to manoeuvre their way back into the championship race, a 4-0 defeat at Parkhead on 1 January allowing Celtic to move five points clear at the top. The gap between the pair at the end of the season was six points as Willie

Tommy Cairns, Rangers captain and inside forward.

50 Greatest Players

ALEC SMITH Outside left

Joined Rangers: May 1894   **From:** Darvel

Debut: v Leith Athletic, League, 3 November 1894

Appearances: 470   **Goals:** 151

Left Rangers: May 1915 (retired)

Honours won with Rangers: 7 league championships;
3 Scottish Cups; 20 caps (Scotland)

The first and arguably the greatest of a glorious tradition
of outstanding left wingers to wear Rangers colours,
Alec Smith was a football superstar long before the
phrase was ever coined.

Smith, a Darvel lace mill worker, was discovered
playing for his local team by Rangers' international full
back Nicol Smith, a native of the same Ayrshire village but no
relation. Nicol asked him to play for Rangers in a friendly against English FA Cup
holders Notts County at the end of the 1893-94 season. The 18-year-old's superb
display in a 3-1 Rangers win ensured he would be signed by the club and begin a
remarkable 21-year career at Ibrox.

Smith's finest quality, and one unusual for a winger, was his remarkable consistency.
Highly skilled and powerful in possession, he created countless chances for team-mates
and was a prolific goalscorer in his own right. He scored in Rangers' Scottish Cup final
victories of 1897 and 1898, claimed another winner's medal in the tournament in
1903 and ended his career with seven league championship winner's medals.

He was also one of the greatest Scotland players of his era, winning 20 caps and
scoring five goals for his country. Among his many outstanding international
performances was as part of the side that defeated England 4-1 at Parkhead in 1900.
Smith won his last Scotland cap in 1911, his final league title with Rangers two years
later before retiring in the summer of 1915 at the age of 39.

Maley's men reclaimed the title. The Scottish Cup brought familiar dismay,
the ever-prolific Willie Reid's goal scant consolation as Rangers lost 2-1 to
eventual finalists Hibs in a third round tie at Easter Road.

The saddest news of the season for Rangers, however, came in May 1914
when Jimmy Wilson, club trainer and confidante of Wilton for the previous
17 years, died. Replacing Wilson, whose input had helped bring seven league
championships and two Scottish Cups to Ibrox, was an onerous
responsibility but Wilton, typically, found the right man for the job.

A New Trainer Arrives

Bill Struth, like Wilson a former professional runner, had attracted much attention with his work as trainer of Clyde. The Shawfield club had reached the Scottish Cup finals of 1910 and 1912, eliminating Rangers on the way in both campaigns, and Edinburgh-born Struth was an integral part of their success. He needed no second invitation to join Wilton at Ibrox.

The first years of the Wilton-Struth partnership were acted out against the grim backdrop of the First World War. Hostilities began 10 days into the 1914-15 season, but the government decided league football should continue as an important form of entertainment. The SFA took a contrary view and suspended the Scottish Cup which, given Rangers' record in it, perhaps upset no one at Ibrox.

Rangers lost five of their first 12 league fixtures and were way off the championship pace set initially by Hearts. The Tynecastle outfit, who would contribute more members of their playing staff to the war effort than any other Scottish club, were caught by Celtic in the closing weeks of the season with Rangers finishing a distant third, 15 points behind the Parkhead men.

It was the final campaign for the great Alec Smith who made his last appearance for the club in October 1914, just a few days short of his 38th birthday. As he bowed out, two Rangers stars of the future arrived in the shape of full back Bert Manderson from Belfast and Andy Cunningham, a precocious inside forward from Kilmarnock.

A good start to the 1915-16 season, which saw nine of the first 10 games won, saw Rangers take an early lead in the wartime championship but they were unable to sustain it. Hampered by poor away form, the Ibrox men were able to win only one of their last six matches as Celtic romped home 11 points clear at the top.

The loss of players to active service made team selection an often arbitrary affair for most clubs through the war years and few were able to count on settled sides. Among the Rangers men who left for active service were James Paterson, a qualified doctor and Willie Reid, their perennial top scorer.

In 1916-17 Rangers once more failed to build on an excellent start that saw them take maximum points from their first seven games. They proceeded to drop five points from their next four matches and eventually finished third in the table behind Celtic and Morton.

Wilton did, however, make two more significant signings in May 1917 when he enlisted the services of right winger Sandy Archibald from Raith Rovers and half back Tommy Muirhead for all of £20 from Hibs. Both men would provide terrific value.

50 Greatest Players

WILLIE REID Forward

Joined Rangers: April 1909   **From:** Portsmouth

Debut: v Celtic, Scottish Cup Final replay, 17 April 1909

Appearances: 230   **Goals:** 195

Left Rangers: May 1920   **For:** Albion Rovers

Honours won with Rangers: 4 league championships;

9 caps (Scotland)

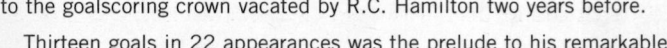

Willie Reid made his debut for Rangers in one of the most infamous matches in Scottish football history, the 1909 Scottish Cup final replay against Celtic which sparked a major riot, causing the trophy to be withheld. Reid played in two more games for Rangers that season, failing to either score or be on a winning side, but the 1909-10 campaign saw him establish his credentials as a successor to the goalscoring crown vacated by R.C. Hamilton two years before.

Thirteen goals in 22 appearances was the prelude to his remarkable haul in 1910-11 as he rattled in 41 goals in 36 games, helping Rangers claim the league championship for the first time in nine years. Reid was equally as prolific in the next two seasons as the title was retained and his marvellous form earned him nine caps for Scotland. He scored four times for his country, including the third in the famous 3-1 win over England at Hampden in 1914, which was watched by an estimated attendance of 130,000.

From 1916 to 1919, Reid served his country in the First World War, but he returned to Rangers for one last season, typically scoring eight goals in his nine appearances during 1919-20 as the league was won. He left Ibrox that summer for Albion Rovers and later managed the Cliftonhill club. Reid died in 1966 at the age of 80.

Final-day Title Battle

The 1917-18 championship was a thrilling affair that deserved to be played out in far happier circumstances than those still engulfing the country. Although Rangers lost two of their first eight games, they found themselves locked in a neck-and-neck battle for the title with defending champions Celtic. It went to the final day, 13 April 1918, with both sides on 54 points. Rangers held their nerves better, goals from Archibald and Bowie earning a 2-1 win over Clyde at Ibrox, while Celtic were held 1-1 at home to Motherwell. It was Rangers' title by a solitary point.

Rangers had won their ninth championship despite joint-top scorers Tommy Cairns and Jimmy Gordon grabbing just 11 goals each. With Reid still absent, Wilton addressed the centre forward problem by signing former Scottish international David McLean from Third Lanark for the 1918-19 season.

McLean was a great success, scoring 29 goals in 24 matches as the title race went to the wire again. Rangers made a brilliant start, winning 11 and drawing one of their first 12 games, but away defeats at Morton, Partick Thistle and Kilmarnock saw them dragged into another tense battle at the top with Celtic.

The Parkhead men started the final day, 10 May 1919, with a one point lead but looked to have the tougher fixture away to Ayr United, where Rangers had dropped a point a few weeks earlier. Ironically, Rangers were in action at Parkhead against Clyde, who were using the ground temporarily, and a McLean hat-trick inspired them to a 4-0 win. Celtic, however, earned a 2-0 victory at Somerset Park to win the title by a point.

With the war now mercifully over, Scottish football resumed normal service for 1919-20 with the return of the Scottish Cup. The First Division

Great Managers – 1899-1920

WILLIAM WILTON

The modern day job description of a football manager would undoubtedly bewilder William Wilton, but this gentleman of the Edwardian era was the first to hold the post at Rangers, and emerged as a hugely significant influence on the development of the club.

Although he joined Rangers as a player in 1883, Wilton's talent on the field was limited and he never progressed beyond the reserve side. It was as an administrator that he would prove to be a colossus for the club, playing a major role in the move to Ibrox in 1887 and then becoming match secretary, the job which preceded the position of manager, two years later.

He was named as Rangers' first manager in 1899 when the club became a limited company and, with the help of outstanding trainers in James Wilson and then Bill Struth, Wilton oversaw seven league championship triumphs and one Scottish Cup success during his reign. Wilton, in his position as the first ever treasurer of the Scottish Football League, also ensured Rangers' voice would be heard in the game's corridors of power during a period which saw the transition from amateur to professional football.

Tragically, Wilton lost his life in a freak accident at sea on 2 May 1920 when he was swept overboard while spending some rare leisure time on a friend's yacht on the Inverclyde coast.

was expanded by four clubs to 22 and it was Rangers who would last the pace best of all in a marathon 42-match campaign. A 1-0 defeat at Motherwell was the only blip in an excellent start by the Ibrox side who won 16 of their opening 19 games to surge clear at the top. Celtic battled admirably to maintain their challenge in the second half of the season but, despite an unexpected 2-1 home defeat to Clydebank, Rangers held onto their advantage and clinched the title with a goalless draw at Dumbarton on 28 April 1920.

Three weeks earlier, their Scottish Cup campaign had ended after an epic three-match semi-final against Albion Rovers, the Coatbridge club winning the second replay 2-0 at Parkhead.

Rangers, content with the championship, could also look to a strengthened side as the end of the season had seen the introduction of goalkeeper Willie Robb from Morton and defender Davie Meiklejohn who would prove an inspired capture from Maryhill Juniors.

Tragically, all the satisfaction gleaned from the campaign was overshadowed by the death of William Wilton on 2 May 1920. Just four days after seeing Rangers win their 14th major honour under his leadership, he lost his life when he was swept overboard and lost at sea while on a yachting break. The Ibrox club were stunned by the sudden loss of such an influential figure but Wilton had ensured his successor was already in place. Bill Struth, brought to the club as trainer six years earlier, was named Rangers manager. It would be as good an appointment as the club would ever make.

Chapter Three: 1920-27
Struth Takes Charge

Bill Struth's maxim, for as long as he was associated with Rangers, was that no player was greater than the club. Few of the men who have worn the light blue jersey through the generations have come closer to challenging that notion than Struth's first signing as manager of the club, Alan Lauder Morton.

An outside left with remarkable close control and mesmerizing trickery, Partick-born Morton was 27 and had already been capped twice for Scotland when Struth brought him to Ibrox from Queen's Park in the summer of 1920 as a replacement for James Paterson whose medical career took him to London and Arsenal.

The Rangers No. 11 jersey had gathered something of a mystical air, having been worn for so long with such distinction by Alec Smith. Although Paterson had proved an able replacement, Morton would go on to stake a powerful claim as the finest exponent of left wing play ever to represent the club.

As Morton arrived, Rangers said farewell to Jimmy Gordon who, at 32, moved on to join Dunfermline after an outstanding 14-year Ibrox career which had brought him five championship medals and 10 caps for Scotland.

With Morton's influence immediate, Rangers made a breathtaking start to their defence of the championship. They dropped just two points in drawn games at Aberdeen and Ayr United in their opening 23 matches of the campaign and opened up a commanding lead at the top of the table.

Even the disappointment of a 2-0 home defeat at the hands of Celtic on New Year's Day could take nothing away from an otherwise unstoppable surge to Rangers' 11th title triumph. George Henderson, a centre forward signed from Forfar Athletic, had been one of William Wilton's last signings for the club towards the end of the 1919-20 season and he soon proved a shrewd acquisition.

Bill Struth built as fine a team as Ibrox has ever seen.

After scoring four times in a 5-0 win over Dundee at Ibrox in November, Henderson went on to grab 21 goals in 23 league appearances in 1920-21. Also making his Ibrox bow in that match against Dundee was Billy McCandless, a Northern Ireland international full back, who had been signed from Linfield and would emerge as a reliable and highly effective servant.

The championship was wrapped up with four games to spare when Clyde were beaten 3-1 at Ibrox on 19 April 1921 with goals from Meiklejohn, Archibald and Henderson. Rangers eventually romped home a full 10 points clear of Celtic. The impact of new manager Struth and the players he had brought to Ibrox encouraged the belief among Rangers supporters that the club's barren run in the Scottish Cup, now stretching into an 18th season, would be brought to an end.

Endless Heartache in the Scottish Cup

Although Alloa Athletic unexpectedly troubled Rangers in the second round, the then non-league side forcing a replay, progress to the final was otherwise relatively stress-free for Struth's side who crushed Albion Rovers 4-1 in the semi-final at Parkhead to book a final showdown at the same venue against Partick Thistle on 16 April 1921.

Having beaten the Firhill side home and away in the league, scoring five goals without reply, Rangers were understandably the warmest of favourites to win the cup. Once more, however, the script was ripped up on a day when a crowd of less than 30,000, a consequence of a controversial SFA decision to double admission prices to two shillings, saw Thistle lift the Scottish Cup for the only time in their history.

Rangers, playing in their white strip as Thistle wore blue, dominated much of the contest, but were let down by poor finishing. The only goal of the final was scored by Thistle right winger John Blair after 20 minutes, with Rangers temporarily down to 10 men while left half Jimmy Bowie replaced a ripped pair of shorts. The Ibrox men's dreams of Scottish Cup success had been torn apart just as effectively.

When Rangers won their first nine matches of the 1921-22 season, a third successive championship seemed a likely prospect. Although a 2-0 home defeat by Hearts brought the sequence to an end, Rangers were still able to enter the New Year out in front in the title race. Struth had stuck by the previous season's squad, although he did make one interesting addition to the playing staff in October 1921.

Carl Hansen, a centre forward who had caught Struth's eye during Rangers' three-match trip to Copenhagen in June that year, became the first overseas player ever signed by the club. Hansen made a positive impact, scoring on his debut in a 2-1 win over Dundee at Ibrox on Boxing Day, and ended the season with eight goals from 11 appearances.

Rangers' title defence, however, floundered in January and February when they dropped eight points in nine matches to hand Celtic the initiative going into the final stages of the campaign. On the final day, April 29 1922, Celtic had a one-point lead and appeared to have the tougher fixture, away to Morton. Rangers were also on their travels but strongly fancied to beat Clyde at Shawfield.

Despite dominating the match, though, Rangers could only draw 0-0. Hope filtered through from Greenock with the news that Morton were leading Celtic 1-0, but a goal two minutes from time by Andy McAtee earned the Parkhead men the point which was good enough to take the title.

It was a painful blow for Rangers, coming just two weeks after they had suffered another dose of apparently endless heartache in the Scottish Cup. Having negotiated replays against Albion Rovers and St Mirren in earlier rounds, Rangers avenged the previous year's final defeat when they eclipsed Partick Thistle 2-0 in the semi-final at Ibrox.

Rangers' 1921-22 'nearly men'. From left. Back row: McDermid, Reid, Roberts, Morton, Lawson, Kirkwood, Fowler, Johnston, Low. Middle row: Robb, Archibald, Manderson, Nicholson, Bowie, McKenna, Walls, Smith, Gould. Front row: McCandless, Cairns, Muirhead, Cunningham, Dixon, Henderson, Meiklejohn, Morton.

Davie Meiklejohn, already an Ibrox hero in 1923, would have another 12 successful years with the club.

Once more, Struth's men went into the final as huge favourites when they lined up against Morton at Hampden on 15 April 1922. Not for the first time, a Rangers side were left feeling the fates had conspired against them.

Alan Morton struck a post during a ceaseless early spell of pressure from the favourites, before Rangers' goalkeeper Willie Robb conceded a free-kick, sliding outside his penalty area to collect a weakly struck pass-back from Billy McCandless. Jimmy Gourlay, the Morton right half, stepped up to sweep the kick high into the net to give the Greenock side a 12th minute lead.

Despite being reduced to 10 men just eight minutes later, when Andy Cunningham was hospitalised with a broken jaw, Rangers managed to exert considerable pressure on the Morton goal, but were unable to force an equalizer. The long wait to lift the Scottish Cup again would continue.

Champions Again

Rangers made a slipshod start to the 1922-23 season, dropping four points in their first six league matches. A 3-1 win over Celtic at Parkhead in October, Cunningham scoring twice, put them back on course and by the time the rivals met again, Rangers' 2-0 victory at Ibrox on New Year's Day with strikes from Hansen and Archibald gave them a clear lead at the top.

Airdrie, however, had emerged as surprise challengers and they eclipsed Celtic as the biggest threat to Rangers' championship hopes when they defeated Bill Struth's men 1-0 at Broomfield in February. When Rangers suffered further defeats at Raith Rovers, Albion Rovers and Hibs, the Lanarkshire side entertained genuine hopes of becoming Scottish champions for the first time. But Rangers, held their nerve to wrap up the title with a game to spare, Henderson scoring the only goal of the game against Kilmarnock at Ibrox on 21 April which put them out of Airdrie's reach.

In the Scottish Cup, Rangers had been put out of their annual misery at an early stage when they rather dismally lost 2-0 to Ayr United at Somerset Park in the second round. Although both the Glasgow and Charity Cups were collected, the trophy which mattered most continued to tease Rangers mercilessly.

In May 1923, Struth made another smart addition to his squad, paying Alloa a sum of £750 to recruit left half Tully Craig. A former Celtic player, the man from Stirling would go on to enjoy an outstanding Ibrox career.

Rangers made an irresistible start to the 1923-24 campaign, seizing the initiative in the championship race from the off. They recorded 14 wins and six draws in their first 20 league games, affording them the luxury of maintaining an eight point lead at the top when they drew 2-2 with Celtic at Parkhead on New Year's Day.

Airdrie once again surpassed Celtic as the closest challengers to Rangers but, despite some slips in the second half of the season, including a 1-0 home defeat at the hands of Raith Rovers, the Ibrox side retained their title fairly comfortably. It was formally clinched with a 2-1 win over Hibs at Ibrox on 5 April, Rangers eventually finishing nine points clear of runners-up Airdrie.

The Scottish Cup drought extended to a 21st year, however, Hibs coming from behind at Easter Road to defeat Rangers 2-1 in a third round tie.

With Celtic plagued by inconsistency, it was no longer a surprise when the outstanding Airdrie side boasting talents such as Hughie Gallacher and Bob McPhail, again laid down the most effective title challenge to Rangers in 1924-25. A 1-0 win over the champions at Broomfield in September helped Airdrie forge an early lead, but Rangers stormed back with a lengthy unbeaten run which included a 4-1 win over Celtic at Ibrox on New Year's Day.

Struth's men then hit a worrying spell, however, dropping eight points in seven matches, culminating in a 4-1 defeat against Hibs at Easter Road on 11 March. Rangers' season, in fact, was in danger of falling apart at this time as, 10 days later, Celtic hammered them 5-0 in the Scottish Cup semi-final at Hampden. It was an ignominious performance by the Ibrox players in front of the first six-figure attendance in Scottish football history, 101,714 fans thronging to Mount Florida for the occasion.

Rangers recovered well enough to ensure the title race went down to the wire. They held a one-point lead over Airdrie on the final day as Ayr United visited Ibrox. Billy McCandless scored the only goal of the match, Airdrie lost 1-0 at St Johnstone and Rangers were champions for the 14th time, by a three-point margin.

Lowest-ever Placing

They started 1925-26 as most people's favourites to win a fourth successive championship but, despite winning their first three matches, Rangers unexpectedly found themselves mired in one of the worst seasons in the club's history. They lost six of their next 10 games and by the time they drew 2-2 with Celtic at Parkhead on 1 January 1926, Rangers were well off the pace. Clearly not assisted by a lengthy injury list, which saw key men like Meiklejohn, Cairns, Cunningham, Archibald and Morton sidelined for significant periods, Rangers had nonetheless slipped badly below the standards set by Struth.

They eventually finished sixth in the table, a lowest ever placing, a humbling 14 points behind new champions Celtic. Not surprisingly, the Scottish Cup failed to lift the gloom as Rangers lost 1-0 to eventual winners St Mirren in the semi-final at Parkhead.

Followers of the club looking for positive aspects of the season could at least consider the signing of Jimmy Fleming from St Johnstone in October 1925. The forward scored 20 goals in 25 appearances, while 17-year-old James Marshall served notice of his potential with seven goals in four games. Dougie Gray, a 20-year-old spotted by Struth's scouting network in the North-east playing for Aberdeen Mugiemoss, was another new arrival who would enjoy a memorable career at Ibrox.

Willie Robb moved from Rangers to Hibs in July 1926.

Rangers also ended the season with a new first-choice goalkeeper in the shape of Tom Hamilton, an imposing keeper enlisted three years earlier from Kirkintilloch Rob Roy. He replaced Willie Robb, who moved to Hibs in July 1926, and like him would earn international recognition while at Ibrox.

It was, then, a Rangers side revitalised by youth but with a backbone of experience which set out to reclaim the championship in 1926-27. They discovered fresh challengers in their way in the shape of an emerging

Motherwell side who revealed themselves as a new major force in the league.

Defeats at St Johnstone and at home to Queen's Park blighted an otherwise solid start to the campaign for Rangers. Then a dreadful December saw them surrender the initiative totally as they dropped six points from the four games that month, including a 4-1 thumping at Hamilton.

Goals from Sandy Archibald and teenager Marshall stopped the rot in earning a 2-1 win when Celtic first-footed Ibrox, the first of six straight wins which put Rangers back on course. They lost just once more, 1-0 at Cowdenbeath in March, to hold off Motherwell's impressive challenge and eventually finish

Dougie Gray arrived at Ibrox in 1925 and stayed for 20 years.

five points clear of the Fir Park side. Jimmy Fleming, top scorer for the season with 21 goals, effectively clinched the title for Rangers with two games to spare when he notched the winner against Celtic at Parkhead on 18 April 1927.

Six Titles in Eight Seasons

A sixth championship success in eight seasons underlined Rangers position as the dominant force in Scottish football, but it could not totally ease the continuing frustration of their awful Scottish Cup record. The quarter-final was as far as they progressed this time, a Falkirk side inspired by former Celtic hero Patsy Gallacher winning 1-0 at Ibrox in a replay watched by a crowd of 80,000 on 9 March 1927.

Manager Struth, however, was assembling one of the finest teams in Rangers' history and to that end made another signing of huge significance in April 1927 when he brought Scotland international forward Bob McPhail to Ibrox from Airdrie. Two goals in a 4-1 win over Celtic in the semi-final of the Charity Cup at Parkhead at the end of the season was simply a foretaste of what was to come from McPhail, who would go on to become one of Rangers' greatest ever goalscorers.

In his first full season, he would also have a major role to play in arguably the most famous and celebrated victory in the club's history. Rangers, at last, were about to wake from their Scottish Cup nightmare.

Chapter Four: 1927-39
End of the Jinx

Bill Struth's team could hardly have sent out a clearer signal as they opened the 1927-28 campaign with a 10-match unbeaten league run. The only point dropped was in a 1-1 draw with championship contenders Motherwell at Fir Park. It proved to be a statement of intent in what would prove one of the most famous seasons in Rangers' history,

The Rangers line-up was missing some familiar faces, long serving club captain Tommy Cairns, at the age of 36, having moved to England to join Bradford City where, remarkably, he would extend his senior career for a further five seasons. Bert Manderson, another terrific Ibrox servant, joined him at Valley Parade. In Bob McPhail's first full season at the club, he gelled superbly in an exciting forward line alongside Sandy Archibald, Andy Cunningham, Jimmy Fleming and Alan Morton.

Their first league defeat was surprisingly suffered against strugglers Queen's Park at Hampden on 29 October. Rangers' response was to reel off a nine match unbeaten sequence, before they were edged out 1-0 by Celtic at Parkhead on 2 January 1928. Despite that defeat, Rangers still had a handy lead in the championship race and were not threatened again until an excellent Motherwell side won 2-0 at Ibrox in February.

Jock Buchanan, an experienced right half who had helped Morton defeat Rangers in the 1922 Scottish Cup final, had been added to the squad just before Christmas and he settled in quickly to help see the title defence through to a successful conclusion. One further defeat at Hibernian allowed Celtic and Motherwell to maintain their pursuit of the leaders into the closing weeks of the campaign but Rangers always had the edge, eventually clinching the title in style with a 5-1 win over Kilmarnock at Ibrox on 21 April. Fleming's hat-trick in that match gave him a tremendous strike rate of 37 goals from 40 appearances for the season.

The championship triumph, however, was almost of secondary importance to what Rangers had achieved at Hampden seven days earlier in front of a record crowd of 118,115. After an impressive run to reach the final, only Albion Rovers in the quarter-final tie causing any real concern, Rangers at last ended their Scottish Cup jinx.

Sandy Archibald (left) tracks Falkirk's Jock McIllwain in Rangers' 4-1 away win in November 1928. Rangers were midway through their 10-match winning run.

In the absence of injured captain Tommy Muirhead, Davie Meiklejohn played the role of a true leader when he stepped forward to convert the penalty kick to open the scoring for Rangers in the final against Celtic. A double from Archibald and one from McPhail saw the Ibrox side go on to record a famous 4-0 victory. Rangers had finally beaten the Scottish Cup jinx and when the title was clinched the following Saturday, it meant they had won the league and Scottish Cup double for the first time in their history.

'Wee Blue Devil'

It was a golden period for the club with several of their leading players at the peak of their powers, none more so than winger Morton who earned his nickname of the 'Wee Blue Devil' that very season when he inspired Scotland's 'Wembley Wizards' to their stunning 5-1 win over England.

Rangers moved almost seamlessly into season 1928-29 and turned the championship race into little more than a carefree romp. A free-scoring start, in which the remarkably prolific Jimmy Fleming scored no fewer than six hat-tricks by the middle of December, saw them win 16 of their first

Great Matches

SCOTTISH CUP FINAL   **Hampden Park, 14 April 1928**

Rangers 4   **Celtic 0**   **Attendance 118,115**
Meiklejohn (pen)
McPhail
Archibald 2

For a generation of Rangers supporters in the massive crowd which thronged to Hampden for the 50th Scottish Cup final, seeing their team lift the trophy was a brand new experience. On one of the greatest days in the club's history, a 25-year hoodoo was laid to rest in spectacular fashion. While Celtic came into the match as Cup holders, Rangers were out in front in the league title race and optimistic they would finally capture the famous old trophy once again.

Yet in a torrid first half for Bill Struth's side, they were grateful to goalkeeper Tom Hamilton for keeping them in the match. Hamilton was in inspired form and one save to deny Celtic right winger Connolly from point-blank range was breathtaking. Rangers were relieved to reach half-time with the scoreline still blank.

The second half could hardly have provided a starker contrast. Rangers suddenly moved up a gear and signalled their fresh intent when Andy Cunningham forced a brilliant save from Celtic's precocious young keeper John Thomson two minutes after the restart. With 55 minutes gone, one of the most famous moments in Rangers' history arrived. Alan Morton's cross from the left picked out Jimmy Fleming and his shot beat Thomson and appeared to clearly cross the line before being punched away by Celtic captain Willie McStay.

Referee Willis Bell, however, awarded a penalty kick. Rangers captain Davie Meiklejohn, outstanding in defence during Celtic's first-half dominance, stepped forward to take the onerous responsibility from the spot. Taking only a short run-up, Meiklejohn coolly drilled the ball wide of Thomson into the corner of the net.

Rangers would not be denied now and proceeded to stun Celtic with some magical football. After Cunningham struck the crossbar, Bob McPhail made it 2-0 from close range in 68 minutes after Thomson dropped a high ball. Two minutes later, Sandy Archibald made it three with a sweetly struck 25 yard shot and the right winger, so often a thorn in Celtic's flesh, produced another long range effort to complete the rout 10 minutes from time.

Rangers: T. Hamilton, Gray, R. Hamilton, Buchanan, Meiklejohn, Craig, Archibald, Cunningham, Fleming, McPhail, Morton

Celtic: J. Thomson, W. McStay, Donoghue, Wilson, J. McStay, McFarlane, Connolly, A. Thomson, McGrory, McInally, McLean

Referee: Willis Bell (Glasgow)

17 games. By the time they defeated Celtic 3-0 at Ibrox on New Year's Day, they were virtually out of sight of their nearest rivals.

That Old Firm victory was a special day all round for the club as the new Main Stand at Ibrox, which remains today as a listed building, was officially opened. There was also a touch of sadness in January 1929, however, when Andy Cunningham left Rangers after 14 hugely successful years to join Newcastle United in a £2,500 deal. He would eventually manage the English club.

But even without him, Rangers cruised to their third successive championship, suffering only one defeat all season when they went down 3-1 at Hamilton Accies. The title had been clinched as early as 16 March when James Marshall's goal earned a 1-1 draw against Falkirk at Ibrox, and put Rangers out of reach of both Celtic and Motherwell with fully eight games remaining.

Rangers finished a monumental 16 points clear at the top and their form led many to predict that the Cup would follow in another 'double' season. Indeed, their progress to the final was smooth enough, save for a nail-biting 3-2 win over St Mirren in the semi-final, and Rangers became clear favourites to defeat Kilmarnock in the showpiece fixture at Hampden on 6 April 1929.Killie, who had beaten Celtic 1-0 in the semi-finals, found themselves under siege in the opening stages. In the 15th minute the pressure told when keeper Sam Clemie fouled Jock Buchanan and conceded a penalty kick. Tully Craig volunteered to take the kick, but was defied by a spectacular Clemie save. The Killie goalkeeper was in simply inspired form and a series of fabulous saves kept the scoreline blank at half-time. Three minutes into the second half, the Rugby Park side stunned the Rangers' fans as John Aitken beat Tom Hamilton from close range. Then, in the 73rd minute, it became clear the Ibrox men were heading for a shock defeat when Jimmy Williamson made it 2-0 for Kilmarnock.

It was all too much for Jock Buchanan and he earned a piece of unwanted history when he became the first player sent off in a Scottish Cup final, receiving his marching orders two minutes from time for arguing with the referee.

The defeat was especially disappointing for Rangers' captain Tommy Muirhead. Having missed the previous year's final because of injury, his ambition to play in a Scottish Cup-winning side remained unfulfilled. Season 1929-30 would be the last one at Ibrox for Muirhead who had proved more than worth the £20 fee paid to Hibs for his transfer back in 1917. Sadly for him, he played only slightly more than a marginal role in what was another memorable campaign for Rangers.

Although George Brown, an intelligent left half from Ashfield, was added to the squad, Rangers failed to match the staggering consistency of the previous season and dropped five points in their first 10 matches. Still, a 1-0 win over Celtic at Ibrox in October gave them the edge in the title race, and they went on to record a telling 11 consecutive victories from December to February. That sequence included a 2-1 win at Parkhead; Rangers' first New Year's Day triumph on Celtic's ground for 28 years.

Club captain Muirhead at least had the pleasure of scoring one of the goals in the 3-0 win over Clyde at Ibrox on 29 March 1930 which saw Rangers

50 Greatest Players

ANDY CUNNINGHAM Inside forward

Joined Rangers: April 1915   **From:** Kilmarnock

Debut: v Partick Thistle, League, 5 April 1915

Appearances: 389   **Goals:** 182

Left Rangers: January 1929   **For:** Newcastle United

Honours won with Rangers: 7 league championships,
1 Scottish Cup, 12 caps (Scotland)

In his third appearance for Rangers, their final League fixture of the 1914-1915 season, Andy Cunningham scored twice in a 4-0 win over Queen's Park at Hampden. It was the first hint of the talent of the most successful and effective inside forwards to play for the club.

Cunningham, a native of Ayrshire, began his career with local team Newmilns before turning professional with Kilmarnock. In his first full season with Rangers he scored 18 goals in 20 appearances, but was absent for the next two years as he served in the First World War. He returned to reclaim his place in 1918-19 and never looked back.

A fair-haired, intelligent footballer who created as many goals as he scored, Cunningham went on to win seven League championship medals. Twice a losing Scottish Cup finalist, perhaps the most satisfying moment of his Rangers career came when he was part of the side which defeated Celtic 4-0 in the 1928 final at Hampden. He earned 12 caps for Scotland, his five goals for his country including one in the 3-0 win over England at Hampden in 1921.

Remarkably, Cunningham extended his career into English football at the age of 38 when he joined Newcastle United in a £2,500 move in January 1929. He later managed Newcastle and Dundee before becoming a sportswriter. Cunningham died in 1973 at the age of 82.

The Grand Slam team in May 1930. From left. Back row: McDonald, Marshall, McPhail, Dawson, Simpson, Hamilton, Fleming, Smith, Archibald. Front row: Manager B. Struth, Main, Gray, Meiklejohn, Brown, Nicholson, Craig, Coach A. Dixon. In foreground: the Glasgow Cup, Scottish Cup, Charity Cup.

clinch a fourth successive title with five games to spare, eventually finishing five points clear of runners-up Motherwell.

Muirhead, though, played no part in Rangers' successful Scottish Cup campaign. The tournament, still more prestigious than the league championship, saw Struth's side require a replay to oust Cowdenbeath in the second round, but thereafter they made comfortable progress and thumped Hearts 4-1 in the semi-final at Hampden.

Spectacular Winner

Partick Thistle were their opponents when they returned to Mount Florida for the final on 12 April 1930 and a crowd of 107,457 saw two well-matched sides – Rangers had won both league games that season by the odd goal – battle out a tense but absorbing goalless draw. The replay four days later, watched by another six-figure attendance, was just as closely fought.

Despite being reduced to 10 men after 15 minutes when Alan Morton was injured, Rangers took the lead through James Marshall only for Torbet to level. A second replay looked likely until Tully Craig scored one of the great Scottish Cup goals, lobbing in a spectacular winner with just five minutes left.

Rangers had done the double for the second time in three seasons and with the Glasgow and Charity Cups also added to the Ibrox trophy room, this vintage crop of players became known as the 'Grand Slam Team'.

50 Greatest Players

ALAN MORTON Winger

Joined Rangers: June 1920   **From:** Queen's Park

Debut: v Airdrie, League, 17 August 1920

Appearances: 440   **Goals:** 105

Left Rangers: May 1933 (retired)

Honours won with Rangers: 9 league championships;
3 Scottish Cups; 29 caps (Scotland)

The fleet-footed and diminutive outside left was, in the
modern parlance, a player who put 'bums on seats'.
Destined to be one of the greatest Scottish international
footballers of all time, Alan Morton had already been
capped twice by his country when he moved to Ibrox
from Queen's Park in the summer of 1920. Possessed
of terrific dribbling skills in the great Scottish tradition
of the time, he tortured full backs with his seemingly endless range of flicks, shimmies
and dummies. He was so much more than just a showman, however, and more often
than not there was a devastating end product to his play.

Far stronger than his 5ft 4in frame suggested, the Partick-born player was never
intimidated by his larger opponents. Wearing boots with only three studs on them to aid
his balance, Morton won nine league championship medals and three Scottish Cup
winner's medals during his 13-year career with Rangers. He won 31 caps for Scotland,
a staggering tally for that time. His most famous performance came in 1928 when he
inspired the 'Wembley Wizards' 5-1 win over England, earning him the nickname of the
'Wee Blue Devil'.

Morton was a part-time player throughout his career, retaining his trade as a mining
engineer. He retired at the end of the 1932-33 season, becoming a director at Ibrox.
He remained on the club's board until his death in 1971 at the age of 78.

The success continued in 1930-31 but this time Rangers didn't have such
an easy ride in the championship. They dropped seven points in their first 11
games, including a 2-0 defeat at Parkhead, and it was Celtic who set the early
pace with the ever more impressive Motherwell making it a thrilling three
horse race.

A new regular in the Rangers attack this season was Jimmy Smith, a
bustling 19-year-old centre forward who had been signed from East Stirling
two years earlier and who was showing immense promise. Smith scored 21
goals in as many appearances, a tally which included five in an 8-0 defeat of

From left. Rangers' Robert Main, Jerry Dawson, Jimmy Simpson and Sandy Archibald pose for a picture during training in August 1932.

Clyde at Shawfield in February 1931. That rout actually came during a worrying spell of form for Rangers, which saw them drop six points in five games, but they recovered to produce a run of nine consecutive wins which saw the title race go to their final game of the season. Protecting a three-point lead over Celtic, who had a game in hand, Rangers ensured they could not be caught when goals from McPhail, Smith, Marshall and Archibald claimed a 4-0 win over East Fife at Bayview Park on 25 April 1931. With Celtic drawing their game in hand three days later, the final winning margin was two points and Rangers had won a club record, fifth consecutive championship.

Hopes of another double had been washed away in farcical conditions, adapted to better by Dundee, when Rangers lost 2-1 to the Dark Blues in the second round of the Scottish Cup at a sodden Ibrox.

Rangers went into 1931-32 seeking to emulate Celtic's record achievement of six consecutive title wins and Struth added one significant fresh face to his squad, that of 21-year-old Irish centre forward Sam English. The Coleraine-born player had scored an extraordinary 293 goals in just three seasons with Glasgow junior side Yoker Athletic to attract Struth's attention. He scored twice on his debut as the league campaign opened with a 4-1 win over Dundee at Ibrox and went on to notch a remarkable 53 goals in 42 appearances. His tally of 44 League goals is a Rangers record to this day but, tragically, English's debut season with the club is remembered for his desperately unfortunate part in the tragic death of Celtic and Scotland goalkeeper John Thomson at the age of 23.

Old Firm Tragedy

Celtic visited Ibrox on 5 September 1931 for a typically tense Old Firm fixture watched by a crowd of 80,000. At the start of the second half, Thomson, a marvellously agile and incredibly brave keeper, dived at English's feet as the striker raced onto a Jimmy Fleming pass. In the collision which followed, Thomson suffered a depressed fracture of the skull. He was taken to hospital but died later that night. It was a tragedy which touched the whole of Scottish football and the entire Rangers staff attended Thomson's funeral in Fife. Although completely exonerated by the enquiry into the incident, English never fully recovered from the trauma of Thomson's death. He later described his football career after the incident as 'seven years of joyless sport'.

The Thomson tragedy shrouded everything else in Scottish football that season, a campaign which saw both Rangers and Celtic eclipsed by an increasingly effective Motherwell side who won the championship for the only time in their history. They had signalled their intent by beating Rangers 4-2 at Fir Park in the third game of the season and when the Ibrox men suffered a shock home defeat at the hands of Queen's Park in October, they found themselves playing catch-up. Rangers' fate was sealed with defeats at both Third Lanark and Airdrie in the closing weeks of the season and Motherwell were deserving champions as they finished five points clear of Struth's squad.

The Rangers fans were compensated for the loss of the title when the Scottish Cup was won for the seventh time. A barrage of 21 goals had been scored in dismissing Brechin City, Raith Rovers,

Although cleared of any blame, Sam English never recoverd from the tragic incident at Ibrox on 5 September 1931.

50 Greatest Players

SANDY ARCHIBALD Winger

Joined Rangers: May 1917   **From:** Raith Rovers

Debut: v Kilmarnock, league, 18 August 1917

Appearances: 580   **Goals:** 148

Left Rangers: November 1934 **For:** Raith Rovers

Honours won with Rangers: 13 league championships, 3 Scottish Cups,

8 caps (Scotland)

Willie Maley, the legendary Celtic manager of the time, once said of Sandy Archibald: 'So long as he is on the pitch, we can never be sure of victory over Rangers, no matter the score.' His outstanding performances were not just reserved for Old Firm games. Over an incredible span of 17 years, outside right Archibald proved himself a truly great Rangers player.

The Fifer joined the club from Raith Rovers as a 19-year-old and in his first full season with the club earned a league championship medal. Amazingly, Archibald went on to play a part in 12 more title-winning sides for Rangers, although some records rather cruelly deprive him of credit for the 1933-34 success, when he made a significant 15 appearances in what was his last season for the club.

There was Scottish Cup glory too, for the powerful and athletic ex-miner from Aberdour. Most notably, he scored twice in the famous 4-0 win over Celtic in the 1928 final. He went on to collect two further winner's medals in the competition.

Archibald made eight appearances for Scotland between 1921 and 1932, his international honours restricted by being in direct competition for a place with the brilliant Huddersfield Town outside right Alex Jackson for much of that time. On leaving Rangers after hanging up his boots, Archibald returned to Fife to manage both Raith Rovers and Dunfermline Athletic before his untimely death at the age of 49 in 1946.

Hearts, Motherwell and Hamilton Accies to reach the final against Kilmarnock at Hampden on 16 April 1932. The underdogs went in front, but Bob McPhail's second-half goal earned Rangers a replay four days later. It was a far more one-sided affair, goals from Fleming, McPhail and English giving Rangers a stylish 3-0 win.

A 2-0 defeat at home to St Mirren on the opening day of the 1932-33 season was hardly a promising sign for Rangers but they recovered to win eight and draw three of their next 11 matches and engage champions Motherwell in another tremendous battle for the title. It was also a season that saw Alan Morton make his final appearance for Rangers, scoring in the 5-1 win over Airdrie at Ibrox on 7 January 1933. The peerless outside left formally retired at the end of the season, after 13 years of outstanding service, and became a Rangers director.

The pivotal result in the championship race came in February when two goals from Jimmy Fleming and a Jimmy Smith penalty gave Rangers a 3-1 win over Motherwell at Fir Park and a clear advantage. The Ibrox side's tremendous consistency, winning 11 and drawing two of their last 13 games, was just too much for their Lanarkshire rivals and the title came back to Ibrox by a three-point margin. The Scottish Cup, however, saw Kilmarnock gain revenge for their final defeat the previous year when they knocked Rangers out with the only goal of a third round tie at Rugby Park.

By the end of the season, Jerry Dawson had established himself as Rangers' new first choice keeper. The 23-year-old, who had been signed from Camelon Juniors three years earlier, had already proved himself as an able deputy to the excellent Tom Hamilton and had now overtaken the older man in the pecking order.

The haunted Sam English, desperate to escape the cruel taunts that still came his way at several grounds in the wake of the John Thomson tragedy, was sold to Liverpool for £8,000 at the start of the 1933-34 season. He would eventually retire from football, his spirit broken, at the age of just 28.

Jimmy Smith, top scorer the previous campaign with 35 goals from 39 appearances, set himself up for another prolific season when he scored four and six times respectively in the 5-1 and 9-1 defeats of Airdrie and Ayr United as Rangers made a powerful start to their defence of the title.

Bob McPhail in action in September 1935.

Jimmy Simpson heads clear from Celtic's John Crum in the Old Firm league fixture at Ibrox in September 1935, a match which Celtic won 2-1.

It would be no cruise to the championship, however, for a Rangers side which further bolstered their attacking options with the signing of Alec Venters from Cowdenbeath in November 1933. Motherwell were desperate to reclaim the title and carved out an early lead over Rangers courtesy of a 2-1 win when the teams met at Fir Park in September. Even though Rangers won 14 of their next 16 games, they found themselves matched by opponents displaying a similar level of consistency. It was a compelling two-horse race, with Celtic a distant third.

Motherwell eventually cracked, and when Rangers defeated Falkirk 3-1 at Brockville on 25 April 1934, they were champions again with two games to spare, eventually finishing four points clear of the Lanarkshire side. It was a glorious season all round for Rangers who were recognised as the best of British when they defeated English champions Arsenal 5-1 on aggregate in what was billed as the 'British Championship'.

The Scottish Cup campaign was also successful, both starting and ending with a rout. The 14-2 hammering of non-league Blairgowrie in the first round, with Jimmy Fleming scoring a record nine times, equalled the scoreline recorded against Whitehill 50 years earlier. Hearts, Aberdeen and St Johnstone all put up far stiffer resistance in subsequent rounds, but in the final at Hampden on 21 April 1934, St Mirren found Rangers in unstoppable form. Billy Nicholson, who had the daunting task of taking over Alan Morton's No. 11 jersey, scored twice in a 5-0 win with the other goals coming from Bob McPhail, Bobby Main and Jimmy Smith, the latter claiming 46 goals in 38 appearances that season.

James Marshall, known as 'Doc' because of his medical qualifications, left Rangers after nine successful years that summer to join Arsenal, but the strength of the Ibrox squad was such that this period of dominating Scottish football was not about to end.

50 Greatest Players

DAVIE MEIKLEJOHN Defender

Joined Rangers: September 1919   **From:** Maryhill Juniors

Debut: v Aberdeen, League, 20 March 1920

Appearances: 563   **Goals:** 46

Left Rangers: May 1936 (retired)

Honours won with Rangers: 12 league championships, 5 Scottish Cups, 15 caps (Scotland)

Rangers have had many inspiring captains throughout their history and Davie Meiklejohn may just have been the greatest of them all. Born in Govan, 'Meek' was also born to lead Rangers.

An imposing figure at either right half or centre half, Meiklejohn was a cultured footballer with an advanced perception of how the game should be played. Signed from Maryhill Juniors as a teenager, he made 10 appearances at the end of the 1919-20 title-winning season and was virtually established as a first-teamer from then onwards.

Meiklejohn went on to play in 12 more league championship teams and added five Scottish Cup winner's medals for good measure. Perhaps his seminal moment in a Rangers jersey came in the 1928 final when, assuming responsibility as captain, he stepped forward to convert the penalty kick which sent the Ibrox men on their way to a 4-0 win over Celtic and the club's first Scottish Cup triumph for 25 years.

Naturally, Meiklejohn found himself captaining his country, one highlight of his 15 caps coming in 1931 when he led Scotland to a memorable 2-0 win over England at Hampden. Meiklejohn retired at the end of the 1935-36 season, initially becoming a newspaper columnist and then returning to football as manager of Partick Thistle. He died in 1959 at the age of 59.

The Double – Again

Season 1934-35 saw Torry Gillick, signed from Petershill a year earlier, begin to emerge as the outstanding and hugely popular performer he would become. Dunfermline were swatted 7-1 at East End Park on the opening day, the incredible Smith scoring six of them, and there were narrow wins over potential title rivals Motherwell and Hearts in the next two fixtures.

Rangers opened an early lead but dropped six points in six games during December to offer hope to the chasing pack. Celtic were discouraged when they lost 2-1 at Ibrox on New Year's Day and despite losing to Partick Thistle the next day, Rangers then won eight in a row to emerge as clear favourites.

The title was clinched on 13 April 1935 with a 3-1 win over Aberdeen at Pittodrie, with three games to spare. Celtic finished in the top two for the first time in four seasons, three points behind.

Rangers emerged from a testing Scottish Cup campaign to win the double for the second successive season. Third Lanark, St Mirren and Motherwell were beaten before a replay was needed to edge past Hearts in an epic semi-final watched by a combined attendance of over 193,000 at Hampden.

Hamilton Accies, who finished fourth in the championship, were Rangers' final opponents at Hampden on 20 April 1935. The Douglas Park side produced an admirable display, their young goalkeeper Morgan saving a Bob McPhail penalty, but eventually succumbed 2-1. Rangers were yet again indebted to Jimmy Smith who scored both goals and finished the season with a tally of 44 from 37 appearances.

When Smith scored 14 goals in the first eight League games of 1935-36, earning Rangers six wins and a draw, the Ibrox men appeared on course to win a fourth consecutive championship. Celtic, however, were enjoying something of a revival and won 2-1 at Ibrox in the next match to open up a lead.

By November, the Parkhead men were five points clear and Rangers did not appear to be helped by the sale of Torry Gillick to Everton for £8,000 the following month. However, Struth's men did hit back with a thrilling 4-3 win over Celtic – McPhail and Smith both claiming doubles – on New Year's Day 1936. They eventually drew level with Celtic but blew their title chances when they lost 1-0 at Hamilton on 11 April. Celtic eventually finished five points clear and won their first title since 1926.

For Rangers, the Scottish Cup which tormented them for so long had become a close friend and the pain of losing the title was eased when, for the first time in their history, they lifted the famous old trophy for a third successive year.

Mid-table Third Lanark were their surprise opponents in the final at Hampden on 18 April 1936 and Bob McPhail scored the only goal of a largely undistinguished match after only 90 seconds. It was a poignant day for Davie Meiklejohn as one of Rangers' greatest captains lifted his last trophy for the club before retiring at the end of the season.

Rude Shock

The championship was reclaimed in some style in 1936-37, a season which saw the debut of 16-year-old Willie Thornton. The young striker from Winchburgh in West Lothian would become one of the finest goalscorers in Rangers' history.

Unbeaten in their opening 17 matches, Rangers suffered something of a rude shock at Tynecastle in December when they were hammered 5-2 by a Hearts side who the following month completed a double over the league leaders with a 1-0 win at Ibrox. However, they were the only two defeats Rangers would suffer until they went down 3-2 at Clyde on the final day of the season. By then, their 23rd championship had already been sewn up and they finished seven points clear of runners-up Aberdeen, a new force in Scottish football.

If Rangers were worthy champions, it was also a season when they endured one of their most embarrassing results. On 30 January 1937, hopes of a fourth consecutive Scottish Cup triumph were high when they were drawn against Queen of the South at Palmerston Park. Such hopes were dashed in dramatic fashion as the unfancied Doonhamers edged a 1-0 victory. The Dumfries side, who would be knocked out of the tournament themselves by Second Division Morton, finished the season third bottom of the First Division. It would stand for 30 years as the biggest shock result in Rangers' history.

When Rangers were unbeaten in their first 16 matches of 1937-38, there was no reason for the club's supporters to expect anything less than the retention of the title. Alarm bells sounded, however, when the team lost 3-0 to Celtic at Parkhead in the Ne'erday fixture and then 3-1 to Partick Thistle at Ibrox two days later. It was the start of a catastrophic spell which saw Rangers win just once in eight games, including a stunning 6-1 defeat at Dundee.

Rangers eventually finished third in the table, a distant 12 points behind champions Celtic and nine adrift of runners-up Hearts. There was no solace to be found in the Scottish Cup where the Ibrox men found themselves on the wrong side of a 4-3 scoreline in a thrilling semi-final against Kilmarnock at Hampden.

Manager Struth sensed the need to strengthen his squad and two significant fresh faces were added at the start of the 1938-39 season. Jock Shaw, a tenacious 25-year-old full back, was signed from Airdrie for £2,000 and would become one of Rangers' most popular and effective captains. The other new recruit, wing half Scot Symon from Portsmouth, was to make his name at the club as both player and manager.

Both made solid contributions as Rangers reclaimed the title, a prospect which had seemed fanciful in the extreme when the team were crushed 6-2 by reigning champs Celtic at Parkhead in September. Displaying admirable resilience, Rangers recovered to produce a run of 12 wins from 13 games between 29 October and 11 January which included a 2-1 success against Celtic at Ibrox on 2 January.

Adding great excitement to Rangers' performances was a 17-year-old right winger called Willie Waddell, who had made a dramatic entrance to the first team picture at the start of the season when he scored the only goal of a friendly against Arsenal at Ibrox watched by 41,000. Few could have predicted the massive influence the teenager would have on Rangers' history in years to come. He amassed 29 first team appearances that season, chipping in with seven goals, as Rangers won the championship by an 11-point margin from runners-up Celtic. It made up for an abject exit from the Scottish Cup at the third round stage, Rangers losing 4-1 to Clyde at Ibrox. That the Shawfield club went on to win the trophy was of scant consolation.

Nonetheless, Rangers approached the end of the 1930s as unquestionably the leading light in Scottish football. Sadly, the game was about to be cast into insignificance by the dark shadows gathering over Europe.

Chapter Five: 1939-54
The Iron Age

On 2 September 1939, a crowd of 30,000 at Cathkin Park saw Rangers defeat Third Lanark 2-1, the Ibrox men making it nine points out of 10 from their first five league fixtures of the season as they sought to retain their title. Just 24 hours later, all thoughts of football glory were tossed into the periphery of people's lives when Britain declared war on Germany.

The suspension of football on 6 September was an understandable reaction by the SFA as the country got its priorities in order. The hiatus lasted less than three weeks, the authorities soon recognizing the value of sport as a welcome diversion to the grim events unfolding across the globe.

The duration of the war meant seven seasons of unofficial, if not uncompetitive, football. After playing a couple of friendly matches, Rangers returned to semi-meaningful action when two regional leagues, divided on a west-south and north-east basis, began at the end of October.

Rangers won their first nine fixtures, setting up a platform to win the competition with a degree of comfort. Public interest was confirmed by an attendance of 40,000 at Ibrox on New Year's Day 1940 for the 1-1 draw with Celtic. If the austerity of the time lent a surreal air to proceedings, Rangers nonetheless pleased their supporters when they defeated Falkirk, winners of the North-east league, 2-1 with goals from Alec Venters and Adam Little in a championship play-off at Ibrox on 1 June.

It completed a 'double' of sorts, a remarkable crowd of 90,000 having converged at Hampden the previous month to see Jimmy Smith score the only goal of the match as Rangers edged out Dundee United in the final of the Scottish Emergency War Cup.

Football, of course, took a distant second place to the war effort and Rangers' players, like those of all other clubs, found themselves either working in the Clydeside shipyards and munitions factories or on active service. First team luminaries such as Willie Thornton, who earned the Military Medal for his part in the Italian campaign, Davie Kinnear, Eddie Rutherford and Willie Paton all did their bit on foreign fields along with several lesser-known reserve team players.

Jock Shaw, seen here in action in December 1940, was a stalwart of Rangers' wartime team.

Inevitably, team line-ups were wildly unpredictable from one week to the next and most clubs looked to recruit guest players on occasion to stimulate interest among the supporters. Among those who turned out for Rangers during the Second World War was the legendary England winger Stanley Matthews. He wore the No. 7 jersey twice for the club, in a 1-0 regional league win over Morton which drew 20,000 to Ibrox on 30 March 1940 and then in the 3-0 Charity Cup final win against Partick Thistle at Hampden on 31 May 1941.

That 1940-41 season had seen the leagues split on a more practical and economic north and south basis. With the Scottish Cup suspended for the duration of the war, a new competition, the Southern League Cup, was introduced, while the Summer Cup was added to fill out the close season.

Southern League Champions

Jimmy Smith's 24 goals in 19 appearances helped Rangers win the initial Southern League, while Hearts were beaten 4-2 in a replay after a 1-1 draw in the final of the Southern League Cup. The two matches at Hampden drew a combined attendance of 145,000. Rangers also reached the Summer Cup final where they were beaten 3-2 by Hibs.

The Southern League Cup also remained at Ibrox, Torry Gillick scoring the only goal of the Hampden final against Morton, and Rangers added the Summer Cup to their collection, albeit only on the toss of a coin after 120 minutes had failed to produce a goal in the final against Hibs on 4 July 1942.

Among the exciting young players to emerge at Ibrox during the Second World War was Jimmy Duncanson, a direct and dynamic inside forward who helped fill the void left by the retirement of Bob McPhail. Duncanson was an impressive contributor in 1942-43 as the Southern League was again won. One of his 14 league goals came in an extraordinary Old Firm fixture on

50 Greatest Players

BOB McPHAIL Inside forward

Joined Rangers: April 1927   **From:** Airdrie

Debut: v Aberdeen, League, 13 August 1927

Appearances: 408   **Goals:** 261

Left Rangers: January 1941 (retired)

Honours won with Rangers: 9 league championships, 6 Scottish Cups,

16 caps (Scotland)

The six Scottish Cup winner's medals Bob McPhail won as a Rangers player form one of the prize exhibits in the Ibrox trophy room. Even before he joined the club in 1927, the precocious inside forward had tasted success in the tournament, having played in Airdrie's 1924 Cup final win over Hibernian when he was just 18.

Rangers paid £5,000 for McPhail's services, a considerable fee, but one which proved tremendous value for money. A powerful player with an admirable work ethic, the Barrhead-born McPhail had an almost unerring eye for goal. It brought him 230 league goals for Rangers, a club record which stood until broken by Ally McCoist some 50 years later.

McPhail's prolific strike rate, and his fine left wing partnerships with Alan Morton and then Davie Kinnear, helped him win nine league championship medals for Rangers before the war effectively brought his career to an end. He played for Scotland on 17 occasions, scoring seven goals, two of them coming in the 3-1 win over England at Hampden in 1937. He officially retired in 1941, although did make a handful of wartime appearances for St Mirren before returning to Rangers as reserve team trainer.

New Year's Day. Even allowing for Celtic's poor form that season – they would eventually finish 10th in the table – it was a memorable afternoon for the Rangers supporters in the 30,000 crowd at Ibrox as Bill Struth's side romped to an 8-1 victory. Torry Gillick claimed a hat-trick, Willie Waddell and George Young each scored twice with Duncanson completing the rout.

The Southern League Cup was also lifted again, this time on a corner kick countback after a 1-1 draw with Falkirk at Hampden, but the Summer Cup was lost to St Mirren who won by the only goal of the final on 10 July 1943.

The Summer Cup was dropped from the schedule for 1943-44, one which saw the Southern League title comfortably retained by a Rangers side who won 17 of their first 20 fixtures. Top scorer was Willie McIntosh, a guest player from St Johnstone, who claimed an impressive tally of 30 goals in 25 appearances. Rangers reached the Southern League Cup final again but the trophy had new name engraved upon it, Hibernian winning on a

50 Greatest Players

JERRY DAWSON Goalkeeper

Joined Rangers: November 1929   **From:** Camelon Juniors

Debut: v St Mirren, League, 24 January 1931

Appearances: 271

Left Rangers: May 1946   **For:** Falkirk

Honours won with Rangers: 5 league championships;
3 Scottish Cups; 14 caps (Scotland)

Signed as understudy to Tom Hamilton, Jerry Dawson was 20
when he was recruited from Camelon Juniors. The Falkirk-born
custodian had to be patient, but in the 1932-33 season, he made
the number one position his own and went on to be regarded as
one of the club's greatest keepers of all time.

Dawson, real name James, was given the moniker Jerry by his team-mates who likened
him to the brilliant Burnley and England goalkeeper Jeremiah Dawson. In time, the
Rangers' Dawson would prove every bit as good, if not better. He was blessed with stunning
reflexes but his greatest gift was in minimizing the need to use them, thanks to an unerring
positional sense which allowed him to make the most difficult saves appear run of the mill.

Five league championships and two Scottish Cup winners' medals were the Dawson haul
from his Ibrox career which continued through the Second World War when he also helped
Rangers dominate the various wartime competitions. Dawson was capped on 14 occasions
by Scotland, labelled 'Prince of Goalkeepers' by the press, and appeared for his country a
further nine times during the Second World War. He left Rangers in the summer of 1946
and played for another three years for Falkirk. Later, he became manager of East Fife.
Dawson died in 1977 at the age of 67.

corner kick count after a goalless draw in front of 63,000 at Hampden on
20 May 1944.

Old Firm fixtures retained huge popularity during these troubled times. In
season 1944-45, a combined attendance of almost 230,000 watched the four
games played between Rangers and Celtic. Although Rangers lost 1-0 at
Ibrox on New Year's Day, they had the upper hand in the three other
fixtures, winning 4-0 at Parkhead in the reverse league game and 3-2 and
2-1 respectively in the Hampden finals of the Glasgow and Charity Cups.

In winning their last nine fixtures, Rangers ensured the Southern League
title was captured again and they also reclaimed the Southern League Cup,
goals from Torry Gillick and Alec Venters defeating Motherwell 2-1 in the
final at Hampden on 12 May 1945.

The Allies' hard won victory in Europe meant 1945-46 would be the last of the Second World War seasons and there was understandably an air of celebration as supporters flocked to football grounds in even greater numbers. Although Germany and Italy had already surrendered when the new campaign got underway, the continuation of the war in the Pacific prompted the football authorities to proceed on an unofficial basis, although the clubs were re-organized into a Division A and B of the Scottish League. As it turned out, Japan surrendered just a few weeks into the season.

Rangers shrugged off the loss of two of their first three games to win Division A by eight points from the emerging Hibs side. Rangers had won all seven of the unofficial championships during the wartime period.

50 Greatest Players

JIMMY SMITH Centre forward

Joined Rangers: August 1928 **From:** East Stirling

Debut: v Hamilton Accies, League, 27 March 1929

Appearances: 259   **Goals:** 249

Left Rangers: May 1946 (retired)

Honours won with Rangers: 5 league championships;
3 Scottish Cups; 2 caps (Scotland)

It was on the club's close season North American tour in 1929 that Jimmy Smith first served notice of the incredibly prolific contribution he would make to Rangers' history. The young centre forward netted 18 goals in seven matches against Canadian and US opponents to stake his claim for a regular first team place.

Season 1929-30 duly saw Smith become a first choice No. 9 for manager Bill Struth and he responded by scoring 21 goals in as many appearances as Rangers won the league championship. Not, perhaps, the most cultured player ever to wear the light blue jersey, Smith could certainly lay claim to be one of the most effective. A typical battering-ram type centre forward of the era, he used his terrific physical presence to plough his way through opposition defenders. Complemented by more gifted forwards such as McPhail and Gillick, Smith was every bit as crucial to Rangers' success. He also earned three Scottish Cup winner's medals, scoring both goals in the 1935 final against Hamilton Accies. Capped twice by Scotland – scoring against Ireland in 1937 – he continued his scoring exploits for Rangers throughout the Second World War before retiring in 1946. Smith remained at Ibrox as first team trainer, then as a scout until 1967.

The Russians are coming! Dinamo Moscow's keeper, Alexei 'Tiger' Khomich, punches the ball clear in the 1945 friendly at Ibrox. The match ended in a 2-2 draw.

They were unable to add to their four Southern League Cup successes, Aberdeen defeating them 3-2 in a memorable final at Hampden on 11 May 1946, watched by a staggering attendance of 135,000. Rangers, though, did end the last unofficial season on a high as they won the Victory Cup, a celebratory tournament which preceded the return of the Scottish Cup. Having defeated Celtic in a semi-final replay, Rangers collected the trophy at Hampden with a 3-1 win over Hibs. Jimmy Duncanson scored twice with Torry Gillick also on target in front of a 100,000 crowd. But perhaps the most notable match of that season occured on 28 November 1945 when, as part of a British tour, Dinamo Moscow visited Ibrox. The Russians, unbeaten against Cardiff, Chelsea and Arsenal, arrived in Glasgow shrouded in an air of mystery which captured the imagination of the supporters. A crowd of 95,000, by some distance the biggest at Ibrox that season, gathered to witness a match which earned an enduring place in the Rangers story. After trailing 2-0, goals from Jimmy Smith, in what would be his last season before retirement, and George Young earned the home side a 2-2 draw.

For men like Smith, goalkeeper Dawson and full back Gray, the war coincided with the end of their Rangers careers. As season 1946-47 dawned, a new-look Ibrox side would dominate the immediate post-war era just as their predecessors had reigned supreme in the era leading up to the hostilities.

The basis of this latest success was built on a defence which, in recognition of the momentous events later to occur in Berlin and beyond, became known as the Iron Curtain. Bobby Brown, a worthy successor to Dawson in goal, had been signed from Queen's Park and proved an outstanding last line in a back division whose names still trip easily off the tongues of Rangers supporters of an older vintage. In full backs George Young and Jock Shaw, wing halves Ian McColl and Sammy Cox and the peerless centre half Willie Woodburn, manager Struth had assembled a defence which many argue was the finest in Scottish football history.

Against an equally famous ensemble, the Famous Five forward line which ensured Hibs were Rangers' most powerful challengers during this period, they had to be good. Of course, Rangers were also endowed with highly effective attacking options of their own in the shape of men such as Willie Waddell, Willie Thornton, Torry Gillick and Jimmy Duncanson.

50 Greatest Players

DOUGIE GRAY Right back

Joined Rangers: June 1925   **From:** Aberdeen Mugiemoss

Debut: v Kilmarnock, League, 3 October 1925

Appearances: 555   **Goals:** 2

Left Rangers: April 1947 (retired)

Honours won with Rangers: 10 league championships; 6 Scottish Cups;
10 caps (Scotland)

Dougie Gray made his final appearance for Rangers on 1 December 1945 in a 3-2 Southern League victory over Hibernian at Ibrox. It was 20 years and two months since his debut for the club, an astonishing example of longevity almost beyond compare in Scottish football. Born in Alford, Aberdeenshire, the powerful full back was signed from his local junior side in the summer of 1925. He made 25 first team appearances in his debut season, announcing himself as a worthy successor to the excellent Bert Manderson as Rangers' right back.

Gray was reliability personified, an incisive tackler who read the game brilliantly and was very seldom bettered by opposition wingers. He won 10 league championships with Rangers and played in six Scottish Cup winning sides. The Second World War saw him earn a further six unofficial championship medals as he clocked up a tally of 940 appearances for the club in all matches, a record no player is ever likely to eclipse. He was capped 10 times by Scotland, his last appearance coming against Wales in 1932. Gray officially retired at the end of the 1946-47 season, 18 months after his final senior appearance for Rangers.

The acrobatic Bobby Brown was the last line of Rangers' defence for almost 10 years.

Hibs laid down their challenge firmly at the start of the 1946-47 season, winning 2-1 at Ibrox in the second league fixture. Rangers responded by winning 12 of their next 14 games to gain an edge on the Edinburgh side. It was tight at the top all the way but Rangers clinched the title with a 4-1 win over Hamilton Accies at Ibrox in their final match on 12 April, Hibs finishing just two points behind them.

The Easter Road men gained revenge in the Scottish Cup, knocking Rangers out in the second round with a 2-0 replay victory after a goalless draw at Ibrox watched by a crowd of 95,000.

Matches between Rangers and Hibs were massive attractions, as witnessed by the 125,154 inside Hampden to see the Ibrox men win a League Cup semi-final 3-1. In the inaugural final of the tournament, a follow-on from the wartime Southern League Cup, Rangers swept Aberdeen aside 4-0 at Hampden on 5 April 1947.

Powerbroker Struth

While his players enjoyed more success on the pitch, manager Struth also increased his power base behind the scenes at the club when former player Jimmy Bowie, who had suggested the 71-year-old may wish to consider retirement, was deposed as chairman for his troubles. John Wilson, a Glasgow councillor and Struth's favoured candidate, became the new chairman.

Maintaining dominance on the field would be a more arduous task for the manager as Hibs illustrated in 1947-48 by winning the league title for the first time since 1903 and only the second time in their history. Rangers had looked a safe bet to retain the championship when they won 17 of their first 19 games but a 1-0 defeat at Easter Road on 31 January derailed them.

They won just two of their next seven games and a 2-1 defeat at home to Hearts in the final league match saw Hibs finish two points clear. The League Cup was also lost, Falkirk producing a shock 1-0 win over Rangers in the semi-final, but the Ibrox boys wouldn't end the season empty-handed.

Willie Thornton scored the only goal of a classic Scottish Cup semi-final against Hibs in front of an amazing 143,570 crowd. Morton, conquerors of Celtic in the other semi, provided stern opposition in the final. Torry Gillick scored Rangers' equalizer in a 1-1 draw at Hampden on 17 April 1947 and the replay four days later was just as closely matched. In front of a record midweek attendance of 133,750, Billy Williamson made the most of a rare appearance heading the game's only goal five minutes from the end of extra time.

The 'Treble'

When Rangers made an uncertain start to the 1948-49 season, dropping seven points in their first eight league matches which included a 4-2 home defeat at the hands of rivals Hibs, few would have predicted the historic feat the team would go on to achieve. They became the first to win the 'treble' of league championship, Scottish Cup and League Cup in one campaign.

The League Cup was the first trophy collected, Rangers emerging from a daunting qualifying section which included Celtic and Hibs en route to the final at Hampden on 12 March 1949 which saw goals from Torry Gillick and Willie Paton earn a 2-0 win over Raith Rovers.

The Scottish Cup was retained in some style, Rangers cruising imperiously to the final where they were convincing 4-1 winners over Clyde. George Young converted two penalty kicks, Billy Williamson again scored in what was his only appearance of the campaign and Jimmy Duncanson completed the ledger.

The league championship had seen Dundee usurp Hibs as Rangers' biggest threat this time around, emphasized by a 3-1 win for the Dark Blues over Struth's men at Dens Park in January. By winning 10 of their final 11 matches, Rangers were able to reel in Dundee in the most dramatic fashion.

Torry Gillick gives chase against Queen's Park at Ibrox in March 1948.

Going into the final day of the season, 30 April 1949, Dundee needed only a point at Falkirk to win the title. Rangers, just seven days after lifting the Scottish Cup, had to win against Albion Rovers at Cliftonhill and hope their rivals would slip up. They did. While Dundee lost 4-1 at Brockville, a Thornton hat-trick inspired Rangers to win by the same scoreline in Coatbridge. The title and the 'treble' were won.

The Best Ever Rangers Team?

It was a hard act to follow in 1949-50 but this outstanding Rangers side, one of the finest in the club's history, did their level best and it was a case of two out of three ain't bad as both the League and Scottish Cup were retained. Having won a League Cup qualifying section which included Celtic, Rangers lost their grip on the trophy when they were beaten 2-1 in the semi-final by an East Fife side managed by former Rangers player Scot Symon and who went on to win the tournament.

Rangers avenged the loss when the teams met again in the final of the Scottish Cup. East Fife never recovered from Willie Findlay's first minute goal and a double from man of the match Thornton saw Rangers earn a 3-0 win in front of 120,015 at Hampden on 22 April 1950.

Seven days later, Rangers were at Ibrox playing hosts to a Hibs side who had re-established themselves as the main contenders in the championship. Rangers had won nine of their first 10 fixtures, losing 1-0 at Easter Road during the sequence, then went down heavily 4-0 to Motherwell at Fir Park. They did not lose another league match, however, and that level of consistency was needed to hold off Hibs. The goalless draw between the teams at Ibrox, witnessed by 101,000, was good enough for Rangers who drew 2-2 at Third Lanark on 1 May 1950 and finished the campaign just one point ahead of Hibs.

For the next two seasons, however, it was the green and white half of Edinburgh's turn to dominate Scottish football. For Struth and Rangers, the uncommon experience of being second best had to be endured as no trophies were delivered to Ibrox during this spell. The warning signs were there when Rangers, for the first time, failed to qualify from their League Cup section, which was won by Aberdeen who defeated Struth's men at Ibrox and Pittodrie. By then dropping eight points in their first eight league games, Rangers allowed Hibs to seize an early advantage in the title race they were simply far too good to surrender. Hibs eventually finished 10 points clear of runners-up Rangers, rubbing in their superiority with a 4-1 win at Easter Road on the final day.

Great Matches

SCOTTISH LEAGUE DIVISION ONE Cliftonhill, 30 April 1949

Albion Rovers 1 Rangers 4 Attendance 15,000
Wallace Thornton 3
Duncanson

Few of the Rangers players who made the short journey to Coatbridge on the final day of the campaign could have been overly optimistic they would return to Glasgow as Scottish champions. While victory over already-relegated Albion Rovers was considered a formality for the Ibrox men, they knew the outcome of the title race was firmly in Dundee's hands. The Dens Park club needed just a point from their match at mid-table Falkirk to clinch the championship and were heavily tipped to do at least as much. Rangers, who had lifted the Scottish Cup the previous week to add to the League Cup they had won in March, initially wore the look of a side going through the motions at Cliftonhill.

They made a feckless start to the match, but they were settled by an opening goal after 20 minutes from top scorer Willie Thornton who planted the ball firmly past Rovers keeper McGregor. Six minutes later, Jimmy Duncanson headed home an Eddie Rutherford cross to put Rangers firmly in command.

The score remained 2-0 at half-time. At Brockville, it was goalless with Dundee's Alex Stott having had a penalty saved by Falkirk keeper George Nicol. The drama was beginning to unfold. Seven minutes into the second half at Cliftonhill, Dougie Wallace pulled a goal back for Rovers, but Thornton restored Rangers' two-goal advantage on the hour with a magnificent solo effort, dummying McGregor and stroking the ball into the empty net.

Dundee, meanwhile, had collapsed as Falkirk romped to an unlikely 4-1 victory. It was left to Thornton to apply the *coup de grâce* for Rangers, lashing the ball home to complete his hat-trick 10 minutes from time. Soon after the final whistle, news filtered through to Bill Struth and his players that they had won the championship and, with it, become the first club to complete the domestic treble.

The feat was recorded in what would be considered today as astonishingly low-key fashion by the newspapers, whose main focus was on how Dundee had thrown the title away. However, as time went on, the significance of Thornton's hat-trick would not be underestimated and the brilliant centre forward went down in history as the man whose goals won the first-ever Scottish treble.

Albion Rovers: McGregor, Muir, Kerr, Martin, English, Hunter, McKinnon, Craig, Wallace, Devlin, Smith

Rangers: Brown, Young, Shaw, McColl, Woodburn, Cox, Waddell, Duncanson, Thornton, Williamson, Rutherford

Referee: J. Jackson (Glasgow)

Rangers captain George Young in a tussle for the ball with Arsenal's Doug Lishman during a match marking the switching-on of the floodlights at Highbury in 1951.

The new champions had also ended Rangers' interest in the Scottish Cup at the second round stage, winning a dramatic tie 3-2 at Ibrox. The scorer of both of Rangers' goals was Billy Simpson, an £11,500 recruit from Linfield who would become a successful and immensely popular player for the club. It was the final campaign for Jimmy Duncanson, who moved to St Mirren, while the squad was strengthened with inside left John Prentice arriving from Hearts.

Rangers made a stronger challenge to Hibs in 1951-52, after recovering from a poor start to the league campaign. Six points behind the champions at the turn of the year, Rangers dragged themselves back into contention only to lose one and draw three of their final four games. Hibs retained the title, finishing four points clear of the Ibrox men.

Rangers' cup ambitions were thwarted by two very fine sides of the era. In the League Cup, after an outstanding performance in beating Celtic 3-0 in the semi-finals, Rangers lost a dramatic final 3-2 to Dundee. George Young made it 2-2 in the 88th minute, only for Alfie Boyd to head home a cross from the great Billy Steel and claim a last minute winner for the Dens Park outfit.

The Scottish Cup saw Rangers paired with Motherwell in the quarter-finals. A late equalizer by Sloan at Ibrox, Thornton having given Rangers an early lead, forced a Fir Park replay. Thornton again fired Rangers in front but this time Motherwell hit back to win 2-1 and went on to defeat Dundee in the final and lift the Scottish Cup for the first time.

Struth and Rangers were determined to avoid a third successive barren season but the omens for 1952-53 looked grim when they lost 5-0 to Hearts at Tynecastle in their opening League Cup qualifying match.

50 Greatest Players

TORRY GILLICK Inside forward

Joined Rangers: May 1933   **From:** Petershill Juniors

Debut: v Partick Thistle, League, 30 September 1933

Appearances: 140   **Goals:** 62

Left Rangers: December 1935   **For:** Everton

Rejoined Rangers: August 1945   **From:** Everton

Left Rangers: May 1950 (retired)

Honours won with Rangers: 2 league championships, 2 Scottish Cups, 2 League Cups

Rangers supporters of a certain vintage would insist that Torrance Gillick was one of the most naturally gifted footballers ever to play for the club. In his two spells at Ibrox Torry delighted as an exquisite passer of the ball as well as a highly adept finisher.

Born in Airdrie, Gillick was just 17 when Rangers signed him from Petershill Juniors in 1933 and he was good enough to earn two first team appearances in the 1933-34 season. The following season found manager Bill Struth picking him on a regular basis and Gillick scored 21 goals in 34 appearances as he helped Rangers retain both the league championship and Scottish Cup.

It came as a surprise, then, when Rangers agreed to sell Gillick to Everton for £8,000 in December 1935. An unqualified success at Goodison Park, Gillick helped his new club win the English championship in 1939 and won all five of his Scotland caps while an Everton player. He returned to Rangers as a 'guest' player during the Second World War, scoring prolifically, and was officially re-signed by the club in 1945. Gillick won a further league championship medal with Rangers in 1947 and set the club on their way to Scottish football's first domestic 'treble' with the first goal of the 1948-49 League Cup final win over Raith Rovers. He retired at the end of the following season and died at the early age of 56 in 1971.

Goalkeeper Bobby Brown was the unfortunate scapegoat, losing his place for the rest of the campaign to George Niven. Rangers recovered sufficiently to win the section, which also included Motherwell and Aberdeen, but were eventually beaten 1-0 by Division B side Kilmarnock in a semi-final upset.

Attention switched to the league where East Fife, managed brilliantly by Scot Symon, were the surprise early leaders. Rangers had lost three of their first five matches, but put together a 15-match unbeaten run from

50 Greatest Players

WILLIE THORNTON Centre forward

Joined Rangers: March 1936   **From:** Winchburgh Albion

Debut: v Partick Thistle, League, 2 January 1937

Appearances: 308   **Goals:** 196

Left Rangers: June 1954 (retired)

Honours won with Rangers: 4 league championships,
3 Scottish Cups; 2 League Cups; 7 caps (Scotland)

As remarkable a man as he was a footballer, Willie Thornton
was one of the most popular and successful centre forwards
ever to play for Rangers. Born in the tiny West Lothian
village of Winchburgh, he was spotted playing for the local
Albion side and went to Ibrox straight from school. Aged just
16 he made his first team debut and scored his first senior
goal for the club in his second appearance. By season 1938-
39, he had displaced Jimmy Smith as the first choice No. 9, claiming 23 goals in 36
league games and winning his first championship medal with the club.

The Second World War stalled the prodigious 19-year-old's blooming career, but on
active service with the Duke of Atholl Highland Regiment, the young soldier's bravery in
the 1943 Italian campaign earned him the Military Medal.

After the war, Thornton began to make up for lost time and 25 goals in 36 games
helped Rangers win the championship and League Cup in 1946-47. He won his first
Scottish Cup the following season and in 1948-49 plundered 34 goals as Rangers won
the domestic 'treble', Thornton's hat-trick in the 4-1 win over Albion Rovers sealing the
feat. He scored twice in the 1950 Scottish Cup final win over East Fife and was
Scotland's Player of the Year two years later. Thornton, never booked or sent off during
his career, retired in 1954 and managed Dundee and Partick Thistle. He returned to
Ibrox as assistant-manager in September 1968 and remained at the club, providing
visitors with guided tours of the trophy room, until his death in 1991 at the age of 71.

1 November to 7 March to haul themselves into a dramatic three-horse race
for the title with the Methil club and Hibs.

It eventually came down to a straight fight between Rangers and Hibs, the
Easter Road club finishing the campaign a week earlier than the Ibrox side.
It left Struth's men heading to Dumfries needing just a point against Queen
of the South to become champions for the 28th time. They trailed 1-0 at half-
time but Waddell's equalizer 15 minutes from time was enough to draw level
on 43 points at the top of the table and depose Hibs on goal average.

Willie Waddell leaps over a challenge from Partick Thistle's Gibb in a 3-0 victory at Ibrox on the opening day of the 1953-54 season.

The title triumph came a week after Rangers had won the Scottish Cup. After an arduous campaign which saw them find a way past Dundee, Celtic and Hearts, they faced Aberdeen in the final. John Prentice's early goal was cancelled out by Harry Yorston for the Dons to necessitate a replay which Rangers won 1-0, Billy Simpson on target three minutes before half-time.

The End of an Era

So Rangers entered 1953-54 still basking in the glow of winning the league and Scottish Cup double for the seventh time in their history. A desperately disappointing season started promisingly enough, Rangers easing through their League Cup qualifying section, but by the time they were disappointingly knocked out 2-0 by Partick Thistle in the semi-finals on 10 October, the pattern for their most dismal campaign in a long time had been set. In their first 11 fixtures, they dropped 11 points and were simply never in the hunt. They eventually finished in fourth place, nine points adrift of a Celtic side who took the title back to Parkhead for the first time in 16 years.

At the age of 79, Bill Struth decided it was time to step down. On 1 April 1954, the man who won a staggering 18 league titles and 10 Scottish Cups in his 34 years at the helm, announced he would be retiring at the end of the season. Despite his advanced years, the news still came as a shock to the

Great Managers – 1920-54

BILL STRUTH

Both in terms of statistical achievement and moulding the club into the institution it remains today, William Struth has to be regarded as the greatest manager in the history of Rangers. Born in Edinburgh in 1875, Struth did not play football at a serious level. He developed his interest in sporting achievement as a professional athlete, and in 1908 was appointed trainer of Clyde. His work with the Shawfield club attracted the attention of Rangers manager William Wilton who recruited Struth as successor to James Wilson as the trainer at Ibrox in 1914. On Wilton's tragic death in 1920, the Rangers board immediately appointed Struth as his successor and could not even have dared to imagine the remarkably successful 34-year reign he would enjoy.

An unflinching disciplinarian, Struth demanded the highest possible standards from his players both on and off the pitch. Dress code was as important as tactics to a man who, for the most part, left the intricacies of strategy in the hands of his senior players or trainers such as the excellent James Kerr.

Under Struth's imposing leadership, Rangers won the league championship 18 times, lifted the Scottish Cup on 10 occasions and collected the league cup twice. In season 1948-49, he guided Rangers to the first domestic 'treble' in Scottish football history. Named a director of the club in 1947, Struth retired as manager in 1954 and remained on the Ibrox board until his death on 21 September 1956 at the age of 81.

Rangers players and supporters, although the recent addition to the board of directors of John Lawrence, a Glasgow builder who would have a considerable impact at the club in the years to come, may have been a factor.

The team's last chance to send Struth into retirement with another trophy was in the Scottish Cup but, just nine days after his announcement, he doubtless looked on in agony as Rangers suffered one of the worst defeats in their history, hammered 6-0 by Aberdeen in the semi-final at Hampden.

The end of the season also saw the culmination of two other outstanding Rangers careers, captain Jock Shaw retiring at the age of 42 and marvellous goalscorer Willie Thornton leaving the club to become manager of Dundee.

Tremendous losses though they were, it was time for a new era at Ibrox. Speculation over Bill Struth's successor was intense. Scot Symon, the former player who had been such a remarkable success as manager of East Fife and was now in charge of Preston North End – steering them to the FA Cup final that very season – was considered the favourite by the Scottish press. Their judgement was sound. On 15 June 1954, Symon returned to Ibrox as only the third manager in Rangers' 82-year history.

Chapter Six: 1954-67
The Symon Years

Just a month into his first season in charge of Rangers, Scot Symon saw his prospects of immediate success in the job badly compromised by one of the harshest decisions ever handed down by the Scottish Football Association's disciplinary committee. On 14 September, Rangers' immensely talented and massively influential centre half Willie Woodburn was given a *sine die* suspension by the SFA – effectively a life ban – in the wake of the fifth sending-off of his 14-year Ibrox career. Woodburn had been dismissed in the final minute of Rangers' 2-0 League Cup qualifying section victory over Stirling Albion at Ibrox on 28 August 1954 for an off-the-ball fracas. It was not untypical for a player who was fiercely committed to Rangers, but never regarded as malicious.

The SFA sentence was exceptionally draconian and all the more difficult to comprehend in light of the outstanding service Woodburn had also given to his country in 24 appearances for Scotland. He was 35 when the suspension was handed down and although it was eventually rescinded in April 1957, there was no way then for Woodburn to resume his career. The loss of such a pivotal figure was a considerable blow for Symon as he looked to reclaim the dominance of Scottish football his predecessor Struth had so often achieved for Rangers.

In the first match without Woodburn, reserve team centre half Duncan Stanners was promoted for the daunting task of a league fixture against Celtic at Parkhead, but Rangers slid to a 2-0 defeat. Symon eventually settled on a switch from right back to centre half for captain George Young and Rangers were able to stay in title contention until January, buoyed by a 4-1 win over Celtic at Ibrox on New Year's Day in which Johnny Hubbard scored a hat-trick.

Seven points were dropped in their next five games, however, as Rangers gradually lost touch with an excellent Aberdeen side who crushed them 4-0 at Pittodrie on 2 April. Rangers eventually finished third, five points behind runners-up Celtic and a further three adrift of Aberdeen who won the championship for the first time.

The cup competitions offered no greater encouragement for Symon in his opening campaign. After winning their League Cup qualifying section,

50 Greatest Players

WILLIE WOODBURN Centre half

Joined Rangers: October 1937   **From:** Edinburgh Ashton

Debut: v Motherwell, League, 20 August 1938

Appearances: 329   **Goals:** 2

Left Rangers: June 1955 (retired)

Honours won with Rangers: 5 league championships; 4 Scottish Cups; 2 League Cups; 24 caps (Scotland)

As a 19-year-old, Willie Woodburn was introduced to the Rangers first-team in the title-winning 1938-39 season, playing a dozen games as understudy to former Scotland captain Jimmy Simpson as the league championship was won. He then lost the best part of his career to the Second World War but when competitive action resumed in 1946-47, he soon established himself as a first-team fixture at Ibrox.

The League Cup and another league championship were won that season as Woodburn emerged as one of the finest, most complete centre halves ever seen in Scottish football. The Edinburgh-born player bucked the trend of 'stoppers' always looking to make a constructive pass rather than an aimless clearance. In 1948-49, he missed only two of Rangers' 44 games as the domestic 'treble' was clinched for the first time. Two more league championships and Scottish Cups were won by Woodburn, along with 24 international caps – an outstanding tally at that time – before his career was ended prematurely by a harsh SFA *sine die* ban in September 1954, imposed after Woodburn had been sent off for the fifth time in his career. The suspension was lifted in April 1957, but the dispirited Woodburn had long since retired. He became a respected newspaper columnist and lived in Edinburgh until his death in 2001 at the age of 82.

Rangers fell at the next hurdle, losing 3-2 on aggregate to Motherwell in the quarter-finals. The Scottish Cup handed Rangers the most difficult assignment possible in the sixth round with a trip to Pittodrie where a 2-1 defeat at the hands of Aberdeen was no great surprise.

One significant plus point of the season was the first team breakthrough of 18-year-old right winger Alex Scott who made a spectacular debut on 9 March 1955 with a hat-trick in the 4-1 league win over his hometown team Falkirk at Ibrox. It proced to be a delicious taste of what was to follow in Scott's excellent Rangers career. Symon also made a notable signing in January 1955 when Jimmy Millar was recruited from Dunfermline Athletic for £5,000. Although initially signed as a midfield player, Millar would eventually become one of the most effective and popular centre forwards in Rangers' history.

The close season of 1955 saw Symon continue to reshape the Rangers' squad, paying his previous club Preston North End £12,000 for the services of midfielder Sammy Baird. The quest to recapture the league title in 1955-56 started badly, however, Rangers dropping six points in their opening six games to slide into an unpromising mid-table position.

The Burly Kitchenbrand

The addition of powerful South African centre forward Don Kichenbrand helped turn the tide, as Rangers then embarked on a 23-match unbeaten run. The burly Kichenbrand, while not universally popular among the Ibrox crowd, was certainly effective and his 24 league goals in 25 appearances went a long way to Rangers winning the championship for the 29th time.

The title was effectively wrapped up with a 1-0 win over Aberdeen at Ibrox on 18 April 1956, Alex Scott scoring the vital goal, and Rangers finished the season six points clear of the deposed Pittodrie side. The rivalry between the clubs was especially keen, Aberdeen having knocked Rangers out of the League Cup in the semi-finals with a tense 2-1 win at Hampden en route to winning the trophy. Rangers did have the satisfaction of beating the Dons 2-1 at Ibrox in the fifth round of the Scottish Cup, but were humbled 4-0 by eventual winners Hearts in a one-sided quarter-final at Tynecastle.

Nonetheless, Scot Symon had landed his first trophy as Rangers manager and was effectively ensuring the club were prepared for the challenges which lay ahead. Another important signing during the season had been that of full back

High kicking: Ian McColl in Scottish Cup action against Dundee in February 1956.

50 Greatest Players

SAMMY COX Full back

Joined Rangers: May 1946   **From:** Dundee

Debut: v Motherwell, League, 10 August 1946

Appearances: 310   **Goals:** 20

Left Rangers: March 1955   **For:** East Fife

Honours won with Rangers: 4 league championships; 3 Scottish Cups; 2 League Cups; 24 caps (Scotland)

Although he is remembered as one of the finest left backs ever to play for Scotland, Sammy Cox initially made his first team breakthrough with Rangers as a right back and then spent much of his Ibrox career as a left half.

Signed from Dundee after spells with Queen's Park and Third Lanark, the Darvel-born player made 13 appearances in helping Rangers win the League championship in 1946-47, his first full season with the club. Bitingly efficient in the tackle and a highly astute reader of the game, Cox soon became a favourite with the Ibrox crowd and was a fixture in the famous 'Iron Curtain' defence.

Winning 25 caps for Scotland, Cox gained a wider reputation as one of the most proficient defenders in world football. This stemmed from his success in direct opposition to England's winger Stanley Matthews who described Cox as 'the most difficult full back I ever faced'. Cox left Rangers towards the end of the 1954-55 season and continued his playing career successfully with East Fife. In 1959, he retired and emigrated to Canada.

Bobby Shearer from Hamilton Accies for £2,000, a resilient and ultrareliable character who would become a tremendous club captain.

The stars of the hugely successful side of the immediate post-war era were gradually leaving Ibrox, and the summer of 1956 saw three more depart. Sammy Cox joined East Fife on a free transfer, Bobby Brown was sold to Falkirk for £2,200 and Willie Waddell retired.

Season 1956-57, then, signalled a new era in many ways, no less so than with Rangers' first venture into European football. It was the second season of the European Cup, Hibs having represented Scotland well in the inaugural tournament when they reached the semi-finals and lost to Reims.

Rangers would also fall to French opposition but, unfortunately, at the initial hurdle. Handed a bye in the first round, Symon's side were paired with Nice. Max Murray, a centre forward signed a year earlier from Queen's Park, claimed the distinction of scoring Rangers' first goal in European competition when he cancelled out Faivre's opener for the visitors in the first leg at Ibrox on 24 October 1956. Billy Simpson grabbed a deserved winner for Rangers who missed a hatful of chances to record a more comfortable victory in front of 65,000 fans.

When Johnny Hubbard scored from the penalty spot five minutes from half-time in Nice on 14 November, opening up a 3-1 aggregate lead, progress to the quarter-finals looked likely. The French side retrieved the situation, however, with two goals in three second-half minutes to level the scores and

50 Greatest Players

WILLIE WADDELL Winger

Joined Rangers: March 1938 **From:** Eastfield Heatherbell

Debut: v Ayr United, League, 3 September 1938

Appearances: 301   **Goals:** 58

Left Rangers: May 1956 (retired)

Honours won with Rangers: 4 league championships; 2 Scottish Cups; 17 caps (Scotland)

On 29 August 1938, a crowd of 41,000 at Ibrox witnessed the birth of a legend when 17-year-old Willie Waddell scored the only goal of the game as Rangers defeated English champions Arsenal in a friendly. Five days later, the Forth-born outside right made his competitive first team debut in a 4-1 win over Ayr United. Waddell went on to score seven times in 27 league appearances in that debut campaign, helping Rangers win the title. So began the most remarkable Rangers career of them all.

Employed as an electrician at the Harland & Wolff Clydeside shipyard during the Second World War, he continued to play for Rangers as they won a multitude of wartime titles and cups. In the first post-war season, 1946-47, Waddell's pace, power and precision crossing from the right wing played a key role in another championship triumph. He was now one of the most dynamic and effective players in Scottish football, perhaps at his peak when Rangers won the first ever domestic 'treble' in 1948-49 (although injury ruled him out of the League Cup final).

Waddell's most satisfying moment came near the end of his playing career when he scored the goal against Queen of the South on 7 May 1953 which clinched Rangers' first title for three years. He was capped 17 times for Scotland, scoring six goals, with one of his finest displays coming in the 3-1 win over England at Wembley in 1949. He hung up his boots in 1956 to become a journalist but would return to football, and eventually Rangers, with dramatic results (see page 120).

Rangers' European dream begins. From left: George Niven, Eric Caldow, Bobby Shearer, Ian McColl and George Young (on floor) watch Muro's shot go over the bar in their opening European Cup tie against OGC Nice at Ibrox. Rangers won the match 2-1.

force a play-off. The closing minutes of the match also saw Willie Logie become the first Rangers player to be sent off in a European tie, when he was dismissed for fighting along with Nice's Bravo.

The play-off was staged two weeks later at the Parc des Princes in Paris, hardly the most neutral venue possible, and Rangers again failed badly in front of goal, eventually losing 3-1 in a hostile atmosphere.

A shaky start to the season had also seen Rangers fail to qualify from their League Cup section, losing out to Celtic, and the start of their defence of the league championship was equally unconvincing. As Hearts set the early pace, Rangers suffered home defeats to Kilmarnock and Motherwell as they dropped five points in their first eight games.

A 5-3 win over Hearts at Ibrox in December hauled Rangers firmly back into contention and from 19 January 1957 to the end of the season, Symon's men reeled off a marvellous 16-match unbeaten run, dropping just two points in the process, to win the title from their Tynecastle rivals by a two point margin.

Rangers' sole defeat in that period of the campaign was a bitterly disappointing one as they made their exit from the Scottish Cup at the hands of Celtic, losing 2-0 in front of 88,000 fans at Ibrox in a sixth round replay after a remarkable 4-4 draw at Parkhead.

A Colossus Leaves

The end of the season saw George Young hang up his boots at the age of 34. The giant defender was a colossus for club and country, winning every domestic honour with Rangers and representing Scotland on a then record 53 occasions.

He was undoubtedly badly missed in 1957-58 as Rangers endured a barren season on all fronts. Hopes of a third successive championship effectively died in only the fourth game of the season when an outstanding Hearts side, on their way to a first title success for 61 years, came to Ibrox and won 3-2. It was one of three defeats Rangers' suffered in their first six league fixtures.

The League Cup provided Rangers with the most chastening experience in the club's history. Their progress to the final at Hampden on 19 October 1957 was fairly straightforward, but how Symon and his players must have wished they had never got there. Rangers were simply a shambles as they were crushed 7-1 by a rampant Celtic side. Billy McPhail, scorer of a hat-trick for the Parkhead men, tortured the unfortunate Rangers centre half John Valentine, who had been signed from Queen's Park at the end of the previous season as a potential replacement for Young.

Valentine was the scapegoat for the humiliating defeat and, although no-one in the Rangers team could reflect on the final with any pride, he never played for the first-team again. The following month, Symon signed veteran stopper Willie Telfer from St Mirren for £10,000 and he would prove a solid and reliable performer in the problem position.

Rangers' second European Cup campaign finally saw a success for Scottish clubs against French opposition. They defeated St Etienne 3-1 at Ibox and held on for a 1-2 defeat in France in the first round. The second round, however, saw the Ibrox team pitched against an altogether higher class of foe in the shape of AC Milan.

Although Max Murray gave Rangers a 1-0 half-time lead in the first leg at Ibrox, the slick Italians stunned the home fans with four goals in the last 15 minutes of the match to make the return a formality. Milan won 2-0 at a sodden San Siro Stadium to complete a 6-1 aggregate victory.

A Scottish Cup semi-final, then, gave Rangers their last hope of silverware from the season. That too ended in disappointment. After a 2-2 draw, the

50 Greatest Players

GEORGE YOUNG Defender

Joined Rangers: August 1941   **From:** Kirkintilloch Rob Roy

Debut: v Motherwell, League, 10 August 1946

Appearances: 428   **Goals:** 31

Left Rangers: May 1957 (retired)

Honours won with Rangers: 6 league championships;
4 Scottish Cups; 2 League Cups; 53 caps (Scotland)

Born in Grangemouth in 1922, George 'Corky' Young signed schoolboy forms with Rangers at 15 and turned professional at 19 after learning his trade in the juniors with Kirkintilloch Rob Roy. A giant of a man in every sense, the 6ft 2ins, hefty defender turned out to be a colossal player for the Ibrox club.

Although more naturally a centre half, Young usually played at right back as Willie Woodburn took the pivotal position. He collected the first of his six league championship medals in 1946-47 and eventually succeeded Jock 'Tiger' Shaw as Rangers captain. Young was a key figure in the famed 'Iron Curtain' defence, not only a powerful physical presence but talented with the ball at his feet and capable of delivering long, raking passes of consistent accuracy.

Young was also a fabulous Scotland player. His haul of 53 caps, 48 as captain, stood as a Scottish record until surpassed by Denis Law. His international career had an abrupt and controversial ending when he was dropped for the World Cup qualifier in Spain in May 1957, the SFA taking umbrage at Young's announcement it would be his last game for Scotland. Young retired at the end of the 1956-57 season, having won his final league championship medal with Rangers, and went into hotel management. He later spent three seasons as manager of Third Lanark. He died in 1997 at the age of 74.

replay, also at Hampden, saw them go down by 2-1 to Hibs. To rub salt in Ranger's wounds, Max Murray was denied a legitimate late equalizer by a linesman's flag.

Dramatic Final Day

A dismal start to 1958-59 offered little hope of a successful season as Rangers made an early exit from the League Cup, finishing second in their qualifying section to eventual winners Hearts who appeared all set to maintain their ascendancy in Scotland.

Rangers dropped six points in their first six league matches as Hearts opened up an early advantage, but on 2 October 1958 Symon made an inspired and crucial signing when Ian McMillan, a 27-year-old Scotland international, was recruited from Airdrie for £10,000. A wonderful midfield player with remarkable vision and almost faultless passing ability, McMillan was the spark Rangers needed. He was pivotal in a 14-match unbeaten run which included a sizzling 5-0 win over Hearts at Ibrox in December, Max Murray scoring a hat-trick and the emerging Ralph Brand a double, as Rangers drove their way back into the title race.

When they lost 2-1 to Celtic at Parkhead in February to bow out of the Scottish Cup in the third round, Rangers turned all of their attention to the championship which went down to a dramatic final day in Glasgow.

It began with Rangers two points clear of Hearts with the teams on exactly the same goal average. Aberdeen were the visitors to Ibrox while Hearts had travelled to face Celtic. When Brand fired Rangers into the lead, they looked likely to claim at least the point which would assure them of the title, but Aberdeen hit back to earn a shock 2-1 win.

Rangers were booed from the field by the 41,000 crowd who were convinced they had blown the championship, but then news came through that Hearts too had failed, losing 2-1 to Celtic. With a little help from their greatest rivals, Rangers were Scottish champions for the 31st time.

It meant a return to the European Cup in 1959-60 and Rangers enjoyed their most successful and thrilling campaign yet, even if it did have a somewhat sobering end. Belgian champions Anderlecht, belligerent and overly physical, were crushed 7-2 on aggregate in the first round and Rangers then carved out a 5-4 aggregate win over admirable Czech side Red Star Bratislava to reach the quarter-finals.

There they found themselves locked in a tense battle with Dutch champions Sparta Rotterdam. Rangers looked to have done the hard work with a 3-2 first leg win in Holland, but Sparta responded by snatching a 1-0 victory at Ibrox. With no away goals rule yet in force, it meant a play-off at Highbury, home of their old friends Arsenal. Sammy Baird scored twice on a memorable night in London as Rangers won 3-2.

The semi-final draw pitted Rangers against Eintracht Frankfurt, but it turned out to be a mis-match. Symon's team simply could not cope with the pace, flair and technique of the Germans, who whipped them 6-1 in the first leg in Frankfurt and then put on another exhibition at Ibrox, winning 6-3 for a staggering 12-4 aggregate victory. That Eintracht subsequently lost 7-3 to Real Madrid in the classic final at Hampden says everything about the gulf in class between Rangers and Europe's elite at the time.

Perhaps not surprisingly, the European Cup run proved something of a distraction to Rangers on the home front. They failed to qualify from their League Cup section for the third time in four seasons, beaten home and away by Motherwell, and in the league they fell away badly after a decent start had seen them win nine of their first 12 games.

Amazingly, Rangers failed to win any of their last eight league fixtures at Ibrox that season, eventually finishing third in the table, 12 points behind champions Hearts and eight adrift of runners-up Kilmarnock who were making great strides under the charge of former Ibrox hero Willie Waddell.

McColl Recalled

The Scottish Cup provided the joy Rangers certainly merited for their strenuous efforts throughout a draining campaign. Despite an impressive 4-1 win over Celtic in their semi-final replay, Rangers actually went into the final at Hampden on 23 April 1960 as slight underdogs in the bookies' eyes against a vibrant Kilmarnock side.

Manager Symon's surprise recall of club captain Ian McColl, whose right half slot had been filled by Harold Davis for much of the season, swung the match in Rangers' favour. McColl was outstanding, orchestrating much of the Ibrox side's best work as the Scottish Cup was won for the first time since 1953. McColl retired the following season to become Scotland manager.

Jimmy Millar, who had been successfully switched to centre forward on a close season tour of Denmark the previous year, scored a goal in each half as Rangers won 2-0 and finished the season as Ranger's top marksman.

The Scottish Cup triumph ensured Rangers' participation in European competition once more and the 1960-61 Cup-Winners' Cup provided some of the many highlights in what turned out to be a memorable campaign.

The catalyst for much of the success was the summer signing of a man destined to become arguably the finest Scottish footballer of all time. On 21 June 1960, Scot Symon sanctioned a Scottish record fee of £17,500 to secure the services of a 20-year-old midfielder called Jim Baxter from Raith Rovers.

Rangers and their supporters would see the best years of an all too brief but brilliant career of an innately gifted, if often self-destructive, left-sided playmaker. Added to talented performers such as Ian McMillan, Jimmy Millar, Ralph Brand and Davie Wilson, Baxter's arrival signalled the start of a golden era for a team still regarded by many as the finest in Ibrox history.

50 Greatest Players

IAN McCOLL Right half

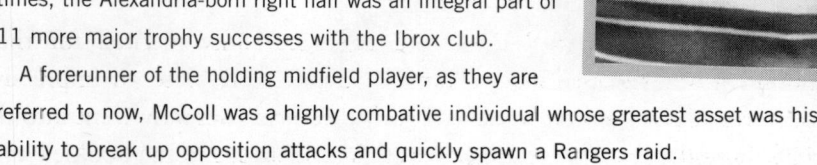

Joined Rangers: June 1946   **From:** Queen's Park

Debut: v St Mirren, League Cup, 12 October 1946

Appearances: 526   **Goals:** 14

Left Rangers: October 1960 (retired)

Honours won with Rangers: 7 league championships;
5 Scottish Cups; 2 League Cups; 14 caps (Scotland)

Ian McColl was 19 when he collected his first winner's
medal as a Rangers player in the 1946-47 League Cup
final and was 32 when he was recalled from the reserves to
earn his last in the 1960 Scottish Cup final. In between
times, the Alexandria-born right half was an integral part of
11 more major trophy successes with the Ibrox club.

A forerunner of the holding midfield player, as they are
referred to now, McColl was a highly combative individual whose greatest asset was his
ability to break up opposition attacks and quickly spawn a Rangers raid.

Signed as a teenager from Queen's Park, McColl reaped a rich harvest of honours in
his early years with Rangers and later was made captain as the exciting side of the late
1950s and early 1960s began to take shape. Although a peripheral figure towards the
end of his playing career, he answered the call brilliantly in the 1960 Scottish Cup final
when he deputised for the injured Harold Davis in the 2-0 win over Kilmarnock.

McColl effectively retired in October that year when he was appointed manager of
Scotland in succession to Andy Beattie. He had a successful four and a half years in
the job, continuing a link with the international team which had seen him win 14 caps
as a player, before spending three years as manager of Sunderland.

Recovering from a couple of early League Cup qualifying section defeats,
Rangers progressed at the expense of Celtic and then defeated a fine Dundee
side 5-3 on aggregate in the quarter-finals. Queen of the South were crushed
7-0 in the last four and Rangers once again found themselves facing
Kilmarnock in a Hampden final on 29 October 1960. As in the Scottish
Cup showpiece the previous season, Rangers ran out 2-0 winners against
Willie Waddell's side. Brand and Scott were the scorers as the League Cup
was placed in the Ibrox trophy room for the first time since 1949.

By the time it was collected, Rangers had advanced beyond the first round
of the European Cup-Winners' Cup with a closely fought 5-4 aggregate
victory over Ferencvaros of Hungary. Their quarter-final assignment proved

European Cup-Winners' Cup final action. Fiorentina's Orzan hacks the ball clear as team-mate Gonfiantini holds off Alex Scott in the first leg at Ibrox.

far easier, with a Baxter-inspired Rangers running riot against Borussia Mönchengladbach, defeating the Germans 3-0 in Düsseldorf then racking up an amazing 8-0 win in the return leg at Ibrox. Brand, who would be top scorer for Rangers that season with 40 goals in 54 appearances, claimed the club's first hat-trick in European football.

The semi-final draw paired Rangers with Wolves, twice English champions in the previous three seasons, in an intriguing 'Battle of Britain' showdown. Despite injury problems which forced them to play recently-signed centre half Doug Baillie at centre forward, Rangers engineered a fine 2-0 win in the first leg at Ibrox and then defied a Wolves onslaught at Molineux to snatch a 1-1 draw and become the first Scottish club to reach a European final.

Fiorentina, 4-2 aggregate winners over Dinamo Zagreb in the other semi-final, stood between Rangers and the honour of becoming the first British club to lift a European trophy.

A penalty miss in the first leg at Ibrox by Rangers captain Eric Caldow, with Fiorentina already leading by Luigi Milan's 11th minute goal, proved crucial as Milan doubled the visitors' lead in the closing moments. The second leg in Florence was clearly a tall order for Rangers, especially when Milan scored his third goal of the final with 12 minutes on the clock.

To their credit, Rangers continued to battle and were rewarded when Alex Scott levelled the scores on the night on the hour mark. Fiorentina were rattled briefly, Rangers coming close to a second goal which would have revived their hopes, but Swedish international forward Kurt Hamrin notched a spectacular goal seven minutes from time to seal a convincing 4-1 aggregate win for the Italian side.

The final was the last match of a strenuous but rewarding season for Rangers which had seen them reclaim the league championship to add to their League Cup success. A powerful start, which included a 5-1 drubbing of Celtic at Parkhead in a run of 10 wins from their first 11 matches, saw them always in front of a chasing pack headed by Kilmarnock.

32nd Championship Victory

The Rugby Park side, in fact, defeated Rangers both home and away and there was genuine concern for the Ibrox men when they lost 6-1 at Aberdeen with the finishing line in sight. Rangers regained their composure, winning their last two matches and clinching the club's 32nd championship in emphatic style with a memorable 7-3 win over Ayr United at Ibrox on 29 April 1961. They finished just one point clear of Kilmarnock.

Hopes of a domestic treble had perished the previous month when Rangers were soundly beaten 5-2 by Motherwell at Ibrox in a Scottish Cup third round replay, but they could only be satisfied by an eventful season.

Billy Ritchie had displaced George Niven as goalkeeper as Rangers began the 1961-62 campaign in confident mood, cruising through a League Cup qualifying section which included a Dundee side who would be their main rivals in the championship race. East Fife and St Johnstone were then dismissed before Rangers fended off a stout challenge from Hearts to retain the League Cup, defeating the Tynecastle men 3-1 in a final replay at Hampden after a 1-1 draw.

Dundee's consistency allowed them to forge an early advantage in the title chase, Rangers forced to play catch-up after dropping nine points in their first 14 fixtures. However, a run of 10 straight wins from 10 January to 3 March 1962 put Symon's side back in the chase. Needing just two wins from their last three fixtures, Rangers suddenly faltered, drawing with Celtic and Kilmarnock and losing to Aberdeen as Dundee came through to win the title for the first and only time in their history by a three point margin.

European competition had again captured the imagination of the Rangers support and there were hopes the team could follow the previous season's

Great Matches

SCOTTISH LEAGUE DIVISION ONE   **Ibrox, 29 April 1961**

Rangers 7   **Ayr United 3**   **Attendance 45,000**
Scott 3   A. McIntyre
Wilson 2   Fulton
Brand 2   Christie

It is hard to imagine a more stylish manner to clinch a championship than that effected by Rangers in sealing the 1960-61 Scottish title. With nearest rivals Kilmarnock having a game in hand, Scot Symon's men knew only victory in their final match against relegated Ayr United at Ibrox would be good enough.

Rangers, with the League Cup already in their possession and the European Cup-Winners' Cup final against Fiorentina to come, scored seven goals, and missed as many clear-cut chances again, in a breathless display orchestrated by midfielder Ian McMillan.

Right winger Alex Scott opened the scoring on 18 minutes when he hooked a shot over his shoulder and beyond the Ayr keeper from 14 yards, and the same player turned and drilled the ball home from the edge of the box to make it 2-0 seven minutes later. A run from the irresistible McMillan created number three for Davie Wilson in 33 minutes and four minutes from the interval, a slick move between McMillan and Scott set up a Ralph Brand tap-in for 4-0. McIntyre beat the unsighted Billy Ritchie to pull one back for Ayr on the stroke of half-time, but Rangers were in no mood to let up.

Scott completed his hat-trick with a brilliant 20-yard free-kick after Brand had been fouled on 53 minutes, but Ayr, refusing to throw in the towel, scored a second eight minutes later through Fulton, after Ritchie fumbled a cross. It was of little consequence, Wilson heading in a McMillan cross to make it 6-2 to Rangers in 75 minutes. The big Ibrox crowd were lapping up the pure entertainment on offer and even appreciated Jim Christie's shot to reply once more for the visitors four minutes from time. It was Rangers' day, however, and they had the final word in the 88th minute. McMillan and Scott combined to great effect again to allow Brand to crack home his 24th league goal of the season from close range.

Kilmarnock had beaten Partick Thistle 4-1, but news of Rangers' thrashing of their rivals rendered their game in hand meaningless. Rangers were champions of Scotland for the 32nd time.

Rangers: Ritchie, Shearer, Caldow, Davis, Paterson, Baxter, Wilson, McMillan, Scott, Brand, Hume

Ayr United: Gallacher, Burn, G. McIntyre, W. McIntyre, Glen, Curlett, Fulton, Gibson, Christie, A. McIntyre, Bradley

Referee: J. Holburn (Edinburgh)

success by reaching the European Cup final this time. With Jim Baxter at his best, Monaco were beaten 6-4 on aggregate in the first round and Rangers encountered few difficulties against Vorwärts Berlin in the second round, recording a 6-2 overall victory despite having to play the second leg against the East Germans on neutral soil in Malmo, Sweden.

The quarter-final against Standard Liege, however, was a huge disappointment. Rangers badly missed the injured Eric Caldow and were well beaten 4-1 in the first leg in Belgium. At Ibrox, the tie was nearly retrieved, but the 2-0 win with goals from Brand and Caldow was mere consolation.

Willie Henderson, an exciting teenage right winger, missed the match after failing to negotiate the traffic to Ibrox in time for kick-off, but the little man made a big impression as he began to emerge as a first team regular. He was the outstanding player as Rangers lifted the Scottish Cup. Aberdeen, Kilmarnock and Motherwell were among their victims en route to the final where St Mirren were beaten more convincingly at Hampden than the 2-0 scoreline suggested. Ralph Brand, scorer of 40 goals for the second successive season, and Davie Wilson were the marksmen as Rangers lifted the famous old trophy for the 16th time.

A jubilant Rangers team led by Eric Caldow (with trophy) and Ralph Brand embark on their lap of honour after beating Hearts 3-1 in the 1962 League Cup final replay.

The season was also notable for the first-team breakthrough of John Greig, a 19-year-old who scored eight goals in 15 appearances at inside forward. He was then the stand-out performer on a ground-breaking close-season tour of the Soviet Union which saw Rangers unbeaten in matches against Lokomotiv Moscow, Dinamo Tbilisi and Dinamo Kiev. It was just the start of a long and extraordinary Rangers career for Greig.

What was becoming an exceptional Rangers side really began to bloom in 1962-63 as the championship was reclaimed. They won eight of their first nine matches to surge into an early lead which was never seriously threatened, even by a severe winter which sent Scottish football into cold storage just after Rangers defeated Celtic 4-0 at Ibrox in the Ne'erday fixture.

Rangers' next game was not until 9 March and they had to squeeze 12 fixtures into the final two months of the season. Unperturbed, they finished nine points clear of Kilmarnock to claim their 33rd championship.

McNamee of Celtic and Jimmy Millar contest a corner kick in the 1963 Scottish Cup final. The match ended in a 1-1 draw, but Rangers went on to win the replay 3-0.

The defence of the League Cup had faltered at the semi-final stage, Rangers losing a dramatic semi-final 3-2 to Bertie Black's late goal for Kilmarnock, while the European Cup-Winners' Cup was also a disappointment. The intimidating tactics of Seville were overcome in the first round as Rangers recorded a 4-2 aggregate win over the Spanish side, but they found themselves way out of their depth against a wonderful Tottenham Hotspur team in the second round. Spurs, England's first 20th-century 'double' winners a year earlier, swamped Rangers 5-2 in the first leg at White Hart Lane then won 3-2 for good measure in the return at Ibrox, Jimmy Greaves on target in both matches. Bill Nicholson's side went on to defeat Atletico Madrid in the final and become the first British club to win a European trophy.

Domestic Domination

Rangers were able to console themselves with domestic domination as they went on to add the Scottish Cup to their league title success. The double was completed with some panache, Celtic swept aside 3-0 in a final replay at Hampden on 15 May 1963. Brand scored twice and Wilson claimed the other.

Henderson had firmly established himself as the first choice right winger to such an extent that Rangers were able to sell the tremendously talented Alex Scott to Everton, then regarded as the 'Bank of England' club, for a lucrative £46,000 fee.

Season 1963-64 saw this Rangers side at their zenith in domestic terms, if still a long way short of fulfilling their desire to compete with Europe's elite. Still, there was no disgrace in their first round European Cup exit at the hands of the peerless Real Madrid side of the time. Although Symon's team was hampered by injury, even at full strength they would have struggled to cope with Alfredo Di Stefano and co. Ferenc Puskas scored the only goal of the first leg at Ibrox three minutes from time, then helped himself to a hat-trick as Real humbled Rangers 6-0 in the return at the Bernabeu.

That left Rangers free to pursue more trophies in their own backyard, and they responded by achieving the 'treble' of league championship, Scottish Cup and League Cup for the second time in the club's history. Celtic were beaten home and away in qualifying from their League Cup section and Rangers eased their way to a final showdown with Morton at Hampden on 26 October 1963. This was Jim Forrest's day, the 19-year-old striker who had made his first-team breakthrough the previous season scoring four times in Rangers' 5-0 win. Alex Willoughby, another promising youngster and Forrest's cousin, got the other goal.

50 Greatest Players

IAN McMILLAN Inside forward

Joined Rangers: October 1958   **From:** Airdrie

Debut: v Raith Rovers, League, 18 October 1958

Appearances: 194   **Goals:** 55

Left Rangers: December 1964   **For:** Airdrie

Honours won with Rangers: 4 league championships; 3 Scottish Cups; 2 League Cups; 1 cap (Scotland)

A goal on his debut after a £10,000 transfer from Airdrie in 1958 began six years of almost unbroken Ibrox success for Ian McMillan. His craft and close control in the inside right position transformed Rangers in his first season, allowing them to clinch the first of four league championships he would win with the club. More success followed as he went on to form a peerless midfield axis with Jim Baxter. The pair thrived on the European stage as Rangers enjoyed their early adventures in continental club competition, culminating in their appearance in the 1961 Cup-Winners' Cup final.

McMillan was already a Scotland international when he joined Rangers at the age of 27 and, surprisingly, he added just one more cap to finish with a meagre tally of six. It was an unjustifiably poor return for a player of his talent, but he reaped a far richer harvest from his glorious spell at Ibrox.

An Airdrie man born and bred, he had won the Second Division championship with his home-town club in 1955 and he returned to Broomfield in a £5,000 transfer midway through the 1964-65 season. McMillan hung up his boots in 1967 and later became manager and then a director of Airdrie.

Rangers opened their title defence strongly with a 13-match unbeaten run but it was Kilmarnock who led the table at the turn of the year. A 2-0 home win over the Ayrshire side on 14 March turned the tide and Rangers eventually finished six points clear of their rivals to claim a 34th league success.

The Scottish Cup saw Rangers fend off Celtic 2-0 in the quarter-finals then squeeze past Jock Stein's fine Dunfermline side when Davie Wilson scored the only goal of the semi-final at Hampden. Dundee stood between Scot Symon and his players as they looked to emulate Bill Struth's treble-winning side of 1948-49. Rangers achieved the feat in some style.

It looked as though the heroics of Dundee keeper Bert Slater would force extra-time with the sides locked at 1-1, but Rangers, at the top of their game, would not be denied. Jimmy Millar scored his second of the match in the 89th minute to regain the lead and Ralph Brand sealed the 3-1 win in the closing moments, scoring in the Scottish Cup final for the third successive year.

Ralph Brand is grabbed by Celtic goalkeeper John Fallon as he heads for goal in the 1965 League Cup final. Rangers won the match 2-1.

Season 1964-65 proved a watershed for Rangers as this fine side began to break up – and for the complexion of Scottish football as a whole. For the Ibrox side, only the League Cup was retained as their supremacy began to wane. Celtic were beaten 2-1 in the final, Jim Forrest scoring both goals, but the Parkhead club were about to be spectacularly revived after a long period in the doldrums. Under new manager Jock Stein, who ended a brief spell at Hibs to take over in February 1965, Celtic won the Scottish Cup for the first time in 11 years. Rangers' defence of the trophy had ended at the quarter-final stage when they lost 2-1 to Hibs at Easter Road.

In the league, Rangers never recovered from a terrible start which saw them drop nine points in their first eight matches. A broken leg sustained by Jim Baxter in December didn't help their cause and they eventually trailed in fifth, six points behind first-time champions Kilmarnock – Rangers' worst ever post-war finishing position.

Rangers had performed creditably in the European Cup when faced with an exceptionally difficult draw. Ronnie McKinnon's last-minute goal in Belgrade forced a play-off against Yugoslav champions Red Star in the first round. Rangers returned to their happy hunting ground of Highbury and won 3-1.

Rapid Vienna provided no less daunting opposition in the second round but after winning the first leg at Ibrox 1-0, Rangers produced one of their finest European displays of all-time in Austria to claim a 2-0 victory and book a quarter-final place. Baxter was fabulous for the Ibrox men but sadly, suffered a broken leg in the final minute of the match.

Stalwart defender Bobby Shearer admires the silverware from Rangers' famous trophy cabinet.

Baxter Absent

His absence from the quarter-final matches against reigning European and World Club champions Inter Milan was a bitter blow. Rangers retained some hope in losing 3-1 in the San Siro Stadium, but an admirable effort in the second leg at Ibrox reaped only a 1-0 win and a narrow aggregate defeat. Inter went on to retain the trophy.

To complete a generally disappointing season for the Rangers supporters, 'Slim' Jim Baxter's itchy feet and desire for better financial terms eventually proved too much for Scot Symon. On 25 May 1965, at the age of 25, Baxter was sold to Sunderland for £72,500.

By the time season 1965-66 began, Rangers were also without long serving Bobby Shearer who was given a free transfer, while Ralph Brand moved to Manchester City for £10,000. Younger players like Greig, Henderson, Willoughby and Forrest would be given the opportunity to become the mainstays of a team in transition. Rangers made a highly acceptable start to the campaign and reached the League Cup final where, with some justification, they felt hard done by in losing 2-1 to Celtic at Hampden in a match where they had enjoyed much of the play. It was a clear sign, however, of the restored competitive edge new manager Stein had given Rangers' greatest rivals.

50 Greatest Players

JIM BAXTER Midfielder

Joined Rangers: June 1960   **From:** Raith Rovers

Debut: v Partick Thistle, League Cup, 13 August 1960

Left Rangers: Summer 1965   **For:** Sunderland

Rejoined Rangers: Summer 1969   **From:** Nottingham Forest

Left Rangers: November 1970 (retired)

Appearances: 254   **Goals:** 24

Honours won with Rangers: 3 league championships;
3 Scottish Cups; 4 Scottish League Cups; 27 caps
(Scotland)

Rangers broke the Scottish transfer record in the summer of 1960 when they paid Raith Rovers £17,500 for 20-year-old Jim Baxter. The Ibrox club have arguably never written a cheque which brought more rewarding dividends. 'Slim Jim', a nickname that stuck even as his girth increased, is widely regarded as the most talented footballer ever to play for the club.

Baxter was not an all-round talent. There were many things he could not do well, tackling notable among them, but his weaknesses became an irrelevance when set against his extraordinary gifts as a player. The former Fife miner possessed exquisite ball control, a bewildering range of passing and a left foot to die for. In a glorious period still cherished by those Rangers fans who witnessed it, Baxter's undiluted brilliance helped the club dominate Scottish football in the early sixties.

Baxter loved the big occasion and was at his arrogant best in Old Firm matches and when playing for Scotland against England. His performances for his country – for whom he won 34 caps, at Wembley in 1963 and 1967 – are still regarded as among the finest of any Scotland player.

Baxter's greatest weakness, sadly, was his indiscipline and a love of the good life which did not marry well with the demands of professional football. He left Rangers for the first time in the summer of 1965 for Sunderland in a £72,500 transfer, and later joined Nottingham Forest for £100,000. He returned to Ibrox in the summer of 1969 but was unable to repeat his former glories.

Baxter retired in November 1970, aged just 31, to become a publican in his adopted home of Glasgow. He died in 2001 at the age of 61.

50 Greatest Players

RALPH BRAND Forward

Joined Rangers: April 1954   **From:** School

Debut: v Kilmarnock, League, 6 November 1954

Appearances: 317   **Goals:** 206

Left Rangers: August 1965   **For:** Manchester City

Honours won with Rangers: 4 league championships;
3 Scottish Cups; 4 Scottish League Cups; 8 caps (Scotland)

A month before his 18th birthday, Ralph Brand made his first team debut for Rangers and scored twice in a 6-0 thrashing of Kilmarnock. It turned out to be a prophetically prolific start to a career which would mark him out as one of the finest forwards to play for the Ibrox club.

The Edinburgh-born youngster's performance for Scotland in the televised under-15 schoolboy international against England in 1952 alerted Rangers to his potential. He signed professionally at Ibrox two years later and, after a two-year absence for National Service, began to establish himself in the Rangers first-team in the 1958-59 season as he won the first of his four league championship medals.

In the early 60s, Brand and Jimmy Millar plundered goals aplenty, forming one of the most revered forward partnerships in Rangers' history. Remarkably, Brand scored in three successive Scottish Cup finals from 1962-64 inclusive, the last of them allowing Rangers to clinch a domestic 'treble' that season.

An incisive and intelligent player, always aware of the movement and position of his team-mates, Brand would have been a success in any era. He was desperately unfortunate only to win eight caps for Scotland, especially as he scored eight goals in those appearances for his country. At the start of the 1965-66 season, Brand was sold to Manchester City for £30,000. He then had spells with Sunderland and Raith Rovers before retiring in 1970.

In the league, Rangers were unbeaten in their first 15 matches but were badly shaken when they fell 5-1 to Celtic at Parkhead on 3 January. Ibrox title hopes all but disappeared with the loss of six points in four games during March and although Rangers won their last seven matches, it wasn't enough to catch Celtic who won their first championship since 1954 by a two-point margin.

The Old Firm found themselves head to head again in the quest for the Scottish Cup and Rangers were able to prevent Celtic winning the 'treble' in Stein's first full season. Following a tense goalless draw at Hampden on 23 April, Rangers lifted the trophy for the 19th time with a dramatic replay victory four days later. Kai Johansen, a Danish full back signed at the start of the season from Morton, spectacularly crashed the only goal of the night beyond Celtic keeper Ronnie Simpson, 20 minutes from time.

It was Scot Symon's 15th and, as it would transpire, final trophy success as Rangers manager. While his track record in 12 seasons since replacing Bill Struth was unarguably successful, Jock Stein's impact at Celtic began to send tremors of concern through the Ibrox boardroom.

It was decided Symon, a traditional manager of the old school, needed a more modern coach to assist him. After failing to lure Eddie Turnbull of Aberdeen as his assistant, Rangers hired Bobby Seith from Dundee to help Symon midway through the 1966-67 season. It was a campaign Rangers would never forget.

They were again unfortunate to lose to Celtic in the League Cup final, Bobby Lennox scoring the only goal of a controversial match, and were

50 Greatest Players

ERIC CALDOW Full back

Joined Rangers: May 1953   **From:** Muirkirk Juniors

Debut: v Ayr United, League Cup, 12 September 1953

Appearances: 407   **Goals:** 25

Left Rangers: April 1966   **For:** Stirling Albion

Honours won with Rangers: 5 league championships;
2 Scottish Cups; 3 Scottish League Cups; 40 caps (Scotland)

Equally adept at right back, where he won 11 of his 40 caps for Scotland and started his Rangers career, Eric Caldow is most instantly recalled as possibly the finest left back ever to play for the Ibrox club. Signed on schoolboy forms, he made his first team debut at the age of 19. He then became an important member of the thrilling early 1960s outfit. In addition to his many winner's medals, Caldow also appeared in the 1961 European Cup-Winners' Cup final against Fiorentina.

Exceptionally quick, tactically astute and totally resolute, Caldow formed a memorable full back partnership with Rangers captain Bobby Shearer. He was a natural leader himself, skippering both club and country at various stages of his career.

His international days came to a cruel end at Wembley in 1963 when a gruesome challenge from England's Bobby Smith left him with a multiple leg fracture. Caldow recovered to play for Rangers again, winning his last winner's medal in the 1964-65 League Cup, before joining Stirling Albion on a free transfer in 1966. After hanging up his boots, Caldow had managerial spells at Corby Town, Hurlford United and Stranraer.

always in contention in the league, losing just three games all season. Celtic, however, sealed the title with a 2-2 draw at Ibrox on 6 May 1967 and finished three points clear of Rangers. By that stage, Rangers were in the curious position of looking forward to their second European final while still suffering the after effects of the worst result in the club's history.

On 28 January 1967, Rangers unthinkably lost 1-0 at Berwick Rangers in the first round of the Scottish Cup. Sammy Reid scored one of the most famous goals in Scottish football history as the Second Division strugglers, inspired by player-manager Jock Wallace, achieved a result that was noted around the globe. Scapegoats were demanded for the humiliation and Rangers' strikers on the day, Jim Forrest and George McLean, were cruelly singled out. Both left Ibrox before the end of the season. In the case of Forrest especially, one of the most prolific scorers Rangers ever employed, it was a decision which smacked of desperation and poor judgement.

Rangers recovered quickly enough to resume their European Cup-Winners' Cup campaign. They had negotiated the challenges of Glentoran and Borussia Dortmund in the first two rounds before the Berwick debacle, and now they faced Real Zaragoza in the quarter-finals.

Both teams won 2-0 on their own ground with extra-time in the second leg in Spain seeing Dave Smith, an astute purchase from Aberdeen at the start of the season, having his penalty saved. The competition rules at the time meant a coin-toss would decide who would reach the semi-finals, and Rangers' captain John Greig got it right.

Slavia Sofia were surprisingly undemanding opposition in the last four, Rangers winning more comfortably than the 2-0 aggregate score suggested, but the final against Bayern Munich clearly represented a massive challenge.

Already up against it with the match being staged on German soil in Nuremberg, Rangers kicked off on 31 May 1967 under the added pressure of Celtic's remarkable 2-1 win over Inter Milan in Lisbon the previous week, which had seen them become the first British club to win the European Cup.

The burden was just too much for Rangers to bear. They were anything but outplayed in a tense match, but badly lacked the kind of natural goalscoring talent which had been sacrificed with the hasty sale of Forrest. Makeshift centre forward Roger Hynd missed an outstanding chance to win it for Rangers, who paid the price when Franz Roth scored the only goal of the final 11 minutes from the end of extra-time.

While there was no disgrace in losing to a team of Bayern's quality in Germany, Rangers' bitter disappointment was intensified by Celtic's success. It wasn't about to get any easier.

Chapter Seven: 1967-72
The Worst of Times, the Best of Times

In the summer of 1967, Rangers had appointed Davie White as assistant-manager. Just 34 years of age at the time, he had earned a reputation as Scotland's most promising and tactically-innovative young manager. In the remarkable season which had just seen Celtic win the European Cup and Rangers reach the Cup-Winners' Cup final, White had guided Clyde to third place behind the Old Firm in the league championship.

As part of his eagerness to absorb the lessons of continental football, he had travelled with both Celtic and Rangers to watch their respective European finals in Lisbon and Nuremberg. Clearly, the Ibrox club saw him as the ideal man to assist Scot Symon in the battle with Jock Stein's ascendant Parkhead side. Few could have predicted that, less than five months after becoming Scot Symon's number two, White would be leading from the front.

Despite the disappointment of failing to qualify from their League Cup section, crucially losing 3-1 to Celtic at Parkhead, Rangers made a good start to their 1967-68 championship bid, winning six and drawing two of their first eight games to lead the table by a point from their great rivals. A place in the second round of the Fairs Cup had also been secured with a 3-2 aggregate victory over Dynamo Dresden of East Germany.

Yet on 1 November 1967, Rangers dropped a bombshell on Scottish football when, for the first time in their history, they sacked their manager. The Ibrox crowd's reaction to the 0-0 draw with Dunfermline four days earlier, added to the pressure of Celtic's increasing status (they were in Argentina playing Racing Club for the World Club Championship), panicked Rangers chairman John Lawrence and his fellow directors, who decided a change was needed. Whatever the merits of the decision, it remains one of the most tawdry episodes in Rangers' history that Symon, an unflinchingly loyal and successful servant as both player and manager, was told the news by a third party. To his great credit, he resisted any temptation to criticise the club.

Davie White was named as the new manager and made an excellent start, winning his first nine league matches to keep Rangers ahead of Celtic in the

Great Managers – 1954-1967

SCOT SYMON

Born in Errol, Perthshire on 9 May 1911, James Scotland Symon was a fine player for Rangers and later became an outstanding manager of the club. An all-round sportsman with a fiercely competitive spirit, Symon achieved the rare distinction of being capped by Scotland at both football and cricket. It was with the larger ball that he truly excelled in a playing career which saw him provide terrific service to Dundee, Portsmouth and Rangers.

A wing half, or defensive midfielder as he would be described in today's game, Symon lost his best days as a player to the Second World War and retired in 1947. He began his managerial career at East Fife, winning both promotion and the League Cup with the Methil club. In 1953, he took the helm at Preston North End, guiding them to the FA Cup final, before being lured back to Ibrox as Bill Struth's replacement in 1954.

His record as Rangers' manager speaks for itself – six league championships, five Scottish Cups and four League Cups. Symon also took the club to the European Cup-Winners' Cup finals of 1961 and 1967. There are those who still maintain his team of the mid-60s was the finest Rangers have ever produced.

How sad, then, that his departure from Ibrox on 1 November 1967 was such a distasteful affair. The Rangers board, panicked by Celtic's rise to pre-eminence under Jock Stein, sent a third party to inform Symon his services as manager were no longer required. He deserved much better but, through later service as a Dumbarton director then manager of Partick Thistle, Symon never said a bad word against Rangers.

He died on 30 April 1985 at the age of 73.

championship and booking a Fairs Cup quarter-final place with a 4-3 aggregate success against Cologne in the second round.

White, in fact, was staggeringly unfortunate not to win the title for Rangers at the first attempt. They remained unbeaten until the final day of the season, but could not shake off an equally consistent Celtic. Rangers were shattered in their last match, losing 3-2 at Ibrox to a last-minute goal against Aberdeen, while Celtic won 2-1 at Dunfermline to seal their third consecutive title by two points. It would be as close as White got.

Rangers finished the season empty-handed again. They exited the Scottish Cup, losing to a late goal against Hearts in a Tynecastle quarter-final replay, and their Fairs Cup bid ended at the same stage. Drawn against English opposition for the third time, Rangers found the emerging Leeds United just too strong and well-organized. After a 0-0 draw at Ibrox, goals from Johnny Giles and Peter Lorimer gave Leeds a 2-0 second leg victory at Elland Road.

White's first and, as it would transpire, only full season in charge, 1968-69, began with another early departure from the League Cup. Rangers lost both home and away to Celtic in their qualifying section and failed to reach the quarter-finals for the second successive year.

They exacted quick revenge over Jock Stein's men with a highly impressive 4-2 win at Parkhead in the second league fixture of the campaign, Willie Johnston netting twice, and stoked some hope among their support that the title was a genuine possibility. That belief was stymied by the loss of six points in their next six games, however, and White responded by paying a Scottish record transfer fee of £100,000 to Hibernian for Colin Stein, a powerful, committed and free scoring centre forward.

50 Greatest Players

JIMMY MILLAR Forward

Joined Rangers: January 1955   **From:** Dunfermline

Debut: v Dundee, League, 29 January 1955

Appearances: 317   **Goals:** 162

Left Rangers: June 1967   **For:** Dundee United

Honours won with Rangers: 3 league championships; 5 Scottish Cups; 3 Scottish League Cups; 2 caps (Scotland)

Edinburgh-born Jimmy Millar was signed by Rangers as a half back of some repute when they paid Dunfermline Athletic £5,000 to bring the 20-year-old to Ibrox at the start of 1955. Yet after four years of sporadic first team action, his career was transformed spectacularly during a close-season trip to Denmark in May 1959. Moved to centre forward for the injured Max Murray during a game against Staevnet, Millar scored all of Rangers' goals in a 4-0 win. Not surprisingly, Scot Symon kept him at No. 9 from the start of the 1959-60 season. Millar soon made the position his own, scoring both goals in the 2-0 Scottish Cup final win over Kilmarnock in that season.

An intensely committed player, who married physical durability with a considerable degree of technical ability, Millar's aerial prowess belied his 5ft 6ins stature. His partnership with Ralph Brand was the stuff of Ibrox legend, Millar setting up almost as many goals for his sidekick as he scored himself.

He went full circle to win the last honour of his Ibrox career, moving back to half back and playing a key role in the tense 1966 Scottish Cup final victory over Celtic. Millar moved to Dundee United the following year and later had a spell as manager of Raith Rovers before becoming a publican.

50 Greatest Players

DAVIE WILSON Winger

Joined Rangers: May 1956   **From:** Baillieston Juniors

Debut: v Dundee, League, 2 January 1957

Appearances: 373   **Goals:** 157

Left Rangers: August 1967   **For:** Dundee United

Honours won with Rangers: 4 league championships;
5 Scottish Cups; 2 Scottish League Cups; 22 caps
(Scotland)

The sight of the blond-haired Davie Wilson sprinting down
the left wing thrilled many a supporter of both Rangers and
Scotland. A first-team debutant at the age of 17 in 1957,
it was not until season 1960-61 that he made the No. 11
jersey his own and became an integral part of what many
still regard as the greatest ever Rangers team.

Wilson was a real crowd pleaser, a pacy and always
positive winger who never held back his instinct to forage
into the penalty area. Such was his finishing prowess, he
could be pressed into service as a centre forward when
needed. On one such occasion, Wilson scored six goals in a 7-1 league win over Falkirk
in 1962. His scoring record of more than one goal every three games for Rangers is
remarkable for a wide man and he matched it on Scotland duty, scoring nine times in 22
appearances for his country. Wilson produced some memorable displays in the dark blue
of Scotland, most notably when filling in at left back for injured team-mate Eric Caldow
for 85 minutes of the famous 2-1 win over England at Wembley in 1963.

It was something of a surprise when Rangers moved him on to Dundee United at the
start of the 1967-68 season. Wilson was still only 28 and went on to provide the
Tannadice club with five years of excellent service. He later played for, then managed,
Dumbarton and had a spell as assistant manager at Kilmarnock.

Colin Stein's impact was immediate and spectacular with hat-tricks in his
first two appearances against Arbroath and Hibernian, but he was also
dogged by indiscipline, being sent off no fewer than three times in that debut
season. Despite beating Celtic again, John Greig scoring the only goal of the
game at Ibrox on 2 January 1969, Rangers were never really able to get
themselves back into firm contention for the title. Their inconsistency in the
new year proved costly, and they finished as runners-up again, this time five
points behind Celtic.

An excellent run in the Inter-Cities Fairs Cup was some consolation for the supporters. Yugoslav side Vojvodina were edged out in the first round, Dundalk of Ireland swamped in round two and Dutch outfit DWS Amsterdam beaten 4-1 on aggregate to claim a last eight berth.

An impressive Ibrox display in the first leg of the quarter-final saw Athletic Bilbao defeated 4-1, providing just enough insurance for the return in Spain which was lost 2-0. The semi-final draw delivered another mouth-watering showdown with English opponents but, as against Leeds the previous year, Rangers were unable to boost Scottish morale as they were knocked out by Newcastle United. Andy Penman's failure from the penalty spot in the goalless first leg at Ibrox, his kick saved by Newcastle keeper Willie McFaul, was crucial. At St James' Park, goals from Scottish players Jim Scott and Jackie Sinclair gave the Geordies a 2-0 win and a place in the final where they defeated Ujpest Dozsa of Hungary to lift the trophy.

Newcastle United keeper Willie McFaul gathers the ball as team-mate John McNamee (No. 5, falling) brings down Willie Henderson for a penalty. Andy Penman missed the subsequent spot kick and the first leg of the Inter-City Fairs Cup semi-final at Ibrox ended goalless.

Willie Henderson gets the better of Celtic's Bobby Lennox at Ibrox in September 1969.

The Scottish Cup delivered the greatest misery of Rangers' season. They found excellent form to reach the final, negotiating the toughest of draws to eliminate Hibs, Hearts, Airdrie and Aberdeen, the latter by a sizzling 6-1 in the semi-final at Parkhead. Inevitably, Celtic were waiting in the final at Hampden on 26 April 1969.

This was a bleak day in the career of Sir Alex Ferguson. The young Alex had been signed by Scot Symon from Dunfermline for £65,000 in the summer of 1967 and had finished that first season at Ibrox as the club's top scorer. Under White, however, in his second season, he found himself used mainly as a substitute.

Suspension to Colin Stein meant Ferguson was called up to lead the Rangers attack against Celtic, his first appearance of the Scottish Cup campaign. The Ibrox side were picked apart by their Old Firm rivals, the 4-0 scoreline indicative of the difference between them. Manager White blamed Ferguson for Celtic's second minute opener, citing his failure to mark Billy McNeill who headed in a Bobby Lennox corner unchallenged. Ferguson did not play for Rangers again. On 21 November 1969, he was sold to Falkirk for £20,000. It was a case of bad timing from his viewpoint as less than a week later, Davie White was sacked as Rangers manager.

The 1969-70 season had started badly for White who had brought Jim Baxter's mercurial, but fading talents back to Ibrox after the former Rangers hero had been released by Nottingham Forest. Baxter was unable to provide the inspiration Davie White hoped for and Rangers were knocked out of the League Cup at the qualifying stage yet again by Celtic.

When they then lost three of their first eight league fixtures, including a 1-0 home defeat against Celtic, alarm bells started to ring in the Ibrox boardroom. The crunch for White came in the second round of the European Cup-Winners' Cup in which Rangers met the Polish side Gornik Zabrze. Two goals from Willie Johnston had seen Rangers through their first round challenge against Steaua Bucharest and they were expected to cope with another Eastern European test. Instead, they were beaten 3-1 in both legs to crash out of the tournament in what was seen as unacceptable fashion. The second leg at Ibrox had also been marred by controversy. Baxter and Willie Henderson had slept in and missed training on the day before the game, yet retained their places in White's line-up.

White Leaves, Waddell Arrives

The day after the Gornik defeat, on 27 November, White was dismissed just over two years since he had been given the job. Rangers' search for a successor would not take long, having already identifed the man they believed could revive the club's fortunes.

On 3 December 1969, Willie Waddell returned to Ibrox 13 years after he had called time on his outstanding playing career with the club. He had found success in management with Kilmarnock, guiding them to the title in 1965, before leaving football for a high-profile journalistic career with the *Scottish Daily Express*.

Waddell, indeed, had been one of Rangers' sternest critics and penned one famous article in which he labelled White as 'the boy David'. Now, at the age of 48, Waddell became the fifth manager in Rangers' 97-year history.

While his appointment was universally acclaimed by the Rangers support, there was no instant cure to the club's ills under Waddell. He galvanized the players enough to win nine and draw two of their first 11 league games under his charge, but they faded badly at the end of the season, winning just one of their last eight to finish 12 points behind Celtic who were champions for a fifth successive season.

The Scottish Cup had offered Waddell his first real opportunity of a trophy as Rangers manager, but Celtic also put paid to that when the sides met in the quarter-finals at Parkhead. Jim Craig's own goal gave Rangers an early lead which Lennox cancelled out before half-time and Alex MacDonald's dismissal handed Celtic the initiative as they won 3-1 with two goals in the last five minutes.

Waddell shook up his squad at the end of the season with Baxter, long serving full back Davie Provan and goalkeepers Norrie Martin and Erik Sorensen among those given free transfers. The number one position was now in the possession of the giant Peter McCloy who had become Waddell's first major signing when he came from Motherwell in March 1970. The most significant change to the Ibrox set-up, however, was behind the scenes. In April 1970, Waddell had recruited the Hearts assistant-manager Jock Wallace to become the new first-team coach at Rangers. The man who had inspired Berwick Rangers to their famous Scottish Cup triumph over the Glasgow giants three years earlier was now charged with the task of whipping the Ibrox side into shape.

Youth to the Fore

Waddell and Wallace decided to give youth its head in 1970-71, as players such as Alfie Conn, Alex Miller and Graham Fyfe had showed plenty enough talent to make the grade. Sandy Jardine, on the fringes of first team action for some time, became a regular as did Alex MacDonald who had been signed by Davie White from St Johnstone for £50,000 in November 1968. If the youthful side were too inconsistent to threaten Celtic's dominance in the championship, the policy paid off dramatically in the League Cup as Rangers won their first trophy for four years.

After cruising through their qualifying section, Waddell's team defeated Hibs in the quarter-finals and surprise packet Cowdenbeath in the semis to set up another final showdown with Celtic at Hampden on 24 October 1970. It would be a day 16-year-old Derek Johnstone would never forget.The Dundee-born teenager had scored twice on his first team debut in a 5-0 league win over Cowdenbeath at Ibrox a month earlier, but few could believe Waddell and Wallace's decision to hand him only his second starting appearance in an Old Firm cup final. Johnstone's prodigious heading ability, however, proved the key to a famous victory as he memorably leapt to head in a Willie Johnston cross for the only goal of the match five minutes before half-time. It was the start of a tremendous Rangers career.

By the time the League Cup was collected, Rangers had gone out of Europe at the first hurdle, although there was no disgrace in their 2-1

Great Matches

SCOTTISH LEAGUE CUP FINAL   **Hampden Park, 24 October 1970**

Rangers 1   **Celtic 0**   **Attendance 106,263**
Johnstone

Having produced an abject display in losing 2-0 at home to Aberdeen in the league seven days earlier, Rangers went into the first showpiece game of the season as firm underdogs against a Celtic side seeking a sixth successive League Cup triumph.

The absence of injured skipper John Greig was another pre-match blow for the Ibrox men and, to many, there seemed to be a hint of desperation in manager Willie Waddell's shock inclusion in the starting line-up of 16-year-old Derek Johnstone. The teenage striker had previously started just one first team match, scoring twice in a 5-0 league win over Cowdenbeath, and it appeared to be a tremendous risk to throw such an inexperienced and youthful player into a high-profile contest.

Johnstone, however, would prove the key to Rangers winning their first major trophy since lifting the Scottish Cup four years earlier. Five minutes from the end of a first half dominated by Rangers, despite playing into the driving wind and rain, Willie Henderson and Alex MacDonald combined to release Willie Johnston on the right wing. His cross towards the penalty spot was aimed for Johnstone who was sandwiched between Celtic's experienced defensive pair of Billy McNeill and Jim Craig. With the kind of prodigious leap which would be his trademark in an outstanding career, Johnstone soared above both men to plant a header firmly beyond keeper Evan Williams.

Celtic pressed hard for an equalizer at the start of the second half, driven on by the craft of Bobby Murdoch, but their best chance was missed by Willie Wallace who drove the ball high over Peter McCloy's crossbar from close range.

In the end, there was no doubting the merit of Rangers' surprise victory over Jock Stein's men and they were desperately unlucky not to double their lead when Colin Stein burst clear and fired in a shot which struck a post and rebounded into the grateful arms of Williams.

The final whistle prompted tremendous celebrations at the Rangers end of a packed Hampden while Willie Waddell savoured his first trophy success at the club since replacing Davie White as manager the previous year.

Rangers: McCloy, Jardine, Miller, Conn, McKinnon, Jackson, Henderson, MacDonald, Johnstone, Stein, Johnston

Celtic: Williams, Craig, Quinn, Murdoch, McNeill, Hay, Johnstone, Connelly, Wallace, Hood (Lennox), Macari

Referee: T. Wharton (Glasgow)

1970 League Cup final action. Colin Stein (second right) strikes the ball past Celtic goalkeeper Evan Williams, only for his shot to hit the post and rebound back into the keeper's hands.

aggregate loss to a tremendous Bayern Munich side who rode their luck in the opening round Fairs Cup tie.

Rangers were already well out of the championship race when Celtic, locked in tight battle for the title with Aberdeen, visited Ibrox on 2 January 1971. It was a day which cast a dark shadow over Rangers and Scottish football as a whole. An unremarkable game had a remarkable ending, Jimmy Johnstone firing Celtic in front a minute from time before Colin Stein equalized for Rangers with almost the last touch of the ball.

After the dramatic finale came an appalling tragedy as 66 people died and 145 were injured in a crush of bodies making their way out of the stadium down stairway 13 at the Copland Road end of the ground. It was initially believed the carnage was caused by fans trying to rush back up the steps on hearing the roar which greeted Stein's goal but the Fatal Accident Inquiry later established the disaster occured some five minutes after the final whistle when some of those leaving stumbled, causing a domino effect.

The rest of the season was played out against an almost surreal backdrop of grief and recrimination, Waddell taking a leading role in organising Rangers' response. The long term outcome of his deliberations would be the reconstruction of Ibrox Stadium into the magnificent and safe arena it is today.

When action resumed on the pitch, Rangers trailed home in fourth place in the championship, a massive 15 points behind Celtic who held off Aberdeenís challenge to win a sixth successive title.

Rangers entertained hopes of a cup double as they beat a path beyond Falkirk, St Mirren, Aberdeen and Hibs to reach the final of the Scottish Cup.

50 Greatest Players

WILLIE HENDERSON Winger

Joined Rangers: June 1960   **From:** School

Debut: v Clyde, League, 11 March 1961

Appearances: 426   **Goals:** 62

Left Rangers: July 1972   **For:** Sheffield Wednesday

Honours won with Rangers: 2 league championships; 4 Scottish Cups; 2 Scottish League Cups; 29 caps (Scotland)

He may have been both myopic and diminutive but anyone who saw him play could see that Willie Henderson was a giant player for Rangers. Just 17 when he made his first team debut, the Airdrie-born schoolboy signing became one of the most exciting talents ever to pass through the Ibrox front door.

An outside right of blistering pace and impossible trickery, the prodigious Henderson won the first of his 29 Scotland caps at the age of 18 and by season 1962-63 had achieved the considerable feat of displacing Alex Scott as the regular Rangers No. 7.

Contact lens-wearing Henderson appeared to possess an in-built radar system as his supply of crosses more often than not found their way to grateful team-mates in the opposition penalty area. A fun-loving character off the pitch, 'Wee Willie' had his share of disciplinary problems but his contributions on the field were beyond reproach.

Henderson played in the 1967 European Cup-Winners' Cup final and five years later, when Rangers won the competition, he scored crucial goals en route to the final but did not play in Barcelona.

Having lost his place in the side to Tommy McLean, Henderson was sold to Sheffield Wednesday in the summer of 1972. Two years later, he moved to Hong Kong Rangers before returning to Scotland to finish his career with home town club Airdrie. He retired in 1979.

Celtic, however, exacted revenge for their League Cup final defeat at the hands of the Ibrox men. Incredibly, Derek Johnstone scored again, this time three minutes from the end of the match to earn a 1-1 draw and force a replay on 12 May 1971.

Celtic took command of the replay with two goals in as many first half minutes from Macari and Hood, Rangers' sole response in the second half coming from Jim Craig's own goal as the Parkhead side lifted the trophy.

In the summer of 1971 Waddell made a significant addition to his squad with the £60,000 capture of Scotland winger Tommy McLean from Kilmarnock. He would prove an inspired buy as Rangers embarked on one of the most memorable seasons in their history.

The campaign started tamely, Rangers losing their grip on the League Cup when they failed to qualify from their section. They lost twice to Celtic, despite both matches being played at Ibrox because of reconstruction work taking place at Parkhead. In the league, the loss of four of their first five matches, including another home defeat at the hands of Celtic, made it fairly clear from an early stage that Rangers' lengthy wait to reclaim the title would be further extended. They did respond by winning 12 of their next 13 games but then lost 2-1 to leaders Celtic on 3 January 1972 to end any lingering hopes. Rangers won just two of their last seven matches to finish in third place, 16 points adrift of champions Celtic.

The Ibrox club's season had become consumed by their efforts in the European Cup-Winners' Cup where they were enjoying a magnficent campaign against high class opposition. French club Rennes had been narrowly beaten in the first round before Rangers secured a dramatic away goals victory over Sporting Lisbon of Portugal in round two. Serie A side Torino were edged out 2-1 on aggregate in the last eight to set up a semi-final showdown with old foes Bayern Munich. It was third time lucky for Rangers, beaten by the Germans in the 1967 Cup-Winners' Cup final and in the first round of the Fairs Cup in 1970-71.

A 1-1 first leg draw in Munich set up a huge night at Ibrox on 19 April 1972, where goals from Jardine and young European debutant Derek Parlane earned Rangers a deserved 2-0 win in front of 80,000 jubilant supporters. Five years on from their great disappointment, Rangers would have another opportunity to win one of the world's most prestigious competitions.

A 2-0 defeat to Hibs in the Scottish Cup semi-final replay at Hampden five days later meant all of Rangers' attention was focused on their third European Cup-Winners' Cup final where they would face Dinamo Moscow in Barcelona on 24 May.

50 Greatest Players

WILLIE JOHNSTON Winger

Joined Rangers: June 1964   **From:** Lochore Welfare

Debut: v St Johnstone, League Cup, 29 August 1964

Left Rangers: December 1972   **For:** West Bromwich Albion

Rejoined Rangers: August 1980   **From:** Vancouver Whitecaps

Left Rangers: March 1982   **For:** Hearts

Appearances: 393   **Goals:** 125

Honours won with Rangers: 1 Scottish Cups; 2 Scottish League Cup; 1 European Cup-Winners' Cup; 9 caps (Scotland)

Another in the seemingly endless line of top-class wingers to appear for Rangers, the Ibrox club perhaps did not get the very best of Johnston. His place among the greats, however, is merited by his two goals in the 1972 European Cup-Winners' Cup final victory alone.

An outside left of exceptional pace and delightful skills, 'Bud' Johnston was still two months short of his 18th birthday when he helped Rangers lift the League Cup in his debut season. League championship success would elude Johnston, however, this genuine entertainer soon became a fans' favourite and enjoyed his finest hour in Barcelona in May 1972. A key performer en route to the final, his double against Dinamo Moscow in the Nou Camp ensured Rangers would lift their first European trophy. A sweet moment for the man who had been in the side beaten by Bayern Munich in the 1967 final.

Bedevilled by on-field indiscipline and clashes with management, Johnston was sold to West Bromwich Albion in 1972 for £135,000. Despite success in English football, his career found its nadir when he was sent home from the 1978 World Cup finals in Argentina after failing a drugs test. He won his 22nd and final cap for Scotland in the infamous 3-1 defeat by Peru.

He moved to Vancouver Whitecaps the following year, returned to Britain for a loan spell with Birmingham City then rejoined an ailing Rangers in 1980. A free transfer in 1982 saw him continue his career with Hearts and Falkirk before retiring in 1985 to become a publican in Kirkcaldy.

Great Matches

EUROPEAN CUP-WINNERS' CUP FINAL   Nou Camp, Barcelona, 24 May 1972

Rangers 3
Stein
Johnston 2

Dinamo Moscow 2
Estrekov
Makovikov

Attendance 45,000

It was a glorious case of third time lucky for Rangers as they finally got their hands on a European trophy. After losing out to Fiorentina and Bayern Munich in the 1961 and 1967 Cup-Winners' Cup finals respectively, victory for the Ibrox club on a heady night in Barcelona tasted all the sweeter.

If Catalonia seemed a long way from home for Dinamo Moscow, with Rangers supporters making up the bulk of the Nou Camp crowd, the Russian side didn't let it show as they made the brighter start to a thrilling contest. Rangers, with goalkeeper Peter McCloy at the top of his game, weathered the early storm and made the crucial breakthrough on 24 minutes. Dave Smith's raking pass over the advancing defence picked out Colin Stein and the centre forward drilled a close range shot beyond keeper Pilgui. McCloy's fine save denied Makovikov a quick equalizer for Dinamo and Rangers took full advantage, doubling their lead five minutes before half-time. Smith was again the creator, finding Willie Johnston with a delightful cross which the winger headed beyond Pilgui from six yards.

Rangers had the European trophy they craved so badly firmly in sight and appeared to put the issue beyond doubt when they made it 3-0 four minutes into the second half. McCloy's booming clearance from his own penalty area soared into the Dinamo box where Johnston reacted quickest to drill home a left-foot shot.

Just before the hour mark Dinamo hopes flickered when they pulled a goal back, Estrekov beating McCloy with a close range header. Three minutes from time Rangers found themselves in a sweat when Makovikov drove a shot high beyond McCloy to reduce the deficit to 3-2 for the Russians.

Happily for manager Willie Waddell, first team coach Jock Wallace and the players, the Spanish referee's final whistle blew without further scoring and Rangers had achieved their greatest triumph at the culmination of a campaign which saw them defeat top quality opposition from France, Portugal, Italy and Germany. Greig and his team-mates had ensured they would be revered for years to come as the men who brought European success to the club.

Rangers: McCloy, Jardine, Mathieson, Greig, Johnstone, Smith, McLean, Conn, Stein, MacDonald, Johnston

Dinamo Moscow: Pilgui, Basalev, Dolmatov, Zykov, Dobbonosov (Gerschkovitch), Zhukov, Baidatchini, Jakubik (Estrekov), Sabo, Makovikov, Evryuzhikbin

Referee: Jose de Mendibil (Spain)

European glory. Above: Colin Stein celebrates after scoring the opening goal. Below left: Alex MacDonald charges through the Moscow defence. Below right: John Greig shows off the cup from the team bus.

It was Willie Waddell's finest hour. Urged on by a huge travelling support, Rangers finally captured the European trophy they craved so badly. Sadly the celebrations of the Rangers fans turned sour in clashes with Franco's ruthless Spanish police. The trophy presentation was cancelled, Greig receiving the cup from UEFA officials out of public view in the bowels of Barcelona's Nou Camp stadium.

Nonetheless, it had been a fine achievement by Rangers and one which set the seal on Waddell's managerial reign. On 7 June 1972 he made the unexpected announcement that he was handing the job over to Jock Wallace. Waddell moved into an administrative role as the club's general manager where his influence on Rangers' affairs would be even more dominant.

His first task was to fight UEFA's decision, in the aftermath of the trouble in Barcelona, to ban Rangers from European competition for two years. Waddell succeeded in having the suspension reduced to just one season. It left Rangers unable to defend their trophy in 1972-73 but, together, Waddell and Wallace would ensure the club built on that success.

Great Managers – 1969-1972

WILLIE WADDELL

When Willie Waddell returned to Ibrox on 3 December 1969, it was to a Rangers in some disarray. The club had not won the league championship since 1964 and were without a major trophy of any description since lifting the Scottish Cup two years later. One of the club's all-time greatest players (see page 85), Waddell's affection for Rangers had remained undiluted since he hung up his boots and left Ibrox in 1956. A year later, he had begun his managerial career at Kilmarnock and enjoyed tremendous success with the Rugby Park club, culminating in the first league championship of their history in 1965. Waddell left Kilmarnock the same year to pursue a career in journalism. Having rejected several high profile offers to return to management, he was finally tempted by his first love when Rangers dismissed the relatively inexperienced David White in 1969.

In October 1970, a revitalised Rangers ended their trophy famine when they defeated Celtic 1-0 in the League Cup final and Waddell went on to steer the club to their greatest triumph, lifting the European Cup-Winners' Cup two years later. Waddell also displayed his gift for strong leadership and cogent administration when dealing with the dark days which followed the Ibrox Disaster in January 1971. He became general manager of the club after the Cup-Winners' Cup success and oversaw the marvellous reconstruction of Ibrox Stadium. Waddell continued to serve Rangers as vice-chairman and managing director until 1984. He died on 14 October 1992 at the age of 71.

Chapter Eight: 1972-86
Trebles and Troubles

Jock Wallace's first season as Rangers manager started well and finished triumphantly, but was not without its problems in-between times. The team emerged safely from a League Cup qualifying section which included Clydebank, St Mirren and Ayr United but their start to the league campaign was far less convincing as they lost three of their first five matches.

There was clearly no time to rest on the laurels of the Cup-Winners' Cup triumph and within six months of the heady evening in Barcelona, Rangers had sold both goalscoring heroes of the final. Colin Stein joined Coventry City in October 1972 in a deal which saw Quinton Young and a cash adjustment of £90,000 come Rangers way, then in December they sold Wille Johnston to West Bromwich Albion for £135,000. Meanwhile, Wallace made his first signing as Rangers manager when defender Tom Forsyth came from Motherwell for what would prove to be a bargain fee of £40,000.

The League Cup bid ended at the semi-final stage, John Brownlie scoring the only goal of a tense affair at Hampden for eventual tournament winners Hibs, but Rangers recovered impressively from their poor start in the league, losing just one more fixture all season. That defeat, at home to Hearts on 2 December 1972, would ultimately prove crucial.

Despite winning 17 of their last 18 matches, dropping a solitary point in their penultimate game against Aberdeen at Pittodrie, Rangers still ended the season as runners-up to Celtic who clinched their eighth successive title by just one point.

General manager Waddell had ensured Rangers would not be completely devoid of European action in 1972-73, despite the UEFA ban. He was a prime mover in the setting up of the European Super Cup which saw Ajax, the European Cup holders, face Cup-Winners' Cup holders Rangers over two legs in the inaugural competition in January 1973. The fabulous Dutch side, which boasted luminaries such as Johann Cruyff, Ruud Krol, Arie Haan, Johnny Rep, Johan Neeskens and Arnold Muhren, won 3-1 at Ibrox before triumphing 3-2 in the Amsterdam return against an outclassed but far from disgraced Rangers team.

The Scottish Cup, in its centenary year, provided the last hope of a trophy for Wallace in his first season and Rangers found their way past Dundee United, Hibs, Airdrie and Ayr United to book another Old Firm final. It turned out to be something of a classic, Tom Forsyth stabbing home a celebrated close range winner for Rangers in a thrilling 3-2 victory.

It gave Rangers their first Scottish Cup win since 1966 and provided Wallace with an ideal platform on which to build. The summer of 1973 also saw a significant boardroom change at Ibrox as Lawrence Marlborough, grandson of retiring chairman John Lawrence, was appointed a director. More than a decade later, Marlborough would be a central figure in one of the great dramas of the Rangers story.

Season 1973-74 started brightly for Rangers, as they topped their League Cup qualifying section which included Celtic. However, a change in the competition format meant the top two progressed to the knock-out stages and it eventually worked against the Ibrox men who were beaten 3-1 at Hampden when the Old Firm, almost inevitably, met again in the semi-finals.

All in all, it was a deeply disappointing campaign for Wallace and his players. They dropped seven points from their first six league matches and, despite winning eight of the next nine, were never likely to sustain a title challenge. A 1-0 defeat at Parkhead on 5 January confirmed as much and Rangers eventually finished third, five points behind nine-in-a-row champions Celtic with Hibs in the runners-up spot.

Alfie Conn (right) beats Brogan and keeper Hunter for Rangers' second goal in the 1973 Cup final.

Great Matches

SCOTTISH CUP FINAL   **Hampden Park, 5 May 1973**

Rangers 3   **Celtic 2**   **Attendance 122,714**
Parlane   Dalglish
Conn   Connelly (pen)
Forsyth

Scottish football's most famous tournament celebrated its 100th birthday and, in front of the last six-figure crowd recorded in the country, the celebrations were savoured by Rangers who won a classic contest to lift the Scottish Cup for the first time since 1966.

Celtic, who had claimed an eighth successive league championship by a solitary point from the Ibrox club just seven days earlier, went into the high profile final as slight favourites. Jock Stein's men set about justifying that status and made the brighter start to a fast-paced and hugely entertaining match. They took a deserved lead in 24 minutes when Davie Hay and Dixie Deans combined to create an opening for Kenny Dalglish which the precocious striker finished superbly, drilling a low shot beyond Rangers keeper Peter McCloy. Jock Wallace's side responded admirably and 10 minutes later restored parity. Alex MacDonald beat George Connelly on the left and swept over a cross which Derek Parlane, at full stretch, headed past Ally Hunter in the Celtic goal.

Remarkably, Rangers went 2-1 ahead just 17 seconds into the second half after Celtic kicked off. Connelly was dispossessed by Quinton Young who fed Parlane. He in turn ushered the ball into the path of Alfie Conn who outstripped Billy McNeill to slam a fierce shot beyond Hunter. Rangers' lead lasted just six minutes. A superb move involving Johnstone, Dalglish and Deans ended with the latter firing in a netbound shot which was blocked on the line by John Greig. Referee Gordon spotted a handball by the Rangers captain and Connelly stepped up to convert the penalty kick to make it 2-2.

It was now pulsating stuff for the huge crowd and it was Rangers who grabbed what proved to be the winner on the hour. Derek Johnstone headed a Tommy McLean free-kick against a post and the ball rolled along the goal-line into the path of Tom Forsyth. The defender, signed earlier in the season from Motherwell, could hardly believe his luck as he bundled the ball home to claim his first goal for the club.

It was enough to ensure Rangers finished their own centenary season on a high and gave Jock Wallace his first trophy since succeeding Willie Waddell as manager at Ibrox.

Rangers: McCloy, Jardine, Mathieson, Greig, Johnstone, MacDonald, McLean, Forsyth, Parlane, Conn, Young

Celtic: Hunter, McGrain, Brogan (Lennox), Murdoch, McNeill, Connelly, Johnstone, Deans, Dalglish, Hay, Callaghan

Referee: J.R.P. Gordon (Newport-on-Tay)

After a comfortable 6-0 aggregate win over Turkish side Ankaragucu in the first round of the European Cup-Winners' Cup, Rangers were convincingly defeated 5-3 by an impressive Borussia Mönchengladbach outfit, boasting German internationals Jupp Heynckes, Berti Vogts and Rainer Bonhof.

The Scottish Cup, won in such style the previous season, was surrendered meekly at the fourth round stage. Playing on a Sunday for the first time, Rangers were humbled 3-0 at Ibrox by Dundee.

Wallace, then, had much to prove when the 1974-75 season got underway and failure to qualify from their League Cup section did little to prove that the team was capable of preventing Celtic claiming a 10th successive title.

Alfie Conn, another of the Barcelona heroes, had been sold to Spurs for £140,000 during the summer and Rangers needed a spark to ignite a credible title challenge. It came in the shape of Bobby McKean, an exciting right-sided midfielder signed from St Mirren for £40,000 in September 1974.

Rangers won 10 and drew two of their first dozen league games, including a 2-1 win over Celtic at Parkhead, but the defending champions fought back to hold a narrow lead at the turn of the year. Rangers, at last finding form and consistency when it mattered most, completed the double over Celtic with a stylish 3-0 win at Ibrox on 4 January 1975 and never looked back.

The Return of Stein

The popular return of Colin Stein from Coventry in March gave the team a boost and, it was the fans' favourite who scored the goal in a 1-1 draw at Easter Road at the end of that month which clinched Rangers' first title since 1964. There were tremendous scenes of celebration, even injured captain John Greig appearing as a substitute for the final minute. Rangers had done it with four games to spare and eventually finished seven points clear of Hibs with Celtic, their long spell of dominance finally over, back in third.

Rangers had failed to extend their Scottish Cup bid beyond their opening tie, losing 2-1 to Aberdeen in an Ibrox replay, and had no European football to enjoy. But, they were to make up for such disappointments in the next season. Having broken Celtic's spell, Wallace and Rangers set out to weave one of their own over Scottish football and they achieved it spectacularly well in 1975-76, repeating the achievements of Bill Struth's 1948-49 squad and Scot Symon's 1963-64 vintage by winning the domestic treble.

The League Cup was collected for the first time in five years, a spectacular diving header from Alex MacDonald was all that separated Rangers from Celtic in a closely-fought final at Hampden on 25 October 1975, in which Tom Forsyth was outstanding in defence for the Ibrox men.

Alex MacDonald's fantastic diving header wins the 1975 League Cup for Rangers.

It was a new era for Scottish football, the inaugural season of the 10-team Scottish Premier Division which, most notably, meant the Old Firm would now face each other four times during each championship campaign. Rangers made the perfect start, defeating Celtic 2-1 at Ibrox on the opening day, but after winning their first three games they then shed 13 points from the next 12. Celtic had a three point lead at the top of the table at the end of 1975 but Rangers started to reel them in with a 1-0 win in the Ne'erday fixture at Ibrox.

Wallace's team were unbeaten for the rest of the season and clinched the title with two games to spare, top scorer Derek Johnstone scoring the only goal of the match against Dundee United at Tannadice on 24 April 1976 after just 22 seconds. Rangers finished six points clear of runners-up Celtic.

Hopes of European Cup success had been extinguished by an admirable St Etienne side, the French team defeating Rangers 4-1 on aggregate in the second round and eventually returning to Glasgow for the final which they lost narrowly to Bayern Munich.

The Rangers support, however, were more than satisfied with their club's rediscovered domestic supremacy and the treble was completed at Hampden on 1 May 1976 when Hearts were comfortably beaten 3-1 in the Scottish Cup final. Johnstone again displayed his liking for early goals, netting the opener in 42 seconds, then struck again late on after Alex MacDonald had claimed the second.

After the feast, a totally unexpected famine struck Rangers in 1976-77 which could not have been in starker contrast to the highs of the previous season. They made a stumbling start to the defence of the title, winning just two of their first eight matches, and were always trailing. Crucially, they lost two and drew two of the four Old Firm fixtures and finished the campaign in second place, nine points behind new champions Celtic.

There was no compensation on offer in the cup competitions. Most disappointing was a first round European Cup exit, losing 2-1 on aggregate to the unremarkable Swiss champions FC Zurich. The League Cup was lost at the semi-final stage, Rangers crushed 5-1 by Ally MacLeod's vibrant Aberdeen side. Wallace's team, perhaps, were still recovering from being pushed to a four-match marathon in the quarter-finals by First Division side Clydebank who were inspired by a young winger called Davie Cooper.

A Second Treble then Tragedy

Rangers did reach the Scottish Cup final, defeating Motherwell and Hearts along the way, but the third of the previous year's trophies was lost in controversial circumstances. The Ibrox men bitterly disputed the penalty award for handball against Derek Johnstone, the kick converted by Andy Lynch to give Celtic the only goal of the match.

It was clear the Rangers squad needed a fresh injection of talent for 1977-78 and they duly arrived. Gordon Smith, an astute striker recruited from Kilmarnock for £65,000, the poised midfield talent of Bobby Russell who was unearthed from junior football and winger Davie Cooper, who cost £100,000 from Clydebank. Together they provided the inspiration which allowed Jock Wallace to match Jock Stein's achievement of winning a second domestic treble.

The loss of their first two games against Aberdeen and Hibs suggested Rangers would struggle in the league again, but they then compiled a 14- match unbeaten run, including 12 wins, to open a healthy lead at the top of the table over the Dons. The Pittodrie club emerged as Rangers' main title challengers, defeating Wallace's side 4-0 in Aberdeen on Christmas Eve and then 3-0 at Ibrox in March 1978. The gap at the top had narrowed but Rangers recovered to win five of their last six fixtures, clinching the title on the final day with a 2-0 win over Motherwell at Ibrox. They finished just two points clear of Aberdeen.

A new knockout format had been introduced in the League Cup and Rangers eliminated holders Aberdeen 7-4 on aggregate in the third round en route to an Old Firm final. Smith scored the winner three minutes from the

50 Greatest Players

COLIN STEIN Centre forward

Joined Rangers: October 1968   **From:** Hibernian

Debut: v Arbroath, league, 2 November 1968

Left Rangers: October 1972   **For:** Coventry City

Rangers: March 1975   **From:** Coventry City

Left Rangers: May 1978 (retired)

Appearances: 206   **Goals:** 97

Honours won with Rangers: 1 league championship; 2 Scottish Cups; 2 Scottish League Cups; 1 European Cup-Winners' Cup; 17 caps (Scotland)

By scoring a remarkable eight goals in his first three games for Rangers, Colin had an impossibly high standard to maintain. However, this rumbustious centre forward, who was Scottish football's first six-figure player when Rangers paid Hibs £100,000 for him, became one of the most popular strikers to play for the club.

The Linlithgow-born Stein was a goal predator who made his physical presence felt against even the most uncompromising defenders. In 1972, he wrote his name indelibly into Ibrox folklore with his contribution to the Cup-Winners' Cup triumph in Barcelona.

Stein scored four goals over the two legs of the extraordinary second round tie against Sporting Lisbon, then grabbed the opener in the final. Just months later, he found himself on his way to Coventry. However, in March 1975, with the English club unable to maintain the payments, Stein returned to Ibrox. In fairytale fashion, he scored the goal at Easter Road which clinched the club's first league championship for 11 years.

Stein was capped 21 times for Scotland, four of his 10 goals for his country coming in one match against Cyprus. Gradually marginalized as a first team contributor, he was offered a free transfer in the summer of 1978, but decided to retire.

---

end of extra time at Hampden, Celtic defender Edvaldsson having cancelled out Cooper's opener for Rangers in normal time. Rangers' joy was laced with great sadness, their 2-1 victory coming just two days after midfielder Bobby McKean was tragically found dead in his car outside his home.

The Cup-Winners' Cup campaign had ended with a disappointing 3-0 aggregate defeat at the hands of Dutch side Twente Enschede in the first round, giving Rangers ample time to concentrate on domestic matters.

Aberdeen stood between them and the completion of a second 'treble' in three seasons when the teams met in the Scottish Cup final on 6 May 1978. Alex MacDonald gave Rangers a half-time lead which Johnstone doubled just before the hour. Ian Ritchie's counter for the Dons five minutes from time ensured a nervy finale but Rangers held out to complete a terrific achievement.

The club's supporters scarcely had time to savour it, however. Just over two weeks later, on 23 May, Jock Wallace dropped a bombshell by resigning as Rangers manager. He moved to England to take charge of Second Division Leicester City with no reason given for his sudden and wholly unexpected departure from a club he clearly loved.

It was suggested the relationship between Willie Waddell and Wallace had been strained and also that the manager had become frustrated by the parsimony of the Rangers' board. Whatever, Wallace never revealed his reasons and never uttered a word of criticism about Rangers.

Greig Takes Over

Waddell wasted no time in appointing Wallace's replacement. On 24 May 1978, John Greig was named as the seventh manager in Rangers' history. The long-serving club captain immediately announced his retirement as a player at the age of 35 as he looked to make the transition from dressing room to manager's office as smoothly as possible.

The initial signs could only be regarded as highly promising. With virtually the same squad which had won the 'treble', Derek Johnstone having been persuaded by Greig to succeed him as captain and withdraw a transfer request, the new boss so nearly kept all three trophies at Ibrox in 1978-79.

Despite a poor start in the league, which saw them win just one of their first nine games and drop 10 points in the process, Rangers clawed their way back into title contention. Dundee United were the early season pace-setters but it ultimately came down to an Old Firm head-to-head title race.

When Rangers defeated Celtic 1-0 on 5 May in a home fixture played at Hampden because of reconstruction work at Ibrox, they moved one point clear with four games to play. When the teams met again at Parkhead 16 days later, Rangers needed just a point to retain the championship while Celtic knew a win would give them the title.

In a pulsating contest, Rangers led 1-0 at half-time through Bobby Russell's goal and when Johnny Doyle was sent off 10 minutes into the second half, the reigning champions appeared to be in firm control. The home side hit back, however, taking a 2-1 lead with goals from Aitken and McCluskey before Alex MacDonald levelled with 14 minutes remaining. Rangers had the point they needed, but with five minutes remaining, Colin Jackson put through his own net. Heartbroken, Rangers' could only watch as Murdo MacLeod added a fourth just before the final whistle.

50 Greatest Players

JOHN GREIG Defender

Joined Rangers: June 1960   **From:** Edina Hearts

Debut: v Airdrie, League Cup, 2 September 1961

Appearances: 755   **Goals:** 120

Left Rangers: May 1978 (retired)

Honours won with Rangers: 5 league championships;
6 Scottish Cups; 4 Scottish League Cups, 1 European
Cup-Winners' Cup; 44 caps (Scotland)

As the 20th century drew to a close, John Greig was voted the
'Greatest Ever Ranger' by the club's supporters. It is an assessment
with which it is difficult to argue. The Edinburgh-born Greig was
part of two great Rangers teams, in the early 1960s and the mid
1970s, but just as crucially in the minds of those fans was his
inspirational commitment to the club during less successful times.

Although not lacking in ability, as his 44 caps for Scotland testify, Greig was not the
most talented player to represent Rangers. He was, however, the most extraordinarily
committed and resolute individual to play for the club.

Greig started out as an inside forward, scoring on his debut, nine days before his
19th birthday. It was soon recognised, however, that his natural position was in defence
and it was from there he utilised his qualities to best effect for Rangers, winning his
first league championship in 1963 and then the domestic 'treble' the following year.

When that Rangers team eventually broke up and the Ibrox club found themselves
overshadowed by Jock Stein's Celtic, Greig came to the fore as an exemplary captain,
who refused to accept second best. His reward was to be the leader of the team who
restored pre-eminence to Rangers under Jock Wallace by winning the 'treble' in both
1976 and 1978. Greig, who had captained his country in the famous 1967 Wembley
victory over England, retired abruptly in the summer of 1978 to replace Wallace as
Rangers manager. Agonizingly close to another 'treble' in his first season in charge,
Greig's reign grew progressively less successful and he resigned in October 1983.

He worked as a radio pundit and in the travel business, until Rangers welcomed one
of their greatest servants back into the fold in 1990 as a public relations manager.

Celtic finished three points clear of Rangers and it would be as close as
Greig would come to winning the title as manager. His first season in charge,
however, was still a success with both domestic cups retained.

Aberdeen were beaten 2-1 in the League Cup final on 31 March 1979,
Celtic having been edged out 3-2 in extra-time in a thrilling semi-final.

PSV Eindhoven's Kees Krijgh (third left) is unable to prevent Derek Parlane getting in a header at goal during the European Cup clash in 1978.

The Scottish Cup campaign was a somewhat tortuous affair, Rangers needing replays against both Kilmarnock and Partick Thistle before engaging Hibs in a marathon three-match final.

The first match at Hampden on 12 May and the replay four days later both finished goalless and were as dull as that suggests. The second replay, delayed until 28 May because of the Old Firm title decider, drew just 30,602 to Hampden but at last provided genuine entertainment. Rangers won 3-2 after extra-time, Hibs left-back Arthur Duncan putting the winner through his own net after Johnstone had scored twice in regulation time.

Rangers also drew great satisfaction from a memorable European Cup campaign. Juventus, one of the tournament favourites, were beaten 2-1 on aggregate in the first round, and Greig's team were equally impressive in defeating Dutch champions PSV Eindhoven 3-2 in Holland in the second round after a goalless draw at Ibrox. The quarter-final draw paired Rangers with Cologne and, hampered by the absence of injured captain Johnstone, the Scots were edged out 2-1 on aggregate by the Bundesliga champions.

Great Matches

EUROPEAN CUP, 2ND ROUND, 2ND LEG   Philips Stadium, 1 November 1978

| **PSV Eindhoven 2** | **Rangers 3** | **Attendance 29,000** |

PSV Eindhoven 2
Lubse
Deijkers

Rangers 3
A. MacDonald
Johnstone
Russell

After a goalless first leg at Ibrox, Rangers travelled to Holland as firm outsiders to claim a place in the quarter-finals of the European Cup. PSV Eindhoven, laced with international players who had featured at the World Cup finals in Argentina a few months before, were expected to finish the job at home.

The Dutch champions could not have made a better start as they opened the scoring after just 34 seconds, striker Harry Lubse taking advantage of some lax defending to drill a low shot beyond Peter McCloy from 14 yards. It was the only goal of the first half and PSV seemed content to sit on their lead.

Rangers, who had beaten one of the pre-tournament favourites Juventus in the first round, knew a scoring draw would be good enough to make further progress and they gradually clawed their way back into the tie. They equalized 12 minutes into the second half with a fine and familiar goal, McLean crossing for Alex MacDonald to head home.

Having worked hard to get back on terms, Rangers were stunned when PSV restored their lead just three minutes later, Gerry Deijkers crashing a spectacular effort past the helpless McCloy. In what was becoming a remarkable match, Rangers responded to make it 2-2 in the 66th minute. McLean touched a free-kick to Kenny Watson whose long range shot was deflected into the net by Derek Johnstone.

As it stood, John Greig's team were already in position to reach the last eight of the European Cup on the away goals rule but, as the Dutchmen surged forward in a desperate search for a winner, it was Rangers who broke away to claim one of their finest ever European victories. Tommy McLean was the creator once again, his threaded pass sending Bobby Russell clear. The young midfielder was coolness personified as he strode forward with the ball and drove it out of reach of the advancing Eindhoven keeper Van Engelen into the corner of the net.

There were only three minutes remaining and the task was now firmly beyond the shattered PSV players.

PSV Eindhoven: Van Engelen, Krijgh (Smits), Stevens, Van Kraay, Brandts, W. Van der Kerkhof, Jansen, Poortvliet, R. Van der Kerkhof, Lubse, Deijkers

Rangers: McCloy, Jardine, A. Forsyth, T. Forsyth, Johnstone, MacDonald, McLean, Russell, Parlane, Smith, Watson

Referee: K. Palotai (Hungary)

The rich promise of the season, however, would not be fulfilled. For Greig and Rangers, 1979-80 was a nightmare and the start of a doleful period in the club's history. Losing seven of their first 15 matches, Rangers were six points off the pace at the turn of the year. The signing of midfielder Ian Redford from Dundee for a record fee of £210,000 in February 1980 sparked a brief spell of better form, but Rangers lost four of their last eight games to drift home in fifth place, 11 points behind Alex Ferguson's Aberdeen who were the first club outside the Old Firm to win the title since 1965.

This time, there was no recompense for Rangers in the cup competitions. The League Cup was surrendered in the third round, losing 5-1 on aggregate to Aberdeen, while the European Cup-Winners' Cup campaign ended with a 4-2 second round aggregate defeat at the hands of an outstanding Valencia side who included Mario Kempes and Rainer Bonhof in their ranks.

Rangers' final chance of salvation came in the Scottish Cup where Celtic, who finished one point behind Aberdeen in the title race, were also out to ensure they did not finish the season empty-handed. For Rangers, 1-0 winners over Aberdeen in the semi-finals, only victory in the Old Firm final would ensure their qualification for European football the following season.

A fine contest at Hampden on 10 May was settled in extra-time when George McCluskey deflected a Danny McGrain shot beyond the wrong-footed Peter McCloy to claim the only goal for Celtic. Rangers' misery and Celtic's celebrations were overshadowed by a pitch invasion and some dreadful violence after the final whistle. The eventual outcome of the government inquiry into the scenes was the introduction of the Criminal Justice Act (Scotland) which banned alcohol from grounds.

Greig Strengthens the Squad

Greig moved to strengthen his squad during the summer, signing striker Colin McAdam from Partick Thistle and midfielder Jim Bett from Belgian side Lokeren. Willie Johnston, now 33, returned to Ibrox from Vancouver Whitecaps while Alex MacDonald, a tremendous servant for almost 12 years, was sold to Hearts.

Both McAdam, who scored 10 goals in his first 12 league games, and Bett made good starts as Rangers underwent a 15 match unbeaten run which included two wins over Celtic. They were unable to sustain it, however, and won only three of their next 12 fixtures, eventually finishing third in the table, 12 points behind Celtic who deposed runners-up Aberdeen as champions.

Things had started to unravel for Rangers with their exits from two cup competitions in the first half of the season. The 3-2 aggregate loss to

Aberdeen in the third round of the League Cup was controversial and certainly no disgrace but the same could not be said of Rangers' elimination from the Anglo-Scottish Cup.

Appearing in the tournament for the first time as a consequence of their failure to qualify for Europe, Rangers defeated Partick Thistle 5-4 on aggregate in the first round to book a quarter-final tie against Chesterfield. The English Third Division side dished out one of the most embarrassing defeats in Rangers' history. After earning a 1-1 draw in the first leg at Ibrox, the Derbyshire club crushed a shame-faced Rangers 3-0 at their Recreation Ground. Two of Chesterfield's goals came from Phil Bonnyman, a Scottish midfielder who had played one first team match for Rangers during a brief spell at the club in the early 1970s.

Greig badly needed something to restore confidence in his stewardship of the club and he got it in the Scottish Cup. Rangers laboured at times en route to the final, notably in needing a replay against First Division St Johnstone, for whom a teenage Ally McCoist was a scorer, in the fourth round, but eventually turned on the style when they got there.

Dundee United were the opponents at Hampden on 9 May 1981 and Hamish McAlpine's last minute save to keep out an Ian Redford penalty kick ensured a goalless draw. The replay, three days later, saw Rangers, with Johnstone, Cooper and emerging young striker John MacDonald all recalled to the starting line-up, discover their finest form of the season. Cooper, who got the opener, and two-goal MacDonald were especially impressive in a 4-1 win every bit as convincing as the scoreline suggests.

The Scottish Cup triumph, giving Greig his third trophy as Rangers manager, allowed the club to end the season with a feelgood factor but it dissipated fairly rapidly in 1981-82 with another lacklustre league campaign. Ten points were dropped in the first 11 matches and Rangers were never in serious contention. They eventually finished third once more, again 12 points adrift of Celtic who held onto the title by two points from Aberdeen.

Rangers' return to Europe was short-lived as they lost 4-2 on aggregate to an unremarkable Dukla Prague side in the first round of the Cup-Winners' Cup, but Greig and his players were boosted by success in the League Cup. A sectional format had been restored and Rangers were not really tested until the semi-finals where they squeezed past St Mirren 4-3 on aggregate.

The final against Dundee United at Hampden on 28 November 1981, found Rangers trailing to a Ralph Milne goal but they they came back to win 2-1 with spectacular strikes from Cooper and Redford.

Rangers' pursuit of a domestic cup double saw them require a replay to defeat Second Division Forfar Athletic in the semi-finals and book a final date against Aberdeen at Hampden on 22 May 1981. John MacDonald headed the Ibrox men into an early lead but Alex McLeish's stunning and unlikely strike for the Dons took the match into extra-time. Rangers wilted badly and were cut apart by Aberdeen who romped to a 4-1 victory.

At the end of the season Greig gave free transfers to Sandy Jardine and Colin Jackson, Tom Forsyth was forced to retire through injury and Tommy McLean hung up his boots to become assistant-manager. New faces for 1982-83 included Swedish international midfielder Robert Prytz, signed from

50 Greatest Players

TOMMY McLEAN Winger

Joined Rangers: June 1971 **From:** Kilmarnock

Debut: v Celtic, League Cup, 14 August 1971

Appearances: 452   **Goals:** 57

Left Rangers: May 1982 (retired)

Honours won with Rangers: 3 league championships,
4 Scottish Cups; 3 Scottish League Cups; 1 European Cup-
Winners' Cup; 1 cap (Scotland)

The £65,000 paid to Kilmarnock for the services of the diminutive Scotland winger in the summer of 1971 must be regarded as Waddell's shrewdest piece of business as manager. A teenage star in Waddell's title-winning Killie side six years earlier, McLean became perhaps the most precise crosser of the ball ever seen at Ibrox. Wonderfully astute and tactically aware, his range of passing was an exceptional asset for Rangers in open play while his delivery of the ball from set pieces was quite outstanding. In his first season he eclipsed Willie Henderson as first choice outside right in the side which won the European Cup-Winners' Cup and later made an immense contribution to the sides which won domestic 'trebles' in 1976 and 1978.

McLean hung up his boots at the end of the 1981-82 season, becoming assistant-manager to John Greig. He was caretaker manager for three games, all of them lost, after Greig's resignation in October 1983 and left the club when Jock Wallace took over. McLean embarked on a managerial career at Morton, won the Scottish Cup in 1991 with Motherwell and had spells in charge of Hearts, Raith Rovers and Dundee United before returning to Rangers in 2001 as youth development coach.

50 Greatest Players

ALEX MacDONALD Midfielder

Joined Rangers: November 1968   **From:** St Johnstone

Debut: v Clyde, League, 23 November 1968

Appearances: 503   **Goals:** 94

Left Rangers: August 1980   **For:** Hearts

Honours won with Rangers: 3 Scottish league championships; 4 Scottish Cups; 4 League Cups; 1 European Cup-Winners' Cup; 1 cap (Scotland)

Few players relished playing for Rangers more than Alex MacDonald. His pride in representing the club was almost tangible as he hustled and harried his way through more than 500 games in a terrific 12-year career at Ibrox.

The Glasgow-born MacDonald made his name in the fine St Johnstone side managed by Willie Ormond, and was 20 when Rangers paid the Perth club £50,000 for him in 1968. Although he did not immediately earn the approval of the Ibrox crowd, by 1970-71 MacDonald had established himself as a first-team regular.

The tenacious midfielder won over the doubters. He scored crucial goals against Rennes and Torino en route to the 1972 European Cup-Winners' Cup final and became the hub of the dominant mid-1970s side. Surprisingly, MacDonald was capped just once by Scotland, in a friendly against Switzerland in 1976.

At the age of 32, MacDonald went to Hearts for £30,000 and the following year became manager of the Tynecastle club, coming agonizingly close to guiding them to a League and Scottish Cup double in 1986. 'Doddie', as he has always been affectionately known, later took Airdrie to the Scottish Cup finals of 1992 and 1995.

Malmo for £100,000, and defender Craig Paterson from Hibs for a record fee of £225,000. Greig looked to Paterson to form a defensive partnership with John McClelland, the excellent Northern Ireland international brought from Mansfield Town the previous season.

Unfortunately, injury disrupted Paterson's debut season and it was another poor one for Greig and Rangers. They won just four of their opening 14 league games and were 10 points off the pace by Christmas, eventually trailing home in fourth place a massive 18 points behind Dundee United who became Scottish champions for the first and only time in their history.

John MacDonald takes on a Dortmund defender in the UEFA Cup second round, second leg at Ibrox in September 1982. Rangers won 2-0 on the night.

Rangers reached the finals of both domestic cup tournaments but failed to bring any joy into a dismal season. The League Cup was lost 2-1 to Celtic at a sodden Hampden on 4 December 1982, Rangers unable to recover fully from a 2-0 half-time deficit.

The Scottish Cup final was reached courtesy of a controversial extra-time goal by Sandy Clark – signed from West Ham United for £160,000 in March 1983 – in the semi-final replay against St Mirren. Rangers faced Aberdeen, now Cup-Winners' Cup holders, at Hampden on 21 May. Despite looking the better side for lengthy spells, Rangers' lack of a cutting edge allowed the below-par Dons to retain the trophy as Eric Black struck the only goal in extra-time.

The UEFA Cup had merely provided further evidence of Rangers' inadequacies when, after a good first round win over Borussia Dortmund, they were thrashed 6-2 on aggregate by another German side, Cologne, in the second round.

The departure of Jim Bett, one of the season's best performers, at the end of the season, left Greig in desperate need of a good start to the 1983-84 campaign. His one major addition to the squad was Ally McCoist, a

£185,000 capture from Sunderland. The striker would make a massive mark on Rangers' history, but not soon enough for the manager who signed him.

Rangers made a terrible start in the league, losing eight of their first 12 games. It was too much for Greig and, under increasing pressure, he resigned as Rangers manager on 28 October 1983, If his departure had seemed inevitable for some time, it was nonetheless the cause of great sadness that one of the club's most dedicated servants had been unable to match the success of his playing career as manager.

A Popular Appointment

After both Jim McLean of Dundee United and Aberdeen's Alex Ferguson turned the job down, Rangers turned to a familiar face. Jock Wallace, then at Motherwell, returned to Ibrox to begin his second spell as manager on 10 November 1983.

His was a popular appointment among the club's supporters who afforded him a warm welcome and hoped he could repeat his previous triumphs at the club. Wallace initially effected a revival of sorts, but although Rangers put together a 15-match unbeaten run from 19 November to 31 March, they were never able to get back into title contention. They won just two of their last nine games and finished fourth, 15 points behind champions Aberdeen.

Rangers were already out of Europe when Wallace took charge, having lost on away goals to Porto in the second round of the Cup-Winners' Cup under the stewardship of caretaker boss Tommy McLean.

At home, the Scottish Cup offered only further disappointment when Rangers lost 3-2 to Dundee at Ibrox in a quarter-final replay on 17 March 1984. Eight days later, Rangers faced Celtic in the League Cup final in dire need of a pick-me-up and, thanks to a hat-trick from Ally McCoist, who was struggling to win over the Rangers' support, they got it. Celtic twice fought back from a goal down to take the match into extra-time which saw McCoist net a rebound from a penalty blocked by Pat Bonner to clinch a dramatic 3-2 victory.

Wallace made a title challenge his priority for 1984-85 and added more depth and quality to his squad by signing two Dundee players, midfielder Cammy Fraser and striker Iain Ferguson, for a combined fee of £365,000.

He was not helped, however, by the strict wage structure which still prevailed at Ibrox. It prompted John McClelland, who had become an excellent captain and defender for the club, to demand a transfer. He was sold to Watford for £265,000 with Craig Paterson replacing him as skipper.

Rangers made a solid start to their title bid, with just two defeats in their first 20 matches they were still in contention at Christmas. That changed with a 2-1 defeat at the hands of Celtic at Ibrox on New Year's Day 1985, sparking a miserable run which saw Wallace's men win just two of their next 10 games. They finished fourth, a gaping 21 points behind Aberdeen.

The retention of the League Cup was the highlight of another disappointing season, Iain Ferguson scoring the only goal of the final against Dundee United in monsoon-like conditions at Hampden on 28 October 1984, four days after Rangers had lost 3-0 to Inter Milan at the San Siro Stadium in the first leg of their UEFA Cup second round tie.

Rangers produced an heroic effort in the return at Ibrox against a side boasting the talents of Liam Brady and Karl-Heinz Rummenigge, but their 3-1 victory, with Iain Ferguson scoring twice, was not quite good enough.

If the morale of the supporters had been raised by that European effort, it was well and truly sunk when Rangers were knocked out of the Scottish Cup in the fourth round by Dundee at Ibrox on 16 February 1985. John Brown scored the only goal of the game for the Tayside club and the Rangers fans gave vent to their frustration with Ally McCoist the main focus of their ire.

The Seeds of Revolution

Things would get worse before they got better, but 1985-86 turned out to be a seminal one for Rangers and for Scottish football as a whole. The seeds of a revolution were sewn in November 1985 when Lawrence Marlborough, who had resigned as a director of the club two years earlier to concentrate on his business affairs in the United States, purchased enough shares to secure a controlling interest. Marlborough appointed David Holmes as a director at Ibrox and his influence would prove to be highly significant.

On the pitch, Rangers had started the season well enough with five wins and a draw against Celtic in their first six league matches, but an all too familiar scenario unfolded as they won just three of their next 15. As another title challenge faded badly, the cup competitions gave Wallace and his players no respite from their troubles.

Their bid for a third successive League Cup triumph faltered in the semi-finals where they lost 2-1 on aggregate to Hibs and there was a similar outcome against unheralded Spanish opponents Atlético Osasuna in the first round of the UEFA Cup. Effectively, Rangers' season ended on 25 January 1986 when they were beaten 3-2 by Hearts at Tynecastle in the third round of the Scottish Cup.

Holmes, now chief executive of the club, had decided on the course of action to be taken. On 7 April 1986, Jock Wallace was sacked by Rangers and 24 hours later Graeme Souness was paraded at a packed Ibrox press conference and introduced as the club's new player-manager.

50 Greatest Players

SANDY JARDINE Full back

Joined Rangers: June 1965   **From:** School

Debut: v Hearts, League, 4 February 1967

Appearances: 674   **Goals:** 77

Left Rangers: May 1982   **For:** Hearts

Honours won with Rangers: 3 league championships, 5 Scottish Cups, 5 Scottish League Cups, 1 European Cup-Winners' Cup, 17 caps (Scotland)

A week after the most infamous defeat in the club's history at Berwick in the Scottish Cup, Rangers handed 18-year-old Sandy Jardine his senior debut. The 5-1 victory was a portent of the influence of one of the club's most reliable and loyal servants.

Edinburgh-born Jardine played in many positions before establishing himself as one of the finest full backs in Rangers' history. With just a Scottish League Cup medal to his name until 1972, Jardine went on to collect 13 more major honours over the next ten years. The highlight was the 1972 European Cup-Winners' Cup triumph, while he was also an essential part of the 'treble' winning sides of 1976 and 1978.

In hindsight, Rangers were premature in giving Jardine a free transfer at the age of 33, in 1982. He played on for another five years with Hearts, passing the 1,000 mark of senior appearances, and winning his second Scottish Player of the Year award in 1986. Jardine was also an outstanding Scotland international, winning 38 caps for his country and appearing in the World Cup finals of 1974 and 1978. On retiring, he became co-manager of Hearts before leaving football in 1988 for a business career. He is now back at Rangers as part of the club's commercial department.

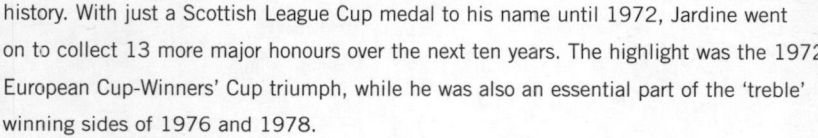

The recruitment of the 32-year-old Scotland captain, whose transfer from Sampdoria at the end of the season would cost £300,000, was a dramatic statement of intent from the new Ibrox regime. Former Liverpool midfielder Souness enjoyed a huge worldwide football profile which would allow him to effect some astonishing changes in playing personnel.

Walter Smith, the highly-rated Dundee United assistant-manager, was named as Souness' right-hand man and his first task was to ensure Rangers achieved European qualification. A 2-0 win over Motherwell at Ibrox on 3 May 1986, the final day of the league campaign, ensured Rangers scraped into the UEFA Cup. They finished fifth in the table, 15 points behind Celtic who edged out Hearts in a dramatic finale to the title race.

Souness, who had spent his whole career outside Scotland, was unable to comprehend the despair among the Rangers supporters that afternoon, the qualification for Europe cast into insignificance for them by the championship triumph of their greatest rivals. He would learn quickly what the Old Firm rivalry was all about, and for the Ibrox fans, things would never be the same again...

Great Managers – 1972-1978 & 1983-1986

JOCK WALLACE

Born and raised in Wallyford, legend has it that the young Jock Wallace would walk the 120-mile round trip from the East Lothian mining village to Ibrox to see Rangers play. Apocryphal or not, the story does justice to a unique man's commitment to the club.

A fine goalkeeper with Airdrie, WBA, Bedford and Hereford, Wallace's first significant imprint on the history of Rangers came in January 1967 when he was player-manager of Berwick as they astonishingly defeated the Ibrox giants 1-0 at Shielfield in the first round of the Scottish Cup. Two years later, he was recruited by Hearts as assistant-manager before the call came in June 1970 from Willie Waddell to become first-team coach at Ibrox. Wallace played a key role in the club's revival under Waddell, culminating in the 1972 European Cup-Winners' Cup triumph, and was installed as manager at the start of the following season when his mentor moved upstairs to become general manager.

Wallace placed great emphasis on fitness and stamina, a legacy of his active army service with the King's Own Scottish Borderers, but also had a keen eye for a player and a sound tactical brain. He was an unqualified success as Rangers manager, winning the Scottish Cup in 1973, the club's first championship for 11 years in 1975 and then completing the 'treble' in both 1975-76 and 1977-78.

Unexpectedly, he resigned in the summer of 1978, his reasons never fully revealed. Wallace became manager of Leicester City, winning the English Second Division title, before returning to Scotland to boss Motherwell in 1982. In October 1983, he became Rangers manager for a second time after John Greig resigned.

Despite two League Cup final wins, Wallace was unable to repeat the great success of his first spell in charge and, in April 1986, he was dismissed. Wallace continued his managerial career with Seville in Spain then Colchester United but his place in the affections of the Rangers fans was undiminished. Troubled by ill health, he died in July 1996 at the age of 61.

Chapter Nine: 1986-98
Souness and Smith

While Graeme Souness and Walter Smith spent part of the 1986 close season in Mexico as captain and assistant manager respectively of Scotland's World Cup squad, the planning for what would be an explosive and unforgettable first season at the Ibrox helm was well underway.

Colin West, purchased from Watford for £200,000, was the first signing of the new regime, but the striker was a mere appetizer of what was to follow for a disbelieving but delighted Rangers support, as David Holmes, Souness and Smith combined to change the club's profile.

There was a distinctly English flavour to the new Ibrox menu, Souness utilizing his profile in the game to reverse the trend of top players leaving Scotland to head south of the border. Defence was set as the priority for the team the new management wanted to build and the first major outlay saw Rangers break the record goalkeeper transfer fee when they paid Norwich City £600,000 for Chris Woods, deputy to England international Peter Shilton.

On the eve of the 1986-87 season came perhaps the most significant and influential capture Souness or Smith ever made when Terry Butcher, the Ipswich Town and England defender coveted by Manchester United and Tottenham, was persuaded to come to Glasgow in a £725,000 move. Butcher was installed as the new Rangers captain and would live up to the reputation of his illustrious predecessors in the role, as he proved an inspirational figure both on and off the pitch.

While success lay ahead, however, Souness and Rangers could hardly have made a worse start. At Easter Road on 9 August 1986, amid a feverish atmosphere, Rangers lost their opening league fixture 2-1 to Hibs, with the new player-manager sent off for a reckless challenge on home striker George McCluskey which sparked a mass brawl.

Graeme Souness calmly questions the linesman's eyesight in the Old Firm clash at Parkhead in April 1987.

50 Greatest Players

PETER McCLOY Goalkeeper

Joined Rangers: March 1970 **From:** Motherwell

Debut: v Dunfermline, League, 14 March 1970

Appearances: 535

Left Rangers: August 1986 (retired)

Honours won with Rangers: 2 league championships;
4 Scottish Cups; 4 Scottish League Cups; 1 European Cup-
Winners' Cup; 4 caps (Scotland)

No goalkeeper in Rangers' history has made more first team
appearances than Peter McCloy and his haul of 11 major
honours in 16 years of service at Ibrox gives him a powerful
claim to be recognized as the finest No. 1 to play for the club.

Signed in 1970 from Motherwell, the 23-year-old McCloy
immediately displaced Gerry Neef as Rangers' first choice keeper. At 6ft 4ins, the
Girvan-born keeper's very presence commanded the respect of opposition forwards.
His prodigious clearances from the hand often found their way into the opposition
penalty area, never more dramatically than when McCloy was able to claim an 'assist'
for Willie Johnston's Cup-Winners' Cup final winner.

After the arrival of Stewart Kennedy in April 1973, McCloy was unable to make the
shirt his own, but his resilience, durability and outstanding fitness enabled him to
extend his career, picking up his final winner's medal in the 1984-85 League Cup final.
He was 39 when he made his last competitive appearance for Rangers in April 1986.
McCloy then became reserve team coach at Ibrox before leaving to become a freelance
goalkeeping coach, combined with business interests in his native Ayrshire.

From such an ignominious beginning, which also saw Rangers lose 3-2 at
home to Dundee United the next Saturday, a recovery was staged. Crucial to
it was a 1-0 win over Celtic at Ibrox at the end of August, Ian Durrant scoring
the goal, in which the home fans began to enthuse at the type of football
Souness was looking to employ.

If the title challenge took some time to click into top gear, Rangers were
sustained by success in the League Cup which saw them defeat Celtic 2-1 in
the final at Hampden on 26 October 1986 with goals from Durrant and Davie
Cooper, the latter netting the winner from the penalty spot.

Although further league defeats were suffered against Dundee, Motherwell
and Aberdeen, Rangers emerged as favourites to win the title when they
compiled a 19-match unbeaten run from 29 November 1986 to 28 March

1987, winning 16 of them. The December signing of no-nonsense defender Graham Roberts from Tottenham for £450,000 proved a pivotal one. A 3-1 defeat at Celtic with five games remaining threw it back into the melting pot, but Rangers were by now determined not to let the club's first title success for nine years pass them by. It was clinched at Pittodrie on 2 May, Butcher's towering header earning a 1-1 draw against Aberdeen in a tempestuous contest which saw Souness sent off again. News of Celtic's shock

50 Greatest Players

DEREK JOHNSTONE Forward/Defender

Joined Rangers: July 1970   **From:** School

Debut: v Cowdenbeath, League, 19 September 1970

Left Rangers: September 1983   **For:** Chelsea

Rejoined Rangers: January 1985   **From:** Chelsea

Left Rangers: June 1986   **For:** Partick Thistle

Appearances: 546   **Goals:** 210

Honours won with Rangers: 3 league championships; 5 Scottish Cups; 5 Scottish League Cups; 1 European Cup-Winners' Cup; 14 caps (Scotland)

To score the only goal in an Old Firm Cup final on your third appearance at the age of 16 is a feat to match any achieved by any player in Rangers' history. But this was to be just the beginning of Derek Johnstone's great career.

If Johnstone's winner against Celtic was the stuff of legend, so too was his appearance at centre half in Rangers' European Cup-Winners' Cup winning side in 1972 when still only 18. Injury to Colin Jackson, who himself had been deputising for leg-break victim Ronnie McKinnon, forced Johnstone's switch to central defence and he was a natural.

The rest of his career saw him feature at both ends of the pitch, and occasionally in midfield, but it was as a goalscorer with both feet and head that he made his mark, helping win two domestic 'trebles' in 1976 and 1978. In the latter season he scored 38 goals for Rangers, was Scottish Player of the Year, yet played no part in Scotland's ill-fated trip to the World Cup finals in Argentina. Johnstone was capped 14 times in all, scoring twice.

In September 1983, he was sold to Chelsea for £30,000 before returning to Ibrox in January 1985 for £25,000. It was an unsuccessful reprise and Rangers gave Johnstone a free transfer in the summer of 1986. He briefly entered management with Partick Thistle before giving up the game for a successful career in the media.

2-1 defeat at home to Falkirk meant the point was enough to crown Rangers champions with one match to spare and spark wild scenes of celebration.

Rangers finished six points clear of deposed champions Celtic and Souness' first season in charge had been an unqualified success. That was despite a shock third round exit from the Scottish Cup in January when Adrian Sprott scored a famous goal for Hamilton Accies at Ibrox whose shock 1-0 win brought to an end a record-breaking sequence of shut-outs for Chris Woods.

If Souness was angry with his team over their Scottish Cup demise, he had saved his fury for the match officials when Rangers were controversially knocked out of the UEFA Cup in the third round on the away goals rule to Borussia Mönchengladbach. The harsh dismissals of Stuart Munro and Davie Cooper in the goalless second leg in Germany were certainly crucial.

The summer of 1987 saw Souness display his ruthless streak with the sale of Dave McPherson, blamed for the Scottish Cup defeat by Hamilton, to Hearts as he continued to reshape the squad. During the 1987-88 season, more big name signings arrived, among them England internationals Trevor Francis and Ray Wilkins, exciting winger Mark Walters and the long coveted defender Richard Gough who came from Spurs for a record £1.1 million. While the emphasis on a high-quality recruitment policy was welcomed, the number of new faces appeared to affect Rangers' consistency as they unsuccessfully defended the Premier Division title.

A poor start saw them lose three of their first five games, including a 1-0 reverse at Celtic, but the most telling blow was the loss of Terry Butcher in November as he suffered a broken leg in a 1-0 defeat at the hands of Aberdeen at Ibrox. Rangers could not cope with the absence of their captain

Ian Durrant strikes the winning penalty in the 1987 League Cup final against Aberdeen.

and eventually finished third in the table, 12 points behind a vibrant Celtic side who were champions in their centenary year.

Rangers did retain the League Cup, defeating Aberdeen in a penalty shoot-out after a 3-3 draw in arguably the finest final in the tournament's history. The Scottish Cup, however, brought dismay for Souness and his team again as they

Great Matches

SCOTTISH LEAGUE CUP FINAL		**Hampden Park, 25 October 1987**
Rangers 3	**Aberdeen 3**	**Attendance 71,961**
Cooper	Bett (pen)	
Durrant	Hewitt	
Fleck	Falconer	

*After extra-time - Rangers won 5-3 on penalties

Handicapped by the suspensions of Woods, Butcher and player-manager Graeme Souness, the Ibrox side were far from overwhelming favourites to defeat a confident and settled Aberdeen outfit at Hampden. When the Pittodrie men took a ninth-minute lead, ex-Ranger Jim Bett stroking home a penalty kick after Nicky Walker had fouled Falconer, the holders' prospects looked even bleaker.

They rallied superbly, however, and equalized with one of the greatest goals ever seen at the famous old stadium. Ally McCoist was fouled by Miller on the edge of the box and Davie Cooper stepped up to lash a stupendous free-kick into the roof of the net.

Five minutes before half-time, Rangers took the lead when Fleck and McCoist combined to set Ian Durrant clear for a cool, low finish. But Aberdeen stormed back in the second half and made it 2-2 on 72 minutes, Hewitt netting with a left-foot shot after Graham Roberts only partially cleared a Miller cross. Ten minutes from time the Dons appeared to have it won when Bett provided the cross for Falconer to head past Walker in the Rangers goal. An amazing match was forced into extra-time, however, when Fleck stabbed home from close range in the 87th minute.

In a draining additional half hour, McCoist missed the best chance to snatch a winner and the first ever League Cup final penalty shoot-out was required. McCoist, Cooper, Fleck and Trevor Francis all scored for Rangers, as did Bett, Peter Weir and Hewitt for Aberdeen. Peter Nicholas then stepped up to crack his effort off the top of the crossbar and over. It was left to Ian Durrant to win the trophy for Rangers and the young midfielder made no mistake, calmly drilling his kick out of Leighton's reach.

Rangers: Walker, Nicholl, Munro, Roberts, Ferguson (Francis), Gough, McGregor (Cohen), Fleck, McCoist, Durrant, Cooper

Aberdeen: Leighton, McKimmie, Connor, Simpson (Weir), McLeish, W. Miller, Hewitt, Bett, J. Miller, P. Nicholas, Falconer

Referee: R. Valentine (Dundee)

slumped to a 2-0 fourth round defeat against Dunfermline at East End Park, which prompted one of the manager's most famous dressing-room tantrums.

In the club's first European Cup campaign for nine years, however, Rangers performed with great credit to reach the quarter-finals. On a heady evening at Ibrox, they overturned a 1-0 first leg deficit against the powerful Soviet champions Dinamo Kiev in the first round. Mark Falco, signed from Watford at the start of the season and sold to Queens Park Rangers before the end of it, and Ally McCoist scored the goals in a 2-0 win.

Gornik Zabrze were beaten 4-2 on aggregate in the second round and Rangers were back in Eastern Europe for a quarter-final against Steaua Bucharest. After losing a difficult first leg 2-0 in the Romanian capital, Rangers failed to turn it around at Ibrox goals from Gough and McCoist gave them a 2-1 win over the 1986 European Champions.

The turnover in playing staff continued, striker Robert Fleck moved on and when Graham Roberts fell out with Souness after a 1-0 home defeat against Aberdeen in the penultimate league game of the season, he discovered that, despite his cult status in the eyes of the supporters, there was only ever one winner in any dispute with the manager.

Roberts moved on to Chelsea at the start of the 1988-89 campaign and Souness made two major signings, capturing the Everton and England right back Gary Stevens for £1 million and paying £600,000 to recruit Kevin Drinkell as a new strike partner for McCoist.

Ally McCoist begins to celebrate as Mark Walters fires the ball past Celtic's McCarthy and Aitken for the fifth goal in the August 1988 massacre.

Great Matches

SCOTTISH LEAGUE PREMIER DIVISION   Ibrox, 27 August 1988

Rangers 5   **Celtic 1**   Attendance 42,858
McCoist 2   McAvennie
Wilkins
Drinkell
Walters

With Celtic having won the League and Scottish Cup double the previous season, the first Old Firm fixture of 1988-89 was seen as crucial to Rangers' hopes of reclaiming the championship. While Graeme Souness' men had made an impressive start to the new campaign, much of the optimism around the Ibrox stands drained away when Celtic took the lead after just five minutes. Peter Grant's shot struck a post and Frank McAvennie was quickest to react and fire the ball beyond Chris Woods.

The response of the Rangers players, inspired by the midfield artistry of Ray Wilkins and the thrilling wing play of Mark Walters, was to simply blow a bewildered Celtic side away with one of the finest Old Firm performances of all time. Rangers equalized in 10 minutes, Ally McCoist shooting home from close range after a John Brown shot was blocked, and set about dominating the contest in emphatic fashion. They earned a deserved half-time lead when Wilkins scored one of the great Old Firm goals, smashing an unstoppable 25 yard volley beyond Ian Andrews in the 36th minute.

For the recently signed Celtic goalkeeper, it was something of a nightmare afternoon and a minute into the second half he blundered badly to allow a backward header from McCoist to loop into the net. Rangers clicked into top gear and made it 4-1 in 59 minutes, the irresistible Walters providing the cross for Kevin Drinkell to head home. Four minutes later, the Rangers fans were in a ferment when McCoist dispossessed Roy Aitken and slipped the ball to Walters who netted number five with a low drive from the edge of the box.

Celtic were reeling and Rangers could have added to their tally in the closing half hour, but appeared content to settle for having imposed such a level of dominance over their greatest rivals. The performance and result had laid down the marker of what would be a convincing championship season for Souness and his players.

Rangers: Woods, Stevens, Brown, Gough, Wilkins, Butcher, Drinkell, I. Ferguson, McCoist, Durrant (Souness), Walters (Cooper)

Celtic: Andrews, Morris, Rogan, Aitken, McCarthy, Grant, Stark (Miller), McStay, McAvennie, Walker, Burns (Whyte)

Referee: K. Hope (Glasgow)

Rangers made a fabulous start to the campaign. They won seven and drew one of their first eight matches, among them a sizzling 5-1 Old Firm victory at Ibrox. That euphoria was severely dampened by a 2-1 defeat to Aberdeen at Pittodrie which saw Ian Durrant, then emerging as one of the finest midfield talents seen in Scottish football for a generation, suffer a career-threatening knee injury from an infamous challenge by Neil Simpson.

Three more defeats in their next 10 games suggested Rangers had been badly shaken by the loss of one of their key men, but they won 14 of the following 16 fixtures to place themselves firmly in pole position to win the championship. It was clinched in style on 29 April 1989, with three games to spare, with a 4-0 win over Hearts at Ibrox.

Mel Sterland, signed the previous month from Sheffield Wednesday and who would move back to Yorkshire to join Leeds United after just 13 games for Rangers, scored twice as did Drinkell who had enjoyed an outstanding debut season. Rangers finished six points clear of runners-up Aberdeen with Celtic four points further back in third place.

The UEFA Cup campaign was a major anti-climax, Rangers losing 3-1 on aggregate to an ordinary Cologne side in the second round, but the League Cup was won for a third consecutive season with a 3-2 win in another memorable final against Aberdeen. Rangers were now bidding for the 'treble' when they faced Celtic at Hampden in the Scottish Cup final on 20 May 1989.

It was not to be. The absence of the injured Wilkins was keenly felt, as a below-par Rangers were beaten 1-0, Joe Miller pouncing on a loose pass back by Gary Stevens following a disputed throw-in to score the winner for Celtic.

Boardroom Changes

The season had also seen a change in the boardroom when, in November 1988, Lawrence Marlborough ended a long family dynasty at Ibrox by selling his controlling interest in the club to Edinburgh businessman David Murray for £6 million. Murray, a self-made millionaire, had been alerted to the club's availability by his friendship with Souness, and when the deal went through, the player-manager also became a director.

In the close season of 1989 new owner Murray sanctioned Souness' most audacious transfer market move yet when Rangers snatched striker Maurice Johnston from under the noses of their Old Firm rivals, who had appeared on the verge of bringing him back to Parkhead from French club Nantes.

Johnston's arrival at Ibrox sparked one of the biggest media frenzies ever seen in Scottish football as he became the first high-profile Catholic player to sign for Rangers since the Second World War. Souness, whose wife was a Catholic, had grasped the thorniest Old Firm nettle of them all and he could not have done so with a more controversial character than Johnston. All that concerned Souness was Johnston's undoubted qualities as a footballer and

50 Greatest Players

DAVIE COOPER Winger

Joined Rangers: June 1977 **From:** Clydebank

Debut: v Aberdeen, League, 13 August 1977

Appearances: 540 **Goals:** 75

Left Rangers: August 1989 **For:** Motherwell

Honours won with Rangers: 3 league championships;
3 Scottish Cups; 7 Scottish League Cups; 24 caps (Scotland)

The untimely death of Davie Cooper in March 1995, just a month after his 39th birthday, brought great sadness to the whole Scottish footballing community.

Under-21 international Cooper signed for £100,000 in the summer of 1977. The previous season, the Clydebank winger with breathtaking ball control had beguiled Rangers manager Jock Wallace in a marathon four-game League Cup quarter-final. Cooper was an instant favourite at Ibrox, his artistry and exquisite left foot establishing him as one of the stars of the excellent side which won the domestic 'treble' in 1977-78.

A cup double followed before Rangers went through a lean period. Jock Wallace's return as manager in 1983 revitalized Cooper, earning him a recall to the Scotland squad after a four-year absence. He went on to win 24 caps, appearing in the 1986 World Cup finals. Cooper again flourished in the early years of the Graeme Souness revolution at Ibrox, as he won more League titles and was only deprived of a place at the 1990 World Cup by injury.

At 33, he was unexpectedly sold to Motherwell for £50,000 and enjoyed a glorious Indian summer to his career, helping them win the Scottish Cup in 1991. Cooper's career turned full circle when he rejoined Clydebank and he planned to retire at the end of the 1994-95 season. On 22 March 1995, Cooper suffered a brain haemorrhage while filming a children's coaching video with Charlie Nicholas. He died in hospital the following day. Tommy Burns, then manager of Celtic, said it all: 'Scotland have lost a national treasure.'

the Scotland international coped remarkably well with the publicity, adverse and otherwise, which surrounded his astonishing move.

Rangers, who had also recruited England midfielder Trevor Steven from Everton for yet another new record fee of £1.525 million, made a shaky start and many fans questioned the sales of the peerless Davie Cooper to Motherwell and the immensely popular Kevin Drinkell to Coventry City.

However, after winning just two of their first eight fixtures, Rangers lost just one of the next 21. Included in the run were two wins over Celtic.

At Ibrox on 4 November 1989, Johnston won over most remaining doubters when he scored late to earn a 1-0 win over his former club. At Parkhead on 2 January 1990, the recently signed Nigel Spackman from QPR netted the only goal of another tense Old Firm battle. Rangers had gained the momentum they required to successfully defend the title and they clinched it with a 1-0 win over Dundee United at Tannadice, Steven the scorer, with two games to spare. They finished seven points clear of closest rivals Aberdeen and Hearts, with Celtic back in fifth place.

50 Greatest Players

RAY WILKINS Midfielder

Joined Rangers: November 1987 **From:** Paris Saint-Germain

Debut: v Hearts, League, 28 November 1987

Appearances: 96   **Goals:** 3

Left Rangers: December 1989   **For:** Queens Park Rangers

Honours won with Rangers: 2 league championships, 1 Scottish League Cup

Although he made fewer than 100 first team appearances for Rangers in little more than two years at the club, many count Ray Wilkins as one of the finest midfielders ever to play at Ibrox. His £250,000 move from Paris Saint-Germain in November 1987 came as a surprise, the then 31-year-old, having already won the last of his 84 England caps, was considered to be at the wrong end of his career.

There was also a preconception that he was an overtly negative player, surely unlikely to fire the imagination of the Rangers supporters. Yet it turned out Graeme Souness had made one of his shrewdest captures as Ibrox boss in persuading Wilkins to come to Glasgow.

An ultimate professional on and off the pitch, Wilkins quickly earned the approval of the Rangers fans with the unerring accuracy and intelligent choice of passes he made. His modus operandi was a simple one – keep the ball and you don't lose the game. More often than not, Wilkins' skills ensured Rangers won the game.

Two league championship medals and a League Cup winner's medal do scant justice to Wilkins' contribution as a Rangers player and his time at the club was all too short. At the end of his final match against Dunfermline in December 1989, he received a tumultuous standing ovation from the four Ibrox stands. Always supremely fit, Wilkins extended his career beyond his 40th birthday and later returned to Scotland for a brief spell at Hibernian before moving into coaching and management.

Mo Johnston wins over another few thousand Rangers fans with a late winner against Celtic in November 1989.

The retention of the title more than compensated for the disappointment experienced in all their cup competitions. Rangers had exited the European Cup in the first round, the damage done with a 3-1 first leg loss to Bayern Munich at Ibrox which rendered a brave goalless draw in Germany useless.

Aberdeen finally turned the tables on Rangers in the League Cup, two Paul Mason goals giving the Pittodrie side a 2-1 win in the third consecutive final between the teams at Hampden, while Celtic took some measure of consolation for a miserable campaign by beating Rangers 1-0 at Parkhead in the fourth round of the Scottish Cup.

As he looked to win a third successive title in 1990-91, Souness busied himself in the transfer market once more. England striker Mark Hateley, Dutch winger Pieter Huistra, Ukrainian defender Oleg Kuznetsov and the uncompromising utility man Terry Hurlock were all added to the squad with varying degrees of success.

50 Greatest Players

TERRY BUTCHER Defender

Joined Rangers: August 1986   **From:** Ipswich Town

Debut: v Hibernian, League, 9 August 1986

Appearances: 176   **Goals:** 11

Left Rangers: November 1990   **For:** Coventry City

Honours won with Rangers: 3 league championships;
2 Scottish League Cups; 32 caps (England)

If just one player typified the transformation effected at Rangers by Graeme Souness, it was Terry Butcher. The recruitment of the England defender from Ipswich Town for £725,000 at the start of the 1986-87 season was a stunning statement of Souness' intent to raise the stakes in Scottish football to unprecedented levels. One of the most highly-rated centre backs in world football, Butcher became one of the most effective and inspirational captains the club has had. He led by example, playing with ferocious commitment and an almost frightening will-to-win. Almost instantly adored by the Ibrox faithful, it was wholly appropriate that Butcher should head the goal against Aberdeen to give Rangers their first championship for nine years.

Capped 77 times by England, many of them as captain, Butcher was also a highly intelligent footballer, with a sweet left foot (which Ally McCoist christened 'The Winchester'). His broken leg in November 1987 was a bitter blow that helped Celtic reclaim the title. But Butcher, and the championship, returned in 1988-89 and he captained Rangers to a third league success the following season.

Butcher left Ibrox in November 1990, but through subsequent managerial and coaching spells at Coventry City, Sunderland, Dundee United and Motherwell, he has retained an affection for Rangers which is reciprocated by their supporters.

A patchy start to the season saw an unhappy ending to the Ibrox career of Terry Butcher who had established himself as one of the most popular captains the club had ever known. His relationship with Souness soured when the manager blamed him for a 2-1 defeat against Dundee United at Tannadice in September and Butcher found himself heading back to England to become player-manager of Coventry City. Butcher's wholehearted approach and dedication to the cause had already guaranteed he would be remembered with nothing less than total affection by the Rangers support.

Having dropped eight points in their first 11 games, Rangers regrouped and a 15-match unbeaten run which included 13 victories, put them firmly back into a dramatic title race which eventually saw them running neck and neck with Alex Smith's determined Aberdeen side.

After another disappointing European Cup elimination, losing 4-1 to Red Star Belgrade in the second round, Rangers had regained their hold on the League Cup with a 2-1 win over Celtic in the final at Hampden with goals from Walters and Gough. The Scottish Cup proved elusive yet again, however, Celtic again knocking Rangers out at Parkhead, this time 2-0 in a combustible fourth round tie which saw Hurlock, Hateley and Walters all sent off for various misdemeanors.

It left Rangers to focus solely on making it three in a row in the league, but their attention was diverted dramatically by the sudden departure of Souness as manager on 16 April 1991. He had been unable to resist the offer to return to Liverpool, the club where he had experienced almost unlimited

Great Managers – 1986-1991

GRAEME SOUNESS

As befits the man's extraordinary character, the reign of Graeme Souness as Rangers manager was unquestionably the most turbulent, controversial and enthralling in the club's history. His appointment at the age of 32 in April 1986 stunned Scottish football. Rangers, whose financial horizons had been broadened by businessman Lawrence Marlborough's takeover of the club, had tempted one of the country's finest midfielders (still at the peak of his playing career with Serie A club Sampdoria) to become player-manager.

Deeply unpopular with opposition fans for his abrasive and arrogant approach, Souness was adored by the Ibrox club's support as he restored Rangers' pre-eminent position in Scottish football. Despite his own playing career suffering as red cards and the pressure of management gradually limited his appearances, the former Tottenham, Middlesbrough and Liverpool player soon recruited English international players such as Terry Butcher, Chris Woods, Graham Roberts, Gary Stevens, Ray Wilkins and Trevor Francis to Ibrox. In 1987 the league championship was won for the first time in nine years and Souness added three more titles and four Scottish League Cup triumphs before his abrupt departure to become Liverpool manager in April 1991.

The Edinburgh-born Souness has since come through major heart surgery to continue his managerial career with varying degrees of success at Galatasaray, Southampton, Torino, Benfica and Blackburn Rovers.

success during his playing career, as their new manager.

There were just four league games of the season remaining and although Souness offered to stay and see out the campaign, Rangers decided to make the change immediate. The search for Souness' successor was brief – the day after he left he was replaced by Walter Smith.

Sandy Robertson earned Smith a priceless victory in his first match in charge with the goal in a 1-0 win over St Mirren at Love Street and Ian Ferguson struck to ensure a similar scoreline at home to Dundee United. Rangers were within touching distance of the title but, in their penultimate match they crashed to a 3-0 defeat against Motherwell at Fir Park.

It opened the door for Aberdeen who came to Ibrox on 11 May 1991 for the final day of the campaign needing only a draw to take the championship on goal difference from Rangers.

Already without injured captain Richard Gough, Rangers suffered another blow in the first half of the match when full back Tom Cowan sustained a broken leg. Aberdeen missed good chances to put the Ibrox men in real trouble, most notably when Van de Ven failed to convert from close range.

Mark Hateley wins another header in the championship decider against Aberdeen at Ibrox in May 1991.

Mark Hateley had struggled to win over the fans since his arrival from Monaco at the start of the season, but the big striker chose his moment to emerge as a hero. Five minutes before half-time he slammed in a header from a Walters cross and then ten minutes after the break he slotted in a half-saved Mo Johnston shot.

Despite another injury blow when John Brown was taken off on a stretcher with knee ligament damage, Rangers held on comfortably enough in the end to record a memorable final day title triumph, celebrated by a capacity crowd and by thousands more locked outside the partially reconstructed stadium.

The Team that Smith Built

Having successfully concluded matters after the unexpected exit of Souness, Smith set about putting his own imprint on the Rangers squad as he prepared for the 1991-92 season. Chris Woods, Mark Walters and Trevor Steven were the most notable departures, the latter sold to Marseille for a record £5.5 million. Among Smith's initial signings were goalkeeper Andy Goram, full back David Robertson, midfielder Stuart McCall and the mercurial Ukrainian Alexei Mikhailichenko. All were top quality players and all would make a positive impression at Ibrox.

There were some early disappointments for Smith as his new-look side struggled to gel, especially in a first round defeat in the European Cup on the away goals rule to Czech side Sparta Prague. The League Cup had already been relinquished, Rangers losing 1-0 to Hibs in the semi-final at Hampden.

In the league, they embarked on a marathon 44-match campaign following the reconstruction of the Premier Division to 12 clubs. Rangers made a solid start, but found themselves in a tight battle at the top with Hearts who lead for a lengthy spell. It took a 16-match unbeaten run, including 14 wins, from 30 November 1991 to 14 March 1992 to put Rangers back in control.

They eventually finished nine points clear of the Tynecastle club, clinching a fourth successive championship – the first time they had achieved the feat since 1930 – with three games to spare when they defeated St Mirren 4-0 at Ibrox on 18 April. Ally McCoist, scorer of 39 goals over the season, netted twice to spark the celebrations.

The party continued at Hampden in May when Rangers won the Scottish Cup for the first time since 1981. After an epic 1-0 semi-final victory over Celtic, when they played with 10 men for 84 minutes following the dismissal of David Robertson, Rangers met Airdrie in the final. It was harder work than expected, but goals from Hateley and McCoist gave them a 2-1 win.

There were two 'new' faces added to the squad for the 1992-93 season, Smith bringing Dave McPherson back from Hearts, where had established himself as a Scotland international, and reclaiming Trevor Steven from Marseille just a year after his sale.

One of the most successful eras in Rangers' history was unfolding under Smith's guidance and it reached its peak this season as his team won the club's first domestic 'treble' for 15 years and came agonizingly close to reaching the European Cup final.

When Rangers lost 4-3 to Dundee at Dens Park in their fourth league match of the campaign and dropped a total of four points from their first five games, there was no hint of the extraordinary run they would embark upon to win a fifth consecutive championship. They went 29 games unbeaten, including 23 wins, before losing 2-1 to Celtic at Parkhead on 20 March 1993. In all competitions, Rangers had compiled a 44-match undefeated sequence during that period.

They secured the title with four games to spare, young striker Gary McSwegan claiming the only goal in the decisive fixture against Airdrie at Broomfield. Rangers cruised home nine points clear of runners-up Aberdeen and also vanquished the Pittodrie club in the finals of both domestic cup tournaments.

In the League Cup, an extra time own goal from Gary Smith was the winner in Rangers' 2-1 success over the Dons at Hampden and the 'treble' was completed on 29 May 1993, this time at Parkhead because of reconstruction work to the national stadium. Neil Murray and Mark Hateley got the historic Rangers goals as Aberdeen were beaten 2-1 again.

European Adventure

It was a momentous finale to one of the club's most memorable seasons. The European Cup had taken centre stage for much of it as Rangers became the first British club to play in the group stages of the new Champions League format.

They did so by beating Leeds United in an epic second round tie. The fancied English champions lost 2-1 in each leg, Rangers rising to the occasion at Ibrox and most notably on English soil.

Rangers were rewarded with a Group A draw which bracketed them with the champions of France, Russia and Belgium. After coming from behind to draw 2-2 with an impressive Marseille at Ibrox in the opening fixture, Rangers defeated CSKA Moscow 1-0 on neutral soil in Bochum, Germany and followed that up with a creditable 1-1 draw away to Bruges.

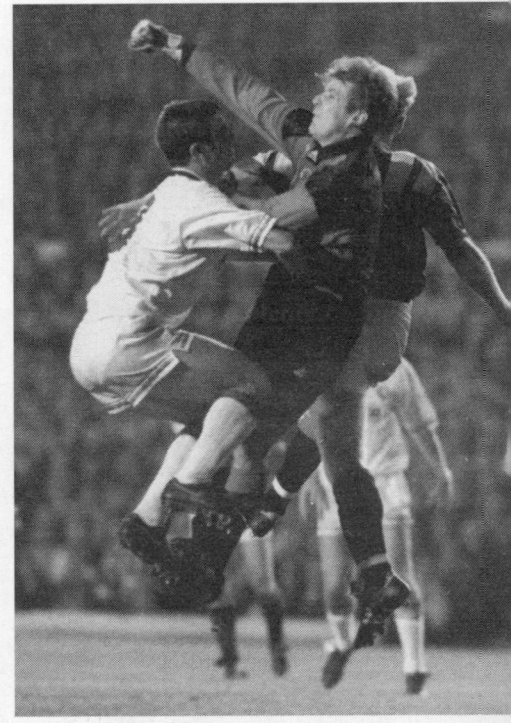

Andy Goram punches the ball away from Eric Cantona in the Champions League second round, second leg at Elland Road.

Great Matches

EUROPEAN CUP, 2ND ROUND, 2ND LEG   **Elland Road, 4 November 1992**

Leeds United   1   Rangers 2   **Attendance 25,118**
Cantona   Hateley
                           McCoist

Although Rangers had responded to the loss of a first-minute Gary McAllister strike to earn a 2-1 first leg victory at Ibrox two weeks earlier, that away goal made Leeds United odds-on favourites in most observers' eyes to win the high profile European Cup tie billed as the 'Battle of Britain'.

The English champions were in extremely confident mood in front of their own fans with the prize on offer of a place in the lucrative group stages of the recently created Champions League.

Rangers, however, were in form and full of determination. After just three minutes, they had wiped out Leeds' away goal to set the platform for one of their most famous and impressive European performances. A long clearance from Andy Goram was flicked on by Ian Durrant into the path of Mark Hateley. The big striker, some 25 yards out, turned and hooked a spectacular shot beyond stunned Leeds keeper John Lukic.

Leeds, who now needed to score at least twice, responded by putting the Rangers goal under some considerable pressure, but the Scottish champions were brilliantly served by keeper Goram and central defenders Richard Gough and John Brown. Goram, in particular, was an inspiration and defied Leeds dangerman Eric Cantona with a series of wonderful saves.

As Leeds' frustration intensified, Rangers simply grew in confidence and took an iron grip on the tie when they made it 2-0 on the night and 4-1 on aggregate in the 58th minute. It was another marvellous goal, Durrant sweeping the ball wide to the rampaging Hateley on the left and his cross was steered beyond Lukic by Ally McCoist's diving header.

Leeds were now a beaten side and when they did finally find a way past Goram, Cantona scoring five minutes from time, it was no more than a consolation. Most of the home fans had long since drifted away from the ground.

Rangers had achieved one of their greatest victories and had boosted the profile of Scottish football by becoming the first British club to reach the group stages of the Champions League.

Leeds United: Lukic, Newsome, Dorigo, Rocastle, Fairclough, Whyte, Strachan, Cantona, Chapman, McAllister, Speed

Rangers: Goram, McCall, Robertson, Gough, McPherson, Brown, Gordon (Mikhailichenko), I. Ferguson, McCoist, Hateley, Durrant

Referee: A. Spirine (Russia)

Scott Nisbet's bizarre winner against the Belgians in a 2-1 victory at Ibrox set up a winner-takes-all match against Marseille in France. Victory for either side would see them go into the European Cup final, but both had to settle for a point, Ian Durrant cancelling out Boksic's opener for the home team. It meant Rangers, still unbeaten, went into their final match at home to CSKA Moscow still hopeful of a combination of results which would see them top the group. While Smith's men were frustrated by the Russians in a goalless draw, however, Marseille won 1-0 in Bruges and went on to defeat AC Milan in the final.

In all, Rangers had won six and drawn four of their 10 matches in the European Cup that season. It was an achievement they could reflect on with some pride and their sense of what might have been was only sharpened by Marseille's subsequent disgrace in being stripped of their European title following a bribes scandal.

The other sour note of the season for Rangers was the broken leg suffered by Ally McCoist in April 1993 during Scotland's disastrous World Cup qualifier against Portugal in Lisbon where they lost 5-0. McCoist was in great form and had scored an incredible 49 goals in 50 games before missing the end of the campaign.

To strengthen his striking options, Smith smashed the Scottish record transfer fee at the start of the 1993-94 season by signing Duncan Ferguson from Dundee United for £4 million. For a variety of reasons, it did not turn out to be one of the club's best investments. The talented young forward was bedevilled by trouble on and off the pitch, eventually serving a jail sentence for a head-butt on John McStay of Raith Rovers during a game at Ibrox which upset Glasgow's Procurator Fiscal more than it did the match referee.

Alexei Mikhailichenko, one of the first of the truly world-class players to come to Ibrox in the 90s.

Ferguson managed just one goal in a debut season which saw him as no more than a marginal figure in the Rangers squad which successfully won a sixth consecutive championship, a new club record. That was despite dropping 10 points in the first 10 matches and facing credible title challenges from both Aberdeen and Motherwell.

Rangers ground it out and the November signing of Scotland striker Gordon Durie from Tottenham proved successful as he contributed 12 goals in 24 league appearances. A 17-match unbeaten run from 18 December 1993 to 22 April 1994 was crucial to Rangers' success.

Although Rangers failed to win any of their last five matches, they clinched the title with two games to spare. Despite losing 1-0 to Hibs at Easter Road, Rangers were confirmed as champions by Motherwell's 2-1 home defeat to Dundee United the same evening. Rangers eventually finished three points clear of Aberdeen with Motherwell a further point back in third place.

There had been no repeat of the previous season's Champions League heroics, Rangers losing out to a last-minute away goal against Levski Sofia as they drew 4-4 on aggregate with the Bulgarian champions in the first round of the tournament.

McCoist Returns in Style

Domestic dominance was less of a problem and the League Cup had been won in the most dramatic fashion. Ally McCoist, just four games into his comeback from his broken leg injury, came on as a substitute to score a spectacular overhead-kick winner as Rangers defeated Hibs 2-1 in the final at Parkhead on 24 October 1993.

Rangers also reached the Scottish Cup final and found themselves with the opportunity to become the first side ever to win back-to-back domestic 'trebles' when they faced Dundee United at Hampden on 21 May 1994. Walter Smith's team were the warmest of favourites to do so but were undone by Ivan Golac's United, Craig Brewster scoring the only goal of the game after a mix-up between Rangers keeper Ally Maxwell and defender Dave McPherson.

Rangers spent heavily once more in the summer of 1994, recruiting two big names in Danish international forward Brian Laudrup from Fiorentina for £3.5 million and the French defender Basile Boli from Marseille. The books were balanced somewhat with the sale of Duncan Ferguson to Everton, while Dave McPherson was moved on to Hearts for the second time in October 1994, this time in a £2 million deal which brought Scotland defender Alan McLaren to Ibrox.

While Laudrup would become one of the most exciting and successful foreign players signed by Rangers, Boli found Scottish football more of a struggle. The Ibrox men made a desperately poor start to the season and Smith faced crisis headlines in the newspapers for the first time when three successive home defeats in August had dramatic consequences.

Rangers lost 1-0 to AEK Athens to go out of the Champions League in the first qualifying round 3-0 on aggregate, lost 2-0 to Celtic in their third League fixture of the campaign and then were beaten 2-1 by Falkirk in the third round of the League Cup. Further defeats at the hands of Hibs and Motherwell, who would be their closest rivals in the title race, maintained the pressure on the manager.

As Laudrup clicked into top gear, however, Rangers put together a 14-match unbeaten run to move comfortably clear at the top of the table. It was the first season of three points for a win in Scottish football and Rangers eventually finished 15 points clear of runners-up Motherwell, managed by Alex McLeish, with Hibs third. It was their seventh successive Premier Division title success and negated the disappointments of the cup competitions for Smith and his players, who had also been knocked out of the Scottish Cup when they lost 4-2 at Hearts in a fourth round tie.

The Rangers supporters had now become accustomed to the club making spectacular close season signings but, by any standards, Walter Smith's £4.3 million swoop for Paul Gascoigne in July 1995 was a breathtaking one. The enormously gifted and endlessly controversial England midfielder was persuaded to come to Ibrox from Lazio and would seldom be out of the headlines in Scotland. Smith also added Yugoslav defender Gordan Petric and Russian striker Oleg Salenko to his squad as Basile Boli and the eventually popular Mark Hateley left the club.

Rangers won 10 of their first 12 league games, including a Gascoigne goal in a 2-0 win over Celtic at Parkhead, and lost only one of their first 12. This would not be another canter to the championship, however, as a Celtic outfit rejuvenated under Tommy Burns locked horns with Rangers in a titanic tussle.

Celtic, in fact, lost just one league game all season but their consistency was matched and just a little bettered by the Ibrox men. Rangers made it eight titles in a row in spectacular fashion when they won their penultimate fixture 3-1 against Aberdeen at Ibrox on 28 April 1996, courtesy of a terrific Gascoigne hat-trick. The final winning margin over Celtic was four points with Aberdeen a staggering 32 points adrift in third place. It was the start of the Old Firm's current stranglehold on Scottish football.

Rangers, who bid a fond farewell to Alexei Mikhailichenko during the course of the campaign and swapped the short-lived presence of Salenko for Dutch international Peter van Vossen, enjoyed mixed fortunes in cup competition during 1995-96.

They lost 2-1 to Aberdeen in the semi-finals of the League Cup, perhaps distracted by their Champions League campaign. They had reached the group stage of the competition for the second time by beating Cypriot side

50 Greatest Players

ANDY GORAM Goalkeeper

Joined Rangers: June 1991   **From:** Hibernian

Debut: v St Johnstone, League, 10 August 1991

Appearances: 261

Left Rangers: June 1998   **For:** Sheffield United

Honours won with Rangers: 6 league championships;
3 Scottish Cups; 3 Scottish League Cups; 28 caps (Scotland)

When Andy Goram performed the half-time draw during Rangers' match against Hearts in 2002, he received an ovation from the home fans which barely abated in time for the restart of the game. Almost four years after he left the club, it showed the depth of affection felt towards arguably Rangers' greatest ever keeper.

Lancashire-born with a Scottish bloodline, Goram won the first of his 43 Scottish caps with Oldham Athletic. He joined Hibernian in 1987 and four years later was brought to Ibrox by Walter Smith for £1 million. Goram suffered some uncomfortable moments in his debut season, notably in the European Cup defeat against Sparta Prague, but his form in 1992-93, when Rangers won the domestic 'treble' and enjoyed a superb Champions League campaign, was at times breathtaking and earned him Scotland's Player of the Year award.

Neither the tallest nor most athletic keeper, Goram more than compensated with his innate positional sense, outstanding reflexes and a command of his penalty area. Often, and especially in Old Firm matches, he seemed able to impose a psychological barrier between himself and opposition strikers. His off-the-field activities, however, often attracted negative publicity and he dismayed many of his admirers by quitting the Scotland squad on the eve of the 1998 World Cup finals. Released by Rangers that summer, he joined Sheffield United then Motherwell. In a surprising career finale, he was signed by Manchester United as cover for Fabien Barthez in March 2001.

Anorthosis 1-0 on aggregate in the qualifying round but found no joy in a section which pitted them against Juventus, Dortmund and Steaua Bucharest. Rangers appeared badly outclassed, especially against the Italian champions who scored four against them both home and away. It was a chastening experience for Smith and his team who finished bottom of Group C without a win from their six matches.

The season at least finished on a considerable high. After clinching the championship, Rangers faced Hearts in the Scottish Cup final at Hampden on 18 May 1996. Although Gordon Durie became the first Rangers player to score a hat-trick in a Scottish Cup final, the day belonged to an imperious Brian Laudrup who simply tore a good Hearts side to pieces with a dazzling display of his skills. The great Dane scored twice and made all three of Durie's goals and even found time to delight the Rangers fans and infuriate the Edinburgh men with his party pieces of ball juggling and close control. Rangers had completed another League and Scottish Cup double in lavish style in a match which would be remembered by their supporters as 'The Laudrup Final'.

Paul Gascoigne playing for England, a month after signing for Rangers.

The 'Nine-in-a-Row' Issue

As Rangers prepared for the 1996-97 season, there was one consuming issue which dominated the thoughts of their fans. Winning the championship would see the club equal the record of nine consecutive titles set by Celtic from 1966 to 1974 under the legendary management of Jock Stein.

Just as Rangers were determined to achieve it, so Celtic were intent on preventing it and another compelling head-to-head race for the title ensued. Smith, who had added Swedish defender Joachim Bjorklund from Vicenza and German midfielder Jorg Albertz from Hamburg, saw his team make the perfect start as they won their first seven games, including a 2-0 success over Celtic at Ibrox with goals from Gough and Gascoigne.

Celtic, however, stayed in touch at the top and perhaps Rangers' most crucial victory of the season came in the second Ibrox Old Firm fixture on 2 January 1997 when Erik Bo Andersen, a Danish striker signed towards the end of the previous season from Aalborg, appeared as a substitute to score twice in a 3-1 success.

Rangers wobbled a little in March, losing to both Dundee United and Kilmarnock, but Celtic were unable to take full advantage as they picked up just one point from their concurrent fixtures. The momentous ninth successive title was secured with one game to spare, Brian Laudrup heading the only goal against Dundee United at Tannadice on 7 May 1997. It was an emotional evening for Richard Gough, unable to play because of injury, but who collected the championship trophy. He had announced earlier in the

50 Greatest Players

STUART McCALL Midfielder

Joined Rangers: August 1991   **From:** Everton

Debut: v Hearts, League, 17 August 1991

Appearances: 265   **Goals:** 20

Left Rangers: June 1998   **For:** Bradford City

Honours won with Rangers: 5 league championships; 3 Scottish Cups; 2 Scottish League Cups; 29 caps (Scotland)

An established Scotland international, having scored for the country of his father's birth in the 1990 World Cup finals in Italy, McCall joined Rangers from Everton for £1.2 million. In no time he became an integral part of the dominant 90s Ibrox side.

Leeds-born McCall's Yorkshire accent never left him but his commitment to the Rangers cause was as fierce as any locally raised player. Famed for his tenacity and ball-winning ability in the middle of the park, he was also far more creative than he was often given credit for. There were few more consistent performers in Smith's nine-in-a-row teams.

McCall followed up the 'double' in his first season at Ibrox by being one of the pivotal players in the side which won the domestic 'treble' in 1992-93 and enjoyed such a laudable European campaign. He collected five league championship medals in all and, although troubled by injury, played a part in the record equalling title win of 1996-97.

His unflinching competitive nature endeared him greatly to the Rangers fans who were genuinely sorry to see him end his Ibrox career in the summer of 1998 when he returned to Bradford City, helping his first club into the English Premiership. He remained there as player and coach until the summer of 2002.

season it would be his last at Ibrox before going to the United States to play for Kansas City Wiz.

Gough had also got his hands on the League Cup earlier in the campaign, Rangers defeating Hearts 4-3 in an epic final at Parkhead on 24 November 1996. Paul Gascoigne and Ally McCoist both scored twice. The defence of the

50 Greatest Players

RICHARD GOUGH Defender

Joined Rangers: October 1987   **From:** Tottenham Hotspur

Debut: v Dundee United, League, 10 October 1987

Left Rangers: May 1997   **For:** Kansas City Wiz

Rejoined Rangers: December 1997   **From:** Kansas City Wiz

Left Rangers: June 1998   **For:** San José Clash

Appearances: 427   **Goals:** 34

Honours won with Rangers: 9 league championships; 3 Scottish Cups; 6 Scottish League Cups; 27 caps (Scotland)

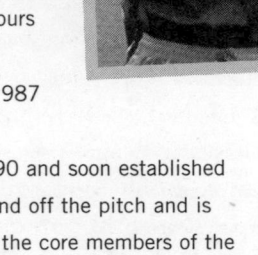

If one player symbolizes Rangers' record-equalling championship run, it would have to be Richard Gough. Not only did he captain the club to the last seven of the title successes, he was a pivotal figure in all nine, a wonderfully committed and consistent defender.

Born in Sweden and raised in South Africa, Gough, having failed to shine in a trial match for Rangers, was signed by Dundee United, becoming an outstanding member of their first and only league-winning team. In 1986, Gough moved to Spurs for £850,000, Dundee United having resisted attempts by Rangers to sign him. He finally arrived at Ibrox in October 1987 for £1.1 million. He would be worth every last penny.

Gough inherited Terry Butcher's captain's armband in 1990 and soon established himself as a worthy successor. He was a natural leader on and off the pitch and is credited with forging the unique bond which existed among the core members of the nine-times champions squad.

Gough left Rangers at the end of the 1996-97 season to join Kansas City Wiz but, midway through the 1997-98 campaign, answered an SOS from manager Walter Smith to return to Ibrox. However, even Gough's presence was unable to prevent Celtic ending the championship run. In the summer of 1998, Gough went back to America to join San José Clash but, remarkably, rejoined Smith again for two seasons in the English Premiership with Everton. He was capped 61 times for Scotland, a tally cut prematurely short by a fall-out with management.

Scottish Cup, however, ended in the quarter-final stage with Tommy Burns for once able to get the better of Rangers as his Celtic side earned a 2-0 home win.

Hopes of an improved Champions League campaign had been raised by an impressive 10-3 aggregate defeat of Russian champions Alania Vladikavkaz in the preliminary round but Group A, which saw Rangers bracketed with Auxerre, Ajax and Grasshoppers Zurich, delivered only further evidence of the gap between the Scottish Champions and Europe's best. Rangers lost five of their six games, including heavy defeats in Switzerland and Holland, and finished six points adrift at the bottom of the section.

Smith up for the Record

At the end of the season, it was announced Walter Smith had signed a new three-year contract as Rangers manager. Aiming for a record-breaking 10th successive championship, he made several summer signings with Italy his favoured recruiting ground. Striker Marco Negri came from Perugia, experienced Swedish midfielder Jonas Thern from Roma and defender Sergio Porrini from Juventus. Another defender, Lorenzo Amoruso, came from Fiorentina but suffered a serious injury on the eve of the season.

There was bitter disappointment for Rangers early in the campaign when they failed to reach the group stage of the Champions League, beaten 4-1 on aggregate by IFK Gothenburg in the second qualifying round. New competition rules meant Rangers were handed the consolation of a switch to the UEFA Cup but they fell there at the first hurdle, losing 2-1 both home and away to Strasbourg.

It intensified the need to win the championship and Rangers made a good start. They were unbeaten in their first eight matches and lost only one of the first 19. Negri was initially a revelation, scoring an astounding 23 goals in his first 10 League appearances for the club. Amoruso's injury prompted Smith to bring Richard Gough back to Ibrox in October and the veteran skipper scored the only goal of the first Old Firm game of the season at Ibrox to hand Rangers the initiative.

In what was already emerging as a dramatic season, Smith added to it when he suddenly announced he would be standing down from his position as manager at the end of the campaign. Smith, who was also a director of the club, had decided it was time for a change and in February 1998, Rangers revealed that former Dutch international coach Dick Advocaat would replace him in the summer.

Before then, Smith and his team, many of them long-serving players approaching the end of their Ibrox careers, were focused on a

50 Greatest Players

PAUL GASCOIGNE Midfielder

Joined Rangers: July 1995   **From:** Lazio

Debut: v Anorthosis Famagusta, European Cup, 9 August 1995

Appearances: 104   **Goals:** 39

Left Rangers: March 1998   **For:** Middlesbrough

Honours won with Rangers: 2 league championships; 1 Scottish
Cup; 1 Scottish League Cup; 22 caps (England)

Despite spending less than three years at Ibrox, Paul
Gascoigne made a lasting impression on Rangers, and Scottish
football in general. The extravagantly gifted and wildly
controversial playmaker was a remarkable capture for Walter
Smith when he recruited him from Lazio for a then record
£4.3 million in the summer of 1995.

Gascoigne's world-class credentials were recognized throughout the game. Only his
notoriously fragile temperament and susceptibility to injury caused some to question
Smith's decision to bring him to Ibrox. Although Rangers, and Smith in particular,
had to endure a fair share of the problems which always seemed to accompany Gascoigne,
it is more than reasonable to assess the player's time in Glasgow as a major success.

He was Scotland's Player of the Year in his first season, capped in memorable
fashion with a devastating hat-trick in the 3-1 win over Aberdeen at Ibrox which
clinched an eighth successive league championship for Rangers. His peerless vision,
ball control and range of passing compensated for his lack of discipline and meant he
was unconditionally adored by the Rangers fans. Unfortunately, if almost inevitably, his
wayward behaviour away from the football pitch eventually became too much for Smith
and Rangers to deal with. In March 1998, Gascoigne was sold to Middlesbrough.
He was later reunited with Smith at Everton but was released towards the end of the
2001-02 season, his footballing future somewhat in doubt.

tremendously tense championship battle with Celtic which went to the last
day of the season.

The Parkhead men, under the guidance of Dutch coach Wim Jansen, forged
into a lead on the back of a 2-0 win over Rangers at Parkhead on 2 January
1998, the first time Celtic had won the New Year Old Firm fixture for 10
years. Rangers reversed the scoreline at Ibrox on 12 April to pull themselves
back into contention but then lost two of their next three games to allow Celtic
to go into the final day on 9 May in pole position.

Rangers were at Tannadice where they had to win and simply hope Celtic slipped up at home to St Johnstone. While Smith's team did their bit, beating Dundee United 2-1, Celtic held their nerve to beat the Perth club 2-0 and win their first championship since 1988 by a two point margin.

50 Greatest Players

BRIAN LAUDRUP Midfielder

Joined Rangers: July 1994   **From:** Fiorentina

Debut: v AEK Athens, European Cup, 10 August 1994

Appearances: 151   **Goals:** 45

Left Rangers: June 1998   **For:** Chelsea

Honours won with Rangers: 3 league championships;
1 Scottish Cup; 1 Scottish League Cup; 20 caps
(Denmark)

Brian Laudrup's fearless diving header that clinched the ninth consecutive championship win at Tannadice in May 1997 would have guaranteed him a place in the club's folklore. In fact, he had already ensured he would be remembered by the Ibrox support in the warmest possible terms.

After Walter Smith's imaginative £3.5 million swoop to sign him from Fiorentina in the summer of 1994, the Danish international was an almost instant hit at Ibrox with his often breathtaking, free-running style of play which truly tormented defences. As adept at taking chances as he was at scoring them, Laudrup's consistency and wonderful skills earned him Scotland's Player of the Year award in both 1995 and 1997. Perhaps his finest display for the club came in the 1996 Scottish Cup final when he almost single-handedly destroyed Hearts in a 5-1 romp.

Notionally an attacking midfielder, Laudrup was almost always given a free role by Rangers. In the historic 1996-97 season, he was pressed into action as an out and out striker because of injuries to others, and responded by finishing the campaign as the club's leading scorer with 20 goals.

Laudrup's form and appetite for the game seemed to wane noticeably during the unsuccessful 1997-98 campaign and he left Rangers at the end of it, enduring a brief and unhappy spell with Chelsea before returning to Denmark to play for FC Copenhagen. Unexpectedly, he retired in 2000 at the age of 31 to concentrate on his business interests, including becoming a players' agent.

50 Greatest Players

IAN DURRANT Midfielder

Joined Rangers: June 1984   **From:** School

Debut: v Morton, League, 20 April 1985

Appearances: 348   **Goals:** 45

Left Rangers: June 1998   **For:** Kilmarnock

Honours won with Rangers: 6 league championships;
3 Scottish Cups; 4 Scottish League Cups;
20 caps (Scotland)

Had his career not been so badly compromised by serious injury, who knows what heights Ian Durrant might have scaled as both a Rangers and Scotland player? As it was, the naturally gifted midfielder was still one of the finest to represent the Ibrox club in the modern era.

Durrant, born and raised little more than a long goal kick away from Ibrox, joined Rangers as a schoolboy. It was quickly apparent Rangers had unearthed a special player who married faultless close control with a terrific sense of timing in making damaging runs into the opposition area. Durrant became a key figure in Graeme Souness' initial championship success, but his career was halted by knee ligament damage caused by Neil Simpson's infamous tackle at Pittodrie in October 1988. Effectively ruled out of top level football for three seasons, Durrant bravely fought back to play a significant role in Rangers' nine-in-a-row championship run. He also proved a consistently adept performer in Europe, most notably in the latter stages of the 1993 Champions League.

After 14 years at the club, he made his last appearance as a substitute in the 1998 Scottish Cup final against Hearts before joining Kilmarnock on a free transfer. His form at Rugby Park was good enough to revive his international career, allowing him to take his final tally of caps to 20. Further injury forced Durrant to formally retire at the end of the 2001-02 season during which he was appointed to the Kilmarnock coaching staff.

Having been knocked out of the League Cup by an extra-time goal from their former striker Gary McSwegan for Dundee United at Ibrox in the quarter-finals, Rangers were left with only the Scottish Cup to save them from the club's first season without a trophy for 12 years. The final at Parkhead on 16 May 1998 saw them face Hearts who had not won a major trophy since 1962. In Smith's last match in charge, Rangers were unable to deliver the victory he craved as a parting gift. Goals from Colin Cameron and Stephane Adam put the Tynecastle side into a 2-0 lead and Ally McCoist's late strike provided a tense finale, but was a mere consolation. Smith's reign was to end not with a bang but a whimper.

Great Managers – 1991-1998

WALTER SMITH

Born in Glasgow's Carmyle district in 1948, Walter Smith dreamed of playing for Rangers. As a boy, he went with his grandfather and father to Ibrox, marvelling at the skills of his idols such as Jimmy Millar and Jim Baxter. A highly competent midfielder or defender, Smith never fulfilled his ambition to wear the light blue jersey, but nonetheless had a playing career to be proud of at Dumbarton and, most of all, Dundee United. It was at Tannadice, under manager Jim McLean, that he developed his coaching talent and was eventually appointed as McLean's assistant in March 1982.

Smith played an important role as United won the league championship for the first time in their history in 1983 and was seen as McLean's eventual successor. In April 1986, however, Smith was finally able to join the club closest to his heart when he was head-hunted by Rangers as assistant to new manager Graeme Souness.

An important calming influence, Smith helped Souness plot Rangers' path back to the summit of Scottish football. The ultimate reward came his way in April 1991 when, after Souness' departure to Liverpool, he was appointed manager at Ibrox. From clinching the desperately close championship from Aberdeen in May 1991, a success he modestly maintained belonged to Souness, Smith brought trophies to Ibrox on an admirably consistent basis. Six more titles, allowing Rangers to equal Celtic's record of nine-in-a-row, three Scottish Cup wins and three Scottish League Cup triumphs was Smith's tremendous haul which included a domestic 'treble' in 1992-93.

Midway through the 1997-98 season, the first Rangers would finish empty-handed for 12 years, Smith announced he would be resigning as manager at the end of the campaign. Although still a director of the club, he decided to fulfil another long-standing ambition to work in English football and in 1998 he left Ibrox to become Everton manager. Financial constraints dogged Smith at Goodison Park where his reign ended in March 2002 with the club embroiled in another relegation battle.

For Ibrox stalwarts McCoist, Ian Durrant, Andy Goram, Richard Gough and Stuart McCall, it was a sad end to their outstanding Rangers careers. It was also Brian Laudrup's final appearance before leaving to join Chelsea under freedom of contract, while Paul Gascoigne had been sold to Middlesbrough in March for £3.45 million.

It was the end of an era for Rangers and their supporters. There are unlikely to be many more dramatic or successful ones than that which was presided over by Souness and Smith.

50 Greatest Players

ALLY McCOIST Forward

Joined Rangers: June 1983   **From:** Sunderland

Debut: v St Mirren, League, 20 August 1983

Appearances: 581   **Goals:** 355

Left Rangers: June 1998   **For:** Kilmarnock

Honours won with Rangers: 9 league championships; 1 Scottish Cup; 9 Scottish League Cups; 59 caps (Scotland)

From unconvincing beginnings in a struggling Rangers team, Ally McCoist became the greatest goalscorer in the club's history. It had already taken three attempts for the Ibrox club to capture him. As a schoolboy the young McCoist opted to hone his skills at St Johnstone; Rangers then lost out to Sunderland when the Perth club sold their prize asset in 1981. Finally in the summer of 1983, the extrovert striker became a Ranger at a cost of £185,000.

Despite finishing his first season as top scorer with 20 goals, including a hat-trick in the 3-2 League Cup final win over Celtic, McCoist initially found approval from Rangers' support difficult to earn. An effervescent, irrepressible character, he soon transformed their opinion in dramatic fashion as he proved himself a peerless sniffer of goals.

Eventually, there was no more popular player at Ibrox than McCoist as he smashed one goalscoring record after another in a glittering 15-year career at the club. He survived a clash of personalities with Graeme Souness to remain a stalwart of the nine-in-a-row squad. McCoist also earned a Scottish record of nine League Cup winner's medals and became the club's all-time leading scorer in both League and European football.

His Rangers career ended on a disappointing note, his final appearance coming in the 1998 Scottish Cup final which was lost 2-1 to Hearts. Given a free transfer, he joined Kilmarnock where he extended his career for a further three seasons. McCoist was also a fine international player, scoring 19 goals in 61 appearances for Scotland. He hung up his boots in the summer of 2001 to pursue a successful television career.

Chapter Ten: 1998-2002
Dutch and Go

Just as Rangers welcomed the arrival of the first foreign manager in their history, so Celtic lost theirs. Wim Jansen left Parkhead in acrimonious circumstances immediately after winning the championship, while his former colleague and compatriot Dick Advocaat took the Ibrox helm.

With Celtic in some disarray, eventually appointing Dr Jozef Venglos as their new head coach on the eve of the 1998-99 season, Advocaat had been planning his debut campaign for several months and performed major surgery on the Rangers squad. Two of his countrymen were signed, bringing experienced international defender Arthur Numan with him from PSV Eindhoven for £5 million and midfielder Giovanni Van Bronckhorst from Feyenoord. The Scottish transfer record was broken with the £5.5 million capture of Andrei Kanchelskis from Fiorentina, striker Rod Wallace joined on a free transfer from Leeds United, Real Mallorca were paid £4.2 million for Spanish forward Gabriel Amato and Scotland's international defender Colin Hendry was signed from Blackburn Rovers for £4 million.

Perhaps not surprisingly, Advocaat's team took time to gel. They lost their opening fixture in the newly formed 12-club Scottish Premier League, 2-1 to Hearts at Tynecastle and dropped six points from their first seven matches. A 5-1 defeat to Celtic at Parkhead on 21 November 1998 was a severe setback for the new manager, but his players responded well to hand him his first piece of silverware eight days later at the same venue. Goals from Stephane Guivarc'h, the French striker signed from Newcastle for £3.5 million earlier in the month, and Jorg Albertz earned a 2-1 win over St Johnstone in the League Cup final.

Advocaat continued to add to his squad, Scotland winger Neil McCann joining from Hearts for £2 million, while the lengthy pursuit of German goalkeeper Stefan Klos was finally concluded when he signed from Borussia Dortmund for £1.7 million.

Rangers compiled a 12-match unbeaten run in the SPL after their heavy loss to Celtic, including 10 victories, to take the initiative in the title race, but back-to-back defeats against Dundee United and St Johnstone offered the Parkhead side some hope of overhauling them.

The Dutch touch. Arthur Numan (above) and Giovanni van Bronckhorst (below) were brought in by Dick Advocaat before the 1998-99 season.

Advocaat's team recovered their poise, however, and they clinched the championship in convincing fashion with three games to spare, defeating their closest rivals 3-0 in a dramatic Old Firm contest at Parkhead on 2 May 1999. Neil McCann netted twice, Albertz completing the job with a penalty, as three players were sent off – Rod Wallace of Rangers and the Celtic pair of Stephane Mahe and Vidar Riseth – by referee Hugh Dallas who was struck on the head by a coin as crowd trouble flared.

Rangers finished six points clear of Celtic at the top of the table with St Johnstone a further 14 points behind in third place. The Perth club had enjoyed an excellent campaign but were beaten 4-0 by Rangers in the semi-finals of the Scottish Cup, a victory which set up the prospect of Advocaat winning the 'treble' in his first season in charge.

Celtic, desperate to salvage something from the campaign, were their final opponents at Hampden on 29 May 1999. It was a tense and closely-fought affair but Rod Wallace netted the only goal to seal the sixth 'treble' in Rangers history. Wallace finished the season as Rangers' leading scorer with 26 goals in all competitions.

Rangers had made positive early strides under Advocaat, and enjoyed a decent run in the UEFA Cup which included a fine 3-2 aggregate win over Bayer Leverkusen before losing 4-2 on aggregate to Parma in the third round.

Making an impact in the Champions League was Advocaat's biggest hope for

1999-2000. Having further strengthened his pool of players with the signing of American midfielder Claudio Reyna towards the end of the previous season, the Dutchman returned to his homeland in the summer to recruit striker Michael Mols from Utrecht for £4 million.

Rangers made a brilliant start to their defence of the SPL, winning their opening eight games and remaining unbeaten in the first 12. That included a 4-2 Ibrox win over Celtic who were under new management again, this time in the shape of John Barnes and Kenny Dalglish.

50 Greatest Players

JORG ALBERTZ Midfielder

Joined Rangers: July 1996   **From:** Hamburg

Debut: v Alania Vladikavkaz, European Cup, 7 August 1996

Appearances: 229   **Goals:** 82

Left Rangers: July 2001   **For:** Hamburg

Honours won with Rangers: 3 league championships; 2 Scottish Cups; 2 Scotiish League Cups; 2 caps (Germany)

With a scoring ratio of better than a goal every three games for Rangers, it is not difficult to understand why Jorg Albertz became such a massively popular player with the club's supporters. The German midfielder, recruited from Hamburg for £4 million in the summer of 1996, developed a knack of scoring vital, often late goals for the club and contributed to significant success during his five years at Ibrox.

A tally of 13 goals from 47 games in his debut season was a foretaste of what Albertz would bring to Rangers, although some fans initially felt his workrate did not always match his ability. It was a harsh assessment, but one which latterly appeared to be shared by Dick Advocaat. The Dutchman's view of the player was difficult to reconcile, given that in his first two seasons at the helm, when five out of six domestic trophies were won, Albertz scored 39 times in 107 appearances.

His thunderous and wonderfully accurate long range free-kicks produced many goals for Rangers and became his trademark. Albertz's place in the fans' affections was also cemented by his ability to turn on the style in Old Firm matches. During season 2000-01, as his first-team starting appearances became less frequent, life at Ibrox began to turn sour for the man from Mönchengladbach. In the summer of 2001, Albertz returned to Hamburg in an acrimonious parting of the ways which met with widespread disapproval from the Rangers fans.

A highly productive first few months of the campaign also saw Rangers progress in the Champions League. A 2-1 aggregate victory over Parma in the third qualifying round landed them in Group F alongside Valencia, Bayern Munich and PSV Eindhoven, a daunting assignment.

A 2-0 defeat in Valencia in their opening fixture was followed by a draw at home to Bayern but Rangers resurrected their hopes of further progress with back-to-back victories over Advocaat's former club PSV. Valencia, the outstanding team in the group, then won at Ibrox to leave Rangers in need of a positive outcome to their final group game in Munich. Despite a good performance, they lost 1-0 to Bayern with their misery compounded by a serious knee injury suffered by Michael Mols.

Domestic Consolation

Third place in Group F did provide the consolation of a place in the third round of the UEFA Cup but, after a 2-0 first leg win at Ibrox, Rangers went down by the same scoreline to Borussia Dortmund in Germany and were knocked out of the competition in a penalty shoot-out.

The two Dortmund fixtures sandwiched the League Cup quarter-final against Aberdeen at Pittodrie which saw an unfamiliar Rangers line-up lose 1-0 in extra-time. The defence of the SPL and the Scottish Cup now concentrated the minds of Advocaat and his players.

Scotland striker Billy Dodds and Turkish midfielder Tugay Kerimoglu were added to the squad as the season progressed, the former scoring Rangers' equalizer in a 1-1 draw with Celtic at Parkhead on 27 December 1999 to protect a comfortable lead at the top of the table.

As Celtic's season fell into disarray, a shock home defeat against Inverness Caledonian Thistle in the Scottish Cup signalling the dismissal of Barnes, Rangers stretched clear in the SPL and compiled a 22-match unbeaten run. A 4-0 Old Firm victory at Ibrox on 26 March 2000 underlined Rangers' superiority and the title was secured with six games to spare.

Billy Dodds, already an international when he joined Rangers in 1999.

Celtic's 1-1 draw against Hibs on 22 April meant Rangers could not be caught and were champions even before they defeated St Johnstone 2-0 at McDiarmid Park the following day. The final winning margin was a record 21 points with Hearts 15 points further behind in third.

50 Greatest Players

BARRY FERGUSON Midfielder

Joined Rangers: July 1994   **From:** School

Debut: v Hearts, League, 10 May 1997

Appearances: 184   **Goals:** 17

Honours won with Rangers: 2 league championships; 2 Scottish Cups; 2 Scottish League Cups; 9 Caps (Scotland)

A born-and-bred Rangers supporter, with an older brother, Derek, playing for the Ibrox club in the 80s, Barry Ferguson always dreamed of playing in the light blue. Having joined Rangers straight from school, Barry earned rave reviews for his performances in the youth and reserve sides before being handed his first team debut by Walter Smith at the age of 19 in the final match of the 1996-97 season.

Ferguson made only 11 appearances the following season, however, and his frustration made him seriously consider quitting Ibrox. Salvation came with the arrival of Dick Advocaat as manager. The Dutch coach placed great faith in Ferguson's ability while also managing to harness the young Scot's often wayward behaviour off the pitch.

His performances helped Rangers win the domestic 'treble' in 1998-99 and, despite missing the Scottish Cup final triumph at the end of the campaign, Ferguson was named Scotland's Young Player of the Year by the Scottish PFA. The following season, he played a major role as Rangers retained the title and was honoured as Scotland's Player of the Year by the Scottish Football Writers' Association. By now a full Scotland international, the composed and technically gifted Ferguson was unexpectedly handed the captaincy of Rangers in October 2000.

Speculation over Ferguson's future reached fever pitch in 2001-02 and for most of the season it seemed he would leave Rangers to pursue his ambition to play in the English Premiership. However, Alex McLeish's arrival as manager gave the player a new lease of life at Ibrox and, after leading Rangers to victory in both the League and Scottish Cups, he announced he would be staying at the club.

Rangers' progress in the Scottish Cup had been untroubled, including a 7-0 thrashing of First Division Ayr United in the semi-final, and they encountered few difficulties in a largely one-sided final against Aberdeen at Hampden on 27 May 2000. Without a substitute keeper, an early injury to Jim Leighton left the Pittodrie side's goal to be tended by striker Robbie Winters. Van Bronckhorst, Vidmar, Dodds and Albertz all found a way past the unfortunate Winters as Rangers cruised to a 4-0 win and Advocaat took his haul of trophies to five from his first two seasons at Ibrox.

Dutch Imports

Having established such a dominance of Scottish football, Advocaat dipped into the Dutch market once more as he looked to further enhance his squad for the 2000-01 season, signing defenders Fernando Ricksen and Bert Konterman from AZ Alkmaar and Feyenoord respectively. Rangers made a highly acceptable start to the campaign, winning their first four league matches and also defeating Danish champions Herfolge 6-0 on aggregate to reach the group stages of the Champions League for the third successive year.

However, the wheels fell off dramatically at Parkhead on 27 August in a match which would prove the turning point of the season for both Rangers and Celtic. The home team, under new management again in the shape of Martin O' Neill, inflicted a 6-2 defeat on Advocaat's shell-shocked outfit. It gave Celtic the initiative in the title race and it was one would they would not relinquish. Rangers spent heavily in an attempt to forge a response, signing Dutch midfielder Ronald de Boer from Barcelona for £4.5 million and then doubling the Scottish transfer record with an astonishing £12 million swoop for Norwegian striker Tore Andre Flo from Chelsea.

Although Flo scored on his debut when Rangers avenged their Old Firm loss by beating Celtic 5-1 at Ibrox on 26 November, a further 13 points had been dropped in the intervening period, including three successive defeats at the hands of Hibs, St Johnstone and Kilmarnock. A 1-0 loss to Celtic at Parkhead on 11 February 2001 effectively sent the trophy to Parkhead.

Celtic clinched the title with five games to spare and then emphasized their ascendancy with a 3-0 win at Ibrox in the final Old Firm league fixture on 29 April. The final winning margin was 15 points with Hibs, now managed by Alex McLeish, a further 16 points back in third place.

Advocaat had hoped to make it third time lucky in the Champions League even though their group presented tough opposition. The manager could not have wished for a better start, an impressive 5-0 Ibrox win over Sturm Graz followed by a 1-0 win over Monaco in France, which saw Tugay shine in an unfamiliar sweeper role. Rangers dropped their first points when they lost 3-2 to Galatasaray in Istanbul but even worse was a goalless draw against the Turkish side at Ibrox.

A poor performance and 2-0 defeat at the hands of Sturm Graz in Austria left Rangers requiring victory over Monaco at Ibrox in their final fixture to make progress. Goals from Kenny Miller, a £2 million signing from Hibs, and Michael Mols put them in sight of the next round, but a late goal from Marco Simone earned the visitors a 2-2 draw. Rangers finished third in the group and once again had to settle for the consolation of a UEFA Cup place. Their stay in the tournament was brief; losing 3-1 on aggregate to Kaiserslautern.

Domestic cup competitions provided further disappointment for Advocaat and his players. They lost a tempestuous League Cup semi-final 3-1 to Celtic at Hampden on 7 February 2001 which saw Claudio Reyna and Michael Mols of Rangers sent off along with the opposition's Lubomir Moravcik.

The following month, Rangers' last hope of silverware from the season disappeared when they lost 1-0 to Dundee United at Tannadice in the quarter-finals of the Scottish Cup. With Celtic going on to win both cup tournaments, completing their first domestic 'treble' since 1969, Advocaat suddenly found himself under intense pressure to redress the balance in 2001-02.

The sales of three midfield players did nothing to aid him. Giovanni van Bronckhorst went to Arsenal for £8.5 million, Tugay joined Blackburn Rovers for £1.3 million and the Rangers fans were particularly upset at the hugely popular Jorg Albertz's return to Germany in a £4 million move to Hamburg.

Neil McCann in action for Scotland against Latvia in 2000.

50 Greatest Players

LORENZO AMORUSO Defender

Joined Rangers: July 1997 **From:** Fiorentina

Debut: v Celtic, Scottish Cup, 5 April 1998

Appearances: 189 **Goals:** 18

Honours won with Rangers: 2 league championships; 2 Scottish Cups; 2 Scottish League Cups

Unquestionably one of the most popular players among the current generation of Rangers supporters, Lorenzo Amoruso has both captured the imagination and divided opinion among Ibrox fans since his arrival from Serie A in the summer of 1997.

Signed by Walter Smith as a potential long-term replacement for central defensive linchpin and inspirational captain Richard Gough, the man from Bari was sidelined for most of his first campaign with a knee injury. Remarkably, his first two appearances were against Celtic in successive weeks in April 1998 and he endeared himself to the club's fans by making significant contributions to back-to-back Old Firm victories.

With Gough's departure, Amoruso was handed both the captaincy and a regular first team place at the start of the 1998-99 season by new manager Dick Advocaat. He responded by leading the team to the domestic 'treble'. Prone to some rash errors of judgement and not averse to taking risks in and around his own penalty area, the big Italian is not everyone's idea of a top class defender and he has not been without his detractors. However, he continued to enjoy success in 1999-2000 as he skippered Rangers to a successful defence of the title before injury ruled him out of the Scottish Cup final win the same season.

Things turned sour for Amoruso in 2000-01 as he was stripped of the captaincy by Advocaat after a loss of form and he appeared certain to leave the club in the summer of 2001. He stayed, however, and in 2001-02 flourished following the arrival of Alex McLeish as Advocaat's replacement, so much so he was named Player of the Year by the Scottish Professional Footballers' Association.

Christian Nerlinger, another German midfielder, was recruited from Borussia Dortmund for £1.7 million and Advocaat also signed Argentinian striker Claudio Caniggia from Dundee for just under £1 million and the Trinidad and Tobago international playmaker Russell Latapy under freedom of contract from Hibs.

Rangers made a good start, all three of the new signings scoring as they defeated Aberdeen 3-0 at Pittodrie. They were unbeaten in their first eight league fixtures but suffered a severe blow when they lost 2-1 to Fenerbahce in the third qualifying round of the Champions League, Scotland having two clubs in the competition for the first time.

Dodgy Dagestan

Rangers' failure to reach the group stage was compounded by an unsettling saga over their first round tie in the UEFA Cup against Russian side Anzhi Makhachkala. Despite safety concerns about the Dagestan area where Anzhi were located, UEFA initially ruled that Rangers must travel. The Ibrox club were prepared to withdraw from the tournament and risk a fine or ban but, eventually, UEFA ordered a one-off tie to be played on neutral soil in Warsaw. Bert Konterman's goal earned Rangers a 1-0 win in a scrappy and historic contest on 27 September 2001.

Three days later, Rangers faced the first acid test of the campaign when Celtic, already ahead in the title race, visited Ibrox for the first Old Firm League game of the season. Despite enjoying plenty of possession, Rangers slipped to a 2-0 defeat as the defending champions took a firm grip of the championship race.

Michael Ball, a £6 million recruit from Everton, and Georgian international striker Shota Arveladze from Ajax had been added to Advocaat's squad who won their next five league games before heading to Parkhead to face Celtic again on 25 November. It was a match Rangers simply could not afford to lose if they wished to retain any genuine hope in the title race but lose it they did, 2-1, with the afternoon also soured by a touchline bust-up between Advocaat and Ball when the English defender was substituted.

Speculation over the future of Advocaat, who was in the final *season of his managerial contract and had consistently declined to*

Team USA star Claudio Reyna made a big impression in a short time at Rangers.

Dutchman Fernando Ricksen (left) and the Dane Peter Lovenkrands – both internationals of quality – have become firm favourites with the Ibrox crowd.

declined to reveal his intentions, intensified. Shortly after Rangers defeated Paris Saint-Germain in a penalty shoot-out to reach the fourth round of the UEFA Cup in December, Advocaat revealed he was resigning as manager.

The Dutchman moved into a director of football role and on 11 December 2001, Alex McLeish was named as the 11th incumbent of the post of Rangers manager. The former Scotland international defender, a Glaswegian native who made his name as a key figure in Alex Feguson's successful Aberdeen side, was recruited from Hibs along with his assistant Andy Watson and charged with the task of trying to rein in Martin O' Neill's dominant Celtic.

He made a promising start, Rangers winning 13 and drawing three of the first 16 league games under him, but the championship was already a lost cause. Celtic wrapped it up with four games to spare on 6 April 2002 and eventually finished a massive 18 points clear of Rangers with surprise packets Livingston a staggering 27 points further adrift in third place.

Alex McLeish had been unable to extend Rangers' eventful UEFA Cup campaign, although there was no shame, only frustration, in a 4-3 aggregate fourth round defeat at the hands of eventual tournament winners Feyenoord.

Great Matches

SCOTTISH CUP FINAL — Hampden Park, 4 May 2002

Rangers 3 — **Celtic 2** — Attendance 51,138

Lovenkrands 2 — Hartson
Ferguson — Balde

Having collected his first piece of silverware as Rangers manager two months earlier in the shape of the League Cup, Alex McLeish cemented a highly-promising start to his Ibrox career when his team completed a domestic cup double in dramatic and memorable fashion.

Celtic, having comfortably retained the league championship title, went into the match as favourites and Rangers appeared to be in some trouble when they lost striker Claudio Caniggia to injury after just 15 minutes then went a goal behind four minutes later as John Hartson took advantage of lax marking to head home.

Rangers responded with the kind of spirit and determination McLeish had instilled in them since taking the Ibrox helm and equalized in 21 minutes, Peter Lovenkrands pouncing on a mix-up between Johan Mjallby and Chris Sutton to drill a low shot beyond Robert Douglas.

Celtic suffered their own injury blow just before half-time when captain Paul Lambert limped off but, five minutes into the second half, they regained the lead. Again there were question marks over the Rangers defending as Bobo Balde rose to head a Neil Lennon free-kick past Stefan Klos.

Rangers, however, were undeterred and noticeably began to dominate possession. Captain Barry Ferguson was on top form and he made it 2-2 in 68 minutes with a brilliantly-struck free-kick awarded for Balde's needless foul on Lorenzo Amoruso on the edge of the box. In the closing stages, Rangers looked by far the likelier side to win it but extra-time looked inevitable. With a matter of seconds left, however, the Ibrox men sent their support into raptures when they went in front for the first time. Neil McCann's cross from the left picked out the run of Lovenkrands and the young Dane grabbed himself a piece of Ibrox folklore as he stooped to head the ball beyond Douglas.

There was barely time for Celtic to restart the match before referee Hugh Dallas blew the final whistle. Alex McLeish savoured a tremendous victory which he hoped would give him the platform to deliver even greater successes to his new club.

Rangers: Klos, Moore, Amoruso, Numan, Ross, Ricksen, Ferguson, De Boer, McCann, Lovenkrands, Caniggia (Arveladze)

Celtic: Douglas, Mjallby, Sutton, Balde, Agathe, Lennon, Petrov, Lambert (McNamara), Thompson, Hartson, Larsson

Referee: H. Dallas (Motherwell)

The season, however, would end with Rangers supporters buoyed by a new sense of optimism as McLeish's rejuvenated side won both domestic cup competitions. The new manager was denied the financial resources of his immediate predecessors in the job and, shortly before his arrival, another midfielder had been sold when Claudio Reyna moved to Sunderland. But even without any new signings, McLeish managed to instil a freshness of spirit among the squad he inherited. He struck a major psychological blow for himself and the team when, in his first Old Firm fixture, an extra-time goal from Bert Konterman earned a 2-1 win over Celtic in the semi-final of the League Cup at Hampden.

Their surprise opponents in the final at Hampden on 17 March were Ayr United, the First Division side having produced a shock win over Hibs in the other semi. Tore Andre Flo, Barry Ferguson and Claudio Caniggia with a double claimed the goals in a 4-0 win, to give McLeish his first trophy success after just three months in charge. It was also a notable afternoon for Ferguson, the midfielder lifting his maiden prize as Rangers captain after replacing Lorenzo Amoruso in the job midway through the previous season.

Rangers negotiated a smooth path to the Scottish Cup final and, on 4 May 2002, McLeish and Ferguson were celebrating again as Celtic were defeated 3-2 in an epic contest. The Ibrox men twice came from behind and won it with an injury time goal from Lovenkrands, his second of the game.

McLeish could hardly have wished for a better or more upbeat start to his Rangers career and was further boosted by Ferguson's decision soon afterwards to stay at the club despite interest from the English Premiership. In the summer, Spanish midfielder Mikel Arteta was signed from Barcelona for £6.2 million and Australian defender Kevin Muscat joined under freedom of contract from Wolves, the manager reinforcing his squad as Kanchelskis, Tony Vidmar and Scott Wilson all left at the end of their contracts.

No-one knew better than McLeish that judgement on his success or otherwise would be delivered on the evidence of his ability to reclaim the championship from Celtic. One hundred and thirty years after a teenager had the bright idea of forming a football club called Rangers, the 2002-03 season dawned with new dreams and ambitions to fulfil.

THE **ESSENTIAL HISTORY** OF
RANGERS

CLUB STATISTICS

The Rangers Directory

Club Information

- Ground: Ibrox Stadium, 150 Edmiston Drive, Glasgow, G51 2XD.
- Tel: 0141 580 8500.
- Tickets: 0870 600 1993.
- Customer Services: 0870 600 1972.
- Website: www.rangers.co.uk
- Ground capacity (2002): 50,444 (all seated).
- Pitch measurements: 115yds x 75yds.
- Year formed: 1872.
- Club nicknames: the Gers, the Light Blues.
- Previous grounds: Flesher's Haugh (1872-75), Burnbank (1875-76), Kinning Park, (1876-87), First Ibrox (1887-99).
- Colours: Royal blue shirts, white shorts, white and royal blue socks.
- Change colours: Tangerine shirts, royal blue shorts, tangerine socks.

Honours

- Scottish League champions: 1890-91 (joint), 1898-99, 1899-1900, 1900-01, 1901-02, 1910-11, 1911-12, 1912-13, 1917-18, 1919-20, 1920-21, 1922-23, 1923-24, 1924-25, 1926-27, 1927-28, 1928-29, 1929-30, 1930-31, 1932-33, 1933-34, 1934-35, 1936-37, 1938-39, 1946-47, 1948-49, 1949-50, 1952-53, 1955-56, 1956-57, 1958-59, 1960-61, 1962-63, 1963-64, 1974-75, 1975-76, 1977-78, 1986-87, 1988-89, 1989-90, 1990-91, 1991-92, 1992-93, 1993-94, 1994-95, 1995-96, 1996-97, 1998-99, 1999-2000. Runners-up: 25 times.
- Scottish Cup winners: 1894, 1897, 1898, 1903, 1928, 1930, 1932, 1934, 1935, 1936, 1948, 1949, 1950, 1953, 1960, 1962, 1963, 1964, 1966, 1973, 1976, 1978, 1979,1981, 1992, 1993, 1996, 1999, 2000, 2002. Runners-up: 17 times.
- Scottish League Cup winners: 1946-47, 1948-49, 1960-61, 1961-62, 1963-64, 1964-65, 1970-71, 1975-76, 1977-78, 1978-79, 1981-82, 1983-84, 1984-85, 1986-87, 1987-88, 1988-89, 1990-91, 1992-93, 1993-94, 1996-97, 1998-99, 2001-02. Runners-up: 7 times.
- European Cup-Winners' Cup winners: 1972. Runners-up: 1961, 1967.
- European Cup semi-finalists: 1960, 1993.
- Fairs (UEFA) Cup semi-finalists: 1969.
- English FA Cup semi-finalists: 1887.
- Glasgow Cup winners: 1892-93, 1893-94, 1896-97, 1897-98, 1899-1900, 1900-01, 1901-02, 1910-11, 1911-12, 1912-13, 1913-14, 1917-18, 1918-19, 1921-22, 1922-23, 1923-24, 1924-25, 1929-30, 1931-32, 1932-33, 1933-34, 1935-36, 1936-37, 1937-38, 1939-40, 1941-42, 1942-43, 1943-44, 1944-45, 1947-48, 1949-50, 1953-54, 1956-57, 1957-58, 1959-60, 1968-69, 1970-71, 1974-75 (joint winners with Celtic), 1975-76, 1978-79, 1983-84, 1985-86, 1986-87.
- Glasgow Charity Cup winners: 1878-79, 1898-97, 1899-1900, 1903-04, 1905-06, 1906-07, 1908-09, 1910-11, 1918-19, 1921-22, 1922-23, 1924-25, 1927-28, 1928-29, 1929-30, 1930-31, 1931-32, 1932-33, 1933-34, 1938-39, 1939-40, 1940-41, 1941-42, 1943-44, 1944-45, 1945-46, 1946-47, 1947-48, 1950-51, 1954-55, 1956-57, 1959-60.
- Glasgow League winners: 1895-96, 1897-98.

- Scottish Regional League, Western Division winners: 1939-40.
- Southern League winners: 1940-41, 1941-42, 1942-43, 1943-44, 1944-45, 1945-46
- Scottish Emergency War Cup winners: 1940.
- Southern League Cup winners: 1940-41, 1941-42, 1942-43, 1944-45
- Summer Cup winners: 1942.
- Victory Cup winners: 1946.
- Drybrough Cup winners: 1979-80.

Records

- World Record: 49 League Championships.
- World Record: 100 Major Domestic Trophies.
- Highest attendance: 118,567 v Celtic, League, 2 January 1939.
- Record victory: 13-0 v Possilpark, Scottish Cup, 6 October 1877 v Uddingston, Scottish Cup, 10 November 1877 and v Kelvinside, Scottish Cup, 28 September 1889.
- Record defeat: 1-7 v Celtic, League Cup final, 19 October 1957.
- Record League victory: 10-0 v Hibs, 24 December 1898.
- Record League defeat: 0-6 v Dumbarton, 4 May 1892.
- Most capped player: Ally McCoist, 60, Scotland.
- Record transfer fee received: £8,500,000 from Arsenal for Giovanni van Bronckhorst, July 2001.
- Record transfer fee paid: £12,500,000 to Chelsea for Tore Andre Flo, November 2000.
- Record appearances: John Grieg, 755, 1960-78.
- Most goals for club: Ally McCoist, 355, 1983-98.
- Record league appearances Sandy Archibald, 513, 1917-1934.
- Most league goals: Ally McCoist, 251.
- Most goals in one season: Sam English, 44, 1931-32.
- Most European Appearances: John Greig, 64.
- Most European Goals: Ally McCoist, 21.
- Most Goalkeeper Appearances: Peter McCloy, 535, 1970-1986.
- Most Scottish Cup Appearances: Alec Smith, 74.
- Most Scottish Cup Goals: Jimmy Fleming, 44.
- Most League Cup Appearances: John Greig, 121.
- Most League Cup Goals: Ally McCoist, 54.

Rangers' record appearance maker, John Greig.

185

50 Greatest Players

This list is not intended to be definitive. Clearly, every Rangers supporter would have their own choices to be included. However, the 50 listed here are representative of the skill, achievement and dedication which makes a great Rangers player. The list is sure to prompt debate and there are many other players who could just as easily be included in it. Hopefully, however, the 50 men here provide an example of the variety of talent to represent Rangers Football Club over 130 years.

No. 1 John Greig (Defender) - 755 appearances, 120 goals. As committed to Rangers as anyone ever was, through good times and bad. Voted 'Greatest Ever Ranger' by the club's supporters, an accolade impossible to contest (see page 128).

No. 2 Alec Smith (Outside left) - 481 appearances, 152 goals. First in a long line of great Rangers wingers, the Darvel marvel served the club for 21 years and was a peerless talent for both club and country (see page 36).

No. 3 Jim Baxter (Inside left) - 254 appearances, 24 goals. Regarded by many as the greatest Scottish player of all time, 'Slim Jim' was a world class performer, if a self-destructive one (see page 101).

No. 4 Alan Morton (Outside left) - 440 appearances, 105 goals. Winner of nine League championship medals during a glory-filled Ibrox career, 'the Wee Blue Devil' attained legendary status with his bewitching wing play for club and country (see page 54).

No. 5 Ally McCoist (Striker) - 581 appearances, 355 goals. Quite simply the greatest goalscorer Rangers have ever known. From difficult beginnings at Ibrox, he became revered by the modern generation of supporters (see page 170).

No. 6 Davie Meiklejohn (Defender) - 563 appearances, 46 goals. A cultured and consistent footballer, 'Meek' was both an outstanding captain and defender who played in 12 championship winning Rangers teams (see page 61).

No. 7 Willie Waddell (Winger) - 301 appearances, 58 goals. Later a legend as manager and administrator, Waddell first found greatness as a Rangers player with 18 years of tormenting defenders with his pace, power and precision crossing (see page 85).

No. 8 Derek Johnstone (Defender/Striker) - 546 appearances, 210 goals. A tremendous goalscorer who proved equally gifted in central defence. A European Cup Winners Cup hero as a teenager, 'DJ' became of Rangers' most effective and popular players (see page 143).

No. 9 John McPherson (Inside forward) - 218 appearances, 121 goals. Rangers' first 'superstar', the outstanding Scottish player of his era. 'Kitey' was a member of the club's first title-winning side in 1891 and later served on the Ibrox board (see page 23).

No. 10 Willie Woodburn (Defender) - 329 appearances, 2 goals. Regarded by many as the finest centre half Scottish football has seen. Committed, constructive and ultra-reliable, his career was prematurely ended by an SFA suspension (see page 82).

No. 11 Davie Cooper (Winger) - 540 appearances, 75 goals. Possibly the most naturally talented player ever to pull on a Rangers jersey. Cooper's magical left foot inspired the treble winning side of 1977-78 and later helped Graeme Souness revitalise the club in 1986 (see page 148).

No. 12 Neil Gibson (Wing half) - 192 appearances, 22 goals. A graceful, sweet-passing midfield player, Gibson was considered the finest footballer in Britain during his 10 trophy-laden years at Ibrox and would be a £30 million man in the modern market (see page 26).

No. 13 Richard Gough (Defender) - 427 appearances, 34 goals. A remarkably consistent defender, Gough was an exemplary captain and infectious motivator during the era which saw him lead Rangers to nine successive championships (see page 164).

No. 14 Willie Thornton (Forward) - 308 appearances, 194 goals. As fearless as he was talented, 'Bustle' was the spearhead of the outstanding Rangers side which emerged immediately after the Second World War (see page 78).

No. 15 Sandy Jardine (Defender) - 674 appearances, 77 goals. A tremendous servant who achieved great success with both Rangers and Scotland. Cool, classy and solid as a full-back or sweeper (see page 139).

No. 16 Brian Laudrup (Forward) - 151 appearances, 45 goals. Few players have made as much of an impact on Scottish football as the free-running Danish star whose world class talent lit up Ibrox in the 1990s (see page 167).

No. 17 Andy Cunningham (Forward) - 389 appearances, 182 goals. As both a creator and taker of goals, Cunningham was the inspiration behind Rangers' successful sides of the 1920s (see page 38).

No. 18 R.C. Hamilton (Forward) - 209 appearances, 184 goals. Rangers' first great goalscoring hero, the man from Elgin scored more against Celtic than any other player until Ally McCoist came along (see page 29).

No. 19 Terry Butcher (Defender) - 176 appearances, 11 goals. An inspirational captain whose commitment and world class defensive skills were the key to the revival effected at Rangers by Graeme Souness in 1986 (see page 153).

No. 20 Bob McPhail (Forward) - 408 appearances, 261 goals. More than just a prolific goalscorer, this hard working and intelligent Ibrox legend was a class act for club and country (see page 67).

No. 21 Sandy Archibald (Winger) - 580 appearances, 148 goals. A powerful and athletic winger who helped Rangers to 13 championship titles (see page 58).

No. 22 Andy Goram (Goalkeeper) - 261 appearances. As effective a goalkeeper as Rangers or Scotland have ever seen with remarkable reflexes and positional awareness (see page 161).

No. 23 Willie Henderson (Winger) - 426 appearances, 2 goals. 'Wee Willie' made light of short-sightedness to become one of the most effective and entertaining wingers in Scottish football (see page 113).

No. 24 George Young (Defender) - 428 appearances, 31 goals. A wonderful captain of Rangers and Scotland, 'Corky' was equally effective as centre half or full-back in the famed 'Iron Curtain' defence (see page 88).

No. 25 Ralph Brand (Forward) - 317 appearances, 206 goals. Incisive and clever forward who brought others into play and plundered goals himself (see page 102).

No. 26 Jimmy Millar (Forward) - 317 appearances, 162 goals. Can hardly be separated from Brand with whom he formed a feared front line partnership (see page 107).

No. 27 Ian McMillan (Inside forward) - 194 appearances, 55 goals. 'The Wee Prime Minister' brilliantly complemented Jim Baxter in the marvellous Rangers team of the early 1960s (see page 98).

No. 28 Tommy McLean (Winger) - 452 appearances, 57 goals. Few players delivered the ball with such consistent accuracy as diminutive dead-ball specialist McLean who lit up European and 'treble' winning sides (see page 134).

No. 29 Ian McColl (Right half) - 526 appearances, 14 goals. His captaincy and highly combative and consistent performances were an integral part of 13 trophy successes (see page 91).

No. 30 Jerry Dawson (Goalkeeper) - 271 appearances. His medal haul was limited by the Second World War but the 'Prince of Goalkeepers' stunning reflexes and unerring positional sense helped Rangers to an array of silverware (see page 68).

No. 31 Eric Caldow (Full back) - 407 appearances, 25 goals. Regarded by many people as the finest left-back to play for Rangers or Scotland, Caldow was a mainstay of two great Rangers teams (see page 103).

No. 32 Jimmy Smith (Forward) - 259 appearances, 249 goals. His goals-per-game ratio says it all. The battering ram striker was a scoring phenomenon for the great Rangers side of the 1930s (see page 69).

No. 33 Dougie Gray (Full back) - 555 appearances, 2 goals. Including wartime matches, the ultra-consistent defender made a staggering 940 appearances in all games for Rangers (see page 71).

No. 34 Willie Reid (Forward) - 230 appearances, 195 goals. One of the most effective goalscorers in Rangers' history, Reid was a key component in the club's pre-First World War successes (see page 38).

No. 35 Alex MacDonald (Midfield) - 503 appearances, 94 goals. Played from the heart for Rangers, 'Doddie' had the tenacity, drive and happy goalscoring knack which made him an outstanding midfield player (see page 135).

No. 36 Ian Durrant (Midfield) - 348 appearances, 45 goals. Despite a career compromised by serious injury, Durrant's talent enabled him to become one of the great midfield players of the modern generation (see page 168).

No. 37 Davie Wilson (Winger) - 373 appearances, 157 goals. A pacy and stylish winger with a tremendous nose for goal, Wilson was adored by fans of Rangers and Scotland alike (see page 108).

No. 38 Willie Johnston (Winger) - 393 appearances, 125 goals. More than just a winger, 'Bud' displayed great skill, pace and shooting ability to become one of Rangers' European legends (see page 117).

No. 39 Paul Gascoigne (Midfield) - 104 appearances, 39 goals. The most gifted English player of his generation made a huge impact in his time at Ibrox with his skill, goals and exuberance (see page 166).

No. 40 Peter McCloy (Goalkeeper) - 535 appearances. 'The Girvan Lighthouse' played more games for Rangers than any other keeper. A European and 'treble' winning hero for the club (see page 142).

No. 41 Sammy Cox (Full back) - 310 appearances, 20 goals. Excelled in all the defensive arts and nullified all the great wingers of his era during a superb career for club and country (see page 84).

No. 42 Jock Drummond (Full back) - 223 appearances, 2 goals. Determined, uncompromising and effective, he formed a legendary full-back partnership with Nicol Smith in Rangers' first great side (see page 24).

No. 43 Torry Gillick (Inside forward) - 140 appearances, 62 goals. A maverick talent who, in two spells at the club, delighted Rangers fans with the finesse and audacity of his passing and finishing (see page 77).

No. 44 Stuart McCall (Midfield) - 265 appearances, 20 goals. The midfield mainstay of Rangers' nine-in-a-row era, Anglo-Scot McCall married a big heart to often underrated technical ability (see page 163).

No. 45 Ray Wilkins (Midfield) - 96 appearances, 3 goals. At Ibrox all too briefly, one of England's great midfielders nonetheless carved a place in Rangers folklore with his class and intelligence (see page 149).

No. 46 Moses McNeil (Winger) - 34 appearances, 9 goals. Not only named and formed the club but was talented enough to become Rangers' first international player (see page 9).

No. 47 Colin Stein (Forward) - 206 appearances, 97 goals. A bustling striker and natural predator, his European exploits made him one of the most popular players ever in the eyes of the Rangers fans (see page 127).

No. 48 Jorg Albertz (Midfield) - 229 appearances, 82 goals. The German free-kick specialist endeared himself to the Rangers support with his commitment to the club and displays in Europe and against Celtic (see page 173).

No. 49 Barry Ferguson (Midfield) - 184 appearances, 18 goals. Named club captain at a relatively young age, the gifted and committed playmaker has already earned a place in Rangers' hall of fame (see page 175).

No. 50 Lorenzo Amoruso (Defender) - 189 appearances, 18 goals. A cult hero for many, less highly regarded by others, but unquestionably as popular with the fans as any modern day Ranger (see page 178).

Results and Tables 1874-2002

The following pages include details of every official match played by Rangers. Each league season has its own page and is dated at the top. League matches appear first, followed by individual cup competitions. The opponents played at home are written in capital letters and appear in upper and lower case for away games. The date of the match, the score, Rangers goalscorers and the match attendance are also included. In the early years of Scottish football, accurate records were not always kept and some details may be missing from the tables. Full League and Cup appearances and the goalscorers are featured separately. The final league table is included at the bottom of each page as well as a Fact File which notes particularly interesting facts and figures for the season as well as any notable transfers in and out.

The results of matches played during the years 1940-45 are not included. During these wartime years the official league programme was suspended. In both the League and Cup Appearances and Goalscorers tables the category 'other' includes matches in the European Cup (and Champions League), European Cup-Winners' Cup, Fairs/UEFA Cup and European Super Cup.

Pre-League FA Cup Results 1874-79

Season 1874-75

Scottish Cup

DATE	OPPONENTS	SCORE		GOALSCORERS
Oct 10	OXFORD	(Rd1)	W 2-0	M.McNeil, Gibb
Nov 28	DUMBARTON	(Rd2)	D 0-0	
Dec 12	Dumbarton	(R)	L 0-1	

Season 1875-76

Scottish Cup

Oct 16	FIRST LANARK	(Rd1)	W 7-0	John Campbell 3 Watson 2, Phillips, P.Campbell
Oct 30	Third Lanark*	(Rd2)	W 1-0	P.Campbell
Nov 13	THIRD LANARK	(R)	L 1-2	M.McNeil

*Third Lanark protest upheld, Rangers kicked off both halves, replay ordered.

Season 1876-77

Scottish Cup

Sep 30	QUEEN'S PARK JNRS	(Rd1)	W 4-1	James Campell, rest unrecorded
Oct 21	Towerhill	(Rd2)	W 8-0	P.Campbell 2, Dunlop 2, Marshall 2, Watson 2
Dec 9	Mauchline	(Rd4)	W 3-0	Marshall, P.Campbell, Watson
Dec 30	Lennox	(QF)	W 3-0	P.Campbell, Marshall, Dunlop
Mar 17	Vale of Leven*	(F)	D 1-1	McDougall o.g.
Apr 7	Vale of Leven*	(R)	D 1-1	Dunlop
Apr 13	Vale of Leven†	(2R)	L 2-3	P.Campbell, M.McNeil

*Played at Hamilton Crescent, Glasgow.
†Played at Hampden Park. Rangers received byes in round three and semi-finals.

Season 1877-78

Scottish Cup

DATE	OPPONENTS	SCORE		GOALSCORERS
Oct 6	POSSILPARK	(Rd1)	W 13-0	Marshall 2, Watson 2, Ricketts, P.Campbell 3, James Campbell 2, Hill 2, M.McNeil
Oct 27	ALEXANDRA ATHLETIC	(Rd2)	W 8-0	Dunlop, P.Campbell 3, M.McNeil 3, James Campbell
Nov 10	UDDINGSTON	(Rd3)	W 13-0	Marshall 4, Watson 4, M.McNeil 2, James Campbell, P.Campbell, Hill
Dec 1	VALE OF LEVEN	(Rd4)	D 0-0	
Dec 15	Vale of Leven	(R)	L 0-5	

Season 1878-79

Scottish Cup

Sep 28	SHAFTESBURY	(Rd1)	W 3-0	Struthers, rest unrecorded
Oct 19	Whitefield	(Rd2)	W 6-1	Unrecorded
Nov 9	PARKGROVE	(Rd3)	W 8-2	Struthers 3, Hill 3, Dunlop, P.Campbell
Nov 30	ALEXANDRA ATHLETIC	(Rd4)	W 3-0	Dunlop, McQuarrie, unrecorded
Mar 8	PARTICK	(Rd5)	W 4-0	Angus 2, Hill, Steel
Mar 22	Queen's Park	(QF)	W 1-0	Dunlop
Apr 19	Vale of Leven	(F)	D 1-1	Struthers

*Played at Hampden Park. Rangers refused to take part in replay of final after protest. Rangers received bye in semi-final.

Pre-League FA Cup Results 1879-90

Season 1879-80

Scottish Cup

DATE	OPPONENTS	SCORE		GOALSCORERS
Sep 20	QUEEN'S PARK	(Rd1) D	0-0	
Sep 27	Queen's Park	(R) L	1-5	Steel

Season 1880-81

Scottish Cup

Sep 11	GOVAN	(Rd1) W	4-1	Unrecorded
Oct 2	Northern	(Rd2) W	1-0	Struthers
Oct 23	PARTICK THISTLE	(Rd3) W	3-0	Angus 3,
Nov 13	CLYDE	(Rd4) W	11-0	Struthers, Steel,
				Pringle, Angus;
				rest unrecorded
Dec 18	Hurlford	(Rd5) W	3-0	Christie, Angus, McNeil
Dec 25	DUMBARTON	(QF) L	1-3	Pringle

Season 1881-82

Scottish Cup

Sep 10	THIRD LANARK	(Rd1) W	2-1	Pringle, Weir
Oct 22	ALEXANDRA ATHLETIC	(Rd3) W	3-1	Pringle 2, Hill
Nov 12	Thornliebank	(Rd4) W	2-0	Hill, opponent o.g.
Dec 3	South Western*	(Rd5) W	2-1	Inglis, McFarlane
Dec 24	SOUTH WESTERN	(Rd5) W	4-0	Christie, Inglis,
				McFarlane, Hill
Jan 28	Dumbarton†	(QF) L	1-2	Pringle
Feb 4	Dumbarton	(QF) L	1-5	Hill

*Replay ordered after South Western protest.
†Replay ordered after Rangers protest.

Season 1882-83

Scottish Cup

Sep 9	Jordanhill	(Rd1) W	4-0	Watson 2, Corbett 2
Sep 30	Queen's Park	(Rd2) L	2-3	Pringle, McIntyre

Season 1883-84

Scottish Cup

Sep 8	Northern	(Rd1) W	1-0	Gossland
Sep 29	WHITEHILL	(Rd2) W	14-2	McHardy,
				rest unrecorded
Oct 20	FALKIRK	(Rd3) W	5-2	McGregor, Hamilton,
				Gossland, McHardy,
				unrecorded
Nov 10	Dunblane	(Rd4) W	6-1	Unrecorded
Dec 1	St. Bernards	(Rd5) W	3-0	McHardy, Gossland,
				Pringle
Dec 22	Cambuslang	(QF) W	5-1	Gossland 2, Pringle,
				Heggie, Inglis
Jan 19	Vale of Leven	(SF) L	0-3	

Season 1884-85

Scottish Cup

Sep 13	WHITEHILL	(Rd1) W	11-0	Unrecorded
Oct 4	Third Lanark	(Rd2) D	2-2	Gossland, Morton
Oct 11	THIRD LANARK	(R) D	0-0	
Oct 25	Third Lanark*	(Rd3) W	3-0	Lawrie, Cook,
				Morton
Nov 15	Arbroath†	(Rd4) L	3-4	Morton, Gossland,
				McKenzie
Dec 20	Arbroath	(R) W	8-1	Unrecorded
Dec 27	Renton	(QF) L	3-4	Gossland, McKenzie,
				Peacock

*Both teams entered in third round after second draw.
†Replay ordered after Rangers protest. Rangers received a bye in fifth round.

Season 1885-86

Scottish Cup

DATE	OPPONENTS	SCORE		GOALSCORERS
Sep 12	Clyde	(Rd1) L	0-1	

Season 1886-87

Scottish Cup

Sep 11	GOVAN ATHLETIC	(Rd1) W	9-1	Gray, J.Gow, Peacock,
				opponent o.g., rest
				unrecorded
Oct 2	WESTBOURNE	(Rd2) W	5-2	Buchanan, McKenzie,
				Duncan, Lawrie,
				unrecorded
Oct 23	CAMBUSLANG	(Rd3) L	0-2	

FA Cup

Oct 30	Everton	(Rd1) W	1-0	Heggie
Nov 20	CHURCH	(Rd2) W	2-1	Lawrie 2
Dec 4	COWLAIRS	(Rd3) W	3-2	Fraser, Lawrie,
				Peacock
Jan 29	LINCOLN CITY	(Rd4) W	3-0	Fraser, Lindsay,
				Peacock
Feb 19	OLD WESTMINSTERS	(QF) W	5-1	Lafferty, Lawrie,
				Lindsay, Fraser,
				unrecorded
Mar 5	Aston Villa*	(SF) L	1-3	Lafferty

*Played at Nantwich Road, Crewe. Rangers received a bye in fourth round.

Season 1887-88

Scottish Cup

Sep 3	BATTLEFIELD	(Rd1) W	4-1	White 2, Brand,
				Lawrie
Sep 24	Partick Thistle	(Rd2) L	1-2	Brand

Season 1888-89

Scottish Cup

Sep 1	PARTICK THISTLE	(Rd1) W	4-2	Sloan 2, Wylie,
				J.Gow
Sep 22	Clyde	(Rd2) D	2-2	Aird, Wylie
Sep 29	CLYDE	(R) L	0-3	

Season 1889-90

Scottish Cup

Sep 7	UNITED ABSTAINERS	(Rd1) W	6-2	Unrecorded
Sep 28	Kelvinside Athletic	(Rd2) W	13-0	Allan 2, Wylie 2,
				Henderson 2,
				McIntyre, Robin,
				Mitchell, rest unrecorded
Oct 19	VALE OF LEVEN	(Rd3) D	0-0	
Oct 26	Vale of Leven	(R) L	2-3	Wylie, D.Gow

Season 1890-91

Scottish League

DATE	OPPONENTS	SCORE	GOALSCORERS	ATTENDANCE
Aug 16	HEARTS	W 5-2	Kerr 2, H.McCreadie, J.McPherson, Adams o.g.	4,000
Aug 23	Cambuslang	W 6-2	McPherson 4, D.Gow, - Marshall	
Sep 13	Dumbarton	L 1-5	Hislop	4,000
Oct 4	ST MIRREN	W 8-2	McPherson 5, Kerr 3	-
Oct 18	COWLAIRS	D 1-1	Hislop	-
Jan 17	Vale of Leven	W 3-1	McPherson, Hislop, Henderson	-
Jan 24	Hearts	W 1-0	Kerr	5,000
Feb 7	Abercorn	D 1-1	Marshall	-
Feb 21	CAMBUSLANG	W 2-1	H.McCreadie, McPherson	2,000
Feb 28	St Mirren	W 7-3	H.McCreadie 2, Henderson 2, Kerr, McPherson, Sloan o.g.	-
Mar 7	Third Lanark	W 4-0	McPherson, rest unrecorded	-
Mar 14	ABERCORN	W 2-0	H.McCreadie, Henderson	5,000
Mar 21	Celtic	D 2-2	A.McCreadie, Hislop	12,000
Mar 28	Cowlairs	W 2-0	Henderson, Hislop	-
Apr 4	VALE OF LEVEN	W 4-0	Hislop 2; rest unrecorded	2,000
Apr 25	DUMBARTON	W 4-2	A.McCreadie, Hislop, Kerr, McPherson	12,000
May 2	CELTIC	L 1-2	Henderson	10,000
May 9	THIRD LANARK	W 4-1	McKenzie 3, Hislop	6,000

Championship Play-off

May 21	Dumbarton*		D 2-2	Hislop, H.McCreadie	10,000

*Played at Cathkin Park, Glasgow. Rangers and Dumbarton declared joint champions.

Scottish Cup

Sep 6	Celtic	(Rd1) L 0-1		16,000

League & Cup Appearances

PLAYER	LEAGUE	CUP COMPETITION S CUP	TOTAL
Gow	17	1	18
Henderson	14		14
Hislop	19	1	20
Hodge	10		10
Kerr	19	1	20
McCreadie A	16	1	17
McCreadie H	15	1	16
McIntyre	9		9
McKenzie	3		3
McPherson	19	1	20
Marshall	17	1	18
Mitchell	19	1	20
Muir	8	1	9
Reid	17	1	18
White	2		2
Wilson	1		1
Wylie	4	1	5

Goalscorers

PLAYER	LEAGUE	CUP COMPETITION S CUP	TOTAL
McPherson	15		15
Hislop	10		10
Kerr	8		8
Henderson	6		6
McCreadie H	6		6
McKenzie	3		3
McCreadie A	2		2
Marshall	2		2
Gow	1		1
Opps' o.gs.	2		2

Goalscorers totals include Championship Play-off match. Two goals in match against Vale of Leven on 4 April were unrecorded.

Fact File

John 'Kitey' McPherson claimed the first Scottish league hat-trick in Rangers history when he scored four goals in the 6-2 win over Cambuslang.

MATCH SECRETARY: William Wilton
CAPTAIN: Davy Mitchell
TOP SCORER: John McPherson
BIGGEST WIN: 8-2 v St Mirren, 4 October 1890, league
HIGHEST ATTENDANCE: 16,000 v Celtic, 6 September 1890, Scottish Cup
MAJOR TRANSFERS IN: John McPherson from Cowlairs

Final Scottish League Table

		P	W	D	L	F	A	Pts
1	DUMBARTON	18	13	3	2	61	21	29
1	RANGERS	18	13	3	2	58	25	29
3	CELTIC	18	11	3	4	48	21	21
4	CAMBUSLANG	18	8	4	6	47	42	20
5	THIRD LANARK	18	8	3	7	38	39	15
6	HEARTS	18	6	2	10	31	37	14
7	ABERCORN	18	5	2	11	36	47	12
8	ST MIRREN	18	5	1	12	39	62	11
8	VALE OF LEVEN	18	5	1	12	27	65	11
10	COWLAIRS	18	3	4	11	24	50	6

DUMBARTON AND RANGERS DECLARED JOINT CHAMPIONS AFTER A 2-2 PLAY-OFF DRAW.
CELTIC, THIRD LANARK AND COWLAIRS DEDUCTED FOUR POINTS FOR RULE INFRINGEMENT.

Season 1891-92

Scottish League

DATE	OPPONENTS	SCORE	GOALSCORERS	ATTENDANCE
Aug 15	Renton	W 4-1	Muir 2, Kerr, McPherson	-
Aug 22	Celtic	L 0-3		12,000
Aug 29	THIRD LANARK	L 2-3	McKenzie 2	5,106
Sep 5	DUMBARTON	L 1-3	Kerr	5,000
Sep 12	Vale of Leven	W 6-1	Unrecorded	-
Sep 26	ABERCORN	W 6-2	Fraser 3, J.McPherson 2, Kerr	3,000
Oct 3	Leith Athletic	L 1-3	Kerr	-
Oct 10	Third Lanark	D 2-2	H.McCreadie, Fraser	5,000
Oct 17	CAMBUSLANG	W 2-1	Marshall, Blyth	3,000
Oct 24	CLYDE	L 1-5	Kerr	5,000
Nov 21	HEARTS	L 0-1		3,000
Dec 5	St Mirren	W 4-3	J.McPherson 2, Kerr, McGowan	-
Feb 13	VALE OF LEVEN	W 7-0	Law 3, McBain, Barker, Kerr, A.McCreadie	2,000
Feb 27	Cambuslang	W 6-0	Barker, J.McPherson, rest unrecorded	-
Mar 19	RENTON	W 5-2	Barker 3, A.McCreadie, J.McPherson	6,000
Mar 26	Abercorn	W 1-0	Law	-
Apr 16	LEITH ATHLETIC	W 3-2	McBain, J.McPherson, A.McCreadie	-
Apr 23	Hearts	L 2-3	Scott, J.McPherson	5,000
May 4	Dumbarton	L 0-6		1,000
May 7	CELTIC	D 1-1	H.McCreadie	-
May 10	ST MIRREN	L 2-3	A.McCreadie, Allan	-
May 21	Clyde	W 3-1	J.McPherson, A.McCreadie (pen), Bowie o.g.	-

Scottish Cup

Nov 28	ST BERNARD'S	(Rd1) W 5-1	Kerr, Blyth, J.McPherson, McBain, unrecorded	3,000
Dec 19	KILMARNOCK	(Rd2) D 0-0		2,000
Dec 26	Kilmarnock	(R) D 1-1	Kerr	3,000
Jan 23	Kilmarnock*	(2R) W 3-2	Henderson 2, J.McPherson	5,000
Jan 30	ANNBANK	(QF) W 2-0	Watt, H.McCreadie	5,000
Feb 6	Celtic	(SF) L 3-5	Law, Henderson, Kerr	12,000

*Played at Westmarch Park, Paisley.

League & Cup Appearances

PLAYER	LEAGUE	CUP COMPETITION S CUP	TOTAL
Allan	3		3
Barker	8		8
Blyth	5	1	6
Cullen	5		5
Drummond	4		4
Dunbar	11	6	17
Fleming	1		1
Fraser	4		4
Glass	1		1
Haddow	22	6	28
Hay	1		1
Henderson	7	5	12
Hodge	15	6	21
Kerr	21	5	26
Law	5	2	7
McBain	3	3	6
McCreadie A	19	5	24
McCreadie H	16	4	20
McGowan	1	2	3
McIntyre	2		2
McKenzie	2		2
McPherson D	2		2
McPherson J	18	6	24
Marshall	20	6	26
Mitchell	17	6	23
Muir	5		5
Scott	12	1	13
Steel	3		3
Tait	6		6
Turnbull	1		1
Watt	2	2	4

Goalscorers

PLAYER	LEAGUE	CUP COMPETITION S CUP	TOTAL
McPherson J	10	2	12
Kerr	7	3	10
Barker	5		5
Law	4	1	5
McCreadie A	5		5
Fraser	4		4
McBain	2	1	3
McCreadie H	2	1	3
Henderson		3	3
Blyth	1	1	2
McKenzie	2		2
Muir	2		2
Allan	1		1
McGowan	1		1
Marshall	1		1
Scott	1		1
Watt		1	1
Opps' o.gs.	1		1

11 goals unrecorded

Fact File

The first attempt to play the home league fixture against Renton, on 7 December 1891, was abandoned after 75 minutes because of heavy snow with the score at 2-2.

MATCH SECRETARY: William Wilton

CAPTAIN: Davy Mitchell

TOP SCORER: John McPherson

BIGGEST WIN: 7-0 v Vale of Leven, 13 February, 1892, league

HIGHEST ATTENDANCE: 12,000 v Celtic, 22 August 1891, league; v Celtic, 6 February 1892, Scottish Cup

MAJOR TRANSFERS IN: Jock Drummond from Kilmarnock

MAJOR TRANSFERS OUT: Tom Wylie to Everton

Final Scottish League Table

		P	W	D	L	F	A	Pts
1	DUMBARTON	22	18	1	3	78	27	37
2	CELTIC	22	16	3	3	62	21	35
3	HEARTS	22	15	4	3	65	35	34
4	LEITH ATH.	22	12	1	9	51	40	25
5	RANGERS	22	11	2	9	59	46	24
6	THIRD LANARK	22	8	5	9	44	47	21
7	RENTON	22	8	5	9	37	43	21
8	CLYDE	22	8	4	10	63	61	20
9	ABERCORN	22	6	5	11	44	59	17
10	ST MIRREN	22	5	5	12	43	60	15
11	CAMBUSLANG	22	2	6	14	21	53	10
12	VALE OF LEVEN	22	0	5	17	24	99	5

Season 1892-93

Scottish League

DATE	OPPONENTS	SCORE	GOALSCORERS	ATTENDANCE
Aug 20	Abercorn	W 4-0	Bruce 2, J.McPherson, Barker	-
Aug 22	LEITH ATHLETIC	W 3-2	McInnes 2, D.McPherson	5,000
Sep 3	DUMBARTON	W 3-2	Bruce 2, Barker	6,000
Sep 10	Third Lanark	W 4-2	A.McCreadie (pen), Bruce, H.McCreadie, unrecorded	8,000
Sep 24	CELTIC	D 2-2	Turnbull, H.McCreadie	14,000
Oct 1	Leith Athletic	W 2-1	H.McCreadie 2	5,000
Oct 15	ST MIRREN	D 0-0		4,000
Oct 22	CLYDE	W 4-1	J.McPherson 2, Kerr, Mitchell	-
Nov 5	Renton	D 2-2	Clark, H.McCreadie	-
Feb 4	ABERCORN	W 4-3	H.McCreadie 2, J.McPherson, Kerr (pen)	-
Mar 11	Clyde	W 3-0	H.McCreadie, Kerr, J.McPherson	-
Mar 18	Hearts	W 2-1	Kerr, Steel	-
Mar 25	St Mirren	D 2-2	J.McPherson, Dick	-
Apr 1	THIRD LANARK	W 2-1	H.McCreadie, Barker	3,000
Apr 15	RENTON	W 2-0	Drummond, Scott	-
Apr 22	Dumbarton	L 0-3		-
Apr 29	Celtic	L 0-3		-
May 6	HEARTS	W 2-1	J.McPherson, H.McCreadie	-

Scottish Cup

Nov 26	ANNBANK	(Rd1) W 7-0	Kerr 4, H.McCreadie 2, Clark	-
Jan 21	Dumbarton	(Rd2) W 1-0	H.McCreadie	-
Jan 28	St Bernard's	(QF) L 2-3	Barker, unrecorded	8,000

League & Cup Appearances

PLAYER	LEAGUE	CUP COMPETITION	TOTAL
		S CUP	
Barker	11	3	14
Bruce	4		4
Clark	1	2	3
Davie	6		6
Dick	2		2
Drummond	17	3	20
Freebairn	2		2
Gow	10	1	11
Haddow	18	3	21
Hay	1		1
Kerr	13	3	16
McCreadie A	14	3	17
McCreadie H	15	3	18
McInnes	4		4
McPherson D	8	1	9
McPherson J	18	3	21
Marshall	18	3	21
Martin	2		2
Mitchell	16	3	19
Muir	1	1	2
Reid	2		2
Scott	10		10
Smith	2		2
Steel	2		2
Turnbull	2		2

Goalscorers

PLAYER	LEAGUE	CUP COMPETITION	TOTAL
		S CUP	
McCreadie H	10	3	13
Kerr	4	4	8
McPherson J	7		7
Bruce	5		5
Barker	3	1	4
Clark	1	1	2
McInnes	2		2
Dick	1		1
Drummond	1		1
McCreadie A	1		1
McPherson D	1		1
Mitchell	1		1
Scott	1		1
Steel	1		1
Turnbull	1		1

2 goals unrecorded

Fact File

On 18 February 1893, Rangers defeated Celtic 3-1 in the Glasgow Cup final at Cathkin Park with goals from John Barker, Neil Kerr and John McPherson. It was the first piece of silverware won by the club.

MATCH SECRETARY: William Wilton

CAPTAIN: Davy Mitchell

TOP SCORER: Hugh McCreadie

BIGGEST WIN: 7-0 v Annbank, 26 November 1892, Scottish Cup

HIGHEST ATTENDANCE: 14,000 v Celtic, 24 September 1892, league

MAJOR TRANSFERS IN: Nicol Smith from Darvel

Final Scottish League Table

		P	W	D	L	F	A	Pts
1	CELTIC	18	14	1	3	54	25	29
2	RANGERS	18	12	4	2	41	27	28
3	ST MIRREN	18	9	2	7	40	39	20
4	THIRD LANARK	18	9	1	8	53	39	19
5	HEARTS	18	8	2	8	39	41	18
6	LEITH ATH.	18	8	1	9	35	31	17
6	DUMBARTON	18	8	1	9	35	35	17
8	RENTON	18	5	5	8	31	44	15
9	ABERCORN	18	5	1	12	35	52	11
10	CLYDE	18	2	2	14	25	55	6

Season 1893-94

Scottish League Division 1

DATE	OPPONENTS	SCORE	GOALSCORERS	ATTENDANCE
Aug 12	Dundee	D 3-3	Gray 3	6,000
Aug 19	RENTON	W 5-3	Gray 2, Kerr, Barker, Steel	5,000
Aug 26	St Bernard's	D 0-0		5,000
Sep 2	CELTIC	W 5-0	Barker 3, McPherson, Gray	18,000
Sep 9	Renton	W 2-1	Steel, Barker	-
Sep 23	DUMBARTON	W 4-0	H.McCreadie 2, Marshall, unrecorded	-
Sep 30	Leith Athletic	D 2-2	Steel 2	4,000
Oct 14	Hearts	L 2-4	Blyth, Gray	8,000
Nov 4	LEITH ATHLETIC	W 1-0	McPherson	3,000
Nov 11	Third Lanark	W 2-1	McPherson, Boyd	-
Dec 23	THIRD LANARK	L 0-3		5,000
Jan 20	Dumbarton	L 0-2		-
Jan 27	St Mirren	D 2-2	Boyd, Crawford o.g.	
Feb 24	Celtic	L 2-3	Gray, Barker	10,000
Mar 10	DUNDEE	W 7-2	Boyd 2, Steel 2, Barker, A.McCreadie, Mitchel	3,000
Apr 14	HEARTS	L 1-2	Boyd	4,000
Apr 21	ST MIRREN	W 5-0	Steel, rest unrecorded	4,000
May 2	ST BERNARD'S	L 1-2	Gray	1,000

Scottish Cup

Nov 25	COWLAIRS	(Rd1) W 8-0	Boyd 3, McPherson 2, H.McCreadie 2, Kerr	5,000
Dec 16	LEITH ATH	(Rd2) W 2-0	McPherson, Blyth	2,500
Jan 13	Clyde	(QF) W 5-0	Steel 4, McPherson	10,000
Feb 3	QUEEN'S PARK	(SF) D 1-1	Boyd	15,000
Feb 10	Queen's Park	(R) W 3-1	Smith, McPherson, Steel	16,000
Feb 17	Celtic*	(F) W 3-1	H.McCreadie, Barker, McPherson	17,000

*Played at Hampden Park.

League & Cup Appearances

PLAYER	LEAGUE	CUP COMPETITION	TOTAL
		S CUP	
Barker	13	3	16
Blyth	5	1	6
Boyd	10	4	14
Davie		1	1
Drummond J	17	6	23
Drummond R	1		1
Gray	18	5	23
Haddow	15	6	21
Johnstone	1		1
Kerr	6	1	7
McCreadie A	18	6	24
McCreadie H	9	5	14
McKenzie	1		1
McPherson	15	6	21
Marshall	18	6	24
Mitchell	15	5	20
Montgomery	1		1
Muir	4		4
Smith	17	6	23
Steel	14	5	19

Goalscorers

PLAYER	LEAGUE	CUP COMPETITION	TOTAL
		S CUP	
Steel	7	5	12
Boyd	5	4	9
Gray	9		9
McPherson	3	6	9
Barker	7	1	8
McCreadie H	2	3	5
Blyth	1	1	2
Kerr	1	1	2
McCreadie A	1		1
Marshall	1		1
Mitchell	1		1
Smith		1	1
Opps' o.gs.	1		1

5 goals unrecorded

Fact File

On 1 January 1894, the first Ne'erday Old Firm fixture took place at Parkhead. Rangers won the friendly match 3-2 with two goals from John Gray and one from John McPherson.

MATCH SECRETARY: William Wilton

CAPTAIN: Davy Mitchell

TOP SCORER: James Steel

BIGGEST WIN: 8-0 v Cowlairs, 25 November 1893, Scottish Cup

HIGHEST ATTENDANCE: 18,000 v Celtic, 2 September 1893, league

MAJOR TRANSFERS IN: John Gray from Albion Rovers

MAJOR TRANSFERS OUT: Donald Gow to Sunderland

Final Scottish League Div 1 Table

		P	W	D	L	F	A	Pts
1	CELTIC	18	14	1	3	53	32	29
2	HEARTS	18	11	4	3	46	32	26
3	ST BERNARD'S	18	11	1	6	53	39	23
4	RANGERS	18	8	4	6	44	30	20
5	DUMBARTON	18	7	5	6	32	35	19
6	ST MIRREN	18	7	3	8	49	47	17
6	THIRD LANARK	18	7	3	8	38	44	17
8	DUNDEE	18	6	3	9	47	59	15
9	LEITH ATH.	18	4	2	12	36	46	10
10	RENTON	18	1	2	15	23	57	4

Season 1894-95

Scottish League Division 1

DATE	OPPONENTS	SCORE	GOALSCORERS	ATTENDANCE
Aug 18	DUMBARTON	W 3-0	Barker 2, unrecorded	-
Aug 25	St Bernard's	W 4-1	McPherson 2, Barker 2	-
Sep 1	DUNDEE	W 1-0	Gibson	4,000
Sep 8	Leith Athletic	W 4-3	Barker 2, Mitchell, Cowan	-
Sep 22	Celtic	L 3-5	Gray, Barker, McPherson	20,000
Sep 29	ST MIRREN	W 4-3	McPherson 2, Cowan, Goldie o.g.	5,000
Oct 13	Third Lanark	W 2-0	Hamilton, unrecorded	10,000
Oct 20	HEARTS	L 0-1		10,000
Nov 3	LEITH ATHLETIC	W 5-1	A.Smith 2, Gray, McPherson, McCreadie	-
Dec 1	Dumbarton	L 0-1		-
Dec 8	Clyde	W 5-1	Barker 2, Gray 2, Cowan	-
Dec 27	CLYDE	W 4-1	McPherson, rest unrecorded	-
Jan 19	Hearts	D 0-0		10,000
Jan 26	Dundee	L 1-2	McCreadie	6,000
Feb 16	THIRD LANARK	L 0-1		4,000
Mar 9	St Mirren	L 2-4	McPherson, Boyd	-
Mar 23	CELTIC	D 1-1	McPherson	-
Apr 27	ST BERNARD'S	W 2-1	Boyd, A.Smith	5,000

Scottish Cup

Nov 24	HEARTS	(Rd1) L 1-2	Cowan		12,000

League & Cup Appearances

PLAYER	LEAGUE	CUP COMPETITION S CUP	TOTAL
Barker	15	1	16
Boyd	13		13
Cowan	16	1	17
Crawford	6		6
Drummond	16	1	17
Gardiner	2		2
Gibson N	8		8
Gibson W	17	1	18
Gray	7	1	8
Haddow	11	1	12
Hamilton	2		2
McCreadie	13	1	14
McPherson	17	1	18
Marshall	15	1	16
Mitchell	11		11
Montgomery	7		7
Pray	3	1	4
Smith A	6		6
Smith N	13	1	14

Goalscorers

PLAYER	LEAGUE	CUP COMPETITION S CUP	TOTAL
Barker	9		9
McPherson	9		9
Cowan	3	1	4
Gray	4		4
Smith A	3		3
Boyd	2		2
McCreadie	2		2
Gibson W	1		1
Hamilton	1		1
Mitchell	1		1
Opps' o.gs.	1		1

5 goals unrecorded

Fact File

Rangers lost 2-0 to Celtic in the Glasgow Cup final on 17 November 1894 in front of 20,000 spectators at Cathkin Park.

MATCH SECRETARY: William Wilton

CAPTAIN: Davy Mitchell

TOP SCORERS: John Barker and John McPherson

BIGGEST WIN: 5-1 v Leith Athletic, 3 November 1894, league; v Clyde, 8 December 1894, league

HIGHEST ATTENDANCE: 20,000 v Celtic, 22 September 1894, league

MAJOR TRANSFERS IN: Neil Gibson from Royal Albert

Final Scottish League Div 1 Table

		P	W	D	L	F	A	Pts
1	HEARTS	18	15	1	2	50	18	31
2	CELTIC	18	11	4	3	50	29	26
3	RANGERS	18	10	2	6	41	26	22
4	THIRD LANARK	18	10	1	7	51	39	21
5	ST MIRREN	18	9	1	8	34	34	19
6	ST BERNARD'S	18	8	1	9	37	40	17
7	CLYDE	18	8	0	10	38	47	16
8	DUNDEE	18	6	2	10	28	33	14
9	LEITH ATH.	18	3	1	14	32	64	7
9	DUMBARTON	18	3	1	14	27	58	7

Season 1895-96

Scottish League Division 1

DATE	OPPONENTS	SCORE	GOALSCORERS	ATTENDANCE
Aug 17	Dumbarton	W 5-3	Miller 2, Barker 2, A.Smith	-
Aug 24	THIRD LANARK	L 0-4		-
Aug 31	Hearts	W 2-1	Oswald, unrecorded	-
Sep 7	CELTIC	L 2-4	Stewart, A.Smith	16,000
Sep 14	St Bernard's	W 4-3	McPherson, Miller, A.Smith, unrecorded	-
Oct 5	St Mirren	W 7-1	A.Smith 4, McPherson, Oswald, McCreadie	-
Oct 12	ST BERNARD'S	W 2-0	A.Smith, McPherson	4,000
Oct 26	Hibernian	D 1-1	Barker	8,000
Nov 9	CLYDE	D 4-4	Oswald 2, McPherson, Mitchell	4,000
Nov 23	HIBERNIAN	W 4-0	Oswald 2, Barker, McPherson	6,000
Nov 30	Dundee	W 3-1	Marshall, Barker, Oswald	3,000
Dec 7	HEARTS	W 7-2	Oswald 3, Gibson, Barker, McPherson, unrecorded	-
Dec 14	Celtic	L 2-6	A.Smith, McCreadie	25,000
Dec 21	Third Lanark	W 3-2	A.Smith, McCreadie, Boyd	5,000
Jan 4	DUMBARTON	W 3-1	Oswald, McCreadie, Miller o.g.	2,000
Feb 8	Clyde	D 2-2	Stewart, A.Smith	-
Feb 22	ST MIRREN	D 3-3	A.Smith 2, Miller	3,000
Feb 29	DUNDEE	W 3-1	McCreadie 2, McPherson	3,000

Scottish Cup

DATE	OPPONENTS		SCORE	GOALSCORERS	ATTENDANCE
Jan 18	Dumbarton	(Rd1)	D 1-1	Stewart	-
Jan 25	DUMBARTON	(R)	W 3-1	A.Smith 2, Oswald	6,000
Feb 1	ST MIRREN	(Rd2)	W 5-0	Oswald 3, McPherson, McCreadie	4,500
Feb 15	HIBERNIAN	(QF)	L 2-3	A.Smith, McCreadie	18,000

League & Cup Appearances

PLAYER	LEAGUE	CUP COMPETITION S CUP	TOTAL
Barker	12		12
Bell	7	4	11
Boyd	4		4
Burns	6		6
Crawford	2	2	4
Drummond	16	2	18
Gibson	17	4	21
McAllan	1		1
McCreadie	10	4	14
McIntyre	3		3
McLeod	5		5
McPherson	16	4	20
Marshall	12	4	16
Mathie	1		1
Miller	8		8
Mitchell	12	4	16
Muir	1		1
Murdoch	1		1
Oswald	17	4	21
Russell	2		2
Smith A	17	4	21
Smith N	17	4	21
Stewart	7	4	11
Wilson	3		3
Yuille	1		1

Goalscorers

PLAYER	LEAGUE	CUP COMPETITION S CUP	TOTAL
Smith A	13	3	16
Oswald	11	4	15
McCreadie	6	2	8
McPherson	7	1	8
Barker	6		6
Miller	4		4
Stewart	2	1	3
Boyd	1		1
Gibson	1		1
Marshall	1		1
Mitchell	1		1
Opps' o.gs.	1		1

3 goals unrecorded

Fact File

Rangers used six goalkeepers in an undistinguished season following the loss of David Haddow to Motherwell – Murdoch, Wilson, McLeod, Bell, Yuille and McAllan.

MATCH SECRETARY: William Wilton

CAPTAIN: Davy Mitchell

TOP SCORER: Alec Smith

BIGGEST WIN: 7-1 v St Mirren, 5 October 1895, league

HIGHEST ATTENDANCE: 25,000 v Celtic, 14 December 1895, league

MAJOR TRANSFERS IN: Matthew Dickie from Renton

MAJOR TRANSFERS OUT: David Haddow to Motherwell

Final Scottish League Div 1 Table

		P	W	D	L	F	A	PTS
1	CELTIC	18	15	0	3	64	25	30
2	RANGERS	18	11	4	3	57	39	26
3	HIBERNIAN	18	11	2	5	58	39	24
4	HEARTS	18	11	0	7	68	36	22
5	DUNDEE	18	7	2	9	33	42	16
6	THIRD LANARK	18	7	1	10	47	51	15
6	ST BERNARD'S	18	7	1	10	36	53	15
8	ST MIRREN	18	5	3	10	31	51	13
9	CLYDE	18	4	3	11	39	59	11
10	DUMBARTON	18	4	0	14	36	74	8

Season 1896-97

Scottish League Division 1

DATE	OPPONENTS	SCORE	GOALSCORERS	ATTENDANCE
Aug 15	ST MIRREN	W 5-1	Turnbull 2, Hyslop, R.Crawford, J.Miller	8,000
Aug 22	Third Lanark	D 1-1	Gibson	15,000
Aug 29	DUNDEE	W 3-1	Hyslop, D.Crawford, Burgess o.g.	13,000
Sep 5	Hibernian	L 3-4	J.Miller 2, Turnbull	-
Sep 12	HEARTS	W 5-0	R.Crawford, A.Smith, Oswald, Hyslop, J.Miller	14,000
Sep 21	Hearts	L 1-2	Gibson	7,000
Sep 26	Abercorn	W 9-2	McPherson 5, Turnbull 2, J.Miller, R.Crawford	-
Oct 3	HIBERNIAN	W 4-3	Turnbull 3, McCreadie	20,000
Oct 10	Celtic	D 1-1	McPherson	24,000
Oct 17	CLYDE	W 2-1	McPherson 2	4,000
Oct 24	THIRD LANARK	W 6-1	Low 3, McPherson 2, Oswald	5,000
Nov 7	St Mirren	D 2-2	A.Smith, Mitchell	-
Nov 28	Dundee	L 2-3	J.Miller, A.Smith	10,000
Dec 5	Clyde	W 7-2	Hyslop 4, rest unrecorded	4,000
Dec 12	ABERCORN	W 6-1	Turnbull 2, Hyslop 2, A.Smith, unrecorded	2,000
Dec 19	CELTIC	W 2-0	Low, J.Miller	15,000
Dec 26	St Bernard's	L 2-3	J.Miller, Hyslop	2,000
Feb 20	ST BERNARD'S	W 3-2	A.Smith, McPherson, Russell o.g.	-

Scottish Cup

Jan 9	Partick Thistle	(Rd1)	W 4-2	Hyslop 2, N.Smith, Gibson	6,000
Jan 23	HIBERNIAN	(Rd2)	W 3-0	Low 2, McPherson	22,000
Feb 13	Dundee	(QF)	W 4-0	Gibson, Hyslop, McCreadie, J.Miller	16,000
Mar 13	Morton	(SF)	W 7-2	McPherson 2, Low, Gibson, J.Miller, Hyslop, A.Smith	12,000
Mar 20	Dumbarton*	(F)	W 5-1	J.Miller 2, Hyslop, McPherson, A.Smith	15,000

*Played at Hampden Park.

League & Cup Appearances

PLAYER	LEAGUE	CUP COMPETITION S CUP	TOTAL
Crawford D	7		7
Crawford R	7		7
Dickie	18	5	23
Drummond	16	5	21
Gibson	17	5	22
Glen	1		1
Hay	1		1
Hyslop	17	5	22
Jackson	1		1
Low	9	5	14
McCreadie A	18	5	23
McPherson	10	4	14
Miller A	2		2
Miller J	15	5	20
Mitchell	17	5	22
Oswald	5	1	6
Smith A	17	5	22
Smith N	9	5	14
Turnbull	11		11

Goalscorers

PLAYER	LEAGUE	CUP COMPETITION S CUP	TOTAL
Hyslop	10	5	15
McPherson	11	4	15
Miller J	8	4	12
Turnbull	10		10
Low	4	3	7
Smith A	5	2	7
Gibson	2	3	5
Crawford R	3		3
McCreadie A	1	1	2
Oswald	2		2
Crawford D	1		1
Mitchell	1		1
Smith N		1	1
Opps' o.gs.	2		2

4 goals unrecorded

Fact File

Andrew McCreadie was the only ever-present in the Rangers side during the season, playing in all 23 competitive fixtures.

MATCH SECRETARY: William Wilton

CAPTAIN: Davy Mitchell

TOP SCORERS: Tom Hyslop and John McPherson

BIGGEST WIN: 9-2 v Abercorn, 26 September 1896, league

HIGHEST ATTENDANCE: 24,000 v Celtic, 10 October 1896, league

MAJOR TRANSFERS IN: Tommy Low from Blackburn, Bobby Neil from Liverpool

Final Scottish League Div 1 Table

		P	W	D	L	F	A	Pts
1	HEARTS	18	13	2	3	47	22	28
2	HIBERNIAN	18	12	2	4	50	20	26
3	RANGERS	18	11	3	4	64	30	25
4	CELTIC	18	10	4	4	42	18	24
5	DUNDEE	18	10	2	6	38	30	22
6	ST MIRREN	18	9	1	8	38	29	19
7	ST BERNARD'S	18	7	0	11	32	40	14
8	THIRD LANARK	18	5	1	12	29	46	11
9	CLYDE	18	4	0	14	27	65	8
10	ABERCORN	18	1	1	16	21	88	3

Season 1897-98

Scottish League Division 1

DATE ATTENDANCE	OPPONENTS	SCORE	GOALSCORERS	
Sep 1	St Bernard's	W 4-2	Hamilton 2, Miller, Hyslop	7,000
Sep 11	HIBERNIAN	W 1-0	Hamilton	15,000
Sep 20	Hearts	D 2-2	Hamilton, A.Smith	13,000
Sep 25	Third Lanark	W 3-0	Hyslop (pen), A.Smith, Hamilton	15,000
Sep 27	CELTIC	L 0-4		30,000
Oct 2	HEARTS	W 2-0	Hamilton 2	15,000
Oct 9	Partick Thistle	W 5-1	Mitchell, Gibson, Neil, Hamilton, Hyslop	8,000
Oct 16	Clyde	W 8-1	A.Smith 3, Miller 2, Hamilton, Hyslop, McPherson	6,000
Oct 23	CLYDE	W 7-0	Hyslop 3 (1 pen), McPherson,Hamilton, Miller, A.Smith	3,000
Nov 6	St Mirren	W 5-1	Turnbull 2, Low, McPherson, Hamilton	-
Dec 4	ST MIRREN	W 9-0	Hamilton 4, McPherson 3, Neil, Miller	5,000
Dec 11	Hibernian	W 5-0	Hamilton 3, Hyslop, A.Smith	9,000
Dec 25	DUNDEE	W 5-0	Miller 4, A.Smith	6,000
Jan 3	PARTICK THISTLE	W 6-1	A.Smith 2, McPherson 2, Miller, Hyslop	4,000
Feb 12	Dundee	L 1-2	A.Smith	11,000
Mar 19	ST BERNARD'S	W 8-1	Hyslop 3, McPherson 2, A.Smith, Neil, Turnbull	5,000
Apr 9	THIRD LANARK	D 0-0		3,000
Apr 11	Celtic	D 0-0		15,000

Scottish Cup

Jan 8	POLTON VALE	(Rd1) W 8-0	Miller 2, McPherson 2, A.Smith, Hamilton, Goudie, Neil	3,000
Jan 22	CARTVALE	(Rd2) W12-0	Hamilton 4, A.Smith 2, Neil (pen), Mitchell, Kerr, Gibson, Miller, Coulrough o.g.	-
Feb 5	Queen's Park	(QF) W 3-1	McPherson, Hamilton, Miller	20,000
Feb 19	THIRD LANARK	(SF) D 1-1	A.Smith	20,000
Feb 26	Third Lanark	(R) D 2-2	Hamilton, A.Smith	16,000
Mar 12	Third Lanark	(2R) W 2-0	McPherson, Gibson (pen)	12,000
Mar 26	Kilmarnock*	(F) W 2-0	A.Smith, Hamilton	14,000

*Played at Hampden Park.

League & Cup Appearances

PLAYER	LEAGUE	CUP COMPETITION S CUP	TOTAL
Crawford	6	4	10
Dickie	17	7	24
Drummond	16	5	21
Gibson	15	6	21
Glen	5		5
Goudie		1	1
Hamilton	15	7	22
Hyslop	13	2	15
Jamieson	1		1
Kerr	1	2	3
Low	12	2	14
McCreadie	4		4
McPherson	12	7	19
Miller	15	7	22
Mitchell	11	6	17
Murray	3		3
Neil	12	7	19
Oswald	4	1	5
Scott		2	2
Smith A	17	7	24
Smith N	13	3	16
Turnbull	4	1	5
Turner	1		1
Yuille	1		1

Goalscorers

PLAYER	LEAGUE	CUP COMPETITION S CUP	TOTAL
Hamilton	18	8	26
Smith A	12	6	18
McPherson	10	4	14
Miller	10	4	14
Hyslop	12		12
Neil	3	2	5
Gibson	1	2	3
Turnbull	3		3
Mitchell	1	1	2
Goudie		1	1
Kerr		1	1
Low	1		1
Opps' o.gs.		1	1

Fact File

The league fixture against Celtic at Parkhead on 1 January 1898 was abandoned after 70 minutes, with the score at 1-1, because of a pitch invasion.

MANAGER: William Wilton
CAPTAIN: Davy Mitchell
TOP SCORER: R.C. Hamilton
BIGGEST WIN: 12-0 v Cartvale, 22 January 1898, Scottish Cup
HIGHEST ATTENDANCE: 30,000 v Celtic, 27 September 1897, league
MAJOR TRANSFERS IN: R.C.Hamilton from Queen's Park

Final Scottish League Div 1 Table

		P	W	D	L	F	A	Pts
1	CELTIC	18	15	3	0	56	13	33
2	RANGERS	18	13	3	2	71	15	29
3	HIBERNIAN	18	10	2	6	47	29	22
4	HEARTS	18	8	4	6	54	33	20
5	THIRD LANARK	18	8	2	8	37	38	18
5	ST MIRREN	18	8	2	8	30	36	18
7	DUNDEE	18	5	3	10	29	36	13
7	PARTICK T	18	6	1	11	34	64	13
9	ST BERNARD'S	18	4	1	13	35	67	9
10	CLYDE	18	1	3	14	21	83	5

Season 1898-99

Scottish League Division 1

DATE	OPPONENTS	SCORE	GOALSCORERS	ATTENDANCE
Aug 20	PARTICK THISTLE	W 6-2	Hamilton 3, J.Sharp, Neil, J.Miller	7,000
Aug 27	St Mirren	W 3-1	A.Smith, Hamilton, McPherson	-
Sep 3	Hearts	W 3-2	Hamilton 2, Wilkie	17,000
Sep 10	THIRD LANARK	W 4-1	J.Miller, McPherson, Campbell, Neil (pen)	18,000
Sep 19	St Bernard's	W 2-0	A.Smith, Neil (pen)	8,000
Sep 24	Celtic	W 4-0	Neil (pen), McPherson, Campbell, J.Miller	45,000
Sep 26	Third Lanark	W 3-2	Campbell 2, McPherson	14,000
Oct 1	HEARTS	W 3-1	Hamilton 2, A.Smith	25,000
Oct 8	Dundee	W 2-1	Hamilton, Wilkie	7,500
Nov 5	Partick Thistle	W 5-0	Hamilton 2, J.Miller 2, A.Sharp	5,000
Nov 19	Hibernian	W 4-3	J.Miller, A.Smith, Hamilton, Neil (pen)	10,000
Nov 26	CLYDE	W 8-0	J.Miller 3, A.Sharp 2, Gibson 2, Watson o.g.	4,000
Dec 3	ST BERNARD'S	W 5-2	Campbell 4, Hamilton	3,000
Dec 17	DUNDEE	W 7-0	Hamilton 3, A.Smith 2, McPherson 2	3,000
Dec 24	HIBERNIAN	W10-0	A.Smith 4, Hamilton 2, McPherson, J.Miller, Gibson (pen), Campbell	7,000
Dec 31	ST MIRREN	W 3-2	Campbell 2, A.Smith	5,000
Jan 2	CELTIC	W 4-1	Hamilton 3, Campbell	30,000
Jan 7	Clyde	W 3-0	A.Smith, J.Miller, Neil (pen)	4,000

Scottish Cup

Jan 14	HEARTS	(Rd1) W 4-1	Gibson 2, Neil (pen), Hamilton	20,000
Feb 11	Ayr Parkhouse	(Rd2) W 4-1	Hamilton 2, Campbell, A.Smith	5,000
Feb 18	CLYDE	(QF) W 4-0	Low, McPherson, Gibson (pen), Hamilton	6,000
Apr 15	St Mirren	(SF) W 2-1	McPherson, J.Miller	10,000
Apr 22	Celtic*	(F) L 0-2		25,000

*Played at Hampden Park.

League & Cup Appearances

PLAYER	LEAGUE	CUP COMPETITION S CUP	TOTAL
Campbell	16	5	21
Crawford	17	5	22
Dickie	18	5	23
Drummond	5	1	6
Gibson	18	4	22
Hamilton	18	5	23
Low		1	1
McPherson	15	5	20
Miller J	16	5	21
Miller JE	5		5
Mitchell	13	5	18
Neil	18	4	22
Oswald		1	1
Sharp A	4		4
Sharp J	1		1
Smith A	18	4	22
Smith N	13	4	17
Wilkie	3	1	4

Goalscorers

PLAYER	LEAGUE	CUP COMPETITION S CUP	TOTAL
Hamilton	21	4	25
Campbell	12	1	13
Smith A	12	1	13
Miller J	11	1	12
McPherson	7	2	9
Neil	6	1	7
Gibson	3	3	6
Sharp A	3		3
Wilkie	2		2
Low		1	1
Sharp J	1		1
Opps' o.gs.	1		1

Fact File

Rangers won all 18 of their league fixtures, a 100 per cent record unequalled to this day.

MANAGER: William Wilton

CAPTAIN: Davy Mitchell

TOP SCORER: R.C. Hamilton

BIGGEST WIN: 10-0 v Hibernian, 24 December 1898, league

HIGHEST ATTENDANCE: 45,000 v Celtic, 24 September 1898, league

MAJOR TRANSFERS IN: John Campbell from Blackburn Rovers.

Final Scottish League Div 1 Table

		P	W	D	L	F	A	Pts
1	RANGERS	18	18	0	0	79	18	36
2	HEARTS	18	12	2	4	56	30	26
3	CELTIC	18	11	2	5	51	33	24
4	HIBERNIAN	18	10	3	5	42	43	23
5	ST MIRREN	18	8	4	6	46	32	20
6	THIRD LANARK	18	7	3	8	33	38	17
7	ST BERNARD'S	18	4	4	10	30	37	12
7	CLYDE	18	4	4	10	23	48	12
9	PARTICK T	18	2	2	14	19	58	6
10	DUNDEE	18	1	2	15	23	65	4

Season 1899-1900

Scottish League Division 1

DATE	OPPONENTS	SCORE	GOALSCORERS	ATTENDANCE
Aug 19	Third Lanark	W 5-1	Campbell 2, J.Miller, Hyslop, N.Smith	16,000
Aug 26	Clyde	W 6-2	Hyslop 2, McPherson, A.Smith, J.Robertson unrecorded	10,000
Sep 2	HEARTS	W 4-3	Campbell 2, Hamilton 2	20,000
Sep 9	Kilmarnock	W 4-2	Campbell, A.Smith, McPherson, Hamilton	10,000
Sep 18	Hearts	D 1-1	Hamilton	15,000
Sep 25	HIBERNIAN	W 3-2	Hamilton, A.Smith, Wilkie	12,000
Oct 7	CELTIC*	D 3-3	Graham 2, A.Smith	40,000
Oct 14	CLYDE	W 7-0	McPherson 3, A.Smith 2, Sharp, Hamilton	5,000
Oct 21	Hibernian	W 2-0	A.Smith 2	16,000
Nov 4	DUNDEE	W 6-0	A.Smith 3, Hamilton, Wilkie, Watson o.g.	6,000
Nov 25	ST BERNARD'S	W 4-3	McPherson 2, Hamilton, J.Robertson	5,000
Dec 2	St Mirren	W 3-1	Hamilton 3	-
Dec 9	KILMARNOCK	W 6-1	Wilkie 2, Hamilton 2, J.Robertson, Graham	5,000
Dec 16	ST MIRREN	W 4-1	Neil 2 (1 pen), A.Smith, Hamilton	2,000
Jan 1	Celtic	L 2-3	A.Smith, Wilkie	20,000
Jan 6	THIRD LANARK	W 2-1	Neil, McPherson	4,000
Jan 20	Dundee	W 3-2	Hamilton 3	12,000
Feb 3	St Bernard's	W 4-1	McPherson, Campbell, Gibson, Wilkie	4,000

*Played at Parkhead.

Scottish Cup

Jan 13	MORTON	(Rd1) W 4-2	McPherson 2, Wilkie, A.Smith	7,000
Jan 27	MAYBOLE	(Rd2) W12-0	Hamilton 4, Wilkie 3, A.Smith, Robertson, Hyslop, Neil, Gibson	3,000
Feb 17	Partick Thistle	(QF) W 6-1	Hamilton 2, A.Smith, McPherson, Wilkie, Graham	10,000
Feb 24	CELTIC	(SF) D 2-2	A.Smith, McPherson	33,000
Mar 10	Celtic	(R) L 0-4		32,000

League & Cup Appearances

PLAYER	LEAGUE	CUP COMPETITION S CUP	TOTAL
Campbell	7		7
Crawford	8	2	10
Dickie	17	5	22
Drummond	15	4	19
Dunlop	6	1	7
Gibson	16	5	21
Graham	13	5	18
Hamilton	16	4	20
Howden	1		1
Hyslop	5	1	6
McKinlay	2		2
McPherson	13	4	17
Miller	7	1	8
Mitchell	2		2
Neil	15	4	19
Robertson	15	5	20
Sharp	3		3
Smith A	16	5	21
Smith N	10	4	14
Wilkie	11	5	16

Goalscorers

PLAYER	LEAGUE	CUP COMPETITION S CUP	TOTAL
Hamilton	17	6	23
Smith A	13	4	17
McPherson	9	4	13
Wilkie	6	5	11
Campbell	6		6
Graham	3	1	4
Hyslop	3	1	4
Neil	3	1	4
Robertson	3	1	4
Gibson	1	1	2
Miller	1		1
Sharp	1		1
Smith N	1		1
Opps' o.gs.	1		1

1 goal unrecorded

Fact File

Rangers' 6-1 win over Kilmarnock on 9 December 1899 was the last match at Ibrox Park; the 4-1 win over St Bernard's on 3 February 1900 was the first to take place at Ibrox Stadium.

MANAGER: William Wilton
CAPTAIN: Jock Drummond
TOP SCORER: R.C. Hamilton
BIGGEST WIN: 12-0 v Maybole, 27 January 1900, Scottish Cup
HIGHEST ATTENDANCE: 40,000 v Celtic, 7 October 1899, league
MAJOR TRANSFERS IN: Jacky Robertson from Southampton

Final Scottish League Div 1 Table

		P	W	D	L	F	A	Pts
1	RANGERS	18	15	2	1	69	27	32
2	CELTIC	18	9	7	2	46	27	25
3	HIBERNIAN	18	9	6	3	43	24	24
4	HEARTS	18	10	3	5	41	24	23
5	KILMARNOCK	18	6	6	6	30	37	18
6	DUNDEE	18	4	7	7	36	39	15
6	THIRD LANARK	18	5	5	8	31	38	15
8	ST MIRREN	18	3	6	9	30	46	12
8	ST BERNARD'S	18	4	4	10	29	47	12
10	CLYDE	18	2	0	16	24	70	4

Season 1900-01

Scottish League Division 1

DATE	OPPONENTS	SCORE	GOALSCORERS	ATTENDANCE
Aug 18	THIRD LANARK	W 4-0	Gibson, Cameron 2, McPherson	10,000
Aug 25	Hearts	W 1-0	Neil	10,000
Sep 1	KILMARNOCK	W 5-1	Campbell 2, Hamilton, Cameron, A.Smith	9,500
Sep 8	Partick Thistle	W 2-1	A.Smith, Cameron	9,000
Sep 17	Hibernian	L 1-4	Campbell	-
Sep 26	HEARTS	W 1-0	A.Smith	6,000
Sep 29	Queen's Park	W 3-2	Robertson (pen), McPherson, Russell o.g.	16,000
Oct 6	Celtic	L 1-2	Cameron	12,000
Oct 13	Third Lanark	D 1-1	McPherson	5,000
Oct 20	DUNDEE	W 4-2	Hamilton 3, A.Smith	9,000
Nov 3	PARTICK THISTLE	W 4-1	Hamilton 3, A.Smith	7,000
Nov 17	Morton	W 3-1	Hamilton, Speedie, McPherson	7,000
Nov 24	ST MIRREN	W 5-2	Hamilton 4, Graham	6,000
Dec 1	Kilmarnock	W 2-1	Speedie, McPherson	10,000
Dec 15	Dundee	W 5-1	Campbell 2, Hamilton, Robertson, A.Smith	10,000
Dec 29	QUEEN'S PARK	W 3-2	Robertson, Graham, Speedie	11,000
Jan 1	CELTIC	W 2-1	Speedie, McPherson	30,000
Jan 5	St Mirren	W 4-1	Hamilton 3, McPherson	6,000
Jan 26	HIBERNIAN	W 6-0	Hamilton 2, Sharp 2, - A.Smith, Handling o.g.	
Feb 16	MORTON	W 3-2	Hamilton 2, Speedie	5,000

Scottish Cup

Jan 12	Celtic	(Rd1) L 0-1		28,000

League & Cup Appearances

PLAYER	LEAGUE	CUP COMPETITION S CUP	TOTAL
Cameron	9		9
Campbell	18	1	19
Crawford	4		4
Dickie	20	1	21
Drummond	18	1	19
Gibson	19	1	20
Graham	5		5
Hamilton	19	1	20
McPherson	18		18
Neil	9	1	10
Robertson	20	1	21
Sharp	2	1	3
Smith A	17	1	18
Smith N	18	1	19
Speedie	11	1	12
Stark	12		12
Tutty	1		1

Goalscorers

PLAYER	LEAGUE	CUP COMPETITION S CUP	TOTAL
Hamilton	20		20
McPherson	7		7
Smith A	7		7
Cameron	5		5
Campbell	5		5
Speedie	5		5
Robertson	3		3
Graham	2		2
Sharp	2		2
Gibson	1		1
Neil	1		1
Opps' o.gs.	2		2

Fact File

Five Rangers players were in the Scotland team which defeated England 4-1 at Parkhead on 7 April 1900 – Nicol Smith, Jock Drummond, Neil Gibson, Jacky Robertson and Alec Smith.

MANAGER: William Wilton
CAPTAIN: Jock Drummond
TOP SCORER: R.C. Hamilton
BIGGEST WIN: 6-0 v Hibernian, 26 January 1901, league
HIGHEST ATTENDANCE: 30,000 v Celtic, 1 January 1901, league
MAJOR TRANSFERS IN: Jamie Stark from Glasgow Perthshire, Finlay Speedie from Clydebank Juniors

Final Scottish League Div 1 Table

		P	W	D	L	F	A	Pts
1	RANGERS	20	17	1	2	60	25	35
2	CELTIC	20	13	3	4	49	28	29
3	HIBERNIAN	20	9	7	4	29	22	25
4	MORTON	20	9	3	8	40	40	21
5	KILMARNOCK	20	7	4	9	35	47	18
5	THIRD LANARK	20	6	6	8	20	29	18
7	DUNDEE	20	6	5	9	36	35	17
7	QUEEN'S PARK	20	7	3	10	33	37	17
9	ST MIRREN	20	5	6	9	33	43	16
10	HEARTS	20	5	4	11	22	30	14
11	PARTICK T	20	4	2	14	28	49	10

Season 1901-02

Scottish League Division 1

DATE	OPPONENTS	SCORE	GOALSCORERS	ATTENDANCE
Aug 17	Kilmarnock	L 2-4	R.C.Hamilton, McDougall	6,000
Aug 24	HEARTS	W 2-1	Speedie, R.C.Hamilton	17,000
Aug 31	Dundee	W 3-0	McDougall 2, Speed e	12,000
Sep 7	KILMARNOCK	W 3-2	Campbell, A.Smith, Gibson	16,000
Sep 16	Hearts	W 2-0	Neil, R.C.Hamilton	
Sep 21	St Mirren	W 5-1	Campbell 2, A.Smith, Wilkie,Jackson o.g.	10,000
Sep 23	HIBERNIAN	L 0-2		10,000
Sep 28	Third Lanark	D 2-2	A.Smith, R.C.Hamilton	16,000
Oct 5	CELTIC	D 2-2	Neil, Speedie	30,000
Oct 19	Hibernian	W 3-2	Wilkie, R.C.Hamilton (pen), Neil	12,000
Nov 2	QUEEN'S PARK	W 2-1	McPherson, R.C.Hamilton	12,000
Nov 9	Morton	W 3-2	McPherson 2, Wilkie	7,000
Nov 16	THIRD LANARK	L 1-4	Robertson	5,000
Dec 7	MORTON	W 2-1	A.Smith, R.C.Hamilton	3,000
Jan 1	Celtic	W 4-2	N.Smith, Campbell, Robertson, R.C.Hamilton	40,000
Jan 4	Queen's Park	W 1-0	Robertson	20,000
Jan 18	ST MIRREN	W 3-2	Speedie 2, Cameron o.g.	12,000
Mar 29	DUNDEE	W 3-1	R.C.Hamilton, A.Smith, Speedie	13,000

Scottish Cup

Jan 11	JOHNSTONE	(Rd1)	W 6-1	Howie o.g., Speedie, A.Smith, J.R.Hamilton, Robertson, Graham	2,000
Jan 25	CALEDONIAN	(Rd2)	W 5-1	Wilkie, A.Smith 2, Campbell, J.R.Hamilton	5,000
Feb 22	KILMARNOCK	(QF)	W 2-0	Speedie, A.Smith	10,000
Mar 22	HIBERNIAN	(SF)	L 0-2		35,000

League & Cup Appearances

PLAYER	LEAGUE	CUP COMPETITION S CUP	TOTAL
Campbell	12	3	15
Crawford	8	1	9
Dickie	15	4	19
Drummond	12	3	15
Gibson	13	4	17
Goudie	1		1
Graham	3	1	4
Hamilton JR	1	2	3
Hamilton RC	16	2	18
McDougall	4		4
McPherson J	5	1	6
McPherson N	2		2
Morton	2	1	3
Neil	16	1	17
Robertson	8	4	12
Smith A	18	4	22
Smith N	15	4	19
Speedie	16	4	20
Stark	16	3	19
Wilkie	14	2	16
Young	1		1

Goalscorers

PLAYER	LEAGUE	CUP COMPETITION S CUP	TOTAL
Hamilton RC	9		9
Smith A	5	4	9
Speedie	6	2	8
Campbell	4	1	5
Robertson	3	1	4
Wilkie	3	1	4
McDougall	3		3
McPherson J	3		3
Neil	3		3
Hamilton JR		2	2
Gibson	1		1
Graham		1	1
Smith N	1		1
Opps' o.gs.	2	1	3

Fact File

On 9 September 1901, Rangers defeated Celtic 3-1 with goals from R.C.Hamilton (2) and Bobby Neil to win the Glasgow Exhibition Cup.

MANAGER: William Wilton
CAPTAIN: Jock Drummond
TOP SCORERS: R.C. Hamilton and Alec Smith
BIGGEST WIN: 6-1 v Johnstone, 11 January 1902, Scottish Cup
HIGHEST ATTENDANCE: 40,000 v Celtic, 1 January 1902, league

Final Scottish League Div 1 Table

		P	W	D	L	F	A	Pts
1	RANGERS	18	13	2	3	43	29	28
2	CELTIC	18	11	4	3	38	28	26
3	HEARTS	18	10	2	6	32	21	22
4	THIRD LANARK	18	7	5	6	30	26	19
4	ST MIRREN	18	8	3	7	29	28	19
6	HIBERNIAN	18	6	4	8	36	23	16
6	KILMARNOCK	18	5	6	7	22	27	16
8	QUEEN'S PARK	18	5	4	9	21	32	14
9	DUNDEE	18	4	5	9	15	31	13
10	MORTON	18	1	5	12	20	41	7

Season 1902-03

Scottish League Division 1

DATE	OPPONENTS	SCORE	GOALSCORERS	ATTENDANCE
Aug 16	Third Lanark	L 2-4	Hamilton 2	13,000
Aug 23	PARTICK THISTLE	W 9-0	Hamilton 4, Neil 2, Lennie 2, Mackie	7,000
Aug 30	Port Glasgow	W 3-0	Stark, Neil (pen), Hamilton	7,000
Sep 6	Hearts	L 1-2	Neil (pen)	14,000
Sep 15	Hibernian	L 0-1		6,500
Sep 20	MORTON	W 4-1	Fraser, Hamilton, McDonald, A.Smith	6,000
Sep 27	Queen's Park	W 2-0	Mackie, Hamilton	12,000
Sep 29	HIBERNIAN	L 2-5	J.Walker, Stark	15,000
Oct 4	HEARTS	W 2-1	Speedie 2	11,000
Oct 11	Morton	W 4-0	J.Robertson, Hamilton, McDonald 2	7,000
Oct 18	Celtic	D 1-1	A.Smith	25,000
Nov 1	THIRD LANARK	W 2-0	Mackie 2	12,000
Nov 8	Partick Thistle	W 4-2	J.Walker, Neil (pen), A.Smith 2	7,000
Nov 15	QUEEN'S PARK	W 3-2	Speedie, J.Robertson, Neil	10,000
Nov 22	St Mirren	W 1-0	A.Smith	-
Nov 29	KILMARNOCK	W 5-0	A.Smith, Hamilton, J.Walker 2, McDonald	4,500
Dec 6	Dundee	L 1-3	Neil	12,000
Dec 13	PORT GLASGOW	W 4-2	Brodie, Hamilton 2, Speedie	3,000
Dec 20	Kilmarnock	D 0-0		4,000
Jan 1	CELTIC	D 3-3	J.Walker 2, Neil	25,000
Jan 3	ST MIRREN	D 2-2	McDonald, J.Walker	6,000
Jan 17	DUNDEE	D 1-1	Gibson	10,000

Scottish Cup

Jan 10	AUCHTERARDER	(Rd1)	W 7-0	Speedie 3, McDonald 2, Hamilton, Gibson	2,000
Jan 24	KILMARNOCK	(Rd2)	W 4-0	J.Walker 2, J.Robertson, McDonald	7,500
Feb 28	Celtic	(QF)	W 3-0	A.Smith, J.Walker, Hamilton	40,000
Mar 7	Stenhousemuir	(SF)	W 4-1	J.Robertson 2, Hamilton 2	8,000
Apr 11	Hearts*	(F)	D 1-1	Stark	30,000
Apr 18	Hearts*	(R)	D 0-0		35,000
Apr 25	Hearts*	(2R)	W 2-0	Mackie, Hamilton	35,000

*Played at Parkhead.

League & Cup Appearances

PLAYER	LEAGUE	CUP COMPETITION S CUP	TOTAL
Brodie	1		1
Crawford	4	1	5
Dickie	21	7	28
Drummond	19	6	25
Fraser	15	7	22
Gibson	17	6	23
Graham	2		2
Hamilton	19	7	26
Henderson	2	1	3
Lennie	5		5
McDonald	13	7	20
McMurray		1	1
Mackie	8	1	9
Neil	17		17
Robertson	20	7	27
Smith A	22	7	29
Smith N	7		7
Speedie	18	7	25
Stark	12	7	19
Walker J	17	5	22
Walker W	2		2
Wallace	1		1

Goalscorers

PLAYER	LEAGUE	CUP COMPETITION S CUP	TOTAL
Hamilton	13	5	18
Walker J	7	3	10
McDonald	5	3	8
Neil	8		8
Smith A	6	1	7
Speedie	4	3	7
Mackie	4	1	5
Robertson	2	3	5
Stark	2	1	3
Gibson	1	1	2
Lennie	2		2
Brodie	1		1
Fraser	1		1

Fact File

Alex Fraser, signed from Clydebank Juniors, scored on his league debut for Rangers against Morton on 20 September 1902. It proved to be the defender's only goal in the four seasons he spent at Ibrox.

MANAGER: William Wilton

CAPTAIN: Jock Drummond

TOP SCORER: R.C. Hamilton

BIGGEST WIN: 9-0 v Partick Thistle, 23 August 1902, league

HIGHEST ATTENDANCE: 40,000 v Celtic, 28 February 1903, Scottish Cup

MAJOR TRANSFERS IN: George Henderson from Dundee

Final Scottish League Div 1 Table

		P	W	D	L	F	A	Pts
1	HIBERNIAN	22	16	5	1	48	18	37
2	DUNDEE	22	13	5	4	31	12	31
3	RANGERS	22	12	5	5	56	30	29
4	HEARTS	22	11	6	5	46	27	28
5	CELTIC	22	8	10	4	36	30	26
6	ST MIRREN	22	7	8	7	39	40	22
7	THIRD LANARK	22	8	5	9	34	27	21
8	PARTICK T	22	6	7	9	34	50	19
9	KILMARNOCK	22	6	4	12	24	43	16
10	QUEEN'S PARK	22	5	5	12	33	48	15
11	PORT GLASGOW A	22	3	5	14	26	49	11
12	MORTON	22	2	5	15	22	55	9

Season 1903-04

Scottish League Division 1

DATE	OPPONENTS	SCORE	GOALSCORERS	ATTENDANCE
Aug 15	THIRD LANARK	W 4-3	Hamilton 3 (1 pen), A.Smith	7,000
Aug 22	Airdrie	W 3-1	Stark, Speedie, Hamilton	10,000
Aug 29	ST MIRREN	D 2-2	Hamilton, Walker	10,000
Sep 5	Motherwell	W 5-2	Hamilton 4, Speedie	6,000
Sep 19	HEARTS	W 5-1	Hamilton 3, Walker 2	9,000
Sep 26	QUEEN'S PARK	W 5-0	Hamilton 2, Robertson (pen), Walker, Mackie	14,000
Sep 28	Partick Thistle	W 4-1	Speedie, Walker, Robertson (pen), A.Smith	8,000
Oct 10	Third Lanark*	L 0-1		25,000
Oct 17	Celtic	D 0-0		25,000
Oct 24	Morton	W 3-1	Speedie, Walker, Robertson	4,000
Oct 31	DUNDEE	W 6-1	Mackie, Walker 2, Hamilton 2, Jeffrey o.g.	10,300
Nov 7	Queen's Park	W 3-2	Speedie, Hamilton, Drummond	16,000
Nov 14	HIBERNIAN	D 1-1	Hamilton	8,000
Nov 21	Dundee	L 1-3	A.Smith	14,400
Nov 28	MORTON†	W 5-0	Hamilton 2, Speedie, Walker 2	3,000
Dec 5	Kilmarnock	D 2-2	N.Smith, unrecorded	3,000
Dec 12	MOTHERWELL	W 3-0	Hamilton, Mackie 2	3,000
Dec 19	Port Glasgow	D 1-1	Mackie	4,000
Dec 26	Hibernian	W 2-1	Hamilton, Robertson	6,000
Jan 1	Celtic	D 2-2	Speedie, Mackie	30,000
Jan 2	PARTICK THISTLE	W 2-0	Walker, Hamilton	6,000
Jan 9	St Mirren	L 4-5	Mackie 2, Hamilton 2 (1 pen)	-
Jan 16	KILMARNOCK	W 3-0	Mackie, Hamilton, Donaghy	4,000
Jan 30	Hearts	L 1-2	Hamilton	12,000
Feb 13	PORT GLASGOW	W 8-1	Speedie 3, A.Smith, Hamilton 2, Campbell, Gibson	3,500
Mar 26	AIRDRIE	W 5-0	Donaghy, Chalk, Mackie 2, Stark	6,000

*Played at Ibrox. †Played at Cappielow.

Scottish Cup

Jan 23	HEARTS	(Rd1) W 3-2	Hamilton, Walker 2	30,000
Feb 6	Hibernian	(Rd2) W 2-1	Mackie, Walker	17,000
Feb 20	St Mirren	(QF) W 1-0	Hamilton	17,000
Mar 5	MORTON	(SF) W 3-0	Walker 2, Hamilton	10,000
Apr 16	Celtic*	(F) L 2-3	Speedie 2	64,472

*Played at Hampden Park.

League & Cup Appearances

PLAYER	LEAGUE	CUP COMPETITION S CUP	TOTAL
Campbell	4		4
Chalk	4		4
Dickie	15		15
Dinsmore	1		1
Donaghy	5	1	6
Drummond	14	1	15
Findlay	1		1
Fraser	14	4	18
Gibson	17		17
Gray	1		1
Hamilton	24	4	28
Hartley	4		4
Henderson	18	5	23
McDonald	1		1
Mackie	23	5	28
Neil	5		5
Paton	2		2
Robertson	18	5	23
Smith A	16	5	21
Smith N	22	5	27
Speedie	23	5	28
Stark	22	5	27
Walker	21	5	26
Watson	11	5	16

Goalscorers

PLAYER	LEAGUE	CUP COMPETITION S CUP	TOTAL
Hamilton	28	3	31
Walker	11	5	16
Mackie	12	1	13
Speedie	10	2	12
Robertson	4		4
Smith A	4		4
Donaghy	2		2
Stark	2		2
Campbell	1		1
Chalk	1		1
Drummond	1		1
Gibson	1		1
Smith N	1		1
Opps' o.gs.	1		1

1 goal unrecorded

Fact File

Jacky Robertson scored twice as Rangers defeated Celtic 5-2 at Hampden on 14 May 1904 to win the Glasgow Charity Cup.

MANAGER: William Wilton
CAPTAIN: Jamie Stark
TOP SCORER: R.C. Hamilton
BIGGEST WIN: 8-1 v Port Glasgow, 13 February 1904, league
HIGHEST ATTENDANCE: 64,472 v Celtic, 16 April 1904, Scottish Cup final
MAJOR TRANSFERS OUT: Matt Dickie to Clyde, Jock Drummond to Falkirk

Final Scottish League Div 1 Table

		P	W	D	L	F	A	Pts
1	THIRD LANARK	26	20	3	3	61	26	43
2	HEARTS	26	18	3	5	63	35	39
3	CELTIC	26	18	2	6	69	28	38
3	RANGERS	26	16	6	4	80	33	38
5	DUNDEE	26	13	2	11	55	46	28
6	ST MIRREN	26	11	5	10	45	38	27
6	PARTICK T	26	10	7	9	43	40	27
8	QUEEN'S PARK	26	6	9	11	28	47	21
9	PORT GLASGOW A	26	8	4	14	33	49	20
10	HIBERNIAN	26	7	5	14	31	42	19
11	MORTON	26	7	4	15	31	51	18
11	AIRDRIEONIANS	26	7	4	15	32	62	18
13	MOTHERWELL	26	6	3	17	26	61	15
14	KILMARNOCK	26	4	5	17	27	66	13

Season 1904-05

Scottish League Division 1

DATE	OPPONENTS	SCORE	GOALSCORERS	ATTENDANCE
Aug 20	Third Lanark	L 1-2	Mackie	20,000
Aug 27	HIBERNIAN	W 4-0	Hamilton 2, Mackie, Kyle	12,000
Sep 3	PARTICK THISTLE	W 8-1	Stark, Speedie 3, Kyle 2, Hamilton 2	7,000
Sep 10	Dundee	W 3-0	Hamilton 2, Chaplin o.g.	14,760
Sep 17	Queen's Park	W 4-0	Kyle 2, A.Smith, Hamilton	30,231
Sep 19	Hibernian	W 2-1	Hamilton, McColl	-
Sep 26	HEARTS	D 1-1	Speedie	20,188
Oct 1	ST MIRREN	L 2-3	Mackie, Turnbull	10,000
Oct 15	Celtic	D 2-2	Hamilton, Mackie	25,000
Oct 22	QUEEN'S PARK	W 5-0	Mackie 2, Walker, McColl, Hamilton	15,000
Oct 29	DUNDEE	W 2-1	McColl, Mackie	13,000
Nov 5	Hearts	W 5-0	A.Smith, Walker 2, Speedie, Hamilton	10,000
Nov 12	St Mirren	L 0-3		-
Nov 19	THIRD LANARK	W 3-1	Kyle 2, A.Smith	
Dec 3	Kilmarnock	W 4-0	Kyle 2, Hamilton, Robertson	6,500
Dec 10	Motherwell	W 2-0	McLean o.g., Hamilton	5,000
Dec 17	AIRDRIE	W 4-1	Speedie, Hamilton, Kyle, Mackie	4,000
Dec 31	Airdrie	D 2-2	May, Speedie (pen)	8,000
Jan 3	Partick Thistle	W 4-1	Kyle, Hamilton 2, Robertson	11,000
Jan 14	MOTHERWELL	W 3-2	Speedie 2 (1 pen), McColl	6,000
Jan 21	KILMARNOCK	W 6-2	May, Walker, Speedie 2, McColl, Mackie	-
Feb 4	Port Glasgow	W 3-0	Walker, McColl 2	7,000
Feb 18	CELTIC	L 1-4	Kyle	30,000
Mar 18	PORT GLASGOW	W 5-1	A.Smith 2, Hamilton, Speedie, Low	5,000
Apr 1	MORTON	W 5-0	Hamilton 2, A.Smith 2, Kyle	5,000
Apr 29	Morton	W 2-0	Speedie, Kyle	3,000

League Championship Play-off

May 6	Celtic*	L 1-2	Robertson	30,000

*Played at Hampden Park.

Scottish Cup

Jan 28	AYR PARKHOUSE	(Rd1) W 2-1	Robertson, Chalmers	7,000
Feb 11	Morton	(Rd2) W 6-0	McColl 2, Speedie 2 (1 pen), Kyle, Walker	9,000
Feb 25	BEITH	(QF) W 5-0	Kyle 2, Speedie 2, Chalmers	4,000
Mar 25	Celtic	(SF) W 2-0	Speedie, Robertson	36,000
Apr 8	Third Lanark	(F)* D 0-0		54,000
Apr 15	Third Lanark	(R)* L 1-3	A.Smith	55,000

*Played at Hampden Park.

League & Cup Appearances

PLAYER	LEAGUE	CUP COMPETITION S CUP	TOTAL
Allan	8		8
Campbell	2	3	5
Chalmers	1	2	3
Craig	4	3	7
Donaghy	2	1	3
Easton	9		9
Fraser	14	3	17
Gilchrist	1		1
Gourlay	4		4
Hamilton	17	1	18
Henderson	14	3	17
Kyle	23	5	28
Low	1	1	2
McColl	13	4	17
McEwan	9	3	12
Mackie	20	1	21
May	23	4	27
Robertson	21	6	27
Sinclair	17	6	23
Smith A	27	6	33
Smith N	12		12
Speedie	27	6	33
Stark	14	6	20
Turnbull	1		1
Walker	12	2	14
Watson	2		2

Goalscorers

PLAYER	LEAGUE	CUP COMPETITION S CUP	TOTAL
Hamilton	19		19
Speedie	13	5	18
Kyle	14	3	17
McColl	7	2	9
Mackie	8		8
Smith A	7	1	8
Walker	5	1	6
Robertson	3	2	5
Chalmers		2	2
May	2		2
Low	1		1
Stark	1		1
Turnbull	1		1
Opps' o.gs.	2		2

Appearances and goalscorers tables include the League Championship Play-off

Fact File

A crowd of 60,000 were at Ibrox on 2 January 1905 for the league fixture against Celtic, but the match was abandoned after an hour because of a pitch invasion.

MANAGER: William Wilton

CAPTAIN: Jamie Stark

TOP SCORER: R.C. Hamilton

BIGGEST WIN: 8-1 v Partick Thistle, 3 September 1904, league

HIGHEST ATTENDANCE: 55,000 v Third Lanark, 15 April 1905, Scottish Cup final replay

MAJOR TRANSFERS IN: RS McColl from Newcastle United, John May from Derby County

MAJOR TRANSFERS OUT: Jacky Robertson to Chelsea

Final Scottish League Div 1 Table

		P	W	D	L	F	A	Pts
1	Celtic	26	18	5	3	68	31	41
1	Rangers	26	19	3	4	83	28	41
3	Third Lanark	26	14	7	5	60	28	35
4	Airdrieonians	26	11	5	10	38	45	27
4	Hibernian	26	9	8	9	39	39	26
5	Partick T	26	12	2	12	36	56	26
7	Dundee	26	10	5	11	38	32	25
7	Hearts	26	11	3	12	43	44	25
9	Kilmarnock	26	9	5	12	29	45	23
10	St Mirren	26	9	4	13	33	36	22
11	Port Glasgow A	26	8	5	13	30	48	21
12	Queen's Park	26	6	8	12	28	45	20
13	Morton	26	7	4	15	27	50	18
14	Motherwell	26	6	2	18	28	53	14

Celtic beat Rangers 2-1 in a play-off for the championship.

Season 1905-06

Scottish League Division 1

DATE	OPPONENTS	SCORE	GOALSCORERS	ATTENDANCE
Aug 19	KILMARNOCK	W 3-2	McColl (pen), Hamilton 2	10,000
Aug 25	ABERDEEN	W 1-0	McMillan	8,000
Sep 2	Airdrie	L 1-5	Hamilton	12,000
Sep 11	Hibernian	W 2-1	Hamilton, Low	6,000
Sep 15	ST MIRREN	W 1-0	Stark	15,000
Sep 25	HEARTS	L 0-5		18,000
Oct 7	Port Glasgow	W 4-1	Kyle, Stark, Hamilton, Speirs	3,000
Oct 14	DUNDEE	D 1-1	Shaw	9,500
Oct 21	CELTIC	W 3-2	Kyle, Shaw, May	30,000
Oct 28	Falkirk	W 6-1	Ruddiman 3, May, Kyle (pen), Shaw	6,000
Nov 4	Queen's Park	W 2-1	Hawthorne o.g., Speirs	13,000
Nov 11	THIRD LANARK	L 2-4	Kyle 2	10,000
Nov 18	Motherwell	D 3-3	Kyle 3 (1 pen)	5,000
Nov 25	MORTON	L 1-2	Hamilton	4,000
Dec 2	QUEEN'S PARK	W 3-1	Kivlichan 2, Smith	7,000
Dec 9	Morton	W 3-0	Speirs, May, Hamilton	5,000
Dec 16	Aberdeen	D 1-1	Rankine	10,000
Dec 23	MOTHERWELL	W 2-1	McColl, Smith	6,000
Dec 30	AIRDRIE	L 1-3	Speirs	8,000
Jan 1	Celtic	L 0-1		40,000
Jan 2	PARTICK THISTLE	W 1-0	McColl	-
Jan 6	Kilmarnock	W 3-1	Hamilton, Dalrymple, McColl	6,000
Jan 13	St Mirren	L 2-3	Smith, McColl	-
Jan 20	PORT GLASGOW	W 4-0	Dalrymple 3, McColl	8,000
Feb 3	Third Lanark	L 0-3		13,000
Feb 17	Dundee	D 1-1	Kivlichan	10,000
Mar 3	HIBERNIAN	D 1-1	Hamilton	7,000
Mar 17	Partick Thistle	D 1-1	Speirs	8,000
Mar 24	FALKIRK	W 3-1	Stark, Kivlichan, McFie	7,000
Apr 7	Hearts	D 2-2	Speirs, unrecorded	6,000

Scottish Cup

Jan 27	Arthurlie	(Rd1) W 7-1	Speirs 3, McColl, Dalrymple 2, May	6,000
Feb 10	Aberdeen	(Rd2) W 3-2	Dalrymple 2, Hamilton	14,000
Mar 10	Port Glasgow	(QF) L 0-1		11,000

League & Cup Appearances

PLAYER	LEAGUE	CUP COMPETITION	TOTAL
		S CUP	
Campbell	6	3	9
Cochrane	10		10
Craig A	25	3	28
Craig J	1		1
Croal	3		3
Dalrymple	13	2	15
Fraser	2		2
Gourlay	6		6
Gray	26	3	29
Hamilton	20	3	23
Kivlichan	9		9
Kyle	22	2	24
Low	2		2
McColl	13	2	15
McFie	4		4
McGhee	1		1
McMillan	9		9
May	21	3	24
Miller	1		1
Rankine	8		8
Ruddiman	4		4
Shaw	6		6
Sinclair	30	3	33
Smith	24	3	27
Speedie	2		2
Speirs	18	3	21
Stark	28	3	31
Steel	2		2
Walker	14		14

Goalscorers

PLAYER	LEAGUE	CUP COMPETITION	TOTAL
		S CUP	
Hamilton	9	1	10
Speirs	6	3	9
Dalrymple	4	4	8
Kyle	8		8
McColl	6	1	7
Kivlichan	4		4
May	3	1	4
Ruddiman	3		3
Shaw	3		3
Smith	3		3
Stark	3		3
Low	1		1
McFie	1		1
McMillan	1		1
Rankine	1		1
Opps' o.gs.	1		1

1 goal unrecorded

Fact File

Rangers' 5-0 defeat by Hearts at Ibrox on 25 September 1905 stands to this day as the club's record home loss in a league fixture.

MANAGER: William Wilton

CAPTAIN: Jamie Stark

TOP SCORER: R.C. Hamilton

BIGGEST WIN: 7-1 v Arthurlie, 27 January 1906, Scottish Cup

HIGHEST ATTENDANCE: 40,000 v Celtic, 1 January 1906, league

MAJOR TRANSFERS IN: R.G. Campbell from Celtic, James Speirs from Maryhill

MAJOR TRANSFERS OUT: R.C. Hamilton to Fulham

Final Scottish League Div 1 Table

		P	W	D	L	F	A	Pts
1	CELTIC	30	24	1	5	76	19	49
2	HEARTS	30	18	7	5	64	27	43
3	AIRDRIEONIANS	30	15	8	7	53	31	38
4	RANGERS	30	15	7	8	58	48	37
5	PARTICK T	30	15	6	9	44	40	36
6	THIRD LANARK	30	16	2	12	62	38	34
6	DUNDEE	30	11	12	7	40	33	34
8	ST MIRREN	30	13	5	12	41	37	31
9	MOTHERWELL	30	9	8	13	50	64	26
9	MORTON	30	10	6	14	35	54	26
11	HIBERNIAN	30	10	5	15	35	40	25
12	ABERDEEN	30	8	8	14	36	48	24
13	FALKIRK	30	9	5	16	52	68	23
14	KILMARNOCK	30	8	4	18	46	68	20
14	PORT GLASGOW A	30	6	8	16	38	68	20
16	QUEEN'S PARK	30	5	4	21	41	88	14

Season 1906-07

Scottish League Division 1

DATE	OPPONENTS	SCORE	GOALSCORERS	ATTENDANCE
Aug 18	FALKIRK	D 2-2	Smith, Speirs	13,000
Aug 25	Port Glasgow	W 2-0	Mainds, Kyle	8,000
Sep 1	ABERDEEN	W 6-2	Stark 2, Kyle, Smith, Rankine, Speirs	10,000
Sep 22	Dundee	L 0-2		14,600
Sep 24	HEARTS	D 1-1	McFie	10,000
Sep 29	PARTICK THISTLE	L 1-2	Hamilton	12,000
Oct 13	Kilmarnock	W 5-1	Speirs 2, Smith, Kyle, Rankine	7,000
Oct 20	MORTON	W 2-0	Kivlichan, Speirs	9,000
Oct 27	Celtic	L 1-2	Kyle	30,000
Nov 3	ST MIRREN	D 1-1	Kyle (pen)	12,000
Nov 10	Third Lanark	W 2-0	Kyle (pen), Law	16,000
Nov 17	QUEEN'S PARK	W 3-2	Dickie, Kyle, Cunningham	14,000
Nov 24	Hibernian	W 3-1	Kyle, McFie, Smith	-
Dec 1	AIRDRIE	W 2-1	Speirs, Smith	13,000
Dec 8	Clyde	W 5-1	Smith 2, Speirs, Kyle, Dickie	-
Dec 15	MOTHERWELL	L 0-1		5,000
Dec 22	Aberdeen	W 3-0	Kyle 2, Smith	7,000
Dec 29	HAMILTON A	L 0-1		5,000
Jan 1	CELTIC	W 2-1	Dickie, Kivlichan	50,000
Jan 2	Partick Thistle	D 2-2	Campbell 2	7,000
Jan 5	Morton	L 1-2	Speirs	5,000
Jan 12	HIBERNIAN	W 1-0	Speirs	7,000
Jan 19	Airdrie	W 3-2	Cunningham, Speirs, Campbell (pen)	8,000
Feb 2	THIRD LANARK	D 0-0		10,000
Feb 9	Hamilton A	W 3-0	Speirs 2, Cunningham	6,000
Feb 23	St Mirren	D 0-0		7,000
Mar 2	Motherwell	L 0-1		5,000
Mar 16	Falkirk	L 1-2	Kivlichan	7,000
Mar 23	CLYDE	W 4-0	Campbell 3, Stark	7,000
Apr 1	DUNDEE	D 2-2	Campbell 2 (1 pen)	12,000
Apr 6	Queen's Park	W 2-1	Livingston, Campbell	18,000
Apr 13	Hearts	W 1-0	Smith	9,000
Apr 20	Kilmarnock	W 3-0	Livingston 2, Speirs	2,500

Scottish Cup

Jan 26	Falkirk	(Rd1) W 2-1	Campbell (pen), McFie	16,000
Feb 16	Galston	(Rd2) W 4-0	Livingston 2, Dickie, Speirs	4,000
Mar 9	CELTIC	(QF) L 0-3		-

League & Cup Appearances

PLAYER	LEAGUE	CUP COMPETITION S CUP	TOTAL
Campbell	26	3	29
Craig	12		12
Cunningham	10		10
Dickie	20	3	23
Galt	21	1	22
Gordon	1		1
Gray	20	3	23
Hamilton	2		2
Hendry	19	3	22
Jackson	16		16
Kivlichan	11		11
Kyle	27	1	28
Law	6		6
Livingston	10	3	13
McColl	1		1
McDonald	5		5
McFarlane	1		1
McFie	12	2	14
Menzies	1		1
Mainds	13		13
May	17	2	19
Newbigging	34	3	37
Rankine	7		7
Ruddiman	3		3
Smith	25	3	28
Speedie	1		1
Speirs	22	3	25
Stark	22	3	25
Taylor	9		9

Goalscorers

PLAYER	LEAGUE	CUP COMPETITION S CUP	TOTAL
Speirs	13	1	14
Campbell	12	1	13
Kyle	13		13
Smith	8		8
Livingston	4	2	6
Dickie	3	1	4
Cunningham	3		3
Kivlichan	3		3
McFie	2	1	3
Stark	3		3
Rankine	2		2
Hamilton	1		1
Law	1		1
Mainds	1		1

Fact File

On Christmas Day 1906, Rangers defeated Preston North End 3-1 in a friendly match at Deepdale. Archie Kyle (2) and Alec Smith scored the goals.

MANAGER: William Wilton

CAPTAIN: Jamie Stark

TOP SCORER: James Speirs

BIGGEST WIN: 5-0 v Port Glasgow, 30 March 1907, league

HIGHEST ATTENDANCE: 60,000 v Celtic, 9 March 1907, Scottish Cup

MAJOR TRANSFERS IN: Alex Newbigging from Reading, George Livingston from Manchester City

MAJOR TRANSFERS OUT: Finlay Speedie to Newcastle United, R.S. McColl to Queen's Park

Final Scottish League Div 1 Table

		P	W	D	L	F	A	PTS
1	CELTIC	34	23	9	2	80	30	55
2	DUNDEE	34	18	12	4	53	26	48
3	RANGERS	34	19	7	8	69	33	45
4	AIRDRIEONIANS	34	18	6	10	59	44	42
5	FALKIRK	34	17	7	10	73	58	41
6	THIRD LANARK	34	15	9	10	57	48	39
7	ST MIRREN	34	12	13	9	50	44	37
8	CLYDE	34	15	6	13	47	52	36
9	HEARTS	34	11	13	10	46	43	35
10	MOTHERWELL	34	12	9	13	45	48	33
11	ABERDEEN	34	10	10	14	48	55	30
11	HIBERNIAN	34	10	10	14	40	49	30
13	MORTON	34	11	6	17	41	50	28
14	PARTICK T	34	9	8	17	40	60	26
15	QUEEN'S PARK	34	9	6	19	51	66	24
16	HAMILTON A	34	8	5	21	40	64	21
16	KILMARNOCK	34	8	5	21	40	72	21
16	PORT GLASGOW A	34	7	7	20	30	67	21

Season 1907-08

Scottish League Division 1

DATE	OPPONENTS	SCORE	GOALSCORERS	ATTENDANCE
Aug 15	MORTON	W 3-0	Smith 2, Campbell	7,000
Aug 17	Port Glasgow	W 6-1	Campbell 2, Livingston 2, McDonald, Thomson o.g.	6,000
Aug 24	ABERDEEN	W 4-0	Campbell 3, Livingston	20,000
Aug 31	Falkirk	D 4-4	Campbell, Galt, May, Livingston	14,000
Sep 7	KILMARNOCK	W 1-0	Campbell	14,000
Sep 21	Morton	W 3-2	Galt, Campbell, Kyle	10,000
Sep 30	QUEEN'S PARK	D 1-1	Livingston	17,000
Oct 5	AIRDRIE	L 1-2	McDonald	22,000
Nov 2	Queen's Park	L 1-3	Livingston	20,000
Nov 9	ST MIRREN	D 2-2	Kyle, Hamilton	15,000
Nov 15	Partick Thistle	W 2-1	Steven, Campbell	8,000
Nov 23	HIBERNIAN	D 1-1	Campbell	11,000
Nov 30	Third Lanark	W 5-3	Kyle 3, Speirs, Hamilton	9,000
Dec 7	Hearts	W 2-1	Kyle, Hamilton	11,000
Dec 14	MOTHERWELL	W 4-2	Speirs 2, May, Kyle	10,000
Dec 21	Dundee	W 2-1	Campbell, May	15,000
Dec 28	FALKIRK	D 2-2	Speirs, Campbell	25,000
Jan 1	Celtic	L 1-2	Kyle	60,000
Jan 2	PARTICK THISTLE	W 3-2	Livingston 2, Kyle	5,000
Jan 4	Airdrie	L 0-3		7,000
Jan 11	THIRD LANARK	W 2-0	Speirs, Kyle	8,000
Jan 18	Aberdeen	D 0-0		10,000
Feb 15	Hamilton A	D 2-2	Livingston, McDonald	6,000
Feb 29	HEARTS	W 2-1	Campbell, Barrie	6,000
Mar 7	Kilmarnock	W 2-0	Livingston, Smith	8,000
Mar 14	Clyde	W 2-0	Kyle, Gordon	9,000
Mar 21	HAMILTON A	W 1-0	Campbell	6,000
Mar 28	Hibernian	W 3-0	Campbell 3	9,000
Apr 4	Motherwell	W 2-1	Campbell 2	3,000
Apr 11	CLYDE	D 1-1	Campbell	6,000
Apr 13	St Mirren	W 2-0	Campbell, Kyle	4,000
Apr 18	PORT GLASGOW	W 5-1	Campbell 3, McDonald, May	2,500
Apr 20	DUNDEE	W 2-0	Noble, May (pen)	12,000
Apr 25	CELTIC	L 0-1		40,000

Scottish Cup

Jan 25	Falkirk	(Rd1) D 2-2	Livingston, May	20,000
Feb 1	FALKIRK	(R) W 4-1	Smith 2, Kyle, Speirs	52,000
Feb 8	CELTIC	(Rd2) L 1-2	Kyle	23,000

League & Cup Appearances

PLAYER	LEAGUE	CUP COMPETITION S CUP	TOTAL
Barrie	11	3	14
Bovill	2		2
Campbell	32		32
Craig	23	3	26
Cunningham	3		3
Dickie	9	3	12
Galt	27	3	30
Gordon	22		22
Hadden	2		2
Hamilton	11		11
Hendry	12	3	15
Jackson	14		14
Kyle	27	3	30
Law	13		13
Livingston	24	3	27
McArthur	6		6
McDonald	19		19
May	26	3	29
Newbigging	26	3	29
Noble	8		8
Sharp	1		1
Smith	22	3	25
Speirs	13	3	16
Steven	9		9
Taylor	12		12

Goalscorers

PLAYER	LEAGUE	CUP COMPETITION S CUP	TOTAL
Campbell	25		25
Kyle	12	2	14
Livingston	10	1	11
May	5	1	6
Speirs	5	1	6
Smith	3	2	5
McDonald	4		4
Hamilton	3		3
Galt	2		2
Barrie	1		1
Gordon	1		1
Noble	1		1
Steven	1		1
Opps' o.gs.	1		1

Fact File

As part of the transfer deal bringing R.C. Hamilton back to Ibrox from Fulham, Rangers played the London side in a friendly at Craven Cottage on Christmas Day 1907. Hamilton scored the only goal of the game for Rangers.

MANAGER: William Wilton

CAPTAIN: R.G. Campbell

TOP SCORER: R.G. Campbell

BIGGEST WIN: 6-1 v Port Glasgow, 17 August 1907, league

HIGHEST ATTENDANCE: 60,000 v Celtic, 1 January 1908, league

MAJOR TRANSFERS IN: R.C. Hamilton from Fulham, Alec Barrie from Sunderland, Harry Rennie from Hibs, James Sharp from Arsenal

MAJOR TRANSFERS OUT: Jamie Stark to Chelsea

Final Scottish League Div 1 Table

		P	W	D	L	F	A	Pts
1	CELTIC	34	24	7	3	86	27	55
2	FALKIRK	34	22	7	5	103	42	51
3	RANGERS	34	21	8	5	74	40	50
4	DUNDEE	34	20	8	6	71	28	48
5	HIBERNIAN	34	17	8	9	55	42	42
6	AIRDRIEONIANS	34	18	5	11	58	41	41
7	ST MIRREN	34	13	10	11	50	59	36
8	ABERDEEN	34	13	9	12	45	44	35
9	THIRD LANARK	34	13	7	14	45	50	33
10	MOTHERWELL	34	12	7	15	61	53	31
11	HAMILTON A	34	10	8	16	55	65	28
11	HEARTS	34	11	6	17	50	62	28
13	MORTON	34	9	9	16	43	66	27
14	PARTICK T	34	8	9	17	43	69	25
14	KILMARNOCK	34	6	13	15	38	61	25
15	QUEEN'S PARK	34	7	8	19	54	84	22
17	CLYDE	34	5	8	21	36	75	18
18	PORT GLASGOW A	34	5	7	22	39	98	17

Season 1908-09

Scottish League Division 1

DATE	OPPONENTS	SCORE	GOALSCORERS	ATTENDANCE
Aug 15	PORT GLASGOW	W 7-0	McDonald 3, McPherson 2, Murray, Bennett	15,000
Aug 22	Partick Thistle	W 2-0	McPherson, Murray	12,000
Aug 29	FALKIRK	W 4-1	A.Smith 2, Bennett, McDonald	30,000
Sep 5	Aberdeen	W 2-0	Campbell, Bennett	9,000
Sep 12	Kilmarnock	W 5-0	Murray 2, A.Smith, Bennett, McPherson	9,000
Sep 19	ST MIRREN	D 1-1	Campbell	27,000
Sep 28	DUNDEE	W 2-0	Bennett, Campbell	35,000
Oct 10	Airdrie	L 3-4	Gordon, Campbell, McPherson	11,000
Oct 17	MOTHERWELL	W 3-1	Livingston, A.Smith, J.Smith	11,000
Oct 24	AIRDRIE	W 2-0	J.Smith 2	18,000
Oct 31	THIRD LANARK	D 2-2	J.Smith, Livingston	24,000
Nov 7	MORTON	W 8-0	Murray 3, Bennett 2, McPherson 2, A.Smith	10,000
Nov 14	Queen's Park	D 1-1	Murray	32,000
Nov 21	Clyde	W 1-0	Bennett	18,000
Nov 28	HEARTS	W 4-3	Campbell 2, May, Bennett	9,000
Dec 5	Falkirk	L 0-1		10,000
Dec 12	Hamilton	W 7-0	Campbell 4, A.Smith, Yuille, Gordon	8,000
Dec 19	KILMARNOCK	D 1-1	May	8,000
Dec 26	St Mirren	W 3-1	Bennett, McPherson, Murray	12,000
Jan 1	CELTIC	L 1-3	Murray	60,000
Jan 2	PARTICK THISTLE	W 6-0	Livingston 4, A.Smith, J.Smith	5,000
Jan 9	Dundee	L 0-4		16,000
Jan 30	Motherwell	W 5-2	McPherson 2, A.Smith, Bennett, Campbell	7,000
Feb 27	Port Glasgow	L 0-2		4,000
Mar 6	HIBERNIAN	D 0-0		4,000
Mar 13	Celtic	W 3-2	Yuille, McDonald, Murray	28,000
Mar 27	ABERDEEN	W 3-1	Bennett, Campbell, Gilchrist	10,000
Mar 30	HAMILTON	W 4-0	Gordon 3, Campbell (pen)	-
Apr 3	Hearts	D 0-0		11,000
Apr 12	CLYDE	D 2-2	Gilchrist, McPherson	15,000
Apr 19	Hibernian	L 0-1		6,000
Apr 24	Third Lanark	L 0-1		11,000
Apr 26	QUEEN'S PARK	L 2-3	Bennett, McPherson	1,000
Apr 28	Morton	W 7-1	Campbell 3, A.Smith, Gordon, Stark, McDonald	2,000

Scottish Cup

Jan 23	St Johnstone	(Rd1) W 3-0	Stark, Bennett, Campbell	7,000
Feb 6	Dundee	(Rd2) D 0-0		31,000
Feb 13	DUNDEE	(R) W 1-0	McPherson	54,500
Feb 20	QUEEN'S PARK	(QF) W 1-0	McPherson	45,000
Mar 20	Falkirk	(SF) W 1-0	McPherson	12,000
Apr 10	Celtic	(F)* D 2-2	Gilchrist, Bennett	70,000
Apr 17	Celtic	(R)* D 1-1	Gordon	60,000

*Played at Hampden Park. Trophy witheld following riot at final replay.

League & Cup Appearances

PLAYER	LEAGUE	CUP COMPETITION S CUP	TOTAL
Bennett	28	7	35
Campbell	22	5	27
Craig	28	7	35
Galt	24	7	31
Gilchrist	8	5	13
Gordon	25	2	27
Jackson	1		1
Law	20	7	27
Livingston	13		13
McArthur	3		3
McDonald	22	2	24
McKenzie	2		2
McLean	1		1
McPherson	26	7	33
May	21	5	26
Miller	1		1
Murray	14	1	15
Noble	2		2
Reid	2	1	3
Rennie	31	7	38
Sharp	18		18
Smith A	28	7	35
Smith J	7		7
Stark	17	7	24
Taylor	6		6
Waddell	1		1
Yuille	3		3

Goalscorers

PLAYER	LEAGUE	CUP COMPETITION S CUP	TOTAL
Campbell	16	1	17
Bennett	13	2	15
McPherson	12	3	15
Murray	11		11
Smith A	9		9
Gordon	6	1	7
Livingston	6		6
McDonald	6		6
Smith J	5		5
Gilchrist	2	1	3
May	2		2
Stark	1	1	2
Yuille	2		2

Fact File

Jimmy Gordon scored seven goals in Rangers' three ties in the Glasgow Charity Cup, including two in the 4-2 win over Celtic at Parkhead in the final.

Final Scottish League Div 1 Table

		P	W	D	L	F	A	Pts
1	CELTIC	34	23	5	6	71	24	51
2	DUNDEE	34	22	6	6	70	32	50
3	CLYDE	34	21	6	7	61	37	48
4	RANGERS	34	19	7	8	91	38	45
5	AIRDRIEONIANS	34	16	9	9	67	46	41
6	HIBERNIAN	34	16	7	11	40	32	39
7	ST MIRREN	34	15	6	13	53	45	36
7	ABERDEEN	34	15	6	13	61	53	36
9	FALKIRK	34	13	7	14	58	56	33
9	KILMARNOCK	34	13	7	14	47	61	33
11	THIRD LANARK	34	11	10	13	56	49	32
11	HEARTS	34	12	8	14	54	49	32
13	PORT GLASGOW A	34	10	8	16	39	52	28
13	MOTHERWELL	34	11	6	17	47	73	28
15	QUEEN'S PARK	34	6	13	15	42	65	25
16	HAMILTON A	34	6	12	16	42	72	24
17	MORTON	34	8	7	19	39	90	23
18	PARTICK T	34	2	4	28	38	102	8

MANAGER: William Wilton

CAPTAIN: Jamie Stark

TOP SCORER: R.G. Campbell

BIGGEST WIN: 8-0 v Morton, 7 November 1908, league

HIGHEST ATTENDANCE: 70,000 v Celtic, 10 April 1909, Scottish Cup final

MAJOR TRANSFERS IN: Billy McPherson from Liverpool, Jamie Stark from Chelsea, Alex Bennett from Celtic, Willie Reid from Portsmouth

MAJOR TRANSFERS OUT: R.C. Hamilton to Morton, George Livingston to Manchester United, James Sharp to Fulham

Season 1909-10

Scottish League Division 1

DATE	OPPONENTS	SCORE	GOALSCORERS	ATTENDANCE
Aug 16	KILMARNOCK	W 3-0	Smith, Reid, Hunter	18,000
Aug 21	Airdrie	L 1-2	Hogg	13,000
Aug 28	ST MIRREN	D 1-1	Bennett	16,000
Sep 4	Dundee	L 2-4	McPherson, Bennett	22,000
Sep 18	ABERDEEN	W 2-1	Gordon, Gilchrist	16,000
Sep 20	Hibernian	L 0-1		10,000
Sep 27	DUNDEE	W 2-1	McPherson, Reid	30,000
Oct 2	Port Glasgow	D 1-1	Hunter	5,000
Oct 16	HAMILTON	W 5-1	Hunter 5	9,000
Oct 23	Kilmarnock	W 2-0	Hunter 2	9,500
Oct 30	CELTIC	D 0-0		45,000
Nov 6	Partick Thistle	D 0-0		30,000
Nov 13	Clyde	L 0-1		18,000
Nov 20	QUEEN'S PARK	W 7-1	Hunter 3, Ramage, May, Gilchrist, McPherson	14,000
Nov 27	MOTHERWELL	W 4-1	Hunter 3, Gilchrist	7,000
Dec 4	Morton	W 4-1	Bennett 2, McPherson, Ramage	6,000
Dec 11	Third Lanark	L 1-2	Hunter	6,000
Dec 18	PARTICK THISTLE	W 2-1	Gilchrist, McPherson	16,000
Dec 25	Falkirk	L 1-3	McPherson	7,000
Jan 1	Celtic	D 1-1	Hogg	47,000
Jan 3	PORT GLASGOW	W 4-0	Reid 2, McLean, McPherson	8,000
Jan 8	HEARTS	W 1-0	McPherson	8,000
Jan 15	Hamilton	W 3-2	Hunter 3 (1 pen)	8,000
Jan 29	Motherwell	W 3-2	Miller, McPherson, Hogg	8,000
Feb 19	MORTON	W 2-1	Hogg, Bennett	8,000
Feb 26	St Mirren	W 6-1	Reid 3, Hogg 2, McPherson	8,000
Mar 5	Aberdeen	D 1-1	Reid	8,000
Mar 12	Queen's Park	L 2-3	Reid 2	16,000
Mar 19	AIRDRIE	W 3-0	Yuille 2, Bennett	5,000
Mar 26	HIBERNIAN	W 1-0	Smith	15,000
Mar 28	THIRD LANARK	W 1-0	McPherson	12,000
Apr 18	Hearts	W 3-1	Reid 2, McPherson	7,000
Apr 23	CLYDE	W 1-0	Gordon	10,000
Apr 30	FALKIRK	L 0-1		15,000

Scottish Cup

DATE	OPPONENTS		SCORE	GOALSCORERS	ATTENDANCE
Jan 22	INVERNESS THISTLE	(Rd1)	W 3-1	Gilchrist, May, Reid	10,000
Feb 5	Clyde	(Rd2)	L 0-2		35,000

League & Cup Appearances

PLAYER	LEAGUE	CUP COMPETITION S CUP	TOTAL
Bell	1		1
Bennett	22	1	23
Campbell	14	1	15
Craig	9		9
Galt	25	2	27
Gilchrist	13	1	14
Gordon	19		19
Hendry	2		2
Hogg	26	1	27
Hunter	17	1	18
Jackson	1		1
Law	22	1	23
Lock	32	2	34
McKenzie	24	2	26
McLean	1		1
McPherson	25	2	27
May	23	2	25
Miller	9		9
Ramage	6		6
Reid	20	2	22
Rennie	2		2
Smith	21	2	23
Stark	24	2	26
Waddell	11		11
Yuille	5		5

Goalscorers

PLAYER	LEAGUE	CUP COMPETITION S CUP	TOTAL
Hunter	19		19
Reid	12	1	13
McPherson	12		12
Bennett	6		6
Hogg	6		6
Gilchrist	4	1	5
Gordon	2		2
May	1	1	2
Ramage	2		2
Smith	2		2
Yuille	2		2
McLean	1		1
Miller	1		1

Fact File

Billy Hogg became the first full English international player signed by Rangers when he moved to Ibrox from Sunderland in May 1909.

MANAGER: William Wilton

CAPTAIN: Jamie Stark

TOP SCORER: Willie Hunter

BIGGEST WIN: 7-1 v Queen's Park, 20 November 1909, league

HIGHEST ATTENDANCE: 47,000 v Celtic, 1 January 1910, league

MAJOR TRANSFERS IN: Billy Hogg from Sunderland, Herbert Lock from Southampton, Willie Hunter from Airdrie

MAJOR TRANSFERS OUT: Jamie Stark to Morton, Harry Rennie to Kilmarnock, John May to Morton

Final Scottish League Div 1 Table

		P	W	D	L	F	A	Pts
1	CELTIC	34	24	6	4	63	22	54
2	FALKIRK	34	22	8	4	71	28	52
3	RANGERS	34	20	6	8	70	35	46
4	ABERDEEN	34	16	8	10	44	29	40
5	CLYDE	34	14	9	11	47	40	37
6	DUNDEE	34	14	8	12	52	44	36
7	THIRD LANARK	34	13	8	13	62	44	34
7	HIBERNIAN	34	14	6	14	33	40	34
9	AIRDRIEONIANS	34	12	9	13	46	57	33
10	MOTHERWELL	34	12	8	14	59	60	32
10	KILMARNOCK	34	12	8	14	53	59	32
12	HEARTS	34	12	7	15	59	50	31
12	ST MIRREN	34	13	5	16	48	58	31
14	QUEEN'S PARK	34	12	6	16	54	74	30
15	HAMILTON A	34	11	6	17	50	67	28
16	PARTICK T	34	8	10	16	45	59	26
17	MORTON	34	11	3	20	38	60	25
18	PORT GLASGOW A	34	3	5	26	25	93	11

Season 1910-11

Scottish League Division 1

DATE	OPPONENTS	SCORE	GOALSCORERS	ATTENDANCE
Aug 20	ST MIRREN	W 1-0	Gordon	25,000
Aug 27	Raith Rovers	W 2-0	Gordon, Smith	10,000
Sep 3	DUNDEE	L 1-2	Reid	30,000
Sep 10	Hamilton A	W 4-2	Gibson 2, Reid, Bennett	10,000
Sep 17	ABERDEEN	L 2-4	Reid 2	19,000
Sep 19	Hearts	W 4-1	Reid 4	9,000
Sep 26	HIBERNIAN	W 4-0	Reid 3, Gibson	15,000
Oct 1	Motherwell	W 2-1	Reid, Hogg	12,000
Oct 15	Third Lanark	D 1-1	Gordon	30,000
Oct 22	MORTON	L 1-5	Reid	15,000
Oct 29	Celtic	W 1-0	Hogg	35,000
Nov 5	AIRDRIE	W 7-1	Hogg 2, Reid 2, Bennett (pen) Gordon, Yuille	12,000
Nov 12	KILMARNOCK	W 3-0	Hogg 2, Reid	7,000
Nov 19	Queen's Park	W 4-0	Reid 2, Hogg, Bennett	18,000
Nov 26	MOTHERWELL	W 7-1	Reid 4, Chapman 2, Hogg	6,000
Dec 3	Aberdeen	L 0-1		14,000
Dec 10	FALKIRK	D 1-1	Reid	10,000
Dec 17	St Mirren	L 1-2	Hogg	10,000
Dec 24	HEARTS	W 2-0	Reid, Galt	9,000
Dec 31	Kilmarnock	W 2-0	Reid, Gibson	12,000
Jan 2	CELTIC	D 1-1	Reid	60,000
Jan 3	Partick Thistle	D 2-2	Bowie, Reid	35,000
Jan 7	CLYDE	W 6-1	Hogg 2, Goodwin 2, Reid, Chapman	10,000
Jan 14	HAMILTON A	W 4-0	Gibson, Smith, Hogg, Hendry	8,000
Jan 21	Airdrie	W 4-1	Reid 2, Bennett (pen), Hogg	10,000
Feb 4	RAITH ROVERS	W 4-1	Reid 2, Bowie, Gordon	8,000
Feb 18	PARTICK THISTLE	W 2-0	Reid, Bennett (pen)	8,000
Mar 11	Hibernian	W 3-1	Smith, Reid, Hogg	12,000
Mar 18	QUEEN'S PARK	W 4-0	A.Brown, Goodwin, Parker, Bowie	6,000
Mar 25	Morton	D 2-2	Reid, Bowie	10,000
Apr 8	Dundee	W 2-0	Goodwin, A.Brown	12,000
Apr 15	Falkirk	D 2-2	Reid, Campbell	10,000
Apr 20	THIRD LANARK	W 3-1	Reid, Bennett, Smith	10,000
Apr 22	Clyde	W 1-0	Reid	10,000

Scottish Cup

Jan 28	KILMARNOCK	(Rd1) W 2-1	Hogg, Reid	40,000
Feb 11	MORTON	(Rd2) W 3-0	Reid 2, Bowie	39,000
Feb 25	Dundee	(QF) L 1-2	Hogg	30,000

League & Cup Appearances

PLAYER	LEAGUE	CUP COMPETITION S CUP	TOTAL
Bennett	23	3	26
Brown A	3		3
Brown R	4		4
Bowie	17	3	20
Campbell	23	2	25
Chapman	28	2	30
Craig	1		1
Galt	18	2	20
Gibson	6		6
Goodwin	10		10
Gordon	28	3	31
Hendry	31	2	33
Hogg	30	3	33
Law	24	3	27
Lock	34	3	37
McAulay	1		1
Parker	2		2
Paterson	2		2
Reid	33	3	36
Richmond	20	1	21
Smith	29	3	32
Taylor	1		1
Yuille	6		6

Goalscorers

PLAYER	LEAGUE	CUP COMPETITION S CUP	TOTAL
Reid	38	3	41
Hogg	14	2	16
Bennett	6		6
Bowie	4	1	5
Gibson	5		5
Gordon	5		5
Goodwin	4		4
Smith	4		4
Chapman	3		3
Brown A	2		2
Campbell	1		1
Galt	1		1
Hendry	1		1
Parker	1		1
Yuille	1		1

Fact File

Willie Reid scored five goals in six matches as Rangers won both the Glasgow and Charity Cups in 1910-11, defeating Celtic in the finals of both competitions at Hampden Park.

MANAGER: William Wilton

CAPTAIN: George Chapman

TOP SCORER: Willie Reid

BIGGEST WIN: 7-1 v Airdrie, 5 November 1910, league; v Motherwell, 26 November 1910, league

HIGHEST ATTENDANCE: 60,000 v Celtic, League, 1 January 1911

MAJOR TRANSFERS IN: George Chapman from Blackburn Rovers, James Bowie from Queen's Park

MAJOR TRANSFERS OUT: Billy McPherson to Hearts, David Taylor to Bradford City

Final Scottish League Div 1 Table

		P	W	D	L	F	A	Pts
1	RANGERS	34	23	6	5	90	34	52
2	ABERDEEN	34	19	10	5	53	28	48
3	FALKIRK	34	17	10	7	65	42	44
4	PARTICK T	34	17	8	9	50	41	42
5	CELTIC	34	15	11	8	48	18	41
5	DUNDEE	34	18	5	11	54	42	41
7	CLYDE	34	14	11	9	45	36	39
7	THIRD LANARK	34	16	7	11	59	53	39
9	HIBERNIAN	34	15	6	13	44	48	36
10	KILMARNOCK	34	12	10	12	42	45	34
11	AIRDRIEONIANS	34	12	9	13	49	53	33
12	ST MIRREN	34	12	7	15	46	57	31
13	MORTON	34	9	11	14	49	51	29
14	HEARTS	34	8	8	18	42	59	24
14	RAITH R	34	7	10	17	36	55	24
16	HAMILTON A	34	8	5	21	31	60	21
17	MOTHERWELL	34	8	4	22	37	66	20
18	QUEEN'S PARK	34	5	4	25	28	80	14

Season 1911-12

Scottish League Division 1

DATE	OPPONENTS	SCORE	GOALSCORERS	ATTENDANCE
Aug 16	RAITH ROVERS	W 5-0	Reid 2, Hogg, Bennett, Galt	11,000
Aug 19	MORTON	W 6-1	Reid 2, Bennett 2, Hogg, Gordon	25,000
Aug 26	Clyde	W 2-0	Bennett, Hogg	35,000
Sep 2	DUNDEE	W 2-1	Bennett 2	30,000
Sep 16	Aberdeen	W 2-1	Goodwin, Reid	16,000
Sep 25	HIBERNIAN	W 2-0	Bennett (pen), Chapman	40,000
Sep 30	THIRD LANARK	W 4-0	Reid 4	22,000
Oct 14	Airdrie	D 2-2	Hogg, Reid	18,000
Oct 21	CELTIC	W 3-1	Bowie 2, Gordon	47,000
Oct 28	Partick Thistle	W 1-0	Reid	30,000
Nov 4	ST MIRREN	W 4-1	Bowie, Goodwin, Reid, Hogg	13,000
Nov 11	Motherwell	W 2-1	Hogg, Reid	15,000
Nov 18	QUEEN'S PARK	W 1-0	Goodwin	20,000
Nov 25	HAMILTON A	W 7-0	Reid 4, Hogg, Bowie, Goodwin	12,000
Dec 2	Morton	L 1-2	Hogg	15,000
Dec 9	St Mirren	W 5-1	Reid 3, Hogg, Goodwin	15,000
Dec 16	HEARTS	W 2-1	Reid, Hogg	22,000
Dec 23	Falkirk	W 2-0	Bennett, Smith	10,000
Dec 30	KILMARNOCK	W 6-1	Hogg 3, Bennett, A.Brown, Reid	15,000
Jan 1	Celtic	L 0-3		70,000
Jan 2	PARTICK THISTLE	W 4-1	Reid 3, Galt	20,000
Jan 6	Hibernian	L 0-5		13,000
Jan 13	CLYDE	L 1-2	Reid	30,000
Jan 20	ABERDEEN	W 2-0	Parker, Goodwin	20,000
Feb 3	Hamilton A	D 1-1	Reid	10,000
Feb 17	Third Lanark	W 3-1	Reid, Hogg, Bowie	25,000
Feb 24	AIRDRIE	W 4-1	Hogg 2, Reid, Smith	15,000
Mar 2	Queen's Park	D 0-0		25,000
Mar 9	FALKIRK	W 4-0	Hogg 2, Reid 2	8,000
Mar 16	Dundee	L 1-2	Parker	8,000
Mar 23	Raith Rovers	W 1-0	Goodwin	6,000
Mar 30	Kilmarnock	L 2-3	Reid, Goodwin	4,000
Apr 15	Hearts	L 1-2	Reid	8,000
Apr 27	MOTHERWELL	W 3-1	Bennett 2, Hendry	6,000

Scottish Cup

Jan 27	STENHOUSEMUIR	(Rd1) W 3-1	Paterson 2, Reid	7,500
Feb 10	Clyde*	(Rd2) L 1-3	Hendry	52,000

*Match abandoned after 75 mins because of pitch invasion – Rangers conceded tie.

League & Cup Appearances

PLAYER	LEAGUE	CUP COMPETITION S CUP	TOTAL
Allan	1	1	2
Bennett	25	2	27
Bowie	24	2	26
Brown A	8		8
Brown J	1		1
Brown R	5		5
Campbell	32	2	34
Chapman	2		2
Farrington	1		1
Galt	26	2	28
Goodwin	17		17
Gordon	29	2	31
Hendry	32	2	34
Hogg	30	1	31
Law	11		11
Lock	33	2	35
Ormond	12		12
Paterson	4	1	5
Parker	3		3
Reid	32	2	34
Richmond	12	1	13
Robertson	2		2
Smith	27	2	29
Waddell	5		5

Goalscorers

PLAYER	LEAGUE	CUP COMPETITION S CUP	TOTAL
Reid	33	1	34
Hogg	18		18
Bennett	11		11
Goodwin	8		8
Bowie	5		5
Galt	2		2
Gordon	2		2
Hendry	1	1	2
Paterson		2	2
Parker	2		2
Smith	2		2
Brown A	1		1
Chapman	1		1

Fact File

Jimmy Gordon missed Rangers' title-clinching win at Raith Rovers on 23 March 1912 as he was playing for Scotland in their 1-1 draw with England at Hampden Park on the same day.

MANAGER: William Wilton
CAPTAIN: R.G. Campbell
TOP SCORER: Willie Reid
BIGGEST WIN: 7-0 v Hamilton, 25 November 1911, league
HIGHEST ATTENDANCE: 70,000 v Celtic, 1 January 1912, league
MAJOR TRANSFERS OUT: George Law to Leeds City

Final Scottish League Div 1 Table

		P	W	D	L	F	A	Pts
1	RANGERS	34	24	3	7	86	34	51
2	CELTIC	34	17	11	6	58	33	45
3	CLYDE	34	19	4	11	56	32	42
4	HEARTS	34	16	8	10	54	40	40
5	PARTICK T	34	16	8	10	47	40	40
6	MORTON	34	14	9	11	44	44	37
7	FALKIRK	34	15	6	13	46	43	36
8	DUNDEE	34	13	9	12	52	41	35
8	ABERDEEN	34	14	7	13	44	44	35
10	AIRDRIEONIANS	34	12	8	14	40	41	32
11	THIRD LANARK	34	12	7	15	40	57	31
12	HAMILTON A	34	11	8	15	32	44	30
13	HIBERNIAN	34	12	5	17	44	47	29
14	MOTHERWELL	34	11	5	18	34	44	27
14	RAITH R	34	9	9	16	39	59	27
16	KILMARNOCK	34	11	4	19	38	60	26
17	QUEEN'S PARK	34	8	9	17	29	53	25
18	ST MIRREN	34	7	10	17	32	59	24

Season 1912-13

Scottish League Division 1

DATE	OPPONENTS	SCORE	GOALSCORERS	ATTENDANCE
Aug 17	AIRDRIE	W 4-2	Montgomery, Hogg, Reid, Gordon	25,000
Aug 24	Hamilton A	W 2-0	Reid, A.Brown	18,000
Aug 31	DUNDEE	D 3-3	Reid 2, Hogg	40,000
Sep 7	St Mirren	W 3-0	Smith, Montgomery, Hogg	20,000
Sep 14	Motherwell	W 2-1	Bennett, Smith	20,000
Sep 21	HEARTS	L 2-4	Reid 2	50,000
Sep 30	KILMARNOCK	W 3-0	Parker, Hogg, Bowie	14,000
Oct 5	Aberdeen	W 3-1	Reid 2, A.Brown	20,000
Oct 19	Hibernian	W 1-0	Reid	16,000
Oct 26	Celtic	L 2-3	Reid 2	45,000
Nov 2	MORTON	D 1-1	Reid	18,000
Nov 9	Queen's Park	W 3-2	Reid, Bowie, Smith	10,000
Nov 16	THIRD LANARK	W 2-1	Reid, Bowie	20,000
Nov 23	CLYDE	W 3-1	Paterson, Reid, Bowie	18,000
Nov 30	Falkirk	L 0-2		15,000
Dec 7	Raith Rovers	D 2-2	Reid, Smith	12,000
Dec 14	ST MIRREN	W 2-1	Reid, Smith	12,000
Dec 21	Airdrie	L 0-3		7,000
Dec 28	ABERDEEN	W 3-1	Goodwin, Bowie, Parker (pen)	15,000
Jan 1	CELTIC	L 0-1		67,000
Jan 2	Partick Thistle	W 3-2	Bowie, A.Brown, Goodwin	25,000
Jan 4	HIBERNIAN	W 5-3	Parker 3, Paterson, A.Brown	20,000
Jan 11	MOTHERWELL	W 3-1	Parker 3	8,000
Jan 25	Morton	W 3-0	Goodwin, Paterson, Reid	15,000
Feb 1	RAITH ROVERS	W 4-0	Reid 2, Goodwin 2	8,000
Mar 1	Kilmarnock	W 3-2	Parker, Paterson	6,000
Mar 8	HAMILTON A	W 3-2	Goodwin, Reid, Bennett	12,000
Mar 15	Hearts	D 1-1	Logan	18,000
Mar 22	PARTICK THISTLE	W 2-0	Bennett, Paterson	12,000
Mar 24	Third Lanark	W 1-0	Hogg	25,000
Apr 5	QUEEN'S PARK	W 4-0	Parker 2, Paterson 2	10,000
Apr 15	Clyde	W 1-0	Reid	10,000
Apr 19	Dundee	D 0-0		12,000
Apr 26	FALKIRK	W 2-1	Goodwin, Bennett (pen)	16,000

Scottish Cup

Feb 8	Hamilton	(Rd2)	D 1-1	Reid	16,000
Feb 15	HAMILTON	(R)	W 2-0	Goodwin, Parker (pen)	37,000
Feb 22	FALKIRK	(Rd3)	L 1-3	Parker	48,000

League & Cup Appearances

PLAYER	LEAGUE	CUP COMPETITION S CUP	TOTAL
Bennett	22		22
Bowie	22	1	23
Brown A	6		6
Brown R	12	3	15
Campbell	22		22
Galt	27	3	30
Gibson	3		3
Goodwin	19	3	22
Gordon	28	3	31
Hempsey	17	3	20
Hendry	13		13
Hogg	16		16
Farrington	7		7
Lock	6		6
Logan	24	3	27
Montgomery	7		7
Muir	2		2
Ormond	24	3	27
Paterson	21	3	24
Parker	9	2	11
Ramsay	3		3
Reid	25	3	28
Riddell	1		1
Robertson	12		12
Smith	22	3	25
Waddell	4		4

Goalscorers

PLAYER	LEAGUE	CUP COMPETITION S CUP	TOTAL
Reid	22	1	23
Parker	12	2	14
Goodwin	7	1	8
Paterson	7		7
Bowie	6		6
Hogg	5		5
Smith	5		5
Bennett	4		4
Brown A	4		4
Montgomery	2		2
Gordon	1		1
Logan	1		1

Fact File

Rangers lost 5-1 to a Scotland XI at Ibrox on 6 January 1913 with a crowd of 35,000 turning up to watch Alec Smith's benefit match.

MANAGER: William Wilton

CAPTAIN: R.G. Campbell

TOP SCORER: Willie Reid

BIGGEST WIN: 4-0 v Raith Rovers, League, 1 February 1913; v Queen's Park, 5 April 1913, league

HIGHEST ATTENDANCE: 67,000 v Celtic, 1 January 1913, league

MAJOR TRANSFERS IN: Jimmy Logan from Aston Villa, John Hempsey from Morton

MAJOR TRANSFERS OUT: Billy Hogg to Dundee

Final Scottish League Div 1 Table

		P	W	D	L	F	A	Pts
1	RANGERS	34	24	5	5	76	41	53
2	CELTIC	34	22	5	7	53	28	49
3	HEARTS	34	17	7	10	71	43	41
3	AIRDRIEONIANS	34	15	11	8	64	46	41
5	FALKIRK	34	14	12	8	56	38	40
6	MOTHERWELL	34	12	13	9	47	39	37
6	ABERDEEN	34	14	9	11	47	40	37
6	HIBERNIAN	34	16	5	13	63	54	37
9	CLYDE	34	13	9	12	41	44	35
10	HAMILTON A	34	12	8	14	44	47	32
11	KILMARNOCK	34	10	11	13	37	54	31
12	ST MIRREN	34	10	10	14	50	60	30
13	MORTON	34	11	7	16	50	59	29
13	DUNDEE	34	8	13	13	33	46	29
15	THIRD LANARK	34	8	12	14	31	41	28
16	RAITH R	34	8	10	16	46	60	26
17	PARTICK T	34	10	4	20	40	55	24
18	QUEEN'S PARK	34	5	3	26	34	88	13

Season 1913-14

Scottish League Division 1

DATE	OPPONENTS	SCORE	GOALSCORERS	ATTENDANCE
Aug 16	Kilmarnock	W 6-1	Reid 2, Gordon, Paterson, Bowie, Bennett (pen)	9,000
Aug 23	ST MIRREN	W 2-1	Reid, Bowie	35,000
Aug 30	Hamilton A	W 1-0	Reid	20,000
Sep 6	ABERDEEN	W 5-1	Reid 2, Bennett, Bowie, Paterson	20,000
Sep 13	Hearts	L 1-2	Logan	12,000
Sep 15	Hibernian	W 3-0	Reid 2, Logan	12,000
Sep 20	DUNDEE	L 0-1		45,000
Sep 22	Aberdeen	D 0-0		18,000
Sep 29	QUEEN'S PARK	W 3-0	Reid, Hendry, Stewart	25,000
Oct 4	Morton	W 1-0	Duncan	18,000
Oct 18	Third Lanark	W 4-2	Logan, Bowie, Parker, Paterson	30,000
Oct 25	CELTIC	L 0-2		63,500
Nov 1	Raith Rovers	W 3-0	Bennett, Reid, Duncan	14,000
Nov 8	DUMBARTON	W 3-2	Parker, Bowie, Gordon (pen)	12,000
Nov 15	AIRDRIE	W 2-0	Reid, Gordon (pen)	20,000
Nov 22	Motherwell	L 0-1		16,000
Nov 29	Clyde	W 1-0	Reid	26,000
Dec 6	MORTON	W 1-0	Craig o.g.	25,000
Dec 13	FALKIRK	W 3-2	Bowie 2, Paterson	24,000
Dec 20	Dundee	W 2-0	Duncan, Stewart	18,000
Dec 27	HAMILTON A	W 3-0	Reid, Stewart, Duncan	6,000
Jan 1	Celtic	L 0-4		80,000
Jan 3	St Mirren	W 1-0	Fulton	16,000
Jan 5	PARTICK THISTLE	D 0-0		10,000
Jan 10	Ayr United	W 2-1	Reid, Gordon	10,000
Jan 17	MOTHERWELL	D 0-0		25,000
Jan 31	RAITH ROVERS	W 4-0	Reid 2, Stewart 2	10,000
Feb 14	Airdrie	W 3-0	Reid, Cairns, Paterson	15,000
Feb 28	Queen's Park	W 6-0	Reid 4, Stewart, Smith	30,000
Mar 7	CLYDE	W 2-1	Paterson	30,000
Mar 14	Dumbarton	W 3-0	Stewart 3	8,000
Mar 21	KILMARNOCK	W 1-0	Hendry	18,000
Mar 25	AYR UNITED	W 5-2	Reid 3, Duncan, Bennett	10,000
Apr 1	Falkirk	L 1-4	Smith	5,000
Apr 7	HIBERNIAN	D 1-1	Cairns	4,000
Apr 13	Partick Thistle	D 1-1	Smith	12,000
Apr 18	THIRD LANARK	W 2-0	Bennett, Logan	12,000
Apr 25	HEARTS	W 3-2	Smith 2, Logan	10,000

Scottish Cup

Feb 7	ALLOA	W 5-0	Stewart 3, A.Brown, Bowie	8,000
Feb 21	Hibernian	L 1-2	Reid	30,000

League & Cup Appearances

PLAYER	LEAGUE	CUP COMPETITION S CUP	TOTAL
Bennett	27		27
Bowie	28	2	30
Brown A	10	2	12
Brown R	10		10
Cairns	8		8
Campbell	17	1	18
Duncan	21	2	23
Ferguson	1		1
Fulton	14	2	16
Galt	17	1	18
Glenn	4		4
Goodwin	1		1
Gordon	31	2	33
Hempsey	22		22
Hendry	29	1	30
Lock	12	2	14
Logan	31	2	33
Muir	17		17
Ormond	17	1	18
Parker	3		3
Paterson	32		32
Reid	33	2	35
Scott	3		3
Smith	11		11
Stewart	19	2	21

Goalscorers

PLAYER	LEAGUE	CUP COMPETITION S CUP	TOTAL
Reid	24	1	25
Stewart	10	3	13
Bowie	7	1	8
Paterson	6		6
Bennett	5		5
Duncan	5		5
Logan	5		5
Smith	5		5
Gordon	4		4
Cairns	2		2
Hendry	2		2
Parker	2		2
Brown A		1	1
Fulton	1		1
Opps' o.g.s	1		1

Fact File

Jimmy Gordon captained Scotland to a 3-1 win over England at Hampden on 4 April 1914 with his Rangers team-mate Willie Reid scoring the Scots' third goal.

MANAGER: William Wilton
CAPTAIN: R.G. Campbell
TOP SCORER: Willie Reid
BIGGEST WIN: 6-0 v Queen's Park, 28 February 1914, league
HIGHEST ATTENDANCE: 80,000 v Celtic, 1 January 1914, league
MAJOR TRANSFERS IN: Jimmy Stewart from Newcastle United, Scott Duncan from Newcastle United, Tommy Cairns from St Johnstone
MAJOR TRANSFERS OUT: James Galt to Everton

Final Scottish League Div 1 Table

		P	W	D	L	F	A	Pts
1	CELTIC	38	30	5	3	81	14	65
2	RANGERS	38	27	5	6	79	31	59
3	HEARTS	38	23	8	7	70	29	54
3	MORTON	38	26	2	10	76	51	54
5	FALKIRK	38	20	9	9	69	51	49
6	AIRDRIEONIANS	38	18	12	8	72	43	48
7	DUNDEE	38	19	5	14	64	53	43
8	THIRD LANARK	38	13	10	15	42	51	36
9	CLYDE	38	11	11	16	44	44	33
9	AYR U	38	13	7	18	56	72	33
11	RAITH R	38	13	6	19	56	57	32
12	KILMARNOCK	38	11	9	18	48	68	31
13	HIBERNIAN	38	12	6	20	58	75	30
13	ABERDEEN	38	10	10	18	38	55	30
15	PARTICK T	38	10	9	19	37	51	29
15	QUEEN'S PARK	38	10	9	19	52	84	29
17	HAMILTON A	38	11	6	21	49	66	28
17	MOTHERWELL	38	11	6	21	46	65	28
19	DUMBARTON	38	10	7	21	45	87	27
20	ST MIRREN	38	8	6	24	38	73	22

Season 1914-15

Scottish League Division 1

DATE	OPPONENTS	SCORE	GOALSCORERS	ATTENDANCE
Aug 15	HAMILTON A	W 1-0	Reid	20,000
Aug 22	Aberdeen	W 2-0	Reid, Paterson	15,000
Aug 29	KILMARNOCK	W 2-1	Reid, Bennett	15,000
Sep 5	Falkirk	W 3-1	Reid, Cairns, Bennett	10,000
Sep 12	Dundee	D 1-1	Reid	15,000
Sep 19	HEARTS	L 1-2	Bowie	41,000
Sep 28	HIBERNIAN	W 4-2	Bowie, Reid, Cairns, Paterson	14,000
Oct 3	MORTON	L 0-2		16,000
Oct 10	Raith Rovers	W 2-1	Bennett, Gordon	7,000
Oct 17	Ayr United	L 0-2		13,000
Oct 24	RAITH ROVERS	L 1-2	Cairns	14,000
Oct 31	Celtic	L 1-2	Reid	35,000
Nov 7	QUEEN'S PARK	W 4-1	Reid 2, Gordon 2	20,000
Nov 14	Dumbarton	D 1-1	Reid	10,000
Nov 21	Airdrie	W 2-1	Duncan, Reid	8,000
Nov 28	THIRD LANARK	W 3-0	Reid 2, Gordon	6,000
Dec 5	ST MIRREN	W 5-0	Logan, Cairns, Reid, Bowie, Paterson	8,000
Dec 12	Kilmarnock	W 1-0	Cairns	5,000
Dec 19	MOTHERWELL	W 5-0	Gordon 2, Bowie, Reid, Paterson	6,000
Dec 26	Third Lanark	D 1-1	Reid	6,000
Jan 1	CELTIC	W 2-1	Bowie, Reid	50,000
Jan 2	Partick Thistle	L 1-3	Duncan	18,000
Jan 4	AIRDRIE	L 0-5		12,000
Jan 9	CLYDE	L 1-2	Cairns	8,000
Jan 16	Morton	W 1-0	Reid	10,000
Jan 23	DUMBARTON	W 1-0	Cairns	8,000
Jan 30	Hibernian	W 2-1	Anderson, Gordon (pen)	8,000
Feb 6	FALKIRK	W 3-0	Cairns 2, Reid	8,000
Feb 13	AYR UNITED	L 1-3	Reid	10,000
Feb 20	Hearts	W 4-3	Reid 3, Cairns	15,000
Feb 27	Motherwell	W 4-2	Reid 2, Cairns 2	8,000
Mar 6	DUNDEE	W 2-1	Cairns, Paterson	12,000
Mar 13	Clyde	W 2-1	Cairns, Paterson	12,000
Mar 27	ABERDEEN	D 1-1	Hendry	10,000
Apr 3	Hamilton A	L 3-4	Bowie, Cairns, Paterson	6,000
Apr 5	PARTICK THISTLE	L 0-1		12,000
Apr 10	St Mirren	W 2-0	Reid 2	12,000
Apr 24	Queen's Park	W 4-0	Cunningham 2, Reid, Gordon	10,000

League Appearances

PLAYER	TOTAL
Anderson	3
Baird	1
Bennett	17
Bowie	36
Brown R	15
Cairns	36
Craig	37
Cunningham	3
Duncan	19
Gordon	30
Hempsey	12
Hendry	17
Kelso	22
Lock	26
Logan	20
Manderson	1
Muir	15
Paterson	30
Pursell	31
Reid	37
Smith	7
Thomson	3

Goalscorers

PLAYER	TOTAL
Reid	28
Cairns	15
Gordon	8
Paterson	7
Bowie	6
Bennett	3
Cunningham	2
Duncan	2
Anderson	1
Hendry	1
Logan	1

Fact File

Alec Smith made his final league appearance for Rangers against Raith Rovers on 24 October 1914, almost 20 years since his debut in November 1894.

MANAGER: William Wilton

CAPTAIN: Jimmy Gordon

TOP SCORER: Willie Reid

BIGGEST WIN: 5-0 v St Mirren, 5 December 1914, league; v Motherwell, 19 December 1914, league

HIGHEST ATTENDANCE: 50,000 v Celtic, 1 January 1915, league

MAJOR TRANSFERS IN: Andy Cunningham from Kilmarnock, Bert Manderson from Linfield, Peter Pursell from Queen's Park, Tommy Kelso from Dundee

MAJOR TRANSFERS OUT: R.G. Campbell to Kilmarnock

Final Scottish League Div 1 Table

		P	W	D	L	F	A	Pts
1	CELTIC	38	30	5	3	91	25	65
2	HEARTS	38	27	7	4	83	32	61
3	RANGERS	38	23	4	11	74	47	50
4	MORTON	38	18	12	8	74	48	48
4	AYR U	38	20	8	10	55	40	48
6	FALKIRK	38	16	7	15	48	48	39
7	HAMILTON A	38	16	6	16	60	55	38
7	PARTICK T	38	15	8	15	56	58	38
9	ST MIRREN	38	14	8	16	56	65	36
10	AIRDRIEONIANS	38	14	7	17	54	60	35
10	HIBERNIAN	38	12	11	15	59	66	35
12	KILMARNOCK	38	15	4	19	55	59	34
12	DUMBARTON	38	13	8	17	51	66	34
14	ABERDEEN	38	11	11	16	39	52	33
14	DUNDEE	38	12	9	17	43	61	33
16	THIRD LANARK	38	10	12	16	51	57	32
17	CLYDE	38	12	6	20	44	59	30
17	MOTHERWELL	38	10	10	18	49	66	30
19	RAITH R	38	9	10	19	53	68	28
20	QUEEN'S PARK	38	4	5	29	27	90	13

Season 1915-16

Scottish League Division 1

DATE	OPPONENTS	SCORE	GOALSCORERS	ATTENDANCE
Aug 21	Dumbarton	W 3-1	Reid 2, Cunningham	6,000
Aug 28	THIRD LANARK	W 4-0	Cunningham 2, Reid 2	16,000
Sep 4	Kilmarnock	W 3-0	Reid, Cunningham, Cairns	8,000
Sep 18	AYR UNITED	W 5-2	Reid 2, Duncan, Cairns, Cunningham	16,000
Oct 2	Airdrie	W 1-0	Cunningham	7,000
Oct 16	HEARTS	L 0-4		15,000
Oct 23	Raith Rovers	W 3-1	Reid 2, Hendry	3,000
Oct 30	CELTIC	W 3-0	Duncan, Reid, Paterson	45,000
Nov 6	Queen's Park	W 6-0	Cairns 2, Cunningham 2 (1 pen) Fleming, Duncan	14,000
Nov 13	HAMILTON A	W 3-0	Cunningham 2 (1 pen), Duncan	15,000
Nov 20	Falkirk	L 0-2		3,000
Nov 27	HIBERNIAN	W 4-2	Cunningham 3, Paterson	7,000
Dec 4	Morton	L 0-2		10,000
Dec 11	ST MIRREN	W 4-0	Gordon 2, Cunningham 2	6,000
Dec 18	Clyde	W 2-0	Reid, Cairns	12,000
Dec 25	FALKIRK	W 1-0	Paterson	10,000
Jan 1	Celtic	D 2-2	Cunningham, Duncan	40,000
Jan 3	PARTICK THISTLE	L 0-1		20,000
Jan 8	MOTHERWELL	W 4-1	Reid 3, Cairns	10,000
Jan 15	Dundee	L 0-2		10,000
Jan 22	KILMARNOCK	W 3-1	Bennett 2, Gordon	4,000
Jan 29	Motherwell	D 2-2	Cairns, Reid	10,000
Feb 5	MORTON	W 1-0	Cairns	25,000
Feb 12	Hearts	W 2-1	Gordon 2 (1 pen)	15,000
Feb 19	ABERDEEN	W 4-0	Cunningham 2 (1 pen), Reid, Cairns	15,000
Feb 26	Ayr United	L 0-1		7,000
Mar 4	AIRDRIE	W 3-0	Gordon, Duncan, Reid	12,000
Mar 11	Hibernian	W 3-2	Paterson 2, Reid	5,000
Mar 18	Third Lanark	W 1-0	Branscombe	22,000
Apr 1	Hamilton A	W 1-0	Sneddon	10,000
Apr 8	RAITH ROVERS	W 3-0	Gordon 2, Paterson	10,000
Apr 10	DUNDEE	W 3-2	Lister, Cairns, Branscombe	5,000
Apr 15	Partick Thistle	L 2-5	Cairns 2	30,000
Apr 17	St Mirren	D 1-1	Paterson	4,000
Apr 20	DUMBARTON	D 2-2	Duncan, Branscombe	3,000
Apr 22	CLYDE	D 2-2	Duncan, Branscombe	5,000
Apr 24	QUEEN'S PARK	W 6-0	Reid 3, Duncan 2, Branscombe	6,000
Apr 29	Aberdeen	D 0-0		6,000

League Appearances

PLAYER	TOTAL
Ballantyne	1
Bennett	17
Bone	2
Bowie	26
Brander	3
Branscombe	7
Cairns	34
Craig	5
Cunningham	20
Duncan	32
Fleming	4
Gordon	31
Hempsey	21
Hendry	18
Lister	5
Lock	16
Logan	26
McCrae	3
Manderson	32
Muir	30
Parker	1
Paterson	31
Pursell	20
Reid	25
Sneddon	5
Taylor	1

Goalscorers

PLAYER	TOTAL
Reid	21
Cunningham	18
Cairns	12
Duncan	10
Gordon	8
Paterson	7
Branscombe	5
Bennett	2
Fleming	1
Hendry	1
Lister	1
Sneddon	1

Fact File

A crowd of 70,000 saw Rangers lose 2-1 to Celtic in the final of the Glasgow Cup at Hampden on 9 October 1915.

MANAGER: William Wilton
CAPTAIN: Jimmy Gordon
TOP SCORER: Willie Reid
BIGGEST WIN: 6-0 v Queen's Park, 6 November 1915, league;
v Queen's Park, 24 April 1916, league
HIGHEST ATTENDANCE: 45,000 v Celtic, 30 October 1915, league

Final Scottish League Div 1 Table

		P	W	D	L	F	A	Pts
1	CELTIC	38	32	3	3	116	23	67
2	RANGERS	38	25	6	7	87	39	56
3	MORTON	37	22	7	8	86	35	51
4	AYR U	38	20	8	10	72	45	48
5	PARTICK T	38	19	8	11	65	41	46
5	HEARTS	37	20	6	11	66	45	46
7	HAMILTON A	38	19	3	16	68	76	41
8	DUNDEE	38	18	4	16	56	49	40
9	DUMBARTON	38	13	11	14	54	64	37
10	KILMARNOCK	38	12	11	15	46	49	35
11	ABERDEEN	38	11	12	15	51	64	34
12	FALKIRK	38	12	9	17	45	61	33
13	ST MIRREN	38	13	4	21	50	67	30
13	MOTHERWELL	38	11	8	19	55	82	30
13	AIRDRIEONIANS	38	11	8	19	44	74	30
16	THIRD LANARK	38	9	11	18	40	56	29
16	CLYDE	38	11	7	20	49	71	29
18	QUEEN'S PARK	38	11	6	21	53	100	28
19	HIBERNIAN	38	9	7	22	44	71	25
20	RAITH R	38	9	5	24	30	65	23

MORTON AND HEARTS PLAYED ONLY ONCE.

Season 1916-17

Scottish League Division 1

DATE	OPPONENTS	SCORE	GOALSCORERS	ATTENDANCE
Aug 19	DUNDEE	W 3-0	C.Duncan 2, S.Duncan	12,000
Aug 26	Hearts	W 3-1	Cairns, S.Duncan, Archibald	8,000
Sep 2	DUMBARTON	W 6-0	C.Duncan 3, Logan, Cairns, S.Duncan (pen)	10,000
Sep 16	KILMARNOCK	W 3-0	S.Duncan 2 (1 pen), C.Duncan	10,000
Sep 30	ST MIRREN	W 1-0	Cairns	12,000
Oct 7	Ayr United	W 3-1	Paterson 2, S.Duncan	6,000
Oct 14	MOTHERWELL	W 2-1	Cairns 2	5,000
Oct 21	Third Lanark	D 1-1	Paterson	30,000
Oct 28	Celtic	D 0-0		40,000
Nov 4	MORTON	L 0-1		30,000
Nov 11	Hibernian	D 0-0		10,000
Nov 18	CLYDE	W 1-0	S.Duncan	8,000
Nov 25	Raith Rovers	W 4-1	Archibald 2, Riddell, Bennett	5,000
Dec 2	FALKIRK	W 3-1	S.Duncan 2, Cairns	7,000
Dec 9	Airdrie	L 0-2		8,000
Dec 16	HIBERNIAN	W 5-1	Martin 2, Manderson, C.Duncan, Dornan o.g.	10,000
Dec 23	Motherwell	L 1-2	Blair (pen)	8,000
Dec 30	AIRDRIE	W 3-0	C.Duncan 2, Lawson	12,000
Jan 1	CELTIC	D 0-0		50,000
Jan 2	Partick Thistle	W 1-0	Martin	12,000
Jan 6	HEARTS	W 1-0	Martin	12,000
Jan 13	Clyde	W 1-0	Riddell	15,000
Jan 20	PARTICK THISTLE	W 3-0	C.Duncan 2, Riddell	
Jan 27	HAMILTON A	W 2-1	Blair (pen), Pursell	8,000
Feb 3	Aberdeen	L 1-3	C.Duncan	6,000
Feb 10	AYR UNITED	W 1-0	Manderson	12,000
Feb 17	Dumbarton	W 3-0	Bell, Cairns, Croot	5,000
Feb 24	St Mirren	D 1-1	Cairns	12,000
Mar 3	ABERDEEN	W 1-0	Gordon	8,000
Mar 10	Morton	L 0-1		7,000
Mar 17	Falkirk	W 2-0	Cairns 2	5,000
Mar 24	RAITH ROVERS	W 4-3	Livingston 3, Cairns	5,000
Mar 31	Kilmarnock	L 1-4	Cairns	5,000
Apr 7	THIRD LANARK	L 0-2		15,000
Apr 9	Queen's Park	W 4-1	C.Duncan 2, Gray, Rutherford	10,000
Apr 21	Hamilton A	L 1-3	C.Duncan	7,000
Apr 21	QUEEN'S PARK	W 1-0	Harris	7,000
Apr 28	Dundee	L 1-2	Blair (pen)	9,000

League Appearances

PLAYER	TOTAL
Anderson	2
Archibald	12
Bell	14
Bennett	7
Blair	35
Bowie	20
Cairns	24
Croot	9
Dick	1
Duncan C	25
Duncan S	28
Gordon	6
Gray	2
Hamilton	1
Harris	1
Hempsey	21
Hendry	6
Law	4
Lawson	24
Livingston	5
Lock	16
Logan	12
McKenna	24
Manderson	38
Martin	21
Paterson	5
Phillip	1
Pursell	30
Riddell	23
Rutherford	1

Goalscorers

PLAYER	TOTAL
Duncan C	15
Cairns	12
Duncan S	9
Martin	4
Archibald	3
Blair	3
Livingston	3
Paterson	3
Riddell	3
Manderson	2
Bell	1
Bennett	1
Croot	1
Gordon	1
Gray	1
Harris	1
Lawson	1
Logan	1
Pursell	1
Rutherford	1
Opps' o.gs.	1

Final Scottish League Div 1 Table

		P	W	D	L	F	A	Pts
1	CELTIC	38	27	10	1	79	17	64
2	MORTON	38	24	6	8	72	39	54
3	RANGERS	38	24	5	9	68	32	53
4	AIRDRIEONIANS	38	21	8	9	71	38	50
5	THIRD LANARK	38	19	11	8	53	37	49
6	KILMARNOCK	38	18	7	13	69	46	43
7	ST MIRREN	38	15	10	13	49	43	40
8	MOTHERWELL	38	16	6	16	57	59	38
9	PARTICK T	38	14	7	17	44	43	35
9	DUMBARTON	38	12	11	15	56	73	35
9	HAMILTON A	38	13	9	16	54	73	35
12	FALKIRK	38	12	10	16	58	57	34
12	CLYDE	38	10	14	14	41	53	34
14	HEARTS	38	14	4	20	44	59	32
15	AYR U	38	12	7	19	47	59	31
16	DUNDEE	38	13	4	21	58	71	30
16	HIBERNIAN	38	10	10	18	57	72	30
18	QUEEN'S PARK	38	11	7	20	56	81	29
19	RAITH R	38	8	7	23	42	91	23
20	ABERDEEN	38	7	7	24	36	68	21

Fact File

Willie Reid, Rangers' leading scorer for the previous six seasons, missed the whole of the 1916-17 campaign while on active military service.

MANAGER: William Wilton

CAPTAIN: Tommy Cairns

TOP SCORER: Charlie Duncan

BIGGEST WIN: 6-0 v Dumbarton, 2 September 1916, league

HIGHEST ATTENDANCE: 50,000 v Celtic, 1 January 1917, league

MAJOR TRANSFERS IN: Sandy Archibald from Raith Rovers, Tommy Muirhead from Hibernian, James Blair from Sheffield Wednesday

MAJOR TRANSFERS OUT: Alec Bennett to Dumbarton

Season 1917-18

Scottish League Division 1

DATE	OPPONENTS	SCORE	GOALSCORERS	ATTENDANCE
Aug 18	Kilmarnock	W 1-0	McDermid	10,000
Aug 25	THIRD LANARK	W 4-2	Cunningham 3 (1 pen), Cairns	18,000
Sep 1	Partick Thistle	L 0-2		20,000
Sep 15	HIBERNIAN	W 3-0	Bowie, Cairns, Gordon o.g.	10,000
Sep 24	QUEEN'S PARK	W 3-0	Muirhead 2, Lawson	12,000
Sep 29	Dumbarton	W 4-2	Cairns 2, Muirhead 2	8,000
Oct 13	Morton	D 1-1	Brown	10,000
Oct 20	CELTIC	L 1-2	Bowie	45,000
Oct 27	St Mirren	D 0-0		10,000
Nov 3	AYR UNITED	D 0-0		8,000
Nov 10	Hearts	W 3-0	Gordon 2, Archibald	12,000
Nov 17	AIRDRIE	W 4-0	Brown 3, Cairns	12,000
Nov 24	Queen's Park	W 3-2	Gordon (pen), Archibald, Brown	12,000
Dec 1	DUMBARTON	W 2-1	Cairns 2	7,000
Dec 8	Hamilton A	W 2-1	Reid 2	9,000
Dec 15	FALKIRK	W 4-1	Brown 2, Archibald, Bowie	8,000
Dec 22	Third Lanark	W 1-0	Muirhead	12,000
Dec 29	ST MIRREN	W 2-0	Bowie, Cairns	12,000
Jan 1	Celtic	D 0-0		55,000
Jan 2	PARTICK THISTLE	W 1-0	Blair (pen)	18,000
Jan 5	Clydebank	D 1-1	Archibald	14,700
Jan 12	HEARTS	W 2-0	Gordon 2	8,000
Jan 26	Ayr United	W 2-0	Cairns, McDermid	5,000
Feb 2	MORTON	W 4-2	Gordon 4	25,000
Feb 9	Hibernian	W 1-0	McDermid	8,000
Feb 16	Clyde	W 3-0	Brown 2, Cairns	8,000
Feb 23	Motherwell	D 0-0		12,000
Mar 2	KILMARNOCK	W 3-0	Archibald 2, McCulloch	20,000
Mar 9	Falkirk	L 0-2		8,000
Mar 16	HAMILTON A	W 4-2	McDermid, Hart, Archibald, Martin	10,000
Mar 23	Airdrie	W 2-1	Hart, Cairns	10,000
Mar 30	CLYDEBANK	W 1-0	Cunningham	10,000
Apr 6	MOTHERWELL	W 2-1	Gordon 2	25,000
Apr 13	CLYDE	W 2-1	Archibald, Bowie	10,000

League Appearances

PLAYER	TOTAL
Archibald	34
Bell	1
Blair	27
Bowie	33
Brown	11
Cairns	34
Cunningham	4
Dick	1
Dixon	32
Gordon	16
Hart	3
Hempsey	25
Lawson	5
Lock	7
McCulloch	2
McDermid	28
McKenna	12
McQueen	12
Manderson	29
Martin	18
Muirhead	7
Pursell	24
Reid	1
Riddell	2
Singleton	2
Young	4

Goalscorers

PLAYER	TOTAL
Cairns	11
Gordon	11
Brown	9
Archibald	8
Bowie	5
Muirhead	5
Cunningham	4
McDermid	4
Hart	2
Reid	2
Blair	1
Lawson	1
McCulloch	1
Martin	1
Opps' o.gs.	1

Fact File

King George V attended an investiture ceremony for war heroes held at Ibrox Stadium on 18 September 1917.

MANAGER: William Wilton

CAPTAIN: Tommy Cairns

TOP SCORERS: Tommy Cairns and Jimmy Gordon

BIGGEST WIN: 4-0 v Airdrie, 17 November 1917, league

HIGHEST ATTENDANCE: 55,000 v Celtic, 1 January 1918, league

MAJOR TRANSFERS IN: Arthur Dixon from Oldham

Final Scottish League Div 1 Table

		P	W	D	L	F	A	PTS
1	RANGERS	34	25	6	3	66	24	56
2	CELTIC	34	24	7	3	66	26	55
3	KILMARNOCK	34	19	5	10	69	41	43
3	MORTON	34	17	9	8	53	42	43
5	MOTHERWELL	34	16	9	9	70	51	41
6	PARTICK T	34	14	12	8	51	37	40
7	QUEEN'S PARK	34	14	6	14	64	63	34
7	DUMBARTON	34	13	8	13	48	49	34
9	CLYDEBANK	34	14	5	15	55	56	33
10	HEARTS	34	14	4	16	41	58	32
11	ST MIRREN	34	11	7	16	42	50	29
12	HAMILTON A	34	11	6	17	52	63	28
13	THIRD LANARK	34	10	7	17	56	62	27
13	FALKIRK	34	9	9	16	38	58	27
15	AIRDRIEONIANS	34	10	6	18	46	58	26
16	HIBERNIAN	34	8	9	17	42	57	25
17	CLYDE	34	9	2	23	37	72	20
18	AYR U	34	5	9	20	32	61	19

Season 1918-19

Scottish League Division 1

DATE	OPPONENTS	SCORE	GOALSCORERS	ATTENDANCE
Aug 17	FALKIRK	W 1-0	McLean (pen)	30,000
Aug 24	Hearts	W 4-1	McLean 3, Cairns	15,000
Aug 31	ST MIRREN	W 2-0	Aitken, McLean	12,000
Sep 7	Hamilton A	W 3-0	McLean 2, Manderson	12,000
Sep 14	PARTICK THISTLE	W 2-0	McLean 2	25,000
Sep 28	AYR UNITED	W 6-2	Bowie 3, Hart 2, Cairns	10,000
Sep 30	Queen's Park	W 2-0	Hart, Cairns	25,000
Oct 12	DUMBARTON	W 3-0	McLean 2, Aitken	12,000
Oct 19	Celtic	W 3-0	Cairns, Bowie, McDermid	36,000
Oct 26	MOTHERWELL	D 0-0		22,000
Nov 2	Third Lanark	W 2-1	Bowie, McLean	25,000
Nov 9	CLYDE	W 3-0	Cairns 2, McLean	20,000
Nov 16	Airdrie	D 0-0		7,000
Nov 23	Morton	L 0-1		10,000
Dec 7	HIBERNIAN	W 5-1	Bowie 3, McLean, Cairns	12,000
Dec 14	Clydebank	W 5-0	McLean 3, Cairns, Lawson	20,000
Dec 21	KILMARNOCK	W 8-0	McLean 4, Bowie 2, Cairns, Lawson	15,000
Dec 28	Motherwell	W 1-0	Bowie	20,000
Jan 1	CELTIC	D 1-1	Bowie	65,000
Jan 2	Partick Thistle	L 0-1		30,000
Jan 4	AIRDRIE	W 2-1	Blair 2 (2 pens)	18,000
Jan 11	Kilmarnock	L 0-1		10,000
Jan 18	QUEEN'S PARK	W 4-0	Cunningham 3, Gordon	20,000
Jan 25	Hibernian	W 2-1	Archibald, Gordon	12,000
Feb 1	Dumbarton	W 2-0	Cairns, McLean	10,000
Feb 8	MORTON	W 1-0	McLean	40,000
Feb 15	St Mirren	D 2-2	Cairns, Manderson	15,000
Feb 22	CLYDEBANK	W 3-0	Brown 3	14,000
Mar 1	HEARTS	W 3-2	Brown, Archibald, Cunningham	35,000
Mar 8	HAMILTON A	W 3-0	Archibald, Brown, Dixon	15,000
Mar 22	Ayr United	D 1-1	Blair (pen)	12,000
Apr 12	Falkirk	W 4-0	Gordon 2, McLean, Bowie	12,000
Apr 21	THIRD LANARK	W 4-0	McLean 2, Dixon, Gordon	15,000
May 10	Clyde	W 4-0	McLean 3, Bowie	35,000

League Appearances

PLAYER	TOTAL
Aitken	21
Archibald	15
Blair	29
Bowie	26
Brown	9
Cairns	28
Cunningham	15
Dixon	34
Donnachie	5
Duncan S	1
Gordon	16
Hart	3
Hempsey	29
Lawson	9
Lock	4
McDermid	7
McLean	24
McQueen	7
Manderson	30
Miller	1
Pursell	23
Riddell	4
Walls	34

Goalscorers

PLAYER	TOTAL
McLean	29
Bowie	14
Cairns	11
Brown	5
Gordon	5
Cunningham	4
Archibald	3
Blair	3
Hart	3
Aitken	2
Dixon	2
Lawson	2
Manderson	2
McDermid	1

Fact File

In the Victory Cup, a one-off tournament to mark the end of the First World War, Rangers lost 1-0 to Airdrie at Broomfield in the quarter-finals on 29 March 1919.

MANAGER: William Wilton

CAPTAIN: Tommy Cairns

TOP SCORER: David McLean

BIGGEST WIN: 8-0 v Kilmarnock, 21 December 1918, league

HIGHEST ATTENDANCE: 65,000 v Celtic, 1 January 1919, league

MAJOR TRANSFERS IN: David McLean from Third Lanark, James Walls from Baillieston, William Aitken from Queen's Park

MAJOR TRANSFERS OUT: James Blair to Sheffield Wednesday

Final Scottish League Div 1 Table

		P	W	D	L	F	A	Pts
1	CELTIC	34	26	6	2	71	22	58
2	RANGERS	34	26	5	3	86	16	57
3	MORTON	34	18	11	5	76	40	47
4	PARTICK T	34	17	7	10	62	43	41
5	MOTHERWELL	34	14	10	10	51	40	38
5	AYR U	34	15	8	11	62	53	38
7	HEARTS	34	14	9	11	59	52	37
7	QUEEN'S PARK	34	15	5	14	59	57	35
8	KILMARNOCK	34	14	7	13	61	59	35
10	CLYDEBANK	34	12	8	14	54	65	32
10	ST MIRREN	34	10	12	12	43	55	32
12	THIRD LANARK	34	11	9	14	60	62	31
13	AIRDRIEONIANS	34	9	11	14	45	54	29
14	HAMILTON A	34	11	5	18	49	75	27
15	DUMBARTON	34	7	8	19	31	58	22
16	FALKIRK	34	6	8	20	46	73	20
16	CLYDE	34	7	6	21	45	75	20
18	HIBERNIAN	34	5	3	26	30	91	13

Season 1919-20

Scottish League Division 1

DATE	OPPONENTS	SCORE	GOALSCORERS	ATTENDANCE
Aug 16	Airdrie	W 1-0	Bowie	12,000
Aug 23	ABERDEEN	W 3-2	Cunningham 2, Reid	22,000
Aug 26	ALBION ROVERS	W 3-0	Reid 2, Bowie	10,000
Aug 30	St Mirren	W 4-0	Bowie 2, Muirhead, Cairns	20,000
Sep 9	RAITH ROVERS	W 3-2	Archibald, Cunningham, Paterson	12,000
Sep 13	Clyde	D 0-0		12,000
Sep 15	Kilmarnock	W 7-1	Gordon 2 (1 pen), Cunningham 2, Paterson, Bowie, Cairns	15,000
Sep 20	DUMBARTON	W 4-0	Gordon 3, Muirhead	10,000
Sep 27	Motherwell	L 0-1		20,000
Sep 29	HEARTS	W 3-0	Reid 2, Archibald (pen)	40,000
Oct 4	KILMARNOCK	W 5-0	Reid 2, Paterson, Archibald, Bowie	15,000
Oct 11	Raith Rovers	W 2-1	Gordon (pen), Archibald	15,000
Oct 18	CELTIC	W 3-0	Cunningham 2, Paterson	76,000
Oct 25	Dundee	W 2-0	Cunningham 2	30,000
Nov 1	THIRD LANARK	W 6-1	Cunningham 3, Cairns, Paterson, McCormack o.g.	20,000
Nov 8	Partick Thistle	W 2-1	Cunningham, Cairns	45,000
Nov 22	Queen's Park	D 0-0		45,000
Nov 29	Albion Rovers	W 4-0	Cunningham 2, Cairns, Bowie	16,000
Dec 6	HIBERNIAN	W 7-0	Cunningham 4, Muirhead, Archibald, Cairns	14,000
Dec 13	Clydebank	D 0-0		20,000
Dec 20	HAMILTON A	W 4-1	Cunningham 2, Archibald, Muirhead	14,000
Dec 27	Ayr United	W 3-0	Bowie, Muirhead, Cairns	10,000
Jan 1	Celtic	D 1-1	Muirhead	80,000
Jan 3	FALKIRK	W 3-1	Cairns 2, Gordon (pen)	25,000
Jan 5	PARTICK THISTLE	D 2-2	Muirhead, Paterson	15,000
Jan 10	Hamilton A	W 2-1	Bowie, Cairns	10,000
Jan 17	ST MIRREN	W 3-1	Archibald 2, Paterson	10,000
Jan 31	Falkirk	W 3-0	Paterson, Archibald, Gordon	12,000
Feb 14	Morton	W 2-0	Reid, Muirhead	20,000
Feb 28	CLYDE	W 1-0	Walls	20,000
Mar 16	MOTHERWELL	D 0-0		20,000
Mar 20	Aberdeen	W 2-0	Paterson, Walls	24,000
Apr 3	AIRDRIE	W 3-2	Cairns 2, Henderson	25,000
Apr 5	CLYDEBANK	L 1-2	Muirhead	25,000
Apr 10	Hearts	D 0-0		24,000
Apr 13	AYR UNITED	W 2-1	Cunningham, McDonald	15,000
Apr 17	QUEEN'S PARK	W 3-1	Cunningham (pen), Henderson, Muirhead	15,000
Apr 21	Hibernian	D 1-1	Meiklejohn	12,000
Apr 24	DUNDEE	W 6-1	Gordon 2, Bowie 2, Cairns, Paterson	25,000
Apr 27	Third Lanark	W 2-0	Meiklejohn, Bowie	35,000
Apr 28	Dumbarton	D 0-0		6,000
May 1	MORTON	W 3-1	Archibald 2, Paterson	30,000

Scottish Cup

Jan 24	DUMBARTON	(Rd1) D 0-0		28,000
Jan 27	DUMBARTON	(R) W 1-0	Cairns	28,000
Feb 7	ARBROATH	(Rd2) W 5-0	Muirhead 2, Archibald, Bowie, Cunningham	25,000
Feb 21	BROXBURN	(Rd3) W 3-0	Muirhead, Cunningham, Dixon	16,000
Mar 6	CELTIC	(QF) W 1-0	Muirhead	85,000
Mar 27	Albion Rovers*	(SF) D 1-1	Paterson	32,000
Mar 31	Albion Rovers*	(R) D 0-0		40,000
Apr 7	Albion Rovers*	(2R) L 0-2		65,000

*Played at Parkhead.

MANAGER: William Wilton

CAPTAIN: Tommy Cairns

TOP SCORER: Andy Cunningham

BIGGEST WIN: 7-0 v Hibernian, 6 December 1919, league

HIGHEST ATTENDANCE: 85,000 v Celtic, 6 March 1920, Scottish Cup,

MAJOR TRANSFERS IN: David Meiklejohn from Maryhill, Willie Robb from Armadale, George Henderson from Forfar

MAJOR TRANSFERS OUT: Peter Pursell to Port Vale, James Paterson to Arsenal, Willie Reid to Albion Rovers, William Aitken to Newcastle United

League & Cup Appearances

PLAYER	LEAGUE	CUP COMPETITION S CUP	TOTAL
Cairns	35	8	43
Cunningham	39	6	45
Dixon	30	6	36
Gordon	33	7	40
Henderson	6	2	8
Johnston	1		1
Lock	35	8	43
Low	1		1
McDonald	3		3
Manderson	40	8	48
Meiklejohn	10	1	11
Muirhead	34	6	40
Paterson	36	8	44
Reid	9		9
Robb	7		7
Ritchie	21	5	26
Smith	6		6
Walls	39	8	47

Goalscorers

PLAYER	LEAGUE	CUP COMPETITION S CUP	TOTAL
Cunningham	23	2	25
Cairns	13	1	14
Muirhead	10	4	14
Bowie	12	1	13
Archibald	11	1	12
Paterson	11	1	12
Gordon	10		10
Reid	8		8
Henderson	2		2
Meiklejohn	2		2
Walls	2		2
Dixon		1	1
McDonald	1		1
Opps' o.gs.	1		1

Fact File

One day after the death of William Wilton, Rangers defeated a Scotland XI at Ibrox in a benefit match for Jimmy Gordon on 3 May 1920. It was Bill Struth's first game in charge of the team.

Final Scottish League Div 1 Table

		P	W	D	L	F	A	Pts
1	RANGERS	42	31	9	2	106	25	71
2	CELTIC	42	29	10	3	89	31	68
3	MOTHERWELL	42	23	11	8	74	53	57
4	DUNDEE	42	22	6	14	79	65	50
5	CLYDEBANK	42	20	8	14	78	54	48
6	MORTON	42	16	13	13	71	48	45
7	AIRDRIEONIANS	42	17	10	15	57	43	44
8	THIRD LANARK	42	16	11	15	56	62	43
8	KILMARNOCK	42	20	3	19	59	74	43
10	AYR U	42	15	10	17	72	69	40
11	DUMBARTON	42	13	13	16	57	65	39
12	QUEEN'S PARK	42	14	10	18	67	73	38
12	PARTICK T	42	13	12	17	51	62	38
12	ST MIRREN	42	15	8	19	63	81	38
15	CLYDE	42	14	9	19	64	71	37
15	HEARTS	42	14	9	19	57	72	37
17	ABERDEEN	42	11	13	18	46	64	35
18	HIBERNIAN	42	13	7	22	60	79	33
19	RAITH R	42	11	10	21	61	83	32
20	FALKIRK	42	10	11	21	45	74	31
21	HAMILTON A	42	11	7	24	56	86	29
22	ALBION R	42	10	8	24	43	77	28

Season 1920-21

Scottish League Division 1

DATE	OPPONENTS	SCORE	GOALSCORERS	ATTENDANCE
Aug 17	AIRDRIE	W 4-1	Cunningham 2, Archibald, Cairns	12,000
Aug 21	MOTHERWELL	W 2-1	Walls, Cunningham	45,000
Aug 24	ABERDEEN	W 2-1	Cunningham, Cairns	20,000
Aug 28	Kilmarnock	W 2-1	Archibald, Cunningham	15,000
Sep 1	Motherwell	W 2-0	Muirhead, Cunningham	25,000
Sep 7	ALBION ROVERS	W 2-1	Archibald, Cunningham	12,000
Sep 11	MORTON	W 2-0	Cunningham 2	41,000
Sep 20	Hearts	W 4-0	Cunningham 2, Cairns, Bowie	30,000
Sep 25	Aberdeen	D 1-1	Cunningham	21,800
Sep 27	HIBERNIAN	W 1-0	Cairns	20,000
Oct 2	ST MIRREN	W 2-0	Archibald (pen), Cunningham	20,000
Oct 9	Dumbarton	W 5-2	Cunningham 2, Meiklejohn, Cairns, A.Morton	10,000
Oct 16	PARTICK THISTLE	W 3-0	Archibald 2, Cunningham	30,000
Oct 23	Celtic	W 2-1	Cairns, A.Morton	65,269
Oct 30	THIRD LANARK	W 2-1	Cunningham, A.Morton	25,000
Nov 6	DUNDEE	W 5-0	Henderson 4, Archibald	43,000
Nov 16	Clydebank	W 4-2	Henderson 4	22,000
Nov 20	HAMILTON A	W 4-0	Henderson 2, Cunningham, Bowie	25,000
Nov 27	Albion Rovers	W 2-1	Cairns, Muirhead	22,000
Dec 4	QUEEN'S PARK	W 3-1	Muirhead 2, Meiklejohn	30,000
Dec 11	FALKIRK	W 2-0	Henderson, Cunningham	25,000
Dec 18	Ayr United	D 1-1	Cunningham	13,000
Dec 25	Clyde	W 3-1	Walls, Cunningham (pen), Henderson	36,000
Jan 1	CELTIC	L 0-2		69,260
Jan 3	Partick Thistle	W 2-0	Archibald, Cairns	42,000
Jan 8	KILMARNOCK	W 2-0	Henderson 2	15,000
Jan 15	Hamilton A	W 1-0	A.Morton	20,000
Jan 22	DUMBARTON	W 2-0	Cunningham, Cairns	15,000
Jan 29	Airdrie	W 3-0	Archibald, Henderson, A.Morton	17,000
Feb 9	RAITH ROVERS	W 1-0	Archibald	15,000
Feb 12	Dundee	W 2-1	Henderson, Cairns	23,000
Mar 2	Falkirk	W 2-0	Cairns, Cunningham (pen)	9,000
Mar 9	AYR UNITED	W 7-2	Henderson 4, Archibald, Cunningham (pen), Cairns	8,000
Mar 19	CLYDEBANK	W 1-0	Archibald	15,000
Mar 28	Queen's Park	D 1-1	Dixon	18,000
Apr 2	Morton	D 0-0		15,000
Apr 9	Hibernian	D 1-1	Archibald (pen)	18,000
Apr 19	CLYDE	W 3-1	Meiklejohn, Archibald, Henderson	10,000
Apr 21	St Mirren	W 1-0	Meiklejohn	10,000
Apr 23	Third Lanark	W 1-0	A.Morton	30,000
Apr 27	HEARTS	D 0-0		10,000
Apr 30	Raith Rovers	W 1-0	Dixon	15,000

Scottish Cup

Feb 5	MORTON	(Rd2) W 2-0	A.Morton, Henderson	67,000
Feb 19	ALLOA	(Rd3) D 0-0		60,000
Feb 26	ALLOA	(R) W 4-1	Cairns 2, Cunningham, Archibald	55,000
Mar 5	Dumbarton	(QF) W 3-0	Bowie, Cunningham, Henderson	6,000
Mar 26	Albion Rovers*	(SF) W 4-1	Cairns 2, Cunningham, Archibald	65,000
Apr 16	Partick Thistle*	(F) L 0-1		28,294

*Played at Parkhead.

League & Cup Appearances

PLAYER	LEAGUE	CUP COMPETITION S CUP	TOTAL
Archibald	38	6	44
Bowie	23	6	29
Cairns	38	6	44
Cunningham	40	6	46
Dixon	41	6	47
Henderson	23	6	29
Johnston	3		3
Lawson	2		2
Low	3		3
McCandless	26	6	32
McDonald	2		2
McDermid	2		2
McKenna	4		4
McQueen	4		4
Manderson	41	6	47
Meiklejohn	35	6	41
Morton A	39	6	45
Morton J	2		2
Muirhead	19		19
Reid	3		3
Robb	42	6	48
Smith	9		9
Walls	23		23

Goalscorers

PLAYER	LEAGUE	CUP COMPETITION S CUP	TOTAL
Cunningham	24	3	27
Henderson	21	2	23
Archibald	14	2	16
Cairns	12	4	16
Morton A	6	1	7
Meiklejohn	4		4
Muirhead	4		4
Bowie	2	1	3
Dixon	2		2
Walls	2		2

Fact File

Goalkeeper Willie Robb was Rangers' only ever-present player this season, playing in all 48 league and Cup matches.

Final Scottish League Div 1 Table

		P	W	D	L	F	A	Pts
1	RANGERS	42	35	6	1	91	24	76
2	CELTIC	42	30	6	6	86	35	66
3	HEARTS	42	20	10	12	74	49	50
4	DUNDEE	42	19	11	12	54	48	49
5	MOTHERWELL	42	19	10	13	75	51	48
6	PARTICK T	42	17	12	13	53	39	46
7	CLYDE	42	21	3	18	63	62	45
8	THIRD LANARK	42	19	6	17	74	61	44
8	MORTON	42	15	14	13	66	58	44
10	AIRDRIEONIANS	42	17	9	16	71	64	43
11	ABERDEEN	42	14	14	14	53	54	42
11	KILMARNOCK	42	17	8	17	62	68	42
13	HIBERNIAN	42	16	9	17	58	57	41
14	AYR U	42	14	12	16	62	69	40
14	HAMILTON A	42	14	12	16	44	57	40
16	RAITH R	42	16	5	21	54	58	37
17	ALBION R	42	11	12	19	57	68	34
17	FALKIRK	42	11	12	19	54	72	34
19	QUEEN'S PARK	42	11	11	20	45	80	33
20	CLYDEBANK	42	7	14	21	47	72	28
21	DUMBARTON	42	10	4	28	41	89	24
22	ST MIRREN	42	7	4	31	43	92	18

MANAGER: Bill Struth

CAPTAIN: Tommy Cairns

TOP SCORER: Andy Cunningham

BIGGEST WIN: 7-2 v Ayr United, 9 March 1921, league

HIGHEST ATTENDANCE: 69,260 v Celtic, 1 January 1921, league

MAJOR TRANSFERS IN: Alan Morton from Queen's Park, Billy McCandless from Linfield

MAJOR TRANSFERS OUT: Jimmy Gordon to Dunfermline, John Hempsey to Kings Park

Season 1921-22

Scottish League Division 1

DATE	OPPONENTS	SCORE	GOALSCORERS	ATTENDANCE
Aug 16	Third Lanark	W 3-1	Archibald, Cunningham, Morton	29,000
Aug 20	Clydebank	W 7-1	Henderson 3, Cairns 2, Archibald, Morton	22,000
Aug 23	ALBION ROVERS	W 3-1	Cunningham, Cairns, Henderson	31,000
Aug 27	MOTHERWELL	W 2-1	McDermid, Cunningham	40,000
Sep 3	St Mirren	W 2-1	Cunningham, Cairns	35,290
Sep 10	KILMARNOCK	W 1-0	Cunningham	20,000
Sep 19	Hearts	W 2-1	McDermid 2	22,000
Sep 24	ABERDEEN	W 1-0	Henderson	26,000
Sep 26	CLYDE	W 3-0	Henderson 3	38,000
Oct 8	HEARTS	L 0-2		40,000
Oct 15	Airdrie	W 2-1	Henderson, Cunningham	15,000
Oct 22	CELTIC	D 1-1	Henderson	50,000
Oct 29	Queen's Park	W 4-2	Henderson 2, Morton, Cunningham	32,000
Nov 5	Dundee	D 0-0		39,000
Nov 12	DUMBARTON	D 1-1	Cairns	16,000
Nov 19	Morton	W 2-1	Cunningham, Henderson	20,000
Nov 26	HAMILTON A	W 5-0	Archibald 2 (1 pen), Cunningham 2, Henderson	20,000
Dec 3	Falkirk	L 0-1		18,000
Dec 10	THIRD LANARK	W 2-1	Cairns, Bowie	20,000
Dec 17	Albion Rovers	W 5-0	Cairns 3, Henderson, Cunningham	10,000
Dec 24	Hibernian	D 0-0		25,000
Dec 26	DUNDEE	W 2-1	Hansen, Cairns	10,000
Dec 31	ST MIRREN	W 4-1	Henderson 2, Cunningham, Cairns	30,000
Jan 2	Celtic	D 0-0		60,000
Jan 3	PARTICK THISTLE	D 2-2	Cairns, Meiklejohn	35,000
Jan 7	Ayr United	W 1-0	Archibald	12,000
Jan 14	RAITH ROVERS	L 0-1		20,000
Jan 21	Hamilton A	D 0-0		20,000
Feb 4	Motherwell	L 0-2		10,000
Feb 18	Partick Thistle	W 1-0	Morton	53,000
Feb 21	CLYDEBANK	W 6-1	McDermid 2, Cunningham 2, Manderson, Meiklejohn	5,000
Feb 28	FALKIRK	D 0-0		18,000
Mar 4	MORTON	W 3-0	Archibald 2 (1 pen), Smith	18,000
Mar 28	HIBERNIAN	W 2-0	Henderson, Nicholson	13,000
Apr 1	AYR UNITED	W 2-0	Archibald, Hansen	20,000
Apr 3	Raith Rovers	W 3-0	Henderson 2, Archibald	20,000
Apr 5	Aberdeen	D 0-0		20,000
Apr 8	Dumbarton	W 4-0	Meiklejohn, McCandless (pen), Henderson, McDermid	7,000
Apr 17	QUEEN'S PARK	W 2-1	Hansen 2	15,000
Apr 22	AIRDRIE	W 3-0	Hansen 3	18,000
Apr 24	Kilmarnock	W 2-1	Hansen, McDermid	12,000
Apr 29	Clyde	D 0-0		30,000

Scottish Cup

Jan 28	Clachnacuddin	(Rd1) W 5-0	Henderson 3, McDermid, Morton	4,000
Feb 11	Albion Rovers	(Rd2) D 1-1	Archibald	20,000
Feb 15	ALBION ROVERS	(R) W 4-0	Morton 2, Meiklejohn, Archibald	35,000
Feb 25	Hearts	(Rd3) W 4-0	Cunningham 2, Dixon, McDermid	40,000
Mar 11	ST MIRREN	(QF) D 1-1	Henderson	67,700
Mar 14	St Mirren	(R) W 2-0	Henderson, Cunningham	38,027
Mar 25	PARTICK THISTLE	(SF) W 2-0	Henderson, Archibald (pen)	60,000
Apr 15	Morton*	(F) L 0-1		70,000

*Played at Hampden Park.

MANAGER: Bill Struth

CAPTAIN: Tommy Cairns

TOP SCORER: George Henderson

BIGGEST WIN: 7-1 v Clydebank, 20 August 1921, league

HIGHEST ATTENDANCE: 70,000 v Morton, 15 April 1922, Scottish Cup

MAJOR TRANSFERS IN: Carl Hansen from Copenhagen

League & Cup Appearances

PLAYER	LEAGUE	CUP COMPETITION S CUP	TOTAL
Archibald	40	8	48
Bowie	5		5
Cairns	40	8	48
Cunningham	32	6	38
Dixon	42	8	50
Hansen	11		11
Henderson	28	7	35
Jamieson	6	1	7
Laird	2		2
Lawson	2		2
McCandless	41	8	49
McDermid	15	3	18
Manderson	38	7	45
Meiklejohn	32	8	40
Morton	31	8	39
Muirhead	36	8	44
Nicholson	17		17
Robb	42	8	50
Smith	2		2

Goalscorers

PLAYER	LEAGUE	CUP COMPETITION S CUP	TOTAL
Henderson	21	6	27
Cunningham	14	3	17
Archibald	9	3	12
Cairns	12		12
McDermid	7	2	9
Hansen	8		8
Morton	4	3	7
Meiklejohn	3	1	4
Bowie	1		1
Dixon		1	1
McCandless	1		1
Manderson	1		1
Nicholson	1		1
Smith	1		1

Fact File

Former Rangers player James Blair of Cardiff City captained Scotland to a 1-0 win over England at Villa Park on 8 April 1922 – the team also included current Ibrox men Sandy Archibald, Tommy Cairns and Alan Morton.

Final Scottish League Div 1 Table

		P	W	D	L	F	A	Pts
1	Celtic	42	27	13	2	83	20	67
2	Rangers	42	28	10	4	83	26	66
3	Raith R	42	19	13	10	66	43	51
4	Dundee	42	19	11	12	57	40	49
5	Falkirk	42	16	17	9	48	38	49
6	Partick T	42	20	8	14	57	53	48
7	Hibernian	42	16	14	12	55	44	46
8	St Mirren	42	17	12	13	71	61	46
9	Third Lanark	42	17	12	13	58	52	46
10	Clyde	42	16	12	14	60	51	44
11	Albion R	42	17	10	15	55	51	44
12	Morton	42	16	10	16	58	57	42
13	Motherwell	42	16	7	19	63	58	39
14	Ayr U	42	13	12	17	55	63	38
15	Aberdeen	42	13	9	20	48	54	35
16	Airdrieonians	42	12	11	19	46	56	35
17	Kilmarnock	42	13	9	20	56	83	35
18	Hamilton A	42	9	16	17	51	62	34
19	Hearts	42	11	10	21	50	60	32
20	Dumbarton	42	10	10	22	46	81	30
21	Queen's Park	42	9	10	23	38	82	28
22	Clydebank	42	6	8	28	34	103	20

Dundee v Ayr; both games at Dundee.

Season 1922-23

Scottish League Division 1

DATE	OPPONENTS	SCORE	GOALSCORERS	ATTENDANCE
Aug 15	ALLOA	W 2-0	Cunningham, Smith	30,000
Aug 19	THIRD LANARK	W 5-1	Hansen 2, Cunningham, Cairns, Morton	30,000
Aug 26	Motherwell	W 4-0	Cunningham 2, Smith, Cairns	16,000
Sep 9	Falkirk	L 0-2		18,000
Sep 18	Hearts	D 0-0		20,000
Sep 23	MORTON	D 0-0		30,000
Sep 25	Clyde	W 2-1	Muirhead, Cairns	31,000
Oct 7	HIBERNIAN	W 2-0	Cunningham, Henderson	22,000
Oct 14	Aberdeen	D 0-0		26,294
Oct 21	ALBION ROVERS	D 2-2	Dixon, Henderson	18,000
Oct 28	Celtic	W 3-1	Cunningham 2, Henderson	55,000
Nov 4	PARTICK THISTLE	W 4-1	Henderson 2, Muirhead, Cunningham	30,000
Nov 11	Hamilton A	W 3-0	Henderson 2, Cairns	10,000
Nov 18	RAITH ROVERS	W 1-0	Johnston	18,000
Nov 25	St Mirren	L 0-1		30,000
Dec 2	AIRDRIE	W 4-1	Henderson 3, Archibald	30,000
Dec 9	DUNDEE	W 4-1	Henderson 2, Muirhead, Archibald	35,000
Dec 16	Ayr United	D 1-1	Henderson	10,000
Dec 23	Alloa	W 2-0	Henderson, Morton	8,000
Dec 30	ABERDEEN	D 1-1	Cunningham (pen)	22,000
Jan 1	CELTIC	W 2-0	Hansen, Archibald	50,000
Jan 2	Partick Thistle	W 1-0	Archibald	36,000
Jan 6	MOTHERWELL	W 2-1	Meiklejohn, Cairns	35,000
Jan 20	Kilmarnock	W 2-1	Henderson, Cairns	16,000
Feb 3	HAMILTON A	W 3-0	Hansen 2, Cunningham	13,000
Feb 6	Third Lanark	D 2-2	Muirhead, Hansen	10,000
Feb 10	Airdrie	L 0-1		12,000
Feb 24	Morton	D 1-1	Dixon	16,000
Mar 3	CLYDE	W 2-1	Henderson 2	15,000
Mar 10	Raith Rovers	L 0-2		10,000
Mar 14	AYR UNITED	W 2-1	Henderson 2	8,000
Mar 24	Dundee	W 2-1	Henderson, Cairns	20,000
Mar 27	FALKIRK	W 2-0	Cunningham (pen), Henderson	15,000
Mar 31	Albion Rovers	L 1-2	Cairns	10,000
Apr 2	ST MIRREN	D 1-1	Morton	10,000
Apr 7	Hibernian	L 0-2		16,000
Apr 21	KILMARNOCK	W 1-0	Henderson	16,000
Apr 28	HEARTS	W 3-0	Cairns 2, Henderson	8,000

Scottish Cup

Jan 13	Clyde	(Rd1) W 4-0	Cunningham 2, Henderson, Morton	40,000
Jan 27	Ayr United	(Rd2) L 0-2		16,000

League & Cup Appearances

PLAYER	LEAGUE	CUP COMPETITION S CUP	TOTAL
Archibald	34	2	36
Cairns	36	2	38
Cunningham	35	2	37
Dixon	34	2	36
Hansen	10		10
Henderson	28	2	30
Jamieson	13		13
Johnston	9		9
Kilpatrick	1		1
Lawson	3		3
McCandless	22	2	24
Manderson	28	1	29
Meiklejohn	34	2	36
Morton	35	2	37
Muirhead	31	2	33
Nicholson	10		10
Reid	13	1	14
Robb	38	2	40
Smith	3		3
Walls	1		1

Goalscorers

PLAYER	LEAGUE	CUP COMPETITION S CUP	TOTAL
Henderson	23	1	24
Cunningham	11	2	13
Cairns	10		10
Hansen	6		6
Archibald	4		4
Morton	3	1	4
Muirhead	4		4
Dixon	2		2
Smith	2		2
Johnston	1		1
Meiklejohn	1		1

Fact File

Carl Hansen became the first foreign player to score in an Old Firm match when the Danish striker notched the opener in Rangers' 2-0 win at Ibrox on 1 January 1923.

MANAGER: Bill Struth

CAPTAIN: Tommy Cairns

TOP SCORER: George Henderson

BIGGEST WIN: 5-1 v Third Lanark, 19 August 1922, league

HIGHEST ATTENDANCE: 55,000 v Celtic, 28 October 1922, league

MAJOR TRANSFERS IN: Tully Craig from Alloa, Tom Hamilton from Kirkintilloch Rob Roy

Final Scottish League Div 1 Table

		P	W	D	L	F	A	Pts
1	RANGERS	38	23	9	6	67	29	55
2	AIRDRIEONIANS	38	20	10	8	58	38	50
3	CELTIC	38	19	8	11	52	39	46
4	FALKIRK	38	14	17	7	44	32	45
5	ABERDEEN	38	15	12	11	46	34	42
6	ST MIRREN	38	15	12	11	54	44	42
7	DUNDEE	38	17	7	14	51	45	41
8	HIBERNIAN	38	17	7	14	45	40	41
9	RAITH R	38	13	13	12	31	43	39
10	AYR U	38	13	12	13	43	44	38
11	PARTICK T	38	14	9	15	51	48	37
12	HEARTS	38	11	15	12	51	50	37
13	MOTHERWELL	38	13	10	15	59	60	36
14	MORTON	38	12	11	15	44	47	35
15	KILMARNOCK	38	14	7	17	57	66	35
16	CLYDE	38	12	9	17	36	44	33
17	THIRD LANARK	38	11	8	19	40	59	30
18	HAMILTON A	38	11	7	20	43	59	29
19	ALBION R	38	8	10	20	38	64	26
20	ALLOA ATH	38	6	11	21	27	52	23

Season 1923-24

Scottish League Division 1

DATE	OPPONENTS	SCORE	GOALSCORERS	ATTENDANCE
Aug 18	Motherwell	W 3-0	Cunningham 2, Morton	22,000
Aug 21	FALKIRK	D 2-2	Cunningham (pen), Morton	18,000
Aug 25	ST MIRREN	W 5-0	Cairns 2, Muirhead, Henderson, Cunningham	20,000
Sep 8	Morton	W 1-0	Cunningham	15,000
Sep 17	Hearts	D 0-0		24,000
Sep 22	ABERDEEN	W 2-0	Cunningham (pen), Henderson	20,000
Sep 24	CLYDE	W 2-1	Cairns, Craig	12,000
Oct 6	Dundee	W 4-1	Henderson 3, Archibald	22,000
Oct 13	AYR UNITED	W 5-0	Meiklejohn 2, Henderson 2, Craig	15,000
Oct 20	Hibernian	W 3-1	Meiklejohn, Henderson, Morton	22,000
Oct 27	CELTIC	D 0-0		38,000
Nov 3	Partick Thistle	W 6-0	Morton 3, Cunningham, Henderson, Cairns	35,000
Nov 10	THIRD LANARK	W 2-0	Meiklejohn, Muirhead	15,000
Nov 17	Falkirk	W 1-0	Cunningham (pen)	16,000
Nov 24	AIRDRIE	D 0-0		20,000
Dec 1	Clydebank	W 2-1	Cunningham, Cairns	10,000
Dec 8	QUEEN'S PARK	D 1-1	Meiklejohn	15,000
Dec 15	Raith Rovers	W 1-0	Henderson	20,000
Dec 22	HAMILTON A	W 4-0	Henderson 3, Archibald	10,000
Dec 29	St Mirren	D 0-0		12,000
Jan 1	Celtic	D 2-2	Cairns, Archibald	60,000
Jan 2	PARTICK THISTLE	W 1-0	Cunningham	30,000
Jan 5	Ayr United	L 1-2	Cairns	14,000
Jan 12	DUNDEE	D 1-1	Craig	10,000
Jan 19	Hamilton A	W 3-2	Craig 2, Cairns	12,000
Feb 2	MOTHERWELL	W 3-0	Craig 2, Cunningham	20,000
Feb 12	Queen's Park	W 2-0	Henderson 2	10,000
Feb 19	KILMARNOCK	W 2-0	Henderson 2	10,000
Feb 26	CLYDEBANK	W 3-0	Craig 3	6,000
Mar 5	Kilmarnock	D 1-1	Archibald	10,000
Mar 11	HEARTS	W 1-0	Henderson	6,000
Mar 19	Aberdeen	L 0-1		16,000
Mar 22	Third Lanark	W 3-1	Cunningham, Henderson, Cairns	10,000
Mar 29	RAITH ROVERS	L 0-1		10,000
Apr 5	HIBERNIAN	W 2-1	Meiklejohn (pen), Cunningham	12,000
Apr 12	MORTON	W 2-1	Craig, Cairns	8,000
Apr 18	Clyde	L 1-3	Craig	10,000
Apr 26	Airdrie	D 0-0		8,000

Scottish Cup

DATE	OPPONENTS		SCORE	GOALSCORERS	ATTENDANCE
Jan 22	LOCHGELLY	(Rd1)	W 4-1	Henderson 3, Craig	6,000
Feb 9	St Mirren	(Rd2)	W 1-0	Henderson	40,291
Feb 23	HIBERNIAN	(Rd3)	L 1-2	Meiklejohn	54,000

League & Cup Appearances

PLAYER	LEAGUE	CUP COMPETITION S CUP	TOTAL
Archibald	34	3	37
Cairns	31	3	34
Craig	17	3	20
Cunningham	30	1	31
Dixon	37	3	40
Hansen	2		2
Henderson	31	2	33
Jamieson	1		1
Johnston	12		12
Kilpatrick	2		2
Kirkwood	3		3
Lawson	2		2
McCandless	33	3	36
McDonald	1		1
McGregor	2		2
Manderson	32	2	34
Meiklejohn	35	3	38
Morton	34	3	37
Muirhead	27	3	30
Nicholson	3		3
Reid	10	1	11
Robb	38	3	41
Walls	1		1

Goalscorers

PLAYER	LEAGUE	CUP COMPETITION S CUP	TOTAL
Henderson	19	4	23
Craig	12	1	13
Cunningham	13		13
Cairns	10		10
Meiklejohn	6	1	7
Morton	6		6
Archibald	4		4
Muirhead	2		2

Fact File

In a match billed as the British Championship, Rangers defeated English champions Liverpool 2-0 at Anfield on 21 April 1924 with goals from Andy Cunningham and George Henderson in front of 38,000 fans.

MANAGER: Bill Struth

CAPTAIN: Tommy Cairns

TOP SCORER: George Henderson

BIGGEST WIN: 6-0 v Partick Thistle, League, 3 November 1923

HIGHEST ATTENDANCE: 60,000 v Celtic, League, 1 January 1924

MAJOR TRANSFERS OUT: Tommy Muirhead to Boston (USA)

Final Scottish League Div 1 Table

		P	W	D	L	F	A	Pts
1	RANGERS	38	25	9	4	72	22	59
2	AIRDRIEONIANS	38	20	10	8	72	46	50
3	CELTIC	38	17	12	9	56	33	46
4	RAITH R	38	18	7	13	56	38	43
5	DUNDEE	38	15	13	10	70	57	43
6	ST MIRREN	38	15	12	11	53	45	42
7	HIBERNIAN	38	15	11	12	66	52	41
8	PARTICK T	38	15	9	14	58	55	39
9	HEARTS	38	14	10	14	61	50	38
10	MOTHERWELL	38	15	7	16	58	63	37
11	MORTON	38	16	5	17	48	54	37
12	HAMILTON A	38	15	6	17	52	57	36
13	ABERDEEN	38	13	10	15	37	41	36
14	AYR U	38	12	10	16	38	60	34
15	FALKIRK	38	13	6	19	46	53	32
16	KILMARNOCK	38	12	8	18	48	65	32
17	QUEEN'S PARK	38	11	9	18	43	60	31
18	THIRD LANARK	38	11	8	19	54	78	30
19	CLYDE	38	10	9	19	40	70	29
20	CLYDEBANK	38	10	5	23	42	71	25

Season 1924-25

Scottish League Division 1

DATE	OPPONENTS	SCORE	GOALSCORERS	ATTENDANCE
Aug 16	Raith Rovers	W 3-0	Henderson 3	15,000
Aug 20	ST JOHNSTONE	W 3-1	Morton 2, Henderson	30,000
Aug 23	Aberdeen	W 1-0	Meiklejohn	23,000
Aug 26	Queen's Park	W 3-1	Cunningham 2, Archibald	30,000
Aug 30	KILMARNOCK	D 1-1	Henderson	18,000
Sep 13	Ayr United	W 4-0	McCandless (pen), Archibald, Cairns, Morton	20,000
Sep 15	Hearts	W 2-1	Henderson, Morton	22,000
Sep 27	Airdrie	L 0-1		27,000
Sep 29	HEARTS	W 4-1	Cairns 2, Meiklejohn, Archibald	12,000
Oct 11	Cowdenbeath	D 2-2	Cunningham 2	20,000
Oct 18	FALKIRK	W 3-1	Henderson 2 (1 pen), Archibald	10,000
Oct 25	Celtic	W 1-0	Morton	40,000
Nov 1	PARTICK THISTLE	W 4-0	Craig, Cunningham, Henderson, Chalmers	25,000
Nov 8	Third Lanark	D 1-1	Craig	23,000
Nov 15	HIBERNIAN	W 3-0	Meiklejohn, Cunningham (pen), Henderson	30,000
Nov 22	St Johnstone	W 3-1	Henderson 2, Morton	10,000
Nov 29	ST MIRREN	W 3-1	Cairns 2, Archibald	26,000
Dec 6	Dundee	D 0-0		20,000
Dec 13	HAMILTON A	W 2-0	Henderson 2	10,000
Dec 20	St Mirren	W 4-1	Henderson 3, Archibald	20,000
Dec 27	MOTHERWELL	W 1-0	Henderson	15,000
Jan 1	CELTIC	W 4-1	Henderson 2, Cunningham, McCandless (pen)	34,000
Jan 3	MORTON	W 2-0	Cairns, Morton	17,000
Jan 5	Partick Thistle	W 1-0	Henderson	25,000
Jan 10	Morton	D 1-1	Morton	10,000
Jan 17	QUEEN'S PARK	D 1-1	Cairns	20,000
Jan 31	Hamilton A	L 0-1		15,000
Feb 10	DUNDEE	W 2-0	McCandless (pen), Chalmers	5,000
Feb 18	Falkirk	D 1-1	Henderson	12,000
Feb 25	AIRDRIE	D 1-1	Archibald	40,000
Mar 11	Hibernian	L 1-4	Dick	23,000
Mar 25	Raith Rovers	W 4-0	Henderson 3, Archibald	-
Mar 28	Kilmarnock	D 0-0		12,000
Apr 1	COWDENBEATH	W 1-0	McCandless (pen)	5,000
Apr 7	ABERDEEN	W 2-0	Cairns 2	8,000
Apr 11	THIRD LANARK	W 5-2	Henderson 2, Cairns 2, Archibald	12,000
Apr 18	Motherwell	D 1-1	Archibald	7,000
Apr 25	AYR UNITED	W 1-0	McCandless	10,000

Scottish Cup

Jan 24	East Fife	(Rd1) W 3-1	Archibald 2, Henderson	10,000
Feb 7	Montrose	(Rd2) W 2-0	Chalmers 2	4,000
Feb 21	ARBROATH	(Rd3) W 5-3	Henderson 3, Cairns, Cunningham	15,000
Mar 7	Kilmarnock	(QF) W 2-1	Henderson, Cunningham	31,502
Mar 21	Celtic*	(SF) L 0-5		101,714

*Played at Hampden Park.

League & Cup Appearances

PLAYER	LEAGUE	CUP COMPETITION S CUP	TOTAL
Archibald	38	5	q43
Cairns	31	5	36
Chalmers	12	2	14
Craig	21	1	22
Cunningham	33	3	36
Dick	1		1
Dixon	36	5	41
Henderson	37	5	42
Ireland	5	1	6
Jamieson	7		7
Kirkwood	5		5
McCandless	32	5	37
McGregor	1		1
Manderson	34	5	39
Meiklejohn	35	5	40
Morton Alan	36	5	41
Morton Archie	1		1
Muirhead	12	3	15
Reid	3		3
Robb	38	5	43

Goalscorers

PLAYER	LEAGUE	CUP COMPETITION S CUP	TOTAL
Henderson	27	5	32
Archibald	10	2	12
Cairns	11	1	12
Cunningham	7	2	9
Morton Alan	8		8
McCandless	5		5
Chalmers		2	2
Meiklejohn	3		3
Craig	2		2
Dick	1		1

Fact File

Davie Meiklejohn, Tommy Cairns and Alan Morton played in all three of Scotland's matches in 1924-25 as the Home International Championship was won with a clean sweep of victories over Wales, Ireland and England.

MANAGER: Bill Struth
CAPTAIN: Tommy Cairns
TOP SCORER: George Henderson
BIGGEST WIN: 4-0 v Ayr United, 13 September 1924, league; v Partick Thistle, 1 November 1924, league; v Raith Rovers, 25 March 1925, league
HIGHEST ATTENDANCE: 101,714 v Celtic, 21 March 1925, Scottish Cup
MAJOR TRANSFERS IN: Tommy Muirhead from Boston (USA)

Final Scottish League Div 1 Table

		P	W	D	L	F	A	Pts
1	RANGERS	38	25	10	3	76	26	60
2	AIRDRIEONIANS	38	25	7	6	85	31	57
3	HIBERNIAN	38	22	8	8	78	43	52
4	CELTIC	38	18	8	12	77	44	44
5	COWDENBEATH	38	16	10	12	76	65	42
6	ST MIRREN	38	18	4	16	65	63	40
7	PARTICK T	38	14	10	14	60	61	38
8	DUNDEE	38	14	8	16	47	54	36
9	RAITH R	38	14	8	16	53	61	36
10	HEARTS	38	12	11	15	64	68	35
11	ST JOHNSTONE	38	12	11	15	57	72	35
12	KILMARNOCK	38	12	9	17	53	64	33
13	HAMILTON A	38	15	3	20	50	63	33
14	MORTON	38	12	9	17	46	69	33
15	ABERDEEN	38	11	10	17	46	56	32
16	FALKIRK	38	12	8	18	44	54	32
17	QUEEN'S PARK	38	12	8	18	50	71	32
18	MOTHERWELL	38	10	10	18	54	63	30
19	AYR U	38	11	8	19	43	65	30
20	THIRD LANARK	38	11	8	19	53	84	30

Season 1925-26

Scottish League Division 1

DATE	OPPONENTS	SCORE	GOALSCORERS	ATTENDANCE
Aug 15	St Johnstone	W 3-0	Cunningham 2, Henderson	15,848
Aug 22	MOTHERWELL	W 1-0	Cunningham	-
Aug 29	MORTON	W 4-1	Henderson 2, Archibald, Cunningham	-
Sep 5	Airdrie	L 1-2	Henderson	27,000
Sep 12	Aberdeen	L 1-3	McCandless (pen)	26,000
Sep 19	ST MIRREN	W 4-1	Archibald, McKay, Henderson, Cairns	40,000
Sep 21	Hibernian	W 2-0	Cunningham, McKay	20,000
Sep 26	Hearts	L 0-3		30,000
Oct 3	KILMARNOCK	W 3-1	Chalmers 2, McKay	20,000
Oct 10	Partick Thistle	L 0-2		35,000
Oct 17	CELTIC	W 1-0	Chalmers	35,000
Oct 24	DUNDEE	L 1-2	Fleming	12,000
Oct 31	Raith Rovers	L 0-1		10,000
Nov 7	Queen's Park	W 6-3	Fleming 4, Cunningham, Morton	35,000
Nov 14	COWDENBEATH	W 3-0	McKay 2, Fleming	14,000
Nov 25	Motherwell	W 3-1	Morton, Malone, McKay	8,000
Nov 28	FALKIRK	L 2-3	Cunningham 2 (1 pen)	16,000
Dec 5	Kilmarnock	D 2-2	Cunningham 2 (1 pen)	10,000
Dec 12	HIBERNIAN	W 3-1	Fleming 2, Morton	22,000
Dec 19	Dundee United	L 1-2	Cunningham (pen)	12,000
Dec 26	ST JOHNSTONE	L 0-1		7,000
Jan 1	Celtic	D 2-2	Cunningham, Muirhead	60,000
Jan 2	PARTICK THISTLE	W 2-1	Cunningham, Cairns	20,000
Jan 4	CLYDEBANK	W 3-1	Henderson 2, Cunningham	15,000
Jan 9	Hamilton A	D 3-3	Fleming, Cairns, Morton	12,000
Jan 16	HEARTS	D 2-2	Craig, Morton	25,000
Jan 30	Cowdenbeath	W 3-2	Muirhead, Cunningham, Cairns	8,000
Feb 10	AIRDRIE	L 1-2	Cunningham (pen)	14,000
Feb 13	RAITH ROVERS	W 4-2	Fleming 2, Cunningham, J.Hamilton (pen)	15,000
Feb 24	Falkirk	D 1-1	Malone	5,000
Feb 27	Dundee	W 5-1	Fleming 5	14,000
Mar 10	QUEEN'S PARK	L 1-2	J.Hamilton (pen)	6,000
Mar 23	St Mirren	L 2-3	Osborne, Cunningham	6,000
Mar 27	ABERDEEN	L 0-1		12,000
Apr 3	Morton	W 3-1	Marshall 2, Fleming	7,000
Apr 5	DUNDEE UNITED	W 2-1	Craig, Marshall	12,000
Apr 10	Clydebank	D 2-2	Marshall 2	6,000
Apr 17	HAMILTON A	W 2-0	Marshall 2	-

Scottish Cup

Jan 23	LOCHGELLY	(Rd1) W 3-0	Fleming 2, Archibald	5,700
Feb 6	STENHOUSEMUIR	(Rd2) W 1-0	Henderson	14,000
Feb 20	Falkirk	(Rd3) W 2-0	McKay, Cunningham	22,000
Mar 6	Morton	(QF) W 4-0	Morton 2, Fleming, Cunningham (pen)	15,000
Mar 20	St Mirren*	(SF) L 0-1		61,000

*Played at Parkhead.

League & Cup Appearances

PLAYER	LEAGUE	CUP COMPETITION S CUP	TOTAL
Archibald	18	2	20
Cairns	17	2	19
Chalmers	6		6
Craig	31	5	36
Cunningham	31	4	35
Dixon	37	5	42
Fleming	21	4	25
Gray	21	4	25
Hamilton J	29	5	34
Hamilton T	16	5	21
Henderson	13	1	14
Hodge	2		2
Ireland	2		2
Jamieson	5		5
Kirkwood	1		1
McCandless	7		7
McGregor	6		6
McKay	22	4	26
Malone	15	3	18
Manderson	15	1	16
Marshall	4		4
Meiklejohn	12		12
Morton	29	5	34
Muirhead	27	4	31
Osborne	9	1	10
Robb	22		22

Goalscorers

PLAYER	LEAGUE	CUP COMPETITION S CUP	TOTAL
Cunningham	18	2	20
Fleming	17	3	20
Henderson	7	1	8
McKay	6	1	7
Marshall	7		7
Morton	5	2	7
Cairns	4		4
Archibald	2	1	3
Chalmers	3		3
Craig	2		2
Hamilton J	2		2
Malone	2		2
Muirhead	2		2
McCandless	1		1
Osborne	1		1

Fact File

When goalkeeper Tom Hamilton made his debut against Raith Rovers on 31 October 1925, it was the first Rangers match Willie Robb had missed since making his own debut against Ayr United on 13 April 1920 – an unbroken run of 241 appearances.

MANAGER: Bill Struth
CAPTAIN: Tommy Cairns
TOP SCORERS: Andy Cunningham and Jimmy Fleming
BIGGEST WIN: 5-1 v Dundee, League, 27 February 1926
HIGHEST ATTENDANCE: 61,000 v St Mirren, 20 March 1926, Scottish Cup
MAJOR TRANSFERS IN: Dougie Gray from Aberdeen Mugiemoss, Robert McKay from Morton, Jimmy Fleming from St Johnstone, James Marshall from Shettleston
MAJOR TRANSFERS OUT: Willie Robb to Hibernian

Final Scottish League Div 1 Table

		P	W	D	L	F	A	Pts
1	CELTIC	38	25	8	5	97	40	58
2	AIRDRIEONIANS	38	23	4	11	95	54	50
3	HEARTS	38	21	8	9	87	56	50
4	ST MIRREN	38	20	7	11	62	52	47
5	MOTHERWELL	38	19	8	11	67	46	46
6	RANGERS	38	19	6	13	79	55	44
7	COWDENBEATH	38	18	6	14	87	68	42
8	FALKIRK	38	14	14	10	61	57	42
9	KILMARNOCK	38	17	7	14	79	77	41
10	DUNDEE	38	14	9	15	47	59	37
11	ABERDEEN	38	13	10	15	49	54	36
12	HAMILTON A	38	13	9	16	68	79	35
13	QUEEN'S PARK	38	15	4	19	70	81	34
14	PARTICK T	38	10	13	15	64	73	33
15	MORTON	38	12	7	19	57	84	31
16	HIBERNIAN	38	12	6	20	72	77	30
17	DUNDEE U	38	11	6	21	52	74	28
18	ST JOHNSTONE	38	9	10	19	43	78	28
19	RAITH R	38	11	4	23	46	81	26
20	CLYDEBANK	38	7	8	23	55	92	22

Season 1926-27

Scottish League Division 1

DATE	OPPONENTS	SCORE	GOALSCORERS	ATTENDANCE
Aug 14	DUNDEE UNITED	W 2-0	Marshall 2	20,000
Aug 17	DUNFERMLINE	W 2-0	Shaw, Archibald	16,000
Aug 21	Airdrie	D 3-3	Marshall, Cairns, Fleming	20,000
Aug 28	PARTICK THISTLE	W 2-1	Marshall 2	22,000
Sep 4	St Johnstone	L 1-2	Morton	5,000
Sep 11	MOTHERWELL	W 2-0	Archibald, Cunningham	18,000
Sep 18	Hearts	W 2-0	Fleming, Cairns	30,000
Sep 25	ABERDEEN	W 3-2	Shaw, McKay, Cunningham	23,000
Oct 2	St Mirren	W 7-3	Henderson 3, Fleming 2, Craig, Archibald	34,000
Oct 16	QUEEN'S PARK	L 0-1		19,000
Oct 23	Morton	W 8-2	Marshall 5, Morton, Fleming, Cairns	5,000
Nov 6	COWDENBEATH	W 4-1	Morton 2, Craig, Fleming	15,000
Nov 13	Hibernian	D 2-2	Cunningham, Marshall	18,000
Nov 20	FALKIRK	W 2-1	Marshall, Muirhead	25,000
Nov 27	CLYDE	W 6-0	Marshall 3, McCandless (pen), Muirhead, Cunningham	10,000
Dec 4	HAMILTON A	L 1-4	Muirhead	10,000
Dec 11	Dundee	D 1-1	Marshall	20,000
Dec 18	Kilmarnock	D 0-0		12,000
Dec 25	Dundee United	L 0-2		15,000
Jan 1	CELTIC	W 2-1	Archibald, Marshall	63,000
Jan 3	Partick Thistle	W 4-1	McMillan 2, Marshall, Cunningham	40,000
Jan 8	ST JOHNSTONE	W 4-2	Morton 3, Jamieson o.g.	8,000
Jan 15	Motherwell	W 4-1	Meiklejohn, Archibald, Fleming, Cunningham	32,000
Jan 29	HEARTS	W 1-0	McMillan	15,000
Feb 12	ST MIRREN	W 4-0	Fleming 2, Morton 2	20,000
Feb 16	Aberdeen	D 2-2	Hair 2	16,000
Feb 23	Dunfermline	W 3-1	Fleming 3	4,000
Mar 1	Queen's Park	W 2-1	Archibald, McMillan	18,000
Mar 12	AIRDRIE	D 1-1	Fleming	27,000
Mar 16	MORTON	W 2-1	Cunningham, Morton	8,000
Mar 23	Cowdenbeath	L 0-1		3,000
Mar 29	HIBERNIAN	W 2-0	McMillan, Marshall	5,000
Apr 2	Falkirk	D 3-3	McMillan, Marshall, Meiklejohn	5,000
Apr 9	Clyde	D 0-0		20,000
Apr 16	Hamilton A	D 1-1	Fleming	10,000
Apr 18	Celtic	W 1-0	Fleming	40,000
Apr 23	DUNDEE	D 0-0		10,000
Apr 30	KILMARNOCK	W 1-0	Fleming	10,000

Scottish Cup

Jan 22	Leith Athletic	(Rd1) W 4-1	Morton 2, Fleming, Craig	14,130
Feb 5	ST MIRREN	(Rd2) W 6-0	Fleming 2, Morton 2, Archibald, Cunningham	56,000
Feb 19	HAMILTON A	(Rd3) W 4-0	Fleming 2, Cunningham, Archibald	53,000
Mar 5	Falkirk	(QF) D 2-2	Archibald, McCandless (pen)	20,233
Mar 9	FALKIRK	(R) L 0-1		80,000

League & Cup Appearances

PLAYER	LEAGUE	CUP COMPETITION S CUP	TOTAL
Archibald	28	5	33
Cairns	15		15
Craig	30	5	35
Cunningham	29	5	34
Dixon	3		3
Fleming	26	5	31
Gray	30	3	33
Hair	2		2
Hamilton J	6		6
Hamilton R	1		1
Hamilton T	37	5	42
Henderson	4		4
Ireland	3		3
Kirkwood	1		1
McCandless	22	5	27
McKay	3		3
McMillan	13	5	18
Manderson	12	2	14
Marshall	25		25
Meiklejohn	30	2	32
Morton	31	5	36
Moyies	1		1
Muirhead	24	3	27
Purdon	2		2
Shaw	36	5	41
Smith	2		2
Weir	2		2

Goalscorers

PLAYER	LEAGUE	CUP COMPETITION S CUP	TOTAL
Fleming	16	5	21
Marshall	20		20
Morton	10	4	14
Archibald	6	3	9
Cunningham	7	2	9
McMillan	6		6
Cairns	3		3
Craig	2	1	3
Henderson	3		3
Muirhead	3		3
Hair	2		2
McCandless	1	1	2
Meiklejohn	2		2
Shaw	2		2
McKay	1		1
Opps' o.gs.	1		1

Fact File

Just over a year after signing him from Morton for £1,750, Rangers made a smart profit on inside right Robert McKay when they sold him to Newcastle United for £2,750 in November 1926.

MANAGER: Bill Struth
CAPTAIN: Tommy Cairns
TOP SCORER: Jimmy Fleming
BIGGEST WIN: 8-2 v Morton, 23 October 1926, league
HIGHEST ATTENDANCE: 80,000 v Falkirk, 9 March 1927, Scottish Cup,
MAJOR TRANSFERS IN: Bob McPhail from Airdrie
MAJOR TRANSFERS OUT: Robert McKay to Newcastle United

Final Scottish League Div 1 Table

		P	W	D	L	F	A	Pts
1	RANGERS	38	23	10	5	85	41	56
2	MOTHERWELL	38	23	5	10	81	52	51
3	CELTIC	38	21	7	10	101	55	49
4	AIRDRIEONIANS	38	18	9	11	97	64	45
5	DUNDEE	38	17	9	12	77	51	43
6	FALKIRK	38	16	10	12	77	60	42
7	COWDENBEATH	38	18	6	14	74	60	42
8	ABERDEEN	38	13	14	11	73	72	40
9	HIBERNIAN	38	16	7	15	62	71	39
10	ST MIRREN	38	16	5	17	78	76	37
11	PARTICK T	38	15	6	17	89	74	36
12	QUEEN'S PARK	38	15	6	17	74	84	36
13	HEARTS	38	12	11	15	65	64	35
14	ST JOHNSTONE	38	13	9	16	55	69	35
15	HAMILTON A	38	13	9	16	60	85	35
16	KILMARNOCK	38	12	8	18	54	71	32
17	CLYDE	38	10	9	19	54	85	29
18	DUNFERMLINE ATH	38	10	8	20	53	85	28
19	MORTON	38	12	4	22	56	101	28
20	DUNDEE U	38	7	8	23	56	101	22

Season 1927-28

Scottish League Division 1

DATE	OPPONENTS	SCORE	GOALSCORERS	ATTENDANCE
Aug 13	Aberdeen	W 3-2	Fleming 2, Morton	25,000
Aug 20	HEARTS	W 4-1	Fleming 2, Archibald, Morton	25,000
Aug 27	Cowdenbeath	W 4-1	Fleming 3, Morton	12,000
Sep 3	ST JOHNSTONE	W 5-1	Fleming 2, McPhail 2, Morton	25,000
Sep 10	Partick Thistle	W 6-0	Craig, Archibald, Cunningham, Fleming, McPhail, Morton	45,000
Sep 17	AIRDRIE	W 2-1	Meiklejohn, McPhail	37,000
Sep 24	Motherwell	D 1-1	McPhail (pen)	30,000
Oct 1	ST MIRREN	W 4-2	McPhail 2, Cunningham, Fleming	30,000
Oct 15	CELTIC	W 1-0	Fleming	60,000
Oct 22	RAITH ROVERS	W 7-0	Fleming 3, McMillan 2, Archibald, Morton	10,000
Oct 29	Queen's Park	L 1-3	McPhail	25,000
Nov 5	Dunfermline	W 5-0	Archibald 2, Cunningham, Fleming, Morton	-
Nov 12	HIBERNIAN	W 4-1	McMillan 2, Fleming, Cunningham	15,000
Nov 19	Falkirk	W 2-1	Fleming, Morton	15,000
Nov 26	Clyde	W 4-1	McPhail 2 (1 pen), Craig, Fleming	18,000
Dec 3	Hamilton A	D 1-1	Archibald	15,000
Dec 10	DUNDEE	W 5-1	Simpson, Archibald, Fleming, McPhail, Morton	10,000
Dec 17	Kilmarnock	D 1-1	Archibald	14,440
Dec 24	ABERDEEN	W 5-0	Fleming 3, Archibald, Morton	15,000
Dec 31	St Johnstone	W 1-0	Morton	10,000
Jan 2	Celtic	L 0-1		70,000
Jan 3	PARTICK THISTLE	W 2-1	Archibald, Fleming	20,000
Jan 7	COWDENBEATH	D 2-2	Cunningham, Marshall	10,000
Jan 14	Airdrie	W 7-2	McPhail 2, Cunningham, Craig, Fleming, Muirhead, Archibald	8,000
Jan 28	BONESS	W 3-1	Archibald, Marshall, McPhail (pen)	12,000
Feb 11	MOTHERWELL	L 0-2		45,000
Feb 15	St Mirren	D 3-3	Archibald, Cunningham, Marshall	15,000
Feb 28	QUEEN'S PARK	W 4-0	Marshall 2, Cunningham, Morton	10,000
Mar 7	Hearts	D 0-0		20,000
Mar 17	Hibernian	L 1-2	Archibald	18,000
Mar 28	FALKIRK	W 4-0	Fleming 3, Buchanan	10,000
Mar 31	CLYDE	W 3-1	Fleming 2, Marshall	18,000
Apr 2	Raith Rovers	D 0-0		10,000
Apr 7	HAMILTON A	W 3-1	Archibald 2, McPhail	15,000
Apr 9	DUNFERMLINE	W 4-0	Cunningham 3, McPhail	10,000
Apr 18	Dundee	W 1-0	McPhail	12,000
Apr 21	KILMARNOCK	W 5-1	Fleming 3, Cunningham 2	28,000
Apr 28	Boness	D 1-1	Cunningham	4,000

Scottish Cup

Jan 21	East Stirling	(Rd1) W 6-0	Fleming 3, McPhail (pen), Cunningham, Archibald	5,500
Feb 4	COWDENBEATH	(Rd2) W 4-2	McPhail 3, Fleming	30,226
Feb 18	KINGS PARK	(Rd3) W 3-1	Morton 2, Cunningham	20,000
Mar 3	Albion Rovers	(QF) W 1-0	Cunningham	25,000
Mar 24	Hibernian*	(SF) W 3-0	Archibald, McPhail, Simpson	43,129
Apr 14	Celtic†	(F) W 4-0	Archibald 2, Meiklejohn (pen), McPhail	118,115

*Played at Tynecastle. †Played at Hampden Park.

MANAGER: Bill Struth

CAPTAIN: Tommy Muirhead

TOP SCORER: Jimmy Fleming

BIGGEST WIN: 7-0 v Raith Rovers, League, 22 October 1927

HIGHEST ATTENDANCE: 118,115 v Celtic, 14 April 1928, Scottish Cup

MAJOR TRANSFERS IN: Jimmy Simpson from Dundee United, Jock Buchanan from Morton

MAJOR TRANSFERS OUT: Tommy Cairns to Bradford City, Bert Manderson to Bradford City

League & Cup Appearances

PLAYER	LEAGUE	CUP COMPETITION S CUP	TOTAL
Archibald	38	6	44
Buchanan	13	4	17
Chalmers	1		1
Craig	34	6	40
Cunningham	31	5	36
Fleming	34	6	40
Gray	38	6	44
Haddow	1		1
Hamilton R	21	6	27
Hamilton T	33	4	37
McCandless	17		17
McMillan	8		8
McPhail	36	6	42
Marshall	6		6
Meiklejohn	34	6	40
Morton	34	6	40
Moyies	2		2
Muirhead	26	2	28
Osborne	1		1
Simpson	7	1	8
Yuill	3	2	5

Goalscorers

PLAYER	LEAGUE	CUP COMPETITION S CUP	TOTAL
Fleming	33	4	37
McPhail	17	6	23
Archibald	16	4	20
Cunningham	14	3	17
Morton	12	2	14
Marshall	6		6
McMillan	4		4
Craig	3		3
Meiklejohn	1	1	2
Simpson	1	1	2
Buchanan	1		1
Muirhead	1		1

Fact File

Rangers won the double of league championship and Scottish Cup for the first time in their history.

Final Scottish League Div 1 Table

		P	W	D	L	F	A	Pts
1	RANGERS	38	26	8	4	109	36	60
2	CELTIC	38	23	9	6	93	39	55
3	MOTHERWELL	38	23	9	6	92	46	55
4	HEARTS	38	20	7	11	89	50	47
5	ST MIRREN	38	18	8	12	77	76	44
6	PARTICK T	38	18	7	13	85	67	43
7	ABERDEEN	38	19	5	14	71	61	43
8	KILMARNOCK	38	15	10	13	68	78	40
9	COWDENBEATH	38	16	7	15	66	68	39
10	FALKIRK	38	16	5	17	76	69	37
11	ST JOHNSTONE	38	14	8	16	66	67	36
12	HIBERNIAN	38	13	9	16	73	75	35
13	AIRDRIEONIANS	38	12	11	15	59	69	35
14	DUNDEE	38	14	7	17	65	80	35
15	CLYDE	38	10	11	17	46	72	31
16	QUEEN'S PARK	38	12	6	20	69	80	30
17	RAITH R	38	11	7	20	60	89	29
18	HAMILTON A	38	11	6	21	67	86	28
19	BO'NESS	38	9	8	21	48	86	26
20	DUNFERMLINE ATH	38	4	4	30	41	126	12

The Essential History of Rangers

Season 1928-29

Scottish League Division 1

DATE	OPPONENTS	SCORE	GOALSCORERS	ATTENDANCE
Aug 11	KILMARNOCK	W 4-2	Fleming 2, Archibald, Morton	20,000
Aug 18	St Mirren	W 5-1	McPhail 3, Marshall 2	22,000
Aug 25	COWDENBEATH	W 3-1	Morton 2, Meiklejohn (pen)	20,000
Sep 8	Dundee	W 3-2	Meiklejohn 2 (1 pen), Morton	16,000
Sep 15	Hearts	W 1-0	Fleming	45,000
Sep 22	RAITH ROVERS	W 7-1	Fleming 3, McPhail 2, McMillan, Morton	16,000
Sep 29	MOTHERWELL	D 0-0		40,000
Oct 6	Third Lanark	W 5-2	Muirhead 2, Meiklejohn, McPhail, Morton	22,000
Oct 13	ST JOHNSTONE	W 8-0	Fleming 3, Morton 3, Archibald, Muirhead	25,000
Oct 20	Celtic	W 2-1	McMillan, Archibald	35,000
Nov 3	Hibernian	W 2-1	Craig, Archibald	22,000
Nov 10	Falkirk	W 4-1	Fleming 3, Buchanan	15,000
Nov 17	HAMILTON A	W 4-0	Fleming 3, Cunningham	14,000
Nov 24	Clyde	W 3-2	Craig, Fleming, Cunningham	15,000
Dec 1	Ayr United	W 3-1	Fleming 3	18,500
Dec 8	ABERDEEN	W 2-0	Muirhead, McPhail	15,000
Dec 15	Airdrie	W 5-2	Fleming 3, Archibald, Morton	8,000
Dec 22	ST MIRREN	D 1-1	Archibald	15,000
Dec 29	Kilmarnock	W 3-1	Archibald 2, Fleming	30,000
Jan 1	CELTIC	W 3-0	Fleming 2, Archibald	60,000
Jan 2	PARTICK THISTLE	W 1-0	Meiklejohn (pen)	10,000
Jan 5	Cowdenbeath	W 2-0	Fleming, McPhail	5,000
Jan 12	Queen's Park	W 4-0	McPhail 3, Fleming	60,000
Jan 26	AIRDRIE	W 2-0	Archibald, Cunningham	25,000
Feb 9	Raith Rovers	W 3-1	Muirhead, Fleming, McPhail	9,000
Feb 26	THIRD LANARK	W 5-1	Craig 2, McPhail 2, Archibald	6,000
Mar 6	St Johnstone	W 3-1	Craig, Marshall, McPhail	8,000
Mar 9	HIBERNIAN	W 3-0	Buchanan, Fleming, McPhail	15,000
Mar 12	HEARTS	W 2-0	Marshall, Fleming	12,000
Mar 16	FALKIRK	D 1-1	Marshall	20,000
Mar 27	Hamilton A	L 1-3	Morton	12,000
Mar 30	CLYDE	D 0-0		12,000
Apr 1	QUEEN'S PARK	W 2-1	Fleming 2	22,000
Apr 10	AYR UNITED	D 0-0		5,000
Apr 17	Motherwell	W 4-2	Morton 2, Craig, McPhail	6,000
Apr 20	Aberdeen	D 2-2	Archibald, Morton	18,000
Apr 24	Partick Thistle	D 1-1	Muirhead	10,000
Apr 27	DUNDEE	W 3-0	Marshall, Fleming, McPhail	5,000

Scottish Cup

Jan 19	EDINBURGH CITY	(Rd1) W11-1	Fleming 3, Craig 2 (1 pen), McPhail 2, Morton 2, Cunningham, Archibald	10,500
Feb 2	PARTICK THISTLE	(Rd2) W 5-1	Fleming 3, Craig, Morton	67,000
Feb 16	Clyde	(Rd3) W 2-0	Muirhead, Archibald	34,000
Mar 2	DUNDEE UNITED	(QF) W 3-1	Marshall, Fleming, McPhail	49,000
Mar 23	St Mirren*	(SF) W 3-2	Muirhead, Archibald, Morton	69,727
Apr 6	Kilmarnock*	(F) L 0-2		114,780

*Played at Hampden Park.

League & Cup Appearances

PLAYER	LEAGUE	CUP COMPETITION S CUP	TOTAL
Archibald	32	6	38
Buchanan	32	6	38
Craig	34	6	40
Cunningham	8	1	9
Fleming	35	6	41
Gray	35	6	41
Hamilton R	34	5	39
Hamilton T	38	6	44
Ireland	7		7
McDonald	3		3
McMillan	6		6
McPhail	33	6	39
Marshall	18	1	19
Meiklejohn	30	5	35
Morton	37	6	43
Muirhead	28	5	33
Osborne	1		1
Simpson	5	1	6
Smith	2		2

Goalscorers

PLAYER	LEAGUE	CUP COMPETITION S CUP	TOTAL
Fleming	33	7	40
McPhail	18	3	21
Morton	14	4	18
Archibald	12	3	15
Craig	6	3	9
Muirhead	6	2	8
Marshall	6	1	7
Meiklejohn	5		5
Cunningham	3	1	4
Buchanan	2		2
McMillan	2		2

Fact File

On 1 January 1929, Rangers opened their new 10,000 seat Main Stand at Ibrox and marked the occasion with a 3-0 win over Celtic.

Final Scottish League Div 1 Table

		P	W	D	L	F	A	Pts
1	Rangers	38	30	7	1	107	32	67
2	Celtic	38	22	7	9	67	44	51
3	Motherwell	38	20	10	8	85	66	50
4	Hearts	38	19	9	10	91	57	47
5	Queen's Park	38	18	7	13	100	69	43
6	Partick T	38	17	7	14	91	70	41
7	Aberdeen	38	16	8	14	81	68	40
8	St Mirren	38	16	8	14	78	75	40
9	St Johnstone	38	14	10	14	57	70	38
10	Kilmarnock	38	14	8	16	79	74	36
11	Falkirk	38	14	8	16	68	86	36
12	Hamilton A	38	13	9	16	58	83	35
13	Cowdenbeath	38	14	5	19	55	69	33
14	Hibernian	38	13	6	19	54	62	32
15	Airdrieonians	38	12	7	19	56	65	31
16	Ayr U	38	12	7	19	65	84	31
17	Clyde	38	12	6	20	47	71	30
18	Dundee	38	9	11	18	59	69	29
19	Third Lanark	38	10	6	22	71	102	26
20	Raith R	38	9	6	23	52	105	24

MANAGER: Bill Struth

CAPTAIN: Tommy Muirhead

TOP SCORER: Jimmy Fleming

BIGGEST WIN: 11-1 v Edinburgh City, 19 January 1929, Scottish Cup

HIGHEST ATTENDANCE: 114,780 v Kilmarnock, 6 April 1929, Scottish Cup

MAJOR TRANSFERS IN: Jimmy Smith from East Stirling, Bob 'Whitey' McDonald from Bethlehem Steel (USA)

MAJOR TRANSFERS OUT: Andy Cunningham to Newcastle United

Season 1929-30

Scottish League Division 1

DATE	OPPONENTS	SCORE	GOALSCORERS	ATTENDANCE
Aug 10	Motherwell	W 2-0	Archibald, Fleming	25,000
Aug 17	HIBERNIAN	W 3-0	McPhail, Marshall, Nicholson	18,000
Aug 24	St Johnstone	W 1-0	Marshall	10,000
Aug 31	FALKIRK	W 4-0	Fleming, Marshall, McPherson, Craig	28,000
Sep 3	QUEEN'S PARK	W 1-0	Archibald	18,000
Sep 7	Aberdeen	D 1-1	Morton	36,000
Sep 14	ST MIRREN	W 2-1	Marshall, Archibald	25,000
Sep 21	Kilmarnock	L 0-1		23,000
Sep 28	DUNDEE UNITED	W 3-1	Archibald 2, McPhail	20,000
Oct 5	Hearts	L 0-2		41,000
Oct 19	Partick Thistle	W 1-0	Fleming	40,000
Oct 26	CELTIC	W 1-0	Nicholson	50,000
Nov 9	HAMILTON A	W 5-2	Fleming 3, Archibald, McPherson	12,000
Nov 16	AYR UNITED	W 9-0	Fleming 4, Archibald 2, Marshall 2, Brown	12,000
Nov 23	Clyde	D 3-3	Brown, Morton (pen), Fleming	25,000
Nov 30	Morton	D 2-2	Fleming 2	18,000
Dec 7	DUNDEE	W 4-1	Brown, Craig, Fleming, Archibald	12,000
Dec 14	AIRDRIE	W 2-0	McPhail, Brown	11,000
Dec 21	MOTHERWELL	W 4-2	McPhail 2, Brown, Fleming	22,000
Dec 28	Hibernian	W 2-0	Fleming, Brown	18,000
Jan 1	Celtic	W 2-1	Morton (pen), Brown	40,000
Jan 2	PARTICK THISTLE	W 2-1	Archibald, McPhail	35,000
Jan 4	ST JOHNSTONE	W 6-1	Fleming 3, Marshall 2, Morton (pen)	15,000
Jan 25	ABERDEEN	W 3-1	Archibald 2, McPhail	45,000
Feb 8	KILMARNOCK	W 4-0	Morton (pen), Fleming, McPhail, Brown	25,000
Feb 11	St Mirren	W 1-0	Fleming	10,000
Feb 19	Dundee United	W 1-0	Fleming	8,000
Feb 22	HEARTS	L 1-3	McPhail	10,000
Mar 4	Queen's Park	W 3-1	Fleming, McPhail, Marshall	13,000
Mar 8	COWDENBEATH	W 5-0	McPhail 2, Fleming 2, Marshall	12,000
Mar 15	Hamilton A	D 1-1	McPhail	18,000
Mar 26	Ayr United	W 3-0	Marshall (pen), Fleming, Brown	6,000
Mar 29	CLYDE	W 3-0	Marshall 2 (1 pen), Muirhead	10,000
Apr 19	Airdrie	L 0-1		4,000
Apr 21	MORTON	W 3-0	Brown, Fleming, Marshall	10,000
Apr 23	Dundee	W 3-1	McPhail 2, Smith	8,000
Apr 26	Cowdenbeath	L 2-3	McPhail 2	2,500
Apr 30	Falkirk	L 1-2	Brown	5,000

Scottish Cup

Jan 13	Queen's Park	(Rd1) W 1-0	McPhail	95,722
Feb 1	COWDENBEATH	(Rd2) D 2-2	Morton 2	40,000
Feb 5	Cowdenbeath	(R) W 3-0	McPhail 2, Fleming	18,754
Feb 15	Motherwell	(Rd3) W 5-2	Fleming 2, McPhail 2, Archibald	27,500
Mar 1	MONTROSE	(QF) W 3-0	Morton 2, Brown	12,500
Mar 22	Hearts*	(SF) W 4-1	Fleming 3, McPhail	92,084
Apr 12	Partick Thistle*	(F) D 0-0		107,457
Apr 16	Partick Thistle*	(R) W 2-1	Marshall, Craig	103,688

*Played at Hampden Park.

League & Cup Appearances

PLAYER	LEAGUE	CUP COMPETITION		TOTAL
		S CUP		
Archibald	34	8		42
Brown	17	5		22
Buchanan	25	7		32
Craig	27	8		35
Fleming	34	7		41
Gray	34	8		42
Hamilton R	29	8		37
Hamilton T	38	8		46
Ireland	1			1
Lockie	2			2
McCandless	2			2
McDonald	13	1		14
McMillan	5			5
McPhail	23	8		31
McPherson	6			6
Main	1			1
Marshall	26	4		30
Meiklejohn	31	8		39
Morton	24	7		31
Muirhead	20			20
Nicholson	12	1		13
Osborne	1			1
Purdon	4			4
Simpson	8			8
Smith	1			1

Goalscorers

PLAYER	LEAGUE	CUP COMPETITION		TOTAL
		S CUP		
Fleming	27	6		33
McPhail	17	6		23
Marshall	14	1		15
Archibald	12	1		13
Brown	11	1		12
Morton	5	4		9
Craig	2	1		3
McPherson	2			2
Nicholson	2			2
Muirhead	1			1
Smith	1			1

Fact File

Rangers won every trophy available to them in 1929-30, beating Celtic in the finals of both the Glasgow Cup and Charity Cup.

Final Scottish League Div 1 Table

		P	W	D	L	F	A	Pts
1	RANGERS	38	28	4	6	94	32	60
2	MOTHERWELL	38	25	5	8	104	48	55
3	ABERDEEN	38	23	7	8	85	61	53
4	CELTIC	38	22	5	11	88	46	49
5	ST MIRREN	38	18	5	15	73	56	41
6	PARTICK T	38	16	9	13	72	61	41
7	FALKIRK	38	16	9	13	62	64	41
8	KILMARNOCK	38	15	9	14	77	73	39
9	AYR U	38	16	6	16	70	92	38
10	HEARTS	38	14	9	15	69	69	37
11	CLYDE	38	13	11	14	64	69	37
12	AIRDRIEONIANS	38	16	4	18	60	66	36
13	HAMILTON A	38	14	7	17	76	81	35
14	DUNDEE	38	14	6	18	51	58	34
15	QUEEN'S PARK	38	15	4	19	67	80	34
16	COWDENBEATH	38	13	7	18	64	74	33
17	HIBERNIAN	38	9	11	18	45	62	29
18	MORTON	38	10	7	21	67	95	27
19	DUNDEE U	38	7	8	23	56	109	22
20	ST JOHNSTONE	38	6	7	25	48	96	19

MANAGER: Bill Struth

CAPTAIN: Tommy Muirhead

TOP SCORER: Jimmy Fleming

BIGGEST WIN: 9-0 v Ayr United, 16 November 1929, league

HIGHEST ATTENDANCE: 107,475 v Partick Thistle, 12 April 1930, Scottish Cup

MAJOR TRANSFERS IN: George Brown from Ashfield, Bobby Main from Baillieston, Jerry Dawson from Camelon

Season 1930-31

Scottish League Division 1

DATE	OPPONENTS	SCORE	GOALSCORERS	ATTENDANCE
Aug 9	Cowdenbeath	W 3-1	Smith 2, Marshall	12,000
Aug 16	HEARTS	W 4-1	Smith 2, Archibald, Morton (pen)	40,000
Aug 23	Dundee	W 1-0	Smith	22,000
Aug 30	MOTHERWELL	D 1-1	Marshall	40,000
Sep 2	HAMILTON A	W 1-0	Brown	30,000
Sep 6	St Mirren	D 1-1	Smith	20,000
Sep 13	LEITH ATHLETIC	W 4-1	Fleming 2, McPhail 2	15,000
Sep 20	Celtic	L 0-2		70,000
Sep 27	PARTICK THISTLE	W 3-1	Smith 2, Morton	25,000
Oct 4	Airdrie	D 3-3	Smith, McPhail, Gray (pen)	15,000
Oct 18	Kilmarnock	L 0-1		15,000
Nov 1	ABERDEEN	W 4-0	Fleming, Morton, McGowan, McPhail	12,000
Nov 8	Falkirk	W 3-1	McGowan 2, Brown	12,000
Nov 15	Queen's Park	W 2-0	Marshall 2	25,000
Nov 22	MORTON	W 7-1	McGowan 2, McPhail, Craig, Morton, Marshall, Gray (pen)	10,000
Nov 29	CLYDE	W 5-1	McPhail 2, McGowan, Marshall, Fleming	10,000
Dec 6	Hibernian	W 2-1	McPhail 2	20,000
Dec 13	EAST FIFE	W 4-0	Marshall 2, McGowan 2	10,000
Dec 20	COWDENBEATH	W 7-0	McGowan 2, Marshall 2, McPhail 2, Archibald	16,000
Dec 27	Hearts	L 0-3		37,000
Jan 1	CELTIC	W 1-0	Morton	83,500
Jan 3	DUNDEE	W 3-0	Marshall, Fleming, McPhail	20,000
Jan 10	Motherwell	L 0-1		26,000
Jan 24	ST MIRREN	D 1-1	McPhail	15,000
Feb 7	AIRDRIE	L 0-1		14,000
Feb 14	Clyde	W 8-0	Smith 5, Meiklejohn, Marshall, McPhail	15,000
Feb 18	Ayr United	D 2-2	Smith, Marshall	7,000
Feb 21	KILMARNOCK	W 1-0	Marshall	10,000
Feb 28	Hamilton A	W 3-0	Marshall 2, Smith	10,000
Mar 7	Aberdeen	W 3-1	Smith, Archibald, Marshall	10,000
Mar 14	Leith Athletic	W 3-1	McPhail, Archibald, Morton	9,000
Mar 18	FALKIRK	W 1-0	Smith	9,000
Apr 1	QUEEN'S PARK	W 2-0	Smith, McPhail	10,000
Apr 4	Morton	W 2-1	Archibald, Brown	14,000
Apr 6	AYR UNITED	W 5-1	McPhail 2, Marshall 2, Morton	14,000
Apr 18	HIBERNIAN	W 1-0	Smith	10,000
Apr 22	Partick Thistle	D 1-1	McPhail	43,400
Apr 25	East Fife	W 4-0	McPhail, Smith, Marshall, Archibald	8,000

Scottish Cup

Jan 17	Armadale	(Rd1) W 7-1	Fleming 3, McPhail 2, Morton (pen), Marshall	5,527
Jan 31	DUNDEE	(Rd2) L 1-2	Fleming	17,000

League & Cup Appearances

PLAYER	LEAGUE	CUP COMPETITION S CUP	TOTAL
Archibald	28	1	29
Brown	29		29
Buchanan	26	2	28
Conlin	2		2
Craig	14		14
Dawson	1		1
Fleming	13	2	15
Gray	38	2	40
Hamilton R	27	2	29
Hamilton T	37	2	39
McAulay	3		3
McDonald	13	2	15
McGowan	12	1	13
McMillan	1		1
McPhail	34	2	36
Main	2		2
Marshall	32	2	34
Meiklejohn	31	1	32
Morton	32	2	34
Murray	4		4
Nicholson	6		6
Simpson	12	1	13
Smith	21		21

Goalscorers

PLAYER	LEAGUE	CUP COMPETITION S CUP	TOTAL
McPhail	20	2	22
Marshall	20	1	21
Smith	21		21
McGowan	10		10
Fleming	5	4	9
Morton	7	1	8
Archibald	6		6
Brown	3		3
Gray	2		2
Craig	1		1
Meiklejohn	1		1

Fact File

Davie Meiklejohn captained Scotland to a 2-0 win over England at Hampden Park on 28 March 1931 with his Rangers team-mates Sandy Archibald, Bob McPhail and Alan Morton also in the side.

MANAGER: Bill Struth

CAPTAIN: Davie Meiklejohn

TOP SCORER: Bob McPhail

BIGGEST WIN: 8-0 v Clyde, 14 February 1931, league

HIGHEST ATTENDANCE: 83,500 v Celtic, 1 January 1931, league

MAJOR TRANSFERS IN: Bob McAulay from Fall River (USA)

MAJOR TRANSFERS OUT: Jock Buchanan to Linfield

Final Scottish League Div 1 Table

		P	W	D	L	F	A	Pts
1	RANGERS	38	27	6	5	96	29	60
2	CELTIC	38	24	10	4	101	34	58
3	MOTHERWELL	38	24	8	6	102	42	56
4	PARTICK T	38	24	5	9	76	43	53
5	HEARTS	38	19	6	13	90	63	44
6	ABERDEEN	38	17	7	14	79	63	41
7	COWDENBEATH	38	17	7	14	58	65	41
8	DUNDEE	38	17	5	16	65	63	39
9	AIRDRIEONIANS	38	17	5	16	59	66	39
10	HAMILTON A	38	16	5	17	59	57	37
11	KILMARNOCK	38	15	5	18	59	60	35
12	CLYDE	38	15	4	19	60	87	34
13	QUEEN'S PARK	38	13	7	18	71	72	33
14	FALKIRK	38	14	4	20	77	87	32
15	ST MIRREN	38	11	8	19	49	72	30
16	MORTON	38	11	7	20	58	83	29
17	LEITH ATH.	38	8	11	19	51	85	27
18	AYR U	38	8	11	19	53	92	27
19	HIBERNIAN	38	9	7	22	49	81	25
20	EAST FIFE	38	8	4	26	45	113	20

Season 1931-32

Scottish League Division 1

DATE	OPPONENTS	SCORE	GOALSCORERS	ATTENDANCE
Aug 8	DUNDEE	W 4-1	English 2, Marshall, Nicholson	30,000
Aug 11	AIRDRIE	W 2-1	Smith 2	10,000
Aug 15	Motherwell	L 2-4	Fleming, Smith	25,000
Aug 18	MORTON	W 7-3	English 5, McPhail 2	10,000
Aug 22	ST MIRREN	W 4-0	English, Brown, Meiklejohn, Nicholson	25,000
Aug 25	LEITH ATHLETIC	W 4-0	Fleming 2, McPhail, English	6,000
Aug 29	Ayr United	W 3-1	English 2, McPhail	13,000
Sep 2	Falkirk	W 2-1	English, McPhail	13,000
Sep 5	CELTIC	D 0-0		80,000
Sep 12	Partick Thistle	W 3-1	McPhail, Fleming, Calderwood o.g.	30,000
Sep 15	ABERDEEN	W 4-1	Fleming 2, Nicholson, McPhail	10,000
Sep 26	Hearts	D 0-0		32,000
Oct 3	COWDENBEATH	W 6-1	Meiklejohn 2, Marshall 2, English 2	8,000
Oct 17	QUEEN'S PARK	L 0-1		20,000
Oct 24	Hamilton A	W 2-1	English, Marshall	-
Oct 31	DUNDEE UNITED	W 5-0	English 3, Murray 2	-
Nov 14	CLYDE	D 2-2	McPhail, English	6,000
Nov 21	Morton	W 2-1	Meiklejohn, English	15,000
Nov 28	Leith Athletic	W 5-2	English 3, Craig, Fleming	7,000
Dec 5	FALKIRK	W 4-0	English 3, Smith	5,000
Dec 12	Aberdeen	D 0-0		24,000
Dec 19	Dundee	L 2-4	McPhail, English	15,000
Dec 26	MOTHERWELL	W 1-0	English	50,000
Jan 1	Celtic	W 2-1	Archibald, Marshall	55,000
Jan 2	PARTICK THISTLE	W 4-0	Fleming 2, McPhail, Marshall (pen)	20,000
Jan 9	St Mirren	W 2-0	Fleming 2	15,000
Jan 23	AYR UNITED	W 6-1	English 3, McPhail 2, Fleming	15,000
Feb 6	HEARTS	W 4-2	McPhail, Marshall, English, Fleming	30,000
Feb 20	THIRD LANARK	W 6-1	McPhail 2, English 2, Archibald, Marshall	25,000
Feb 27	Queen's Park	W 6-1	English 4, McPhail, Marshall	30,000
Mar 12	Dundee United	W 5-0	English 2, Fleming 2, Archibald	-
Mar 19	KILMARNOCK	W 3-0	McPhail, English, Marshall	25,000
Mar 28	Third Lanark	L 3-4	English 2, Marshall	40,000
Apr 2	Cowdenbeath	W 7-1	McPhail 3, Marshall 2, English, Fleming	7,000
Apr 23	Clyde	D 1-1	Marshall (pen)	15,000
Apr 25	Airdrie	L 0-3		6,000
Apr 27	HAMILTON A	W 1-0	Meiklejohn	6,000
Apr 30	Kilmarnock	W 4-2	McPhail 2, Marshall, Smith	10,000

Scottish Cup

Jan 16	BRECHIN CITY	(Rd1) W 8-2	English 3, McPhail 2, Fleming 2, Marshall	6,000	
Jan 30	Raith Rovers	(Rd2) W 5-0	English 3, Archibald, Fleming	18,052	
Feb 13	Hearts	(Rd3) W 1-0	Marshall	53,496	
Mar 5	MOTHERWELL	(QF) W 2-0	Murray, McPhail	88,000	
Mar 26	Hamilton A*	(SF) W 5-2	Marshall 2, English 2, Archibald	53,000	
Apr 16	Kilmarnock†	(F) D 1-1	McPhail	111,982	
Apr 20	Kilmarnock†	(R) W 3-0	Fleming, McPhail, English	105,695	

*Played at Parkhead. †Played at Hampden Park.

MANAGER: Bill Struth

CAPTAIN: Davie Meiklejohn

TOP SCORER: Sam English

BIGGEST WIN: 8-2 v Brechin City, Scottish Cup, 16 January 1932

HIGHEST ATTENDANCE: 111,982 v Kilmarnock, 16 April 1932, Scottish Cup

MAJOR TRANSFERS IN: Sam English from Coleraine

MAJOR TRANSFERS OUT: Bob McAulay to Chelsea

League & Cup Appearances

PLAYER	LEAGUE	CUP COMPETITION S CUP	TOTAL
Archibald	21	6	27
Brown	32	7	39
Craig	8		8
Dawson	13		13
Deans	1		1
English	35	7	42
Fleming	24	5	29
Gray	35	6	41
Hamilton R	5	1	6
Hamilton T	25	7	32
McAulay	36	7	43
McDonald	7		7
McPhail	35	7	42
Main	1		1
Marshall	34	6	40
Meiklejohn	34	7	41
Morton	14	3	17
Murray	6	1	7
Nicholson	11		11
Simpson	33	7	40
Smith	8		8

Goalscorers

PLAYER	LEAGUE	CUP COMPETITION S CUP	TOTAL
English	44	9	53
McPhail	22	5	27
Fleming	16	4	20
Marshall	15	4	19
Archibald	3	2	5
Meiklejohn	5		5
Smith	5		5
Murray	2	1	3
Nicholson	3		3
Brown	1		1
Craig	1		1
Opps' o.gs.	1		1

Fact File

Rangers won both the Glasgow and Charity Cups in 1931-32, defeating Queen's Park and Third Lanark respectively in the finals at Hampden.

Final Scottish League Div 1 Table

		P	W	D	L	F	A	Pts
1	MOTHERWELL	38	30	6	2	119	31	66
2	RANGERS	38	28	5	5	118	42	61
3	CELTIC	38	20	8	10	94	50	48
4	THIRD LANARK	38	21	4	13	92	81	46
5	ST MIRREN	38	20	4	14	77	56	44
6	PARTICK T	38	19	4	15	58	59	42
7	ABERDEEN	38	16	9	13	57	49	41
8	HEARTS	38	17	5	16	63	61	39
9	KILMARNOCK	38	16	7	15	68	70	39
10	HAMILTON A	38	16	6	16	84	65	38
11	DUNDEE	38	14	10	14	61	72	38
12	COWDENBEATH	38	15	8	15	66	78	38
13	CLYDE	38	13	9	16	58	70	35
14	AIRDRIEONIANS	38	13	6	19	74	81	32
15	MORTON	38	12	7	19	78	87	31
16	QUEEN'S PARK	38	13	5	20	59	79	31
17	AYR U	38	11	7	20	70	90	29
18	FALKIRK	38	11	5	22	70	76	27
19	DUNDEE U	38	6	7	25	40	118	19
20	LEITH ATH.	38	6	4	28	46	137	16

Season 1932-33

Scottish League Division 1

DATE	OPPONENTS	SCORE	GOALSCORERS	ATTENDANCE
Aug 13	St Mirren	L 0-2		25,000
Aug 17	Morton	W 3-1	Smith 2, McPhail	16,000
Aug 20	AYR UNITED	W 4-1	English 2, McPhail, McLeod o.g.	17,000
Aug 23	CLYDE	D 2-2	McPhail, McDonald (pen)	8,000
Aug 27	Airdrie	W 2-1	Fleming 2	12,000
Aug 31	THIRD LANARK	W 5-0	Smith 2, Archibald 2, McPhail	10,000
Sep 3	EAST STIRLING	W 4-0	Smith 3, McPhail	10,000
Sep 10	Celtic	D 1-1	McPhail	60,000
Sep 17	PARTICK THISTLE	W 3-0	Smith 2, Morton	13,000
Sep 24	Cowdenbeath	W 3-2	McPhail, Morton, Smith	5,000
Oct 1	MOTHERWELL	D 2-2	McPhail 2	55,000
Oct 8	Dundee	W 3-0	Smith 2, McPhail	6,600
Oct 22	Hearts	L 0-1		25,000
Oct 29	KILMARNOCK	W 2-0	Archibald, Marshall	9,000
Nov 5	Clyde	W 5-0	Marshall 3, McPhail, English	20,000
Nov 12	MORTON	W 6-1	Meiklejohn, English, McPhail, Marshall, Fleming, Smith	-
Nov 19	ST JOHNSTONE	W 3-0	McPhail 2, Smith	
Nov 26	Falkirk	W 4-1	English, Meiklejohn, Smith, Marshall	12,000
Dec 3	ABERDEEN	W 3-1	English 2, Marshall	20,000
Dec 10	Queen's Park	D 0-0		16,000
Dec 17	HAMILTON A	D 4-4	Marshall 2, McPhail, Smith	8,000
Dec 24	ST MIRREN	W 4-0	Marshall 2, McPhail, English	15,000
Dec 31	Ayr United	D 3-3	Smith, Archibald, Fleming	10,000
Jan 2	CELTIC	D 0-0		42,000
Jan 3	Partick Thistle	D 0-0		40,000
Jan 7	Airdrie	W 5-1	Smith 2 (1 pen), McPhail 2, Morton	7,000
Jan 14	East Stirling	W 3-2	Smith 2, Campbell	5,000
Jan 28	COWDENBEATH	W 4-1	Smith 3, Fleming	7,000
Feb 11	Motherwell	W 3-1	Fleming 2, Smith (pen)	30,000
Feb 25	DUNDEE	W 6-4	Marshall 2, Fleming 2, Smith, Nicholson	8,000
Mar 4	Third Lanark	W 3-1	McPhail 2, English	15,000
Mar 11	HEARTS	D 4-4	McPhail 3, Fleming	28,000
Mar 18	Kilmarnock	W 6-2	Smith 3, McPhail 2, English	7,000
Mar 25	St Johnstone	W 2-0	Smith 2	12,000
Apr 8	FALKIRK	W 5-1	Marshall 2, McPhail, Smith, Fleming	12,000
Apr 15	Aberdeen	D 1-1	Smith	22,000
Apr 22	QUEEN'S PARK	W 1-0	McPhail	22,000
Apr 29	Hamilton A	W 4-2	McPhail 2, Fleming, Marshall	4,000

Scottish Cup

DATE	OPPONENTS		SCORE	GOALSCORERS	ATTENDANCE
Jan 23	ARBROATH	(Rd1)	W 3-1	Marshall 2, Smith	5,000
Feb 4	QUEEN'S PARK	(Rd2)	D 1-1	English	30,006
Feb 8	Queen's Park	(R)	D 1-1	Marshall	31,805
Feb 13	Queen's Park	(2R)	W 3-1	Marshall, Fleming, Smith	45,217
Feb 18	Kilmarnock	(Rd3)	L 0-1		-

League & Cup Appearances

PLAYER	LEAGUE	CUP COMPETITION S CUP	TOTAL
Archibald	28	2	30
Brown	38	2	40
Campbell	2		2
Craig	4	4	8
Dawson	20	5	25
Deans	1		1
English	25	5	30
Fleming	21	2	23
Gray	37	4	41
Hamilton R	4	1	5
Hamilton T	18		18
Kennedy	10	1	11
McDonald	29	5	34
McPhail	31	1	32
Main	3	3	6
Marshall	34	5	39
Mason	2		2
Meiklejohn	31	4	35
Morton	6		6
Nicholson	2	1	3
Russell	5		5
Simpson	32	4	36
Smith	34	5	39
Stevenson	1		1

Goalscorers

PLAYER	LEAGUE	CUP COMPETITION S CUP	TOTAL
Smith	33	2	35
McPhail	29		29
Marshall	16	4	20
Fleming	12	1	13
English	10	1	11
Archibald	4		4
Morton	3		3
Meiklejohn	2		2
Campbell	1		1
McDonald	1		1
Nicholson	1		1
Opps' o.gs.	1		1

Fact File

Rapid Vienna became the first foreign club to play at Ibrox when Rangers drew 3-3 with the Austrian side in a friendly on 21 January 1933.

MANAGER: Bill Struth

CAPTAIN: Davie Meiklejohn

TOP SCORER: Jimmy Smith

BIGGEST WIN: 6-1 v Morton, 12 November 1932, league

HIGHEST ATENDANCE: 60,000 v Celtic, 10 September 1932, league,

MAJOR TRANSFERS IN: Archie MacAuley from Camelon

MAJOR TRANSFERS OUT: Bob McGowan to Bournemouth

Final Scottish League Div 1 Table

		P	W	D	L	F	A	Pts
1	RANGERS	38	26	10	2	113	43	62
2	MOTHERWELL	38	27	5	6	114	53	59
3	HEARTS	38	21	8	9	84	51	50
4	CELTIC	38	20	8	10	75	44	48
5	ST JOHNSTONE	38	17	10	11	70	55	44
6	ABERDEEN	38	18	6	14	85	58	42
7	ST MIRREN	38	18	6	14	73	60	42
8	HAMILTON A	38	18	6	14	90	78	42
9	QUEEN'S PARK	38	17	7	14	78	79	41
10	PARTICK T	38	17	6	15	75	55	40
11	FALKIRK	38	15	6	17	70	70	36
12	CLYDE	38	15	5	18	69	75	35
13	THIRD LANARK	38	14	7	17	70	80	35
14	KILMARNOCK	38	13	9	16	72	86	35
15	DUNDEE	38	12	9	17	60	77	33
16	AYR U	38	13	4	21	62	95	30
17	COWDENBEATH	38	10	5	23	65	111	25
18	AIRDRIEONIANS	38	10	3	25	55	102	23
19	MORTON	38	6	9	23	49	97	21
20	EAST STIRLINGSHIRE	38	7	3	28	55	115	17

Season 1933-34

Scottish League Division 1

DATE	OPPONENTS	SCORE	GOALSCORERS	ATTENDANCE
Aug 12	AIRDRIE	W 5-1	Smith 4, Nicholson	10,000
Aug 15	AYR UNITED	W 9-1	Smith 6, Stevenson 3	8,000
Aug 19	Hibernian	D 0-0		21,000
Aug 22	Clyde	W 6-1	Smith 2, McPhail 2, Archibald, Stevenson	20,000
Aug 25	COWDENBEATH	W 3-1	Archibald, Smith (pen), McPhail	7,000
Sep 2	Motherwell	L 1-2	Stevenson	30,000
Sep 9	CELTIC	D 2-2	McPhail, Smith (pen)	49,000
Sep 13	QUEEN OF THE SOUTH	W 5-1	Nicholson 3, Stevenson, Smith	7,000
Sep 16	Ayr United	W 2-0	Fleming 2	-
Sep 23	DUNDEE	W 1-0	McPhail	14,000
Sep 30	Partick Thistle	W 4-3	Main, Fleming, Brown, Stevenson	20,000
Oct 7	ST MIRREN	W 3-0	McPhail 2, Main	14,000
Oct 21	HEARTS	W 3-1	Smith 2 (1 pen), McPhail	30,000
Oct 28	Kilmarnock	W 3-1	McPhail, Smith, Marshall	16,000
Nov 4	CLYDE	W 3-1	Smith 3	10,000
Nov 11	Queen of the South	W 4-0	Smith 3, McPhail	11,040
Nov 18	St Johnstone	L 1-3	Smith	6,000
Nov 25	FALKIRK	W 3-1	McPhail 2, Smith	12,000
Dec 2	Aberdeen	W 2-1	Marshall, Smith (pen)	21,000
Dec 9	QUEEN'S PARK	W 4-0	Smith 2, McPhail, Meiklejohn	10,000
Dec 23	Airdrie	W 7-2	McPhail 3, Fleming 3, Nicholson	-
Dec 30	HIBERNIAN	W 6-0	Smith 3, McPhail 2, Venters	6,000
Jan 1	Celtic	D 2-2	Venters, McPhail	40,000
Jan 2	PARTICK THISTLE	D 2-2	Marshall, Main	20,000
Jan 6	Cowdenbeath	W 4-3	Fleming, Simpson, McPhail, Nicholson	2,000
Jan 13	MOTHERWELL	W 4-2	McPhail 2, Fleming 2	67,000
Jan 27	Dundee	W 6-0	Fleming 5, Smith	20,000
Feb 24	St Mirren	W 2-1	Marshall, Smith	14,000
Mar 10	Hearts	W 2-1	Smith, Marshall	26,000
Mar 14	Hamilton A	W 2-1	MacAuley, Main	10,000
Mar 17	KILMARNOCK	D 2-2	Nicholson, Fleming	7,000
Mar 21	THIRD LANARK	W 1-0	Venters	4,000
Mar 31	ST JOHNSTONE	W 3-0	Venters, Smith, Fleming	13,000
Apr 2	Third Lanark	W 1-0	Marshall	18,000
Apr 7	ABERDEEN	W 2-1	Smith, Falloon o.g.	18,000
Apr 25	Falkirk	W 3-1	Smith 2, Marshall	15,000
Apr 28	HAMILTON A	W 4-2	Nicholson, Venters, Smith, Meiklejohn	-
Apr 30	Queen's Park	D 1-1	Smith	8,000

Scottish Cup

Jan 20	BLAIRGOWRIE	(Rd1) W14-2	Fleming 9, Venters 2, Marshall 2, Nicholson	5,000
Feb 3	Third Lanark	(Rd2) W 3-0	Smith 3	27,038
Feb 17	HEARTS	(Rd3) D 0-0		69,543
Feb 21	Hearts	(R) W 2-1	McPhail, Fleming	47,453
Mar 3	ABERDEEN	(QF) W 1-0	Smith	53,000
Mar 31	St Johnstone*	(SF) W 1-0	Marshall	60,119
Apr 21	St Mirren*	(F) W 5-0	Nicholson 2, McPhail, Main, Smith	113,403

*Played at Hampden Park.

League & Cup Appearances

PLAYER	LEAGUE	CUP COMPETITION S CUP	TOTAL
Archibald	15		15
Brown	35	6	41
Cheyne	3		3
Craig	8	3	11
Dawson	30	6	36
Fleming	13	5	18
Gillick	2		2
Gray	37	7	44
Hamilton	1	1	2
Jenkins	7		7
Kennedy	7		7
MacAuley	5	1	6
McDonald	38	6	44
McPhail	25	6	31
Main	25	6	31
Marshall	21	7	28
Mason	1		1
Meiklejohn	29	5	34
Nicholson	26	3	29
Russell	3	1	4
Simpson	29	7	36
Smith	32	6	38
Stevenson	11		11
Venters	15	1	16

Goalscorers

PLAYER	LEAGUE	CUP COMPETITION S CUP	TOTAL
Smith	41	5	46
Fleming	16	10	26
McPhail	22	2	24
Nicholson	8	3	11
Marshall	7	3	10
Stevenson	7		7
Venters	5	2	7
Main	4	1	5
Archibald	2		2
Meiklejohn	2		2
Brown	1		1
MacAuley	1		1
Simpson	1		1
Opps' o.gs.	1		1

Fact File

Rangers defeated Arsenal 5-1 on aggregate – 2-0 at Ibrox and 3-1 at Highbury – in 'British Championship' matches on 20 and 27 September 1933.

MANAGER: Bill Struth

CAPTAIN: Davie Meiklejohn

TOP SCORER: Jimmy Smith

BIGGEST WIN: 14-2 v Blairgowrie, 20 January 1934, Scottish Cup

HIGHEST ATTENDANCE: 113,403 v St Mirren, 21 April 1934, Scottish Cup

MAJOR TRANSFERS IN: Torry Gillick from Petershill, Alec Venters from Cowdenbeath

MAJOR TRANSFERS OUT: Sam English to Liverpool

Final Scottish League Div 1 Table

		P	W	D	L	F	A	Pts
1	RANGERS	38	30	6	2	118	41	66
2	MOTHERWELL	38	29	4	5	97	45	62
3	CELTIC	38	18	11	9	78	53	47
4	Q OF S	38	21	3	14	75	78	45
5	ABERDEEN	38	18	8	12	90	57	44
6	HEARTS	38	17	10	11	86	59	44
7	KILMARNOCK	38	17	9	12	73	64	43
8	AYR U	38	16	10	12	87	92	42
9	ST JOHNSTONE	38	17	6	15	74	53	40
10	FALKIRK	38	16	6	16	73	68	38
11	HAMILTON A	38	15	8	15	65	79	38
12	DUNDEE	38	15	6	17	68	64	36
13	PARTICK T	38	14	5	19	73	78	33
14	CLYDE	38	10	11	17	56	70	31
15	QUEEN'S PARK	38	13	5	20	65	85	31
16	HIBERNIAN	38	12	3	23	51	69	27
17	ST MIRREN	38	9	9	20	46	75	27
18	AIRDRIEONIANS	38	10	6	22	59	103	26
19	THIRD LANARK	38	8	9	21	62	103	25
20	COWDENBEATH	38	5	5	28	58	118	15

Season 1934-35

Scottish League Division 1

DATE	OPPONENTS	SCORE	GOALSCORERS	ATTENDANCE
Aug 11	Dunfermline	W 7-1	Smith 6, Main	14,000
Aug 18	MOTHERWELL	W 1-0	Meiklejohn	51,000
Aug 22	HEARTS	W 2-1	Main 2	30,000
Aug 25	Dundee	L 2-3	Craig, Brown	19,000
Sep 1	PARTICK THISTLE	W 4-0	Main, McPhail, MacAuley, Smith	20,000
Sep 4	Kilmarnock	W 3-1	Smith, McPhail, Venters	13,000
Sep 8	Celtic	D 1-1	Smith	40,000
Sep 15	AYR UNITED	W 2-0	McPhail, MacAuley	10,000
Sep 22	St Mirren	W 2-0	McPhail, Smith	10,000
Sep 29	HIBERNIAN	W 4-2	Smith 2, Meiklejohn, Main	10,000
Oct 6	Airdrie	W 2-1	Fleming, Simpson	10,000
Oct 20	Clyde	L 1-2	McPhail	30,000
Oct 27	Queen of the South	W 3-2	Gillick 2, Venters	12,100
Nov 3	ST JOHNSTONE	W 3-1	Venters 2, Gillick	20,000
Nov 10	Albion Rovers	W 5-1	Smith 3, Venters, McPhail	-
Nov 17	ABERDEEN	D 2-2	Smith 2	18,000
Nov 24	Queen's Park	W 4-0	Smith 3, Gillick	16,000
Dec 1	HAMILTON A	D 1-1	Gillick	14,000
Dec 8	Hearts	L 1-4	Gillick	35,000
Dec 15	KILMARNOCK	L 2-3	Venters, Gillick	18,000
Dec 22	DUNFERMLINE	W 8-1	Smith 4, MacAuley, Meiklejohn, Gillick, Crawford o.g.	7,000
Dec 25	FALKIRK	W 1-0	Smith	10,000
Dec 29	Motherwell	D 2-2	Gillick 2	25,000
Jan 1	CELTIC	W 2-1	Venters, Gillick	83,000
Jan 2	Partick Thistle	L 0-1		32,000
Jan 5	DUNDEE	W 3-1	Gillick, Venters, MacAuley (pen)	16,000
Jan 12	Ayr United	W 4-2	Smith 2, Nicholson, Venters	12,000
Jan 19	ST MIRREN	W 1-0	Smith	-
Feb 2	Hibernian	W 2-1	Smith 2	23,000
Feb 16	AIRDRIE	W 3-1	McPhail 2, Roberts	10,000
Mar 2	Falkirk	W 3-0	Smith, Venters, McPhail	15,000
Mar 16	QUEEN OF THE SOUTH	W 5-0	McPhail 3 (1 pen), Smith 2	10,000
Mar 20	CLYDE	W 4-2	Gillick 2, Smith, McPhail	5,000
Mar 23	St Johnstone	L 0-2		11,700
Apr 13	Aberdeen	W 3-1	Smith, McPhail, Gillick	17,000
Apr 24	ALBION ROVERS	D 2-2	Gillick 2	8,000
Apr 27	Hamilton A	L 1-2	Smith	9,000
Apr 30	QUEEN'S PARK	L 0-1		6,000

Scottish Cup

Jan 26	COWDENBEATH	(Rd1) W 3-1	Gillick 2, Main	16,000
Feb 9	THIRD LANARK	(Rd2) W 2-0	Smith 2 (1 pen)	25,000
Feb 23	ST MIRREN	(Rd3) W 1-0	Gillick	42,000
Mar 9	Motherwell	(QF) W 4-1	Smith 4	29,777
Mar 30	Hearts*	(SF) D 1-1	Gillick	102,661
Apr 10	Hearts*	(R) W 2-0	McPhail, Main	90,428
Apr 20	Hamilton A*	(F) W 2-1	Smith 2	87,740

*Played at Hampden Park.

League & Cup Appearances

PLAYER	LEAGUE	CUP COMPETITION S CUP	TOTAL
Brown	34	7	41
Cheyne	6		6
Craig	6		6
Dawson	37	7	44
Fiddes	3		3
Fleming	4		4
Gillick	27	7	34
Gray	36	7	43
Hay	1		1
Jenkins	1		1
Kennedy	13	2	15
Kinnear	4		4
MacAuley	16		16
McDonald	35	7	42
McPhail	30	7	37
Main	27	6	33
Meiklejohn	22	4	26
Nicholson	13		13
Roberts	5	3	8
Simpson	37	7	44
Smith	32	5	37
Venters	28	7	35
Winning	1		1

Goalscorers

PLAYER	LEAGUE	CUP COMPETITION S CUP	TOTAL
Smith	36	8	44
Gillick	17	4	21
McPhail	14	1	15
Venters	10		10
Main	5	2	7
MacAuley	4		4
Meiklejohn	3		3
Brown	1		1
Craig	1		1
Fleming	1		1
Nicholson	1		1
Roberts	1		1
Simpson	1		1
Opps' o.gs.	1		1

Fact File

Jimmy Simpson was captain of Scotland when they defeated England 2-0 at Hampden Park on 6 April 1935 with his Rangers team-mates George Brown and Bob McPhail also in the side.

MANAGER: Bill Struth

CAPTAIN: Davie Meiklejohn

TOP SCORER: Jimmy Smith

BIGGEST WIN: 8-1 v Dunfermline, 22 December 1934, league,

HIGHEST ATTENDANCE: 102,661 v Hearts, 30 March 1935, Scottish Cup

MAJOR TRANSFERS IN: David Kinnear from Raith Rovers

MAJOR TRANSFERS OUT: Jimmy Fleming to Ayr United

Final Scottish League Div 1 Table

		P	W	D	L	F	A	Pts
1	RANGERS	38	25	5	8	96	46	55
2	CELTIC	38	24	4	10	92	45	52
3	HEARTS	38	20	10	8	87	51	50
4	HAMILTON A	38	19	10	9	87	67	48
5	ST JOHNSTONE	38	18	10	10	66	46	46
6	ABERDEEN	38	17	10	11	68	54	44
7	MOTHERWELL	38	15	10	13	83	64	40
8	DUNDEE	38	16	8	14	63	63	40
9	KILMARNOCK	38	16	6	16	76	68	38
10	CLYDE	38	14	10	14	71	69	38
11	HIBERNIAN	38	14	8	16	59	70	36
12	QUEEN'S PARK	38	13	10	15	61	80	36
13	PARTICK T	38	15	5	18	61	68	35
14	AIRDRIEONIANS	38	13	7	18	64	72	33
15	DUNFERMLINE ATH	38	13	5	20	56	96	31
16	ALBION R	38	10	9	19	62	77	29
17	Q OF S	38	11	7	20	52	72	29
18	AYR U	38	12	5	21	61	112	29
19	ST MIRREN	38	11	5	22	49	70	27
20	FALKIRK	38	9	6	23	58	82	24

Season 1935-36

Scottish League Division 1

DATE	OPPONENTS	SCORE	GOALSCORERS	ATTENDANCE
Aug 10	ARBROATH	W 6-0	Smith 3, Gillick, McPhail, Brown	11,000
Aug 14	Albion Rovers	W 2-1	Smith, Kinnear	10,000
Aug 17	Ayr United	D 2-2	McPhail 2	20,000
Aug 24	DUNDEE	W 4-3	Smith 2, Meiklejohn (pen), McPhail	20,000
Aug 28	ST JOHNSTONE	W 7-0	Smith 3, Venters 2, McPhail, Gillick	-
Aug 31	Partick Thistle	W 3-1	Smith 2, McPhail	30,000
Sep 7	AIRDRIE	W 5-3	Smith 2, McPhail, Main, Gillick	18,000
Sep 14	Hibernian	D 1-1	Smith	20,000
Sep 21	CELTIC	L 1-2	Smith	72,000
Sep 28	Motherwell	W 2-0	Smith, Winning	15,000
Oct 5	DUNFERMLINE	W 6-2	McPhail 2, Gillick 2, Venters, Main	12,000
Oct 19	HEARTS	D 1-1	Brown	26,000
Oct 26	Clyde	W 4-1	Venters 2 (1 pen), Drysdale 2	14,000
Nov 2	QUEEN'S PARK	D 3-3	Drysdale 2, Venters	16,000
Nov 9	Queen of the South	W 2-0	McPhail 2	10,700
Nov 16	HAMILTON A	W 3-1	Gillick, Fiddes, Venters	20,000
Nov 23	Aberdeen	L 0-1		34,500
Nov 30	KILMARNOCK	W 2-1	Main, Venters	8,000
Dec 7	St Johnstone	W 2-1	Smith, Gillick	10,000
Dec 14	ALBION ROVERS	W 5-1	Main 3, Smith, Venters	9,000
Dec 21	Arbroath	D 0-0		10,000
Dec 28	AYR UNITED	W 6-1	Smith 5, Turnbull	7,000
Jan 1	Celtic	W 4-3	McPhail 2, Smith 2	65,000
Jan 2	PARTICK THISTLE	W 3-1	Smith 2, McPhail	25,000
Jan 4	Dundee	W 3-0	Venters, McPhail, Smith	25,000
Jan 11	Airdrie	W 2-0	Venters 2	12,000
Feb 1	MOTHERWELL	D 0-0		35,000
Feb 15	Dunfermline	W 6-2	Fiddes 3, Turnbull, Drysdale, McPhail	9,000
Feb 29	THIRD LANARK	W 4-2	Fiddes 2, Meiklejohn (pen), McPhail	15,000
Mar 14	CLYDE	W 4-1	Smith 2, Turnbull, Venters	21,000
Mar 18	HIBERNIAN	W 3-0	Venters, Smith, McPhail (pen)	7,000
Mar 21	Queen's Park	W 3-1	McPhail, Venters, Main	26,000
Apr 8	QUEEN OF THE SOUTH	W 2-1	McPhail, Turnbull	5,000
Apr 11	Hamilton A	L 0-1		12,000
Apr 13	Third Lanark	W 3-1	McPhail 2, Kinnear	15,000
Apr 22	Hearts	D 1-1	Turnbull	48,000
Apr 25	Kilmarnock	W 3-0	Kinnear, Venters, MacAuley	8,000
Apr 29	ABERDEEN	L 2-3	McPhail, Venters	12,000

Scottish Cup

DATE	OPPONENTS		SCORE	GOALSCORERS	ATTENDANCE
Jan 29	EAST FIFE	(Rd1)	W 3-1	Smith 2, Venters	3,000
Feb 8	Albion Rovers	(Rd2)	W 3-1	Smith 3	27,381
Feb 22	St Mirren	(Rd3)	W 2-1	McPhail, Smith	43,308
Mar 7	Aberdeen	(QF)	W 1-0	Turnbull	41,663
Mar 28	Clyde*	(SF)	W 3-0	Meiklejohn, McPhail, Main	56,243
Apr 18	Third Lanark*	(F)	W 1-0	McPhail	88,859

*Played at Hampden Park.

League & Cup Appearances

PLAYER	LEAGUE	CUP COMPETITION S CUP	TOTAL
Brown	28	6	34
Cheyne	19	4	23
Dawson	38	6	44
Drysdale	9		9
Fiddes	17	5	22
Gillick	17		17
Gray	38	6	44
Hill	1		1
Kennedy	10		10
Kinnear	12		12
Latif	1		1
MacAuley	6		6
McDonald	22	2	24
McKillop	2		2
McPhail	26	6	32
Main	20	1	21
Meiklejohn	25	4	29
Roberts	3		3
Simpson	35	6	41
Smith	28	6	34
Turnbull	16	6	22
Venters	32	6	38
Wallace	1		1
Winning	12		12

Goalscorers

PLAYER	LEAGUE	CUP COMPETITION S CUP	TOTAL
Smith	31	6	37
McPhail	23	3	26
Venters	17	1	18
Main	7	1	8
Gillick	7		7
Fiddes	6		6
Turnbull	5	1	6
Drysdale	5		5
Kinnear	3		3
Meiklejohn	2	1	3
Brown	2		2
MacAuley	1		1
Winning	1		1

Fact File

Egyptian international Mohammed Latif became the first non-European to play for Rangers when he made his only senior appearance for the club in the 1-1 league draw against Hibernian on 14 September 1935.

MANAGER: Bill Struth
CAPTAIN: Davie Meiklejohn
TOP SCORER: Jimmy Smith
BIGGEST WIN: 7-0 v St Johnstone, 28 August 1935, league,
HIGHEST ATTENDANCE: 88,859 v Third Lanark, 18 April 1936, Scottish Cup
MAJOR TRANSFERS OUT: Torry Gillick to Everton

Final Scottish League Div 1 Table

		P	W	D	L	F	A	Pts
1	CELTIC	38	32	2	4	115	33	66
2	RANGERS	38	27	7	4	110	43	61
3	ABERDEEN	38	26	9	3	96	50	61
4	MOTHERWELL	38	18	12	8	77	58	48
5	HEARTS	38	20	7	11	88	55	47
6	HAMILTON A	38	15	7	16	77	74	37
7	ST JOHNSTONE	38	15	7	16	70	81	37
8	KILMARNOCK	38	14	7	17	69	64	35
9	THIRD LANARK	38	15	5	18	63	65	35
10	PARTICK T	38	12	10	16	64	72	34
11	ARBROATH	38	11	11	16	46	69	33
12	DUNDEE	38	11	10	17	67	80	32
13	QUEEN'S PARK	38	11	10	17	58	75	32
14	DUNFERMLINE ATH	38	12	8	18	67	92	32
15	Q OF S	38	11	9	18	54	72	31
16	ALBION R	38	13	4	21	69	92	30
17	HIBERNIAN	38	11	7	20	56	82	29
18	CLYDE	38	10	8	20	63	84	28
19	AIRDRIEONIANS	38	9	9	20	68	91	27
20	AYR U	38	11	3	24	53	98	25

Season 1936-37

Scottish League Division 1

DATE	OPPONENTS	SCORE	GOALSCORERS	ATTENDANCE
Aug 8	Dundee	D 0-0		22,000
Aug 15	THIRD LANARK	W 3-1	McPhail 3	16,000
Aug 19	DUNDEE	W 3-0	Smith 2, McPhail	12,000
Aug 22	Falkirk	W 2-0	Smith, McPhail	22,000
Aug 29	HIBERNIAN	W 4-0	Smith 2, McPhail, Main	12,000
Sep 5	Arbroath	D 0-0		7,000
Sep 9	Third Lanark	D 0-0		25,000
Sep 12	MOTHERWELL	W 3-2	Venters 3	45,000
Sep 19	Celtic	D 1-1	Venters	60,000
Sep 26	DUNFERMLINE	W 5-3	McPhail 3 (1 pen), Fiddes, Smith	8,000
Oct 3	St Mirren	W 4-1	Smith 2, Kinnear, Venters	25,000
Oct 17	Queen's Park	D 1-1	Cheyne	18,000
Oct 24	QUEEN OF THE SOUTH	D 1-1	McPhail	5,000
Nov 7	ABERDEEN	W 2-1	McPhail 2	60,000
Nov 14	Kilmarnock	W 2-1	Smith, Main	15,000
Nov 21	ST JOHNSTONE	D 0-0		10,000
Nov 28	Albion Rovers	W 3-2	Kinnear, Smith, Simpson	-
Dec 5	Hearts	L 2-5	Smith, Kinnear	40,000
Dec 12	CLYDE	W 2-0	Smith, Brown	10,000
Dec 19	FALKIRK	W 3-0	Smith 2, McPhail	10,000
Dec 26	Hibernian	W 4-1	McPhail (pen), Smith, Main, Venters	25,000
Jan 1	CELTIC	W 1-0	Venters	95,000
Jan 2	Partick Thistle	W 1-0	Kinnear	25,000
Jan 4	HEARTS	L 0-4		31,000
Jan 9	ARBROATH	W 4-0	Smith 2, McPhail (pen), Thornton	14,000
Jan 16	Motherwell	W 4-1	Smith 2, McKillop, McPhail	22,000
Jan 23	ST MIRREN	W 2-0	Venters, Smith	16,000
Feb 6	Dunfermline	W 3-2	Kinnear, Smith, McPhail	8,000
Feb 20	QUEEN'S PARK	D 1-1	Smith	12,000
Feb 27	KILMARNOCK	W 8-0	Smith 3, McPhail 3, MacAuley, Main	7,000
Mar 6	Queen of the South	W 1-0	Smith	11,000
Mar 20	Aberdeen	D 1-1	Main	30,000
Mar 24	HAMILTON A	W 4-0	Venters, McPhail (pen), Smith, Simpson	6,000
Mar 29	PARTICK THISTLE	W 3-1	Venters, Kinnear, McPhail	18,000
Apr 3	St Johnstone	W 2-1	McPhail, Smith	8,000
Apr 7	Hamilton A	W 5-1	Smith 2, McPhail, Main, Kinnear	5,000
Apr 10	ALBION ROVERS	W 1-0	McPhail (pen)	5,000
Apr 23	Clyde	L 2-3	Smith, Kinnear	9,000

Scottish Cup

Jan 30	Queen of the South	(Rd1) L 0-1		13,000

League & Cup Appearances

PLAYER	LEAGUE	CUP COMPETITION S CUP	TOTAL
Brown	35	1	36
Cheyne	17		17
Dawson	38	1	39
Drysdale	7		7
Fiddes	4		4
Gray	36	1	37
Kennedy	21		21
Kinnear	37	1	38
MacAuley	9		9
McDonald	22	1	23
McKillop	17	1	18
McPhail	33	1	34
Main	23	1	24
Reid	1		1
Simpson	31	1	32
Smith	37	1	38
Soutar	10		10
Thornton	5		5
Venters	33	1	34
Winning	2		2

Goalscorers

PLAYER	CUP COMPETITION S CUP	TOTAL
Smith		31
McPhail		25
Venters		10
Kinnear		8
Main		6
Simpson		2
Brown		1
Cheyne		1
Fiddes		1
MacAuley		1
McKillop		1
Thornton		1

Fact File

Bob McPhail scored twice in Scotland's 3-1 win over England at Hampden in front of a record crowd of 149,547 on 17 April 1937. Rangers team-mates Jerry Dawson, Jimmy Simpson and George Brown were also in the side.

MANAGER: Bill Struth
CAPTAIN: Jimmy Simpson
TOP SCORER: Jimmy Smith
BIGGEST WIN: 8-0 v Kilmarnock, 27 February 1937, league
HIGHEST ATTENDANCE: 95,000 v Celtic, 1 January 1937, league
MAJOR TRANSFERS OUT: Archie MacAuley to West Ham United

Final Scottish League Div 1 Table

		P	W	D	L	F	A	Pts
1	RANGERS	38	26	9	3	88	32	61
2	ABERDEEN	38	23	8	7	89	44	54
3	CELTIC	38	22	8	8	89	58	52
4	MOTHERWELL	38	22	7	9	96	54	51
5	HEARTS	38	24	3	11	99	60	51
6	THIRD LANARK	38	20	6	12	79	61	46
7	FALKIRK	38	19	6	13	98	66	44
8	HAMILTON A	38	18	5	15	91	96	41
9	DUNDEE	38	12	15	11	58	69	39
10	CLYDE	38	16	6	16	59	70	38
11	KILMARNOCK	38	14	9	15	60	70	37
12	ST JOHNSTONE	38	14	8	16	74	68	36
13	PARTICK T	38	11	12	15	73	68	34
14	ARBROATH	38	13	5	20	57	84	31
15	QUEEN'S PARK	38	9	12	17	51	77	30
16	ST MIRREN	38	11	7	20	68	81	29
17	HIBERNIAN	38	6	13	19	54	83	25
18	Q OF S	38	8	8	22	49	95	24
19	DUNFERMLINE ATH	38	5	11	22	65	98	21
20	ALBION R	38	5	6	27	53	116	16

Season 1937-38

Scottish League Division 1

DATE	OPPONENTS	SCORE	GOALSCORERS	ATTENDANCE
Aug 14	FALKIRK	D 0-0		20,000
Aug 18	MOTHERWELL	W 2-1	Smith, McPhail	22,000
Aug 21	Hibernian	D 0-0		31,000
Aug 25	Falkirk	W 1-0	Reid	24,000
Aug 28	ST JOHNSTONE	D 2-2	Thornton, Main	20,000
Sep 4	Motherwell	D 1-1	Main	25,000
Sep 11	CELTIC	W 3-1	Venters 2, Thornton	80,000
Sep 15	HIBERNIAN	W 2-0	Kinnear, Smith (pen)	12,000
Sep 18	Ayr United	D 1-1	McPhail	16,000
Sep 25	ST MIRREN	W 4-0	Smith 2, Kinnear, McPhail	12,000
Oct 2	Third Lanark	W 2-1	Smith, McPhail	19,000
Oct 9	DUNDEE	W 6-0	Smith 4, Kinnear, Venters	30,000
Oct 23	HAMILTON A	D 2-2	Reid, Smith	12,000
Nov 6	KILMARNOCK	W 4-1	Smith 2, Venters 2	12,000
Nov 13	Arbroath	D 1-1	Smith	9,000
Nov 20	MORTON	W 3-1	Smith 2, Kinnear	8,000
Nov 27	HEARTS	L 0-3		51,000
Dec 4	Clyde	D 1-1	Smith	20,000
Dec 11	QUEEN'S PARK	W 2-1	Smith, Venters	10,000
Dec 25	St Johnstone	W 5-1	Venters 3, Kinnear 2	10,000
Jan 1	Celtic	L 0-3		83,500
Jan 3	PARTICK THISTLE	L 1-3	Harrison	20,000
Jan 8	AYR UNITED	D 2-2	Thornton, Reid	20,000
Jan 15	St Mirren	D 1-1	Smith	20,000
Jan 29	THIRD LANARK	W 3-0	Thornton 2, Harrison	12,000
Feb 5	Dundee	L 1-6	Venters	12,000
Feb 19	Hamilton A	D 2-2	McPhail, Smith	-
Feb 26	ABERDEEN	D 2-2	Smith 2	35,000
Mar 5	Queen of the South	W 2-0	Main, Kinnear	
Mar 12	Kilmarnock	L 1-2	Kinnear	25,000
Mar 23	ARBROATH	W 3-1	Lyness (pen), Sowerby, Kinnear	-
Mar 26	Morton	W 3-2	Kinnear, Main, Venters	8,000
Apr 9	CLYDE	W 1-0	McPhail	7,000
Apr 13	ABERDEEN	W 3-0	McPhail, Smith, Main	18,000
Apr 16	Queen's Park	W 3-0	Kinnear, Venters, McPhail	20,000
Apr 18	Partick Thistle	D 1-1	McPhail	20,000
Apr 23	Hearts	L 2-3	Kinnear, Main	25,000
Apr 30	QUEEN OF THE SOUTH	L 2-3	McPhail, Turnbull	12,000

Scottish Cup

Jan 22	Alloa	(Rd1) W 6-1	Smith 3, Venters, McPhail, Reid	9,400
Feb 12	QUEEN OF THE SOUTH	(Rd2) W 3-1	McPhail 2, Reid	50,000
Mar 19	Falkirk	(QF) W 2-1	Venters, Thornton	20,058
Apr 2	Kilmarnock*	(SF) L 3-4	Venters 2, Thornton	70,833

*Played at Hampden Park. Rangers received a bye in the third round.

League & Cup Appearances

PLAYER	LEAGUE	CUP COMPETITION S CUP	TOTAL
Brown	32	4	36
Cheyne	9		9
Dawson	26	2	28
Drysdale	2		2
Galloway	2		2
Gray	35	4	39
Harrison	10	1	11
Fiddes	14	1	15
Jenkins	12	2	14
Kinnear	26	2	28
Lyness	2		2
McDonald	3		3
McKillop	29	4	33
McPhail	25	3	28
Main	29	1	30
Reid	8	2	10
Ross	7		7
Simpson	34	4	38
Sowerby	3		3
Smith	32	2	34
Thornton	14	4	18
Turnbull	3		3
Venters	34	4	38
Winning	27	4	31

Goalscorers

PLAYER	LEAGUE	CUP COMPETITION S CUP	TOTAL
Smith	22	3	25
Venters	12	4	16
McPhail	10	3	13
Kinnear	12		12
Thornton	5	2	7
Main	6		6
Reid	3	2	5
Harrison	2		2
Lyness	1		1
Sowerby	1		1
Turnbull	1		1

Fact File

Rangers lost 2-0 to Everton at Ibrox in the first round of the Empire Exhibition Cup on 30 May 1938. The Goodison side reached the final of the eight-team tournament, losing 1-0 to Celtic at Ibrox.

MANAGER: Bill Struth
CAPTAIN: George Brown
TOP SCORER: Jimmy Smith
BIGGEST WIN: 6-0 v Dundee, 9 October 1937, league
HIGHEST ATTENDANCE: 83,500 v Celtic, 1 January 1938, league

Final Scottish League Div 1 Table

		P	W	D	L	F	A	Pts
1	CELTIC	38	27	7	4	114	42	61
2	HEARTS	38	26	6	6	90	50	58
3	RANGERS	38	18	13	7	75	49	49
4	FALKIRK	38	19	9	10	82	52	47
5	MOTHERWELL	38	17	10	11	78	69	44
6	ABERDEEN	38	15	9	14	74	59	39
7	PARTICK T	38	15	9	14	68	70	39
8	ST JOHNSTONE	38	16	7	15	78	81	39
9	THIRD LANARK	38	11	13	14	68	73	35
10	HIBERNIAN	38	11	13	14	57	65	35
11	ARBROATH	38	11	13	14	58	79	35
12	QUEEN'S PARK	38	11	12	15	59	74	34
13	HAMILTON A	38	13	7	18	81	76	33
14	ST MIRREN	38	14	5	19	58	66	33
15	CLYDE	38	10	13	15	68	78	33
16	Q OF S	38	11	11	16	58	71	33
17	AYR U	38	9	15	14	66	85	33
18	KILMARNOCK	38	12	9	17	65	91	33
19	DUNDEE	38	13	6	19	70	74	32
20	MORTON	38	6	3	29	64	127	15

Season 1938-39

Scottish League Division 1

DATE	OPPONENTS	SCORE	GOALSCORERS	ATTENDANCE
Aug 13	St Johnstone	D 3-3	Venters 2, Brown	15,000
Aug 20	MOTHERWELL	D 2-2	Kinnear 2	25,000
Aug 24	ST JOHNSTONE	W 4-2	Venters 2 (1 pen), McPhail, Thornton	18,000
Aug 27	St Mirren	W 5-1	Thornton 2, Main 2, McPhail	20,000
Sep 3	AYR UNITED	W 4-1	McPhail 2, Thornton, Brown	10,000
Sep 10	Celtic	L 2-6	Smith, Thornton	74,500
Sep 14	Motherwell	W 5-0	Thornton 3, Fiddes, Kinnear	16,000
Sep 17	THIRD LANARK	W 5-1	Venters 2, Thornton 2, Black o.g.	20,000
Sep 24	Arbroath	D 3-3	Venters, Harrison, Main	10,000
Oct 1	HIBERNIAN	W 5-2	Thornton, Symon, Venters, Waddell, Kinnear	15,000
Oct 8	Falkirk	D 2-2	Venters 2	
Oct 15	PARTICK THISTLE	W 4-1	Venters 2, McPhail, Thornton	30,000
Oct 22	Kilmarnock	L 1-3	Kinnear	18,000
Oct 29	RAITH ROVERS	W 4-0	Venters 3, Thornton	12,000
Nov 5	Albion Rovers	W 7-2	Waddell 2, Thornton 2, McPhail, Venters, Kinnear	10,000
Nov 12	Hearts	W 3-1	Waddell, McPhail, Venters	40,000
Nov 19	CLYDE	W 2-0	Venters, Waddell (pen)	13,000
Nov 26	Queen's Park	W 3-1	Kinnear, Waddell, Venters	40,000
Dec 3	QUEEN OF THE SOUTH	W 4-1	McPhail 3, Kinnear	16,000
Dec 10	Hamilton A	L 1-2	Venters	17,500
Dec 17	ABERDEEN	W 5-2	Fiddes 4, Venters	30,000
Dec 26	ST MIRREN	W 3-0	Thornton, Fiddes, Venters	18,000
Dec 31	Ayr United	W 4-3	Thornton 2, Venters, Symon	20,000
Jan 2	CELTIC	W 2-1	Kinnear, Venters	118,730
Jan 3	Partick Thistle	W 4-2	Venters 2, Turnbull, Lyness	35,000
Jan 11	ARBROATH	W 4-2	Thornton 2, Lyness, Venters	5,000
Jan 14	Hibernian	D 1-1	Venters	31,000
Jan 28	FALKIRK	W 2-1	Thornton, Smith	30,000
Feb 11	Third Lanark	W 2-1	Harrison 2	20,000
Feb 25	KILMARNOCK	D 2-2	McPhail, Smith	10,000
Mar 4	Raith Rovers	W 2-0	Thornton, Venters	18,000
Mar 11	ALBION ROVERS	W 5-0	Venters 3, McPhail, Thornton	10,000
Mar 18	HEARTS	D 1-1	Smith	40,000
Mar 28	Clyde	D 1-1	McPhail	10,000
Apr 1	QUEEN'S PARK	W 1-0	Venters (pen)	20,000
Apr 8	Queen of the South	D 1-1	Symon	9,000
Apr 21	HAMILTON A	W 3-2	Venters 2, Waddell	10,000
Apr 29	Aberdeen	L 0-2		15,002

Scottish Cup

Jan 21	Raith Rovers	(Rd1) W 1-0	Venters	21,747
Feb 4	HAMILTON A	(Rd2) W 2-0	Lyness, Venters	75,000
Feb 18	CLYDE	(Rd3) L 1-4	Lyness (pen)	63,000

League & Cup Appearances

PLAYER	LEAGUE	CUP COMPETITION S CUP	TOTAL
Brown	19	2	21
Cheyne	2		2
Dawson	33	3	36
Fiddes	19	1	20
Galloway	2		2
Gilmour	2		2
Gray	35	1	36
Harrison	4		4
Jenkins	5		5
Kinnear	26		26
Little	4		4
Lyness	4	2	6
McKillop	25	3	28
McPhail	23	1	24
Main	8	1	9
Reid	2		2
Ross	1		1
Shaw	36	3	39
Simpson	25	3	28
Smith	7		7
Symon	22	3	25
Thornton	36	3	39
Turnbull	6	3	9
Venters	33	2	35
Waddell	27	2	29
Woodburn	12		12

Goalscorers

PLAYER	LEAGUE	CUP COMPETITION S CUP	TOTAL
Venters	35	2	37
Thornton	23		23
McPhail	13		13
Kinnear	9		9
Waddell	7		7
Fiddes	6		6
Lyness	2	2	4
Smith	4		4
Harrison	3		3
Main	3		3
Symon	3		3
Brown	2		2
Turnbull	1		1
Opps' o.gs.	1		1

Fact File

The all-time Ibrox attendance record was set on 2 January 1939 when 118,730 watched Rangers defeat Celtic 2-1 with goals from Davie Kinnear and Alec Venters.

MANAGER: Bill Struth

CAPTAIN: Jimmy Simpson

TOP SCORER: Alec Venters

BIGGEST WIN: 7-2 v Albion Rovers, 5 November 1938, league

HIGHEST ATTENDANCE: 118,730 v Celtic, 2 January 1939, league

MAJOR TRANSFERS IN: Jock Shaw from Airdrie, Scot Symon from Portsmouth

MAJOR TRANSFERS OUT: Bobby Main to New Brighton

Final Scottish League Div 1 Table

		P	W	D	L	F	A	PTS
1	RANGERS	38	25	9	4	112	55	59
2	CELTIC	38	20	8	10	99	53	48
3	ABERDEEN	38	20	6	12	91	61	46
4	HEARTS	38	20	5	13	98	70	45
5	FALKIRK	38	19	7	12	73	63	45
6	Q OF S	38	17	9	12	69	64	43
7	HAMILTON A	38	18	5	15	67	71	41
8	ST JOHNSTONE	38	17	6	15	85	82	40
9	CLYDE	38	17	5	16	78	70	39
10	KILMARNOCK	38	15	9	14	73	86	39
11	PARTICK T	38	17	4	17	74	87	38
12	MOTHERWELL	38	16	5	17	82	86	37
13	HIBERNIAN	38	14	7	17	68	69	35
14	AYR U	38	13	9	16	76	83	35
15	THIRD LANARK	38	12	8	18	80	96	32
16	ALBION R	38	12	6	20	65	90	30
17	ARBROATH	38	11	8	19	54	75	30
18	ST MIRREN	38	11	7	20	57	80	29
19	QUEEN'S PARK	38	11	5	22	57	83	27
20	RAITH R	38	10	2	26	65	99	22

Season 1946-47

Scottish League Division A

DATE	OPPONENTS	SCORE	GOALSCORERS	ATTENDANCE
Aug 10	Motherwell	W 4-2	Duncanson 2, Thornton, Waddell	30,000
Aug 14	HIBERNIAN	L 1-2	Young (pen)	50,000
Aug 17	KILMARNOCK	W 3-2	Cox, Gillick, Waddell	25,000
Aug 21	Falkirk	W 5-0	Thornton 3, Duncanson, Waddell	-
Aug 28	THIRD LANARK	W 8-1	Thornton 3, Caskie 3, Gillick, Duncanson	22,000
Aug 31	QUEEN'S PARK	W 2-0	Duncanson 2	20,000
Sep 4	Aberdeen	L 0-1		35,000
Sep 7	Celtic	W 3-2	Duncanson 2, Parlane	28,000
Sep 14	ST MIRREN	W 4-0	Duncanson 3, Gillick	15,000
Sep 30	Partick Thistle	L 2-3	Gillick, Duncanson	36,000
Nov 2	MORTON	W 2-1	Thornton, Cox	40,000
Nov 9	Hamilton A	W 6-0	Thornton 3, McNee, Gillick, Duncanson	15,000
Nov 16	Clyde	W 4-2	McNee, McColl, Duncanson, Thornton	27,000
Nov 23	QUEEN OF THE SOUTH	W 2-1	Thornton, Gillick	10,000
Nov 30	Hearts	W 3-0	Duncanson, McNee, Thornton	45,000
Dec 7	MOTHERWELL	W 2-1	Thornton, Young (pen)	35,000
Dec 14	Hibernian	D 1-1	Duncanson	41,378
Dec 21	FALKIRK	W 2-1	Duncanson, Gillick	15,000
Dec 28	Third Lanark	D 1-1	Gillick	35,000
Jan 1	CELTIC	D 1-1	Gillick	85,000
Jan 2	Kilmarnock	W 2-0	Gillick 2	32,325
Jan 4	St Mirren	L 0-1		18,000
Jan 11	PARTICK THISTLE	W 4-0	Waddell, Thornton, Young (pen), Gillick	18,000
Jan 18	ABERDEEN	W 1-0	Waddell	60,000
Feb 1	Queen's Park	D 0-0		40,000
Feb 3	Queen of the South	W 2-0	Young (pen), Arnison	11,000
Feb 15	Morton	W 1-0	Thornton	18,000
Mar 29	CLYDE	W 5-0	Williamson 4, Rutherford	15,000
Apr 7	HEARTS	L 1-2	Thornton	12,000
Apr 12	HAMILTON A	W 4-1	Williamson 2, Parlane, Duncanson	8,000

Scottish Cup

Jan 25	CLYDE	(Rd1) W 2-1	Duncanson, Thornton	74,606
Feb 22	HIBERNIAN	(Rd2) D 0-0		95,000
Mar 8	Hibernian	(R) L 0-2		48,816

Scottish League Cup

Sep 21	ST MIRREN†	W 4-0	Arnison 2, Cox, Stead	20,000
Sep 28	Queen's Park†	W 4-2	Duncanson 2, Gillick, Thornton	30,000
Oct 5	MORTON†	W 3-0	Duncanson, Caskie, Thornton	50,000
Oct 12	St Mirren†	W 4-0	Gillick 2, Thornton 2	20,000
Oct 19	QUEEN'S PARK†	W 1-0	Arnison	20,000
Oct 26	Morton†	W 2-0	Young (pen), Thornton	18,000

†Qualifying Section B - Rangers finished top.

Mar 1	DUNDEE UTD	(QF/FL) W 2-1	Waddell, Caskie	40,000
Mar 5	Dundee Utd	(QF/SL) D 1-1	Duncanson	18,000
Mar 22	Hibernian*	(SF) W 3-1	Gillick, Thornton, Waddell	125,154
Apr 5	Aberdeen*	(F) W 4-0	Duncanson 2, Gillick, Williamson	82,684

*Played at Hampden Park.

League & Cup Appearances

PLAYER	LEAGUE	CUP COMPETITION		TOTAL
		S CUP	SL CUP	
Arnison	7	1	2	10
Brown	30	3	9	42
Caskie	13	1	8	22
Cox	13		5	18
Duncanson	27	3	8	38
Gillick	27	2	8	37
Gray	9		3	12
Lindsay	2			2
McColl	19	3	7	29
McNee	10			10
Parlane	4	2		6
Rae	19	2	6	27
Rutherford	5		2	7
Shaw Jock	28	3	10	41
Shaw John			1	1
Stead	3		1	4
Symon	10		2	12
Thornton	25	3	8	36
Waddell	22	3	7	32
Watkins	6	1	2	9
Williamson	5		4	9
Woodburn	18	3	8	29
Young	28	3	9	40

Goalscorers

PLAYER	LEAGUE	CUP COMPETITION		TOTAL
		S CUP	SL CUP	
Duncanson	18	1	6	25
Thornton	18	1	6	25
Gillick	12		5	17
Waddell	5		2	7
Williamson	6		1	7
Caskie	3		2	5
Young	4		1	5
Arnison	1		3	4
Cox	2		1	3
McNee	3			3
Parlane	2			2
McColl	1			1
Rutherford	1			1
Stead			1	1

Fact File

Dougie Gray and Jimmy Smith, two of Rangers
longest serving players, retired at the end of
the season.

Final Scottish League Div A Table

		P	W	D	L	F	A	Pts
1	RANGERS	30	21	4	5	76	26	46
2	HIBERNIAN	30	19	6	5	69	33	44
3	ABERDEEN	30	16	7	7	58	41	39
4	HEARTS	30	16	6	8	52	43	38
5	PARTICK T	30	16	3	11	74	59	35
6	MORTON	30	12	10	8	58	45	34
7	CELTIC	30	13	6	11	53	55	32
8	MOTHERWELL	30	12	5	13	58	54	29
9	THIRD LANARK	30	11	6	13	56	64	28
10	CLYDE	30	9	9	12	55	65	27
11	FALKIRK	30	8	10	12	62	61	26
12	Q OF S	30	9	8	13	44	69	26
13	QUEEN'S PARK	30	8	6	16	47	60	22
14	ST MIRREN	30	9	4	17	47	65	22
15	KILMARNOCK	30	6	9	15	44	66	21
16	HAMILTON A	30	2	7	21	38	85	11

MANAGER: Bill Struth

CAPTAIN: Jock Shaw

TOP SCORERS: Willie Thornton and Jimmy Duncanson

BIGGEST WIN: 8-1 v Third Lanark, 28 August 1946, league

HIGHEST ATTENDANCE: 125,154 v Hibernian, 22 March 1947,
League Cup

MAJOR TRANSFERS IN: Sammy Cox from Dundee, Bobby Brown from
Queen's Park

MAJOR TRANSFERS OUT: John Galloway to Chelsea

Season 1947-48

Scottish League Division A

DATE	OPPONENTS	SCORE	GOALSCORERS	ATTENDANCE
Aug 13	THIRD LANARK	W 5-2	Thornton 3, Williamson, Waddell	-
Aug 27	Partick Thistle	W 1-0	Thornton	35,000
Sep 20	CELTIC	W 2-0	Williamson, Findlay	50,000
Oct 18	HIBERNIAN	W 2-1	Paton, Williamson	55,000
Oct 25	St Mirren	L 1-2	Thornton	24,000
Nov 1	AIRDRIE	W 3-1	Thornton, Shaw (pen), Marshall	15,000
Nov 8	Queen of the South	W 3-0	Findlay 2, Marshall	21,000
Nov 15	Clyde	W 2-1	Thornton, Marshall	30,000
Nov 22	MORTON	D 1-1	Duncanson	25,000
Nov 29	Queen's Park	W 4-1	Gillick 2, Parlane, Duncanson	28,000
Dec 6	Hearts	W 2-1	Duncanson, Rutherford	40,000
Dec 13	ABERDEEN	W 4-0	Gillick 2, Rutherford, Thornton	30,000
Dec 20	Third Lanark	W 1-0	Gillick	20,000
Dec 25	Dundee	W 3-1	Duncanson 3	25,000
Dec 27	PARTICK THISTLE	W 2-1	Rutherford, Gillick	20,000
Jan 2	Celtic	W 4-0	McColl, Thornton, Rutherford, Duncanson	60,000
Jan 3	DUNDEE	W 2-1	Thornton 2	35,000
Jan 10	Falkirk	W 5-1	Gillick 2, Duncanson 2, Waddell	22,000
Jan 17	MOTHERWELL	W 2-0	Thornton, Young	35,000
Jan 31	Hibernian	L 0-1		52,750
Feb 14	ST MIRREN	W 3-2	Thornton 3	20,000
Feb 28	Queen of the South	L 2-3	Gillick, Thornton	34,000
Mar 13	Morton	W 1-0	Thornton	18,000
Mar 20	QUEEN'S PARK	L 1-2	Rutherford	37,000
Mar 29	FALKIRK	D 1-1	Duncanson	-
Apr 3	Aberdeen	D 1-1	Duncanson	43,800
Apr 24	Motherwell	D 1-1	Duncanson	25,000
Apr 26	CLYDE	W 2-1	McPherson, Cox	
May 1	Airdrie	W 2-1	Findlay 2	18,000
May 3	HEARTS	L 1-2	Findlay	10,000

Scottish Cup

Jan 24	Stranraer	(Rd1)	W 1-0	Thornton	6,000
Feb 7	LEITH ATH	(Rd2)	W 4-0	Thornton, Waddell, Cox, Rutherford	17,000
Feb 21	PARTICK TH	(Rd3)	W 3-0	Young (pen), Duncanson, McGowan o.g.	68,000
Mar 6	EAST FIFE	(QF)	W 1-0	Duncanson	90,000
Mar 27	Hibernian*	(SF)	W 1-0	Thornton	143,570
Apr 17	Morton*	(F)	D 1-1	Gillick	131,975
Apr 21	Morton*	(R)	W 1-0	Williamson	133,750

*Played at Hampden Park.

Scottish League Cup

Aug 9	CELTIC†		W 2-0	Williamson 2	80,000
Aug 16	Third Lanark†		W 3-1	Williamson 2, Duncanson	25,000
Aug 23	DUNDEE†		W 3-0	Williamson, Gillick, Thornton	25,000
Aug 30	Celtic†		L 0-2		60,000
Sep 6	THIRD LANARK†		W 3-0	Findlay 2, Gillick	20,000
Sep 13	Dundee†		D 1-1	Paton	39,000

†Qualifying Section C – Rangers finished top.

Sep 27	STENHOUSEMUIR	(QF)	W 2-0	Findlay, Thornton	25,000
Oct 11	Falkirk*	(SF)	L 0-1		44,432

*Played at Hampden Park.

MANAGER: Bill Struth

CAPTAIN: Jock Shaw

TOP SCORER: Willie Thornton

BIGGEST WIN: 5-1 v Falkirk, 10 January 1948, league,

HIGHEST ATTENDANCE: 143,570 v Hibernian, 27 March 1948, Scottish Cup

MAJOR TRANSFERS IN: Willie Findlay from Albion Rovers

MAJOR TRANSFERS OUT: Jimmy Parlane to Airdrie

League & Cup Appearances

PLAYER	LEAGUE	CUP COMPETITION		TOTAL
		S CUP	SL CUP	
Brown	30	7	8	45
Caskie	12	3		15
Cox	30	7	8	45
Duncanson	29	7	8	44
Findlay	7	1	4	12
Gillick	21	7	7	35
Johnson	1			1
Lindsay	3			3
Little	1			1
McColl	29	7	7	43
McPherson	1			1
Marshall	4			4
Parlane	1			1
Paton	4		1	5
Rae	19	1	4	24
Rutherford	20	6	1	27
Shaw	28	7	8	43
Thornton	30	7	8	45
Waddell	12	3	7	22
Watkins	3		1	4
Williamson	7	1	4	12
Woodburn	23	6	8	37
Young	15	7	4	26

Goalscorers

PLAYER	LEAGUE	CUP COMPETITION		TOTAL
		S CUP	SL CUP	
Thornton	17	3	2	22
Duncanson	12	2	1	15
Gillick	9	1	2	12
Findlay	6		3	9
Williamson	3	1	5	9
Rutherford	5	1		6
Marshall	3			3
Waddell	2	1		3
Cox	1	1		2
Paton	1		1	2
Young	1	1		2
McColl	1			1
McPherson	1			1
Parlane	1			1
Shaw	1			1
Opps' o.g.s.		1		1

Fact File

Jimmy Smith was appointed first team trainer at Ibrox, taking over the role vacated by another former player, Bob 'Whitey' McDonald.

Final Scottish League Div A Table

		P	W	D	L	F	A	Pts
1	HIBERNIAN	30	22	4	4	86	27	48
2	RANGERS	30	21	4	5	64	28	46
3	PARTICK T	30	16	4	10	61	42	36
4	DUNDEE	30	15	3	12	67	51	33
5	ST MIRREN	30	13	5	12	54	58	31
6	CLYDE	30	12	7	11	52	57	31
7	FALKIRK	30	10	10	10	55	48	30
8	MOTHERWELL	30	13	3	14	45	47	29
9	HEARTS	30	10	8	12	37	42	28
10	ABERDEEN	30	10	7	13	45	45	27
11	THIRD LANARK	30	10	6	14	56	73	26
12	CELTIC	30	10	5	15	41	56	25
13	Q OF S	30	10	5	15	49	74	25
14	MORTON	30	9	6	15	47	43	24
15	AIRDRIEONIANS	30	7	7	16	40	78	21
16	QUEEN'S PARK	30	9	2	19	45	75	20

Season 1948-49

Scottish League Division A

DATE	OPPONENTS	SCORE	GOALSCORERS	ATTENDANCE
Aug 14	Motherwell	D 1-1	Thornton	35,000
Aug 18	FALKIRK	W 4-3	Gillick 2, Thornton, Findlay	40,000
Aug 21	Celtic	W 1-0	Findlay	50,000
Aug 28	DUNDEE	D 1-1	Findlay	55,000
Sep 1	Partick Thistle	D 1-1	Thornton	40,000
Sep 4	THIRD LANARK	W 2-1	Williamson, Duncanson	35,000
Oct 23	Hearts	L 0-2		42,000
Nov 6	HIBERNIAN	L 2-4	Thornton, Gillick	50,000
Nov 13	St Mirren	W 2-0	Gillick, Waddell	40,000
Nov 27	East Fife	W 2-1	Thornton, Duncanson	20,737
Dec 4	Clyde	W 3-1	Thornton 2, Paton	25,000
Dec 11	MORTON	W 4-1	Thornton 2, Findlay, Rutherford	25,000
Dec 18	Queen of the South	W 2-0	Thornton, Rutherford	20,200
Dec 25	Falkirk	D 2-2	Paton, Waddell	21,000
Jan 1	CELTIC	W 4-0	Duncanson 3, Thornton	95,000
Jan 3	Dundee	L 1-3	Marshall	39,000
Jan 8	MOTHERWELL	W 2-0	Paton, Thornton	55,000
Jan 15	Third Lanark	L 1-2	Thornton	35,000
Jan 29	PARTICK THISTLE	D 2-2	Thornton, Cox	55,000
Feb 12	Aberdeen	W 2-0	Thornton, Paton	42,000
Feb 19	Hibernian	W 1-0	Paton	50,000
Feb 26	ST MIRREN	W 2-1	Thornton, Duncanson	40,000
Mar 19	CLYDE	W 4-1	Paton 2, Thornton, Duncanson	50,000
Apr 2	QUEEN OF THE SOUTH	W 3-0	Thornton 2, Duncanson	28,000
Apr 5	HEARTS	W 2-1	Cox, Paton	45,000
Apr 13	EAST FIFE	W 3-1	Young 2 (2 pens), Paton	35,000
Apr 16	ABERDEEN	D 1-1	Duncanson	45,000
Apr 18	ALBION ROVERS	W 3-1	Williamson, Waddell, Young (pen)	16,000
Apr 25	Morton	W 1-0	Thornton	40,000
Apr 30	Albion Rovers	W 4-1	Thornton 3, Duncanson	15,000

Scottish Cup

Jan 22	ELGIN CITY	(Rd1)	W 6-1	Thornton 2, Duncanson 2, Cox, Rutherford	29,000
Feb 5	Motherwell	(Rd2)	W 3-0	Young (pen), Paton, Thornton	31,000
Mar 5	PARTICK TH	(QF)	W 4-0	Thornton 2, Duncanson, Paton	65,000
Mar 26	East Fife*	(SF)	W 3-0	Thornton 3	104,958
Apr 23	Clyde*	(F)	W 4-1	Young 2 (2 pens), Williamson, Duncanson	120,162

*Played at Hampden Park. Rangers received a bye in third round.

Scottish League Cup

Sep 11	CLYDE†		D 1-1	Findlay	50,000
Sep 18	Hibernian†		D 0-0		47,000
Sep 25	Celtic†		L 1-3	Findlay	65,000
Oct 2	Clyde†		W 3-1	Waddell 3 (2 pens)	27,000
Oct 9	HIBERNIAN†		W 1-0	Thornton	76,466
Oct 16	CELTIC†		W 2-1	Williamson, Waddell	105,000

†Qualifying Section A – Rangers finished top.

Oct 30	ST MIRREN	(QF)	W 1-0	Thornton	50,000
Nov 20	Dundee*	(SF)	W 4-1	Rutherford, McColl, Duncanson, Thornton	50,996
Mar 12	Raith Rovers*	(F)	W 2-0	Gillick, Paton	57,450

*Played at Hampden Park.

MANAGER: Bill Struth

CAPTAIN: Jock Shaw

TOP SCORER: Willie Thornton

BIGGEST WIN: 6-1 v Elgin City, 22 January 1949, Scottish Cup

HIGHEST ATTENDANCE: 120,162 v Clyde, 23 April 1949, Scottish Cup

MAJOR TRANSFERS OUT: Billy Arnison to Luton Town, Charlie Watkins to Luton Town

League & Cup Appearances

PLAYER	LEAGUE	CUP COMPETITION		TOTAL
		S CUP	SL CUP	
Brown	30	5	9	44
Caskie	1		1	2
Cox	29	5	9	43
Duncanson	24	5	8	37
Findlay	12		4	16
Frame	1			1
Gillick	8		4	12
Lindsay	4		2	6
McColl	30	5	6	41
Marshall	3		3	6
Paton	19	4	1	24
Rae	1		3	4
Rutherford	27	5	3	35
Shaw	27	5	9	41
Thornton	29	5	9	43
Waddell	20	5	8	33
Walmsley	1			1
Williamson	6	1	4	11
Woodburn	30	5	7	42
Young	28	5	9	42

Goalscorers

PLAYER	LEAGUE	CUP COMPETITION		TOTAL
		S CUP	SL CUP	
Thornton	23	8	3	34
Duncanson	10	4	1	15
Paton	9	2	1	12
Waddell	3		4	7
Findlay	4		2	6
Young	3	3		6
Gillick	4		1	5
Rutherford	2	1	1	4
Williamson	2	1	1	4
Cox	2	1		3
McColl			1	1
Marshall	1			1

Fact File

George Young captained the Scotland team which defeated England 3-1 at Wembley on 9 April 1949. Four of his Rangers team-mates also played in the match – Sammy Cox, Willie Woodburn, Willie Waddell and Willie Thornton.

Final Scottish League Div A Table

		P	W	D	L	F	A	Pts
1	RANGERS	30	20	6	4	63	32	46
2	DUNDEE	30	20	5	5	71	48	45
3	HIBERNIAN	30	17	5	8	75	52	39
4	EAST FIFE	30	16	3	11	64	46	35
5	FALKIRK	30	12	8	10	70	54	32
6	CELTIC	30	12	7	11	48	40	31
7	THIRD LANARK	30	13	5	12	56	52	31
8	HEARTS	30	12	6	12	64	54	30
9	ST MIRREN	30	13	4	13	51	47	30
10	Q OF S	30	11	8	11	47	53	30
11	PARTICK T	30	9	9	12	50	63	27
12	MOTHERWELL	30	10	5	15	44	49	25
13	ABERDEEN	30	7	11	12	39	48	25
14	CLYDE	30	9	6	15	50	67	24
15	MORTON	30	7	8	15	39	51	22
16	ALBION R	30	3	2	25	30	105	8

Season 1949-50

Scottish League Division A

DATE	OPPONENTS	SCORE	GOALSCORERS	ATTENDANCE
Sep 10	PARTICK THISTLE	W 2-0	Waddell, Findlay	60,000
Sep 24	CELTIC	W 4-0	Rutherford, Findlay, Waddell (pen), Williamson	64,000
Oct 15	Falkirk	W 2-0	Williamson, Rutherford	20,000
Oct 22	HEARTS	W 1-0	Findlay	50,000
Oct 29	Aberdeen	W 3-1	Findlay, Thornton, Rutherford	40,000
Nov 5	Hibernian	L 0-1		51,500
Nov 12	ST MIRREN	W 1-0	Johnson	45,000
Nov 19	Raith Rovers	W 3-1	Williamson 2, Thornton	24,800
Nov 26	STIRLING ALB	W 2-1	Thornton, Williamson	45,000
Dec 3	CLYDE	W 5-4	Thornton 2, Cox 2, Johnson	25,000
Dec 10	Motherwell	L 0-4		28,000
Dec 17	QUEEN OF THE SOUTH	W 1-0	Thornton	18,000
Dec 24	Partick Thistle	W 3-1	Johnson 2, Thornton	35,000
Dec 31	DUNDEE	D 2-2	Thornton, Findlay	35,000
Jan 2	Celtic	D 1-1	McCulloch	65,000
Jan 3	THIRD LANARK	W 3-1	Thornton 2, Johnson	30,000
Jan 7	East Fife	W 2-0	Williamson, Rutherford	18,674
Jan 14	FALKIRK	W 3-0	Young (pen), Rutherford, Williamson	35,000
Jan 21	Hearts	W 1-0	Findlay	49,000
Feb 4	ABERDEEN	D 2-2	Young 2 (2 pens)	50,000
Feb 18	St Mirren	W 2-1	Rutherford, Waddell	40,000
Feb 25	RAITH ROVERS	W 2-0	Williamson, Waddell	35,000
Mar 4	Stirling Albion	W 2-0	Williamson, Paton	25,000
Mar 18	MOTHERWELL	W 2-0	Findlay, Rutherford	38,000
Mar 25	Queen of the South	W 2-1	Thornton, Williamson	18,000
Apr 8	EAST FIFE	D 2-2	Cox, Findlay	40,000
Apr 10	Clyde	W 2-1	Rae, Cox	25,000
Apr 17	Dundee	W 1-0	Duncanson	32,000
Apr 29	HIBERNIAN	D 0-0		101,000
May 1	Third Lanark	D 2-2	Williamson, Paton	32,800

Scottish Cup

Jan 28	Motherwell	(Rd1) W 4-2	Williamson, Paton, McCulloch, Findlay	32,000
Feb 11	COWDENBEATH	(Rd2) W 8-0	McCulloch 2, Williamson 2, Johnson 2, Paton, Rutherford	24,000
Mar 11	RAITH ROVERS	(QF) D 1-1	Findlay	43,080
Mar 15	Raith Rovers	(R) D 1-1	Williamson	28,500
Mar 27	RAITH ROVERS	(2R) W 2-0	Findlay, Cox	63,000
Apr 1	Queen of the South*	(SF) D 1-1	Rutherford	52,924
Apr 5	Queen of the South*	(R) W 3-0	Williamson, Young (pen), Findlay	58,975
Apr 22	East Fife*	(F) W 3-0	Findlay, Thornton 2	120,015

*Played at Hampden Park. Rangers received a bye in third round.

Scottish League Cup

Aug 13	Celtic†	L 2-3	Waddell (pen), Thornton	71,000
Aug 17	ST MIRREN†	W 5-1	Waddell 2 (1 pen), Rutherford, Findlay, Thornton	50,000
Aug 20	ABERDEEN†	W 4-2	Findlay 2, Duncanson 2	50,000
Aug 27	CELTIC†	W 2-0	Findlay, Waddell	95,000
Aug 30	St Mirren†	D 1-1	Duncanson	45,000
Sep 3	Aberdeen†	D 1-1	Findlay	43,000

†Qualifying Section A - Rangers finished top.

Sep 17	COWDENBEATH	(QF/FL) L 2-3	Williamson, Marshall	46,670
Sep 21	Cowdenbeath	(QF/SL) W 3-1	Cox 2, Rutherford	25,586
Oct 8	East Fife*	(SF) L 1-2	Marshall	74,507

*Played at Hampden Park.

MANAGER: Bill Struth

CAPTAIN: Jock Shaw

TOP SCORER: Willie Findlay

BIGGEST WIN: 8-0 v Cowdenbeath, 11 February 1950, Scottish Cup

HIGHEST ATTENDANCE: 120,015 v East Fife, 22 April 1950, Scottish Cup

MAJOR TRANSFERS IN: Johnny Hubbard from Pretoria

League & Cup Appearances

PLAYER	LEAGUE	CUP COMPETITION		TOTAL
		S CUP	SL CUP	
Brown	30	8	9	47
Cox	30	8	9	47
Duncanson	12	2	6	20
Findlay	20	7	9	36
Gillick	2		1	3
Hubbard	2			2
Johnson	20	2		22
Lindsay	2	1		3
McColl	30	8	8	46
McCulloch	10	2		12
McIntyre	2			2
Marshall	1		2	3
Paton	7		3	10
Rae	7	3	2	12
Rutherford	22	5	8	35
Shaw	29	7	9	45
Thornton	19	6	4	29
Waddell	7	3	9	19
Williamson	19	7	5	31
Woodburn	29	8	9	46
Young	30	8	9	47

Goalscorers

PLAYER	LEAGUE	CUP COMPETITION		TOTAL
		S CUP	SL CUP	
Findlay	8	5	5	18
Williamson	11	5	1	17
Thornton	11	2	2	15
Rutherford	7	2	2	11
Waddell	4		4	8
Cox	4	1	2	7
Johnson	5	2		7
Duncanson	1		3	4
McCulloch	1	3		4
Paton	2	2		4
Young	3	1		4
Marshall			2	2
Rae	1			1

Fact File

Four of the Rangers 'Iron Curtain' defence – Brown, Young, McColl and Cox – were ever-presents in the league while the other two, Shaw and Woodburn, missed just one match each.

Final Scottish League Div A Table

		P	W	D	L	F	A	Pts
1	RANGERS	30	22	6	2	58	26	50
2	HIBERNIAN	30	22	5	3	86	34	49
3	HEARTS	30	20	3	7	86	40	43
4	EAST FIFE	30	15	7	8	58	43	37
5	CELTIC	30	14	7	9	51	50	35
6	DUNDEE	30	12	7	11	49	46	31
7	PARTICK T	30	13	3	14	55	45	29
8	ABERDEEN	30	11	4	15	48	56	26
9	RAITH R	30	9	8	13	45	54	26
10	MOTHERWELL	30	10	5	15	53	58	25
11	ST MIRREN	30	8	9	13	42	49	25
12	THIRD LANARK	30	11	3	16	44	62	25
13	CLYDE	30	10	4	16	56	73	24
14	FALKIRK	30	7	10	13	48	72	24
15	Q OF S	30	5	6	19	31	63	16
16	STIRLING A	30	6	3	21	38	77	15

Season 1950-51

Scottish League Division A

DATE	OPPONENTS	SCORE	GOALSCORERS	ATTENDANCE
Sep 9	East Fife	W 3-0	Thornton, Findlay, Waddell	26,000
Sep 16	DUNDEE	D 0-0		40,000
Sep 23	Celtic	L 2-3	Rae, Thornton	53,789
Sep 30	AIRDRIE	W 4-1	Thornton 2, R.Simpson 2	20,000
Oct 7	Partick Thistle	L 1-2	Thornton	33,000
Oct 14	THIRD LANARK	W 2-1	Cox, Rutherford	35,000
Oct 28	ABERDEEN	L 1-2	Thornton	50,000
Nov 4	HIBERNIAN	D 1-1	Paterson o.g.	80,000
Nov 11	St Mirren	W 2-0	Paton, Thornton	20,000
Nov 18	RAITH ROVERS	W 4-1	Thornton, Paton, Williamson, Young (pen)	25,000
Nov 25	Falkirk	D 1-1	Thornton	20,000
Dec 2	Clyde	L 1-2	Williamson	22,000
Dec 9	MORTON	W 2-0	Paton 2	35,000
Dec 23	EAST FIFE	W 5-0	W.Simpson 3, Rae, Hubbard	25,000
Dec 30	Dundee	L 0-2		37,400
Jan 1	CELTIC	W 1-0	Waddell	55,000
Jan 6	PARTICK THISTLE	L 1-3	Waddell	40,000
Jan 20	HEARTS	W 2-1	Thornton, W.Simpson	54,000
Feb 3	Aberdeen	W 4-2	Thornton 2, Paton, W.Simpson	42,000
Feb 17	ST MIRREN	D 1-1	W.Simpson	20,000
Feb 24	Raith Rovers	L 1-3	Waddell	25,000
Mar 3	FALKIRK	W 5-2	Findlay 3, W.Simpson, Marshall	20,000
Mar 10	CLYDE	W 4-0	Findlay 2, McColl, Waddell	20,000
Mar 17	Morton	W 2-0	Marshall, Findlay	22,000
Mar 24	MOTHERWELL	W 3-0	Findlay, Hubbard, W.Simpson	30,000
Mar 31	Airdrie	L 1-2	Waddell	20,000
Apr 7	Motherwell	W 3-2	Rutherford, Woodburn, Findlay	18,000
Apr 21	Hearts	W 1-0	Findlay	35,000
Apr 25	Third Lanark	W 5-1	W.Simpson 4, Rutherford	25,000
Apr 28	Hibernian	L 1-4	W.Simpson	40,000

Scottish Cup

Jan 27	QUEEN OF THE SOUTH	(Rd1) W 2-0	W.Simpson, Waddell	40,000
Feb 10	HIBERNIAN	(Rd2) L 2-3	W.Simpson 2	102,342

Scottish League Cup

Aug 12	Morton†	W 2-1	Rutherford, Findlay	18,500
Aug 16	ABERDEEN†	L 1-2	Findlay	40,000
Aug 19	CLYDE†	W 4-0	Thornton 3, J.Dunn o.g.	45,000
Aug 26	MORTON†	W 6-1	Thornton 2, Findlay 2, Paton 2	35,000
Aug 30	Aberdeen†	L 0-2		42,000
Sep 2	Clyde†	W 5-1	Thornton 2, Findlay 2, Paton	31,000

†Qualifying Section D - Rangers finished second and failed to reach quarter-finals.

League & Cup Appearances

PLAYER	LEAGUE	CUP COMPETITION		TOTAL
		S CUP	SL CUP	
Beckett	1			1
Brown	30	2	6	38
Cox	19	2	6	27
Duncanson	1			1
Dunlop	2			2
Findlay	16	1	6	23
Hubbard	8			8
Johnson	2			2
Lindsay	6		2	8
Little	1			1
McColl	25	1	6	32
Marshall	5			5
Paton	19	1	6	26
Prentice	1			1
Rae	25	2		27
Rutherford	17	1	6	24
Simpson R	2			2
Simpson W	19	2		21
Shaw	18	2	6	26
Thornton	21	2	6	29
Waddell	28	2	6	36
Williamson	6			6
Woodburn	28	2	5	35
Young	30	2	5	37

Goalscorers

PLAYER	LEAGUE	CUP COMPETITION		TOTAL
		S CUP	SL CUP	
Thornton	12		7	19
Findlay	10		6	16
Simpson W	13	3		16
Paton	5		3	8
Waddell	6	1		7
Rutherford	3		1	4
Hubbard	2			2
Marshall	2			2
Rae	2			2
Simpson R	2			2
Williamson	2			2
Cox	1			1
McColl	1			1
Woodburn	1			1
Young	1			1
Opps' o.gs.	1		1	2

Fact File

Rangers failed to qualify from their League Cup section for the first time since the tournament's inception.

MANAGER: Bill Struth

CAPTAIN: Jock Shaw

TOP SCORER: Willie Thornton

BIGGEST WIN: 6-1 v Morton, 26 August 1950, League Cup

HIGHEST ATTENDANCE: 102,342 v Hibernian, 10 February 1951, Scottish Cup

MAJOR TRANSFERS IN: Billy Simpson from Linfield, John Prentice from Hearts

MAJOR TRANSFERS OUT: Jimmy Duncanson to St Mirren

Final Scottish League Div A Table

		P	W	D	L	F	A	Pts
1	HIBERNIAN	30	22	4	4	78	26	48
2	RANGERS	30	17	4	9	64	37	38
3	DUNDEE	30	15	8	7	47	30	38
4	HEARTS	30	16	5	9	72	45	37
5	ABERDEEN	30	15	5	10	61	50	35
6	PARTICK T	30	13	7	10	57	48	33
7	CELTIC	30	12	5	13	48	46	29
8	RAITH R	30	13	2	15	52	52	28
9	MOTHERWELL	30	11	6	13	58	65	28
10	EAST FIFE	30	10	8	12	48	66	28
11	ST MIRREN	30	9	7	14	35	51	25
12	MORTON	30	10	4	16	47	59	24
13	THIRD LANARK	30	11	2	17	40	51	24
14	AIRDRIEONIANS	30	10	4	16	52	67	24
15	CLYDE	30	8	7	15	37	57	23
16	FALKIRK	30	7	4	19	35	81	18

Season 1951-52

Scottish League Division A

DATE	OPPONENTS	SCORE	GOALSCORERS	ATTENDANCE
Sep 8	PARTICK THISTLE	W 4-1	Findlay 3, Rutherford	60,000
Sep 22	CELTIC	D 1-1	Findlay	86,000
Sep 29	Aberdeen	L 0-1		31,000
Oct 10	EAST FIFE	D 1-1	Waddell	20,000
Oct 20	HEARTS	W 2-0	Findlay, Waddell	40,000
Nov 3	Hibernian	D 1-1	Findlay	55,000
Nov 10	ST MIRREN	W 5-1	Thornton 3, Johnson, Findlay	25,000
Nov 17	Raith Rovers	L 1-3	Liddell	21,000
Nov 24	STIRLING ALBION	W 3-0	Johnson 2, Waddell	20,000
Dec 1	THIRD LANARK	D 1-1	Thornton	20,000
Dec 8	Morton	W 1-0	McColl	14,000
Dec 15	MOTHERWELL	W 3-0	Thornton, Liddell, Cox	40,000
Dec 22	Partick Thistle	W 3-1	Cox 2, Paton	35,000
Dec 29	QUEEN OF THE SOUTH	W 3-2	Thornton 2, Young (pen)	30,000
Jan 1	Celtic	W 4-1	Paton 2, Liddell, Waddell	45,000
Jan 2	DUNDEE	L 1-2	Thornton	35,000
Jan 5	East Fife	L 1-2	Thornton	18,000
Jan 12	AIRDRIE	W 1-0	Thornton	45,000
Jan 19	Hearts	D 2-2	Findlay 2	47,600
Jan 26	St Mirren	W 5-0	Thornton 2, Liddell 2, Paton	32,000
Feb 2	ABERDEEN	W 3-2	Thornton, Paton, Young (pen)	40,000
Feb 13	HIBERNIAN	D 2-2	McCulloch, Young (pen)	45,000
Feb 16	Airdrie	W 1-0	Thornton	24,000
Feb 27	RAITH ROVERS	W 1-0	Thornton	20,000
Mar 1	Stirling Albion	W 5-1	Prentice, Waddell, Rae, Cox (pen), Thornton	14,000
Mar 15	MORTON	W 1-0	Thornton	35,000
Mar 22	Motherwell	L 1-2	Simpson	22,200
Mar 29	Queen of the South	D 2-2	Marshall, Thornton	12,000
Apr 16	Third Lanark	D 1-1	Prentice	15,000
Apr 19	Aberdeen	D 1-1	Liddell	20,000

Scottish Cup

Feb 9	ELGIN CITY	(Rd2) W 6-1	Findlay 2, Paton, Waddell, Liddell, Thornton	36,324
Feb 23	Arbroath	(Rd3) W 2-0	Thornton 2	13,510
Mar 8	MOTHERWELL	(QF) D 1-1	Thornton	82,000
Mar 12	Motherwell	(R) L 1-2	Thornton	36,632

Rangers received a bye in first round.

Scottish League Cup

Aug 11	East Fife†	D 0-0		18,500
Aug 15	ABERDEEN†	W 2-1	Rutherford, Paton	60,000
Aug 18	Queen of the South†	W 3-0	Simpson 2, Waddell	19,000
Aug 25	EAST FIFE†	W 4-1	Simpson 2, Waddell (pen), Findlay	28,000
Aug 29	Aberdeen†	L 1-2	Simpson	28,000
Sep 1	QUEEN OF THE SOUTH†	W 5-2	Thornton 3, McColl, Simpson	40,000

†Qualifying Section D - Rangers finished top.

Sep 15	Dunfermline	(QF/FL) L 0-1		20,000
Sep 19	DUNFERMLINE	(QF/SL) W 3-1	Findlay 2, Gardiner	45,000
Oct 13	Celtic*	(SF) W 3-0	Thornton, Johnson, Findlay	83,235
Oct 27	Dundee*	(F) L 2-3	Findlay, Young	95,235

*Played at Hampden Park.

MANAGER: Bill Struth

CAPTAIN: Jock Shaw

TOP SCORER: Willie Thornton

BIGGEST WIN: 6-1 v Elgin City, 9 February 1952, Scottish Cup

HIGHEST ATTENDANCE: 95,325 v Dundee, 27 October 1951, League Cup

MAJOR TRANSFERS IN: Johnny Little from Queen's Park, Colin Liddell from Hearts

MAJOR TRANSFERS OUT: Billy Williamson to St Mirren, Torry Gillick to Partick Thistle, Eddie Rutherford to Hearts

League & Cup Appearances

PLAYER	LEAGUE	CUP COMPETITION		TOTAL
		S CUP	SL CUP	
Boyd	2			2
Brown	29	4	10	43
Cox	23	3	8	34
Findlay	14	1	10	25
Gardiner	4		2	6
Hubbard	1			1
Johnson	9		2	11
Liddell	24		4	28
Little	28	4	10	42
Marshall	1			1
McColl	29	4	10	43
McCulloch	6	2		8
Neillands	3			3
Niven	1			1
Paton	15	4	5	24
Prentice	19	4	1	24
Pryde	3			3
Rae	2	1	3	6
Rutherford	4		8	12
Shaw	2			2
Simpson	3		6	9
Stanners	1			1
Thornton	28	4	6	38
Waddell	24	3	10	37
Woodburn	27	2	10	39
Young	28	4	9	41

Goalscorers

PLAYER	LEAGUE	CUP COMPETITION		TOTAL
		S CUP	SL CUP	
Thornton	18	5	4	27
Findlay	9	2	5	16
Waddell	5	1	2	8
Liddell	6	1		7
Paton	5	1	1	7
Simpson	1		6	7
Cox	4			4
Johnson	3		1	4
Young	3		1	4
McColl	1		1	2
Prentice	2			2
Rutherford	1		1	2
Gardiner			1	1
Marshall	1			1
McCulloch	1			1
Rae	1			1

Fact File

Rangers lost 3-2 to Arsenal on 17 October 1951 in a friendly match to mark the opening of the floodlights at Highbury. The match was watched by a crowd of 62,000.

Final Scottish League Div A Table

		P	W	D	L	F	A	Pts
1	HIBERNIAN	30	20	5	5	92	36	45
2	RANGERS	30	16	9	5	61	31	41
3	EAST FIFE	30	17	3	10	71	49	37
4	HEARTS	30	14	7	9	69	53	35
5	RAITH R	30	14	5	11	43	42	33
6	PARTICK T	30	12	7	11	48	51	31
7	MOTHERWELL	30	12	7	11	51	57	31
8	DUNDEE	30	11	6	13	53	52	28
9	CELTIC	30	10	8	12	52	55	28
10	Q OF S	30	10	8	12	50	60	28
11	ABERDEEN	30	10	7	13	65	58	27
12	THIRD LANARK	30	9	8	13	51	62	26
13	AIRDRIEONIANS	30	11	4	15	54	69	26
14	ST MIRREN	30	10	5	15	43	58	25
15	MORTON	30	9	6	15	49	56	24
16	STIRLING A	30	5	5	20	36	99	15

Season 1952-53

Scottish League Division A

DATE	OPPONENTS	SCORE	GOALSCORERS	ATTENDANCE
Sep 6	St Mirren	W 3-2	Grierson 2, Thornton	45,000
Sep 20	Celtic	L 1-2	Liddell	48,000
Sep 27	THIRD LANARK	W 4-1	Thornton 2, Grierson 2	25,000
Oct 11	HIBERNIAN	L 1-2	Grierson	65,000
Oct 18	East Fife	L 2-3	Thornton, Grierson	20,000
Nov 1	QUEEN OF THE SOUTH	W 3-1	Liddell, Simpson, Paton	20,000
Nov 8	Falkirk	W 2-1	Prentice, Simpson	18,500
Nov 15	Clyde	W 6-4	Simpson 3, Prentice, Waddell, Grierson	28,000
Nov 22	RAITH ROVERS	W 3-2	Grierson 2, Prentice	30,000
Dec 6	ABERDEEN	W 4-0	McCulloch 2, Simpson, Young (pen)	35,000
Dec 13	Hearts	D 2-2	Simpson, Grierson	27,000
Dec 20	ST MIRREN	W 4-0	Simpson 4	35,000
Dec 27	Airdrie	D 2-2	Grierson, Simpson	20,000
Jan 1	CELTIC	W 1-0	Simpson	80,000
Jan 3	Third Lanark	W 2-0	Prentice 2	20,581
Jan 10	PARTICK THISTLE	D 2-2	Paton, Grierson	30,000
Jan 17	Hibernian	D 1-1	Grierson	60,500
Jan 31	EAST FIFE	W 4-0	McColl 2, Simpson, Grierson	52,000
Feb 14	Dundee	D 1-1	Cowie o.g.	24,000
Feb 23	FALKIRK	W 4-0	Simpson 3, Prentice	35,000
Mar 7	CLYDE	L 1-2	Young (pen)	55,000
Mar 18	Raith Rovers	L 1-3	Simpson	18,000
Mar 21	MOTHERWELL	W 4-1	Grierson 2, McCulloch, Simpson	35,000
Mar 28	Aberdeen	D 2-2	Grierson, Gardiner	35,000
Apr 6	HEARTS	W 3-0	Simpson, Prentice, McColl	40,000
Apr 11	Partick Thistle	W 2-1	Gardiner, Young (pen)	25,500
Apr 15	AIRDRIE	W 8-2	Grierson 4, Prentice, Paton, Young (pen), Cross o.g.	20,000
Apr 20	Motherwell	W 3-0	Paton 2, Young (pen)	30,720
May 2	DUNDEE	W 3-1	Grierson 2, Simpson	45,000
May 7	Queen of the South	D 1-1	Waddell	17,000

Scottish Cup

Jan 24	ARBROATH	(Rd1)	W 4-0	Hubbard, Prentice, McCulloch, Simpson	44,000
Feb 7	Dundee	(Rd2)	W 2-0	Hubbard, Grierson	43,024
Feb 21	Morton	(Rd3)	W 4-1	Grierson 2, Simpson, Prentice	23,000
Mar 14	CELTIC	(QF)	W 2-0	Prentice, Grierson	95,000
Apr 4	Hearts*	(SF)	W 2-1	Grierson, Prentice	116,262
Apr 25	Aberdeen*	(F)	D 1-1	Prentice	129,762
Apr 29	Aberdeen*	(R)	W 1-0	Simpson	113,700

*Played at Hampden Park.

Scottish League Cup

Aug 9	Hearts†		L 0-5		41,000
Aug 13	MOTHERWELL†		W 2-0	Thornton, Liddell	50,000
Aug 16	ABERDEEN†		W 3-1	Grierson 2, Thornton	40,000
Aug 23	HEARTS†		W 2-0	Thornton, Liddell	75,000
Aug 27	Motherwell†		D 3-3	Prentice, Thornton, Paton	35,000
Aug 30	Aberdeen†		W 2-1	Waddell, Thornton	35,000

†Qualifying Section C - Rangers finished top.

Sep 13	THIRD LANARK	(QF/FL)	D 0-0		50,000
Sep 17	Third Lanark	(QF/SL)	W 2-0	Grierson, Prentice	42,000
Oct 4	Kilmarnock*	(SF)	L 0-1		45,715

*Played at Hampden Park.

MANAGER: Bill Struth

CAPTAIN: Jock Shaw

TOP SCORER: Derek Grierson

BIGGEST WIN: 8-2 v Airdrie, 15 April 1953, league

HIGHEST ATTENDANCE: 129,762 v Aberdeen, 25 April 1953, Scottish Cup

MAJOR TRANSFERS IN: Derek Grierson from Queen's Park

MAJOR TRANSFERS OUT: Joe Johnson to Lincoln City

League & Cup Appearances

PLAYER	LEAGUE	CUP COMPETITION		TOTAL
		S CUP	SL CUP	
Brown			1	1
Cox	23	5	9	37
Dunlop	1			1
Gardiner	2			2
Grierson	30	7	7	44
Hubbard	24	7	1	32
Liddell	6		8	14
Little	30	7	9	46
Marshall			1	1
McColl	29	7	9	45
McCulloch	12	1		13
Niven	30	7	8	45
Paton	6	3	3	12
Prentice	30	6	7	43
Pryde	3	2		5
Rae	3			3
Shaw	1			1
Simpson	21	6		27
Stanners	3	1		4
Thornton	4		9	13
Waddell	16	5	9	30
Woodburn	27	6	9	42
Young	29	7	9	45

Goalscorers

PLAYER	LEAGUE	CUP COMPETITION		TOTAL
		S CUP	SL CUP	
Grierson	23	5	3	31
Simpson	21	3		24
Prentice	8	5	2	15
Thornton	4		5	9
Paton	5		1	6
Young	5			5
Liddell	2		2	4
McCulloch	3	1		4
McColl	3			3
Waddell	2		1	3
Gardiner	2			2
Hubbard		2		2
Opps' o.gs.	2			2

Fact File

Rangers lost 2-1 to Manchester United at Hampden in the first round of the Coronation Cup on 13 May 1953. Hunter McMillan scored their goal in front of 75,546.

Final Scottish League Div A Table

		P	W	D	L	F	A	Pts
1	RANGERS	30	18	7	5	80	39	43
2	HIBERNIAN	30	19	5	6	93	51	43
3	EAST FIFE	30	16	7	7	72	48	39
4	HEARTS	30	12	6	12	59	50	30
5	CLYDE	30	13	4	13	78	78	30
6	ST MIRREN	30	11	8	11	52	58	30
7	DUNDEE	30	9	11	10	44	37	29
8	CELTIC	30	11	7	12	51	54	29
9	PARTICK T	30	10	9	11	55	63	29
10	Q OF S	30	10	8	12	43	61	28
11	ABERDEEN	30	11	5	14	64	68	27
12	RAITH R	30	9	8	13	47	53	26
13	FALKIRK	30	11	4	15	53	63	26
14	AIRDRIEONIANS	30	10	6	14	53	75	26
15	MOTHERWELL	30	10	5	15	57	80	25
16	THIRD LANARK	30	8	4	18	52	75	20

Season 1953-54

Scottish League Division A

DATE	OPPONENTS	SCORE	GOALSCORERS	ATTENDANCE
Sep 5	PARTICK THISTLE	W 3-0	Grierson, Paton, Prentice	60,000
Sep 19	CELTIC	D 1-1	Paton	60,000
Sep 26	Stirling Albion	L 0-2		24,000
Oct 17	EAST FIFE	W 2-0	Simpson, Grierson	40,000
Oct 24	Dundee	L 0-1		34,000
Oct 31	HEARTS	L 0-1		30,000
Nov 7	Aberdeen	D 1-1	Simpson	30,000
Nov 14	HAMILTON A	W 8-1	Thornton 3, Waddell 2 (1 pen), Paton, Hubbard, Simpson	25,000
Nov 21	Raith Rovers	W 2-1	Thornton, Simpson	18,000
Nov 28	CLYDE	D 1-1	Thornton	40,000
Dec 12	Queen of the South	L 1-2	McColl	18,500
Dec 19	Partick Thistle	W 1-0	Thornton	20,000
Dec 26	HIBERNIAN	W 3-1	Gardiner 2, Prentice	28,000
Jan 1	Celtic	L 0-1		65,000
Jan 2	STIRLING ALBION	W 3-1	Paton, Prentice, McCulloch	28,000
Jan 9	St Mirren	W 1-0	Paton	37,500
Jan 16	AIRDRIE	W 3-0	Gardiner 2, Thornton	19,000
Jan 23	East Fife	L 1-2	Grierson	18,000
Feb 6	DUNDEE	W 2-0	Grierson, McCulloch	38,000
Feb 20	Hearts	D 3-3	Waddell, Gardiner, Paton	49,000
Mar 6	Hamilton A	D 1-1	Little	16,500
Mar 17	RAITH ROVERS	D 2-2	Caldow (pen), Paton	12,000
Mar 20	Clyde	W 5-2	Simpson 2, Prentice 2, Grierson	29,919
Mar 27	Falkirk	L 3-4	Simpson 2, Grierson	20,000
Apr 3	QUEEN OF THE SOUTH	W 2-0	Simpson, McColl	10,000
Apr 14	ST MIRREN	D 1-1	Simpson	12,000
Apr 17	ABERDEEN	L 1-3	Paton	45,000
Apr 21	FALKIRK	W 3-0	Caldow (pen), Simpson, Grierson	22,000
Apr 24	Airdrie	L 0-2		8,000
Apr 26	Hibernian	D 2-2	Grierson, Paton	17,300

Scottish Cup

Jan 30	QUEEN'S PARK	(Rd1) W 2-0	Waddell, Gardiner	34,133
Feb 13	KILMARNOCK	(Rd2) D 2-2	Grierson, Gardiner	40,000
Feb 17	Kilmarnock	(R) W 3-1	Paton 2, McCulloch	33,545
Feb 27	Third Lanark	(Rd3) D 0-0		45,591
Mar 3	THIRD LANARK	(R) D 4-4	Prentice 2, Simpson 2	17,000
Mar 8	THIRD LANARK	(2R) W 3-2	Caldow (pen), Paton, Prentice	31,000
Mar 13	BERWICK	(QF) W 4-0	Simpson, Paton, Liddell, Caldow (pen)	60,245
Apr 10	Aberdeen*	(SF) L 0-6		110,939

*Played at Hampden Park.

Scottish League Cup

Aug 8	Raith Rovers†	W 4-0	Young (pen), Prentice, Simpson, Grierson	24,807
Aug 12	HEARTS†	W 4-1	Simpson, Hubbard, Young (pen), Grierson	60,000
Aug 15	HAMILTON†	W 5-1	Grierson 3, Paton 2	35,000
Aug 22	RAITH ROVERS†	W 3-1	Paton 2, McCulloch	38,000
Aug 26	Hearts†	D 1-1	Grierson	35,000
Aug 29	Hamilton A†	W 5-0	Paton 4, Waddell	25,000

†Qualifying Section C - Rangers finished top.

Sep 12	AYR UNITED	(QF/FL) W 4-2	Prentice 3, Grierson	20,000
Sep 16	Ayr United	(QF/SL) L 2-3	Waddell (pen), Paton	20,000
Oct 10	Partick Thistle*	(SF) L 0-2		48,064

*Played at Hampden Park.

MANAGER: Bill Struth

CAPTAIN: Jock Shaw

TOP SCORER: Willie Paton

BIGGEST WIN: 8-1 v Hamilton, 14 November 1953, League

HIGHEST ATTENDANCE: 110, 939 v Aberdeen, 10 April 1954, League Cup

MAJOR TRANSFERS IN: Alex Scott from Bo'ness United

League & Cup Appearances

PLAYER	LEAGUE	CUP COMPETITION		TOTAL
		S CUP	SL CUP	
Brown	21	4		25
Caldow	8	3	2	13
Cox	28	7	9	44
Findlay	1	1		2
Gardiner	8	2		10
Grierson	21	6	9	36
Hubbard	15	1	9	25
Liddell	5	2		7
Little	25	8	9	42
McColl	27	8	9	44
McCulloch	9	7	1	17
McMillan	1			1
Neillands	2			2
Niven	9	4	9	22
Paton	19	6	7	32
Prentice	18	5	9	32
Rae	8	1		9
Rodger	1			1
Simpson	18	4	2	24
Stanners	8			8
Thornton	8			8
Waddell	29	6	8	43
Woodburn	21	6	9	36
Young	20	7	7	34

Goalscorers

PLAYER	LEAGUE	CUP COMPETITION		TOTAL
		S CUP	SL CUP	
Paton	9	4	9	22
Grierson	8	1	7	16
Simpson	11	3	2	16
Prentice	5	3	4	12
Gardiner	5	2		7
Thornton	7			7
Waddell	3	1	2	6
Caldow	2	2		4
McCulloch	2	1	1	4
Hubbard	1		1	2
McColl	2			2
Young			2	2
Liddell		1		1
Little	1			1

Fact File

Rangers lost 2-1 to Arsenal at Ibrox on 8 December 1953 in a British Championship match to officially open the stadium's floodlights. Willie McCulloch scored the Rangers goal in front of an 80,000 attendance.

Final Scottish League Div A Table

		P	W	D	L	F	A	Pts
1	CELTIC	30	20	3	7	72	29	43
2	HEARTS	30	16	6	8	70	45	38
3	PARTICK T	30	17	1	12	76	54	35
4	RANGERS	30	13	8	9	56	35	34
5	HIBERNIAN	30	15	4	11	72	51	34
6	EAST FIFE	30	13	8	9	55	45	34
7	DUNDEE	30	14	6	10	46	47	34
8	CLYDE	30	15	4	11	64	67	34
9	ABERDEEN	30	15	3	12	66	51	33
10	Q OF S	30	14	4	12	72	58	32
11	ST MIRREN	30	12	4	14	44	54	28
12	RAITH R	30	10	6	14	56	60	26
13	FALKIRK	30	9	7	14	47	61	25
14	STIRLING A	30	10	4	16	39	62	24
15	AIRDRIEONIANS	30	5	5	20	41	92	15
16	HAMILTON A	30	4	3	23	29	94	11

Season 1954-55

Scottish League Division A

DATE	OPPONENTS	SCORE	GOALSCORERS	ATTENDANCE
Sep 11	HIBERNIAN	D 1-1	Grierson	54,000
Sep 18	Celtic	L 0-2		45,000
Oct 2	East Fife	W 7-2	Grierson 2, Paton 2, Gardiner, Young (pen), McCulloch	16,500
Oct 9	STIRLING ALBION	W 6-1	Gardiner 4, Grierson 2	20,000
Oct 16	Partick Thistle	W 5-2	Simpson 2, Grierson Hubbard 2 (1 pen),	35,741
Oct 23	DUNDEE	W 3-0	Grierson, Hubbard (pen), Rae	30,000
Oct 30	St Mirren	L 1-2	Hubbard (pen)	35,054
Nov 6	KILMARNOCK	W 6-0	Simpson 2, Brand 2, Paton, Hubbard (pen)	40,000
Nov 13	Falkirk	W 3-0	Simpson 2, Prentice	20,000
Nov 20	Clyde	D 1-1	Gardiner	32,000
Nov 27	RAITH ROVERS	W 1-0	Hubbard (pen)	25,000
Dec 4	Queen of the South	W 2-1	Simpson 2	12,500
Dec 11	ABERDEEN	W 3-1	Simpson 2, Grierson	45,800
Dec 18	Hearts	W 4-3	Grierson 2, Simpson 2	40,000
Dec 25	Hibernian	L 1-2	Grierson	43,000
Jan 1	CELTIC	W 4-1	Hubbard 3 (1 pen), Simpson	65,000
Jan 3	Motherwell	L 0-2		25,000
Jan 8	EAST FIFE	W 2-0	Gardiner, Simpson	28,000
Jan 29	Dundee	L 1-2	Simpson	28,000
Feb 12	ST MIRREN	D 1-1	McCulloch	40,000
Feb 26	Kilmarnock	L 0-1		25,000
Mar 5	Stirling Albion	W 2-0	Prentice, Gardiner	9,000
Mar 9	FALKIRK	W 4-1	Scott 3, Gardiner	8,000
Mar 12	CLYDE	W 1-0	Simpson	60,000
Mar 19	Raith Rovers	L 0-1		14,500
Mar 26	QUEEN OF THE SOUTH	W 1-0	Hubbard (pen)	15,000
Apr 2	Aberdeen	L 0-4		32,000
Apr 9	HEARTS	W 2-1	Hubbard, Simpson	30,000
Apr 11	PARTICK THISTLE	W 3-1	Hubbard 2 (1 pen), Simpson	28,000
Apr 30	MOTHERWELL	W 2-0	Hubbard, McMillan	30,000

Scottish Cup

Feb 5	DUNDEE	(Rd5) D 0-0		58,000
Feb 9	Dundee	(R) W 1-0	Gallagher o.g.	25,600
Feb 19	Aberdeen	(Rd6) L 1-2	Neillands	44,647

Scottish League Cup

Aug 14	Stirling Albion†	W 5-0	Simpson 3, Prentice 2	24,000
Aug 18	PARTICK THISTLE†	D 1-1	Davidson o.g.	45,000
Aug 21	CLYDE†	L 1-3	Grierson	50,000
Aug 28	STIRLING ALBION†	W 2-0	Paton, Hubbard (pen)	30,000
Sep 1	Partick Thistle†	W 2-1	Prentice, Simpson	26,883
Sep 4	Clyde†	W 2-1	Simpson, Paton	32,700

†Qualifying Section C – Rangers finished top.

Sep 22	Motherwell	(QF/FL) L 1-2	Prentice	24,000
Sep 25	MOTHERWELL	(QF/SL) D 1-1	Paton	55,000

Fact File

After the fifth dismissal of his career, centre half Willie Woodburn was suspended indefinitely by the Scottish Football Association on 14 September 1954 at the age of 35 and never played again.

MANAGER: Scot Symon

CAPTAIN: George Young

TOP SCORER: Billy Simpson

BIGGEST WIN: 6-0 v Kilmarnock, 6 November 1954, league

HIGHEST ATTENDANCE: 65,000 v Celtic, 1 January 1955, league,

MAJOR TRANSFERS IN: Jimmy Millar from Dunfermline, Billy Ritchie from Bathgate Thistle

MAJOR TRANSFERS OUT: Willie Findlay to Albion Rovers, Colin Liddell to Morton

League & Cup Appearances

PLAYER	LEAGUE	CUP COMPETITION		TOTAL
		S CUP	SL CUP	
Brand	3	1		4
Brown	8			8
Caldow	11		1	12
Cox	12	3		15
Cunning	3		2	5
Gardiner	11	1	1	13
Grierson	18		5	23
Hubbard	23	3	3	29
Liddell			3	3
Little	21	3	8	32
Millar	2		1	3
McColl	26	3	6	35
McCulloch	12	2	4	18
McKenzie, George	1		2	3
McKenzie, Gordon	9			9
McMillan	4			4
Menzies			1	1
Neillands	1	1		2
Niven	22	3	8	33
Paton	19	3	5	27
Prentice	18	1	8	27
Pryde	5			5
Rae	19	3	7	29
Rodger	2			2
Scott	7			7
Simpson	25	2	5	32
Stanners	7		2	9
Waddell	11		4	15
Woodburn	1		6	7
Woods	1			1
Young	28	3	7	38

Goalscorers

PLAYER	LEAGUE	CUP COMPETITION		TOTAL
		S CUP	SL CUP	
Simpson	18		5	23
Hubbard	14	1		15
Gardiner	9			9
Grierson	11		1	12
Paton	3		3	6
Prentice	2		4	6
Scott	3			3
Brand	2			2
McCulloch	2			2
McMillan	1			1
Neillands		1		1
Rae	1			1
Young	1			1
Opps' o.gs.		1	1	2

Final Scottish League Div A Table

		P	W	D	L	F	A	Pts
1	ABERDEEN	30	24	1	5	73	26	49
2	CELTIC	30	19	8	3	76	37	46
3	RANGERS	30	19	3	8	67	33	41
4	HEARTS	30	16	7	7	74	45	39
5	HIBERNIAN	30	15	4	11	64	54	34
6	ST MIRREN	30	12	8	10	55	54	32
7	CLYDE	30	11	9	10	59	50	31
8	DUNDEE	30	13	4	13	48	48	30
9	PARTICK T	30	11	7	12	49	61	29
10	KILMARNOCK	30	10	6	14	46	58	26
11	EAST FIFE	30	9	6	15	51	62	24
12	FALKIRK	30	8	8	14	42	54	24
13	Q OF S	30	9	6	15	38	56	24
14	RAITH R	30	10	3	17	49	57	23
15	MOTHERWELL	30	9	4	17	42	62	22
16	STIRLING A	30	2	2	26	29	105	6

Season 1955-56

Scottish League Division A

DATE	OPPONENTS	SCORE	GOALSCORERS	ATTENDANCE
Sep 10	STIRLING ALBION	D 0-0		25,000
Sep 24	CELTIC	D 0-0		47,000
Oct 8	AIRDRIE	D 4-4	Hubbard 2 (1 pen), Murray, Baird	25,000
Oct 15	Partick Thistle	W 3-1	Hubbard, Scott, Baird	40,000
Oct 22	Stirling Albion	D 2-2	Scott, Kichenbrand	15,000
Oct 29	Queen of the South	L 1-2	Simpson	16,500
Nov 5	Falkirk	W 2-1	Paton, Scott	20,000
Nov 12	HEARTS	W 4-1	Kichenbrand 2, Baird, Simpson	51,000
Nov 19	Kilmarnock	W 2-1	Kichenbrand, Baird	25,600
Nov 26	MOTHERWELL	D 2-2	Hubbard (pen), Kichenbrand	40,000
Dec 3	RAITH ROVERS	W 4-0	Simpson 2, Kichenbrand, Scott	26,000
Dec 10	Aberdeen	D 0-0		25,000
Dec 17	HIBERNIAN	W 4-1	Hubbard 2 (1 pen), Kichenbrand, Simpson	50,000
Dec 24	DUNFERMLINE	W 6-0	Kichenbrand 2, Baird 2, Scott, Hubbard	30,000
Dec 31	Clyde	W 4-0	Scott, Simpson, Kichenbrand, Baird	31,000
Jan 2	Celtic	W 1-0	Hubbard	47,000
Jan 7	DUNDEE	W 3-1	Hubbard 2 (1 pen), Scott	46,000
Jan 9	St Mirren	W 1-0	Paton	37,500
Jan 21	EAST FIFE	W 3-0	Baird, Hubbard (pen), Kichenbrand	30,000
Jan 28	Airdrie	W 4-0	Baird 3, Hubbard	22,000
Feb 11	PARTICK THISTLE	W 1-0	Hubbard	45,000
Feb 25	St Mirren	W 1-0	Kichenbrand	43,000
Mar 7	QUEEN OF THE SOUTH	W 8-0	Kichenbrand 5, Simpson 2, Scott	30,000
Mar 10	FALKIRK	W 4-0	McColl, Simpson, Baird, Rae	45,000
Mar 17	Hearts	D 1-1	Hubbard (pen)	50,000
Mar 21	ST MIRREN	W 4-1	Kichenbrand 3, Prentice	30,000
Mar 24	KILMARNOCK	W 3-2	Kichenbrand 2, Hubbard (pen)	30,000
Mar 31	Motherwell	W 2-1	Murray 2	27,500
Apr 2	Dundee	W 3-0	Hubbard 2, Simpson	18,500
Apr 7	Raith Rovers	W 5-0	Murray 2, Leigh o.g. Hubbard 2 (1 pen),	20,000
Apr 9	East Fife	L 1-2	Baird	10,000
Apr 18	ABERDEEN	W 1-0	Scott	45,000
Apr 21	Hibernian	D 2-2	Murray, Baird	30,000
Apr 25	Dunfermline	L 0-1		-
Apr 28	CLYDE	L 0-1		25,000

Scottish Cup

Feb 5	ABERDEEN	(Rd5) W 2-1	Scott, Kichenbrand	66,000
Feb 18	Dundee	(Rd6) W 1-0	Kichenbrand	42,500
Mar 3	Hearts	(QF) L 0-4		47,258

Scottish League Cup

Aug 13	Falkirk†	W 5-0	Hubbard 2, Scott, Murray, McMillan	21,000
Aug 17	FALKIRK†	W 4-3	Hubbard 2 (1 pen), Scott, Murray	35,000
Aug 20	Queen of the South†	W 2-1	Hubbard, Scott	15,000
Aug 27	CELTIC†	L 1-4	Scott	75,000
Aug 31	Celtic†	W 4-0	Baird 2, Simpson, Murray	61,000
Sep 3	QUEEN OF THE SOUTH†	W 6-0	Arnison 2, Scott 2, Hubbard, Simpson	50,000

†Qualifying Section Four – Rangers finished top.

Sep 14	Hamilton A	(QF/FL) W 2-1	Hubbard, Simpson	18,000
Sep 17	HAMILTON A	(QF/SL) W 8-0	Scott 3, Simpson 2, Hubbard 2, Prentice	40,000
Oct 1	Aberdeen*	(SF) L 1-2	Hubbard	79,500

*Played at Hampden Park.

League & Cup Appearances

PLAYER	LEAGUE	CUP COMPETITION		TOTAL
		S CUP	SL CUP	
Arnison			2	2
Baird	33	3	7	43
Brown	3			3
Caldow	26		9	35
Elliott	2			2
Hubbard	34	3	9	46
Kichenbrand	25	3		28
Little	25	3	9	37
McColl	34	3	9	46
McMillan			3	3
Millar	1		1	2
Murray	8		5	13
Niven	31	3	9	43
Paton	1			1
Prentice	10		5	15
Queen	1			1
Rae	27	3	5	35
Scott	34	3	9	46
Shearer	16	3		19
Simpson	32	3	8	43
Stanners	1			1
Thomson	1			1
Young	29	3	9	42

Goalscorers

PLAYER	LEAGUE	CUP COMPETITION		TOTAL
		S CUP	SL CUP	
Hubbard	17		10	27
Kichenbrand	24	2		26
Scott	9	1	9	19
Baird	14		2	16
Simpson	10		5	15
Murray	6		3	9
Arnison			2	2
Prentice	1		1	2
McColl	1			1
McMillan			1	1
Paton	1			1
Rae	1			1
Opps' o.gs.	1			1

MANAGER: Scot Symon

CAPTAIN: George Young

MAJOR TRANSFERS IN: Max Murray from Queen's Park, Sammy Baird from Preston North End, Don Kichenbrand from Delfos, Bobby Shearer from Hamilton

MAJOR TRANSFERS OUT: Willie Gardiner to Leicester City, Bobby Brown to Falkirk

Final Scottish League Div A Table

		P	W	D	L	F	A	Pts
1	RANGERS	34	22	8	4	85	27	52
2	ABERDEEN	34	18	10	6	87	50	46
3	HEARTS	34	19	7	8	99	47	45
4	HIBERNIAN	34	19	7	8	86	50	45
5	CELTIC	34	16	9	9	55	39	41
6	Q OF S	34	16	5	13	69	73	37
7	AIRDRIEONIANS	34	14	8	12	85	96	36
8	KILMARNOCK	34	12	10	12	52	45	34
9	PARTICK T	34	13	7	14	62	60	33
10	MOTHERWELL	34	11	11	12	53	59	33
11	RAITH R	34	12	9	13	58	75	33
12	EAST FIFE	34	13	5	16	61	69	31
13	DUNDEE	34	12	6	16	56	65	30
14	FALKIRK	34	11	6	17	58	75	28
15	ST MIRREN	34	10	7	17	57	70	27
16	DUNFERMLINE ATH	34	10	6	18	42	82	26
17	CLYDE	34	8	6	20	50	74	22
18	STIRLING A	34	4	5	25	23	82	13

Fact File

Rangers' 8-0 win over Queen of the South at Ibrox on 7 March 1956 was the first Scottish league fixture to be played under floodlights.

Season 1956-57

Scottish League Division 1

DATE	OPPONENTS	SCORE	GOALSCORERS	ATTENDANCE
Sep 8	Airdrie	D 3-3	Murray 2, Hubbard	18,000
Sep 15	KILMARNOCK	L 0-1		30,000
Sep 22	Celtic	W 2-0	Murray, Scott	53,000
Sep 29	AYR UNITED	W 3-1	Scott 2, Hubbard (pen)	27,000
Oct 6	St Mirren	W 2-1	Baird, Scott	28,700
Oct 13	PARTICK THISTLE	W 4-1	Simpson 2, Baird, Hubbard (pen)	38,000
Nov 3	HIBERNIAN	W 5-3	Murray 2, Scott, Hubbard (pen), Simpson	45,000
Nov 10	MOTHERWELL	L 2-3	Baird 2	63,000
Nov 17	Falkirk	W 2-0	Murray 2	19,000
Nov 24	ABERDEEN	W 3-1	Simpson, Hubbard (pen), Murray	29,100
Dec 1	EAST FIFE	W 6-1	Scott 2, Baird 2, Hubbard 2	26,000
Dec 8	Raith Rovers	L 1-5	Simpson	20,000
Dec 15	HEARTS	W 5-3	Murray 2, Hubbard, Davis, Simpson	45,000
Dec 22	Kilmarnock	L 2-3	Simpson, Murray	22,436
Dec 29	QUEEN OF THE SOUTH	W 4-0	Simpson 2, Murray 2	30,000
Jan 1	CELTIC	W 2-0	Murray, Simpson	60,000
Jan 2	Dundee	W 3-1	Scott, Simpson, Young (pen)	28,500
Jan 12	Ayr United	L 0-1		15,000
Jan 19	ST MIRREN	W 1-0	Murray	33,000
Jan 26	Partick Thistle	W 3-0	Murray 2, Simpson	35,000
Feb 9	DUNFERMLINE	W 2-1	Murray, Simpson	40,000
Feb 23	QUEEN'S PARK	D 3-3	Murray, Morrison, Hubbard (pen)	19,000
Mar 2	Hibernian	W 3-2	Murray 2, Morrison	40,000
Mar 9	Motherwell	W 5-2	Murray 2, Morrison, Hubbard, Wilson	30,000
Mar 16	FALKIRK	D 1-1	Murray	35,000
Mar 20	DUNDEE	W 4-0	Simpson, Murray, Baird, Ferguson o.g.	25,000
Mar 23	Aberdeen	W 2-1	Hubbard, Simpson	26,500
Mar 30	East Fife	W 3-0	Morrison 2, Simpson	13,000
Apr 2	RAITH ROVERS	W 3-1	Morrison, Scott, Simpson	50,000
Apr 13	Hearts	W 1-0	Simpson	49,000
Apr 17	AIRDRIE	W 3-2	Baird 2, Simpson	25,000
Apr 22	Queen's Park	W 6-4	Murray 2, Hubbard 2, Simpson, Scott	33,786
Apr 27	Queen of the South	W 3-0	Murray 2, Hubbard (pen)	14,500
Apr 29	Dunfermline	W 4-3	Scott 2, Hubbard, Simpson	10,000

Scottish Cup

Feb 2	Hearts	(Rd5) W 4-0	Hubbard (pen), Murray, Scott, Simpson	47,484
Feb 16	Celtic	(Rd6) D 4-4	Morrison, Simpson, Hubbard (pen), Murray	55,000
Feb 20	CELTIC	(R) L 0-2		88,000

Scottish League Cup

Aug 11	EAST FIFE†	W 3-0	Simpson 2, Hubbard (pen)	51,000
Aug 15	Celtic†	L 1-2	Murray	45,000
Aug 18	Aberdeen†	W 6-2	Simpson 2, Murray 2, Shearer, Hubbard	35,000
Aug 25	East Fife†	W 4-1	Murray, Simpson, Hubbard (pen), Rae	18,000
Aug 29	CELTIC†	D 0-0		84,000
Sep 1	ABERDEEN†	W 4-1	Simpson 2, Hubbard (pen), Scott	48,000

†Qualifying Section Two – Rangers finished second and failed to qualify.

European Cup

Oct 24	NICE	(Rd2/FL) W 2-1	Murray, Simpson	65,000
Nov 14	Nice	(Rd2/SL) L 1-2	Hubbard (pen)	12,000
Nov 28	Nice*	(R) L 1-3	Bonvin o.g.	15,000

*Played in Paris. Rangers received a bye in first round.

League & Cup Appearances

PLAYER	LEAGUE	CUP COMPETITION			TOTAL
		S CUP	SL CUP	E CUP	
Baird	32	3	3	3	41
Caldow	30	3	4	3	40
Davis	20	3		1	24
Grierson	3				3
Hubbard	33	3	6	3	45
Little		5	6		11
Logie	16		3		19
McColl	34	3	6	3	46
Morrison	5	2			7
Murray	30	3	6	3	42
Niven	34	3	5	3	45
Paton	1			2	3
Rae			3		3
Ritchie			1		1
Scott	29	3	6	3	41
Shearer	34	3	6	3	46
Simpson	32	3	6	3	44
Walker	2				2
Wilson	6				6
Young	28	1	6	2	37

Goalscorers

PLAYER	LEAGUE	CUP COMPETITION			TOTAL
		S CUP	SL CUP	E CUP	
Murray	29	2	4	1	36
Simpson	21	2	7	1	31
Hubbard	15	2	4	1	22
Scott	12	1	1		14
Baird	9				9
Morrison	6	1			7
Davis	1				1
Rae			1		1
Shearer			1		1
Wilson	1				1
Young	1				1
Opps' o.gs.	1			1	2

MANAGER: Scot Symon

CAPTAIN: George Young

TOP SCORER: Max Murray

BIGGEST WIN: 6-1 v East Fife, 1 December 1956, league

HIGHEST ATTENDANCE: 88,000 v Celtic, 20 February 1957, Scottish Cup

MAJOR TRANSFERS IN: Harold Davis from East Fife

MAJOR TRANSFERS OUT: John Prentice to Falkirk, Willie Paton to Ayr United, Derek Grierson to Falkirk

---

Final Scottish League Div 1 Table

		P	W	D	L	F	A	Pts
1	RANGERS	34	26	3	5	96	48	55
2	HEARTS	34	24	5	5	81	48	53
3	KILMARNOCK	34	16	10	8	57	39	42
4	RAITH R	34	16	7	11	84	58	39
5	CELTIC	34	15	8	11	58	43	38
6	ABERDEEN	34	18	2	14	79	59	38
7	MOTHERWELL	34	16	5	13	72	66	37
8	PARTICK T	34	13	8	13	53	51	34
9	HIBERNIAN	34	12	9	13	69	56	33
10	DUNDEE	34	13	6	15	55	61	32
11	AIRDRIEONIANS	34	13	4	17	77	89	30
12	ST MIRREN	34	12	6	16	58	72	30
13	QUEEN'S PARK	34	11	7	16	55	59	29
14	FALKIRK	34	10	8	16	51	70	28
15	EAST FIFE	34	10	6	18	59	82	26
16	Q OF S	34	10	5	19	54	96	25
17	DUNFERMLINE ATH	34	9	6	19	54	74	24
18	AYR U	34	7	5	22	48	89	19

Fact File

Team captain George Young retired in May 1957 at the age of 34. He had spent 16 years at Ibrox.

Season 1957-58

Scottish League Division 1

DATE	OPPONENTS	SCORE	GOALSCORERS	ATTENDANCE
Sep 7	QUEEN OF THE SOUTH	W 4-2	Simpson 2, Shearer, Hubbard (pen)	25,000
Sep 21	CELTIC	L 2-3	Simpson 2	60,000
Oct 12	St Mirren	W 3-1	Baird, Hubbard, Murray	30,000
Oct 26	HEARTS	L 2-3	Simpson 2	62,000
Nov 2	Queen's Park	W 4-2	Baird, Kichenbrand, Hubbard (pen), Simpson	30,824
Nov 9	KILMARNOCK	L 3-4	Hubbard 2 (1 pen), Kichenbrand	45,000
Nov 16	CLYDE	W 2-0	Baird 2	65,000
Nov 23	Falkirk	W 4-0	Hubbard 4 (2 pens)	22,000
Nov 30	EAST FIFE	D 3-3	Murray, Baird, Davis	26,000
Dec 7	Motherwell	D 2-2	Baird, Murray	25,000
Dec 14	Dundee	W 2-1	Hubbard (pen), Cowie o.g.	20,000
Dec 21	THIRD LANARK	W 5-1	Murray 2, Shearer, Wilson, Brand	22,000
Dec 28	Aberdeen	W 2-1	Brand, Scott	21,000
Jan 1	Celtic	W 1-0	Scott	50,000
Jan 2	PARTICK THISTLE	W 2-0	Murray, Scott	30,000
Jan 4	Queen of the South	D 1-1	Murray	13,000
Jan 11	HIBERNIAN	W 3-1	Baird, Simpson, Muir o.g.	47,000
Jan 18	Airdrie	W 4-3	Brand, Scott, Murray, Simpson	20,000
Feb 22	QUEEN'S PARK	W 5-1	Murray 2, Hubbard 2 (1 pen), Brand	30,000
Mar 8	Clyde	W 3-1	Duncan 2, Brand	31,500
Mar 10	Kilmarnock	D 3-3	Hubbard 2 (2 pens), Murray	15,335
Mar 19	FALKIRK	W 3-2	McColl, Brand, Millar	25,000
Mar 22	East Fife	W 1-0	Brand	12,000
Mar 29	MOTHERWELL	D 2-2	Millar, Duncan	40,000
Apr 12	Third Lanark	W 5-1	Hubbard 2 (2 pens), Simpson 2, Brand	36,000
Apr 16	RAITH ROVERS	W 4-1	Murray 2, Hubbard, Millar	16,000
Apr 21	Hibernian	L 1-3	Murray	25,000
Apr 23	Raith Rovers	W 3-1	Millar 2, Baird	10,000
Apr 26	ABERDEEN	W 5-0	Murray 3, Brand 2	15,000
Apr 28	ST MIRREN	W 1-0	Murray	-
Apr 30	Hearts	L 1-2	Brand	30,000
May 3	AIRDRIE	L 1-2	Hubbard (pen)	25,000
May 5	Partick Thistle	W 2-1	Murray, Wilson	6,500
May 10	DUNDEE	L 0-1		11,000

Scottish Cup

Feb 1	Cowdenbeath	(Rd1) W 3-1	Murray 2, Simpson	16,866
Feb 15	Forfar	(Rd2) W 9-1	Murray 3, Brand 2, Simpson 2, Hubbard, McColl	8,066
Mar 1	Dunfermline	(Rd3) W 2-1	Murray, Brand	24,377
Mar 15	Queen of the South	(QF) W 4-3	Murray 2, Millar 2	23,000
Apr 5	Hibernian*	(SF) D 2-2	Millar, Murray	76,727
Apr 9	Hibernian*	(R) L 1-2	Baird (pen)	75,000

*Played at Hampden Park.

Scottish League Cup

Aug 10	ST MIRREN†	W 6-0	Murray 3, Simpson 3	55,000
Aug 14	Partick Thistle†	W 1-0	Baird	35,000
Aug 17	RAITH ROVERS†	W 4-3	Scott, Hubbard, Murray, Simpson	47,000
Aug 24	St Mirren†	W 4-0	Murray 2, Scott, Baird	23,000
Aug 28	PARTICK THISTLE†	L 0-3		40,000
Aug 31	Raith Rovers†	L 3-4	Scott 2, Hubbard (pen)	24,000

†Qualifying Section Two - Rangers finished top.

Sep 11	Kilmarnock	(QF/FL) L 1-2	Kichenbrand	26,803
Sep 14	KILMARNOCK	(QF/SL) W 3-1	Hubbard (pen), Scott, Simpson	78,000
Sep 28	Brechin City*	(SF) W 4-0	Melrose 2, Shearer (pen), Paterson og	28,453
Oct 19	Celtic*	(F) L 1-7	Simpson	82,293

*Played at Hampden Park.

European Cup

Sep 4	ST ETIENNE	(Rd1/FL) W 3-1	Kichenbrand, Scott, Simpson	85,000
Sep 25	St Etienne	(Rd1/SL) L 1-2	Wilson	35,000
Nov 27	AC MILAN	(Rd2/FL) L 1-4	Murray	85,000
Dec 11	AC Milan	(Rd2/SL) L 0-2		3,000

League & Cup Appearances

PLAYER	LEAGUE	CUP COMPETITION			TOTAL
		S CUP	SL CUP	E CUP	
Austin		1			1
Baird	31	6	8	4	49
Brand	22	6			28
Caldow	29	6	10	4	49
Davis	9	8	1		18
Duncan	8	2			10
Hubbard	24	2	7	3	36
Kichenbrand	4	3	2		9
Little	12		1		13
McColl	32	6	10	4	52
Melrose		1			1
Millar	25	3	3	3	34
Moles	3		2		5
Morrison			1		1
Murray	28	6	9	3	46
Niven	5	7	2		14
Queen	1				1
Ritchie	29	6	3	2	40
Robertson			1		1
Scott	23	4	9	4	40
Shearer	28	6	10	3	47
Simpson	16	3	9	3	31
Smith	2				2
Telfer	28	6	2		36
Valentine	2	6	1		9
Wilson	12	4	3	2	21

Goalscorers

PLAYER	LEAGUE	CUP COMPETITION			TOTAL
		S CUP	SL CUP	E CUP	
Murray	19	9	6	1	35
Hubbard	18	1	3		22
Simpson	11	3	6	1	21
Brand	11	3			14
Baird	8	1	2		11
Scott	4		5	1	10
Millar	5		3		8
Kichenbrand	2		1	1	4
Duncan	3				3
Shearer	2		1		3
Wilson	2			1	3
McColl	1	1			2
Melrose			2		2
Davis	1				1
Opps' o.gs.	2				2

MANAGER: Scot Symon

CAPTAIN: Ian McColl

MAJOR TRANSFERS IN: Willie Telfer from St Mirren

MAJOR TRANSFERS OUT: Don Kichenbrand to Sunderland

Final Scottish League Div 1 Table

		P	W	D	L	F	A	Pts
1	HEARTS	34	29	4	1	132	29	62
2	RANGERS	34	22	5	7	89	49	49
3	CELTIC	34	19	8	7	84	47	46
4	CLYDE	34	18	6	10	84	61	42
5	KILMARNOCK	34	14	9	11	60	55	37
6	PARTICK T	34	17	3	14	69	71	37
7	RAITH R	34	14	7	13	66	56	35
8	MOTHERWELL	34	12	8	14	68	67	32
9	HIBERNIAN	34	13	5	16	59	60	31
10	FALKIRK	34	11	9	14	64	82	31
11	DUNDEE	34	13	5	16	49	65	31
12	ABERDEEN	34	14	2	18	68	76	30
13	ST MIRREN	34	11	8	15	59	66	30
14	THIRD LANARK	34	13	4	17	69	88	30
15	Q OF S	34	12	5	17	61	72	29
16	AIRDRIEONIANS	34	13	2	19	71	92	28
17	EAST FIFE	34	10	3	21	45	88	23
18	QUEEN'S PARK	34	4	1	29	41	114	9

Season 1958-59

Scottish League Division 1

DATE	OPPONENTS	SCORE	GOALSCORERS	ATTENDANCE
Aug 20	THIRD LANARK	D 2-2	Baird (pen), Millar	35,000
Sep 6	Celtic	D 2-2	Hubbard (pen), Brand	50,000
Sep 13	PARTICK THISTLE	W 2-1	Hubbard (pen), Brand	41,000
Sep 20	Airdrie	L 4-5	Hubbard 3 (1 pen), Hogg	20,000
Sep 27	DUNDEE	L 1-2	Baird	35,000
Oct 4	Dunfermline	W 7-1	Hubbard 3 (1 pen), Brand, Baird, Duncan, Scott	17,000
Oct 11	ST MIRREN	W 2-1	Duncan, Brand	40,000
Oct 18	RAITH ROVERS	D 4-4	McMillan, Scott, Baird, Hubbard	35,000
Oct 25	Stirling Albion	D 2-2	Brand, McMillan	17,475
Nov 1	HIBERNIAN	W 4-0	Simpson 4	20,000
Nov 8	Clyde	W 4-1	Brand 2, Davis, Simpson	25,000
Nov 15	FALKIRK	W 3-0	Simpson 2, Scott	35,000
Nov 22	Kilmarnock	W 3-0	Brand 2, Wilson	25,672
Nov 29	Motherwell	D 2-2	Brand, Hubbard	42,977
Dec 6	Queen of the South	W 6-3	Brand 3, Scott, Murray, McMillan	10,000
Dec 13	HEARTS	W 5-0	Murray 3, Brand 2	66,000
Dec 20	Aberdeen	W 3-1	Murray, Brand, Scott	18,000
Dec 27	Third Lanark	W 3-2	Murray 2, Brand	30,000
Jan 1	CELTIC	W 2-1	Matthew, Caldow (pen)	55,000
Jan 3	Partick Thistle	L 0-2		37,000
Jan 21	AIRDRIE	W 2-1	Davis, McMillan	40,000
Jan 24	DUNFERMLINE	W 1-0	Murray	30,000
Jan 28	Dundee	W 3-1	Murray 2, Millar	16,000
Feb 7	St Mirren	W 3-1	Matthew, Scott, Murray	29,000
Feb 18	Raith Rovers	D 2-2	Matthew 2	8,000
Feb 21	STIRLING ALBION	W 3-0	Caldow (pen), Wilson, Murray	30,000
Mar 4	Hibernian	D 2-2	Matthew, McMillan	32,000
Mar 7	CLYDE	W 3-1	McMillan, Scott, Murray	33,000
Mar 14	Falkirk	D 5-5	Murray 2, Caldow (pen), Brand, McMillan	15,000
Mar 21	KILMARNOCK	W 1-0	Murray	30,000
Mar 28	MOTHERWELL	W 2-1	Brand, Murray	50,000
Apr 6	QUEEN OF THE SOUTH	W 3-1	Brand, McMillan, Caldow (pen)	15,000
Apr 11	Hearts	L 0-2		30,000
Apr 18	ABERDEEN	L 1-2	Brand	41,000

Scottish Cup

Jan 31	Forfar	(Rd1) W 3-1	Murray, Millar, Scott	9,813
Feb 14	HEARTS	(Rd2) W 3-2	Matthew 2, Kirk o.g.	55,000
Feb 28	Celtic	(Rd3) L 1-2	Murray	45,500

Scottish League Cup

Aug 9	HEARTS†	W 3-0	Wilson, Hubbard, Millar	65,000
Aug 13	Raith Rovers†	L 1-3	Hubbard (pen)	12,000
Aug 16	THIRD LANARK†	D 2-2	Brand, Murray	40,000
Aug 23	Hearts†	L 1-2	Hubbard (pen)	42,000
Aug 27	RAITH ROVERS†	W 6-0	Simpson 3, Murray, Wilson, Hubbard (pen)	25,000
Aug 30	Third Lanark†	W 3-0	Murray 3	28,000

†Qualifying Section One – Rangers finished second and failed to qualify.

League & Cup Appearances

PLAYER	LEAGUE	CUP COMPETITION		TOTAL
		S CUP	SL CUP	
Baird	6		4	10
Brand	25	1	1	27
Caldow	32	3	6	41
Davis	29	3	2	34
Duncan	3			3
Hogg	2			2
Hubbard	8		6	14
Little	1			1
Martin			1	1
Matthew	18	3		21
McColl	11		6	17
McEwan	1			1
McMillan	26	3		29
Millar	5	1	3	9
Murray	22	3	6	31
Niven	34	3	5	42
Orr	1			1
Paterson	3			3
Provan	1			1
Scott	34	3	6	43
Shearer	34	3	6	43
Simpson	6		2	8
Stevenson	26	3		29
Telfer	31	3	6	40
Wilson	15	1	6	22

Goalscorers

PLAYER	LEAGUE	CUP COMPETITION		TOTAL
		S CUP	SL CUP	
Murray	17	2	5	24
Brand	21		1	22
Hubbard	10		4	14
Simpson	7		3	10
McMillan	8			8
Scott	7	1		8
Matthew	5	2		7
Baird	4			4
Caldow	4			4
Millar	2	1	1	4
Wilson	2		2	4
Davis	2			2
Duncan	2			2
Hogg	1			1
Opps' o.gs.		1		1

Fact File

Rangers defeated Arsenal 3-0 at Highbury in a challenge match on 21 April 1959 with two goals from Ralph Brand and an Eric Caldow penalty.

MANAGER: Scot Symon
CAPTAIN: Ian McColl
TOP SCORER: Max Murray
BIGGEST WIN: 7-1 v Dunfermline, 4 Ocober 1958, league
HIGHEST ATTENDANCE: 66,000 v Hearts, 13 December 1958, league
TRANSFERS IN: Andy Matthew from East Fife, Bill Paterson from Newcastle United, Ian McMillan from Airdrie
MAJOR TRANSFERS OUT: Billy Simpson to Stirling Albion, Johnny Hubbard to Bury

Final Scottish League Div 1 Table

		P	W	D	L	F	A	Pts
1	RANGERS	34	21	8	5	92	51	50
2	HEARTS	34	21	6	7	92	51	48
3	MOTHERWELL	34	18	8	8	83	50	44
4	DUNDEE	34	16	9	9	61	51	41
5	AIRDRIEONIANS	34	15	7	12	64	62	37
6	CELTIC	34	14	8	12	70	53	36
7	ST MIRREN	34	14	7	13	71	74	35
8	KILMARNOCK	34	13	8	13	58	51	34
9	PARTICK T	34	14	6	14	59	66	34
10	HIBERNIAN	34	13	6	15	68	70	32
11	THIRD LANARK	34	11	10	13	74	83	32
12	STIRLING A	34	11	8	15	54	64	30
13	ABERDEEN	34	12	5	17	63	66	29
14	RAITH R	34	10	9	15	60	70	29
15	CLYDE	34	12	4	18	62	66	28
16	DUNFERMLINE ATH	34	10	8	16	68	87	28
17	FALKIRK	34	10	7	17	58	79	27
18	Q OF S	34	6	6	22	38	101	18

Season 1959-60

Scottish League Division 1

DATE	OPPONENTS	SCORE	GOALSCORERS	ATTENDANCE
Aug 19	Stirling Albion	W 3-2	Millar 2, Wilson	-
Sep 5	CELTIC	W 3-1	Wilson, Scott, Millar	65,000
Sep 12	Hibernian	W 1-0	Millar	31,500
Sep 19	AYR UNITED	L 0-3		32,000
Sep 26	Partick Thistle	W 3-0	Matthew, McMillan, Scott	30,500
Oct 3	DUNFERMLINE	W 4-1	McMillan 2, Millar, Scott	25,000
Oct 10	Dundee	W 3-1	Baird (pen), Millar, Matthew	22,000
Oct 17	ST MIRREN	L 1-3	Millar	45,000
Oct 24	Aberdeen	W 5-0	Scott 2, Brand, Millar, McMillan	25,000
Oct 31	HEARTS	L 0-2		70,000
Nov 7	CLYDE	W 6-0	Millar 3, Caldow (pen), Baird, McMillan	40,000
Nov 14	Arbroath	W 4-0		6,025
Nov 21	RAITH ROVERS	L 2-3	Wilson, Scott	30,000
Nov 28	Motherwell	L 1-2	Baird	22,000
Dec 5	KILMARNOCK	W 5-0	McMillan 2, Wilson, Scott, Murray	20,000
Dec 12	Third Lanark	W 2-0	McMillan, Millar	25,000
Dec 19	Airdrie	W 5-0	Scott 2, Stevenson, Hume, Millar	20,000
Dec 26	STIRLING ALBION	W 3-0	Scott, Wilson, Hume	21,000
Jan 1	Celtic	W 1-0	Millar	50,000
Jan 2	HIBERNIAN	D 1-1	McMillan	60,000
Jan 9	Ayr United	W 4-2	Millar 2, Hume, McMillan	23,000
Jan 16	PARTICK THISTLE	D 1-1	Caldow (pen)	40,000
Jan 23	Dunfermline	W 5-0	Scott 2, Millar, McMillan, Wilson	16,000
Feb 9	DUNDEE	D 0-0		22,000
Mar 1	ABERDEEN	D 2-2	Caldow (pen), McMillan	
Mar 5	Hearts	L 0-2		45,000
Mar 19	ARBROATH	D 1-1	McMillan	15,000
Mar 26	Raith Rovers	W 2-1	McMillan, Baird	11,000
Apr 16	Kilmarnock	D 1-1	Caldow (pen)	26,925
Apr 18	MOTHERWELL	L 0-2		30,000
Apr 25	St Mirren	D 1-1	Wilson	14,000
Apr 27	Clyde	L 1-4	Brand (pen)	10,000
Apr 30	AIRDRIE	D 0-0		13,000
May 7	THIRD LANARK	L 1-2	Wilson	8,500

Scottish Cup

Jan 30	Berwick	(Rd1) W 3-1	Wilson 3	16,000
Feb 13	ARBROATH	(Rd2) W 2-0	Scott, McMillan	30,000
Feb 27	Stenhousemuir	(Rd3) W 3-0	Millar, McMillan, Wilson	12,300
Mar 12	HIBERNIAN	(QF) W 3-2	Baird, Wilson, Millar	63,000
Apr 2	Celtic*	(SF) D 1-1	Millar	79,786
Apr 6	Celtic*	(R) W 4-1	Wilson 2, Millar 2	70,977
Apr 23	Kilmarnock*	(F) W 2-0	Millar 2	108,017

*Played at Hampden Park.

Scottish League Cup

Aug 8	Hibernian†	W 6-1	Brand 4, Matthew, Millar	44,700
Aug 12	MOTHERWELL†	L 1-2	Scott	65,000
Aug 15	DUNDEE†	W 2-0	Brand, Wilson	37,000
Aug 22	HIBERNIAN†	W 5-1	Wilson 2, Millar 2, Baird	35,000
Aug 26	Motherwell†	L 1-2	Millar	37,000
Aug 29	Dundee†	W 3-2	Millar, Wilson, Baird	20,000

†Qualifying Section Four - Rangers finished second and failed to qualify.

European Cup

Sep 16	ANDERLECHT	(Rd1/FL) W 5-2	Baird 2 (1 pen), Millar, Scott, Matthew	80,000
Sep 23	Anderlecht	(Rd1/SL) W 2-0	Matthew, McMillan	40,000
Nov 11	RS BRATISLAVA	(Rd2/FL) W 4-3	McMillan, Scott, Wilson, Millar	80,000
Nov 18	RS Bratislava	(Rd2/SL) D 1-1	Scott	60,000
Mar 9	Sparta Rotterdam	(QF/FL) W 3-2	Wilson, Baird, Murray	50,000
Mar 16	SPARTA ROTTERDAM	(QF/SL) L 0-1		82,587
Mar 30	Sparta Rotterdam*	(R) W 3-2	Baird 2, Millar	34,176
Apr 13	Eintracht Frankfurt	(SF/FL) L 1-6	Caldow (pen)	80,000
May 5	EINTRACHT FRANKFURT	(SF/SL) L 3-6	McMillan 2, Wilson	70,000

*Played at Highbury.

Fact File

Rangers won the Charity Cup for the last time before the tournament was abandoned, defeating Partick Thistle 2-0 in the final at Hampden in front of just 8,296 on 11 May 1960.

League & Cup Appearances

PLAYER	LEAGUE	CUP COMPETITION S CUP	SL CUP	E CUP	TOTAL
Anderson	1				1
Baird	19	4	3	9	35
Brand	9	1	4	1	15
Caldow	16	7	4	6	33
Davis	26	6	5	8	45
Duncan	1	1			2
Franks	3				3
Grant	1				1
Hume	12		3		15
Little	31	7	2	9	49
Matthew	10	4	2		16
McColl	5	1	1		7
McLean	2				2
McMillan	27	6	3	8	44
Millar	30	7	6	7	50
Murray	2		2		4
Niven	33	6	6	8	53
Paterson	23	7	5		35
Ritchie	1	1	1		3
Scott	29	7	5	9	50
Shearer	21	6	3		30
Stevenson	34	7	5	9	55
Telfer	11	6	4		21
Wilson	27	7	5	8	47

Goalscorers

PLAYER	LEAGUE	CUP COMPETITION S CUP	SL CUP	E CUP	TOTAL
Millar	21	7	5	3	36
Wilson	8	7	4	3	22
McMillan	14	2		4	20
Scott	12	1	1	3	17
Baird	4	1	2	5	12
Brand	2		5		7
Caldow	4		1		5
Matthew	2	1	2		5
Hume	3				3
Murray	1		1		2
Stevenson	1				1

MANAGER: Scot Symon

CAPTAIN: Ian McColl

TOP SCORER: Jimmy Millar

BIGGEST WIN: 6-0 v Clyde, 7 November 1959, league

HIGHEST ATTENDANCE: 108,017 v Kilmarnock, 23 April 1960, Scottish Cup

MAJOR TRANSFERS IN: Albert Franks from Newcastle United

Final Scottish League Div 1 Table

		P	W	D	L	F	A	Pts
1	HEARTS	34	23	8	3	102	51	54
2	KILMARNOCK	34	24	2	8	67	45	50
3	RANGERS	34	17	8	9	72	38	42
4	DUNDEE	34	16	10	8	70	49	42
5	MOTHERWELL	34	16	8	10	71	61	40
6	CLYDE	34	15	9	10	77	69	39
7	HIBERNIAN	34	14	7	13	106	85	35
8	AYR U	34	14	6	14	65	73	34
9	CELTIC	34	12	9	13	73	59	33
10	PARTICK T	34	14	4	16	54	78	32
11	RAITH R	34	14	3	17	64	62	31
12	THIRD LANARK	34	13	4	17	75	83	30
13	DUNFERMLINE ATH	34	10	9	15	72	80	29
14	ST MIRREN	34	11	6	17	78	86	28
15	ABERDEEN	34	11	6	17	54	72	28
16	AIRDRIEONIANS	34	11	6	17	56	80	28
17	STIRLING A	34	7	8	19	55	72	22
18	ARBROATH	34	4	7	23	38	106	15

Season 1960-61

Scottish League Division 1

DATE	OPPONENTS	SCORE	GOALSCORERS	ATTENDANCE
Aug 24	PARTICK THISTLE	W 6-3	Wilson 2, Caldow (pen), Davis, Millar, Brown o.g.	17,000
Sep 10	Celtic	W 5-1	Scott, Millar, Brand, Wilson, Davis	43,000
Sep 17	AIRDRIE	W 3-0	Wilson 2, Brand (pen)	25,000
Sep 24	St Johnstone	W 5-2	Scott 2, Brand, Millar, McMillan	19,000
Oct 1	Third Lanark	W 4-2	Brand 2 (1 pen), Scott, Wilson	32,500
Oct 8	DUNDEE	L 0-1		45,000
Oct 15	DUNFERMLINE	W 3-0	Brand 2, Millar	30,000
Oct 26	Hearts	W 3-1	Scott, Brand, Wilson	30,000
Nov 2	RAITH ROVERS	W 3-0	McMillan, Wilson, McNaught o.g.	10,000
Nov 5	Clyde	W 3-1	Scott, Baxter, Brand	27,000
Nov 12	DUNDEE UNITED	W 4-0	Millar 2, McMillan, Scott	25,000
Nov 26	KILMARNOCK	L 2-4	Wilson, McMillan	55,000
Dec 3	ABERDEEN	W 4-0	McMillan 2, Wilson, Brand	25,132
Dec 10	Hibernian	W 2-1	Wilson, Brand	35,000
Dec 17	ST MIRREN	W 5-1	Millar 2, Wilson, Brand, Clunie o.g.	35,000
Dec 24	Ayr United	L 0-1		15,500
Dec 26	Motherwell	W 2-1	Millar, Brand	22,000
Dec 31	Partick Thistle	W 3-0	Wilson, Millar, Brand	31,478
Jan 2	CELTIC	W 2-1	Brand, Wilson	79,000
Jan 7	Airdrie	D 1-1	Wilson	26,000
Jan 14	ST JOHNSTONE	W 1-0	Caldow (pen)	42,000
Jan 21	THIRD LANARK	W 4-3	Brand 3, Murray	40,000
Jan 28	St Mirren	D 1-1	Murray	34,000
Feb 8	Dundee	L 2-4	Murray 2	22,000
Feb 18	Dunfermline	D 0-0		20,000
Mar 4	Raith Rovers	W 3-2	Brand 2, Wilson	14,000
Mar 8	HEARTS	W 3-0	McLean 2, Brand	35,000
Mar 11	CLYDE	W 2-1	Wilson, McLean	22,000
Mar 18	Dundee United	D 1-1	Brand	17,300
Mar 25	MOTHERWELL	D 2-2	Scott, Murray	42,000
Apr 1	Kilmarnock	L 0-2		29,528
Apr 8	Aberdeen	L 1-6	Scott	21,000
Apr 11	HIBERNIAN	W 1-0	McMillan	45,000
Apr 29	AYR UNITED	W 7-3	Scott 3, Wilson 2, Brand 2	45,000

Scottish Cup

Feb 11	Dundee	(Rd2) W 5-1	Murray 2, Brand 2, Scott	32,000
Feb 25	Motherwell	(Rd3) D 2-2	Murray 2	31,958
Mar 1	MOTHERWELL	(R) L 2-5	Wilson, McMillan	90,000

Scottish League Cup

Aug 13	PARTICK THISTLE†	W 3-1	Millar 2, Scott	51,000
Aug 17	Third Lanark†	L 1-2	Millar	-
Aug 20	CELTIC†	L 2-3	Millar, Brand	60,000
Aug 27	Partick Thistle†	W 4-1	McMillan 2, Millar, Brand	35,000
Aug 31	THIRD LANARK†	W 3-2	Millar 2, Brand	-
Sep 3	Celtic†	W 2-1	Davis, Brand	50,000

†Qualifying Section 2 – Rangers finished top.

Sep 14	DUNDEE	(QF/FL) W 1-0	Scott	40,000
Sep 21	Dundee	(QF/SL) W 4-3	McMillan 2, Wilson, Brand	32,000
Oct 19	Queen of the South*	(SF) W 7-0	Brand 3, Millar 2, McMillan, Scott	17,000
Oct 29	Kilmarnock#	(F) W 2-0	Brand, Scott	82,063

*Played at Parkhead. #Played at Hampden.

European Cup-Winners' Cup

Sep 28	FERENCVAROS	(Rd1/FL) W 4-2	Millar 2, Davis, Brand	36,000
Oct 12	Ferencvaros	(Rd1/SL) L 1-2	Wilson	25,000
Nov 15	Borussia MG	(QF/FL) W 3-0	Millar, Scott, McMillan	50,000
Nov 30	BORUSSIA MG	(QF/SL) W 8-0	Brand 3, Millar 2, Baxter, Scott, Davis	38,174
Mar 29	WOLVERHAMPTON W	(SF1) W 2-0	Scott, Brand	79,229
Apr 19	Wolverhampton W	(SF2) D 1-1	Scott	45,163
May 17	FIORENTINA	(F1) L 0-2		80,000
May 27	Fiorentina	(F2) L 1-2	Scott	50,000

Fact File

Ian McColl was appointed as Scotland manager in November 1960 and officially retired as a Rangers player at the end of the season.

League & Cup Appearances

PLAYER	LEAGUE	CUP COMPETITION			TOTAL
		S CUP	SL CUP	ECWC	
Baillie	5	1	1		7
Baird	1				1
Baxter	27	2	10	8	47
Brand	34	3	9	8	54
Caldow	33	3	10	8	54
Davis	31	3	10	8	52
Henderson	3				3
Hume	2			3	5
Little		2			2
McKinnon	2				2
McLean	6				6
McMillan	28	3	8	7	46
Millar	21	10	5		36
Murray	5	3			8
Niven	22	3	2	2	29
Paterson	30	3	9	8	50
Penman	3				3
Provan	2				2
Ritchie	12	8	6		26
Scott	33	3	10	8	54
Shearer	33	3	8	8	52
Stevenson	8	1	2		11
Wilson	34	3	10	8	55

Goalscorers

PLAYER	LEAGUE	CUP COMPETITION			TOTAL
		S CUP	SL CUP	ECWC	
Brand	24	2	9	5	40
Millar	9		9	5	23
Scott	12	1	4	5	22
Wilson	19	1	1	1	22
McMillan	8	1	5	1	15
Murray	5	4			9
Davis	2		1	2	5
McLean	3				3
Baxter	1		1		2
Caldow	2				2
Opps' o.gs.	3				3

MANAGER: Scot Symon

CAPTAIN: Eric Caldow

TOP SCORER: Ralph Brand

BIGGEST WIN: 8-0 v Borussia Mönchengladbach, 30 November 1960, European Cup-Winners' Cup

HIGHEST ATTENDANCE: 90,000 v Motherwell, 1 March 1961, Scottish Cup

MAJOR TRANSFERS IN: Jim Baxter from Raith Rovers, Doug Baillie from Airdrie

MAJOR TRANSFERS OUT: Andy Matthew to Raith Rovers, Sammy Baird to Hibernian

Final Scottish League Div 1 Table

		P	W	D	L	F	A	Pts
1	RANGERS	34	23	5	6	88	46	51
2	KILMARNOCK	34	21	8	5	77	45	50
3	THIRD LANARK	34	20	2	12	100	80	42
4	CELTIC	34	15	9	10	64	46	39
5	MOTHERWELL	34	15	8	11	70	57	38
6	ABERDEEN	34	14	8	12	72	72	36
7	HEARTS	34	13	8	13	51	53	34
8	HIBERNIAN	34	15	4	15	66	69	34
9	DUNDEE U	34	13	7	14	60	58	33
10	DUNDEE	34	13	6	15	61	53	32
11	PARTICK T	34	13	6	15	59	69	32
12	DUNFERMLINE ATH	34	12	7	15	65	81	31
13	AIRDRIEONIANS	34	10	10	14	61	71	30
14	ST MIRREN	34	11	7	16	53	58	29
15	ST JOHNSTONE	34	10	9	15	47	63	29
16	RAITH R	34	10	7	17	46	67	27
17	CLYDE	34	6	11	17	55	77	23
18	AYR U	34	5	12	17	51	81	22

Season 1961-62

Scottish League Division 1

DATE	OPPONENTS	SCORE	GOALSCORERS	ATTENDANCE
Aug 23	HIBERNIAN	W 3-0	Brand 2 (1 pen), Wilson	40,000
Sep 9	Partick Thistle	W 4-1	Wilson, Millar, Scott, Brand	31,500
Sep 16	CELTIC	D 2-2	Christie, Baxter	70,000
Sep 23	St Mirren	D 1-1	Scott	34,000
Sep 30	STIRLING ALBION	W 4-1	Millar 2, McMillan, Brand	30,000
Oct 14	RAITH ROVERS	W 6-0	Brand 4, Wilson, McMillan	34,500
Oct 21	Motherwell	D 2-2	Wilson, Brand	24,000
Nov 4	Third Lanark	D 3-3	Christie 2, Brand	30,000
Nov 11	DUNDEE	L 1-5	Brand	38,000
Nov 18	FALKIRK	W 4-0	Millar 3, Brand	35,000
Nov 25	Dundee United	W 3-2	Caldow (pen), Greig, Murray	20,000
Dec 2	ST JOHNSTONE	W 2-0	Wilson, Brand	30,000
Dec 16	Dunfermline	L 0-1		16,000
Dec 23	ABERDEEN	L 2-4	Brand, Greig	28,000
Dec 30	Kilmarnock	W 1-0	Millar	21,992
Jan 6	Hibernian	D 0-0		35,000
Jan 10	HEARTS	W 2-1	Scott, Holt o.g.	25,000
Jan 13	ST MIRREN	W 4-0	Caldow (pen), McMillan, Henderson, Murray	36,000
Jan 20	Stirling Albion	W 6-0	Millar 3, Brand 2, Caldow (pen)	20,000
Jan 24	PARTICK THISTLE	W 2-1	Brand, Millar	-
Jan 31	Airdrie	W 5-2	Greig 2, Millar 2, Brand	12,000
Feb 3	AIRDRIE	W 4-0	Brand 2, Millar, Greig	22,000
Feb 10	Raith Rovers	W 3-1	Brand 2, Scott	13,000
Feb 24	Hearts	W 1-0	McMillan	30,000
Feb 28	MOTHERWELL	W 2-1	Millar, Scott	40,000
Mar 3	THIRD LANARK	W 3-1	Brand, Baxter, Scott	35,000
Mar 14	Dundee	D 0-0		35,000
Mar 17	Falkirk	W 7-1	Wilson 6, Scott	18,000
Mar 24	DUNDEE UNITED	L 0-1		35,000
Apr 4	St Johnstone	W 4-0	Greig 2, Wilson, Brand	15,500
Apr 7	DUNFERMLINE	W 1-0	Murray	41,000
Apr 9	Celtic	D 1-1	Wilson	50,000
Apr 25	Aberdeen	L 0-1		22,000
Apr 28	KILMARNOCK	D 1-1	Wilson	39,848

Scottish Cup

Dec 13	Falkirk	(Rd1)	W 2-1	Millar, Wilson	11,500
Jan 27	ARBROATH	(Rd2)	W 6-0	Millar 4, Brand 2	31,908
Feb 17	Aberdeen	(Rd3)	D 2-2	Caldow (pen), Brand	41,359
Feb 21	ABERDEEN	(R)	W 5-1	Millar 2, McMillan, Wilson, Brand	57,600
Mar 10	Kilmarnock	(QF)	W 4-2	McMillan 2, Caldow (pen), Brand	35,995
Mar 31	Motherwell*	(SF)	W 3-1	Murray 2, Wilson	84,321
Apr 21	St Mirren*	(F)	W 2-0	Brand, Wilson	127,940

*Played at Hampden Park.

Scottish League Cup

Aug 12	Third Lanark†		W 2-0	Wilson 2	37,000
Aug 16	DUNDEE†		W 4-2	Brand 2, Wilson, Millar	40,000
Aug 19	Airdrie†		W 2-1	Brand, Davis	20,000
Aug 26	THIRD LANARK†		W 5-0	Wilson 3, Millar, Brand	40,000
Aug 30	Dundee†		D 1-1	Brand	20,000
Sep 2	AIRDRIE†		W 4-1	Brand 2, Greig, Christie	35,000

†Qualifying Section Three – Rangers finished top.

Sep 13	EAST FIFE	(QF/FL)	W 3-1	Christie 2, Davis	20,000
Sep 20	East Fife	(QF/SL)	W 3-1	Wilson, Scott, Brand	15,000
Oct 11	St Johnstone*	(SF)	W 3-2	Wilson 2, Caldow (pen)	41,000
Oct 28	Hearts#	(F)	D 1-1	Millar	88,635
Dec 18	Hearts#	(R)	W 3-1	Millar, Brand, McMillan	47,522

*Played at Parkhead. #Played at Hampden Park.

European Cup

Sep 5	Monaco	(Rd1/FL)	W 3-2	Scott 2, Baxter	6,024
Sep 12	MONACO	(Rd1/SL)	W 3-2	Christie 2, Scott	67,501
Nov 15	Vorwarts	(Rd2/FL)	W 2-1	Caldow (pen), Brand	14,268
Nov 23	VORWARTS*	(Rd2/SL)	W 4-1	McMillan 2, Henderson, Kalinke o.g.	1,781
Feb 7	Standard Liege	(QF/FL)	L 1-4	Wilson	35,891
Feb 14	STANDARD LIEGE	(QF/SL)	W 2-0	Brand, Caldow (pen)	76,730

*Played in Malmo, Sweden.

Fact File

Rangers lost 3-2 to Eintracht Frankfurt on 18 October 1961 in front of a 104,679 crowd in a challenge match to officially open the floodlights at Hampden Park.

League & Cup Appearances

PLAYER	LEAGUE	CUP COMPETITION			TOTAL
		S CUP	SL CUP	E CUP	
Baillie	16	4	1	1	22
Baxter	29	5	11	6	51
Brand	33	7	11	6	57
Caldow	29	7	11	5	52
Christie	3	4	1		8
Davis	33	7	9	6	55
Greig	11	1	2	1	15
Henderson	15	5	2		22
Hume	3				3
King	2		1		3
McKinnon	6	2			8
McMillan	24	6	9	5	44
Millar	23	6	7	5	41
Murray	8	1			9
Paterson	11	2	10	5	28
Provan	3				3
Ritchie	34	7	11	6	58
Scott	23	2	11	4	40
Shearer	34	7	11	6	58
Stevenson	5	1	2		8
Wilson	29	7	11	6	53

Goalscorers

PLAYER	LEAGUE	CUP COMPETITION			TOTAL
		S CUP	SL CUP	E CUP	
Brand	23	6	9	2	40
Wilson	15	4	9	1	29
Millar	15	7	4		26
Scott	7		1	3	11
McMillan	4	3	1	2	10
Caldow	3	2	1	2	8
Christie	3		3	2	8
Greig	7		1		8
Murray	3	2			5
Baxter	2			1	3
Davis	2				2
Henderson	1			1	2
Opps' o.gs.	1			1	2

MANAGER: Scot Symon

CAPTAIN: Eric Caldow

TOP SCORER: Ralph Brand

BIGGEST WIN: 7-1 v Falkirk, 17 March 1961, league

HIGHEST ATTENDANCE: 127,940 v St Mirren, 21 April 1962, Scottish Cup

MAJOR TRANSFERS IN: Jim Christie from Ayr United

MAJOR TRANSFERS OUT: George Niven to Partick Thistle, George McLean to Norwich City

---

Final Scottish League Div 1 Table

		P	W	D	L	F	A	PTS
1	DUNDEE	34	25	4	5	80	46	54
2	RANGERS	34	22	7	5	84	31	51
3	CELTIC	34	19	8	7	81	37	46
4	DUNFERMLINE ATH	34	19	5	10	77	46	43
5	KILMARNOCK	34	16	10	8	74	58	42
6	HEARTS	34	16	6	12	54	49	38
7	PARTICK T	34	16	3	15	60	55	35
8	HIBERNIAN	34	14	5	15	58	72	33
9	MOTHERWELL	34	13	6	15	65	62	32
10	DUNDEE U	34	13	6	15	70	71	32
11	THIRD LANARK	34	13	5	16	59	60	31
12	ABERDEEN	34	10	9	15	60	73	29
13	RAITH R	34	10	7	17	51	73	27
14	FALKIRK	34	11	4	19	45	68	26
15	AIRDRIEONIANS	34	9	7	18	57	78	25
16	ST MIRREN	34	10	5	19	52	80	25
17	ST JOHNSTONE	34	9	7	18	35	61	25
18	STIRLING A	34	6	6	22	34	76	18

Season 1962-63

Scottish League Division 1

DATE	OPPONENTS	SCORE	GOALSCORERS	ATTENDANCE
Aug 22	ST MIRREN	W 3-0	Brand, Millar, J.Wilson o.g.	46,000
Sep 8	Celtic	W 1-0	Henderson	72,000
Sep 15	PARTICK THISTLE	W 2-1	Millar 2	52,000
Sep 22	Hibernian	W 5-1	Millar 2, Wilson 2 (1 pen), Baxter	28,000
Sep 29	DUNDEE	D 1-1	Millar	57,000
Oct 6	Queen of the South	W 4-0	Millar 2, Brand 2	20,000
Oct 13	AIRDRIE	W 5-2	Millar 2, Wilson (pen), McMillan, Greig	28,000
Oct 23	Third Lanark	W 4-1	Henderson 2, Wilson, Brand	20,000
Oct 27	Aberdeen	W 3-2	Millar, Wilson, Greig	40,000
Nov 3	DUNFERMLINE	D 1-1	Wilson (pen)	38,000
Nov 10	Dundee United	L 1-2	Greig	24,000
Nov 17	FALKIRK	W 4-0	Millar 2, Wilson, Greig	20,000
Nov 24	CLYDE	W 3-1	Brand 2, Millar	28,000
Dec 1	Motherwell	D 1-1	Davis	18,000
Dec 8	KILMARNOCK	W 6-1	Brand 3, Wilson, Millar, Henderson	40,319
Dec 15	RAITH ROVERS	W 4-2	Brand 3 (1 pen), Wilson	20,000
Dec 29	St Mirren	W 2-0	Scott, Millar	28,000
Jan 1	CELTIC	W 4-0	Davis, Millar, Greig, Wilson	55,000
Mar 9	Dunfermline	W 2-1	Wilson, Millar	22,500
Mar 16	DUNDEE UNITED	W 5-0	Millar 4, Brand	35,000
Mar 23	Falkirk	W 2-0	Henderson, McLean	16,500
Mar 27	Hearts	W 5-0	Millar 2, Wilson 2, McLean	35,000
Apr 10	HIBERNIAN	W 3-1	Wilson 2, Brand	25,000
Apr 17	Partick Thistle	W 4-1	Wilson 4	32,000
Apr 20	Raith Rovers	D 2-2	Baxter, Millar	11,000
Apr 27	HEARTS	W 5-1	Baxter 2, Brand, Wilson, Holt o.g	40,000
Apr 29	MOTHERWELL	D 1-1	Wilson	25,000
May 6	Airdrie	W 2-0	Baxter, Brand	6,500
May 11	THIRD LANARK	W 1-0	Brand	34,000
May 13	Kilmarnock	L 0-1		12,801
May 18	QUEEN OF THE SOUTH	W 3-1	Millar 2, Brand	20,000
May 22	Clyde	W 3-1	Willoughby 2, Brand	6,000
May 25	Dundee	D 0-0		18,000
May 27	ABERDEEN	D 2-2	Wilson 2	14,000

Scottish Cup

Mar 13	Airdrie	(Rd2) W 6-0	Wilson 3, Brand (pen), Henderson, Thompson o.g.	17,823
Mar 20	EAST STIRLING	(Rd3) W 7-2	Brand 4, Wilson, Millar, McLean	35,000
Mar 30	Dundee	(QF) D 1-1	Brand (pen)	36,839
Apr 3	DUNDEE	(R) W 3-2	Brand 2 (1 pen), Hamilton o.g.	81,190
Apr 13	Dundee United*	(SF) W 5-2	Millar 3, Brand, McLean	56,391
May 4	Celtic*	(F) D 1-1	Brand	129,643
May 15	Celtic*	(R) W 3-0	Brand 2, Wilson	120,273

*Played at Hampden Park.

Scottish League Cup

Aug 11	Hibernian†	W 4-1	Brand 2 (1 pen), Henderson, Wilson	36,500
Aug 15	THIRD LANARK†	W 5-2	Millar 3, Scott, Wilson	25,000
Aug 18	St Mirren†	L 1-2	Murray	37,000
Aug 25	HIBERNIAN†	D 0-0		45,000
Aug 29	Third Lanark†	W 5-2	Millar 3, Scott 2	25,000
Sep 1	ST MIRREN†	W 4-0	Greig 3, Millar	50,000

†Qualifying Section Four - Rangers finished top.

Sep 12	Dumbarton	(QF/FL) W 3-1	Millar, Greig, Wilson (pen)	19,000
Sep 19	DUMBARTON	(QF/SL) D 1-1	Greig	17,500
Oct 10	Kilmarnock*	(SF) L 2-3	Brand 2	76,043

*Played at Hampden Park.

European Cup-Winners' Cup

Sep 5	SEVILLE	(Rd1/FL) W 4-0	Millar 3, Brand	60,500
Sep 26	Seville	(Rd1/SL) L 0-2		25,000
Oct 31	Tottenham H	(Rd2/FL) L 2-5	Henderson, Millar	58,859
Dec 11	TOTTENHAM H	(Rd2/SL) L 2-3	Brand, Wilson	80,000

Fact File

John Lawrence was appointed as Rangers chairman in February 1963 following the death of John Wilson.

League & Cup Appearances

PLAYER	LEAGUE	CUP COMPETITION			TOTAL
		S CUP	SL CUP	ECWC	
Baillie	6				6
Baxter	32	7	9	4	52
Brand	32	7	9	4	52
Caldow	20	4	9	4	37
Davis	16	8	4		28
Forrest	4				4
Greig	27	7	5	2	41
Henderson	27	7	8	4	46
Hunter	1				1
Martin	1				1
McKinnon	32	7	9	4	52
McLean	9	5			14
McMillan	12	2	2	2	18
Millar	31	7	8	4	50
Murray			1		1
Provan	12	3			15
Ritchie	33	7	9	4	53
Scott	4		6		10
Shearer	34	7	9	4	54
Watson	6				6
Willoughby	3				3
Wilson	32	7	7	4	50

Goalscorers

PLAYER	LEAGUE	CUP COMPETITION			TOTAL
		S CUP	SL CUP	ECWC	
Millar	27	4	8	4	43
Brand	19	12	4	2	37
Wilson	23	5	3	1	32
Greig	5		5		10
Henderson	5	1	1	1	8
Baxter	5				5
McLean	2	2			4
Scott	1		3		4
Davis	2				2
Willoughby	2				2
McMillan	1				1
Murray			1		1
Opps' o.gs.	2	2			4

MANAGER: Scot Symon

CAPTAIN: Eric Caldow

TOP SCORER: Jimmy Millar

BIGGEST WIN: 6-0 v Airdrie, 13 March 1963, Scottish Cup

HIGHEST ATTENDANCE: 129,643 v Celtic, 4 May 1963, Scottish Cup

MAJOR TRANSFERS IN: George T. McLean from St Mirren

MAJOR TRANSFERS OUT: Alex Scott to Everton, Bobby Hume to Middlesbrough, Billy Stevenson to Liverpool, Max Murray to West Bromwich Albion, Willie Penman to Newcastle

Final Scottish League Div 1 Table

		P	W	D	L	F	A	Pts
1	RANGERS	34	25	7	2	94	28	57
2	KILMARNOCK	34	20	8	6	92	40	48
3	PARTICK T	34	20	6	8	66	44	46
4	CELTIC	34	19	6	9	76	44	44
5	HEARTS	34	17	9	8	85	59	43
6	ABERDEEN	34	17	7	10	70	47	41
7	DUNDEE U	34	15	11	8	67	52	41
8	DUNFERMLINE ATH	34	13	8	13	50	47	34
9	DUNDEE	34	12	9	13	60	49	33
10	MOTHERWELL	34	10	11	13	60	63	31
11	AIRDRIEONIANS	34	14	2	18	52	76	30
12	ST MIRREN	34	10	8	16	52	72	28
13	FALKIRK	34	12	3	19	54	69	27
14	THIRD LANARK	34	9	8	17	56	68	26
15	Q OF S	34	10	6	18	36	75	26
16	HIBERNIAN	34	8	9	17	47	67	25
17	CLYDE	34	9	5	20	49	83	23
18	RAITH R	34	2	5	27	35	118	9

Season 1963-64

Scottish League Division 1

DATE	OPPONENTS	SCORE	GOALSCORERS	ATTENDANCE
Aug 21	Dundee	D 1-1	Brand (pen)	34,500
Sep 7	CELTIC	W 2-1	McLean, Brand	57,000
Sep 14	Partick Thistle	W 3-0	Forrest 3	35,000
Sep 21	HIBERNIAN	W 5-0	Brand 2, McLean, Forrest, Henderson	50,000
Sep 28	Third Lanark	W 5-0	Forrest 4, Baxter	25,000
Oct 5	FALKIRK	W 4-0	McLean 3, Henderson	36,000
Oct 12	St Mirren	W 3-0	Brand, Willoughby, Forrest	35,000
Oct 19	EAST STIRLING	W 3-1	Forrest 2, Watson	20,000
Oct 30	QUEEN OF THE SOUTH	W 2-0	Forrest, Brand	15,000
Nov 2	Airdrie	W 4-0	Willoughby, Forrest, Baxter, Watson	20,000
Nov 9	ABERDEEN	D 0-0		34,000
Nov 16	Kilmarnock	D 1-1	Brand (pen)	27,624
Nov 23	Dunfermline	W 4-1	Watson 2, Henderson, Forrest	21,000
Nov 30	HEARTS	L 0-3		25,000
Dec 7	Dundee United	W 3-2	McLean 2, Brand	20,000
Dec 14	Motherwell	D 3-3	Provan (pen), Greig, Brand	16,500
Dec 21	St Johnstone	L 2-3	Brand, Provan (pen)	14,000
Dec 28	DUNDEE	W 2-1	Forrest, Provan (pen)	43,000
Jan 1	Celtic	W 1-0	Millar	65,000
Jan 2	PARTICK THISTLE	W 4-3	Brand 2, Greig, Millar	30,000
Jan 4	Hibernian	W 1-0	Millar	19,000
Jan 18	THIRD LANARK	W 2-1	Brand 2	17,000
Feb 1	Falkirk	W 1-0	Brand	16,000
Feb 8	ST MIRREN	L 2-3	Millar, Wilson	35,000
Feb 19	East Stirling	W 5-0	Wilson 2, Forrest 2, Miller o.g.	6,000
Feb 22	Queen of the South	W 4-1	Forrest 2, Wilson, Willoughby	9,500
Feb 29	AIRDRIE	W 4-1	Forrest 2, Baxter (pen), Greig	26,500
Mar 11	Aberdeen	D 1-1	Baxter (pen)	22,000
Mar 14	KILMARNOCK	W 2-0	McLean, Wilson	45,870
Mar 21	Dunfermline	W 2-1	Wilson, McMillan	30,000
Apr 1	Hearts	W 2-1	Brand, Millar	29,000
Apr 4	DUNDEE UNITED	W 2-0	Brand, McLean	28,000
Apr 18	MOTHERWELL	W 5-1	Brand 2, Greig, Millar, McLean	39,000
Apr 29	St Johnstone	L 0-1		12,000

Scottish Cup

Jan 11	Stenhousemuir	(Rd1) W 5-2	Greig 2, Millar, Provan (pen), Brand	10,384
Jan 25	DUNS	(Rd2) W 9-0	Millar 4, Brand 3, McLean, Henderson	17,350
Feb 15	PARTICK TH	(Rd3) W 2-0	Wilson 2, Forrest	62,000
Mar 7	CELTIC	(QF) W 2-0	Forrest, Henderson	84,724
Mar 28	Dunfermline*	(SF) W 1-0	Wilson	67,823
Apr 25	Dundee*	(F) W 3-1	Millar 2, Brand	120,982

*Played at Hampden Park.

Scottish League Cup

Aug 10	Celtic†	W 3-0	Forrest 2, McLean	60,000
Aug 14	QUEEN OF THE SOUTH†	W 5-2	Wilson 2, McLean, Forrest, Provan	30,800
Aug 17	Kilmarnock†	W 4-1	Brand 2, Henderson, McLean	34,246
Aug 24	CELTIC†	W 3-0	Wilson, Brand (pen), Forrest	70,000
Aug 28	Queen of the South†	W 5-2	Forrest 4, Wilson	10,000
Aug 31	KILMARNOCK†	D 2-2	Wilson, Forrest	34,750

†Qualifying Section Four – Rangers finished top.

Sep 11	East Fife	(QF/FL) D 1-1	Forrest	15,000
Sep 18	EAST FIFE	(QF/SL) W 2-0	Brand (pen), Forrest	25,000
Oct 2	Berwick*	(SF) W 3-1	Wilson, Brand, Forrest	16,000
Oct 26	Morton*	(F) W 5-0	Forrest 4, Willoughby	105,907

*Played at Hampden Park.

European Cup

Sep 25	REAL MADRID	(Rd1/FL) L 0-1		81,215
Oct 9	Real Madrid	(Rd1/SL) L 0-6		90,000

Fact File

Rangers were beaten 4-2 on aggregate by Everton in a British Championship contest, losing 3-1 at Ibrox in the first leg on 27 November 1963 then drawing 1-1 at Goodison Park on 2 December 1963.

League & Cup Appearances

PLAYER	LEAGUE	CUP COMPETITION			TOTAL
		S CUP	SL CUP	E CUP	
Baillie	4		1		5
Baxter	26	6	10	2	44
Brand	31	6	10	1	48
Caldow	3	1			4
Davis	4	1			5
Forrest	24	2	10	2	38
Greig	34	6	10	2	52
Henderson	30	5	10	2	47
Hynd	1				1
McKinnon	32	6	9	2	49
McLean	19	3	7	2	31
McMillan	10	3			13
Millar	22	4	2		28
Provan	33	6	10	2	51
Ritchie	34	6	10	2	52
Shearer	31	5	10	2	48
Traill	3	1			4
Watson	7	1	1	1	10
Willoughby	6	1	1		8
Wilson	16	4	9	1	30
Wood	4				4

Goalscorers

PLAYER	LEAGUE	CUP COMPETITION			TOTAL
		S CUP	SL CUP	E CUP	
Forrest	21	2	16		39
Brand	19	5	5		29
Wilson	6	3	6		15
McLean	10	1	3		14
Millar	6	7			13
Greig	4	2			6
Henderson	3	2	1		6
Provan	3	1	1		5
Baxter	4				4
Watson	4				4
Willoughby	3		1		4
McMillan	1				1
Opps' o.gs.	1				1

MANAGER: Scot Symon
CAPTAIN: Bobby Shearer
TOP SCORER: Jim Forrest
BIGGEST WIN: 9-0 v Duns, 25 January 1964, Scottish Cup
HIGHEST ATTENDANCE: 120,982 v Dundee, 25 April 1964, Scottish Cup

Final Scottish League Div 1 Table

		P	W	D	L	F	A	Pts
1	RANGERS	34	25	5	4	85	31	55
2	KILMARNOCK	34	22	5	7	77	40	49
3	CELTIC	34	19	9	6	89	34	47
4	HEARTS	34	19	9	6	74	40	47
5	DUNFERMLINE ATH	34	18	9	7	64	33	45
6	DUNDEE	34	20	5	9	94	50	45
7	PARTICK T	34	15	5	14	55	54	35
8	DUNDEE U	34	13	8	13	65	49	34
9	ABERDEEN	34	12	8	14	53	53	32
10	HIBERNIAN	34	12	6	16	59	66	30
11	MOTHERWELL	34	9	11	14	51	62	29
12	ST MIRREN	34	12	5	17	44	74	29
13	ST JOHNSTONE	34	11	6	17	54	70	28
14	FALKIRK	34	11	6	17	54	84	28
15	AIRDRIEONIANS	34	11	4	19	52	97	26
16	THIRD LANARK	34	9	7	18	47	74	25
17	Q OF S	34	5	6	23	40	92	16
18	EAST STIRLINGSHIRE	34	5	2	27	37	91	12

Season 1964-65

Scottish League Division 1

DATE	OPPONENTS	SCORE	GOALSCORERS	ATTENDANCE
Aug 19	DUNFERMLINE	D 0-0		30,000
Sep 5	Celtic	L 1-3	Wilson	58,000
Sep 12	PARTICK THISTLE	D 1-1	McLean	35,000
Sep 19	Dundee	L 1-4	Forrest	28,700
Sep 26	AIRDRIE	W 9-2	Forrest 3, Brand 3, Greig, Wilson, Baxter (pen)	30,000
Oct 7	St Johnstone	W 1-0	Baxter	
Oct 10	HIBERNIAN	L 2-4	Johnston 2	40,000
Oct 17	Hearts	D 1-1	Johnston	35,000
Oct 27	St Mirren	W 7-0	Forrest 4, Baxter, Millar, Brand	15,000
Oct 31	CLYDE	W 6-1	Millar 2, Forrest, Greig, Johnston, Wood	35,000
Nov 7	ABERDEEN	D 2-2	Baxter, Forrest	40,000
Nov 14	Kilmarnock	D 1-1	Baxter	32,021
Nov 21	MOTHERWELL	D 1-1	Forrest	33,000
Nov 28	Falkirk	W 5-0	Forrest 2, Greig, Baxter, Wilson	14,000
Dec 12	Dundee United	W 3-1	Forrest 3	25,000
Dec 19	THIRD LANARK	W 5-0	Forrest 2, Wilson 2, Beck	22,000
Jan 1	CELTIC	W 1-0	Forrest	64,400
Jan 2	Partick Thistle	D 1-1	Caldow (pen)	28,700
Jan 9	DUNDEE	W 4-0	Forrest 3, Millar	30,000
Jan 16	Airdrie	W 4-0	Wilson, Johnston, Caldow (pen), Forrest	18,000
Jan 30	Hibernian	L 0-1		44,300
Feb 13	HEARTS	D 1-1	Forrest	50,000
Feb 27	ST MIRREN	W 1-0	Wood	30,000
Mar 10	Clyde	W 3-0	McLean 2, Greig	18,000
Mar 13	Aberdeen	L 0-2		25,000
Mar 20	KILMARNOCK	D 1-1	Brand (pen)	30,574
Mar 24	St Johnstone	W 2-1	Wilson, Forrest	5,800
Mar 30	MORTON	L 0-1		25,000
Apr 3	FALKIRK	W 6-1	Forrest 4, Willoughby 2	14,000
Apr 7	Morton	W 3-1	Wilson 2, Forrest	18,000
Apr 14	Dunfermline	L 1-3	Wilson	16,000
Apr 17	DUNDEE UNITED	L 0-1		15,000
Apr 21	Motherwell	W 3-1	McLean, Wood, Henderson	10,000
Apr 23	Third Lanark	W 1-0	Brand	5,000

Scottish Cup

Feb 6	HAMILTON	(Rd1) W 3-0	Brand, Millar, Forrest	22,184
Feb 20	Dundee United	(Rd2) W 2-0	Forrest 2	23,000
Mar 6	Hibernian	(QF) L 1-2	Hynd	47,363

Scottish League Cup

Aug 8	ABERDEEN†	W 4-0	McLean 2, Forrest, Wilson	45,000
Aug 12	St Mirren†	D 0-0		21,000
Aug 15	St Johnstone†	W 9-1	Forrest 4, McLean 2, Brand 2, Baxter	15,000
Aug 22	Aberdeen†	W 4-3	Forrest 3, Brand	30,000
Aug 26	ST MIRREN†	W 6-2	Baxter, Forrest, McLean, Brand, Henderson, Wilson	35,000
Aug 29	ST JOHNSTONE†	W 3-1	Forrest 3	28,000

†Qualifying Section One – Rangers finished top.

Sep 14	Dunfermline	(QF/FL) W 3-0	Brand, Forrest, McLean o.g.	20,000
Sep 16	DUNFERMLINE	(QF/SL) D 2-2	Millar, Forrest	30,000
Sep 30	Dundee United*	(SF) W 2-1	Forrest 2	39,584
Oct 24	Celtic*	(F) W 2-1	Forrest 2	91,423

*Played at Hampden Park.

European Cup

Sep 2	RS BELGRADE	(Rd1/FL) W 3-1	Brand 2, Forrest	77,669
Sep 9	RS Belgrade	(Rd1/SL) L 2-4	Greig, McKinnon	42,939
Nov 4	RS Belgrade*	(R) W 3-1	Forrest 2, Brand	34,428
Nov 18	RAPID VIENNA	(Rd2/FL) W 1-0	Wilson	50,788
Dec 8	Rapid Vienna	(Rd2/SL) W 2-0	Forrest, Wilson	69,272
Feb 17	Inter Milan	(QF/FL) L 1-3	Forrest	49,520
Mar 3	INTER MILAN	(QF/SL) W 1-0	Forrest	78,872

*Played at Highbury.

Fact File

After 10 years at Ibrox, full back and captain Bobby Shearer was given a free transfer by Rangers in April 1965. He joined Queen of the South as player-coach the following month.

League & Cup Appearances

PLAYER	LEAGUE	CUP COMPETITION			TOTAL
		S CUP	SL CUP	E CUP	
Baxter	22	1	10	5	38
Beck	9	1			10
Brand	17	1	10	4	32
Caldow	26	2	1	5	34
Forrest	30	3	10	7	50
Greig	34	3	7	7	51
Henderson	18	3	7	4	32
Hynd	10	2	3	2	17
Johnston	17	3	2	4	26
Martin	9		2		11
Mathieson	1				1
McKinnon	34	3	10	7	54
McLean	8	6	2		16
Millar	21	2	4	6	33
Provan	34	3	10	7	54
Ritchie	25	3	8	7	43
Shearer	3	6	1		10
Watson C	1	1			2
Watson R		3			3
Willoughby	5				5
Wilson	25	9	5		39
Wood	26	2	1	4	33

Goalscorers

PLAYER	LEAGUE	CUP COMPETITION			TOTAL
		S CUP	SL CUP	E CUP	
Forrest	30	3	18	6	57
Brand	6	1	5	3	15
Wilson	10		2	2	14
McLean	4		5		9
Baxter	6		2		8
Millar	4	1	1		6
Greig	4			1	5
Johnston	5				5
Wood	3				3
Caldow	2				2
Henderson	1		1		2
Willoughby	2				2
Beck	1				1
Hynd		1			1
McKinnon				1	1
Opps' o.gs.			1		1

MANAGER: Scot Symon
CAPTAIN: Bobby Shearer
TOP SCORER: Jim Forrest
MAJOR TRANSFERS IN: Thorolf Beck from St Mirren
MAJOR TRANSFERS OUT: Jim Baxter to Sunderland, Ian McMillan to Airdrie, Doug Baillie to Third Lanark

---

Final Scottish League Div 1 Table

		P	W	D	L	F	A	Pts
1	KILMARNOCK	34	22	6	6	62	33	50
2	HEARTS	34	22	6	6	90	49	50
3	DUNFERMLINE ATH	34	22	5	7	83	36	49
4	HIBERNIAN	34	21	4	9	75	47	46
5	RANGERS	34	18	8	8	78	35	44
6	DUNDEE	34	15	10	9	86	63	40
7	CLYDE	34	17	6	11	64	58	40
8	CELTIC	34	16	5	13	76	57	37
9	DUNDEE U	34	15	6	13	59	51	36
10	MORTON	34	13	7	14	54	54	33
11	PARTICK T	34	11	10	13	57	58	32
12	ABERDEEN	34	12	8	14	59	75	32
13	ST JOHNSTONE	34	9	11	14	57	62	29
14	MOTHERWELL	34	10	8	16	45	54	28
15	ST MIRREN	34	9	6	19	38	70	24
16	FALKIRK	34	7	7	20	43	85	21
17	AIRDRIEONIANS	34	5	4	25	48	110	14
18	THIRD LANARK	34	3	1	30	22	99	7

Season 1965-66

Scottish League Division 1

DATE	OPPONENTS	SCORE	GOALSCORERS	ATTENDANCE
Aug 25	ST JOHNSTONE	W 3-2	Forrest 2, Johnston	25,000
Sep 11	Partick Thistle	D 1-1	McLean	29,789
Sep 18	CELTIC	W 2-1	Forrest, McLean (pen)	76,000
Sep 25	Dundee	D 1-1	McLean	22,000
Oct 2	STIRLING ALBION	W 6-0	Wilson 2, Sorensen, Willoughby, Wood, Johnston	20,000
Oct 9	St Mirren	W 6-1	Forrest 3, Johnston McLean 2 (1 pen),	22,500
Oct 16	Hibernian	W 2-1	Willoughby 2	38,000
Oct 27	DUNDEE UNITED	W 2-0	Johnston, Forrest	19,000
Oct 30	Hamilton A	W 7-1	Forrest 5, Henderson, Wilson	12,000
Nov 6	FALKIRK	W 3-0	McLean, Henderson, Markie o.g.	18,000
Nov 13	Hearts	W 2-0	Henderson, McLean	33,225
Nov 20	KILMARNOCK	W 5-0	McLean 3 (1 pen), Johnston 2	30,000
Nov 27	Motherwell	W 3-0	Forrest 2 (1 pen), R.Watson	18,000
Dec 11	MORTON	W 3-1	Greig 2, McLean	25,000
Dec 18	Clyde	D 2-2	McLean, Forrest	18,000
Dec 25	DUNFERMLINE	L 2-3	Forrest, McLean	35,000
Jan 1	PARTICK THISTLE	W 4-0	Johnston, Greig, Willoughby, McLean	15,000
Jan 3	Celtic	L 1-5	Wilson	65,000
Jan 8	St Johnstone	W 3-0	McLean 3	12,500
Jan 22	Stirling Albion	W 2-0	Forrest, Willoughby	18,000
Jan 29	ST MIRREN	W 4-1	McLean 2, Beck, Greig	20,000
Feb 12	HIBERNIAN	W 2-0	McLean, Sorensen	27,000
Feb 26	HAMILTON A	W 4-0	Forrest 2, McLean 2	25,000
Mar 9	Falkirk	L 2-3	Forrest, Markie o.g.	10,000
Mar 12	HEARTS	D 1-1	Forrest	40,000
Mar 19	Kilmarnock	D 1-1	Forrest	25,372
Mar 21	Dundee United	L 0-1		17,000
Apr 6	DUNDEE	W 1-0	Greig	15,000
Apr 9	ABERDEEN	W 1-0	Greig	18,000
Apr 13	Aberdeen	W 2-1	Johnston, Willoughby	20,000
Apr 16	Morton	W 5-0	Johnston, Wilson, Forrest, Greig, Madsen o.g.	15,000
Apr 19	MOTHERWELL	W 2-1	Sorensen, Forrest	15,000
Apr 30	Dunfermline	W 2-1	R.Watson, McLean	16,000
May 4	CLYDE	W 4-0	McLean 2, Millar, Wilson	12,000

Scottish Cup

Feb 5	AIRDRIE	(Rd1)	W 5-1	McLean 3 (1 pen), Wilson, Johnston	16,500
Feb 28	Ross County	(Rd2)	W 2-0	Johnston, McLean	8,500
Mar 5	ST JOHNSTONE	(QF)	W 1-0	Willoughby	32,000
Mar 26	Aberdeen*	(SF)	D 0-0		49,360
Mar 29	Aberdeen*	(R)	W 2-1	Forrest, McLean	40,852
Apr 23	Celtic*	(F)	D 0-0		126,599
Apr 27	Celtic*	(R)	W 1-0	Johansen	98,202

*Played at Hampden Park.

Scottish League Cup

Aug 14	Hearts†		L 2-4	Forrest 2 (1 pen)	32,859
Aug 18	CLYDE†		W 3-0	Willoughby 2, Forrest	25,000
Aug 21	Aberdeen†		L 0-2		25,000
Aug 28	HEARTS†		W 1-0	Johnston	40,000
Sep 1	Clyde†		W 3-1	Johnston, Willoughby, Forrest	15,000
Sep 4	ABERDEEN†		W 4-0	McLean 3, Forrest	45,000

†Qualifying Section Two – Rangers finished top.

Sep 15	Airdrie	(QF/FL)	W 5-1	McLean 2, Greig, Forrest, Willoughby	15,000
Sep 22	AIRDRIE	(QF/SL)	W 4-0	Forrest 3, McLean	10,000
Oct 6	Kilmarnock*	(SF)	W 6-4	McLean 3 (1 pen), Willoughby, Forrest, Henderson	54,702
Oct 23	Celtic*	(F)	L 1-2	Young o.g.	107,609

*Played at Hampden Park.

MANAGER: Scot Symon

CAPTAIN: Eric Caldow

TOP SCORER: George McLean

BIGGEST WIN: 7-1 v Hamilton, 30 October 1965, league

HIGHEST ATTENDANCE: 126,599 v Celtic, 23 April 1966, Scottish Cup

MAJOR TRANSFERS IN: Kai Johansen from Morton

MAJOR TRANSFERS OUT: Ralph Brand to Manchester City

League & Cup Appearances

PLAYER	LEAGUE	CUP COMPETITION		TOTAL
		S CUP	SL CUP	
Beck	2	1	1	4
Caldow	2		1	3
Forrest	30	4	10	44
Greig	32	7	10	49
Henderson	28	5	6	39
Hynd	4			4
Jackson	1			1
Johansen	32	7	10	49
Johnston	31	7	10	48
Martin	1		3	4
Mathieson	3	1		4
McKinnon	33	7	10	50
McLean	24	5	5	34
Millar	10	4	1	15
Provan	33	7	9	49
Ritchie	33	7	7	47
Setterington	1			1
Sorensen	12	4		16
Traill	1			1
Watson C			2	2
Watson R	21	5	6	32
Willoughby	23	2	9	34
Wilson	12	4	5	21
Wood	5		5	10

Goalscorers

PLAYER	LEAGUE	CUP COMPETITION		TOTAL
		S CUP	SL CUP	
McLean	25	5	9	39
Forrest	24	1	10	35
Johnston	9	2	2	13
Willoughby	6	1	5	12
Greig	7		1	8
Wilson	6	1		7
Henderson	3		1	4
Sorensen	3			3
Watson R	2			2
Beck	1			1
Johansen	1			1
Millar	1			1
Wood	1			1
Opps' o.gs.	3		1	4

Fact File

John Greig was named Scotland's Player of the Year for season 1965-66 — the first Rangers player to win the award which had been introduced the previous year.

Final Scottish League Div 1 Table

		P	W	D	L	F	A	Pts
1	CELTIC	34	27	3	4	106	30	57
2	RANGERS	34	25	5	4	91	29	55
3	KILMARNOCK	34	20	5	9	73	46	45
4	DUNFERMLINE ATH	34	19	6	9	94	55	44
5	DUNDEE U	34	19	5	10	79	51	43
6	HIBERNIAN	34	16	6	12	81	55	38
7	HEARTS	34	13	12	9	56	48	38
8	ABERDEEN	34	15	6	13	61	54	36
9	DUNDEE	34	14	6	14	61	61	34
10	FALKIRK	34	15	1	18	48	72	31
11	CLYDE	34	13	4	17	62	64	30
12	PARTICK T	34	10	10	14	55	64	30
13	MOTHERWELL	34	12	4	18	52	69	28
14	ST JOHNSTONE	34	9	8	17	58	81	26
15	STIRLING A	34	9	8	17	40	68	26
16	ST MIRREN	34	9	4	21	44	82	22
17	MORTON	34	8	5	21	42	84	21
18	HAMILTON A	34	3	2	29	27	117	8

Season 1966-67

Scottish League Division 1

DATE	OPPONENTS	SCORE	GOALSCORERS	ATTENDANCE
Sep 10	PARTICK THISTLE	W 6-1	McLean 4, A.Smith, D.Smith	24,000
Sep 17	Celtic	L 0-2		70,000
Sep 24	ABERDEEN	W 3-0	Henderson, Johnston, McLean	40,000
Oct 1	Dundee United	W 3-2	Johansen, A.Smith, Setterington	18,000
Oct 8	FALKIRK	W 5-0	Provan (pen), Millar, Henderson, Johnston, A.Smith	25,000
Oct 15	Hearts	D 1-1	Millar	30,000
Nov 2	St Mirren	W 6-1	Henderson 2, Johnston 2, A.Smith, Provan (pen)	10,000
Nov 5	MOTHERWELL	W 5-1	Forrest 2, A.Smith 2, Setterington	30,000
Nov 9	KILMARNOCK	W 3-0	A.Smith, Setterington, Provan (pen)	28,839
Nov 12	St Johnstone	D 1-1	Forrest	12,500
Nov 19	AYR UNITED	W 4-0	A.Smith 2, Forrest, Provan (pen)	22,000
Nov 26	Hibernian	W 2-1	Forrest 2	25,798
Dec 3	Dunfermline	L 2-3	A.Smith	18,000
Dec 10	STIRLING ALBION	W 4-0	Henderson 2, Greig, Forrest	25,000
Dec 17	AIRDRIE	W 3-0	A.Smith 2, Keenan o.g.	18,000
Dec 31	DUNDEE	D 2-2	McKinnon, A.Smith	25,000
Jan 2	Partick Thistle	D 1-1	A.Smith	27,000
Jan 14	DUNDEE UNITED	W 3-1	Greig, Johnston, McLean	36,000
Jan 18	Aberdeen	W 2-1	McLean 2	31,000
Jan 21	Falkirk	W 1-0	A.Smith	17,000
Feb 4	HEARTS	W 5-1	Willoughby 3, Henderson, Wilson	33,087
Feb 8	Clyde	W 5-1	Henderson, Willoughby 3, Wilson	20,000
Feb 11	Kilmarnock	W 2-1	Wilson, Willoughby	31,551
Feb 25	ST MIRREN	W 3-0	Reid 2, A.Smith	23,000
Mar 4	Motherwell	W 5-1	Willoughby 4, A.Smith	25,000
Mar 7	Airdrie	W 1-0	D.Smith (pen)	20,000
Mar 18	Ayr United	W 4-1	Willoughby 2, Jardine, Oliphant o.g	18,000
Mar 25	HIBERNIAN	W 1-0	A.Smith	30,000
Mar 29	ST JOHNSTONE	W 4-3	Wilson 2, A.Smith, Willoughby	20,000
Apr 1	DUNFERMLINE	L 0-1		30,000
Apr 8	Stirling Albion	W 1-0	Willoughby	8,500
Apr 22	CLYDE	D 1-1	Wilson	25,000
Apr 29	Dundee	D 1-1	Willoughby	20,000
May 6	CELTIC	D 2-2	Jardine, Hynd	78,000

Scottish Cup

Jan 28	Berwick	(Rd1) L 0-1		13,283

Scottish League Cup

Aug 13	HIBERNIAN†	W 1-0	McLean	40,000
Aug 17	Stirling Albion†	W 8-0	Forrest 5, McLean 2 (1 pen), Wilson	16,000
Aug 20	KILMARNOCK†	D 0-0		51,765
Aug 27	Hibernian†	L 2-3	McLean, A.Smith	32,913
Aug 31	STIRLING ALBION†	D 1-1	A.Smith	20,000
Sep 3	Kilmarnock†	W 1-0	Forrest	29,743

†Qualifying Section Two – Rangers finished top.

Sep 14	Ayr United	(QF/FL) D 1-1	Johnston	14,250
Sep 21	AYR UNITED	(QF/SL) W 3-0	McLean 2, Greig	32,000
Oct 19	Aberdeen*	(SF) D 2-2	Henderson 2	38,623
Oct 24	Aberdeen*	(R) W 2-0	Johnston, A.Smith	38,086
Oct 29	Celtic*	(F) L 0-1		94,532

*Played at Hampden Park.

European-Cup Winners' Cup

Sep 27	Glentoran	(Rd1/FL) D 1-1	McLean	40,000
Oct 5	GLENTORAN	(Rd1/SL) W 4-0	Johnston, D.Smith, Setterington, McLean	33,473
Nov 23	B.DORTMUND	(Rd2/FL) W 2-1	Johansen, A.Smith	65,000
Dec 6	B.Dortmund	(Rd2/SL) D 0-0		45,000
Mar 1	REAL ZARAGOZA	(QF/FL) W 2-0	D.Smith, Willoughby	65,000
Mar 22	Real Zaragoza	(QF/SL) L 0-2#		40,000
Apr 19	S.avia Sofia	(SF/FL) W 1-0	Wilson	48,000
May 3	S.AVIA SOFIA	(SF2/SL) W 1-0	Henderson	71,000
May 31	Bayern Munich*	(F) L 0-1		69,500

#Aggregate scores 2-2 – Rangers won on toss of coin. *Played in Nuremberg.

League & Cup Appearances

PLAYER	LEAGUE	S CUP	SL CUP	ECWC	TOTAL
Forrest	17	1	7	2	27
Greig	32	1	8	9	50
Henderson	32	1	9	9	51
Hynd	1 (1)			2	3 (1)
Jackson	4 (1)			1	5 (1)
Jardine	14			5	19
Johansen	33	1	10	9	53
Johnston	21	1	9	6	37
Martin	28	1	2	7	38
Mathieson	1				1
McKinnon	31	1	11	8	51
McLean	9	1	10	2	22
Millar	5 (1)		9	1	15 (1)
Paul	0 (1)				0 (1)
Provan	33	1	9	9	52
Reid	2 (1)				2 (1)
Ritchie	6	9	2		17
Setterington		6		1	7
Smith A	33	1	11	9	54
Smith D	34	1	11	9	55
Watson	4	2	2		8
Willoughby	11 (1)			3	14 (1)
Wilson	17 (2)	(1)	4 (2)	3	24 (5)

Goalscorers

PLAYER	LEAGUE	S CUP	SL CUP	ECWC	TOTAL
Smith A	19		3	1	23
Willoughby	16			1	17
McLean	8		6	2	16
Forrest	8		6		14
Henderson	8		2	1	11
Johnston	5		2	1	8
Wilson	6		1	1	8
Provan	4				4
Setterington	3		1		4
Smith D	2			2	4
Greig	2		1		3
Jardine	2				2
Johansen	1		1		2
Millar	2				2
Reid	2				2
Hynd	1				1
McKinnon	1				1
Opps' o.gs.	2				2

MANAGER: Scot Symon
CAPTAIN: John Greig
MAJOR TRANSFERS IN: Alex Smith from Dunfermline, Dave Smith from Aberdeen, Andy Penman from Dundee
MAJOR TRANSFERS OUT: Jim Forrest to Preston North End, George McLean to Dundee

---

Final Scottish League Div 1 Table

		P	W	D	L	F	A	Pts
1	CELTIC	34	26	6	2	111	33	58
2	RANGERS	34	24	7	3	92	31	55
3	CLYDE	34	20	6	8	64	48	46
4	ABERDEEN	34	17	8	9	72	38	42
5	HIBERNIAN	34	19	4	11	72	49	42
6	DUNDEE	34	16	9	9	74	51	41
7	KILMARNOCK	34	16	8	10	59	46	40
8	DUNFERMLINE ATH	34	14	10	10	72	52	38
9	DUNDEE U	34	14	9	11	68	62	37
10	MOTHERWELL	34	10	11	13	59	60	31
11	HEARTS	34	11	8	15	39	48	30
12	PARTICK T	34	9	12	13	49	68	30
13	AIRDRIEONIANS	34	11	6	17	41	53	28
14	FALKIRK	34	11	4	19	33	70	26
15	ST JOHNSTONE	34	10	5	19	53	73	25
16	STIRLING A	34	5	9	20	31	85	19
17	ST MIRREN	34	4	7	23	25	81	15
18	AYR U	34	1	7	26	20	86	9

Season 1967-68

Scottish League Division 1

DATE	OPPONENTS	SCORE	GOALSCORERS	ATTENDANCE
Sep 9	Partick Thistle	W 2-0	Penman 2	31,000
Sep 16	CELTIC	W 1-0	Persson	90,000
Sep 23	Falkirk	W 1-0	Penman	25,000
Sep 30	HEARTS	D 1-1	Ferguson	40,000
Oct 7	Motherwell	W 2-0	Ferguson, Greig	20,500
Oct 14	Clyde	W 3-1	Greig, Persson, Ferguson	26,000
Oct 23	DUNDEE	W 2-0	Mathieson, Hynd	30,000
Oct 28	DUNFERMLINE	D 0-0		40,000
Nov 4	St Johnstone	W 3-2	Johnston, Ferguson, Persson	20,000
Nov 11	MORTON	W 1-0	Johnston	30,000
Nov 18	Stirling Albion	W 4-2	McKinnon, Penman, Henderson, Persson	22,000
Nov 25	HIBERNIAN	W 2-0	Greig (pen), Willoughby	55,000
Dec 2	AIRDRIE	W 2-1	Johnston, Ferguson	35,000
Dec 16	RAITH ROVERS	W10-2	Ferguson 3, Johnston 2, Persson 2, Greig 2 (1 pen), Willoughby	35,000
Dec 23	KILMARNOCK	W 4-1	Willoughby 2, Johnston, Greig	33,239
Dec 30	Aberdeen	W 4-1	Penman, Watson, Johnston, Willoughby	23,000
Jan 1	PARTICK THISTLE	W 5-2	Hynd 2, Johnston 2, Penman	31,000
Jan 2	Celtic	D 2-2	Johnston, Johansen	75,000
Jan 6	FALKIRK	W 2-0	Ferguson, Penman	37,000
Jan 13	Hearts	W 3-2	Johnston 2, Ferguson	40,000
Jan 20	MOTHERWELL	W 2-0	Willoughby, Greig (pen)	40,000
Feb 3	CLYDE	W 1-0	Greig	45,000
Feb 10	Dundee	W 4-2	Johnston 2, Greig (pen), Persson	30,000
Mar 2	ST JOHNSTONE	W 6-2	Ferguson 4 (1 pen), Willoughby, Persson	35,000
Mar 6	Dunfermline	W 2-1	Ferguson, Persson	24,000
Mar 16	STIRLING ALBION	W 5-0	Persson 3, Ferguson, Corrigan o.g.	18,000
Mar 23	Hibernian	W 3-1	Persson, Henderson, Johnston	27,195
Mar 30	Airdrie	W 2-1	Johnston, A.Smith	18,000
Apr 3	Dundee United	D 0-0		10,000
Apr 6	DUNDEE UNITED	W 4-1	Ferguson 2, Willoughby, Johnston	33,000
Apr 13	Raith Rovers	W 3-2	D.Smith, Willoughby, Penman	24,000
Apr 17	Morton	D 3-3	Greig 2, Johnston	18,500
Apr 20	Kilmarnock	W 2-1	Persson, Willoughby	17,286
Apr 27	ABERDEEN	L 2-3	D.Smith, Ferguson	50,000

Scottish Cup

Jan 27	HAMILTON	(Rd1) W 3-1	Greig 2, Johnston	27,500
Feb 17	Dundee	(Rd2) D 1-1	Stewart o.g.	33,000
Mar 4	DUNDEE	(R) W 4-1	Watson 2, Persson, Easton o.g.	53,875
Mar 9	HEARTS	(QF) D 1-1	Persson	57,521
Mar 13	Hearts	(R) L 0-1		44,094

Scottish League Cup

Aug 12	Aberdeen†	D 1-1	Persson	44,000
Aug 16	CELTIC†	D 1-1	Penman	94,168
Aug 19	DUNDEE UNITED†	W 1-0	Johansen (pen)	55,000
Aug 26	ABERDEEN†	W 3-0	Penman 2, Jardine	50,000
Aug 30	Celtic†	L 1-3	Henderson	75,000
Sep 2	Dundee United†	W 3-0	Ferguson 2, Johnston	18,000

†Qualifying Section Two - Rangers finished second and failed to qualify.

Inter-Cities Fairs Cup

Sep 20	D.Dresden	(Rd1/FL) D 1-1	Ferguson	50,000
Oct 4	D.DRESDEN	(Rd1/SL) W 2-1	Penman, Greig	60,000
Nov 8	COLOGNE	(Rd2/FL) W 3-0	Ferguson 2, Henderson	60,000
Nov 28	Cologne	(Rd2/SL) L 1-3	Henderson	46,000
Mar 6	LEEDS UNITED	(QF/FL) D 0-0		85,000
Apr 9	Leeds United	(QF/SL) L 0-2		50,498

Fact File

Scot Symon was dismissed as manager of Rangers on 1 November 1967.

League & Cup Appearances

PLAYER	LEAGUE	CUP COMPETITION			TOTAL
		S CUP	SL CUP	ICF CUP	
Ferguson	29	5	6	6	46
Greig	32	4	6	6	48
Henderson	20	4	6	6	36
Hynd	3 (1)		2		5 (1)
Jardine	6 (3)	1	6	1	14 (3)
Johansen	33	5	6	6	50
Johnston	30 (1)	4	2	6	42 (1)
Martin	4				4
Mathieson	26	4	5		35
McKinnon	34	4	6	6	50
Penman	24 (2)	2	6	4 (1)	36 (3)
Persson	32	5	4	6	47
Provan		2	6		8
Semple	2				2
Smith A	6 (2)		0 (1)	1 (1)	7 (4)
Smith D	34	5	6	6	51
Sorensen	30	5	6	6	47
Watson	7 (2)	3	0 (1)		10 (3)
Willoughby	20 (3)	2	1		23 (3)

Goalscorers

PLAYER	LEAGUE	CUP COMPETITION			TOTAL
		S CUP	SL CUP	ICF CUP	
Ferguson	19		2	3	24
Johnston	18	1	1		20
Persson	14	2	1		17
Greig	11	2		1	14
Penman	8		3	1	12
Willoughby	10				10
Henderson	2		1	2	5
Hynd	3				3
Watson	1	2			3
Johansen	1	1			2
Smith D	2				2
Jardine	1		1		1
Mathieson	1				1
McKinnon	1				1
Smith A	1				1
Opps' o.gs.	1	2			3

MANAGER: Scot Symon/Davie White

CAPTAIN: John Greig

TOP SCORER: Alex Ferguson

BIGGEST WIN: 10-2 v Raith Rovers, 16 December 1967, league

HIGHEST ATTENDANCE: 94,168 v Celtic Cup, 16 August 1967, league

MAJOR TRANSFERS IN: Alex Ferguson from Dunfermline, Erik Sorensen from Morton, Orjan Persson from Dundee United

MAJOR TRANSFERS OUT: Jimmy Millar to Dundee United, Davie Wilson to Dundee United

Final Scottish League Div 1 Table

		P	W	D	L	F	A	Pts
1	CELTIC	34	30	3	1	106	24	63
2	RANGERS	34	28	5	1	93	34	61
3	HIBERNIAN	34	20	5	9	67	49	45
4	DUNFERMLINE ATH	34	17	5	12	64	41	39
5	ABERDEEN	34	16	5	13	63	48	37
6	MORTON	34	15	6	13	57	53	36
7	KILMARNOCK	34	13	8	13	59	57	34
8	CLYDE	34	15	4	15	55	55	34
9	DUNDEE	34	13	7	14	62	59	33
10	PARTICK T	34	12	7	15	51	67	31
11	DUNDEE U	34	10	11	13	53	72	31
12	HEARTS	34	13	4	17	56	61	30
13	AIRDRIEONIANS	34	10	9	15	45	58	29
14	ST JOHNSTONE	34	10	7	17	43	52	27
15	FALKIRK	34	7	12	15	36	50	26
16	RAITH R	34	9	7	18	58	86	25
17	MOTHERWELL	34	6	7	21	40	66	19
18	STIRLING A	34	4	4	26	29	105	12

Season 1968-69

Scottish League Division 1

DATE	OPPONENTS	SCORE	GOALSCORERS	ATTENDANCE
Sep 7	PARTICK THISTLE	W 2-0	Jardine 2	32,000
Sep 14	Celtic	W 4-2	Johnston 2, Penman, Persson	75,000
Sep 21	KILMARNOCK	D 3-3	Johnston, Jardine, Henderson	39,407
Sep 28	Hearts	D 1-1	Penman	33,000
Oct 5	FALKIRK	W 2-1	Persson, Johnston	40,000
Oct 12	St Johnstone	L 0-2		20,000
Oct 19	DUNFERMLINE	W 3-0	Persson, Jardine, Ferguson	35,000
Oct 26	ABERDEEN	L 2-3	Ferguson, Henderson	40,000
Nov 2	Arbroath	W 5-1	Stein 3, Johnston 2	9,653
Nov 9	HIBERNIAN	W 6-1	Stein 3, Johnston, Henderson, Persson	60,000
Nov 16	St Mirren	L 0-1		43,500
Nov 23	Clyde	D 1-1	Stein	25,000
Nov 30	AIRDRIE	D 1-1	Stein	20,000
Dec 7	Raith Rovers	W 3-0	MacDonald, Stein, Watson	15,000
Dec 14	DUNDEE UNITED	W 2-1	Greig, Johnston	32,000
Dec 28	Morton	W 2-0	Penman, Johnston	21,000
Jan 1	Partick Thistle	W 2-0	Johnston, Stein	24,000
Jan 2	CELTIC	W 1-0	Greig (pen)	85,000
Jan 4	Kilmarnock	D 3-3	Penman, Johnston, Persson	32,893
Jan 11	HEARTS	W 2-0	Penman, Johnston	50,000
Jan 18	Falkirk	W 3-0	Penman 2, Johnston	22,000
Feb 1	ST JOHNSTONE	W 3-0	Penman, Ferguson, Henderson	33,000
Mar 5	Hibernian	W 2-1	Greig (pen), Johnston	31,000
Mar 8	ST MIRREN	W 6-0	Johansen, D.Smith, Greig (pen), Ferguson, Persson, Penman	40,000
Mar 11	ARBROATH	W 2-0	Persson, Penman	25,000
Mar 15	CLYDE	W 6-0	Stein 3, D.Smith, Penman, Ferguson	42,000
Mar 24	Airdrie	L 2-3	Penman, Caldwell o.g.	20,000
Mar 29	RAITH ROVERS	W 2-1	Penman, Johnston	28,000
Apr 5	Dundee United	L 1-2	Greig	21,000
Apr 9	Aberdeen	D 0-0		23,000
Apr 19	MORTON	W 3-0	Ferguson, Persson, Penman	28,000
Apr 22	Dundee	L 2-3	Grieg, Henderson	7,000
Apr 28	DUNDEE	D 1-1	Johnston	6,800
Apr 30	Dunfermline	W 3-0	Johnston 2, Penman	11,700

Scottish Cup

Jan 25	HIBERNIAN	(Rd 1) W 1-0	Stein	58,141
Feb 24	HEARTS	(Rd 2) W 2-0	Johnston, Persson	47,337
Mar 1	AIRDRIE	(QF) W 1-0	Greig (pen)	46,726
Mar 22	Aberdeen*	(SF) W 6-1	Johnston 3, Penman 2, Henderson	66,197
Apr 26	Celtic#	(F) L 0-4		132,870

*Played at Parkhead. #Played at Hampden.

Scottish League Cup

Aug 10	CELTIC†	L 0-2		35,000
Aug 14	Partick Thistle†	W 5-1	A.Smith 2, Ferguson 2, Persson	28,000
Aug 17	MORTON†	W 2-0	Jackson 2	45,000
Aug 24	Celtic†	L 0-1		75,000
Aug 28	PARTICK THISTLE†	W 2-1	Henderson, Jardine	25,000
Aug 31	Morton†	W 5-0	Jardine 2, Henderson 2, Penman	15,000

†Qualifying Section Four – Rangers finished second and failed to qualify.

Inter-Cities Fairs Cup

Sep 18	VOJVODINA	(Rd1/FL) W 2-0	Greig (pen), Jardine	70,000
Oct 2	Vojvodina	(Rd1/SL) L 0-1		12,000
Oct 30	DUNDALK	(Rd2/FL) W 6-1	Henderson 2, Ferguson 2, Greig, Brennan o.g.	30,000
Nov 13	Dundalk	(Rd2/SL) W 3-0	Stein 2, Henderson	10,000
Jan 15	DWS Amsterdam	(Rd2/FL) W 2-0	Johnston, Henderson	18,000
Jan 22	DWS AMSTERDAM	(Rd2/SL) W 2-1	D.Smith, Stein	62,000
Mar 19	A.Bilbao	(QF/FL) W 4-1	Ferguson, Penman, Persson, Stein	62,842
Apr 2	A.Bilbao	(QF/SL) L 0-2		40,000
May 14	NEWCASTLE Utd	(SF1) D 0-0		75,518
May 21	Newcastle Utd	(SF2) L 0-2		60,000

Fact File

Willie Thornton returned to Ibrox on 7 September 1968 when he was appointed assistant manager to Davie White.

League & Cup Appearances

PLAYER	LEAGUE	CUP COMPETITION			TOTAL
		S CUP	SL CUP	ICF CUP	
Conn	1 (1)		0 (1)		1 (2)
Ferguson	7 (5)	1	4	3	15 (5)
Greig	33	5	6	9	53
Henderson	32	5	4	10	51
Hynd	10	3	3		16
Jackson	10	6	5		21
Jardine	15 (3)		1 (1)	3 (1)	19 (5)
Johansen	27	5	8		40
Johnston	29	5	3	9	46
MacDonald	8 (1)	0 (1)	1		9 (2)
Martin	31	5	6	8	50
Mathieson	26	5	6	8	45
McKinnon	28	4	6	8	46
McPhee			2		2
Miller	0 (1)				0 (1)
Neef	3		2		5
Penman	26	5	5 (1)	9	45 (1)
Persson	28 (3)	5	6	7 (1)	46 (4)
Provan		8	1 (1)		9 (1)
Smith A			3		3
Smith D	22 (1)	3 (2)	4	7 (2)	36 (5)
Stein	18	4	7		29
Watson	10	3	2		15
Willoughby	2 (1)		1		3 (1)

Goalscorers

PLAYER	LEAGUE	CUP COMPETITION			TOTAL
		S CUP	SL CUP	ICF CUP	
Johnston	18	4		1	23
Penman	15	2	1	1	19
Stein	13	1		4	18
Henderson	5	1	3	3	12
Ferguson	6		2	3	11
Persson	8	1	1	1	11
Greig	6	1		2	9
Jardine	4		3	1	8
Smith D	2			1	3
Jackson			2		2
Smith A			2		2
MacDonald	1				1
Mathieson				1	1
Watson	1				1
Opps' o.gs.	1		1	2	

MANAGER: Davie White

CAPTAIN: John Greig

MAJOR TRANSFERS IN: Colin Stein from Hibernian, Alex MacDonald from St Johnstone

MAJOR TRANSFERS OUT: Alex Willoughby to Aberdeen, Roger Hynd to Crystal Palace, Alex Smith to Aberdeen

---

Final Scottish League Div 1 Table

		P	W	D	L	F	A	Pts
1	Celtic	34	23	8	3	89	32	54
2	Rangers	34	21	7	6	81	32	49
3	Dunfermline Ath	34	19	7	8	63	45	45
4	Kilmarnock	34	15	14	5	50	32	44
5	Dundee U	34	17	9	8	61	49	43
6	St Johnstone	34	16	5	13	66	59	37
7	Airdrieonians	34	13	11	10	46	44	37
8	Hearts	34	14	8	12	52	54	36
9	Dundee	34	10	12	12	47	48	32
10	Morton	34	12	8	14	58	68	32
11	St Mirren	34	11	10	13	40	54	32
12	Hibernian	34	12	7	15	60	59	31
13	Clyde	34	9	13	12	35	50	31
14	Partick T	34	9	10	15	39	53	28
15	Aberdeen	34	9	8	17	50	59	26
16	Raith R	34	8	5	21	45	67	21
17	Falkirk	34	5	8	21	33	69	18
18	Arbroath	34	5	6	23	41	82	16

Season 1969-70

Scottish League Division 1

DATE	OPPONENTS	SCORE	GOALSCORERS	ATTENDANCE
Aug 30	Dundee United	D 0-0		22,000
Sep 3	ABERDEEN	W 2-0	Provan (pen), Stein	45,000
Sep 6	ST MIRREN	W 2-0	Johnston, Provan (pen)	41,000
Sep 13	Ayr United	L 1-2	Stein	25,250
Sep 20	CELTIC	L 0-1		84,000
Sep 27	Partick Thistle	W 2-1	Henderson, Johnston	21,000
Oct 4	St Johnstone	W 3-1	Stein 2, Baxter	20,000
Oct 11	HIBERNIAN	L 1-3	Johnston	54,000
Oct 25	DUNFERMLINE	W 2-0	Penman, Johansen	32,998
Oct 29	Motherwell	D 2-2	Stein 2	25,000
Nov 1	DUNDEE	W 3-1	Penman 2 (1 pen), Johnston	30,000
Nov 8	Airdrie	W 3-1	Penman, Henderson, Johnston	12,200
Nov 15	KILMARNOCK	W 5-3	Stein 3, Penman (pen), Johnston	35,499
Nov 22	Morton	D 2-2	Stein, Johnston	18,000
Nov 29	RAITH ROVERS	W 3-0	Johnston, Stein, A.MacDonald	25,000
Dec 6	Hearts	W 2-1	Stein, Johnston	36,000
Dec 13	DUNDEE UNITED	W 2-1	Henderson, Stein	45,000
Dec 20	Aberdeen	W 3-2	Stein 2, Johnston	22,000
Dec 27	CLYDE	W 3-0	Setterington, Penman (pen), Greig	35,000
Jan 1	PARTICK THISTLE	W 3-1	Johnston, Semple, Stein	40,000
Jan 3	Celtic	D 0-0		75,000
Jan 17	AYR UNITED	W 3-0	Stein, Greig, I.MacDonald	32,000
Jan 31	St Mirren	W 4-0	Stein 2, Greig, A.MacDonald	48,000
Feb 25	ST JOHNSTONE	W 3-1	Greig 2, Semple	25,000
Feb 28	Hibernian	D 2-2	Stein, Greig	31,332
Mar 7	MOTHERWELL	W 2-1	Stein 2	31,000
Mar 11	Raith Rovers	L 1-2	Penman	6,500
Mar 14	Dunfermline	L 1-2	Stein	16,000
Mar 21	Dundee	L 1-2	Stein	17,000
Mar 25	HEARTS	W 3-2	Penman 2, Johnston	14,000
Mar 28	AIRDRIE	D 1-1	Penman	16,700
Mar 31	Clyde	L 0-1		14,000
Apr 4	Kilmarnock	D 2-2	Greig, Henderson	11,135
Apr 18	MORTON	L 0-2		20,000

Scottish Cup

Jan 24	HIBERNIAN	(Rd1) W 3-1	A.MacDonald 2, Penman	73,716
Feb 7	Forfar	(Rd2) W 7-0	Greig 2, A.MacDonald, Stein, Penman, Johansen (pen), Jardine	10,800
Feb 21	Celtic	(QF) L 1-3	Craig o.g.	75,000

Scottish League Cup

Aug 9	Raith Rovers†	W 3-2	Johansen, Stein, A.MacDonald	21,000
Aug 13	CELTIC†	W 2-1	Persson, Johnston	71,645
Aug 16	Airdrie†	W 3-0	Persson, Jardine, Watson	23,000
Aug 20	Celtic†	L 0-1		70,000
Aug 23	RAITH ROVERS†	D 3-3	Penman, A.MacDonald, Polland o.g.	40,000
Aug 27	AIRDRIE†	W 3-0	Stein, Johnston, Penman	18,000

†Qualifying Section One – Rangers finished second and failed to qualify.

European Cup-Winners' Cup

Sep 17	STEAUA BUCHAREST	(Rd1/FL) W 2-0	Johnston 2	43,346
Oct 1	Steaua Bucharest	(Rd1/SL) D 0-0		90,000
Nov 12	Gornik Zabrze	(Rd2/FL) L 1-3	Persson	72,000
Nov 26	GORNIK ZABRZE	(Rd2/SL) L 1-3	Baxter	70,000

MANAGER: Davie White/Willie Waddell

CAPTAIN: John Greig

TOP SCORER: Colin Stein

BIGGEST WIN: 7-0 v Forfar Athletic, 7 February 1970, Scottish Cup

HIGHEST ATTENDANCE: 90,000 v Steaua Bucharest, 1 October 1969, European Cup-Winners' Cup

MAJOR TRANSFERS IN: Jim Baxter from Nottingham Forest, Peter McCloy from Motherwell

MAJOR TRANSFERS OUT: Alex Ferguson to Falkirk, Bobby Watson to Motherwell

League & Cup Appearances

PLAYER	LEAGUE	CUP COMPETITION			TOTAL
		S CUP	SL CUP	ECWC	
Baxter	14	4	4		22
Conn	8 (4)	2 (1)			10 (5)
Fyfe	4				4
Greig	30	3	6	4	43
Henderson	27	1 (1)	2 (1)	4	34 (2)
Heron	7		2		9
Jackson	3				3
Jardine	10 (4)	0 (1)	4	2 (1)	16 (6)
Johansen	33	3	6	4	46
Johnston	29	2	6	4	41
MacDonald A	15	3	3 (1)		21 (1)
MacDonald I	1	1			2
Martin	1				1
Mathieson	14	3			17
McCloy	7				7
McKinnon	30	3	6	4	43
McPhee	1				1
Neef	26	3	6	4	39
Penman	25 (5)	3	2 (1)	2	32 (6)
Persson	9	3 (1)	3		15 (1)
Provan	9	6	2		17
Semple	4				4
Setterington	4 (2)				4 (2)
Smith	22 (3)	3	4 (1)	0 (2)	29 (6)
Stein	33	3	6	4	46
Watson K	2 (1)				2 (1)
Watson R	5 (3)		2 (1)	1	8 (4)
White	1				1

Goalscorers

PLAYER	LEAGUE	CUP COMPETITION			TOTAL
		S CUP	SL CUP	ECWC	
Stein	24	1	2		27
Johnston	12		2	2	16
Penman	10	2	2		14
Greig	7	2			9
MacDonald A	2	3	2		7
Henderson	4				4
Johansen	1	1	1		3
Persson			2	1	3
Baxter	1			1	2
Jardine		1	1		2
Provan	2				2
Semple	2				2
MacDonald I	1				1
Setterington	1				1
Watson R			1		1
Opps' o.gs.		1	1		2

Fact File

Jim Baxter was given a free transfer at the end of the 1969-70 season. He retired from football in November 1970 at the age of 31.

Final Scottish League Div 1 Table

		P	W	D	L	F	A	Pts
1	CELTIC	34	27	3	4	96	33	57
2	RANGERS	34	19	7	8	67	40	45
3	HIBERNIAN	34	19	6	9	65	40	44
4	HEARTS	34	13	12	9	50	36	38
5	DUNDEE U	34	16	6	12	62	64	38
6	DUNDEE	34	15	6	13	49	44	36
7	KILMARNOCK	34	13	10	11	62	57	36
8	ABERDEEN	34	14	7	13	55	45	35
9	MORTON	34	13	9	12	52	52	35
10	DUNFERMLINE ATH	34	15	5	14	45	45	35
11	MOTHERWELL	34	11	10	13	49	51	32
12	AIRDRIEONIANS	34	12	8	14	59	64	32
13	ST JOHNSTON	34	11	9	14	50	62	31
14	AYR U	34	12	6	16	37	52	30
15	ST MIRREN	34	8	9	17	39	54	25
16	CLYDE	34	9	7	18	34	56	25
17	RAITH R	34	5	11	18	32	67	21
18	PARTICK T	34	5	7	22	41	82	17

Season 1970-71

Scottish League Division 1

DATE	OPPONENTS	SCORE	GOALSCORERS	ATTENDANCE
Aug 29	St Mirren	D 0-0		27,400
Sep 5	FALKIRK	W 2-0	Johnston 2 (1 pen)	39,000
Sep 12	Celtic	L 0-2		75,000
Sep 19	COWDENBEATH	W 5-0	Johnstone 2, Greig 2, A.MacDonald	31,000
Sep 26	Dundee United	W 2-0	Conn, Fyfe	23,000
Oct 3	MOTHERWELL	W 3-1	A.MacDonald, Stein, Johnston	37,000
Oct 10	Hearts	W 1-0	Johnston (pen)	32,500
Oct 17	ABERDEEN	L 0-2		39,763
Oct 31	AIRDRIE	W 5-0	Johnston 2 (1 pen), Stein 2, Conn	28,788
Nov 7	Dunfermline	D 1-1	Jackson	20,000
Nov 14	CLYDE	W 5-0	Stein 2, Johnston (pen), Johnstone, Mulheron o.g.	25,915
Nov 21	Ayr United	L 1-2	Young o.g.	20,000
Nov 25	Hibernian	L 2-3	Johnstone, Stein	18,770
Nov 28	Morton	W 2-1	Conn, Fyfe	15,000
Dec 5	DUNDEE	D 0-0		25,420
Dec 12	St Johnstone	L 1-2	Fyfe	10,500
Dec 19	KILMARNOCK	W 4-2	Johnstone 2, Jackson, A.MacDonald	19,450
Dec 26	ST MIRREN	W 1-0	Greig	25,000
Jan 1	Falkirk	L 1-3	Conn	18,000
Jan 2	CELTIC	D 1-1	Stein	85,000
Jan 16	DUNDEE UNITED	D 1-1	Greig	27,776
Jan 30	Motherwell	W 2-1	Mathieson, Stein	22,500
Feb 6	HEARTS	W 1-0	Henderson	29,398
Feb 20	Aberdeen	D 0-0		36,000
Feb 27	HIBERNIAN	D 1-1	Greig	30,644
Mar 10	Airdrie	L 3-4	A.MacDonald 2, Stein	15,000
Mar 13	DUNFERMLINE	W 2-0	Henderson, Greig	21,580
Mar 20	Clyde	D 2-2	Johnston, Stein	10,500
Mar 27	AYR UNITED	W 2-0	Greig, Johnston	22,000
Apr 3	MORTON	D 0-0		13,986
Apr 10	Dundee	L 0-1		18,000
Apr 14	Cowdenbeath	W 3-1	Jardine, Greig, Stein	3,396
Apr 17	ST JOHNSTONE	L 0-2		17,566
Apr 24	Kilmarnock	W 4-1	Miller, Henderson, A.MacDonald, Stein	8,544

Scottish Cup

Jan 23	FALKIRK	(Rd3) W 3-0	Johnston 2, Conn	42,000
Feb 13	St Mirren	(Rd4) W 3-1	Stein 2, Johnston (pen)	32,373
Mar 6	ABERDEEN	(QF) W 1-0	Jackson	60,584
Mar 31	Hibernian*	(SF) D 0-0		69,429
Apr 5	Hibernian*	(R) W 2-1	Henderson, Conn	54,435
May 8	Celtic*	(F) D 1-1	Johnstone	120,092
May 12	Celtic*	(R) L 1-2	Craig o.g.	103,332

*Played at Hampden Park.

Scottish League Cup

Aug 8	DUNFERMLINE†	W 4-1	Stein 2, Jardine, Johnston (pen)	45,056
Aug 12	Motherwell†	W 2-0	Fyfe, Henderson	25,000
Aug 15	MORTON†	D 0-0		45,000
Aug 19	MOTHERWELL†	W 2-0	Penman, Stein	35,000
Aug 22	Dunfermline†	W 6-0	Johnston 3 (1 pen), Jackson, Fyfe, Stein	17,000
Aug 26	Morton†	W 2-0	Johnston, Conn	18,000

†Qualifying Section Two – Rangers finished top.

Sep 9	Hibernian	(QF/FL) W 3-1	Fyfe 2, Conn	37,365
Sep 23	HIBERNIAN	(QF/SL) W 3-1	A.MacDonald, Greig, Fyfe	54,000
Oct 14	Cowdenbeath*	(SF) W 2-0	Johnston (pen), Stein	35,000
Oct 24	Celtic*	(F) W 1-0	Johnstone	106,263

*Played at Hampden Park.

Inter-Cities Fairs Cup

Sep 16	Bayern Munich	(Rd1/FL) L 0-1		30,000
Sep 30	BAYERN MUNICH	(Rd1/SL) D 1-1	Stein	82,743

MANAGER: Willie Waddell
CAPTAIN: John Greig
TOP SCORER: Colin Stein
BIGGEST WIN: 6-0 v Dunfermline, 22 August 1970, League Cup
HIGHEST ATTENDANCE: 120,092 v Celtic, 8 May 1971, Scottish Cup
MAJOR TRANSFERS OUT: Orjan Persson to Orgryte

League & Cup Appearances

PLAYER	LEAGUE	CUP COMPETITION			TOTAL
		S CUP	SL CUP	ICF CUP	
Alexander	2				2
Conn	23 (2)	5	9 (1)	2	39 (3)
Denny			1		1
Fyfe	11 (3)		6	2	19 (3)
Greig	26	7	8	2	43
Henderson	29	7	6 (1)	0 (2)	42 (3)
Jackson	34	7	9	2	52
Jardine	32	5	10	2	49
Johnston	25	7	10	2	44
Johnstone	13 (4)	(2)	1 (1)		14 (7)
MacDonald A	27 (6)	4 (1)	7 (1)	2	40 (8)
MacDonald I	3		1		4
Mathieson	14	7	2		23
McCallum	1				1
McCloy	31	7	9	2	49
McKinnon	32	7	10	2	51
Miller	21	1	8 (1)	2	32 (1)
Neef	3				3
Parlane	2 (2)				2 (2)
Penman	3 (5)	2	1		6 (5)
Semple	2	1			3
Smith	9 (2)	3	1		13 (2)
Stein	30	7	10	2	49
Watson K	1				1
Watson RM			1		1

Goalscorers

PLAYER	LEAGUE	CUP COMPETITION			TOTAL
		S CUP	SL CUP	ICF CUP	
Stein	12	2	5	1	20
Johnston	9	3	6		18
Greig	8		1		9
Conn	4	2	2		8
Fyfe	3		5		8
Johnstone	6	1	1		8
MacDonald A	6		1		7
Henderson	3	1	1		5
Jackson	2	1	1		4
Jardine	1		1		2
Mathieson	1				1
Miller	1				1
Penman			1		1
Opps' o.gs.	2		1		3

Fact File

Jim Denny became the first Rangers player since Willie Reid in 1909 to make his debut in a Scottish Cup final, when he played against Celtic in the replay on 12 May 1971.

Final Scottish League Div 1 Table

		P	W	D	L	F	A	Pts
1	CELTIC	34	25	6	3	89	23	56
2	ABERDEEN	34	24	6	4	68	18	54
3	ST JOHNSTONE	34	19	6	9	59	44	44
4	RANGERS	34	16	9	9	58	34	41
5	DUNDEE	34	14	10	10	53	45	38
6	DUNDEE U	34	14	8	12	53	54	36
7	FALKIRK	34	13	9	12	46	53	35
8	MORTON	34	13	8	13	44	44	34
9	MOTHERWELL	34	13	8	13	43	47	34
10	AIRDRIEONIANS	34	13	8	13	60	65	34
11	HEARTS	34	13	7	14	41	40	33
12	HIBERNIAN	34	10	10	14	47	53	30
13	KILMARNOCK	34	10	8	16	43	67	28
14	AYR U	34	9	8	17	37	54	26
15	CLYDE	34	8	10	16	33	59	26
16	DUNFERMLINE ATH	34	6	11	17	44	56	23
17	ST MIRREN	34	7	9	18	38	56	23
18	COWDENBEATH	34	7	3	24	33	77	17

Season 1971-72

Scottish League Division 1

DATE	OPPONENTS	SCORE	GOALSCORERS	ATTENDANCE
Sep 4	Partick Thistle	L 2-3	A.MacDonald, Stein	30,000
Sep 11	CELTIC	L 2-3	Johnston (pen), Stein	80,000
Sep 18	Falkirk	W 3-0	Greig 2, Stein	24,000
Sep 25	ABERDEEN	L 0-2		41,236
Oct 2	Hearts	L 1-2	Johnston	29,000
Oct 9	EAST FIFE	W 3-0	Jardine (pen), Fyfe, A.MacDonald	25,000
Oct 16	Dundee United	W 5-1	A.MacDonald 2, Stein, Greig, Jardine	17,000
Oct 23	MOTHERWELL	W 4-0	Fyfe 2, A.MacDonald, Jardine	25,000
Oct 30	KILMARNOCK	W 3-1	A.MacDonald 2, Stein	25,442
Nov 6	St Johnstone	W 4-1	Johnston 3 (2 pens), A.MacDonald	27,000
Nov 13	DUNDEE	L 2-3	Johnston 2	33,200
Nov 20	Morton	W 2-1	Johnston, Greig	12,500
Nov 27	Ayr United	W 2-1	Stein, Henderson	15,100
Dec 4	CLYDE	W 1-0	Stein	25,000
Dec 11	Dunfermline	W 2-0	Greig, Johnston	13,500
Dec 18	AIRDRIE	W 3-0	Stein, Jardine (pen), Fyfe	25,000
Dec 25	Hibernian	W 1-0	Stein	30,000
Jan 1	PARTICK THISTLE	W 2-1	Greig, Johnston	38,200
Jan 3	Celtic	L 1-2	Stein	77,811
Jan 8	FALKIRK	W 3-1	Greig, Jackson, I. MacDonald	23,000
Jan 15	Aberdeen	D 0-0		33,608
Jan 22	HEARTS	W 6-0	Johnstone 3, Johnston, Greig, Conn	35,000
Jan 29	East Fife	W 1-0	Johnstone	12,018
Feb 12	DUNDEE UNITED	W 1-0	Smith	25,000
Feb 19	Motherwell	L 0-2		16,192
Mar 4	Kilmarnock	W 2-1	Jardine, Conn	14,707
Mar 11	ST JOHNSTONE	W 2-0	Johnstone, McLean	25,000
Mar 25	MORTON	L 1-2	Jackson	20,000
Apr 8	Clyde	D 1-1	Johnston	7,500
Apr 10	Dundee	L 0-2		13,000
Apr 22	Airdrie	W 3-0	Penman 2, Fyfe	10,000
Apr 27	DUNFERMLINE	L 3-4	A.MacDonald 2, Stein	5,000
Apr 29	HIBERNIAN	L 1-2	Johnston	11,000
May 1	AYR UNITED	W 4-2	Conn, Penman, A.MacDonald, Fyfe	4,000

Scottish Cup

Feb 5	Falkirk	(Rd1) D 2-2	Johnstone, Greig	20,000
Feb 9	FALKIRK	(R) W 2-0	Stein, McLean	43,000
Feb 26	St Mirren	(Rd2) W 4-1	McLean 2 (1 pen), A.MacDonald, Stein	29,376
Mar 18	Motherwell	(QF) D 2-2	A.MacDonald, Stein	28,577
Mar 27	MOTHERWELL	(R) W 4-2	Stein 2, McLean, Fallon o.g.	44,800
Apr 15	Hibernian*	(SF) D 1-1	A.MacDonald	75,884
Apr 24	Hibernian*	(R) L 0-2		67,547

*Played at Hampden Park.

Scottish League Cup

Aug 14	Celtic†	L 0-2		72,500
Aug 18	AYR UNITED†	W 4-0	Johnstone 2, Stein, McLean (pen)	33,000
Aug 21	MORTON†	W 2-0	Johnstone, A.MacDonald	41,000
Aug 25	Ayr United†	W 4-0	Stein 2, A.MacDonald, Johnstone	20,000
Aug 28	CELTIC†	L 0-3		85,000
Sep 1	Morton†	W 1-0	Stein	7,000

†Qualifying Section Four – Rangers finished second and failed to qualify.

European Cup-Winners' Cup

Sep 15	Rennes	(Rd1/FL) D 1-1	Johnston	13,993
Sep 28	RENNES	(Rd1/SL) W 1-0	A.MacDonald	42,000
Oct 20	SPORTING LISBON	(Rd2/FL) W 3-2	Stein 2, Henderson	50,000
Nov 3	Sporting Lisbon	(Rd2/SL) L 3-4	Stein 2, Henderson	60,000
Mar 8	Torino	(QF/FL) D 1-1	Johnston	40,000
Mar 22	TORINO	(QF/SL) W 1-0	A.MacDonald	75,000
Apr 5	Bayern Munich	(SF/FL) D 1-1	Zobel o.g.	44,000
Apr 19	BAYERN MUNICH	(SF/SL) W 2-0	Jardine, Parlane	80,000
May 24	Dinamo Moscow*	(F) W 3-2	Johnston 2, Stein	45,000

*Played in Barcelona.

Fact File

Rangers defender Dave Smith was named Scotland's Player of the Year for the 1971-72 season.

League & Cup Appearances

PLAYER	LEAGUE	CUP COMPETITION			TOTAL
		S CUP	SL CUP	ECWC	
Conn	21 (2)	3	2 (2)	3 (1)	29 (5)
Denny	7 (2)	0 (1)		1 (1)	8 (4)
Fyfe	9 (5)			1	10 (5)
Greig	28	6	6	8	48
Henderson	13 (2)		3		16 (2)
Jackson	24 (1)	5	6	7	42 (1)
Jardine	31	7	6	9	53
Johnston	23 (1)	7	6	8	44 (1)
Johnstone	16 (1)	7	6	5	34 (1)
MacDonald A	31 (1)	7	4 (2)	9	51 (3)
MacDonald I	7				7
Mathieson	30	7	6	9	52
McCloy	34	7	6	9	56
McKinnon	7	6	4		17
McLean	21 (1)	7	6	6 (1)	40 (2)
Miller	2				2
Parlane	2	1	1		4
Penman	10 (1)		0 (1)	2	12 (3)
Smith	30	7	6 (1)		43 (1)
Stein	28	6	5 (1)	9	48 (1)

Goalscorers

PLAYER	LEAGUE	CUP COMPETITION			TOTAL
		S CUP	SL CUP	ECWC	
Stein	11	5	4	5	25
MacDonald A	11	3	2	2	18
Johnston	11			4	15
Johnstone	7	1	4		12
Greig	8	1			9
Fyfe	6				6
Jardine	5			1	6
McLean	1	4	1		6
Conn	3				3
Henderson	1		2		3
Penman	3				3
Jackson	2				2
MacDonald I	1				1
Parlane			1		1
Smith	1				1
Opps' o.gs.		1		1	2

MANAGER: Willie Waddell

CAPTAIN: John Greig

TOP SCORER: Colin Stein

BIGGEST WIN: 6-0 v Hearts, 22 January 1972, league

HIGHEST ATTENDANCE: 85,000 v Celtic, 28 August 1971, League Cup

MAJOR TRANSFERS IN: Tommy McLean from Kilmarnock

Final Scottish League Div 1 Table

		P	W	D	L	F	A	PTS
1	CELTIC	34	28	4	2	96	28	60
2	ABERDEEN	34	21	8	5	80	26	50
3	RANGERS	34	21	2	11	71	38	44
4	HIBERNIAN	34	19	6	9	62	34	44
5	DUNDEE	34	14	13	7	59	38	41
6	HEARTS	34	13	13	8	53	49	39
7	PARTICK T	34	12	10	12	53	54	34
8	ST JOHNSTONE	34	12	8	14	52	58	32
9	DUNDEE U	34	12	7	15	55	70	31
10	MOTHERWELL	34	11	7	16	49	69	29
11	KILMARNOCK	34	11	6	17	49	64	28
12	AYR U	34	9	10	15	40	58	28
13	MORTON	34	10	7	17	46	52	27
14	FALKIRK	34	10	7	17	44	60	27
15	AIRDRIEONIANS	34	7	12	15	44	76	26
16	EAST FIFE	34	5	15	14	34	61	25
17	CLYDE	34	7	10	17	33	66	24
18	DUNFERMLINE ATH	34	7	9	18	31	50	23

Season 1972-73

Scottish League Division 1

DATE	OPPONENTS	SCORE	GOALSCORERS	ATTENDANCE
Sep 2	Ayr United	L 1-2	Johnston	14,500
Sep 9	PARTICK THISTLE	W 2-1	A.MacDonald, Johnston	35,000
Sep 16	Celtic	L 1-3	Greig	50,416
Sep 23	FALKIRK	W 1-0	McLean (pen)	18,000
Sep 30	Kilmarnock	L 1-2	McLean	10,643
Oct 7	MORTON	D 1-1	Fyfe	30,000
Oct 14	Motherwell	W 2-0	Young, Parlane (pen)	17,621
Oct 21	Arbroath	W 2-1	Parlane, Mason	8,400
Oct 28	ST JOHNSTONE	W 5-1	Conn 2, Parlane 2, Johnstone	21,000
Nov 4	Dundee	D 1-1	Conn	19,600
Nov 11	AIRDRIE	W 1-0	Conn	17,000
Nov 18	HIBERNIAN	W 2-1	Conn, Fyfe	33,356
Nov 25	DUMBARTON	W 3-1	Young, Conn, Parlane	14,500
Dec 2	HEARTS	L 0-1		30,000
Dec 9	Dundee United	W 4-1	Parlane 2, Conn, Jardine	12,500
Dec 16	ABERDEEN	D 0-0		26,375
Dec 23	East Fife	W 4-0	Johnstone 2, Young, Parlane	8,608
Dec 30	AYR UNITED	W 2-1	Conn, Parlane	17,653
Jan 1	Partick Thistle	W 1-0	Young	18,500
Jan 6	CELTIC	W 2-1	Parlane, Conn	72,000
Jan 13	Falkirk	W 4-2	Young 2, Parlane (pen), Conn	17,000
Jan 20	KILMARNOCK	W 4-0	Parlane 2, Young, Greig	14,515
Jan 27	Morton	W 2-1	A.MacDonald, Young	16,000
Feb 10	MOTHERWELL	W 2-1	Young, Jardine	27,000
Feb 19	ARBROATH	W 5-0	Parlane 2, Young, Greig, Miller	15,000
Mar 3	St Johnstone	W 2-1	Miller, Mason	12,000
Mar 10	DUNDEE	W 3-1	Parlane 2, A.MacDonald	32,500
Mar 20	Airdrie	W 6-2	Parlane, Greig, Johnston, McLean, A.MacDonald, Young	20,000
Mar 24	HIBERNIAN	W 1-0	McLean	51,200
Mar 31	Dumbarton	W 2-1	Young, Parlane	13,000
Apr 7	Hearts	W 1-0	Greig	24,000
Apr 14	DUNDEE UNITED	W 2-1	Greig 2	38,000
Apr 21	Aberdeen	D 2-2	McLean, Conn	33,000
Apr 28	EAST FIFE	W 2-0	Young, Conn	27,544

Scottish Cup

Feb 3	DUNDEE UNITED	(Rd3) W 1-0	Young		35,657
Feb 24	HIBERNIAN	(Rd4) D 1-1	Johnston		63,889
Feb 28	Hibernian	(R) W 2-1	McLean 2 (1 pen)		49,007
Mar 17	AIRDRIE	(QF) W 2-0	Parlane (pen), Young		35,500
Apr 4	Ayr United*	(SF) W 2-0	Parlane 2		51,815
May 5	Celtic*	(F) W 3-2	Parlane, Conn, Forsyth		122,714

*Played at Hampden Park.

Scottish League Cup

Aug 12	CLYDEBANK†	W 2-0	Conn, A.MacDonald		26,240
Aug 16	St Mirren†	W 4-0	Johnston, Greig, Stein, Conn		15,000
Aug 19	AYR UNITED†	W 2-1	Johnston, Parlane		25,000
Aug 23	ST MIRREN†	L 1-4	Conn		20,000
Aug 26	Clydebank†	W 5-0	Greig, McLean (pen), Smith, Johnstone, Stein		9,000
Aug 30	Ayr United†	W 2-1	Johnston, Johnstone		15,000

†Qualifying Section Three – Rangers finished top.

Sep 20	Stenhousemuir	(Rd2/FL) W 5-0	Johnstone 3, Parlane, Greig		3,650
Oct 4	STENHOUSEMUIR	(Rd2/SL) L 1-2	Fyfe		6,000
Oct 11	ST JOHNSTONE	(QF/FL) D 1-1	Parlane		15,000
Nov 1	St Johnstone	(QF/SL) W 2-0	Young, Parlane (pen)		12,300
Nov 22	Hibernian*	(SF) L 0-1			46,513

*Played at Hampden Park.

European Super Cup

Jan 16	AJAX	(F1) L 1-3	A.MacDonald		60,000
Jan 24	Ajax	(F2) L 2-3	A.MacDonald, Young		43,000

MANAGER: Jock Wallace

CAPTAIN: John Greig

TOP SCORER: Derek Parlane

MAJOR TRANSFERS IN: Quinton Young from Coventry City, Tom Forsyth from Motherwell, Stewart Kennedy from Stenhousemuir

MAJOR TRANSFERS OUT: Willie Henderson to Sheffield Wednesday, Colin Stein to Coventry City, Willie Johnston to West Bromwich Albion

League & Cup Appearances

PLAYER	LEAGUE	CUP COMPETITION			TOTAL
		S CUP	SL CUP	ES CUP	
Bonnyman			1		1
Conn	18 (2)	1 (1)	7	1	27 (3)
Denny	6		2 (1)		8 (1)
Donaldson	3 (2)			3 (1)	6 (3)
Forsyth	21	6	2		29
Fyfe	3 (3)		6 (1)		9 (4)
Greig	30	6	10	2	48
Jackson	7	7			14
Jardine	34	6	11	2	53
Johnston	4	5			9
Johnstone	31	6	8	2	47
MacDonald A	27 (2)	5	9	2	43 (2)
MacDonald I			0 (1)		0 (1)
Mason	12 (4)	0 (1)			12 (5)
Mathieson	34	6	11	2	53
McCloy	33	6	11	2	52
McLean	22 (2)	6	6	1 (1)	35 (3)
Miller	2 (1)	1			3 (1)
Neef	1				1
Parlane	29 (1)	6	6 (1)	2	43 (2)
Penman			2		2
Smith	29	5	9	2	45
Stein	2 (1)		5		7 (1)
Young	26	6	2 (1)	2	36 (1)

Goalscorers

PLAYER	LEAGUE	CUP COMPETITION			TOTAL
		S CUP	SL CUP	ES CUP	
Parlane	19	4	4		27
Young	13	2	1	1	17
Conn	12	1	3		16
Greig	7	3			10
Johnstone	4	1	5		10
McLean	5	2	1		8
MacDonald A	4	1		2	7
Johnston	2	3			5
Fyfe	2	1			3
Jardine	2				2
Mason	2				2
Miller	2				2
Stein			2		2
Forsyth	1				1
Smith	1				1

Fact File

Central defender Ronnie McKinnon was given a free transfer at the end of the 1972-73 season after 13 years of outstanding service to Rangers.

Final Scottish League Div 1 Table

		P	W	D	L	F	A	Pts
1	CELTIC	34	26	5	3	93	28	57
2	RANGERS	34	26	4	4	74	30	56
3	HIBERNIAN	34	19	7	8	74	33	45
4	ABERDEEN	34	16	11	7	61	34	43
5	DUNDEE	34	17	9	8	68	43	43
6	AYR U	34	16	8	10	50	51	40
7	DUNDEE U	34	17	5	12	56	51	39
8	MOTHERWELL	34	11	9	14	38	48	31
9	EAST FIFE	34	11	8	15	46	54	30
10	HEARTS	34	12	6	16	39	50	30
11	ST JOHNSTONE	34	10	9	15	52	67	29
12	MORTON	34	10	8	16	47	53	28
13	PARTICK T	34	10	8	16	40	53	28
14	FALKIRK	34	7	12	15	38	56	26
15	ARBROATH	34	9	8	17	39	63	26
16	DUMBARTON	34	6	11	17	43	72	23
17	KILMARNOCK	34	7	8	19	40	71	22
18	AIRDRIEONIANS	34	4	8	22	34	75	16

Season 1973-74

Scottish League Division 1

DATE	OPPONENTS	SCORE	GOALSCORERS	ATTENDANCE
Sep 1	AYR UNITED	D 0-0		30,000
Sep 8	Partick Thistle	W 1-0	Scott	22,000
Sep 15	CELTIC	L 0-1		70,000
Sep 29	HEARTS	L 0-3		35,000
Oct 6	Arbroath	W 2-1	O'Hara 2	7,710
Oct 13	EAST FIFE	L 0-1		25,000
Oct 20	Dundee United	W 3-1	Conn 2, O'Hara	11,000
Oct 27	HIBERNIAN	W 4-0	Jardine 2 (2 pens), Conn, Greig	35,000
Nov 3	Dunfermline	D 2-2	Jackson, O'Hara	20,000
Nov 10	MORTON	W 1-0	Greig	20,000
Nov 17	FALKIRK	W 2-1	Greig 2	15,000
Nov 24	Clyde	W 2-0	Jackson, MacDonald	15,000
Dec 15	ST JOHNSTONE	W 5-1	Conn, Young, MacDonald, Parlane, Smith	8,200
Dec 22	Dumbarton	W 2-0	Parlane, Young	7,500
Dec 29	Ayr United	W 1-0	Parlane	17,000
Jan 1	PARTICK THISTLE	D 1-1	Parlane (pen)	20,000
Jan 5	Celtic	L 0-1		55,000
Jan 12	ABERDEEN	D 1-1	McLean	16,000
Jan 19	Hearts	W 4-2	Parlane 4	25,000
Feb 2	ARBROATH	L 2-3	McLean, Parlane (pen)	22,000
Feb 9	East Fife	W 3-0	Hamilton, Scott, McLean	8,499
Feb 23	DUNDEE UNITED	W 3-1	Parlane 2 (1 pen), Young	15,500
Mar 2	Hibernian	L 1-3	McLean	23,149
Mar 16	Morton	W 3-2	Jackson 2, Parlane (pen)	9,000
Mar 23	Falkirk	D 0-0		10,000
Mar 30	CLYDE	W 4-0	Johnston, Greig, MacDonald, Scott	15,000
Apr 2	DUNFERMLINE	W 3-0	Parlane (pen), Scott, Fyfe	12,000
Apr 6	Motherwell	W 4-1	Young 2, Scott, Fyfe	13,346
Apr 13	DUNDEE	L 1-2	Jardine (pen)	25,000
Apr 17	Aberdeen	D 1-1	Greig	18,000
Apr 20	St Johnstone	W 3-1	Fyfe 2, Young	7,500
Apr 24	MOTHERWELL	W 2-1	Scott, Parlane	10,000
Apr 27	DUMBARTON	W 3-1	Scott 2, Fyfe	20,000
Apr 29	Dundee	W 3-2	Fyfe 2, Young	10,578

Scottish Cup

Jan 26	QUEEN'S PARK	(Rd3) W 8-0	Parlane 3, McLean 3, Scott, Morris	19,000
Feb 17	DUNDEE	(Rd4) L 0-3		64,672

Scottish League Cup

Aug 11	FALKIRK†	W 3-1	Scott 2, Conn	35,000
Aug 15	Arbroath†	W 2-1	Conn, Parlane	6,677
Aug 18	CELTIC†	L 1-2	Scott	63,173
Aug 22	ARBROATH†	W 3-0	MacDonald, Conn, Smith	14,000
Aug 25	Celtic†	W 3-1	MacDonald, Parlane, Conn	65,000
Aug 29	Falkirk†	W 5-1	Conn 2, O'Hara, McLean, Forsyth	12,000
	†Qualifying Section One – Rangers finished top.			
Sep 12	DUMBARTON	(Rd2/FL) W 6-0	Parlane 3 (1 pen), Young 2, Greig (pen)	25,000
Oct 10	Dumbarton	(Rd2/SL) W 2-1	Scott, Fyfe	6,000
Oct 31	HIBERNIAN	(QF/FL) W 2-0	Greig, Schaedler o.g.	35,000
Nov 21	Hibernian	(QF/SL) D 0-0		19,245
Dec 5	Celtic*	(SF) L 1-3	MacDonald	54,864
	*Played at Hampden Park.			

European Cup-Winners' Cup

Sep 19	Ankaragucu	(Rd1/FL) W 2-0	Conn, McLean	45,000
Oct 3	ANKARAGUCU	(Rd1/SL) W 4-0	Greig 2, O'Hara, Johnston	30,000
Oct 24	Borussia MG	(Rd2/FL) L 0-3		35,000
Nov 7	BORUSSIA MG	(Rd2/SL) W 3-2	Conn, Jackson, MacDonald	40,000

MANAGER: Jock Wallace

CAPTAIN: John Greig

TOP SCORER: Derek Parlane

BIGGEST WIN: 8-0 v Queen's Park, 26 January 1974, Scottish Cup

HIGHEST ATTENDANCE: 70,000 v Celtic, 15 September, 1973, League

MAJOR TRANSFERS IN: Doug Houston from Dundee United, Johnny Hamilton from Hibernian, Ally Scott from Queen's Park

League & Cup Appearances

PLAYER	LEAGUE	CUP COMPETITION			TOTAL
		S CUP	SL CUP	ECWC	
Conn	7 (4)	5 (5)	4		16 (9)
Denny	0 (1)				0 (1)
Donaldson	1				1
Forsyth	18		11	4	33
Fyfe	7 (6)		1		8 (6)
Greig	30 (2)	1	10	4	45 (2)
Hamilton	4 (3)	2 (1)			6 (4)
Houston	9 (1)	4	3		16 (1)
Hunter	3	1			4
Jackson	18	1	3	2	24
Jardine	34	2	11	4	51
Johnstone	31	2	8 (1)	2	43 (1)
Kennedy	1	2			3
MacDonald	29 (1)		11	3	43 (1)
Mason			2		2
Mathieson	26	2	11	4	43
McCloy	30	1	9	4	44
McDougall	8 (1)				8 (1)
McLean	21 (3)	2	11	4	38 (3)
Morris	5 (1)	1	1		7 (1)
O'Hara	18 (1)	2	2	2 (1)	24 (2)
Parlane	28 (1)	2	8 2		40 (1)
Scott	21 (3)	2	6 (2)		29 (5)
Smith	7 (2)	1	1 (5)	1	10 (7)
Young	19 (1)		(1) 3	1 (1)	23 (3)

Goalscorers

PLAYER	LEAGUE	CUP COMPETITION			TOTAL
		S CUP	SL CUP	ECWC	
Parlane	14	3	5		22
Scott	8	1	4		13
Conn	4		6	2	12
Greig	6		2	2	10
McLean	4	3	1	1	9
Young	7		2		9
Fyfe	7		1		8
MacDonald	3		3	1	7
O'Hara	4		1	1	6
Jackson	4			1	5
Jardine	3				3
Johnstone	1		1		2
Smith	1		1		2
Forsyth			1		1
Hamilton	1				1
Morris		1			1
Opps' o.gs.			1		1

Fact File

Sandy Jardine was the only Rangers player in the Scotland squad for the 1974 World Cup finals in Germany. He played in all three matches against Zaire, Brazil and Yugoslavia.

Final Scottish League Div 1 Table

		P	W	D	L	F	A	Pts
1	CELTIC	34	23	7	4	82	27	53
2	HIBERNIAN	34	20	9	5	75	42	49
3	RANGERS	34	21	6	7	67	34	48
4	ABERDEEN	34	13	16	5	46	26	42
5	DUNDEE	34	16	7	11	67	48	39
6	HEARTS	34	14	10	10	54	43	38
7	AYR U	34	15	8	11	44	40	38
8	DUNDEE U	34	15	7	12	55	51	37
9	MOTHERWELL	34	14	7	13	45	40	35
10	DUMBARTON	34	11	7	16	43	58	29
11	PARTICK T	34	9	10	15	33	46	28
12	ST JOHNSTONE	34	9	10	15	41	60	28
13	ARBROATH	34	10	7	17	52	69	27
14	MORTON	34	8	10	16	37	49	26
15	CLYDE	34	8	9	17	29	65	24
16	DUNFERMLINE ATH	34	8	8	18	43	65	24
17	EAST FIFE	34	9	6	19	26	51	24
18	FALKIRK	34	4	14	16	33	58	22

Season 1974-75

Scottish League Division 1

DATE	OPPONENTS	SCORE	GOALSCORERS	ATTENDANCE
Aug 31	Ayr United	D 1-1	Jardine (pen)	20,000
Sep 7	PARTICK THISTLE	W 3-2	Fyfe 2, Young	25,000
Sep 14	Celtic	W 2-1	McDougall, Jackson	65,000
Sep 21	DUMBARTON	W 3-2	Johnstone 2, Scott	18,000
Sep 28	Kilmarnock	W 6-0	Young 2, Jardine (pen), McKean, Johnstone, McLean	19,609
Oct 5	MORTON	W 2-0	Forsyth, McLean	25,000
Oct 12	Dunfermline	W 6-0	Parlane 5, Johnstone	18,000
Oct 19	CLYDE	W 3-1	Jardine (pen), Fyfe, Johnstone	25,000
Oct 26	Hearts	D 1-1	Jardine (pen)	29,000
Nov 2	St Johnstone	W 2-1	McLean, Young	13,260
Nov 9	DUNDEE	W 1-0	McKean	25,000
Nov 16	Motherwell	W 5-0	Johnstone, Young, MacDonald, Parlane, McKean	19,409
Nov 23	HIBERNIAN	L 0-1		31,500
Nov 30	DUNDEE UNITED	W 4-2	Jardine 2 (1 pen), Parlane, McLean	26,000
Dec 7	Aberdeen	W 2-1	Johnstone, McLean	26,000
Dec 14	ARBROATH	W 3-0	Parlane 2, Jackson	20,000
Dec 21	Airdrie	L 3-4	Jardine 2 (1 pen), Johnstone	19,500
Dec 28	AYR UNITED	W 3-0	McLean, Jardine (pen), Parlane	22,000
Jan 1	Partick Thistle	W 4-0	Jackson, McLean, McDougall, Greig	22,000
Jan 4	CELTIC	W 3-0	Johnstone, McLean, Parlane	71,000
Jan 11	Dumbarton	W 5-1	McLean 3, Parlane, Johnstone	15,800
Feb 1	Morton	D 1-1	Fyfe	17,000
Feb 8	DUNFERMLINE	W 2-0	McLean, MacDonald	23,500
Feb 15	KILMARNOCK	D 3-3	Parlane 3	27,157
Feb 22	Clyde	W 2-1	McKean, O'Hara	20,000
Mar 1	HEARTS	W 2-1	McKean, McLean	40,000
Mar 8	ST JOHNSTONE	W 1-0	Young	42,500
Mar 15	Dundee	W 2-1	McLean, Parlane	22,700
Mar 22	MOTHERWELL	W 3-0	Johnstone 2, Miller	36,500
Mar 29	Hibernian	D 1-1	Stein	38,585
Apr 5	Dundee United	D 2-2	McLean, Johnstone	12,000
Apr 12	ABERDEEN	W 3-2	Johnstone, Stein, Miller (pen)	41,000
Apr 19	Arbroath	W 2-1	Stein, Parlane	6,393
Apr 26	AIRDRIE	L 0-1		65,000

Scottish Cup

Jan 25	Aberdeen	(Rd3) D 1-1	Scott	30,000
Feb 10	ABERDEEN	(R) L 1-2	McKean	53,000

Scottish League Cup

Aug 7	ST JOHNSTONE†	W 3-2	Scott, Jardine, Parlane	25,000
Aug 10	Hibernian†	L 1-3	Scott	23,539
Aug 14	St Johnstone†	W 6-3	Young 2, Jardine 2, Scott, Forsyth	5,800
Aug 17	Dundee†	W 2-0	Jardine, Fyfe	18,548
Aug 24	DUNDEE†	W 4-0	Johnstone 2, Jardine (pen), Scott	35,000
Aug 28	HIBERNIAN†	L 0-1		60,000

†Qualifying Section Two – Rangers finished second and failed to qualify.

League & Cup Appearances

PLAYER	LEAGUE	CUP COMPETITION		TOTAL
		S CUP	SL CUP	
Denny	6 (1)		4 (1)	10 (2)
Forsyth	30	2	5	37
Fyfe	6 (4)	0 (1)	6	12 (5)
Greig	21 (1)		1	22 (1)
Hamilton	2 (1)			2 (1)
Jackson	33	2	5	40
Jardine	34	2	6	43
Johnstone	27	2	6	35
Kennedy	34	2	6	43
MacDonald	29 (1)	2	1	32 (1)
Mathieson			2	2
McDougall	11 (3)	1		12 (3)
McKean	25 (1)	1 (1)		26 (2)
McLean	32 (1)	2	6	40 (1)
Miller	15 (3)	2	4 (1)	21 (4)
O'Hara	2 (1)	0 (1)	1 (1)	3 (4)
Parlane	30 (1)	2	1 (1)	33 (2)
Scott	7 (2)	2	6	15 (2)
Sharp			1	1
Stein	8			8
Young	22 (6)		5 (1)	27 (7)

Goalscorers

PLAYER	LEAGUE	CUP COMPETITION		TOTAL
		S CUP	SL CUP	
Parlane	17		1	18
Johnstone	14		2	16
McLean	15			15
Jardine	9		5	14
Young	6		2	8
McKean	5	1		6
Scott	1	1	4	6
Fyfe	4		1	5
Jackson	3			3
Stein	3			3
Forsyth	1		1	2
MacDonald	2			2
McDougall	2			2
Miller	2			2
Greig	1			1
O'Hara	1			1

Fact File

Rangers undertook an eight-match tour of Canada, New Zealand and Australia in the summer of 1975 with matches in Vancouver, Auckland, Christchurch, Sydney, Brisbane, Melbourne, Adelaide and Perth.

Final Scottish League Div 1 Table

		P	W	D	L	F	A	Pts
1	RANGERS	34	25	6	3	86	33	56
2	HIBERNIAN	34	20	9	5	69	37	49
3	CELTIC	34	20	5	9	81	41	45
4	DUNDEE U	34	19	7	8	72	43	45
5	ABERDEEN	34	16	9	9	66	43	41
6	DUNDEE	34	16	6	12	48	42	38
7	AYR U	34	14	8	12	50	61	36
8	HEARTS	34	11	13	10	47	52	35
9	ST JOHNSTONE	34	11	12	11	41	44	34
10	MOTHERWELL	34	14	5	15	52	57	33
11	AIRDRIEONIANS	34	11	9	14	43	55	31
12	KILMARNOCK	34	8	15	11	52	68	31
13	PARTICK T	34	10	10	14	48	62	30
14	DUMBARTON	34	7	10	17	44	55	24
15	DUNFERMLINE ATH	34	7	9	18	46	66	23
16	CLYDE	34	6	10	18	40	63	22
17	MORTON	34	6	10	18	31	62	22
18	ARBROATH	34	5	7	22	34	66	17

FIRST TEN CLUBS FORMED A NEW PREMIER DIVISION; REMAINING EIGHT PLUS TOP SIX FROM DIVISION 2 FORMED NEW DIVISION 1.

MANAGER: Jock Wallace

CAPTAIN: John Greig

TOP SCORER: Derek Parlane

BIGGEST WIN: 6-0 v Kilmarnock, 28 September 1974, league

HIGHEST ATTENDANCE: 71,000 v Celtic, 4 January 1975, league

MAJOR TRANSFERS IN: Bobby McKean from St Mirren, Colin Stein from Coventry City

MAJOR TRANSFERS OUT: Alfie Conn to Tottenham Hotspur, Dave Smith to Arbroath

Season 1975-76

Scottish League Premier Division

DATE	OPPONENTS	SCORE	GOALSCORERS	ATTENDANCE
Aug 30	CELTIC	W 2-1	Johnstone, Young	69,594
Sep 6	Hearts	W 2-0	Anderson o.g., Murray o.g.	28,000
Sep 13	ST JOHNSTONE	W 2-0	Stein, Johnstone	25,000
Sep 20	HIBERNIAN	D 1-1	Blackley o.g.	37,000
Sep 27	Dundee	D 0-0		15,087
Oct 4	ABERDEEN	W 1-0	McDougall	22,000
Oct 11	Ayr United	L 0-3		20,000
Oct 18	Motherwell	L 1-2	Johnstone	18,925
Nov 1	Celtic	D 1-1	Parlane	60,000
Nov 8	HEARTS	L 1-2	Henderson	30,000
Nov 12	DUNDEE UNITED	W 4-1	Parlane, Johnstone, Jackson, MacDonald	11,000
Nov 15	St Johnstone	W 5-1	Parlane, McKean, McLean, Jardine, McDonald o.g.	9,500
Nov 22	Hibernian	L 1-2	Young	26,547
Nov 29	DUNDEE	W 2-1	Henderson 2	16,500
Dec 6	Aberdeen	L 0-1		19,565
Dec 13	AYR UNITED	W 3-0	Jardine (pen), Henderson, McKean	15,500
Dec 20	MOTHERWELL	W 3-2	Johnstone 2, Henderson	25,000
Dec 27	Dundee United	D 0-0		11,500
Jan 1	CELTIC	W 1-0	Johnstone	57,839
Jan 3	Hearts	W 2-1	Henderson 2	24,000
Jan 10	ST JOHNSTONE	W 4-0	Miller (pen), Hamilton, Johnstone, McKean	20,000
Jan 17	HIBERNIAN	W 2-0	Parlane, McLean	40,000
Jan 31	Dundee	D 1-1	Johnstone	14,407
Feb 7	ABERDEEN	W 2-1	Henderson, MacDonald	35,000
Feb 21	Ayr United	W 1-0	McKean	18,000
Feb 28	Motherwell	W 1-0	Johnstone	25,241
Mar 20	HEARTS	W 3-1	Johnstone, Jackson, McLean	30,000
Mar 27	St Johnstone	W 3-0	Johnstone 2, Greig	9,079
Apr 3	Hibernian	W 3-0	MacDonald, Henderson, Johnstone	18,820
Apr 10	DUNDEE	W 3-0	McKean, Greig, Johnstone	25,000
Apr 14	Aberdeen	D 0-0		17,968
Apr 17	AYR UNITED	W 2-1	MacDonald, Parlane	25,000
Apr 21	MOTHERWELL	W 2-1	McLean, Henderson	27,000
Apr 24	Dundee United	W 1-0	Johnstone	17,000
Apr 26	Celtic	D 0-0		51,000
May 4	DUNDEE UNITED	D 0-0		50,000

Scottish Cup

Jan 24	EAST FIFE	(Rd3)	W 3-0	MacDonald, Henderson, Hamilton	30,000
Feb 14	ABERDEEN	(Rd4)	W 4-1	Johnstone, MacDonald, Henderson, Parlane	60,000
Mar 6	Queen of the South	(QF)	W 5-0	McKean 2, Johnstone 2, Henderson	18,700
Mar 31	Motherwell*	(SF)	W 3-2	Johnstone 2, Miller (pen)	48,915
May 1	Hearts*	(F)	W 3-1	Johnstone 2, MacDonald	85,354

*Played at Hampden Park.

Scottish League Cup

Aug 9	AIRDRIE†		W 6-1	Jardine 3 (2 pens), Stein, Parlane, Miller (pen)	45,000
Aug 13	Clyde†		W 1-0	Johnstone	28,000
Aug 16	MOTHERWELL†		D 1-1	Greig	31,500
Aug 20	CLYDE†		W 6-0	Parlane 2, Jackson, Miller (pen), Young, Johnstone	16,000
Aug 23	Motherwell†		D 2-2	Jardine, Miller (pen)	20,561
Aug 27	Airdrie†		W 2-1	Johnstone, Young	20,000

†Qualifying Section One - Rangers finished top.

Sep 10	QUEEN OF THE SOUTH	(QF/FL)	W 1-0	Johnstone	12,000
Sep 24	Queen of the South	(QF/SL)	D 2-2	Johnstone, MacDonald	7,500
Oct 8	Montrose*	(SF)	W 5-1	Parlane, Johnstone, Miller (pen), Scott, Jardine	20,319
Oct 25	Celtic*	(F)	W 1-0	MacDonald	58,806

*Played at Hampden Park.

European Cup

Sep 17	BOHEMIANS	(Rd1/FL)	W 4-1	Fyfe, O'Hara, Johnstone, Burke o.g.	25,000
Oct 1	Bohemians	(Rd1/SL)	D 1-1	Johnstone	8,000
Oct 22	St Etienne	(Rd2/FL)	L 0-2		28,394
Nov 5	ST ETIENNE	(Rd2/SL)	L 1-2	MacDonald	51,000

League & Cup Appearances

PLAYER	LEAGUE	CUP COMPETITION			TOTAL
		S CUP	SL CUP	E CUP	
Boyd	1				1
Dawson	3	2	1		6
Denny	6 (3)	1 (1)	1		8 (4)
Forsyth	28	5	2	2	37
Fyfe	1 (2)	1	2		4 (2)
Greig	36	5	10	4	55
Hamilton	22	5			27
Henderson	23 (3)	5	0 (2)		28 (5)
Jackson	33	5	10	4	52
Jardine	18 (7)	0 (3)	7	2	27 (10)
Johnstone	32 (1)	4	10	4	50 (1)
Kennedy	11	1	2		14
MacDonald	34 (1)	5	9	3	51 (1)
McCloy	25	5	9	2	41
McDougall	3 (1)	2 (1)			5 (2)
McKean	32 (1)	5	5		42 (1)
McLean	34 (1)	5	9	3	51 (1)
Miller	25 (2)	5	9	3	42 (2)
O'Hara	1 (3)	1 (1)	1		3 (4)
Parlane	17 (7)	1 (2)	9	4	31 (9)
Scott	1 (1)		1		2 (1)
Stein	3 (3)		5 (1)	3	11 (4)
Young	7 (1)		7	3 (1)	17 (2)

Goalscorers

PLAYER	LEAGUE	CUP COMPETITION			TOTAL
		S CUP	SL CUP	E CUP	
Johnstone	16	7	6	2	31
Henderson	10	3			13
MacDonald	4	3	2	1	10
Parlane	5	1	4		10
Jardine	2		5		7
McKean	5	2			7
Miller	1	1	4		6
McLean	4				4
Young	2		2		4
Greig	2		1		3
Jackson	2		1		3
Hamilton	1	1			2
Stein	1		1		2
Fyfe				1	1
McDougall	1				1
O'Hara				1	1
Scott			1		1
Opps' o.gs.	4			1	5

MANAGER: Jock Wallace

CAPTAIN: John Greig

TOP SCORER: Derek Johnstone

BIGGEST WIN: 6-0 v Clyde, 20 August 1975, League Cup

HIGHEST ATTENDANCE: 85,354 v Hearts, 1 May 1976, Scottish Cup

MAJOR TRANSFERS IN: Kenny Watson from Montrose, Iain Munro from Hibs

MAJOR TRANSFERS OUT: Graham Fyfe to Hibs, Ally Scott to Hibs

Final Scottish Premier Division Table

		P	W	D	L	F	A	Pts
1	RANGERS	36	23	8	5	60	24	54
2	CELTIC	36	21	6	9	71	42	48
3	HIBERNIAN	36	18	7	11	55	43	43
4	MOTHERWELL	36	16	8	12	57	49	40
5	HEARTS	36	13	9	14	39	45	35
6	AYR U	36	14	5	17	46	59	33
7	ABERDEEN	36	11	10	15	49	50	32
8	DUNDEE U	36	12	8	16	46	48	32
9	DUNDEE	36	11	10	15	49	62	32
10	ST JOHNSTONE	36	3	5	28	29	79	11

Season 1976-77

Scottish League Premier Division

DATE	OPPONENTS	SCORE	GOALSCORERS	ATTENDANCE
Sep 4	Celtic	D 2-2	Johnstone, Parlane	62,000
Sep 11	KILMARNOCK	D 0-0		23,430
Sep 18	Hibernian	D 1-1	Parlane	19,606
Sep 25	HEARTS	W 4-2	Hamilton, Miller (pen), Parlane, Johnstone	25,000
Oct 2	Ayr United	D 1-1	Parlane	18,000
Oct 15	ABERDEEN	W 1-0	MacDonald	21,800
Oct 23	Motherwell	L 1-3	Hamilton	15,857
Oct 30	Partick Thistle	L 1-2	Watson	16,900
Nov 9	DUNDEE UNITED	W 3-0	Jackson, McKean, Parlane	16,000
Nov 13	Kilmarnock	W 4-0	Jackson 2, McKean, Parlane	14,717
Nov 20	HIBERNIAN	D 1-1	Parlane	24,621
Nov 24	CELTIC	L 0-1		43,500
Nov 27	Hearts	W 1-0	Parlane	19,000
Dec 26	MOTHERWELL	W 1-0	O'Hara	28,000
Jan 1	PARTICK THISTLE	W 1-0	Johnstone	20,000
Jan 8	KILMARNOCK	W 3-0	Parlane 2, O'Hara	18,189
Jan 11	Celtic	L 0-1		60,000
Jan 19	Aberdeen	D 3-3	Miller (pen), MacDonald, Johnstone	25,591
Jan 22	HEARTS	W 3-2	MacDonald 2, Johnstone	19,700
Feb 5	Ayr United	W 2-0	Johnstone, McLean	12,800
Feb 12	DUNDEE UNITED	L 2-3	Jackson, MacDonald	16,000
Feb 16	Hibernian	D 0-0		12,452
Feb 19	ABERDEEN	W 1-0	Miller (pen)	17,000
Mar 5	Motherwell	W 2-0	MacDonald, Watson	15,468
Mar 8	Dundee United	D 0-0		10,250
Mar 15	Partick Thistle	L 3-4	Johnstone, Watson, Parlane	17,000
Mar 19	CELTIC	D 2-2	Parlane 2	55,500
Mar 23	AYR UNITED	D 1-1	Johnstone	10,000
Mar 26	Kilmarnock	L 0-1		8,037
Apr 2	HIBERNIAN	W 2-1	Parlane, Johnstone	11,500
Apr 9	Hearts	W 3-1	Johnstone, Parlane, Jardine (pen)	12,500
Apr 13	PARTICK THISTLE	W 2-1	Johnstone, Jardine (pen)	8,000
Apr 16	AYR UNITED	W 5-1	MacDonald 2, Johnstone, Hamilton, Miller (pen)	10,000
Apr 20	MOTHERWELL	W 4-1	Johnstone, MacDonald, Parlane, Robertson (pen)	8,000
Apr 23	Dundee United	W 1-0	Johnstone	8,000
Apr 30	Aberdeen	L 1-2	Johnstone	13,484

Scottish Cup

Jan 29	FALKIRK	(Rd3) W 3-1	Jardine (pen), Johnstone, MacDonald	17,500
Feb 26	ELGIN CITY	(Rd4) W 3-0	Jackson, McLean (pen), MacDonald	18,000
Mar 12	MOTHERWELL	(QF) W 2-0	McKean, Watson	35,572
Mar 30	Hearts*	(SF) W 2-0	Jackson, Jardine (pen)	23,222
May 7	Celtic*	(F) L 0-1		54,252

Scottish League Cup

Aug 14	ST JOHNSTONE†	W 5-0	Jardine 2, Johnstone, Miller (pen), Henderson	31,000
Aug 18	Hibernian†	D 1-1	Munro	26,000
Aug 21	MONTROSE†	W 4-0	Johnstone 2, Jardine, MacDonald	18,500
Aug 25	HIBERNIAN†	W 3-0	Miller (pen), Jardine, McLean	45,000
Aug 28	Montrose†	W 3-0	Johnstone, Parlane, Jardine	8,000
Sep 1	St Johnstone†	W 1-0	Jardine	4,070

†Qualifying Section Four - Rangers finished top.

Sep 22	CLYDEBANK	(QF/FL) D 3-3	Johnstone, MacDonald, Hamilton	15,000
Oct 6	Clydebank	(QF/SL) D 1-1	Greig	10,000
Oct 18	CLYDEBANK	(R) D 0-0		15,000
Oct 19	Clydebank*	(2R) W 2-1	Parlane, McLean	14,000
Oct 27	Aberdeen#	(SF) L 1-5	MacDonald	20,990

*Played at Firhill. #Played at Hampden Park.

European Cup

Sep 15	FC ZURICH	(Rd1/FL) D 1-1	Parlane	35,000
Sep 29	FC Zurich	(Rd1/SL) L 0-1		28,500

League & Cup Appearances

PLAYER	LEAGUE	S CUP	SL CUP	E CUP	TOTAL
Armour	0 (1)				0 (1)
Dawson	1	1			2
Denny	5	8 (1)	1 (1)		14 (2)
Forsyth	25	5	8	2	40
Greig	30	5	11	2	48
Hamilton	22 (1)	3	2 (2)	1	28 (3)
Henderson	4 (3)		1 (4)		5 (7)
Jackson	30	5	4	1	40
Jardine	36	5	11	2	54
Johnstone	27	5	8	2	42
Kennedy	31	5	4		40
MacDonald	29 (1)	5	11	2	47 (1)
McCloy	5		7	2	14
McDougall	1 (3)	1 (1)			2 (4)
McKean	14 (8)	1	6 (2)	1 (1)	22 (11)
McLean	36	5	10	2	53
Miller	17 (7)		10	2	29 (7)
Morris		1			1
Munro	3 (2)		6		9 (2)
O'Hara	5				5
Parlane	31 (2)	4	11	2	48 (2)
Robertson	7 (4)	1 (1)			8 (5)
Steele	5				5
Stein	1 (1)				1 (1)
Watson	30	5	2 (1)		37 (1)

Goalscorers

PLAYER	LEAGUE	S CUP	SL CUP	E CUP	TOTAL
Johnstone	15	1	5		21
Parlane	16		2	1	19
MacDonald	9	2	3		14
Jardine	2	2	6		10
Jackson	4	2			6
Miller	4		2		6
Hamilton	3		1		4
McKean	2	1	1		4
Watson	3	1			4
McLean	1	1	1		3
O'Hara	2				2
Greig			1		1
Henderson			1		1
Munro			1		1
Robertson	1				1

MANAGER: Jock Wallace

CAPTAIN: John Greig

TOP SCORER: Derek Johnstone

BIGGEST WIN: 5-0 v St Johnstone, 14 August 1976, League Cup

HIGHEST ATTENDANCE: 62,000 v Celtic, 4 September 1976, league

---

Fact File

Rangers' friendly match against Aston Villa at Villa Park on 9 October 1976 was abandoned after 51 minutes because of crowd trouble.

Final Scottish Premier Division Table

		P	W	D	L	F	A	Pts
1	CELTIC	36	23	9	4	79	39	55
2	RANGERS	36	18	10	8	62	37	46
3	ABERDEEN	36	16	11	9	56	42	43
4	DUNDEE U	36	16	9	11	54	45	41
5	PARTICK T	36	11	13	12	40	44	35
6	HIBERNIAN	36	8	18	10	34	35	34
7	MOTHERWELL	36	10	12	14	57	60	32
8	AYR U	36	11	8	17	44	68	30
9	HEARTS	36	7	13	16	49	66	27
10	KILMARNOCK	36	4	9	23	32	71	17

Season 1977-78

Scottish League Premier Division

DATE	OPPONENTS	SCORE	GOALSCORERS	ATTENDANCE
Aug 13	Aberdeen	L 1-3	Russell	21,500
Aug 20	HIBERNIAN	L 0-2		20,800
Aug 27	Partick Thistle	W 4-0	Smith 2, Miller (pen), Russell	18,584
Sep 10	CELTIC	W 3-2	Smith 2, Johnstone	48,788
Sep 17	St Mirren	3-3	Jardine, Cooper, Johnstone	26,000
Sep 24	AYR UNITED	W 2-0	Smith 2	20,000
Oct 1	CLYDEBANK	W 4-1	Cooper 2, Smith 2	13,250
Oct 8	Dundee United	W 1-0	Russell	18,658
Oct 15	Motherwell	W 4-1	Johnstone 3, Smith	20,050
Oct 22	ABERDEEN	W 3-1	Jardine (pen), Smith, MacDonald	40,000
Oct 29	Hibernian	W 1-0	Jardine (pen)	22,750
Nov 5	PARTICK THISTLE	D 3-3	Parlane 2, MacDonald	28,200
Nov 12	Celtic	D 1-1	Johnstone	57,000
Nov 19	ST MIRREN	W 2-1	Johnstone, Miller (pen)	25,000
Nov 26	Ayr United	W 5-0	Johnstone 3, Jackson, Parlane	15,300
Dec 10	DUNDEE UNITED	W 2-0	McLean, Smith	25,000
Dec 17	MOTHERWELL	W 3-1	Smith 2, Johnstone	19,750
Dec 24	Aberdeen	L 0-4		21,000
Dec 31	HIBERNIAN	D 0-0		25,000
Jan 2	Partick Thistle	W 2-1	Johnstone, Smith	30,000
Jan 7	CELTIC	W 3-1	Smith, Greig, Parlane	54,000
Jan 14	St Mirren	W 2-0	Johnstone, Smith	24,300
Feb 4	CLYDEBANK	W 1-0	Johnstone	16,492
Feb 19	Clydebank	W 3-0	Johnstone 2, Cooper	10,000
Feb 25	Motherwell	W 5-3	Johnstone 2, Smith, Cooper, McVie o.g.	20,387
Mar 4	ABERDEEN	L 0-3		34,500
Mar 21	PARTICK THISTLE	W 2-1	MacDonald, Jardine	20,000
Mar 25	Celtic	L 0-2		51,000
Mar 29	Hibernian	D 1-1	Parlane	21,245
Apr 1	ST MIRREN	D 1-1	Johnstone	20,500
Apr 8	Ayr United	W 5-2	Johnstone 2, Smith 2, Greig	13,400
Apr 12	AYR UNITED	D 1-1	Johnstone	12,282
Apr 5	Clydebank	W 2-0	Johnstone 2	9,800
Apr 19	Dundee United	W 1-0	Johnstone	17,293
Apr 22	DUNDEE UNITED	W 3-0	Jackson, Jardine (pen), Cooper	27,050
Apr 29	MOTHERWELL	W 2-0	Jackson, Smith	43,500

Scottish Cup

Jan 28	Berwick	(Rd3)	W 4-2	Jackson 2, Johnstone 2	10,500
Feb 18	STIRLING	(Rd4)	W 1-0	Johnstone	15,500
Mar 11	KILMARNOCK	(QF)	W 4-1	Johnstone, Hamilton, MacDonald, Cooper (pen)	28,000
Apr 5	Dundee United*	(SF)	W 2-0	Johnstone, Greig	25,619
May 6	Aberdeen*	(F)	W 2-1	MacDonald, Johnstone	61,563

*Played at Hampden Park.

Scottish League Cup

Aug 24	ST JOHNSTONE	(Rd2/FL)	W 3-1	Johnstone 2, Miller (pen)	10,000
Sep 3	St Johnstone	(Rd2/SL)	W 3-0	Parlane, Miller (pen), Smith	11,200
Oct 5	ABERDEEN	(Rd2/FL)	W 6-1	Smith 3, Johnstone, Miller (pen), MacDonald	25,000
Oct 26	Aberdeen	(Rd2/SL)	L 1-3	Smith	15,600
Nov 9	DUNFERMLINE	(QF/FL)	W 3-1	McLean 2, Jackson	12,000
Nov 16	Dunfermline	(QF/SL)	W 3-1	Greig, Jardine (pen), Johnstone	8,274
Feb 27	Forfar*	(SF)	W 5-2	Johnstone 2, Parlane 2, MacDonald	12,799
Mar 18	Celtic*	(F)	W 2-1	Cooper, Smith	60,168

*Played at Hampden Park.

European Cup-Winners' Cup

Aug 17	YOUNG BOYS	(PR/FL)	W 1-0	Greig	30,000
Aug 31	Young Boys	(PR/SL)	D 2-2	Johnstone, Smith	21,000
Sep 14	TWENTE ENSCHEDE	(Rd1/FL)	D 0-0		40,000
Sep 28	Twente Enschede	(Rd1/SL)	L 0-3		20,000

Fact File

Colin Stein, who had spent part of the season on loan to Kilmarnock, was offered a free transfer in April 1978 and retired from football at the age of 31.

League & Cup Appearances

PLAYER	LEAGUE	CUP COMPETITION			TOTAL
		S CUP	SL CUP	ECWC	
Cooper	34 (1)	5	8	4	51 (1)
Dawson	1 (1)				1 (1)
Forsyth	31	4	7	4	46
Greig	28 (1)	5	5	2	40 (1)
Hamilton	3 (1)	1	1		5 (1)
Henderson		0 (1)	1		1 (1)
Jackson	35	5	7	4	51
Jardine	32	5	7	4	48
Johnstone	33	5	8	1	47
Kennedy	22	3	6	1	32
MacDonald	34	5	7	3	49
Mackay	1	1	0 (1)		2 (1)
McCloy	14	2	2	3	21
McKean	6 (4)		1 (1)	2 (1)	9 (6)
McLean	29 (2)	5	6	2	42 (2)
Miller	16 (8)	1 (1)	5 (2)	2 (1)	24 (12)
Morris			(1)		0 (1)
Parlane	6 (16)	0 (3)	1 (3)	2	9 (22)
Robertson	2 (1)			1	3 (1)
Russell	33	4	7	4	48
Smith	34 (1)	5	8	3 (1)	50 (2)
Watson	2 (2)	0 (1)	1 (1)	1	4 (4)

Goalscorers

PLAYER	LEAGUE	CUP COMPETITION			TOTAL
		S CUP	SL CUP	ECWC	
Johnstone	25	6	6	1	38
Smith	20	6	1		27
Cooper	6	1	1		8
Parlane	5	3			8
MacDonald	3	2	2		7
Jackson	3	2	1		6
Jardine	5		1		6
Greig	2	1	1	1	5
Miller	2	3			5
McLean	1	2			3
Russell	3				3
Hamilton			1		1
Opps' o.gs.	1				1

MANAGER: Jock Wallace

CAPTAIN: John Greig

TOP SCORER: Derek Johnstone

BIGGEST WIN: 6-1 v Aberdeen, League Cup, 5 October 1977

HIGHEST ATTENDANCE: 61,563 v Aberdeen, Scottish Cup final, 6 May 1978

MAJOR TRANSFERS IN: Davie Cooper from Clydebank, Gordon Smith from Kilmarnock

MAJOR TRANSFERS OUT: Ian McDougall to Dundee, Alex O'Hara to Partick Thistle, Martin Henderson to Philadelphia Furies

Final Scottish Premier Division Table

		P	W	D	L	F	A	Pts
1	RANGERS	36	24	7	5	76	39	55
2	ABERDEEN	36	22	9	5	68	29	53
3	DUNDEE U	36	16	8	12	42	32	40
4	HIBERNIAN	36	15	7	14	51	43	37
5	CELTIC	36	15	6	15	63	54	36
6	MOTHERWELL	36	13	7	16	45	52	33
7	PARTICK T	36	14	5	17	52	64	33
8	ST MIRREN	36	11	8	17	52	63	30
9	AYR U	36	9	6	21	36	68	24
10	CLYDEBANK	36	6	7	23	23	64	19

Scottish League Premier Division

DATE	OPPONENTS	SCORE	GOALSCORERS	ATTENDANCE
Aug 12	ST MIRREN	L 0-1		28,000
Aug 19	Hibernian	D 0-0		23,000
Aug 26	PARTICK THISTLE	D 0-0		24,500
Sep 9	Celtic	L 1-3	Parlane	60,000
Sep 16	ABERDEEN	D 1-1	A.Forsyth (pen)	27,000
Sep 23	Morton	D 2-2	Parlane, Johnstone	16,500
Sep 30	MOTHERWELL	W 4-1	Smith 2, McLean, Johnstone	26,000
Oct 7	DUNDEE UNITED	D 1-1	A.MacDonald	27,000
Oct 14	Hearts	D 0-0		18,159
Oct 21	St Mirren	W 1-0	A.Forsyth (pen)	26,000
Oct 28	HIBERNIAN	W 2-1	A.Forsyth (pen), Smith	24,750
Nov 4	Partick Thistle	L 0-1		20,641
Nov 11	CELTIC	D 1-1	A.Forsyth (pen)	52,330
Nov 18	Aberdeen	D 0-0		26,000
Nov 25	MORTON	W 3-0	Johnstone, Cooper, Smith	21,500
Dec 9	Dundee United	L 0-1		15,247
Dec 16	HEARTS	W 5-3	Johnstone 4, Watson	16,250
Dec 23	ST MIRREN	W 1-0	Johnstone	22,500
Jan 20	Morton	W 2-0	A.MacDonald, Watson	16,500
Feb 10	DUNDEE UNITED	W 1-0	Robertson	23,500
Feb 24	Hearts	L 2-3	Smith, Parlane	16,500
Mar 14	HIBERNIAN	W 1-0	Smith	16,000
Mar 17	Partick Thistle	W 2-0	Cooper, Urquhart	18,685
Mar 27	St Mirren	W 2-1	Urquhart 2	20,000
Apr 7	MORTON	D 1-1	Cooper	15,750
Apr 10	MOTHERWELL	W 3-0	Cooper, A.MacDonald, Smith	12,000
Apr 14	Motherwell	L 0-2		14,612
Apr 21	Dundee United	W 2-1	Dawson, Smith	20,264
Apr 25	Aberdeen	L 1-2	Smith	20,000
Apr 28	HEARTS	W 4-0	Russell 3, Parlane	20,050
May 2	Motherwell	W 2-1	Smith, Jackson	13,052
May 5	CELTIC	W 1-0	A.MacDonald	52,841
May 7	ABERDEEN	W 2-0	Smith, Cooper	32,000
May 21	Celtic	L 2-4	A.MacDonald, Russel	52,000
May 23	PARTICK THISTLE	W 1-0	Johnstone	6,000
May 31	Hibernian	L 1-2	Urquhart	5,000

Scottish Cup

Feb 12	MOTHERWELL	(Rd3) W 3-1	Johnstone, Jackson, Cooper	19,000
Feb 21	KILMARNOCK	(Rd4) D 1-1	A.MacDonald	17,500
Feb 26	Kilmarnock	(R) W 1-0	Urquhart	19,493
Mar 10	DUNDEE	(QF) W 6-3	Jardine (pen), T.Forsyth, Russell, A.MacDonald, Smith,	28,000
Apr 4	Partick Thistle*	(SF) D 0-0		26,232
Apr 16	Partick Thistle*	(R) W 1-0	Johnstone	32,294
May 12	Hibernian*	(F) D 0-0		50,610
May 16	Hibernian*	(R) D 0-0		33,504
May 28	Hibernian*	(2R) W 3-2	Johnstone 2, Duncan o.g.	30,602

*Played at Hampden Park.

Scottish League Cup

Aug 16	ALBION ROVERS	(Rd1/FL) W 3-0	Parlane, Johnstone, Smith	10,000
Aug 23	Albion Rovers	(Rd1/SL) W 1-0	Parlane	6,500
Aug 30	FORFAR	(Rd2/FL) W 3-0	Cooper, McLean, Smith	9,000
Sep 2	Forfar	(Rd2/SL) W 4-1	Smith 2, A.MacDonald, Cooper	5,919
Oct 4	ST MIRREN	(Rd2/FL) W 3-2	Cooper, Miller, Johnstone	20,000
Oct 11	St Mirren	(Rd2/SL) D 0-0		24,000
Nov 8	ARBROATH	(QF/FL) W 1-0	Wells o.g.	10,000
Nov 15	Arbroath	(QF/SL) W 2-1	Smith, Russell	4,000
Dec 13	Celtic*	(SF) W 3-2	Jardine (pen), Jackson, Casey o.g.	49,432
Mar 31	Aberdeen*	(F) W 2-1	A.MacDonald, Jackson	60,000

*Played at Hampden Park.

European Cup

Sep 13	Juventus	(Rd1/FL) L 0-1		70,000
Sep 27	JUVENTUS	(Rd1/SL) W 2-0	A.MacDonald, Smith	44,000
Oct 18	PSV EINDHOVEN	(Rd2/FL) D 0-0		44,000
Nov 1	PSV Eindhoven	(Rd2/SL) W 3-2	A.MacDonald, Johnstone, Russell	29,000
Mar 6	Cologne	(QF/FL) L 0-1		50,000
Mar 22	COLOGNE	(QF/SL) D 1-1	McLean	44,000

Fact File

Rangers won the Tennent Caledonian Cup for the first time, defeating Southampton 4-1 in the final at Ibrox on 6 August 1978.

League & Cup Appearances

PLAYER	LEAGUE	CUP COMPETITION			TOTAL
		S CUP	SL CUP	E CUP	
Armour		0 (2)		0 (2)	0 (4)
Cooper	26 (4)	9	5 (3)	1 (1)	41 (8)
Dawson	23	9	2	2	36
Denny			1 (1)	1	2 (1)
Forsyth A	16	0 (1)	8	4	28 (1)
Forsyth T	17	4	6	6	33
Jackson	28	8	5	5	46
Jardine	35	9	10	6	60
Johnstone	31	8	10	3 (1)	52 (1)
MacDonald A	33	9	9 (1)	6	57 (1)
MacDonald J	0 (2)				0 (2)
Mackay	0 (1)				0 (1)
McCloy	36	9	10	6	61
McLean	34 (1)	8	8	5	55 (1)
Miller	10 (8)	0 (4)	5 (3)	1 (2)	16 (17)
Morris	1				1
Parlane	21 (3)	4	7 (2)	5 (1)	37 (6)
Robertson		0 (2)			0 (2)
Russell	36	9	10	6	61
Smith	31 (2)	6 (2)	8 (2)	6	51 (6)
Strickland	1		1		2
Urquhart	6 (4)	3	3 (2)	1 (1)	13 (7)
Watson	11 (2)	3	3 (1)	2	19 (3)

Goalscorers

PLAYER	LEAGUE	CUP COMPETITION			TOTAL
		S CUP	SL CUP	E CUP	
Smith	11	1	5	1	18
Johnstone	9	4	2	1	16
MacDonald A	5	2	2	2	11
Cooper	5	2	3		10
Russell	4	1	1	1	7
Parlane	4	2			6
Urquhart	4	1			5
Forsyth A	4				4
Jackson	1	1	2		4
McLean	1	1	1		3
Jardine		1	1		2
Watson	2				2
Dawson	1				1
Forsyth T		1			1
Miller			1	1	1
Robertson	1				1
Opps' o.gs.		1	2		3

MANAGER: John Greig

CAPTAIN: Derek Johnstone

TOP SCORER: Gordon Smith

BIGGEST WIN: 4-0 v Hearts, League, 28 April 1979

HIGHEST ATTENDANCE: 70,000 v Juventus, European Cup, 13 September 1978

MAJOR TRANSFERS IN: Alex Forsyth from Manchester United, Billy Urquhart from Inverness Caley

---

Final Scottish Premier Division Table

		P	W	D	L	F	A	Pts
1	CELTIC	36	21	6	9	61	37	48
2	RANGERS	36	18	9	9	52	35	45
3	DUNDEE U	36	18	8	10	56	37	44
4	ABERDEEN	36	13	14	9	59	36	40
5	HIBERNIAN	36	12	13	11	44	48	37
6	ST MIRREN	36	15	6	15	45	41	36
7	MORTON	36	12	12	12	52	53	36
8	PARTICK T	36	13	8	15	42	39	34
9	HEARTS	36	8	7	21	39	71	23
10	MOTHERWELL	36	5	7	24	33	86	17

Season 1979-80

Scottish League Premier Division

DATE	OPPONENTS	SCORE	GOALSCORERS	ATTENDANCE
Aug 11	Hibernian	W 3-1	A.MacDonald, Cooper, Russell	17,731
Aug 18	CELTIC	D 2-2	J.MacDonald, Russell	36,000
Aug 25	Partick Thistle	L 1-2	Johnstone	20,000
Sep 8	ST MIRREN	W 3-1	Johnstone, Smith, Miller (pen)	31,000
Sep 15	Aberdeen	L 1-3	Johnstone	25,000
Sep 22	DUNDEE	W 2-0	Johnstone, Glennie o.g.	25,000
Sep 29	Kilmarnock	L 1-2	Johnstone	15,479
Oct 6	Dundee United	D 0-0		19,464
Oct 13	MORTON	D 2-2	Johnstone 2	25,000
Oct 20	HIBERNIAN	W 2-0	Smith, Miller (pen)	25,000
Oct 27	Celtic	L 0-1		61,000
Nov 3	PARTICK THISTLE	W 2-1	Urquhart 2	18,400
Nov 10	St Mirren	L 1-2	A.Forsyth	17,362
Nov 17	ABERDEEN	L 0-1		18,500
Nov 24	Dundee	L 1-3	Jackson	13,342
Dec 1	KILMARNOCK	W 2-1	Johnstone, Russell	16,557
Dec 8	Morton	W 1-0	Johnstone	14,750
Dec 15	DUNDEE UNITED	W 2-1	Johnstone, Kopel o.g	19,240
Dec 22	Hibernian	L 1-2	McLean	18,740
Dec 29	CELTIC	D 1-1	Johnstone	34,500
Jan 5	ST MIRREN	L 1-2	Jardine (pen)	19,000
Jan 12	Aberdeen	L 2-3	J.MacDonald, Jackson	19,250
Feb 23	MORTON	W 3-1	Russell, Smith, J.MacDonald	28,000
Mar 1	HIBERNIAN	W 1-0	Johnstone	29,500
Mar 12	DUNDEE	W 1-0	Stevens	17,000
Mar 15	PARTICK THISTLE	D 0-0		22,000
Mar 19	Dundee United	D 0-0		9,533
Mar 29	ABERDEEN	D 2-2	Jardine (pen), J.MacDonald	25,000
Apr 2	Celtic	L 0-1		60,000
Apr 5	Dundee	W 4-1	Johnstone 2, Cooper, Smith	12,948
Apr 19	Morton	W 1-0	Russell	15,000
Apr 23	Kilmarnock	L 0-1		8,504
Apr 26	DUNDEE UNITED	W 2-1	Jardine (pen), McLean	19,000
Apr 30	KILMARNOCK	W 1-0	J.MacDonald	7,655
May 3	Partick Thistle	L 3-4	Russell 2, Johnstone	15,000
May 7	St Mirren	L 1-4	Miller	12,000

Scottish Cup

Jan 26	Clyde	(Rd3) D 2-2	Jardine (pen), Jackson	12,500
Jan 30	CLYDE	(R) W 2-0	J.MacDonald 2	12,000
Feb 16	DUNDEE UNITED	(Rd4) W 1-0	Johnstone	29,000
Mar 8	HEARTS	(QF) W 6-1	J.MacDonald 2, Cooper, Jardine (pen), Russell, Johnstone	36,000
Apr 12	Aberdeen*	(SF) W 1-0	Johnstone	50,000
May 10	Celtic*	(F) L 0-1		70,303

*Played at Hampden Park.

Scottish League Cup

Aug 29	Clyde	(Rd2/FL) W 2-1	Dawson, Robertson	5,021
Sep 1	CLYDE	(Rd2/SL) W 4-0	Mackay 2, Smith, O'Neill o.g.	16,000
Sep 26	Aberdeen	(Rd2/FL) L 1-3	Johnstone	22,000
Oct 10	ABERDEEN	(Rd2/SL) L 0-2		35,000

European Cup-Winners' Cup

Aug 21	LILLESTROM	(PR/FL) W 1-0	Smith	25,000
Sep 5	Lillestrom	(PR/SL) W 2-0	A.MacDonald, Johnstone	6,175
Sep 19	FORTUNA DUSSELDORF	(Rd1/FL) W 2-1	A.MacDonald, McLean	36,000
Oct 3	Fortuna Dusseldorf	(Rd1/SL) D 0-0		47,000
Oct 24	Valencia	(Rd2/FL) D 1-1	McLean	61,000
Nov 7	VALENCIA	(Rd2/SL) L 1-3	Johnstone	36,000

MANAGER: John Greig

CAPTAIN: Derek Johnstone

TOP SCORER: Derek Johnstone

BIGGEST WIN: 6-1 v Hearts, Scottish Cup, 8 March 1980

HIGHEST ATTENDANCE: 70,303 v Celtic, Scottish Cup final, 10 May 1980

MAJOR TRANSFERS IN: Gregor Stevens from Leicester City, Ian Redford from Dundee

MAJOR TRANSFERS OUT: Derek Parlane to Leeds United, Jim Denny to Hearts

League & Cup Appearances

PLAYER	LEAGUE	CUP COMPETITION			TOTAL
		S CUP	SL CUP	ECWC	
Cooper	25 (5)	5 (1)	4	4 (2)	38 (8)
Dalziel	1		0 (1)		1 (1)
Dawson	32	5	4	4 (1)	45 (1)
Forsyth A	8		2 (1)		10 (1)
Forsyth T	16	6			22
Jackson	29	5	4	4	42
Jardine	35	6	4	6	51
Johnstone	31 (2)	6	2	6	45 (2)
MacDonald A	23 (3)	1 (2)	4	6	34 (5)
MacDonald J	21 (6)	6	1 (1)		28 (7)
Mackay	0 (2)		1 (1)	0 (1)	1 (4)
McCloy	34	6	4	6	50
McLean	22 (6)	1 (2)	1 (1)	6	30 (9)
Miller	13 (5)	3 (1)	1 (2)	5	22 (8)
Parlane	2 (1)		1	1 (2)	4 (3)
Redford	13				13
Robertson		2	0 (1)		2 (1)
Russell	22 (1)	5	2	3	32 (1)
Smith	20 (10)	4 (1)	3 (1)	6	33 (12)
Stevens	31	6	2		39
Urquhart	4		2		6
Watson	12 (3)	1	4	5 (1)	22 (4)
Young	2				2

Goalscorers

PLAYER	LEAGUE	CUP COMPETITION			TOTAL
		S CUP	SL CUP	ECWC	
Johnstone	15	3	1	2	21
MacDonald J	5	4			9
Russell	7	1			8
Smith	4	1	1		6
Jardine	3	2			5
McLean	2		2		4
Cooper	2	1			3
Jackson	2	1			3
MacDonald A	1		2		3
Miller	3				3
Mackay			2		2
Urquhart	2				2
Dawson			1		1
Forsyth A	1				1
Robertson			1		1
Stevens	1				1
Opps' o.gs.	2	1			3

Fact File

Rangers won the Drybrough Cup pre-season tournament, beating Celtic 3-1 in the final at Hampden on 4 August 1979 with goals from John MacDonald, Sandy Jardine and Davie Cooper.

Final Scottish Premier Division Table

		P	W	D	L	F	A	Pts
1	ABERDEEN	36	19	10	7	68	36	48
2	CELTIC	36	18	11	7	61	38	47
3	ST MIRREN	36	15	12	9	56	49	42
4	DUNDEE U	36	12	13	11	43	30	37
5	RANGERS	36	15	7	14	50	46	37
6	MORTON	36	14	8	14	51	46	36
7	PARTICK T	36	11	14	11	43	47	36
8	KILMARNOCK	36	11	11	14	36	52	33
9	DUNDEE	36	10	6	20	47	73	26
10	HIBERNIAN	36	6	6	24	29	67	18

Season 1980-81

Scottish League Premier Division

DATE	OPPONENTS	SCORE	GOALSCORERS	ATTENDANCE
Aug 9	Airdrie	D 1-1	J.MacDonald	16,000
Aug 16	PARTICK THISTLE	W 4-0	Cooper, McAdam, J.MacDonald, Jardine	25,898
Aug 23	Celtic	W 2-1	Bett, Miller	58,000
Sep 6	Dundee United	W 4-2	Cooper, McAdam. J.MacDonald, Hegarty o.g.	16,269
Sep 13	ABERDEEN	D 1-1	McAdam	34,000
Sep 20	Kilmarnock	W 8-1	J.MacDonald 3, Redford 2 (1 pen), McAdam, Jardine, Bett	15,021
Sep 27	ST MIRREN	W 2-0	Bett, Cooper	30,000
Oct 4	Morton	D 2-2	Miller (pen), McAdam	15,000
Oct 11	HEARTS	W 3-1	McAdam 2, Jefferies o.g.	23,350
Oct 18	AIRDRIE	D 0-0		23,000
Oct 25	Partick Thistle	D 1-1	McAdam	14,250
Nov 1	CELTIC	W 3-0	McAdam 2, J.MacDonald	35,000
Nov 8	St Mirren	D 0-0		17,362
Nov 15	KILMARNOCK	W 2-0	Johnston, Jardine	15,791
Nov 22	Hearts	D 0-0		16,315
Nov 29	MORTON	L 0-1		20,000
Dec 13	Aberdeen	L 0-2		22,500
Dec 20	Kilmarnock	D 1-1	Russell	9,172
Jan 1	PARTICK THISTLE	D 1-1	McAdam	18,000
Jan 3	Airdrie	D 1-1	Dawson	11,800
Jan 10	Morton	W 2-0	J.MacDonald, Redford	13,000
Jan 31	ABERDEEN	W 1-0	Johnston	32,500
Feb 7	Dundee United	L 1-2	J.MacDonald	14,328
Feb 21	Celtic	L 1-3	Johnston	52,800
Feb 28	AIRDRIE	W 2-0	J.MacDonald, Redford	12,200
Mar 14	Hearts	L 1-2	Redford	11,500
Mar 18	DUNDEE UNITED	L 1-4	McAdam	14,000
Mar 21	KILMARNOCK	W 2-0	Redford, Russell	8,488
Mar 28	St Mirren	L 1-2	Dawson	9,988
Apr 1	MORTON	W 4-0	Johnstone 2, Redford, J.MacDonald	7,000
Apr 4	DUNDEE UNITED	W 2-1	Russell, Redford (pen)	16,000
Apr 15	ST MIRREN	W 1-0	Russell	10,000
Apr 18	CELTIC	L 0-1		35,000
Apr 22	Aberdeen	D 0-0		11,500
Apr 25	Partick Thistle	D 1-1	Russell	7,077
May 2	HEARTS	W 4-0	Bett, Russell, Redford, Johnston	8,000

Scottish Cup

Jan 24	Airdrie	(Rd3) W 5-0	Johnstone 2, Stevens, Redford, Bett	16,054
Feb 14	St Johnstone	(Rd4) D 3-3	Redford 2, McAdam	17,595
Feb 18	ST JOHNSTONE	(R) W 3-1	McAdam 2, Stevens	30,000
Mar 7	HIBERNIAN	(QF) W 3-1	Russell, McAdam, J.MacDonald	26,345
Apr 11	Morton*	(SF) W 2-1	Jackson, Russell	27,050
May 9	Dundee United#	(F) D 0-0		53,346
May 12	Dundee United#	(R) W 4-1	J.MacDonald 2, Cooper, Russell	43,099

*Played at Parkhead. #Played at Hampden Park.

Scottish League Cup

Aug 27	Forfar	(Rd2/FL) W 2-0	McAdam 2	4,500
Aug 30	FORFAR	(Rd2/SL) W 3-1	Miller (pen), Johnstone, McAdam (pen)	15,500
Sep 3	ABERDEEN	(Rd3/FL) W 1-0	McAdam	33,000
Sep 24	Aberdeen	(Rd3/SL) L 1-3	McAdam	23,926

Anglo-Scottish Cup

Jul 30	PARTICK THISTLE	(Rd1/FL) W 3-1	J.MacDonald 2, Jardine (pen)	10,000
Aug 6	Partick Thistle	(Rd1/SL) L 2-3	McAdam, Russell	11,000
Oct 13	CHESTERFIELD	(QF/FL) D 1-1	Dalziel	13,000
Oct 28	Chesterfield	(QF/SL) L 0-3		13,914

Fact File

Rangers defeated Arsenal 2-0 at Ibrox on 1 August 1980 in a friendly match to mark the opening of the new Broomloan Road Stand at the Stadium. John MacDonald scored both goals.

League & Cup Appearances

PLAYER	LEAGUE	CUP COMPETITION			TOTAL
		S CUP	SL CUP	AS CUP	
Bett	34	7	4	2	47
Clark	0 (1)				0 (1)
Cooper	17 (8)	1 (4)	4	2	24 (12)
Dalziel				1	1
Dawson	22	7	1		30
Forsyth A	1		2		3
Forsyth T	15 (7)	4	4	3	26 (7)
Jackson	29	5	4	2	40
Jardine	29 (3)	6	4	4	43 (3)
Johnston	21 (6)	6	3 (1)	1	31 (7)
Johnstone	23 (3)	4	2 (1)	4	33 (4)
MacDonald A			0 (1)		0 (1)
MacDonald J	26 (4)	4 (1)	2 (1)	1 (3)	33 (9)
Mackay	0 (6)		1		1 (6)
McAdam	31	4 (1)	4	4	43 (1)
McCloy	26	4	4	4	38
McLean	23 (5)	2	1 (3)	2 (1)	28 (9)
Miller	24 (1)	3 (1)	4	1	32 (2)
Redford	35	7	4	4	50
Russell	23 (5)	6	(1)	3	32 (6)
Stevens	7 (2)	4	(1)	2	13 (3)
Stewart	10	3			13

Goalscorers

PLAYER	LEAGUE	CUP COMPETITION			TOTAL
		S CUP	SL CUP	AS CUP	
McAdam	12	4	5	1	22
MacDonald J	11	3		2	16
Redford	9	3			12
Russell	6	3		1	10
Johnstone	4	2	1		7
Bett	4	1			5
Cooper	3	1			4
Jardine	3			1	4
Miller	2		1		3
Dawson	2				2
Johnston	2				2
Stevens		2			2
Dalziel				1	1
Jackson		1			1
Opps' o.gs.	2				2

MANAGER: John Greig

CAPTAIN: Ally Dawson

TOP SCORER: Colin McAdam

BIGGEST WIN: 8-1 v Kilmarnock, League, 20 September 1980

HIGHEST ATTENDANCE: 58,000 v Celtic, League, 23 August 1980

MAJOR TRANSFERS IN: Jim Bett from Lokeren, Colin McAdam from Partick Thistle, Willie Johnston from Vancouver Whitecaps, Jim Stewart from Middlesbrough

MAJOR TRANSFERS OUT: Gordon Smith to Brighton, Alex MacDonald to Hearts, Billy Urquhart to Wigan

Final Scottish Premier Division Table

		P	W	D	L	F	A	Pts
1	CELTIC	36	26	4	6	84	37	56
2	ABERDEEN	36	19	11	6	61	26	49
3	RANGERS	36	16	12	8	60	32	44
4	ST MIRREN	36	18	8	10	56	47	44
5	DUNDEE U	36	17	9	10	66	42	43
6	PARTICK T	36	10	10	16	32	48	30
7	AIRDRIEONIANS	36	10	9	17	36	55	29
8	MORTON	36	10	8	18	36	58	28
9	KILMARNOCK	36	5	9	22	23	65	19
10	HEARTS	36	6	6	24	27	71	18

Season 1981-82

Scottish League Premier Division

DATE	OPPONENTS	SCORE	GOALSCORERS	ATTENDANCE
Aug 29	Partick Thistle	W 1-0	McLean (pen)	15,352
Sep 5	HIBERNIAN	D 2-2	Bett, Cooper	23,500
Sep 12	St Mirren	D 1-1	MacDonald	15,652
Sep 19	CELTIC	L 0-2		40,900
Oct 3	AIRDRIE	W 4-1	Bett 2, Johnstone, Jardine	12,500
Oct 10	ABERDEEN	D 0-0		30,000
Oct 17	Dundee	W 3-2	MacDonald 2, Russell	11,956
Oct 24	MORTON	D 1-1	Russell	21,000
Oct 31	PARTICK THISTLE	L 0-2		17,000
Nov 7	Hibernian	W 2-1	Bett 2 (1 pen)	14,685
Nov 11	Dundee United	L 0-2		16,138
Nov 14	ST MIRREN	W 4-1	Johnstone, Russell, Bett (pen), Cooper	18,000
Nov 21	Celtic	D 3-3	Dalziel, Bett, MacDonald	48,600
Dec 5	Airdrie	D 2-2	MacDonald, Russell	13,750
Dec 19	DUNDEE	W 2-1	Bett, McAdam	11,000
Jan 9	CELTIC	W 1-0	Bett (pen)	44,000
Jan 16	DUNDEE UNITED	W 2-0	Dalziel, Cooper	23,000
Jan 30	HIBERNIAN	D 1-1	Johnstone	20,000
Feb 17	Partick Thistle	L 0-2		6,513
Feb 20	Dundee United	D 1-1	Dawson	12,945
Feb 27	MORTON	W 3-0	MacDonald, Dalziel, Mackay	10,200
Mar 10	St Mirren	W 3-2	Johnstone 2, Bett (pen)	8,633
Mar 13	ABERDEEN	L 1-3	Johnstone	25,000
Mar 17	Morton	D 0-0		4,579
Mar 20	PARTICK THISTLE	W 4-1	Johnstone, Russell, Bett (pen), MacDonald	13,000
Mar 27	Hibernian	D 0-0		12,390
Mar 31	AIRDRIE	W 1-0	MacDonald	8,000
Apr 10	Celtic	L 1-2	Johnstone	49,144
Apr 14	Dundee	L 1-3	MacDonald	7,975
Apr 17	Airdrie	W 1-0	MacDonald	10,000
Apr 21	Aberdeen	L 1-3	Johnstone	15,700
Apr 24	DUNDEE UNITED	D 1-1	MacDonald	12,000
May 1	Morton	W 3-1	MacDonald 2, Russell	6,500
May 5	ST MIRREN	W 3-0	MacDonald, McAdam, Redford	6,000
May 8	DUNDEE	W 4-0	Dalziel 3, Redford	8,500
May 15	Aberdeen	L 0-4		16,200

Scottish Cup

Feb 6	ALBION ROVERS	(Rd3) W 6-2	Johnstone, MacDonald, Russell, McAdam, McPherson (pen), Redford	9,200
Feb 13	DUMBARTON	(Rd4) W 4-0	Jardine 2, McAdam, Johnstone	15,000
Mar 6	DUNDEE	(QF) W 2-0	Johnstone, McAdam	16,500
Apr 3	Forfar*	(SF) D 0-0		15,878
Apr 6	Forfar*	(R) W 3-1	Johnstone, Bett, Cooper	11,864
May 22	Aberdeen*	(F) L 1-4	MacDonald	53,788

*Played at Hampden Park.

Scottish League Cup

Aug 8	Morton†	D 1-1	McAdam	11,500
Aug 12	DUNDEE†	W 4-1	McAdam, Johnstone, Miller, MacDonald	13,500
Aug 15	RAITH ROVERS†	W 8-1	Redford 4, Russell 2, Jardine, McAdam	18,000
Aug 19	Dundee†	W 2-1	Stevens, McGeachie o.g.	9,124
Aug 22	MORTON†	W 1-0	Johnstone	30,000
Aug 26	Raith Rovers†	W 3-1	Redford, Johnstone, MacDonald	6,000

†Qualifying Section Two - Rangers finished top.

Sep 2	Brechin City	(QF/FL) W 4-0	Russell, Jackson, McLean (pen), Redford	7,000
Sep 23	BRECHIN CITY	(QF/SL) W 1-0	Johnstone	5,000
Oct 7	St Mirren	(SF/FL) D 2-2	McAdam, MacDonald	14,058
Oct 28	ST MIRREN	(SF/SL) W 2-1	Bett (pen), MacDonald	28,000
Nov 28	Dundee United*	(F) W 2-1	Cooper, Redford	53,777

*Played at Hampden Park.

European Cup-Winners' Cup

Sep 16	Dukla Prague	(Rd1/FL) L 0-3		22,500
Sep 30	DUKLA PRAGUE	(Rd1/SL) W 2-1	Bett, MacDonald	35,000

Fact File

Rangers lost 2-0 to Liverpool at Ibrox on 22 December 1981 in a match to mark the completion of the redeveloped stadium.

League & Cup Appearances

PLAYER	LEAGUE	CUP COMPETITION			TOTAL
		S CUP	SL CUP	ECWC	
Bett	35	5	9	2	51
Black	7 (2)		1		8 (2)
Cooper	29 (1)	5	11	1	46 (1)
Dalziel	14 (4)	2 (2)	2		18 (6)
Davies	1 (5)	0 (1)	0 (1)		1 (7)
Dawson	25	6	4 (1)	2	37 (1)
Forsyth	12	7	2		21
Jackson	21	5	4 (1)	1	31 (1)
Jardine	36	6	8	2	52
Johnston	6 (2)		4 (4)	1	11 (6)
Johnstone	27 (1)	4	7 (1)	1 (1)	39 (3)
Lyall	3 (1)				3 (1)
MacDonald	32 (4)	6	6 (4)	1	45 (8)
Mackay	1 (6)	0 (2)	(1)		1 (9)
McAdam	15 (7)	4 (1)	7	2	28 (8)
McClelland	14	3	3	2	22
McCloy	10	2	1		13
McIntyre	0 (1)				0 (1)
McLean	2 (2)	0 (1)	6	1	9 (3)
McPherson		1	1		2
Miller	14 (2)	2 (2)	6 (1)		22 (3)
Redford	20 (12)	4 (1)	8 (3)	0 (2)	32 (18)
Robertson	1 (1)	0 (1)			1 (2)
Russell	32	6	9	2	49
Stevens	13	8	0 (1)		21 (1)
Stewart	26	6	9	1	42

Goalscorers

PLAYER	LEAGUE	CUP COMPETITION			TOTAL
		S CUP	SL CUP	ECWC	
MacDonald	14	2	5	1	22
Johnstone	9	4	3		16
Bett	11	1	1	1	14
Redford	2	1	7		10
Russell	6	1	3		10
McAdam	2	3	4		9
Dalziel	6				6
Cooper	3	1	1		5
Jardine	1	2	1		4
McLean	1		1		2
Dawson	1				1
Jackson			1		1
Mackay	1				1
McPherson		1			1
Miller			1		1
Stevens		1			1
Opps' o.gs.		1			1

MANAGER: John Greig

CAPTAIN: Ally Dawson

TOP SCORER: John MacDonald

BIGGEST WIN: 8-1 v Raith Rovers, League Cup, 15 August 1981

HIGHEST ATTENDANCE: 53,788 v Aberdeen, Scottish Cup final, 22 May 1982

MAJOR TRANSFERS IN: John McClelland from Mansfield Town

Final Scottish Premier Division Table

		P	W	D	L	F	A	PTS
1	CELTIC	36	24	7	5	79	33	55
2	ABERDEEN	36	23	7	6	71	29	53
3	RANGERS	36	16	11	9	57	45	43
4	DUNDEE U	36	15	10	11	61	38	40
5	ST MIRREN	36	14	9	13	49	52	37
6	HIBERNIAN	36	11	14	11	38	40	36
7	MORTON	36	9	12	15	31	54	30
8	DUNDEE	36	11	4	21	46	72	26
9	PARTICK T	36	6	10	20	35	59	22
10	AIRDRIEONIANS	36	5	8	23	31	76	18

Season 1982-83

Scottish League Premier Division

DATE	OPPONENTS	SCORE	GOALSCORERS	ATTENDANCE
Sep 4	Motherwell	D 2-2	Prytz (pen), Redford	19,159
Sep 11	DUNDEE UNITED	D 0-0		22,200
Sep 18	KILMARNOCK	W 5-0	MacDonald 2, Russell, Johnstone, McClelland	17,350
Sep 25	Aberdeen	W 2-1	Johnstone, Prytz	20,300
Oct 2	DUNDEE	D 1-1	Johnstone	18,100
Oct 9	Morton	D 0-0		11,500
Oct 16	St Mirren	D 2-2	Bett, MacKinnon	12,121
Oct 23	HIBERNIAN	W 3-2	Johnstone 2, McNamara o.g.	16,250
Oct 30	Celtic	L 2-3	Prtyz, Cooper	60,408
Nov 6	MOTHERWELL	W 4-0	MacDonald 2, Dalziel 2	17,000
Nov 13	Dundee United	L 2-4	Cooper, Johnstone	16,470
Nov 20	Kilmarnock	D 0-0		9,194
Nov 27	ABERDEEN	L 0-1		27,000
Dec 11	MORTON	D 1-1	Prytz (pen)	9,500
Dec 18	ST MIRREN	W 1-0	MacDonald	10,500
Dec 27	Hibernian	D 0-0		15,900
Jan 1	CELTIC	L 1-2	Black	45,000
Jan 3	Motherwell	L 0-3		11,383
Jan 8	DUNDEE UNITED	W 2-1	Prytz, Kennedy	15,500
Jan 15	KILMARNOCK	D 1-1	MacDonald	11,223
Jan 22	Aberdeen	L 0-2		21,600
Feb 5	DUNDEE	D 1-1	McPherson	8,500
Feb 12	Morton	W 5-0	Bett 2, Kennedy 2, MacDonald	6,900
Feb 26	St Mirren	L 0-1		11,484
Mar 2	Dundee	L 0-1		6,624
Mar 5	HIBERNIAN	D 1-1	Dalziel	10,975
Mar 19	MOTHERWELL	W 1-0	McClelland	18,000
Mar 23	Celtic	D 0-0		51,062
Mar 26	Kilmarnock	W 1-0	MacDonald	6,648
Apr 2	Dundee United	L 1-3	Clark	14,142
Apr 9	ABERDEEN	W 2-1	Redford, Bett	19,800
Apr 23	MORTON	W 2-0	MacDonald, Redford	9,500
Apr 30	ST MIRREN	W 4-0	Bett 2, MacDonald, Clark	9,321
May 4	Dundee	L 1-2	Clark	4,788
May 7	Hibernian	W 2-1	Cooper 2	10,500
May 14	CELTIC	L 2-4	Clark 2	40,500

Scottish Cup

Jan 29	Falkirk	(Rd3) W 2-0	Kennedy, Oliver o.g.	14,700
Feb 19	FORFAR	(Rd4) W 2-1	MacDonald 2	14,500
Mar 12	Queen's Park	(QF) W 2-1	Dalziel, Cooper	13,716
Apr 16	St Mirren*	(SF) D 1-1	Clark	31,102
Apr 19	St Mirren†	(R) W 1-0	Clark	25,725
May 21	Aberdeen†	(F) L 0-1		62,979

*Played at Parkhead. †Played at Hampden Park.

Scottish League Cup

Aug 14	Hibernian†	D 1-1	MacDonald	15,980
Aug 18	AIRDRIE†	W 3-1	Bett, Paterson, Black	9,500
Aug 21	Clydebank†	W 4-1	MacDonald 2, Prytz, McClelland	7,090
Aug 25	Airdrie†	W 2-1	Dalziel, Paterson	6,476
Aug 28	HIBERNIAN†	D 0-0		17,600
Sep 1	CLYDEBANK†	W 3-2	MacDonald, Prytz (pen), Redford	6,300

†Qualifying Section Three – Rangers finished top.

Sep 22	Kilmarnock	(QF/FL) W 6-1	Cooper 4, MacDonald 2	7,903
Oct 6	KILMARNOCK	(QF/SL) W 6-0	MacDonald 2, Johnstone 2, McPherson, Bett (pen)	5,342
Oct 27	HEARTS	(SF/FL) W 2-0	Cooper, Bett	25,500
Nov 10	Hearts	(SF/SL) W 2-1	Bett (pen), Johnstone	18,983
Dec 4	Celtic*	(F) L 1-2	Bett	55,372

*Played at Hampden Park.

UEFA Cup

Sep 15	B.Dortmund	(Rd1/FL) D 0-0		54,000
Sep 29	B.DORTMUND	(Rd1/SL) W 2-0	Cooper, Johnstone	44,500
Oct 20	COLOGNE	(Rd2/FL) W 2-1	Johnstone, McClelland	30,420
Nov 3	Cologne	(Rd2/SL) L 0-5		61,000

Fact File

Derek Ferguson was just 15 years old when he made his first senior appearance for Rangers as a substitute in the 6-3 win over Swansea City at Ibrox on 27 March 1983 in Tom Forsyth's testimonial match.

League & Cup Appearances

PLAYER	LEAGUE	CUP COMPETITION			TOTAL
		S CUP	SL CUP	UEFA	
Bett	35	6	11	4	56
Black	11 (4)	2	5 (1)		18 (5)
Bruce	1				1
Clark	10	3			13
Cooper	26 (5)	5	9	4	44 (5)
Dalziel	7 (8)	2 (2)	2 (1)		11 (11)
Davies	2 (2)	0 (1)	0 (3)		2 (6)
Dawson	24 (1)	5	3 (3)	4	36 (4)
Johnstone	16	1	5	4	26
Kennedy	12 (1)	3	1 (1)		16 (2)
Lyall	2	2 (1)	0 (1)		2 (4)
MacDonald	27 (3)	2 (1)	9 (2)	1 (2)	39 (8)
Mackay	3	0 (2)			2 (5)
MacKinnon	30 (1)	4	11	4	49
McAdam	2 (2)	0 (1)	5 (1)	0 (1)	7 (5)
McClelland	35	6	11	4	56
McCloy	17	6			23
McPherson	15 (5)	2	3	1	21 (6)
Miller		1		0 (1)	1 (1)
Paterson	20	4	9	3	36
Prytz	24 (7)	3 (1)	9	4	42 (8)
Redford	29 (5)	5	10 (1)	3 (1)	47 (7)
Robertson	2 (2)	0 (1)			2 (3)
Russell	18 (3)	3	5	4	30 (3)
Smith	1 (1)	1			2 (1)
Stevens	10	1	2	1 (1)	14 (1)
Stewart	18	11	4		33

Goalscorers

PLAYER	LEAGUE	CUP COMPETITION			TOTAL
		S CUP	SL CUP	UEFA	
MacDonald	10	2	8		20
Bett	6		5		11
Cooper	4	1	5	1	11
Johnstone	6		3	2	11
Clark	5	2			7
Prytz	5		2		7
Dalziel	3	1	1		5
Kennedy	3	1			4
McClelland	2		1	1	4
Redford	3		1		4
Black	1		1		2
McPherson	1		1		2
Paterson			2		2
MacKinnon	1				1
Russell	1				1
Opps' o.gs.	1	1			2

MANAGER: John Greig

CAPTAIN: John McClelland

TOP SCORER: John MacDonald

BIGGEST WIN: 6-0 v Kilmarnock, League Cup, 6 October 1982

HIGHEST ATTENDANCE: 62,979 v Aberdeen, Scottish Cup final, 21 May 1983

MAJOR TRANSFERS IN: Robert Prytz from Malmo, Craig Paterson from Hibs, Dave MacKinnon from Partick Thistle, Sandy Clark from West Ham United

MAJOR TRANSFERS OUT: Willie Johnston to Hearts, Jim Bett to Lokeren

Final Scottish Premier Division Table

		P	W	D	L	F	A	PTS
1	DUNDEE U	36	24	8	4	90	35	56
2	CELTIC	36	25	5	6	90	36	55
3	ABERDEEN	36	25	5	6	76	24	55
4	RANGERS	36	13	12	11	52	41	38
5	ST MIRREN	36	11	12	13	47	51	34
6	DUNDEE	36	9	11	16	42	53	29
7	HIBERNIAN	36	7	15	14	35	51	29
8	MOTHERWELL	36	11	5	20	39	73	27
9	MORTON	36	6	8	22	30	74	20
10	KILMARNOCK	36	3	11	22	28	91	17

Season 1983-84

Scottish League Premier Division

DATE	OPPONENTS	SCORE	GOALSCORERS	ATTENDANCE
Aug 20	ST MIRREN	D 1-1	Prytz (pen)	21,500
Sep 3	Celtic	L 1-2	McCoist	50,662
Sep 10	Hearts	L 1-3	Mitchell	16,173
Sep 17	ABERDEEN	L 0-2		27,500
Sep 24	ST JOHNSTONE	W 6-3	McCoist 2, McClelland, Prytz (pen), Cooper, Clark	12,500
Oct 1	Dundee United	W 2-0	Clark, Hegarty o.g.	16,738
Oct 8	HIBERNIAN	W 1-0	McClelland	21,800
Oct 15	Dundee	L 2-3	Russell, Redford	11,945
Oct 22	MOTHERWELL	L 1-2	McCoist (pen)	15,000
Oct 29	St Mirren	L 0-3		12,068
Nov 5	CELTIC	L 1-2	Clark	42,000
Nov 12	Aberdeen	L 0-3		22,771
Nov 19	DUNDEE UNITED	D 0-0		27,800
Nov 26	St Johnstone	W 1-0	Redford	9,740
Dec 3	HEARTS	W 3-0	Clark 2, MacDonald	22,500
Dec 10	Motherwell	W 3-0	McAdam, Cooper, Mitchell	13,586
Dec 17	DUNDEE	W 2-1	Russell, Williamson	16,500
Dec 27	Hibernian	W 2-0	Williamson, Cooper	20,820
Dec 31	ST MIRREN	D 1-1	Clark	21,200
Jan 7	ABERDEEN	D 1-1	Cooper (pen)	37,500
Jan 21	ST JOHNSTONE	W 2-0	Clark, Russell	18,001
Feb 4	MOTHERWELL	W 2-1	McCoist, Prytz (pen)	17,000
Feb 11	Hearts	D 2-2	McCoist, Williamson	18,063
Feb 25	Dundee	W 3-1	Russell, Cooper, McPherson	11,750
Mar 3	HIBERNIAN	D 0-0		17,000
Mar 6	St Johnstone	W 4-1	Redford, Clark, Davies, McCoist	5,293
Mar 31	Motherwell	W 3-0	Paterson, McPherson, Burns	8,574
Apr 2	CELTIC	L 0-3		53,229
Apr 7	HEARTS	D 0-0		22,000
Apr 21	CELTIC	W 1-0	Williamson	40,260
Apr 28	St Mirren	D 1-1	Williamson	8,092
May 2	DUNDEE UNITED	D 2-2	Clark, Williamson	7,500
May 5	DUNDEE	D 2-2	Redford, Cooper	17,000
May 9	Aberdeen	D 0-0		16,200
May 12	Hibernian	D 0-0		10,567
May 14	Dundee United	W 2-1	Prytz (pen), McCoist	6,457

Scottish Cup

Jan 21	DUNFERMLINE	(Rd3) W 2-1	McAdam, McCoist	17,500
Feb 18	Inverness Caley	(Rd4) W 6-0	Williamson 2, McCoist 2, Redford, Russell	5,500
Mar 10	Dundee	(QF) D 2-2	Russell, McGeachie o.g.	17,097
Mar 17	DUNDEE	(R) L 2-3	McPherson, McClelland	25,000

Scottish League Cup

Aug 24	QUEEN OF THE SOUTH	(Rd2/FL) W 4-0	MacDonald 2, Clark, Prytz (pen)	8,000
Aug 27	Queen of the South	(Rd2/SL) W 4-1	Mitchell, MacKinnon, Cooper, McCoist	7,350
Aug 31	CLYDEBANK†	W 4-0	McCoist 2, Russell, Prytz	8,500
Sep 7	Hearts†	W 3-0	Clark 2, Gauld o.g.	11,287
Oct 5	ST MIRREN†	W 5-0	McCoist 2, Clark, McClelland, Paterson	11,500
Oct 26	HEARTS†	W 2-0	Prytz, Mitchell	12,000
Nov 9	Clydebank†	W 3-0	Cooper, McCoist, McPherson	3,612
Nov 30	St Mirren†	W 1-0	Cooper	5,446

†Qualifying Section Two – Rangers finished top.

Feb 15	Dundee United	(SF/FL) D 1-1	Mitchell	14,569
Feb 22	DUNDEE UNITED	(SF/SL) W 2-0	Clark, Redford	35,950
Mar 25	Celtic*	(F) W 3-2	McCoist 3 (1 pen)	66,369

*Played at Hampden Park.

European Cup-Winners' Cup

Sep 14	Valletta	(Rd1/FL) W 8-0	McPherson 4, Prytz 2 (1 pen), Paterson, MacDonald	18,213
Sep 28	VALLETTA	(Rd1/SL) W 10-0	MacDonald 3 (1 pen), Mitchell 2, Redford 2, Dawson, Mackay, Davies	11,500
Oct 19	PORTO	(Rd2/FL) W 2-1	Clark, Mitchell	27,800
Nov 2	Porto	(Rd2/SL) L 0-1		63,000

MANAGER: John Greig/Jock Wallace

CAPTAIN: John McClelland

TOP SCORER: Ally McCoist

League & Cup Appearances

PLAYER	LEAGUE	CUP COMPETITION			TOTAL
		S CUP	SL CUP	ECWC	
Black			0 (1)		0 (1)
Burns	(5)		0 (2)		0 (7)
Clark	27 (3)	1 (3)	8	3	39 (6)
Cooper	32 (2)	3	9 (1)	4	48 (3)
Davies	0 (3)	0 (1)	0 (1)	1 (1)	1 (6)
Dawson	28	3	10	4	45
Ferguson D	1		1 (1)	0 (2)	2 (3)
Ferguson E	2 (2)				2 (2)
Fleck	1				1
Fraser	7	1			8
Kennedy	0 (2)				(2)
Lyall	1		1		2
MacDonald	2 (16)	1	4 (2)	2 (1)	9 (19)
Mackay	1 (1)		1 (1)	0 (1)	2 (3)
MacKinnon	12 (5)		4	2	18 (5)
McAdam	8	1	1 (1)		10 (1)
McClelland	36	4	11	4	55
McCloy	26	1	10	3	40
McCoist	29 (1)	3 (1)	10	2 (1)	44 (3)
McPherson	32 (4)	3 (1)	9 (1)	4	48 (6)
Mitchell	7 (5)	0 (1)	6 (2)	1 (2)	14 (10)
Munro	2 (3)				2 (3)
Nicholl	17	4	5		26
Paterson	21	1	8	4	34
Prytz	22 (4)	3 (1)	6 (2)	4	35 (7)
Redford	28 (4)	4	7 (1)	3	42 (5)
Russell	27 (4)	4	9 (2)	2	42 (6)
Stevens	1		1		2
Stewart	2		1	1	4
Walker	8	3			11
Williamson	16 (1)	3			19 (1)

Goalscorers

PLAYER	LEAGUE	CUP COMPETITION			TOTAL
		S CUP	SL CUP	ECWC	
McCoist	8	3	9		20
Clark	9		5	1	15
Cooper	6		3		9
Prytz	4		3	2	9
McPherson	2	1	1	4	8
Mitchell	2		3	3	8
Redford	4	1	1	2	8
Williamson	6	2			8
MacDonald	1		2	4	7
Russell	4	2	1		7
McClelland	2		1	1	4
Paterson	1		1	1	3
Davies	1		1		2
McAdam	1	1			2
Burns	1				1
Dawson				1	1
Mackay				1	1
MacKinnon			1		1
Opps' o.gs.	1	1	1		3

Fact File

Rangers defeated Hearts 3-2 at Tynecastle on 15 May 1984 in a testimonial for Alex MacDonald. Kevin Keegan appeared as a guest for Hearts.

Final Scottish Premier Division Table

		P	W	D	L	F	A	Pts
1	ABERDEEN	36	25	7	4	78	21	57
2	CELTIC	36	21	8	7	80	41	50
3	DUNDEE U	36	18	11	7	67	39	47
4	RANGERS	36	15	12	9	53	41	42
5	HEARTS	36	10	16	10	38	47	36
6	ST MIRREN	36	9	14	13	55	59	32
7	HIBERNIAN	36	12	7	17	45	55	31
8	DUNDEE	36	11	5	20	50	74	27
9	ST JOHNSTONE	36	10	3	23	36	81	23
10	MOTHERWELL	36	4	7	25	31	75	15

Season 1984-85

Scottish League Premier Division

DATE	OPPONENTS	SCORE	GOALSCORERS	ATTENDANCE
Aug 11	ST MIRREN	D 0-0		22,398
Aug 18	Dumbarton	W 2-1	McCoist, Redford	9,607
Aug 25	CELTIC	D 0-0		43,500
Sep 1	Dundee	W 2-0	I.Ferguson, Redford	14,156
Sep 8	HIBERNIAN	W 2-0	Paterson, MacDonald	22,601
Sep 15	Aberdeen	D 0-0		23,500
Sep 22	MORTON	W 2-0	McCoist, C.Fraser	16,995
Sep 29	DUNDEE UNITED	W 1-0	Paterson	29,232
Oct 6	Hearts	L 0-1		18,097
Oct 13	St Mirren	W 2-0	Redford, I.Ferguson	14,389
Oct 20	DUMBARTON	D 0-0		16,521
Nov 3	DUNDEE	D 0-0		14,588
Nov 10	Hibernian	D 2-2	C.Fraser, Cooper	14,000
Nov 17	ABERDEEN	L 1-2	Mitchell	44,000
Nov 24	Morton	W 3-1	Redford 2, Dawson	11,000
Dec 1	Dundee United	D 1-1	Mitchell	16,477
Dec 8	HEARTS	D 1-1	Mitchell	16,700
Dec 15	ST MIRREN	W 2-0	C.Fraser, MacDonald	12,763
Dec 22	Celtic	D 1-1	Cooper	43,748
Dec 29	Dumbarton	W 4-2	I.Ferguson, McMinn, Mitchell, Cooper	7,800
Jan 1	CELTIC	L 1-2	Cooper	45,000
Jan 5	Dundee	D 2-2	I.Ferguson 2	11,991
Jan 12	HIBERNIAN	L 1-2	I.Ferguson	18,500
Jan 19	Aberdeen	L 1-5	Prytz	23,000
Feb 2	MORTON	W 2-0	MacDonald, Johnstone	14,121
Feb 9	DUNDEE UNITED	D 0-0		19,370
Feb 23	Hearts	L 0-2		14,004
Mar 2	DUMBARTON	W 3-1	McCoist 2, E.Ferguson	8,424
Mar 16	St Mirren	L 1-2	McCoist	8,608
Mar 23	DUNDEE	L 1-3	McCoist	9,954
Apr 6	ABERDEEN	L 1-2	Prytz	23,437
Apr 20	Morton	W 3-0	McCoist 3	7,000
Apr 27	HEARTS	W 3-1	McCoist, Prytz (pen), Cooper	12,913
May 1	Celtic	D 1-1	McCoist (pen)	40,079
May 4	Dundee United	L 1-2	McCoist	10,251
May 11	Hibernian	L 0-1		7,149

Scottish Cup

Jan 26	Morton	(Rd3) D 3-3	Prytz, MacDonald, McPherson	12,012
Jan 30	MORTON	(R) W 3-1	Mitchell, C.Fraser, MacDonald	18,166
Feb 16	DUNDEE	(Rd4) L 0-1		26,619

Scottish League Cup

Aug 22	FALKIRK	(Rd2) W 1-0	McPherson	10,429
Aug 29	RAITH ROVERS	(Rd3) W 4-0	McCoist 2 (1 pen), Paterson, Redford	10,132
Sep 5	Cowdenbeath	(QF) W 3-1	I.Ferguson, Russell, Redford	9,925
Sep 26	MEADOWBANK	(SF/FL) W 4-0	McCoist 2, I.Ferguson, C.Fraser	12,600
Oct 9	Meadowbank*	(SF/SL) D 1-1	McCoist	5,100
Oct 28	Dundee United†	(F) W 1-0	I.Ferguson	44,698

*Played at Tynecastle. †Played at Hampden Park.

UEFA Cup

Sep 18	Bohemians	(Rd1/FL) L 2-3	McCoist, McPherson	10,000
Oct 3	BOHEMIANS	(Rd1/SL) W 2-0	Paterson, Redford	31,000
Oct 24	Inter Milan	(Rd2/FL) L 0-3		65,591
Nov 7	INTER MILAN	(Rd2/SL) W 3-1	I.Ferguson 2, Mitchell	30,594

MANAGER: Jock Wallace

CAPTAIN: John McClelland/Craig Paterson

TOP SCORER: Ally McCoist

BIGGEST WIN: 4-0 v Raith Rovers, League Cup, 29 August 1984 and v Meadowbank Thistle, League Cup, 26 September 1984

HIGHEST ATTENDANCE: 65,591 v Inter Milan, UEFA Cup, 24 October 1984

MAJOR TRANSFERS IN: Iain Ferguson from Dundee, Cammy Fraser from Dundee, Ted McMinn from Queen of the South, Derek Johnstone from Chelsea

MAJOR TRANSFERS OUT: Sandy Clark to Hearts, John McClelland to Watford

---

League & Cup Appearances

PLAYER	LEAGUE	CUP COMPETITION			TOTAL
		S CUP	SL CUP	UEFA	
Burns	11 (4)	0 (1)			11 (5)
Bruce	1				1
Clark	1	1 (1)	1		3 (1)
Cooper	32	3	5 (1)	3	43 (1)
Dawson	25 (1)		5	4	34 (1)
Durrant	5				5
Ferguson D	7 (1)				7 (1)
Ferguson E	8 (1)				8 (1)
Ferguson I	24 (4)	0 (1)	6	2 (2)	32 (7)
Fleck	1 (7)	0 (2)		0 (1)	1 (10)
Fraser C	27 (1)	3	6	3 (1)	39 (2)
Fraser S	0 (2)				0 (2)
Johnstone	11	1			12
MacDonald	8 (10)	3	0 (1)	0 (1)	11 (12)
MacFarlane	1 (1)	1			2 (1)
MacKinnon	30	3	5	3	41
McClelland	11	5	4		20
McCloy	21	1	3	3	28
McCoist	22 (3)	3	6	3 (1)	34 (4)
McMinn	13 (7)				13 (7)
McPherson	27 (4)	3	4 (2)	4	38 (6)
Mitchell	11 (3)	2 (3)	1 (1)		14 (7)
Munro	13	3	1 (1)		17 (1)
Paterson	22	2	5	4	33
Prytz	17 (4)	2 (1)	1 (1)	2	22 (6)
Redford	24 (2)	1	6	4	35 (2)
Russell	9 (9)	0 (1)	4 (1)	2	15 (11)
Walker	14	2	3	1	20
Williamson	0 (1)				0 (1)

Goalscorers

PLAYER	LEAGUE	CUP COMPETITION			TOTAL
		S CUP	SL CUP	ECWC	
McCoist	12		5	1	18
Ferguson I	6		3	2	11
Redford	5		2	1	8
Mitchell	4	1		1	6
Cooper	5				5
Fraser C	3	1	1		5
MacDonald	3	2			5
Paterson	2		1	1	4
Prytz	3	1			4
McPherson	1	1	1	1	3
Dawson	1				1
Ferguson E	1				1
Johnstone	1				1
McMinn	1				1
Russell			1		1

Fact File

Rangers undertook a three-match trip to the Middle East in March 1985, playing twice in Iraq and once in Jordan.

Final Scottish Premier Division Table

		P	W	D	L	F	A	Pts
1	ABERDEEN	36	27	5	4	89	26	59
2	CELTIC	36	22	8	6	77	30	52
3	DUNDEE U	36	20	7	9	67	33	47
4	RANGERS	36	13	12	11	47	38	38
5	ST MIRREN	36	17	4	15	51	56	38
6	DUNDEE	36	15	7	14	48	50	37
7	HEARTS	36	13	5	18	47	64	31
8	HIBERNIAN	36	10	7	19	38	61	27
9	DUMBARTON	36	6	7	23	29	64	19
10	MORTON	36	5	2	29	29	100	12

Season 1985-86

Scottish League Premier Division

DATE	OPPONENTS	SCORE	GOALSCORERS	ATTENDANCE
Aug 10	DUNDEE UNITED	W 1-0	McCoist	28,035
Aug 17	Hibernian	W 3-1	McCoist, McPherson, Williamson	14,500
Aug 24	HEARTS	W 3-1	Williamson 2, Burns	35,483
Aug 31	Celtic	D 1-1	McCoist	58,365
Sep 7	ST MIRREN	W 3-0	Fleck, Cooper, Burns	27,707
Sep 14	Clydebank	W 1-0	Williamson	9,980
Sep 21	DUNDEE	L 0-1		23,600
Sep 28	ABERDEEN	L 0-3		37,599
Oct 5	Motherwell	W 3-0	McCoist 2, McPherson	12,711
Oct 12	Dundee United	D 1-1	McCoist	15,821
Oct 19	HIBERNIAN	L 1-2	Cooper (pen)	23,478
Oct 26	St Mirren	L 1-2	McCoist	13,911
Nov 2	CLYDEBANK	D 0-0		16,943
Nov 9	CELTIC	W 3-0	Durrant, Cooper, McCoist	42,045
Nov 16	Hearts	L 0-3		23,083
Nov 23	Dundee	L 2-3	McCoist 2	10,798
Dec 7	MOTHERWELL	W 1-0	McCoist	12,872
Dec 14	DUNDEE UNITED	D 1-1	McCoist	17,786
Dec 21	Hibernian	D 1-1	Cooper	10,823
Dec 28	HEARTS	L 0-2		33,410
Jan 1	Celtic	L 0-2		49,812
Jan 4	DUNDEE	W 5-0	McCoist 3, Williamson, Fleck	13,954
Jan 11	CLYDEBANK	W 4-2	Paterson, McPherson, Williamson, McCoist	12,731
Jan 18	ST MIRREN	W 2-0	McCoist, McPherson	17,528
Feb 1	ABERDEEN	D 1-1	Burns	29,887
Feb 8	Motherwell	L 0-1		11,619
Feb 19	Aberdeen	L 0-1		19,500
Feb 22	Dundee United	D 1-1	McCoist	14,644
Mar 1	HIBERNIAN	W 3-1	McCoist 3 (1 pen)	16,574
Mar 15	Dundee	L 1-2	McCoist	10,965
Mar 22	CELTIC	D 4-4	Fraser 2, McCoist, Fleck	41,006
Mar 29	Hearts	L 1-3	McCoist (pen)	24,735
Apr 12	Clydebank	L 1-2	Durrant	7,027
Apr 19	St Mirren	L 1-2	Dawson	9,760
Apr 26	Aberdeen	D 1-1	McMinn	17,000
May 3	MOTHERWELL	W 2-0	McPherson, McCoist (pen)	21,500

Scottish Cup

Jan 25	Hearts	(Rd3) L 2-3	McCoist, Durrant	27,500

Scottish League Cup

Aug 21	CLYDE	(Rd2) W 5-0	Williamson 3 (1 pen), McCoist, Paterson	11,350
Aug 27	Forfar	(Rd3)* D 2-2	Cooper (pen), Williamson *Rangers won 6-5 on penalties.	7,823
Sep 4	Hamilton	(QF) W 2-1	Williamson 2	12,392
Sep 25	Hibernian	(SF/FL) L 0-2		17,916
Oct 9	HIBERNIAN	(SF/SL) W 1-0	Cooper	39,282

UEFA Cup

Sep 18	OSASUNA	(Rd1/FL) W 1-0	Paterson	29,479
Oct 2	Osasuna	(Rd1/SL) L 0-2		25,600

League & Cup Appearances

PLAYER	LEAGUE	CUP COMPETITION			TOTAL
		S CUP	SL CUP	UEFA	
Beattie	5				5
Bell	20 (3)		4	2	26 (3)
Burns	26 (2)	1	4	2	33 (2)
Cooper	28 (4)	1	4	2	35 (4)
Dawson	23 (1)	1	1		25 (1)
Durrant	30	1	5	1	37
Ferguson D	12 (7)	1	0 (1)		13 (8)
Ferguson E	0 (1)				0 (1)
Ferguson I	1 (3)		1 (1)		2 (4)
Fleck	9 (6)		0 (1)		9 (7)
Fraser	7 (1)		0 (1)	1	8 (2)
Johnstone	8		1	1 (1)	10 (1)
MacDonald	2		0 (2)		2 (2)
MacKinnon	18 (6)		2 (1)		20 (7)
McCloy	2				2
McCoist	33	1	4	2	40
McMinn	15 (13)		1 (1)	0 (2)	16 (16)
McPherson	34	1	5	2	42
Miller	2	1			3
Munro	28 (1)		5	2	35 (1)
Nisbet	4 (1)				4 (1)
Paterson	18	4	1	2	25
Russell	17 (10)	0 (1)	4 (1)	2	23 (12)
Walker	34	1	5	2	42
Williamson	20 (3)	1	5	1 (1)	27 (4)

Goalscorers

PLAYER	LEAGUE	CUP COMPETITION			TOTAL
		S CUP	SL CUP	UEFA	
McCoist	25	1	1		27
Williamson	6		6		12
Cooper	4		2		6
McPherson	5				5
Burns	3				3
Durrant	2	1			3
Fleck	3				3
Paterson	1		1	1	3
Fraser	2				2
Dawson	1				1
McMinn	1				1

Fact File

Ally McCoist scored a hat-trick when Rangers defeated Celtic 3-2 at Ibrox on 9 May 1986 in front of a 40,741 crowd in the Glasgow Cup final.

MANAGER: Jock Wallace/Graeme Souness

CAPTAIN: Craig Paterson

TOP SCORER: Ally McCoist

BIGGEST WIN: 5-0 v Clyde, League Cup, 21 August 1985 and v Dundee, League, 4 January 1986

HIGHEST ATTENDANCE: 58,365 v Celtic, League, 31 August 1985

MAJOR TRANSFERS IN: Dougie Bell from Aberdeen

MAJOR TRANSFERS OUT: Robert Prytz to IFK Gothenburg, Ian Redford to Dundee United

Final Scottish Premier Division Table

		P	W	D	L	F	A	Pts
1	CELTIC	36	20	10	6	67	38	50
2	HEARTS	36	20	10	6	59	33	50
3	DUNDEE U	36	18	11	7	59	31	47
4	ABERDEEN	36	16	12	8	62	31	44
5	RANGERS	36	13	9	14	53	45	35
6	DUNDEE	36	14	7	15	45	51	35
7	ST MIRREN	36	13	5	18	42	63	31
8	HIBERNIAN	36	11	6	19	49	63	28
9	MOTHERWELL	36	7	6	23	33	66	20
10	CLYDEBANK	36	6	8	22	29	77	20

Season 1986-87

Scottish League Premier Division

DATE	OPPONENTS	SCORE	GOALSCORERS	ATTENDANCE
Aug 9	Hibernian	L 1-2	McCoist (pen)	24,576
Aug 13	FALKIRK	W 1-0	McCoist (pen)	27,362
Aug 16	DUNDEE UNITED	L 2-3	McCoist 2	43,995
Aug 23	Hamilton	W 2-1	Fraser, West	10,000
Aug 31	CELTIC	W 1-0	Durrant	43,502
Sep 6	Motherwell	W 2-0	Cooper, McPherson	17,013
Sep 13	CLYDEBANK	W 4-0	Fleck 3, McMinn	26,433
Sep 20	Dundee	L 0-1		17,132
Sep 27	ABERDEEN	W 2-0	Souness, McCoist	40,155
Oct 4	Hearts	D 1-1	Cooper	28,637
Oct 8	St Mirren	W 1-0	Cooper	16,861
Oct 11	HIBERNIAN	W 3-0	McPherson, Fleck, Bell	38,196
Oct 18	Falkirk	W 5-1	Fleck 3 (1 pen), Cooper (pen), McCoist	16,800
Oct 29	Dundee United	D 0-0		20,179
Nov 1	Celtic	D 1-1	McCoist	60,000
Nov 8	MOTHERWELL	L 0-1		33,966
Nov 15	Clydebank	W 4-1	McCoist 2, McPherson, Durrant	9,906
Nov 19	DUNDEE	W 2-1	McCoist, McPherson	22,992
Nov 22	Aberdeen	L 0-1		21,733
Nov 29	HEARTS	W 3-0	McCoist, Cooper, Durrant	38,733
Dec 3	ST MIRREN	W 2-0	McPherson, Cooper	23,110
Dec 6	Hibernian	D 0-0		18,536
Dec 13	FALKIRK	W 4-0	Fleck 2, Cooper, Butcher	24,177
Dec 20	Hamilton	W 2-0	Fleck, McCoist	10,000
Dec 27	DUNDEE UNITED	W 2-0	McCoist, Fleck	42,165
Jan 1	CELTIC	W 2-0	Fleck, McCoist	43,206
Jan 6	Motherwell	W 1-0	Roberts	19,658
Jan 10	CLYDEBANK	W 5-0	Fleck 3, McCoist 2 (1 pen)	36,397
Jan 17	HAMILTON	W 2-0	Durrant, McCoist	43,052
Jan 24	ABERDEEN	D 0-0		43,211
Feb 7	Hearts	W 5-2	Fleck 2, Roberts, McCoist, Black o.g	29,000
Feb 14	St Mirren	W 3-1	McCoist 3 (1 pen)	21,399
Feb 28	HIBERNIAN	D 1-1	McPherson	38,630
Mar 7	Falkirk	W 2-1	McCoist 2	18,000
Mar 14	HAMILTON	W 2-0	Cooper, McCoist	33,486
Mar 17	Dundee	W 4-0	McCoist 2, McPherson, Fleck	18,723
Mar 21	Dundee United	W 1-0	McPherson	21,275
Mar 28	MOTHERWELL	W 1-0	McCoist	37,305
Apr 4	Celtic	L 1-3	McCoist	60,800
Apr 14	DUNDEE	W 2-0	Cooper, McCoist	42,427
Apr 18	Clydebank	W 3-0	McCoist 2 (1 pen), West	9,950
Apr 25	HEARTS	W 3-0	McCoist 3 (1 pen)	43,205
May 2	Aberdeen	D 1-1	Butcher	22,568
May 9	ST MIRREN	W 1-0	Fleck	43,510

Scottish Cup

Jan 31	HAMILTON	(Rd3) L 0-1		35,462

Scottish League Cup

Aug 20	Stenhousemuir	(Rd2) W 4-1	Souness, West, Cooper, McCoist	9,052
Aug 27	East Fife	(Rd3) D 0-0		8,835

(Rangers won 5-4 on penalties)

Sep 3	DUNDEE	(QF) W 3-1	Fraser, Souness, McMinn	33,750
Sep 24	Dundee United*	(SF) W 2-1	McCoist, McMinn	45,249
Oct 26	Celtic*	(F) W 2-1	Durrant, Cooper (pen)	74,219

*Played at Hampden Park.

UEFA Cup

Nov 17	ILVES TAMPERE	(Rd1/FL) W 4-0	Fleck 3, McCoist	27,436
Oct 1	Ilves Tampere	(Rd1/SL) L 0-2		2,109
Oct 23	BOAVISTA	(Rd2/FL) W 2-1	McPherson, McCoist	38,772
Nov 4	Boavista	(Rd2/SL) W 1-0	Ferguson	23,000
Nov 26	BORUSSIA MG	(Rd3/FL) D 1-1	Durrant	44,000
Dec 10	Borrusia MG	(Rd3/SL) D 0-0		36,000

Fact File

Between 26 November 1986 and 31 January 1987, Rangers goalkeeper Chris Woods set a new British record of 1,196 minutes without conceding a goal.

League & Cup Appearances

PLAYER	LEAGUE	CUP COMPETITION			TOTAL
		S CUP	SL CUP	UEFA	
Bell	7 (5)			2 (1)	9 (6)
Burns	4		1		5
Butcher	43	1	5	6	55
Cooper	42	1	5	6	54
Dawson	6 (1)		3	1	10 (1)
Durrant	39	1	5	5	50
Ferguson	26 (4)		2 (1)	4	32 (5)
Fleck	35 (5)		1 (3)	3 (1)	39 (9)
Fraser	16		5	3	24
Kirkwood	0 (1)				0 (1)
MacFarlane	2 (2)		0 (1)		2 (3)
McCoist	44	1	5	6	56
McMinn	9 (6)		3 (1)	2 (2)	14 (9)
McPherson	42	1	4	6	53
Miller			0 (1)		0 (1)
Munro	43	1	3 (1)	6	53 (1)
Nicholl	33 (1)	1	4	5	43 (1)
Nisbet	0 (1)			0 (2)	0 (3)
Paterson	2				2
Phillips	0 (6)				0 (6)
Roberts	18	1			19
Russell	1		1		2
Souness	24 (1)	1	3	3	31 (1)
Walker	2				2
West	4 (5)		0 (1)	2 (2)	6 (8)
Woods C	42	1	5	6	54
Woods N	0 (3)				0 (3)

Goalscorers

PLAYER	LEAGUE	CUP COMPETITION			TOTAL
		S CUP	SL CUP	UEFA	
McCoist	34		2	2	38
Fleck	19			3	22
Cooper	9		2		11
McPherson	8			1	9
Durrant	4		1	1	6
McMinn	1		2		3
Souness	1		2		3
West	2		1		3
Butcher	2				2
Fraser	1		1		2
Roberts	2				2
Bell	1				1
Ferguson				1	1
Opps' o.gs.	1				1

MANAGER: Graeme Souness

CAPTAIN: Terry Butcher

MAJOR TRANSFERS IN: Terry Butcher from Ipswich Town, Chris Woods from Norwich City, Graham Roberts from Tottenham, Jimmy Nicholl from West Bromwich Albion

MAJOR TRANSFERS OUT: Ted McMinn to Seville, Craig Paterson to Motherwell, Iain Ferguson to Dundee United, Bobby Williamson to West Bromwich Albion

Final Scottish Premier Division Table

		P	W	D	L	F	A	Pts
1	RANGERS	44	31	7	6	85	23	69
2	CELTIC	44	27	9	8	90	41	63
3	DUNDEE U	44	24	12	8	66	36	60
4	ABERDEEN	44	21	16	7	63	29	58
5	HEARTS	44	21	14	9	64	43	56
6	DUNDEE	44	18	12	14	74	57	48
7	ST MIRREN	44	12	12	20	36	51	36
8	MOTHERWELL	44	11	12	21	43	64	34
9	HIBERNIAN	44	10	13	21	44	70	33
10	FALKIRK	44	8	10	26	31	70	26
11	CLYDEBANK	44	6	12	26	35	93	24
12	HAMILTON A	44	6	9	29	39	93	21

Season 1987-88

Scottish League Premier Division

DATE	OPPONENTS	SCORE	GOALSCORERS	ATTENDANCE
Aug 8	DUNDEE UNITED	D 1-1	McCoist (pen)	39,120
Aug 12	Hibernian	L 0-1		22,000
Aug 15	Aberdeen	L 0-2		22,568
Aug 22	FALKIRK	W 4-0	McCoist 3, Falco	32,340
Aug 29	Celtic	L 0-1		60,800
Sep 5	DUNDEE	W 2-1	Fleck, McCoist	38,302
Sep 12	DUNFERMLINE	W 4-0	McCoist 3, Souness	38,749
Sep 19	Motherwell	W 1-0	Philliben o.g.	19,480
Sep 26	MORTON	W 7-0	McCoist 3, Falco 3, Fleck	35,843
Oct 3	Hearts	D 0-0		29,000
Oct 6	ST MIRREN	W 3-1	Falco, Butcher, Souness	39,298
Oct 10	Dundee United	L 0-1		18,214
Oct 17	CELTIC	D 2-2	McCoist, Gough	44,500
Oct 28	Dunfermline	W 4-0	Durrant 2, McCall (pen), McCoist	18,070
Oct 31	MOTHERWELL	W 1-0	McCoist	36,583
Nov 7	HIBERNIAN	W 1-0	Fleck	37,571
Nov 14	St Mirren	D 2-2	McCoist 2	20,649
Nov 17	ABERDEEN	L 0-1		41,371
Nov 21	Falkirk	W 1-0	Fleck	17,500
Nov 24	Morton	W 3-0	D.Ferguson, Fleck, McCoist	16,500
Nov 28	HEARTS	W 3-2	Fleck, Durrant, Levein o.g.	43,557
Dec 5	DUNDEE UNITED	W 1-0	McCoist (pen)	41,159
Dec 12	Hibernian	W 2-0	Gough, Fleck	21,000
Dec 15	DUNFERMLINE	D 2-2	D.Ferguson, McCoist	31,687
Dec 19	Motherwell	W 2-0	McCoist (pen), Philliben o.g.	15,436
Dec 26	DUNDEE	W 2-0	McCoist 2 (1 pen)	40,938
Jan 2	Celtic	L 0-2		60,800
Jan 6	Dundee	W 1-0	McCoist	17,450
Jan 9	MORTON	W 5-0	McCoist 3, Durrant 2	38,349
Jan 16	Hearts	D 1-1	Durrant (pen)	28,967
Jan 23	FALKIRK	W 3-1	Bartram, Brown, Durrant (pen)	41,088
Feb 6	Aberdeen	W 2-1	McCoist, Gough	22,500
Feb 13	ST MIRREN	W 4-0	Cooper, Walters, Wilkins, Gough	41,664
Feb 27	Dundee United	D 1-1	Walters	20,846
Mar 5	Dunfermline	W 3-0	McCoist (pen), Walters, Gough	19,017
Mar 12	MOTHERWELL	W 1-0	Durrant	39,650
Mar 20	CELTIC	L 1-2	Bartram	43,650
Mar 26	Dundee	W 3-2	Roberts, Walters, Durrant (pen)	14,879
Apr 2	HEARTS	L 1-2	Bartram	41,125
Apr 9	Morton	L 2-3	I.Ferguson, Durrant	12,000
Apr 16	HIBERNIAN	D 1-1	D.Ferguson	32,218
Apr 23	St Mirren	W 3-0	Walters, Brown, McCoist	13,809
Apr 30	ABERDEEN	L 0-1		36,010
May 7	Falkirk	W 5-0	Walters 2, D.Ferguson McCoist 2 (1 pen)	14,500

Scottish Cup

Feb 8	Raith Rovers	(Rd3) D 0-0		9,500
Feb 10	RAITH ROVERS	(R) W 4-1	Durrant 2 (1 pen), Walters, McCoist	35,144
Feb 20	Dunfermline	(Rd4) L 0-2		19,360

Scottish League Cup

Aug 19	Stirling Albion	(Rd2) W 2-1	Falco, McCoist	13,000
Aug 26	Dunfermline	(Rd3) W 4-1	McCoist 3 (1 pen), Falco	18,070
Sep 2	HEARTS	(QF) W 4-1	Falco, McCoist 2 (1 pen)	39,303
Sep 23	Motherwell*	(SF) W 3-1	Fleck, Falco, Kirk o.g.	45,938
Oct 25	Aberdeen*†	(F) D 3-3	Cooper, Durrant, Fleck	71,961

*Played at Hampden Park. †Rangers won 5-3 on penalties.

European Cup

Sep 16	Dinamo Kiev	(Rd1/FL) L 0-1		100,000
Sep 30	DINAMO KIEV	(Rd1/SL) W 2-0	Falco, McCoist	44,500
Oct 21	GORNIK ZABRZE	(Rd2/FL) W 3-1	McCoist, Durrant, Falco	41,366
Nov 4	Gornik Zabrze	(Rd2/SL) D 1-1	McCoist	23,250
Mar 2	Steaua Bucharest	(QF/FL) L 0-2		33,000
Mar 16	STEAUA BUCHAREST	(QF/SL) W 2-1	Gough, McCoist (pen)	44,000

MANAGER: Graeme Souness   **CAPTAIN:** Terry Butcher

MAJOR TRANSFERS IN: Richard Gough from Tottenham, Trevor Francis from Atalanta, Ray Wilkins from PSG, Mark Walters from Aston Villa, John Brown from Dundee, Ian Ferguson from St Mirren

MAJOR TRANSFERS OUT: Robert Fleck to Norwich City, Mark Falco to QPR

League & Cup Appearances

PLAYER	LEAGUE	CUP COMPETITION			TOTAL
		S CUP	SL CUP	E CUP	
Bartram	11	3			14
Brown	9	3			12
Butcher	11		3	4	18
Cohen	4 (3)	0 (2)	2 (1)		6 (6)
Cooper	21 (12)	2 (1)	4	3	30 (13)
Durrant	39 (1)	3	5	6	53 (1)
Falco	9 (5)		2 (1)	2	13 (6)
Ferguson D	31 (1)	3	3	4 (1)	41 (2)
Ferguson I	8				8
Fleck	15 (6)		3 (1)		18 (10)
Francis	8 (10)	0 (1)	1 (1)	2 (2)	11 (14)
Gough	31	2	1	2	36
Kirkwood	3 (1)			1 (2)	4 (3)
MacFarlane	1				1
McCall	8 (4)				8 (4)
McCoist	40	2	5	6	53
McGregor	20 (5)		2 (2)	3	25 (7)
McSwegan	0 (1)				0 (1)
Munro	16 (1)		3	2	21 (1)
Nicholl	21 (1)	1	5	5	32 (1)
Nisbet	22 (3)		1 (1)	2	25 (4)
Phillips	19		4	4	27
Roberts	37	3	5	5	50
Souness	14 (4)	1 (2)	3	6	24 (6)
Walker	5	1			6
Walters	18	3			21
West	0 (1)				0 (1)
Wilkins	24	3	2		29
Woods	39	3	4	6	52

Goalscorers

PLAYER	LEAGUE	CUP COMPETITION			TOTAL
		S CUP	SL CUP	E CUP	
McCoist	31	1	6	4	42
Durrant	10	2	3	1	16
Falco	5		3	2	10
Fleck	7		2		9
Walters	7	1			8
Gough	5			1	6
Ferguson D	4				4
Bartram	3				3
Brown	2				2
Cooper	1		1		2
Souness	2				2
Butcher	1				1
Ferguson I	1				1
McCall	1				1
Roberts	1				1
Wilkins	1				1
Opps' o.gs.	3		1		4

Fact File

Rangers defeated Everton 8-7 on penalties after a 2-2 draw in a match between the reigning Scottish and English champions played in Dubai on 8 December 1987.

Final Scottish Premier Division Table

		P	W	D	L	F	A	Pts
1	CELTIC	44	31	10	3	79	23	72
2	HEARTS	44	23	16	5	74	32	62
3	RANGERS	44	26	8	10	85	34	60
4	ABERDEEN	44	21	17	6	56	25	59
5	DUNDEE U	44	16	15	13	54	47	47
6	HIBERNIAN	44	12	19	13	41	42	43
7	DUNDEE	44	17	7	20	70	64	41
8	MOTHERWELL	44	13	10	21	37	56	36
9	ST MIRREN	44	10	15	19	41	64	35
10	FALKIRK	44	10	11	23	41	75	31
11	DUNFERMLINE ATH	44	8	10	26	41	84	26
12	MORTON	44	3	10	31	27	100	16

Season 1988-89

Scottish League Premier Division

DATE	OPPONENTS	SCORE	GOALSCORERS	ATTENDANCE
Aug 13	Hamilton	W 2-0	Stevens, McCoist	10,500
Aug 20	HIBERNIAN	D 0-0		41,955
Aug 27	CELTIC	W 5-1	McCoist 2, Wilkins, Drinkell, Walters	42,858
Sep 3	Motherwell	W 2-0	Drinkell, Durrant	20,102
Sep 17	Hearts	W 2-1	Durrant (pen), Nisbet	25,501
Sep 24	ST MIRREN	W 2-1	D.Cooper (pen), Walters	35,523
Sep 27	Dundee United	W 1-0	I.Ferguson	20,071
Oct 1	DUNDEE	W 2-0	Drinkell, Walters	40,768
Oct 8	Aberdeen	L 1-2	N.Cooper	23,370
Oct 12	Hibernian	W 1-0	McCoist	26,000
Oct 29	St Mirren	D 1-1	Gray	20,903
Nov 1	HEARTS	W 3-1	Gough, Walters (pen), Gray	36,505
Nov 5	MOTHERWELL	W 2-1	Brown, Drinkell	36,060
Nov 12	Celtic	L 1-3	Walters	60,113
Nov 16	HAMILTON	W 3-1	Gray, I.Ferguson, Drinkell	33,864
Nov 19	Dundee	D 0-0		16,514
Nov 26	ABERDEEN	W 1-0	Gough	42,239
Dec 3	DUNDEE UNITED	L 0-1		39,123
Dec 10	Hearts	L 0-2		26,424
Dec 17	HIBERNIAN	W 1-0	McCall	36,672
Dec 31	Hamilton	W 1-0	D.Ferguson	10,500
Jan 3	CELTIC	W 4-1	Walters 2 (1 pen), Butcher, I.Ferguson	42,515
Jan 7	Motherwell	L 1-2	Drinkell	19,275
Jan 14	Aberdeen	W 2-1	Munro, D.Ferguson	23,000
Feb 11	Dundee United	D 1-1	Munro	22,019
Feb 25	ST MIRREN	W 3-1	I.Ferguson, McCoist, Walters	39,021
Mar 11	HAMILTON	W 3-0	I.Ferguson, Sterland, Gough	35,733
Mar 25	Hibernian	W 1-0	Drinkell	23,321
Apr 1	Celtic	W 2-1	Drinkell, I.Ferguson	60,171
Apr 8	MOTHERWELL	W 1-0	McCoist	33,782
Apr 22	St Mirren	W 2-0	I.Ferguson, McCoist	22,096
Apr 29	HEARTS	W 4-0	Sterland 2, Drinkell 2	42,856
May 2	DUNDEE UNITED	W 2-0	Drinkell, McCoist	39,068
May 6	Dundee	W 2-1	Gray 2	14,889
May 13	ABERDEEN	L 0-3		42,480

Scottish Cup

Jan 28	Raith Rovers	(Rd3) D 1-1	I.Ferguson	10,500
Feb 1	RAITH ROVERS	(R) W 3-0	Walters, Drinkell, Fraser o.g.	40,307
Feb 18	STRANRAER	(Rd4) W 8-0	Drinkell 2, Brown 2, McCoist 2 (1 pen), I.Ferguson, Walters	41,198
Mar 21	DUNDEE UNITED	(QF) D 2-2	Drinkell, McCoist	42,177
Mar 27	Dundee United	(R) W 1-0	McCoist	21,872
Apr 15	St Johnstone*	(SF) D 0-0		47,374
Apr 18	St Johnstone*	(R) W 4-0	Walters, Stevens, Drinkell, McCoist	44,205
May 20	Celtic#	(F) L 0-1		72,069

*Played at Parkhead. #Played at Hampden Park.

Scottish League Cup

Aug 17	Clyde	(Rd2) W 3-0	Drinkell, Walters, D.Ferguson	14,699
Aug 24	CLYDEBANK	(Rd3) W 6-0	McCoist, Gough, Walters, Wilkins, Drinkell, Durrant	34,376
Aug 31	DUNDEE	(QF) W 4-1	McCoist (pen), Walters, I.Ferguson, Forsyth o.g.	39,667
Sep 21	Hearts*	(SF) W 3-0	Walters 2, Nisbet	53,623
Oct 23	Aberdeen*	(F) W 3-2	McCoist 2 (1 pen), I.Ferguson	72,122

*Played at Hampden Park.

UEFA Cup

Sep 7	GKS KATOWICE	(Rd1/FL) W 1-0	Walters	41,120
Oct 5	GKS Katowice	(Rd1/SL) W 4-2	Butcher 2, Durrant, I.Ferguson	40,000
Oct 26	Cologne	(Rd2/FL) L 0-2		42,000
Nov 9	COLOGNE	(Rd2/SL) D 1-1	Drinkell	42,204

Fact File

Rangers defeated Bordeaux 3-1 at Ibrox on 9 August 1988 in Davie Cooper's testimonial match in front of a 43,027 attendance.

League & Cup Appearances

PLAYER	LEAGUE	CUP COMPETITION			TOTAL
		S CUP	SL CUP	UEFA	
Brown	29	6 (1)	5	1	41 (1)
Butcher	34	8	5	4	51
Cooper D	9 (14)	0 (3)	1 (3)	3	13 (20)
Cooper N	11 (3)		2	1	14 (3)
Cowan	3 (1)				3 (1)
Drinkell	32	8	4	3	47
Durrant	8		4	2	14
Ferguson D	12 (4)		4 (1)	2 (1)	18 (6)
Ferguson I	30	6	3	4	43
Gough	35	7	5	4	51
Gray	3 (11)		0 (1)	0 (1)	3 (13)
Kirkwood	2				2
MacDonald	2 (1)				2 (1)
McCall	2 (1)		0 (1)	0 (1)	2 (5)
McCoist	18 (1)	7 (1)	4	2	31 (2)
McGregor				0 (1)	0 (1)
McSwegan	0 (1)				0 (1)
Munro	21 (1)	6 (2)	2	3	32 (3)
Nicholl	1	1	1		3
Nisbet	5 (2)		1 (2)		6 (4)
Robertson	1 (1)				1 (1)
Souness	0 (6)		0 (1)	0 (3)	0 (10)
Sterland	7 (2)		4		11 (2)
Stevens	35	8	5	4	52
Walker	12	2			14
Walters	30 (1)	8	5	4	47 (1)
Wilkins	30 (1)	5 (1)	5	3	43 (2)
Woods	24	6	5	4	39

Goalscorers

PLAYER	LEAGUE	CUP COMPETITION			TOTAL
		S CUP	SL CUP	UEFA	
Drinkell	11	5	2	1	19
McCoist	9	5	4		18
Walters	8	3	5	1	17
Ferguson I	8	2	2	1	13
Gray	5				5
Butcher	2			2	4
Durrant	2		1	1	4
Gough	3		1		4
Brown	1	2			3
Ferguson D	2		1		3
Sterland	3				3
Munro	2				2
Nisbet	1		1		2
Stevens	1	1			2
Wilkins	1		1		2
Cooper D	1				1
Cooper N	1				1
McCall	1				1
Opps' o.gs.		1	1		2

MANAGER: Graeme Souness

CAPTAIN: Terry Butcher

MAJOR TRANSFERS IN: Kevin Drinkell from Norwich City, Gary Stevens from Everton, Neale Cooper from Aston Villa, Mel Sterland from Sheffield Wednesday

MAJOR TRANSFERS OUT: Graham Roberts to Chelsea

Final Scottish Premier Division Table

		P	W	D	L	F	A	PTS
1	RANGERS	36	26	4	6	62	26	56
2	ABERDEEN	36	18	14	4	51	25	50
3	CELTIC	36	21	4	11	66	44	46
4	DUNDEE U	36	16	12	8	44	26	44
5	HIBERNIAN	36	13	9	14	37	36	35
6	HEARTS	36	9	13	14	35	42	31
7	ST MIRREN	36	11	7	18	39	55	29
8	DUNDEE	36	9	10	17	34	48	28
9	MOTHERWELL	36	7	13	16	35	44	27
10	HAMILTON A	36	6	2	28	19	76	14

Season 1989-90

Scottish League Premier Division

DATE	OPPONENTS	SCORE	GOALSCORERS	ATTENDANCE
Aug 12	ST MIRREN	L 0-1		39,951
Aug 19	Hibernian	L 0-2		22,500
Aug 26	Celtic	D 1-1	Butcher	54,000
Sep 9	ABERDEEN	W 1-0	Johnston	40,283
Sep 16	DUNDEE	D 2-2	McCoist 2	35,836
Sep 23	Dunfermline	D 1-1	McCoist	17,765
Sep 30	HEARTS	W 1-0	Johnston	39,554
Oct 3	Motherwell	L 0-1		17,667
Oct 14	DUNDEE UNITED	W 2-1	Johnston, McCoist	36,062
Oct 25	St Mirren	W 2-0	McCoist, Johnston	15,130
Oct 28	HIBERNIAN	W 3-0	McCoist 2, Johnston (pen)	35,260
Nov 4	CELTIC	W 1-0	Johnston	41,598
Nov 18	Dundee	W 2-0	Johnston, Walters	14,536
Nov 22	Aberdeen	L 0-1		22,500
Nov 25	DUNFERMLINE	W 3-0	Johnston, Butcher, McCoist	39,131
Dec 2	Hearts	W 2-1	Walters, Steven	24,771
Dec 9	MOTHERWELL	W 3-1	Butcher, McCoist, Brown	33,549
Dec 16	Dundee United	D 1-1	Johnston	15,947
Dec 23	ST MIRREN	W 1-0	Dodds	31,797
Dec 30	Hibernian	D 0-0		24,500
Jan 2	Celtic	W 1-0	Spackman	54,000
Jan 6	ABERDEEN	W 2-0	Walters, McCoist	41,351
Jan 13	DUNDEE	W 3-0	McCoist, Dodds, Johnston	36,993
Jan 27	Dunfermline	W 1-0	Stevens	17,380
Feb 3	DUNDEE UNITED	W 3-1	Walters, McCoist, Johnston	39,058
Feb 10	Motherwell	D 1-1	Johnston	17,647
Feb 17	HEARTS	D 0-0		41,884
Mar 3	Dundee	D 2-2	Johnston, Dodds	12,743
Mar 17	St Mirren	D 0-0		16,129
Mar 24	HIBERNIAN	L 0-1		37,542
Apr 1	CELTIC	W 3-1	Walters (pen), Johnston, McCoist (pen)	41,926
Apr 8	Aberdeen	D 0-0		23,000
Apr 14	MOTHERWELL	W 2-1	Steven, Johnston	39,305
Apr 21	Dundee United	W 1-0	Steven	15,995
Apr 28	DUNFERMLINE	W 2-0	McCoist, Dodds	40,769
May 5	Hearts	D 1-1	Munro	20,283

Scottish Cup

Jan 20	ST JOHNSTONE	(Rd3) W 3-0	Johnston, Brown, Walters	39,003
Feb 25	Celtic	(Rd4) L 0-1		52,565

Scottish League Cup

Aug 15	ARBROATH	(Rd2) W 4-0	McCoist 3, I.Ferguson	31,762
Aug 23	Morton	(Rd3) W 2-1	Walters, Pickering o.g.	11,821
Aug 30	Hamilton	(QF) W 3-0	Walters 2 (1 pen), Steven	9,162
Sep 19	Dunfermline*	(SF) W 5-0	Steven, Johnston, Walters, McCoist, I.Ferguson	41,643
Oct 22	Aberdeen*	(F) L 1-2	Walters (pen)	61,190
			*Played at Hampden Park.	

European Cup

Sep 13	BAYERN MUNICH	(Rd1/FL) L 1-3	Walters (pen)	40,253
Sep 27	Bayern Munich	(Rd1/SL) D 0-0		40,000

League & Cup Appearances

PLAYER	LEAGUE	CUP COMPETITION			TOTAL
		S CUP	SL CUP	E CUP	
Brown	24 (3)		2	1	27 (3)
Butcher	34	2	5	2	43
Cooper	2 (1)				2 (1)
Cowan	1 (2)			1	2 (2)
Dodds	4 (10)	0 (1)			4 (11)
Drinkell	2 (2)		1 (1)	1	4 (3)
Ferguson D	3 (2)		1 (1)	1	5 (3)
Ferguson I	21 (3)	1	4 (1)	2	28 (4)
Ginzburg	4		3	1	8
Gough	26	1	3	1	31
Johnston	36	2	5	2	45
McCall	2 (2)		0 (1)		2 (3)
McCoist	32 (2)		2	4	38 (2)
Munro	36	2	5	2	45
Nisbet	4 (3)		1	1	6 (3)
Robertson	0 (1)				0 (1)
Souness	0 (1)				0 (1)
Spackman	21		2		23
Steven	34	2	5	2	43
Stevens	35	2	5	2	44
Vinnicombe	1 (6)		0 (2)		1 (8)
Walters	27	2	5	2	36
Wilkins	15		5	2	22
Woods	32	2	2	1	37

Goalscorers

PLAYER	LEAGUE	CUP COMPETITION			TOTAL
		S CUP	SL CUP	E CUP	
McCoist	14		4		18
Johnston	15	1	1		17
Walters	5	1	5	1	12
Steven	3		2		5
Dodds	4				4
Butcher	3				3
Brown	1	1			2
Ferguson I			2		2
Munro	1				1
Spackman	1				1
Stevens	1				1
Opps' o.gs.			1		1

Fact File

Rangers lost 2-1 to Arsenal at Ibrox on 19 December 1989 in a Zenith Data Systems sponsored match for the British Championship. Maurice Johnston scored the Rangers goal in front of a 31,118 attendance.

MANAGER: Graeme Souness

CAPTAIN: Terry Butcher

TOP SCORER: Ally McCoist

BIGGEST WIN: 5-0 v Dunfermline, League Cup, 19 September 1989

HIGHEST ATTENDANCE: 61,190 v Aberdeen, League Cup final, 22 October 1989

MAJOR TRANSFERS IN: Maurice Johnston from Nantes, Trevor Steven from Everton, Nigel Spackman from QPR

MAJOR TRANSFERS OUT: Ray Wilkins to QPR, Kevin Drinkell to Coventry City, Mel Sterland to Leeds United

Final Scottish Premier Division Table

		P	W	D	L	F	A	Pts
1	RANGERS	36	20	11	5	48	19	51
2	ABERDEEN	36	17	10	9	56	33	44
3	HEARTS	36	16	12	8	54	35	44
4	DUNDEE U	36	11	13	12	36	39	35
5	CELTIC	36	10	14	12	37	37	34
6	MOTHERWELL	36	11	12	13	43	47	34
7	HIBERNIAN	36	12	10	14	34	41	34
8	DUNFERMLINE ATH	36	11	8	17	37	50	30
9	ST MIRREN	36	10	10	16	28	48	30
10	DUNDEE	36	5	14	17	41	65	24

Season 1990-91

Scottish League Premier Division

DATE	OPPONENTS	SCORE	GOALSCORERS	ATTENDANCE
Aug 25	DUNFERMLINE	W 3-1	Hateley, Johnston, Walters	39,951
Sep 1	Hibernian	D 0-0		17,500
Sep 8	Hearts	W 3-1	McCoist 2, Huistra	22,101
Sep 15	CELTIC	D 1-1	Hurlock	38,543
Sep 22	Dundee United	L 1-2	Johnston	
Sep 29	MOTHERWELL	W 1-0	Brown	34,863
Oct 6	Aberdeen	D 0-0		19,500
Oct 13	ST MIRREN	W 5-0	McCoist 2 (1 pen), Walters 2, Johnston	38,031
Oct 20	St Johnstone	D 0-0		10,504
Nov 3	HIBERNIAN	W 4-0	Hateley 2, Walters, Steven	35,925
Nov 10	DUNDEE UNITED	L 1-2	McCoist	36,995
Nov 17	Motherwell	W 4-2	Stevens 2, Walters, Johnston	16,457
Nov 20	Dunfermline	W 1-0	Hateley	14,480
Nov 25	Celtic	W 2-1	Johnston, McCoist	52,565
Dec 1	HEARTS	W 4-0	Johnston, Hurlock, McCoist, Walters (pen)	37,623
Dec 8	ST JOHNSTONE	W 4-1	Walters 2, Johnston (pen), Stevens	34,610
Dec 15	St Mirren	W 3-0	Walters, Johnston (pen), Hateley	15,197
Dec 22	ABERDEEN	D 2-2	McCoist 2	37,998
Dec 29	Dundee United	W 2-1	Johnston, Walters	17,564
Jan 2	CELTIC	W 2-0	Walters, Hateley	38,399
Jan 5	Hearts	W 1-0	Hateley	20,956
Jan 12	DUNFERMLINE	W 2-0	Huistra, Johnston	35,120
Jan 19	Hibernian	W 2-0	Johnston, Houchen o.g	15,500
Feb 9	ST MIRREN	W 1-0	McCoist	31,769
Feb 15	MOTHERWELL	W 2-0	McCoist, Hateley	32,192
Feb 25	St Johnstone	D 1-1	Huistra	10,721
Mar 2	Aberdeen	L 0-1		22,500
Mar 9	HEARTS	W 2-1	Steven, Walters	36,128
Mar 24	Celtic	L 0-3		52,000
Mar 30	Dunfermline	W 1-0	Stevens	14,256
Apr 6	HIBERNIAN	D 0-0		35,507
Apr 13	ST JOHNSTONE	W 3-0	Durrant, Spencer, Huistra	35,930
Apr 20	St Mirren	W 1-0	Robertson	18,473
Apr 24	DUNDEE UNITED	W 1-0	Ferguson	32,397
May 4	Motherwell	L 0-3		17,672
May 11	ABERDEEN	W 2-0	Hateley 2	37,652

Scottish Cup

Jan 29	DUNFERMLINE	(Rd3) W 2-0	Huistra, Spackman	29,003
Feb 23	COWDENBEATH	(Rd4) W 5-0	Hateley 2, Nisbet, McCoist, Walters (pen)	29,527
Mar 17	Celtic	(QF) L 0-2		52,286

Scottish League Cup

Aug 21	EAST STIRLING	(Rd2) W 5-0	Hateley 2, Steven, Walters, Johnston	25,595
Aug 28	KILMARNOCK	(Rd3) W 1-0	Johnston	32,671
Sep 4	RAITH ROVERS	(QF) W 6-2	McCoist 3, Johnston, Butcher, Steven	31,320
Sep 26	Aberdeen*	(SF) W 1-0	Steven	40,855
Oct 28	Celtic*	(F) W 2-1	Walters, Gough	62,817

*Played at Hampden Park.

European Cup

Sep 19	Valletta	(Rd1/FL) W 4-0	Johnston 2, McCoist (pen), Hateley	8,000
Oct 2	VALLETTA	(Rd1/SL) W 6-0	Johnston 3 (1 pen), Dodds, Spencer, McCoist	20,627
Oct 24	RS Belgrade	(Rd2/FL) L 0-3		82,500
Nov 7	RS BELGRADE	(Rd2/SL) D 1-1	McCoist	23,831

MANAGER: Graeme Souness/Walter Smith

CAPTAIN: Terry Butcher/Richard Gough   **TOP SCORER:** Maurice Johnston

BIGGEST WIN: 6-0 v Valletta, European Cup, 2 October 1990

HIGHEST ATTENDANCE: 82,500 v Red Star Belgrade, European Cup, 24 October 1990

MAJOR TRANSFERS IN: Mark Hateley from Monaco, Oleg Kuznetsov from Dinamo Kiev, Pieter Huistra from Twente Enschede, Terry Hurlock from Millwall

MAJOR TRANSFERS OUT: Terry Butcher to Coventry City, Derek Ferguson to Hearts, Stuart Munro to Blackburn Rovers

---

League & Cup Appearances

PLAYER	LEAGUE	CUP COMPETITION			TOTAL
		S CUP	SL CUP	E CUP	
Brown	25 (2)	1	4	3 (1)	33 (3)
Butcher	5	3	1		9
Cowan	4 (1)	0 (1)		1	5 (2)
Dodds	3	0 (1)		2	5 (1)
Durrant	3 (1)				3 (1)
Ferguson	10 (1)	1	1 (1)	1	13 (2)
Gough	26	3	5	3	37
Hateley	30 (3)	3	3 (1)	2	38 (4)
Huistra	10 (17)	1 (2)	3 (1)	2	16 (20)
Hurlock	29	2	3 (1)		34 (1)
Johnston	29	2 (1)	4	3	38 (1)
Kuznetsov	2				2
McCoist	15 (11)	1 (1)	4	2 (2)	22 (14)
McSwegan	1 (2)				1 (2)
Munro	14	1	2	4	21
Nisbet	15	3		0 (1)	18 (1)
Reid	3				3
Robertson	7 (8)		1	0 (2)	8 (10)
Spackman	35	2	5	3	45
Spencer	3 (2)			1	4 (2)
Steven	19	3	5	4	31
Stevens	36	3	5	4	48
Vinnicombe	10	1			11
Walters	26 (4)	2	3	4	35 (4)
Woods	36	3	5	4	48

Goalscorers

PLAYER	LEAGUE	CUP COMPETITION			TOTAL
		S CUP	SL CUP	E CUP	
Johnston	11		3	5	19
McCoist	11	1	3	3	18
Hateley	10	2	2	1	15
Walters	12	1	2		15
Huistra	4	1			5
Steven	2		3		5
Stevens	4				4
Hurlock	2				2
Spencer	1			1	2
Brown	1				1
Butcher			1		1
Dodds				1	1
Durrant	1				1
Ferguson	1				1
Gough			1		1
Nisbet		1			1
Robertson	1				1
Spackman			1		1
Opps' o.gs.	1				1

Fact File

Richard Gough was appointed captain of Rangers in November 1990 when Terry Butcher left the club to become player-manager of Coventry City.

Final Scottish Premier Division Table

		P	W	D	L	F	A	Pts
1	RANGERS	36	24	7	5	62	23	55
2	ABERDEEN	36	22	9	5	62	27	53
3	CELTIC	36	17	7	12	52	38	41
4	DUNDEE U	36	17	7	12	41	29	41
5	HEARTS	36	14	7	15	48	55	35
6	MOTHERWELL	36	12	9	15	51	50	33
7	ST JOHNSTONE	36	11	9	16	41	54	31
8	DUNFERMLINE ATH	36	8	11	17	38	61	27
9	HIBERNIAN	36	6	13	17	24	51	25
10	ST MIRREN	36	5	9	22	28	59	19

Season 1991-92

Scottish League Premier Division

DATE	OPPONENTS	SCORE	GOALSCORERS	ATTENDANCE
Aug 10	ST JOHNSTONE	W 6-0	Hateley 3, Johnston 2 (2 pens), Ferguson	35,109
Aug 13	MOTHERWELL	W 2-0	Steven, Maaskant o.g.	35,322
Aug 17	Hearts	L 0-1		22,534
Aug 24	DUNFERMLINE	W 4-0	Huistra, Johnston, Spencer, McCoist	35,559
Aug 31	Celtic	W 2-0	Hateley 2	51,382
Sep 7	Falkirk	W 2-0	Nisbet, Huistra	13,088
Sep 14	DUNDEE UNITED	D 1-1	McCoist	36,347
Sep 21	St Mirren	W 2-1	Huistra, Nisbet	14,503
Sep 28	ABERDEEN	L 0-2		36,330
Oct 5	AIRDRIE	W 4-0	McCoist 2, Nisbet, Johnston	11,101
Oct 8	HIBERNIAN	W 4-2	McCoist 2, Huistra, Tortolano o.g.	35,368
Oct 12	St Johnstone	W 3-2	McCoist 2, Nisbet	10,323
Oct 19	HEARTS	W 2-0	McCoist, Mikhailichenko	36,481
Oct 26	FALKIRK	D 1-1	Johnston	36,441
Oct 29	Dundee United	L 2-3	McCoist 2	15,041
Nov 2	CELTIC	D 1-1	McCoist	37,387
Nov 9	Dunfermline	W 5-0	Gordon 2, Gough, Hateley, McCoist	13,351
Nov 16	AIRDRIE	W 4-0	Hateley 2, D.Robertson, McCoist	36,934
Nov 19	Hibernian	W 3-0	McCoist 2, Hateley	16,833
Nov 23	ST MIRREN	L 0-1		36,272
Nov 30	Motherwell	W 2-0	Gordon, Gough	15,350
Dec 4	Aberdeen	W 3-2	Hateley 2, McCoist	20,081
Dec 7	ST JOHNSTONE	W 3-1	Mikhailichenko, Brown, Hateley	35,784
Dec 14	Falkirk	W 3-1	McCoist, Hateley, McCall	11,801
Dec 21	DUNDEE UNITED	W 2-0	McCoist 2	41,448
Dec 28	DUNFERMLINE	W 2-1	Stevens, Gordon	41,328
Jan 1	Celtic	W 3-1	McCoist, Hateley (pen), Brown	51,789
Jan 4	Airdrie	D 0-0		12,276
Jan 11	HIBERNIAN	W 2-0	Gordon, McCoist	40,616
Jan 18	MOTHERWELL	W 2-0	McCoist, Mikhailichenko	38,217
Feb 1	Hearts	W 1-0	McCoist	24,356
Feb 8	St Mirren	W 2-1	McCoist, Mikhailichenko	16,638
Feb 25	ABERDEEN	D 0-0		38,513
Feb 29	AIRDRIE	W 5-0	Hateley 3 (2 pens), Brown, Rideout	40,568
Mar 10	Hibernian	W 3-1	Hateley 2 (1 pen), McCoist	13,387
Mar 14	Dunfermline	W 3-1	Mikhailichenko 2, Nisbet	12,274
Mar 21	CELTIC	L 0-2		42,160
Mar 28	St Johnstone	W 2-1	Hateley 2	9,697
Apr 7	FALKIRK	W 4-1	McCoist 3, Mikhailichenko	36,832
Apr 11	Dundee United	W 2-1	Mikhailichenko, Brown	11,713
Apr 18	ST MIRREN	W 4-0	McCoist 2, Stevens, Huistra	40,362
Apr 23	Motherwell	W 2-1	Mikhailichenko 2	12,515
Apr 28	HEARTS	D 1-1	McCoist	36,129
May 2	Aberdeen	W 2-0	McCoist 2	16,580

Scottish Cup

Jan 22	Aberdeen	(Rd3) W 1-0	McCoist	23,000
Feb 15	MOTHERWELL	(Rd4) W 2-1	Mikhailichenko 2	38,444
Mar 3	St Johnstone	(QF) W 3-0	McCoist, Gough, Hateley	10,107
Mar 31	Celtic*	(SF) W 1-0	McCoist	45,191
May 9	Airdrie*	(F) W 2-1	Hateley, McCoist	44,045

*Played at Hampden Park.

Scottish League Cup

Aug 20	QUEEN'S PARK	(Rd2) W 6-0	Johnston 4, Durrant, Spackman	32,230
Aug 28	Partick Thistle	(Rd3) W 2-0	Johnston, D.Robertson	12,587
Sep 4	Hearts	(QF) W 1-0	McCoist	22,878
Sep 25	Hibernian*	(SF) L 0-1		40,901

*Played at Hampden Park.

European Cup

Sep 18	Sparta Prague	(QR1/FL) L 0-1		11,053
Oct 2	SPARTA PRAGUE	(QR1/SL) W 2-1	McCall 2	34,260

Fact File

Ally McCoist won the European Golden Boot award as the leading scorer in all European leagues for season 1991-92.

League & Cup Appearances

PLAYER	LEAGUE	CUP COMPETITION			TOTAL
		S CUP	SL CUP	E CUP	
Brown	18 (7)	5	1	1 (1)	25 (8)
Durrant	9 (4)		2	3 (2)	14 (6)
Ferguson	12 (4)	3	1 (1)	1	17 (5)
Gough	33	5	3	1	42
Goram	44	5	4	2	55
Gordon	23	4 (1)			27 (1)
Hateley	29 (1)	2	2	1	34 (1)
Huistra	25 (7)	2 (1)	3 (1)	1	31 (9)
Johnston	10 (1)		4	1	15 (1)
Kuznetsov	16 (2)		1		17 (2)
McCall	35 (1)	3	4	2	44 (1)
McCoist	37 (1)	5	1 (3)	2	45 (4)
McGregor	1				1
McSwegan	0 (4)	0 (1)			0 (5)
Mikhailich'ko	24 (3)	3		1	28 (3)
Morrow	3				3
Nisbet	20		4	2	26
Pressley	0 (1)				0 (1)
Rideout	7 (4)		1 (1)		8 (5)
Robertson D	42	5	4	2	53
Robertson L	1				1
Robertson S	3 (3)		0 (1)		3 (4)
Spackman	42	5	4	2	53
Spencer	4 (4)		2 (1)		6 (5)
Steven	2				2
Stevens	43	5	4	2	54
Vinnicombe	1 (1)				1 (1)

Goalscorers

PLAYER	LEAGUE	CUP COMPETITION			TOTAL
		S CUP	SL CUP	E CUP	
McCoist	34	4	1		39
Hateley	21	2			23
Mikhailich'ko	10	2			12
Johnston	5		5		10
Gordon	5				5
Huistra	5				5
Nisbet	5				5
Brown	4				4
Gough	2	1			3
McCall	1			2	3
Robertson D	1		1		2
Stevens	2				2
Durrant	1		1		2
Ferguson	1				1
Rideout	1				1
Spackman	1		1		1
Spencer	1				1
Steven	1				1
Opps' o.gs.	2				2

MANAGER: Walter Smith **CAPTAIN:** Richard Gough

MAJOR TRANSFERS IN: Andy Goram from Hibernian, Stuart McCall from Everton, Alexei Mikhailichenko from Sampdoria, Dale Gordon from Norwich City

MAJOR TRANSFERS OUT: Chris Woods to Sheffield Wednesday, Mark Walters to Liverpool, Trevor Steven to Marseille, Maurice Johnston to Everton, Terry Hurlock to Southampton

Final Scottish Premier Division Table

		P	W	D	L	F	A	Pts
1	RANGERS	44	33	6	5	101	31	72
2	HEARTS	44	27	9	8	60	37	63
3	CELTIC	44	26	10	8	88	42	62
4	DUNDEE U	44	19	13	12	66	50	51
5	HIBERNIAN	44	16	17	11	53	45	49
6	ABERDEEN	44	17	14	13	55	42	48
7	AIRDRIEONIANS	44	13	10	21	50	70	36
8	ST JOHNSTONE	44	13	10	21	52	73	36
9	FALKIRK	44	12	11	21	54	73	35
10	MOTHERWELL	44	10	14	20	43	61	34
11	ST MIRREN	44	6	12	26	33	73	24
12	DUNFERMLINE ATH	44	4	10	30	22	80	18

Season 1992-93

Scottish League Premier Division

DATE	OPPONENTS	SCORE	GOALSCORERS	ATTENDANCE
Aug 1	ST JOHNSTONE	W 1-0	McCoist	38,036
Aug 4	AIRDRIE	W 2-0	Gordon, Hateley	34,613
Aug 8	Hibernian	D 0-0		17,044
Aug 15	Dundee	L 3-4	McCoist 2, Ferguson	12,807
Aug 22	CELTIC	D 1-1	Durrant	42,239
Aug 29	ABERDEEN	W 3-1	Durrant, McCoist, Mikhailichenko	41,636
Sep 2	Motherwell	W 4-1	McCoist 3, Brown	10,074
Sep 12	Partick Thistle	W 4-1	McPherson, McCall, Gough, Hateley	18,460
Sep 19	HEARTS	W 2-0	McCall, McCoist	41,888
Sep 26	Dundee United	W 4-0	Huistra 2, Steven, McCoist	13,515
Oct 3	FALKIRK	W 4-0	McCoist 4	40,691
Oct 7	St Johnstone	W 5-1	McCoist 2, Hateley 2, Ferguson	9,532
Oct 17	HIBERNIAN	W 1-0	McCoist	40,978
Oct 31	MOTHERWELL	W 4-2	McCoist 3 (1 pen), Brown	38,719
Nov 7	Celtic	W 1-0	Durrant	51,958
Nov 11	DUNDEE	W 3-1	McCoist 2, Hateley	33,497
Nov 21	Hearts	D 1-1	McCoist	20,831
Nov 28	PARTICK THISTLE	W 3-0	Steven, McSwegan, McPherson	40,939
Dec 1	Airdrie	D 1-1	Brown	8,000
Dec 12	Falkirk	W 2-1	Hateley, McCoist	12,000
Dec 19	ST JOHNSTONE	W 2-0	Gough, D.Robertson	35,369
Dec 26	Dundee	W 3-1	Hateley 2, McCoist	13,983
Jan 2	CELTIC	W 1-0	Steven	46,039
Jan 5	DUNDEE UNITED	W 3-2	Hateley, McCall, McCoist	40,239
Jan 30	Hibernian	W 4-3	Hateley 2, Steven, McCoist	17,444
Feb 2	Aberdeen	W 1-0	Hateley	15,500
Feb 9	FALKIRK	W 5-0	Hateley 2, D.Robertson, Steven, Huistra	34,780
Feb 13	AIRDRIE	D 2-2	McCoist 2	39,816
Feb 20	Dundee United	D 0-0		13,234
Feb 23	Motherwell	W 4-0	Hateley 2, McCoist, Mikhailichenko	14,006
Feb 27	HEARTS	W 2-1	McCoist, D.Robertson	42,128
Mar 10	St Johnstone	D 1-1	McCoist	9,210
Mar 13	HIBERNIAN	W 3-0	Hagen, Hateley, McCoist	41,076
Mar 20	Celtic	L 1-2	Hateley	53,241
Mar 27	DUNDEE	W 3-0	McCall, McCoist, Ferguson	40,294
Mar 30	ABERDEEN	W 2-0	Ferguson, McCoist	44,570
Apr 10	MOTHERWELL	W 1-0	Brown	41,353
Apr 14	Hearts	W 3-2	Hateley, McCall	14,622
Apr 17	PARTICK THISTLE	W 3-1	McSwegan 2, Hagen	42,636
May 1	Airdrie	W 1-0	McSwegan	11,830
May 4	Partick Thistle	L 0-3		9,834
May 8	DUNDEE UNITED	W 1-0	Huistra	42,917
May 12	Aberdeen	L 0-1		13,500
May 15	Falkirk	W 2-1	Mikhailichenko, Hateley	8,517

Scottish Cup

Jan 9	Motherwell	(Rd3) W 2-0	McCoist 2	14,314
Feb 6	Ayr United	(Rd4) W 2-0	McCoist, Gordon	13,176
Mar 6	Arbroath	(QF) W 3-0	Hateley, Murray, McCoist (pen)	6,488
Apr 3	Hearts*	(SF) W 2-1	McPherson, McCoist	41,738
May 29	Aberdeen*	(F) W 2-1	Murray, Hateley	50,715

*Played at Parkhead.

Scottish League Cup

Aug 11	Dumbarton	(Rd2) W 5-0	Durrant, Gordon, Hateley, McCoist, Mikhailichenko	11,091
Aug 19	Stranraer	(Rd3) W 5-0	McCoist 3, Hateley 2	4,500
Aug 26	Dundee United	(QF) W 3-2	McCoist, Gough, Huistra	15,716
Sep 22	St Johnstone*	(SF) W 3-1	McCoist 3	30,062
Oct 25	Aberdeen*	(F) W 2-1	McCall, Smith o.g.	45,298

*Played at Hampden Park.

European Cup

Sep 16	LYNGBY	(PR-1-1) W 2-0	Hateley, Huistra	40,036
Sep 30	Lyngby	(PR-1-2) W 1-0	Durrant	4,273
Oct 21	LEEDS UTD	(QR1/FL) W 2-1	McCoist, Lukic o.g.	43,251
Nov 4	Leeds Utd	(QR1/SL) W 2-1	Hateley, McCoist	25,118
Nov 25	MARSEILLE	(Gp A) D 2-2	McSwegan, Hateley	41,624
Dec 9	CSKA Moscow*	(Gp A) W 1-0	Ferguson	9,000
Mar 3	Bruges	(Gp A) D 1-1	Huistra	19,000
Mar 17	BRUGES	(Gp A) W 2-1	Durrant, Nisbet	42,731
Apr 7	Marseille	(Gp A) D 1-1	Durrant	46,000
Apr 21	CSKA MOSCOW†	(Gp A) D 0-0		43,142

*Played in Bochum, Germany. †Rangers failed to qualify from Group A.

League & Cup Appearances

PLAYER	LEAGUE	CUP COMPETITION			TOTAL
		S CUP	SL CUP	E CUP	
Brown	39	5	3 (2)	10	57
Durrant	19 (11)	1 (2)	5	9	34 (13)
Ferguson	29 (1)	2	4	7	42 (1)
Goram	34	4	4	10	52
Gordon	18 (4)	2	1 (1)	1	22 (5)
Gough	25	2	5	7	39
Hagen	5 (3)		1	0 (1)	6 (4)
Hateley	36 (1)	5	4	8	53 (1)
Huistra	27 (3)	2 (1)	3	5 (1)	37 (5)
Kuznetsov	8 (1)				8 (1)
Maxwell	10	1	1		12
McCall	35 (1)	5	4	9	53 (1)
McCoist	32 (2)	4	5	9	50 (2)
McPherson	34	4	5	10	53
McSwegan	8 (1)	0 (1)	1	(3)	9 (5)
Mikhailich'ko	16 (13)	3	1 (1)	4 (1)	24 (15)
Murray	11 (5)	2	1	3 (1)	17 (6)
Nisbet	10	3	1 (1)	2	16 (1)
Pressley	8	0 (1)	(2)		8 (3)
Reid	2				2
Rideout	0 (1)	0 (1)			0 (2)
Robertson D	39	5	5	9	58
Robertson L	1				1
Robertson S	0 (2)				0 (2)
Spackman	2		1		3
Steven	24	3	1 (1)	7	35 (1)
Stevens	9	1			10
Watson	3				3

Goalscorers

PLAYER	LEAGUE	CUP COMPETITION			TOTAL
		S CUP	SL CUP	E CUP	
McCoist	34	5	8	2	49
Hateley	21	2	3	3	29
Durrant	3		1	3	7
Huistra	4		1	2	7
McCall	5		1		6
Ferguson	4			1	5
McSwegan	4			1	5
Steven	5				5
Brown	4				4
Mikhailich'ko	3			1	4
Gordon	1	1	1		3
Gough	2		1		3
McPherson	2	1			3
Robertson D	3				3
Hagen	2				2
Murray	2				2
Nisbet				1	1
Opps' o.gs.			1	1	2

MANAGER: Walter Smith

CAPTAIN: Richard Gough

MAJOR TRANSFERS IN: Dave McPherson from Hearts, Ally Maxwell from Motherwell, Trevor Steven from Marseille

MAJOR TRANSFERS OUT: Nigel Spackman to Chelsea, John Spencer to Chelsea, Paul Rideout to Everton

Final Scottish Premier Division Table

		P	W	D	L	F	A	PTS
1	RANGERS	44	33	7	4	97	35	73
2	ABERDEEN	44	27	10	7	87	36	64
3	CELTIC	44	24	12	8	68	41	60
4	DUNDEE U	44	19	9	16	56	49	47
5	HEARTS	44	15	14	15	46	51	44
6	ST JOHNSTONE	44	10	20	14	52	66	40
7	HIBERNIAN	44	12	13	19	54	64	37
8	PARTICK T	44	12	12	20	50	71	36
9	MOTHERWELL	44	11	13	20	46	62	35
10	DUNDEE	44	11	12	21	48	68	34
11	FALKIRK	44	11	7	26	60	86	29
12	AIRDRIEONIANS	44	6	17	21	35	70	29

Season 1993-94

Scottish League Premier Division

DATE	OPPONENTS	SCORE	GOALSCORERS	ATTENDANCE
Aug 7	HEARTS	W 2-1	Hagen, Hateley	43,261
Aug 14	St Johnstone	W 2-1	Gough, I.Ferguson	10,152
Aug 21	Celtic	D 0-0		47,942
Aug 28	KILMARNOCK	L 1-2	Pressley	44,243
Sep 4	Dundee	D 1-1	Hateley	14,211
Sep 11	PARTICK THISTLE	D 1-1	Hateley	40,988
Sep 18	Aberdeen	L 0-2		19,138
Sep 25	HIBERNIAN	W 2-1	Steven, Hateley	43,200
Oct 2	Raith Rovers	D 1-1	Hetherston o.g.	8,161
Oct 6	MOTHERWELL	L 1-2	I.Ferguson	39,816
Oct 9	Dundee United	W 3-1	Huistra 2, Hateley	11,262
Oct 16	ST JOHNSTONE	W 2-0	Huistra, Hateley	41,960
Oct 30	CELTIC	L 1-2	McCoist	47,522
Nov 3	Hearts	D 2-2	Hateley 2	18,370
Nov 6	Kilmarnock	W 2-0	I.Ferguson, Huistra	19,162
Nov 10	DUNDEE	W 3-1	McCoist 2 (1 pen), I.Ferguson	38,477
Nov 13	RAITH ROVERS	D 2-2	Hateley 2	42,611
Nov 20	Hibernian	W 1-0	Gough	16,506
Nov 27	Partick Thistle	D 1-1	Huistra	17,292
Dec 1	ABERDEEN	W 2-0	Hateley 2	45,182
Dec 4	Motherwell	W 2-0	Durie 2	14,069
Dec 11	DUNDEE UNITED	L 0-3		43,058
Dec 18	St Johnstone	W 4-0	Hateley 2, Steven, Durie	10,056
Dec 27	HEARTS	D 2-2	Hateley 2	45,116
Jan 1	Celtic	W 4-2	Mikhailichenko 2, Hateley, Kuznetsov	48,506
Jan 8	KILMARNOCK	W 3-0	Hateley 2, Huistra	44,919
Jan 15	Dundee	D 1-1	Durie	11,014
Jan 22	Aberdeen	D 0-0		20,267
Feb 5	PARTICK THISTLE	W 5-1	Durie 2, Mikhailichenko, McCall, Steven	42,606
Feb 12	HIBERNIAN	W 2-0	Durie, Steven	43,265
Feb 26	Raith Rovers	W 2-1	I.Ferguson, Durie	8,988
Mar 5	MOTHERWELL	W 2-1	Durie, Hateley (pen)	43,669
Mar 19	ST JOHNSTONE	W 4-0	McCall, Hateley, McPherson, Durie	43,228
Mar 26	Hearts	W 2-1	McCoist, Hateley	18,108
Mar 29	Partick Thistle	W 2-1	Gough, McCoist	14,706
Apr 2	ABERDEEN	D 1-1	McCall	45,888
Apr 5	Dundee United	D 0-0		11,352
Apr 16	RAITH ROVERS	W 4-0	D.Robertson, McCoist, D.Ferguson, Mikhailichenko	42,545
Apr 22	DUNDEE UNITED	W 2-1	Durie 2	44,766
Apr 26	Motherwell	L 1-2	McCoist	14,050
Apr 30	CELTIC	D 1-1	Mikhailichenko	47,018
May 3	Hibernian	L 0-1		14,517
May 7	Kilmarnock	L 0-1		18,012
May 14	DUNDEE	D 0-0		41,620

Scottish Cup

Jan 29	DUMBARTON	(Rd3) W 4-1	Durie, Hateley (pen), Steven, D.Robertson	36,809
Feb 19	ALLOA	(Rd4) W 6-0	McCoist 3 (1 pen), I.Ferguson, McPherson, Newbigging o.g.	37,804
Mar 12	HEARTS	(QF) W 2-0	Brown, Hateley	41,666
Apr 10	Kilmarnock*	(SF) D 0-0		35,144
Apr 13	Kilmarnock*	(R) W 2-1	Hateley 2	29,860
May 21	Dundee United*	(F) L 0-1		37,450

*Played at Hampden Park.

Scottish League Cup

Aug 11	DUMBARTON	(Rd2) W 1-0	I.Ferguson	36,309
Aug 25	Dunfermline	(Rd3) W 2-0	Steven, I.Ferguson	12,993
Sep 1	ABERDEEN	(QF) W 2-1	Hateley (pen), I.Ferguson	45,604
Sep 22	CELTIC	(SF) W 1-0	Hateley	47,420
Oct 24	Hibernian*	(F) W 2-1	Durrant, McCoist	47,632

*Played at Hampden Park.

European Cup

Sep 15	LEVSKI SOFIA	(QR1/FL) W 3-2	Hateley 2, McPherson	37,013
Sep 29	Levski Sofia	(QR1/SL) L 1-2	Durrant	50,000

Fact File

Rangers lost 2-1 to Newcastle United at Ibrox on 3 August 1993 in Ally McCoist's testimonial match. Mark Hateley scored Rangers' goal in front of a 42,623 crowd.

League & Cup Appearances

PLAYER	LEAGUE	CUP COMPETITION			TOTAL
		S CUP	SL CUP	E CUP	
Brown	24	4			28
Durie	23 (1)		5		28 (1)
Durrant	14 (9)	1	5	2	22 (9)
Ferguson D	7 (3)	0 (3)	1 (1)	1	9 (7)
Ferguson I	35	5	5	2	47
Goram	8	2			10
Gough	37	5	5	1	48
Hagen	4 (2)		1	1	6 (2)
Hateley	40 (2)	6	5	2	53 (2)
Huistra	10 (11)		0 (1)	3 (1)	13 (13)
Kuznetsov	4 (2)				4 (2)
Maxwell	31 (1)	4	5	2	42 (1)
McCall	34	6	2	2	44
McCoist	16 (5)	4 (2)	0 (1)		20 (8)
McPherson	27 (1)	5	2	2	36 (1)
Mik'lichenko	24 (10)	3 (2)	1		28 (12)
Miller	2 (1)				2 (1)
Moore	1				1
Morrow	2		0 (1)		2 (1)
Murray	20 (2)	3	2		25 (2)
Pressley	17 (6)	1 (1)	3	1	22 (7)
Robertson	32	6	4	1	43
Scott	5 (1)				5 (1)
Steven	32	3	5	2	42
Stevens	28 (1)	3	3	2	36 (1)
Vinnicombe	2 (2)		1		3 (2)
Wishart	5	2 (1)	1		8 (2)

Goalscorers

PLAYER	LEAGUE	CUP COMPETITION			TOTAL
		S CUP	SL CUP	E CUP	
Hateley	22	4	2	2	30
Durie	12	1			13
McCoist	7	3	1		11
Ferguson I	5	1	3		9
Huistra	6				6
Steven	4	1	1		6
Mik'lichenko	5				5
Gough	3				3
McCall	3				3
McPherson	1	1		1	3
Durrant			1	1	2
Robertson	1	1			2
Brown		1			1
Ferguson D	1				1
Hagen	1				1
Kuznetsov	1				1
Pressley	1				1
Opps' o.gs.	1	1			2

MANAGER: Walter Smith

CAPTAIN: Richard Gough

MAJOR TRANSFERS IN: Duncan Ferguson from Dundee United, Gordon Durie from Tottenham Hotspur

MAJOR TRANSFERS OUT: Dale Gordon to West Ham United, Gary McSwegan to Notts County

Final Scottish Premier Division Table

		P	W	D	L	F	A	Pts
1	RANGERS	44	22	14	8	74	41	58
2	ABERDEEN	44	17	21	6	58	36	55
3	MOTHERWELL	44	20	14	10	58	43	54
4	CELTIC	44	15	20	9	51	38	50
5	HIBERNIAN	44	16	15	13	53	48	47
6	DUNDEE U	44	11	20	13	47	48	42
7	HEARTS	44	11	20	13	37	43	42
8	KILMARNOCK	44	12	16	16	36	45	40
9	PARTICK T	44	12	16	16	46	57	40
10	ST JOHNSTONE	44	10	20	14	35	47	40
11	RAITH R	44	6	19	19	46	80	31
12	DUNDEE	44	8	13	23	42	57	29

Season 1994-95

Scottish League Premier Division

DATE	OPPONENTS	SCORE	GOALSCORERS	ATTENDANCE
Aug 13	MOTHERWELL	W 2-1	Hateley, D.Ferguson	43,750
Aug 20	Partick Thistle	W 2-0	Hateley, Byrne o.g.	15,030
Aug 27	CELTIC	L 0-2		45,466
Sep 11	HEARTS	W 3-0	Hateley 2, Durie	41,041
Sep 17	Falkirk	W 2-0	Boli, Laudrup	12,500
Sep 24	Aberdeen	D 2-2	Hateley, Moore	21,000
Oct 1	DUNDEE UNITED	W 2-0	Hateley, Laudrup	43,030
Oct 8	Hibernian	L 1-2	Boli	12,118
Oct 15	KILMARNOCK	W 2-0	Miller, D.Robertson	44,099
Oct 22	Motherwell	L 1-2	Philliben o.g.	11,160
Oct 30	Celtic*	W 3-1	Hateley 2, Laudrup	32,171
Nov 5	PARTICK THISTLE	W 3-0	Miller, Hateley, Laudrup	43,696
Nov 9	Hearts	D 1-1	Hateley	12,347
Nov 19	Falkirk	D 1-1	Hateley	44,018
Nov 25	ABERDEEN	W 1-0	McCoist	45,072
Dec 4	Dundee United	W 3-0	Laudrup, Huistra, Durrant	10,692
Dec 10	Kilmarnock	W 2-1	McLaren, Laudrup	17,283
Dec 26	HIBERNIAN	W 2-0	Hateley, Gough	44,892
Dec 31	Motherwell	W 3-1	McCall, Laudrup, Durie	11,500
Jan 4	CELTIC	D 1-1	I.Ferguson	45,794
Jan 7	Partick Thistle	D 1-1	D.Robertson	19,351
Jan 14	Falkirk	W 3-2	Huistra 2 (1 pen), McCall	13,495
Jan 21	HEARTS	W 1-0	Miller	44,231
Feb 4	DUNDEE UNITED	D 1-1	D.Robertson	44,197
Feb 12	Aberdeen	L 0-2		20,000
Feb 25	KILMARNOCK	W 3-0	Durie, Laudrup, Durrant	44,859
Mar 4	Hibernian	D 1-1	McCall	12,059
Mar 11	FALKIRK	D 2-2	Brown, Laudrup	43,359
Mar 18	Hearts	L 1-2	Laudrup	9,806
Apr 1	Dundee United	W 2-1	Durie, McLaren	11,500
Apr 8	ABERDEEN	W 3-2	Durrant, Murray, Hateley	44,460
Apr 16	HIBERNIAN	W 3-1	Durie, Durrant, Mikhailichenko	44,193
Apr 20	Kilmarnock	W 1-0	Mikhailichenko	16,086
Apr 29	MOTHERWELL	L 0-2		43,576
May 7	Celtic*	L 0-3		31,025
May 13	PARTICK THISTLE	D 1-1	Moore	45,280

*Played at Hampden Park.

Scottish Cup

Feb 6	Hamilton	(Rd3) W 3-1	Steven, Boli, Laudrup	18,379
Feb 20	Hearts	(Rd4) L 2-4	Laudrup, Durie	12,375

Scottish League Cup

Aug 17	Arbroath	(Rd2) W 6-1	D.Ferguson 3, Hateley 2, McCall	4,665
Aug 31	FALKIRK	(Rd3) L 1-2	Laudrup	40,697

European Cup

Aug 10	AEK Athens	(QR1/FL) L 0-2		30,000
Aug 24	AEK ATHENS	(QR1/SL) L 0-1		44,789

League & Cup Appearances

PLAYER	LEAGUE	CUP COMPETITION			TOTAL
		S CUP	SL CUP	E CUP	
Boli	28	1	1	1	31
Bollan	5 (1)				5 (1)
Brown	10 (3)	0 (2)	1		11 (5)
Caldwell	1				1
Cleland	10	1			11
Durie	16 (4)	2	1	2	21 (4)
Durrant	16 (10)	0 (1)	2 (2)		18 (13)
Ferguson D	1 (3)	1 (1)	1		3 (4)
Ferguson I	13 (3)		2	2	17 (3)
Goram	18 (1)		1	2	21 (1)
Gough	25	2	2	2	31
Hagen	0 (2)				0 (2)
Hateley	23	1	2	2	28
Huistra	15				15
Laudrup	33	2	1	2	38
Maxwell	10	2	1		13
McCall	30	2	2	2	36
McCoist	4 (5)				4 (5)
McGinty	1				1
McKnight	0 (1)				0 (1)
McLaren	24	1			25
McPherson	9		2	1	12
Mik'lichenko	4 (5)				4 (5)
Miller	21	2			23
Moore	19 (2)		2	2	23 (2)
Murray	14 (6)		0 (1)	1	15 (7)
Pressley	2		1		3
Robertson D	23	2	1	2	28
Robertson L	(1)				(1)
Scott	3 (1)				3 (1)
Steven	10 (1)		2		12 (1)
Stevens				1	1
Thomson	5				5
Wishart	3 (1)				3 (1)

Goalscorers

PLAYER	LEAGUE	CUP COMPETITION			TOTAL
		S CUP	SL CUP	E CUP	
Hateley	13		2		15
Laudrup	10	2	1		13
Durie	5	1			6
Durrant	4				4
Ferguson D	1		3		4
McCall	3		1		4
Boli	2	1			3
Huistra	3				3
Miller	3				3
Robertson D	3				3
McLaren	2				2
Mik'lichenko	2				2
Moore	2				2
Brown	1				1
Ferguson I	1				1
Gough	1				1
McCoist	1				1
Murray	1				1
Steven		1			1
Opps' o.gs.	2				2

Fact File

Rangers hosted their own Ibrox International Challenge pre-season tournament in August 1994, losing 4-2 to Sampdoria then defeating Manchester United 1-0.

MANAGER: Walter Smith

CAPTAIN: Richard Gough

TOP SCORER: Mark Hateley

BIGGEST WIN: 6-1 v Arbroath, League Cup, 17 August 1994

HIGHEST ATTENDANCE: 45,794 v Celtic, League, 4 January 1995

MAJOR TRANSFERS IN: Brian Laudrup from Fiorentina, Basile Boli from Marseille, Alan McLaren from Hearts, Alex Cleland from Dundee United

MAJOR TRANSFERS OUT: Duncan Ferguson to Everton, Dave McPherson to Hearts, Gary Stevens to Tranmere Rovers, Oleg Kuznetsov to Maccabi Haifa, Pieter Huistra to Sanfrecce Hiroshima

Final Scottish Premier Division Table

		P	W	D	L	F	A	Pts
1	RANGERS	36	20	9	7	60	35	69
2	MOTHERWELL	36	14	12	10	50	50	54
3	HIBERNIAN	36	12	17	7	49	37	53
4	CELTIC	36	11	18	7	39	33	51
5	FALKIRK	36	12	12	12	48	47	48
6	HEARTS	36	12	7	17	44	51	43
7	KILMARNOCK	36	11	10	15	40	48	43
8	PARTICK T	36	10	13	13	40	50	43
9	ABERDEEN	36	10	11	15	43	46	41
10	DUNDEE U	36	9	9	18	40	56	36

Season 1995-96

Scottish League Premier Division

DATE	OPPONENTS	SCORE	GOALSCORERS	ATTENDANCE
Aug 26	KILMARNOCK	W 1-0	McCall	44,686
Sep 9	RAITH ROVERS	W 4-0	McCoist 2, Miller, Robertson	43,535
Sep 16	Falkirk	W 2-0	Salenko, Robertson	11,445
Sep 23	HIBERNIAN	L 0-1		44,364
Sep 30	Celtic	W 2-0	Cleland, Gascoigne	34,500
Oct 3	MOTHERWELL	W 2-1	Gascoigne, McCoist	37,348
Oct 7	Aberdeen	W 1-0	Moore	22,500
Oct 14	Partick Thistle	W 4-0	Durie 3, Gough	16,346
Oct 21	HEARTS	W 4-1	Salenko 2, Gascoigne, Durie	45,155
Oct 28	Raith Rovers	D 2-2	Gough, Petric	9,200
Nov 4	FALKIRK	W 2-0	McCoist 2	42,059
Nov 8	Kilmarnock	W 2-0	McLaren, Salenko	14,823
Nov 11	Aberdeen	D 1-1	Salenko	45,427
Nov 19	CELTIC	D 3-3	Laudrup, McCoist, McKinlay o.g.	46,640
Nov 25	Hibernian	W 4-1	McCoist, Miller, Durie, Dods o.g.	13,558
Dec 2	Hearts	W 2-0	McCoist (pen), Gascoigne	15,105
Dec 9	PARTICK THISTLE	W 1-0	Durie	43,173
Dec 19	Motherwell	D 0-0		10,179
Dec 26	KILMARNOCK	W 3-0	Salenko, Durie (pen), Gascoigne	45,173
Dec 30	HIBERNIAN	W 7-0	Durie 4, Miller, Gascoigne, Salenko	44,692
Jan 3	Celtic	D 0-0		37,000
Jan 6	Falkirk	W 4-0	McCoist 2 (1 pen), Durie, Robertson	10,581
Jan 13	RAITH ROVERS	W 4-0	Durie 2, McCoist, Ferguson	42,498
Jan 20	HEARTS	L 0-3		45,096
Feb 3	Partick Thistle	W 2-1	Gascoigne 2	16,523
Feb 10	MOTHERWELL	W 3-2	Ferguson, McLaren, McCoist (pen)	45,566
Feb 25	Aberdeen	W 1-0	Gascoigne (pen)	21,000
Mar 3	Hibernian	W 2-0	Laudrup (pen), Mitchell o.g.	11,954
Mar 17	CELTIC	D 1-1	McLaren	47,312
Mar 23	FALKIRK	W 3-2	Andersen 2, Gascoigne	46,014
Mar 30	Raith Rovers	W 4-2	McCoist 3 (1 pen), Durie (pen)	9,300
Apr 10	Hearts	L 0-2		15,350
Apr 13	PARTICK THISTLE	W 5-0	Andersen 3, McCall, Gough	46,438
Apr 20	Motherwell	W 3-1	McCall, Andersen, Gascoigne	13,128
Apr 28	ABERDEEN	W 3-1	Gascoigne 3 (1 pen)	47,247
May 4	Kilmarnock	W 3-0	Durie 2, McCoist	17,056

Scottish Cup

Jan 27	Keith	(Rd3) W 10-1	Ferguson 3, Cleland 3, Durie (pen), Robertson, Miller, Mikhailichenko	14,000
Feb 15	Clyde	(Rd4) W 4-1	Miller 2, van Vossen, Gascoigne	5,722
Mar 9	Caledonian Thistle	(QF) W 3-0	Gascoigne 2, Thomson o.g.	12,000
Apr 7	Celtic*	(SF) W 2-1	McCoist, Laudrup	36,333
May 18	Hearts*	(F) W 5-1	Durie 3, Laudrup 2	37,730

*Played at Hampden Park.

Scottish League Cup

Aug 19	MORTON	(Rd2) W 3-0	McCoist, Hateley, Gascoigne	42,941
Aug 30	STIRLING ALBION	(Rd3) W 3-2	Hateley, McCall, McCoist	46,686
Sep 19	Celtic	(QF) W 1-0	McCoist	32,789
Oct 24	Aberdeen*	(SF) L 1-2	Salenko	26,131

*Played at Hampden Park.

Champions League

Aug 9	ANORTHOSIS	(QR1/FL) W 1-0	Durie	43,519
Aug 23	Anorthosis	(QR1/SL) D 0-0		12,000
Sep 13	Steaua Bucharest	(Gp C) L 0-1		26,000
Sep 27	B.DORTMUND	(Gp C) D 2-2	Gough, Ferguson	33,209
Oct 18	Juventus	(Gp C) L 1-4	Gough	49,825
Nov 1	JUVENTUS	(Gp C) L 0-4		42,523
Nov 22	STEAUA BUCHAREST	(Gp C) D 1-1	Gascoigne	30,800
Dec 6	B.Dortmund*	(Gp C) D 2-2	Laudrup, Durie	35,800

*Rangers failed to qualify from Group C.

MANAGER: Walter Smith **CAPTAIN:** Richard Gough

MAJOR TRANSFERS IN: Paul Gascoigne from Lazio, Gordan Petric from Dundee United, Peter van Vossen from Istanbulspor, Erik Bo Andersen from Aalborg

MAJOR TRANSFERS OUT: Mark Hateley to QPR, Alexei Mikhailichenko to Kiev

League & Cup Appearances

PLAYER	LEAGUE	S CUP	SL CUP	CL	TOTAL
Andersen	6				6
Bollan	4			2 (1)	6 (1)
Brown	8 (6)	3 (1)	1	2 (1)	14 (8)
Cleland	21 (4)	3 (1)	1 (2)	4	29 (7)
Durie	21 (6)	3	1 (1)	4 (2)	29 (9)
Durrant	6 (9)	0 (3)	0 (2)	2 (4)	8 (18)
Ferguson	16 (2)	3	1	2 (1)	22 (3)
Gascoigne	27 (1)	4	3	7	41 (1)
Goram	30	5	4	8	47
Gough	29	2	3	8	42
Hateley			2	2	4
Laudrup	22	5	1	5	33
McCall	19 (2)	4	1	7	31 (2)
McCoist	18 (7)	2	4	4 (2)	28 (9)
McGinty	2				2
McInnes	5 (1)				5 (1)
McLaren	36	5	3	5	49
Mik'lichenko	6 (5)	0 (1)	2 (1)		8 (7)
Miller	17 (6)	3	3	5 (2)	28 (8)
Moore	9 (2)	2	2	1	14 (2)
Murray	2 (3)		0 (4)		2 (7)
Petric	32 (1)	4	3	6	45 (1)
Reid	1				1
Robertson	25	5	3	5	38
Salenko	14 (2)		2	2	18 (2)
Scott	3				3
Shields	1				1
Snelders	2				2
Steven	5 (1)	0 (1)			5 (2)
Thomson	1	0 (1)			1 (1)
van Vossen	3 (4)	2			5 (4)
Wright	6		4	6	16

Goalscorers

PLAYER	LEAGUE	S CUP	SL CUP	CL	TOTAL
Durie	17	4		2	23
McCoist	16	1	3		20
Gascoigne	14	3	1	1	19
Salenko	7		1		8
Andersen	6				6
Ferguson	2	3		1	6
Laudrup	2	3		1	6
Miller	3	3			6
Gough	3			2	5
Cleland	1	3			4
McCall	3		1		4
Robertson	3	1			4
McLaren	3				3
Hateley			2		2
Mik'lichenko		1			1
Moore	1				1
Petric	1				1
van Vossen		1			1
Opps' o.gs.	3	1			4

Fact File

Rangers had three players sent off during their 1995-96 Champions League campaign – Alan McLaren, Alex Cleland and Paul Gascoigne.

Final Scottish Premier Division Table

		P	W	D	L	F	A	Pts
1	RANGERS	36	27	6	3	85	25	87
2	CELTIC	36	24	11	1	74	25	83
3	ABERDEEN	36	16	7	13	52	45	55
4	HEARTS	36	16	7	13	55	53	55
5	HIBERNIAN	36	11	10	15	43	57	43
6	RAITH R	36	12	7	17	41	57	43
7	KILMARNOCK	36	11	8	17	39	54	41
8	MOTHERWELL	36	9	12	15	28	39	39
9	PARTICK T	36	8	6	22	29	62	30
10	FALKIRK	36	6	6	24	31	60	24

Season 1996-97

Scottish League Premier Division

DATE	OPPONENTS	SCORE	GOALSCORERS	ATTENDANCE
Aug 10	RAITH ROVERS	W 1-0	Steven	46,221
Aug 17	Dunfermline	W 5-2	van Vossen 2, McCoist 3 (1 pen)	16,782
Aug 24	DUNDEE UNITED	W 1-0	Gascoigne	48,285
Sep 7	Motherwell	W 1-0	Gough	12,288
Sep 14	HEARTS	W 3-0	Durie, Gascoigne, McCoist	47,240
Sep 21	Kilmarnock	W 4-1	Gascoigne 2 (1 pen), van Vossen 2	14,812
Sep 28	CELTIC	W 2-0	Gough, Gascoigne	50,124
Oct 12	Hibernian	L 1-2	Albertz	12,438
Oct 19	ABERDEEN	D 2-2	Gascoigne, Laudrup (pen)	50,076
Oct 26	MOTHERWELL	W 5-0	Laudrup 2, Gascoigne 3	48,160
Nov 2	Raith Rovers	D 2-2	van Vossen, McCoist	9,722
Nov 14	Celtic	W 1-0	Laudrup	50,009
Dec 1	Aberdeen	W 3-0	Robertson, Laudrup, Miller	19,168
Dec 7	HIBERNIAN	W 4-3	Ferguson, McCoist 2, Laudrup	48,053
Dec 10	Dundee United	L 0-1		12,417
Dec 14	DUNFERMLINE	W 3-1	McCoist, Gough, Andersen	45,878
Dec 17	KILMARNOCK	W 4-2	Andersen 3, Robertson	39,469
Dec 21	Hearts	W 4-1	Robertson, Laudrup, Albertz (pen), Gascoigne	15,139
Dec 26	RAITH ROVERS	W 4-0	Gough, Gascoigne, Albertz, McCoist	48,322
Jan 2	CELTIC	W 3-1	Albertz, Andersen 2	50,019
Jan 4	Hibernian	W 2-1	Andersen, Albertz (pen)	12,650
Jan 12	ABERDEEN	W 4-0	Andersen 2, Albertz (pen), Laudrup	47,509
Jan 15	Kilmarnock	D 1-1	Gascoigne	15,662
Jan 18	Motherwell	W 3-1	Albertz, Laudrup, Gascoigne	13,166
Feb 1	HEARTS	D 0-0		50,024
Feb 8	Dunfermline	W 3-0	Durie, Albertz, Laudrup	16,153
Feb 23	HIBERNIAN	W 3-1	Gough, Albertz, Laudrup	47,618
Mar 1	Aberdeen	D 2-2	Laudrup, Moore	16,331
Mar 12	DUNDEE UNITED	L 0-2		49,192
Mar 16	Celtic	W 1-0	Laudrup	49,733
Mar 22	KILMARNOCK	L 1-2	Durie	50,036
Apr 5	DUNFERMLINE	W 4-0	Albertz, Petric, Laudrup, Hateley	49,832
Apr 15	Raith Rovers	W 6-0	Petric, Durie 2, Robertson, Laudrup, McCoist	9,745
May 5	MOTHERWELL	L 0-2		50,059
May 7	Dundee United	W 1-0	Laudrup	12,180
May 10	Hearts	L 1-3	McInnes	13,097

Scottish Cup

Jan 23	ST JOHNSTONE	(Rd3) W 2-0	Andersen, Rozental	45,037
Feb 15	EAST FIFE	(Rd4) W 3-0	Robertson, Steven, McCoist	41,064
Mar 6	Celtic	(QF) L 0-2		49,284

Scottish League Cup

Aug 14	Clydebank	(Rd2) W 3-0	van Vossen 2, McCoist	6,376
Sep 4	AYR UNITED	(Rd3) W 3-1	Albertz, Gascoigne, McInnes	44,732
Sep 17	HIBERNIAN	(QF) W 4-0	Durie, van Vossen 2, Albertz	45,104
Oct 22	Dunfermline*	(SF) W 6-1	Laudrup 2, McInnes, Andersen 2, Albertz	16,791
Nov 24	Hearts*	(F) W 4-3	McCoist 2, Gascoigne 2	48,559

*Played at Parkhead.

Champions League

Aug 7	ALANIA	(QR1/SL) W 3-1	McInnes, McCoist, Petric	44,799
Aug 21	Alania	(QR1/SL) W 7-2	McCoist 3, van Vossen, Laudrup 2, Miller	32,000
Sep 11	Grasshoppers	(Gp A) L 0-3		20,030
Sep 25	AUXERRE	(Gp A) L 1-2	Gascoigne	37,344
Oct 16	Ajax	(Gp A) L 1-4	Durrant	47,000
Oct 30	AJAX	(Gp A) L 0-1		42,265
Nov 20	GRASSHOPPERS	(Gp A) W 2-1	McCoist 2 (1 pen)	34,192
Dec 4	Auxerre*	(Gp A) L 1-2	Gough	21,300

*Rangers failed to qualify from Group A.

Fact File

Ally McCoist's two goals in the 4-3 win over Hibernian at Ibrox on 7 December 1996 broke the Scottish League post-war scoring record of 264 goals held by Gordon Wallace.

League & Cup Appearances

PLAYER	LEAGUE	S CUP	SL CUP	CL	TOTAL
Albertz	31 (1)	3	5	7	46 (1)
Andersen	6 (11)	2 (1)	1	1 (3)	10 (15)
Bjorklund	28	2	4	6	40
Boyack	0 (1)				0 (1)
Cleland	32	3	4	6	45
Dibble	7				7
Durie	14 (2)	1 (1)	2	3 (1)	20 (4)
Durrant	4 (4)		(2)	2 (1)	1 (2)	7 (9)
Ferguson	18 (6)	3	0 (1)	2 (1)	23 (8)
Fitzgerald	(1)				(1)
Gascoigne	23 (3)	1		3	31 (3)
Goram	25	3	4	6	38
Gough	27	2	5	7	41
Hateley	4				4
Laudrup	33	2	2	6	43
McCall	7	2	4		13
McCoist	13 (12)	1 (2)	2 (1)	4 (2)	20 (15)
McGinty	0 (1)				0 (1)
McInnes	10 (11)	2	2 (2)	5 (2)	17 (16)
McKnight	0 (1)				0 (1)
McLaren	17 (1)	2			19
Miller	7 (6)		3	2 (3)	12 (9)
Moore	23	2	2	4	31
Petric	23 (1)	1	5	6	35 (3)
Robertson	21 (1)	3	1 (1)	3	28 (2)
Rozental	(1)	1			1 (1)
Shields		6	1 (1)	2	9 (1)
Snelders	4	1	2		7
Steven	5 (3)	1	1		7 (3)
van Vossen	6 (8)		(1)	2 (1)	4 (4)	12 (14)
Wilson	1				3 (1)
Wright	1	1			2

Goalscorers

PLAYER	LEAGUE	S CUP	SL CUP	CL	TOTAL
Laudrup	16		2	2	20
McCoist	10	1	3	6	20
Gascoigne	13		3	1	17
Albertz	10			3	13
Andersen	9	1	2		12
van Vossen	5		4	1	10
Durie	5		1		6
Gough	5			1	6
Robertson	4	1			5
McInnes	1		2	1	4
Petric	2		1		3
Miller	1		1		2
Steven	1	1			2
Durrant			1		1
Ferguson	1				1
Hateley	1				1
Moore	1				1
Rozental		1			1

MANAGER: Walter Smith CAPTAIN: Richard Gough
MAJOR TRANSFERS IN: Jorg Albertz from Hamburg, Joachim Bjorklund from Vicenza, Sebastian Rozental from Universidad Catolica, Mark Hateley from QPR
MAJOR TRANSFERS OUT: Richard Gough to Kansas City Wiz, Neil Murray to Sion, Alex Cleland to Everton

Final Scottish Premier Division Table

		P	W	D	L	F	A	Pts
1	RANGERS	36	25	5	6	85	33	80
2	CELTIC	36	23	6	7	78	32	75
3	DUNDEE U	36	17	9	10	46	33	60
4	HEARTS	36	14	10	12	46	43	52
5	DUNFERMLINE ATH	36	12	9	15	52	65	45
6	ABERDEEN	36	10	14	12	45	54	44
7	KILMARNOCK	36	11	6	19	41	61	39
8	MOTHERWELL	36	9	11	16	44	55	38
9	HIBERNIAN	36	9	11	16	38	55	38
10	RAITH R	36	6	7	23	29	73	25

Season 1997-98

Scottish League Premier Division

DATE	OPPONENTS	SCORE	GOALSCORERS	ATTENDANCE
Aug 4	HEARTS	W 3-1	Negri 2, Cleland	48,257
Aug 23	DUNDEE UNITED	W 5-1	Negri 5	48,599
Sep 13	ABERDEEN	D 3-3	Negri (pen), Albertz, Laudrup	50,030
Sep 20	St Johnstone	W 2-0	Negri 2	10,093
Sep 24	Kilmarnock	W 3-0	Negri 2, Stensaas	15,367
Sep 27	MOTHERWELL	D 2-2	Negri, Porrini	48,672
Oct 4	Hibernian	W 4-3	Negri 2 (1 pen), Gascoigne, Albertz	15,169
Oct 18	DUNFERMLINE	W 7-0	Laudrup, Negri 4, Gascoigne 2	49,696
Oct 25	Dundee United	L 1-2	Negri	12,051
Nov 1	KILMARNOCK	W 4-1	Negri 3 (1 pen), Porrini	49,413
Nov 8	CELTIC	W 1-0	Gough	50,082
Nov 15	Aberdeen	D 1-1	Albertz	18,117
Nov 19	Celtic	D 1-1	Negri	49,427
Nov 22	Motherwell	D 1-1	McCoist	12,018
Nov 29	ST JOHNSTONE	W 3-2	Gattuso, Negri 2	49,142
Dec 7	HIBERNIAN	W 1-0	Negri	48,070
Dec 13	Dunfermline	D 0-0		12,443
Dec 20	Hearts	W 5-2	Durie 3, Negri (pen), Albertz	17,092
Dec 27	DUNDEE UNITED	W 4-1	Laudrup, Cleland, Negri 2 (1 pen)	50,017
Jan 2	Celtic	L 0-2		49,396
Jan 10	ABERDEEN	W 2-0	Porrini, Laudrup	49,502
Jan 27	MOTHERWELL	W 1-0	Cleland	49,443
Jan 31	St Johnstone	L 0-2		10,441
Feb 7	DUNFERMLINE	D 1-1	Porrini	49,019
Feb 21	Hibernian	W 2-1	Negri, Albertz	13,968
Feb 24	Kilmarnock	D 1-1	Thern	15,931
Feb 28	HEARTS	D 2-2	Albertz 2	50,046
Mar 14	Motherwell	L 1-2	McCoist	11,779
Mar 21	ST JOHNSTONE	W 2-1	Negri, Thern	49,788
Mar 28	Dunfermline	W 3-2	McCoist 2, Thern	11,531
Apr 1	HIBERNIAN	W 3-0	McCoist, Thern, Durie	48,488
Apr 12	CELTIC	W 2-0	Thern, Albertz	50,042
Apr 19	Aberdeen	L 0-1		17,981
Apr 25	Hearts	W 3-0	Gattuso 2, Albertz	17,415
May 2	KILMARNOCK	L 0-1		50,116
May 9	Dundee United	W 2-1	Laudrup, Albertz (pen)	14,200

Scottish Cup

Jan 24	Hamilton	(Rd3)	W 2-1	Durie, Gough	11,915
Feb 14	Motherwell	(Rd4)	D 2-2	Negri, Durie	12,602
Feb 17	MOTHERWELL	(R)	W 3-0	Albertz 2, Durie	42,011
Mar 9	DUNDEE	(QF)	D 0-0		40,309
Mar 18	Dundee	(R)	W 2-1	McCoist 2	12,418
Apr 5	Celtic*	(SF)	W 2-1	McCoist, Albertz	48,993
May 16	Hearts*	(F)	L 1-2	McCoist	48,946

*Played at Parkhead.

Scottish League Cup

Aug 7	Hamilton	(Rd2)	W 1-0	McCoist	8,866
Aug 19	FALKIRK	(Rd3)	W 4-1	McCoist 3 (1 pen), Stensaas	43,317
Sep 9	DUNDEE UNITED	(QF)	L 0-1		44,155

Champions League

Jul 23	Gotu	(PRI/FL)	W 5-0	Negri, Durie 2, McCoist 2	2,200
Jul 30	GOTU	(PRI/SL)	W 6-0	Durie, Negri 2, McCoist, Albertz, I.Ferguson	44,433
Aug 13	IFK Gothenburg	(QR/FL)	L 0-3		20,000
Aug 27	IFK GOTHENBURG	(QR/SL)	D 1-1	Miller	45,585

UEFA Cup

Sep 16	Strasbourg	(Rd1/FL)	L 1-2	Albertz (pen)	12,450
Sep 30	STRASBOURG	(Rd1/SL)	L 1-2	Gattuso	40,145

League & Cup Appearances

PLAYER	LEAGUE	CUP COMPETITION			TOTAL
		S CUP	SL CUP	CL/UEFA	
Albertz	27 (4)	4 (1)	1	3 (2)	35 (7)
Amoruso	4	1 (1)			5 (1)
Andersen			1 (2)		1 (2)
Bjorklund	31	6	6		43
Bollan	0 (1)		1		1 (1)
Cleland	27 (2)	6	3	3 (1)	39 (3)
Durie	14 (12)	4 (1)	2	5 (1)	25 (14)
Durrant	1 (7)	1 (1)	1 (1)		3 (9)
Ferguson B	6 (1)	3 (1)			9 (2)
Ferguson I	9 (2)	2	2	3 (1)	16 (3)
Gascoigne	14 (6)	2 (1)		5	21 (7)
Gattuso	22 (7)	4	2 (1)	2	30 (8)
Goram	24	7	2	3	36
Gough	24	6			30
Johansson	1 (5)		1 (2)	0 (1)	2 (8)
Laudrup	26 (2)		4	3 (1)	33 (3)
McCall	26 (4)	5 (2)	(1)	2	33 (7)
McCoist	7 (8)	2 (2)	1 (2)	2 (2)	12 (14)
McInnes			1		1
Miller	5 (2)		3	1 (2)	9 (4)
Moore	8 (2)	1 (1)	2	4	15 (3)
Negri	28 (1)	4	2	5	39 (1)
Niemi	5		2		7
Petric	6	3	1	1	11
Porrini	26	4	2	5	37
Rozental	1 (1)	0 (2)			1 (3)
Snelders	7	1	1		9
Stensaas	17 (3)	2	3	3	25 (3)
Thern	22	3	4		29
van Vossen			0 (2)		0 (3)
Vidmar	8 (4)	1	2	4	15 (4)
Wright		(1)			(1)

Goalscorers

PLAYER	LEAGUE	CUP COMPETITION			TOTAL
		S CUP	SL CUP	CL/UEFA	
Negri	32	1		3	36
McCoist	5	4	4	3	16
Albertz	10	3		2	15
Durie	4	3		3	10
Laudrup	5				5
Thern	5				5
Gattuso	3		1		4
Porrini	4				4
Cleland	3				3
Gascoigne	3				3
Gough	1	1			2
Stensaas	1		1		2
Ferguson I				1	1
Miller				1	1

MANAGER: Walter Smith

CAPTAIN: Brian Laudrup/Richard Gough

MAJOR TRANSFERS IN: Marco Negri from Perugia, Jonas Thern from Roma, Sergio Porrini from Juventus, Lorenzo Amoruso from Fiorentina, Jonatan Johansson from Flora Tallin, Richard Gough from Kansas City Wiz, Stale Stensaas from Rosenborg

MAJOR TRANSFERS OUT: Paul Gascoigne to Middlesbrough, David Robertson to Leeds United, Erik Bo Andersen to Odense

---

Final Scottish Premier Division Table

		P	W	D	L	F	A	Pts
1	CELTIC	36	22	8	6	64	24	74
2	RANGERS	36	21	9	6	76	38	72
3	HEARTS	36	19	10	7	70	46	67
4	KILMARNOCK	36	13	11	12	40	52	50
5	ST JOHNSTONE	36	13	9	14	38	42	48
6	ABERDEEN	36	9	12	15	39	53	39
7	DUNDEE U	36	8	13	15	43	51	37
8	DUNFERMLINE ATH	36	8	13	15	43	68	37
9	MOTHERWELL	36	9	7	20	46	64	38
10	HIBERNIAN	36	6	12	18	38	59	30

Fact File

Marco Negri set a new record by scoring in 10 consecutive Premier Division matches in 1997-98, beating the previous run of eight by Hibs' striker Ally McLeod.

Season 1998-99

Scottish Premier League

DATE	OPPONENTS	SCORE	GOALSCORERS	ATTENDANCE
Aug 2	Hearts	L 1-2	Wallace	15,272
Aug 15	MOTHERWELL	W 2-1	Wallace, Albertz (pen)	49,275
Aug 22	Kilmarnock	W 3-1	Wallace, Albertz (pen), Miller	17,608
Aug 29	ST JOHNSTONE	W 4-0	Kanchelskis, Van Bronckhorst, Wallace, Albertz (pen)	48,732
Sep 12	Dundee United	D 0-0		12,088
Sep 20	CELTIC	D 0-0		50,026
Sep 23	Aberdeen	D 1-1	Wallace	17,862
Sep 26	Dunfermline	W 2-0	Johansson, B.Ferguson	11,507
Oct 4	DUNDEE	W 1-0	Albertz	48,348
Oct 17	HEARTS	W 3-0	Johansson, Wallace 2	49,749
Oct 28	Motherwell	L 0-1		11,777
Oct 31	DUNDEE UNITED	W 2-1	Wallace, Amoruso	49,503
Nov 8	St Johnstone	W 7-0	Wallace, Johansson, Albertz 2 (2 pens) Kanchelskis, Guivarcíh 2	9,660
Nov 14	ABERDEEN	W 2-1	van Bronckhorst, Kanchelskis	49,479
Nov 21	Celtic	L 1-5	van Bronckhorst	59,783
Dec 5	DUNFERMLINE	D 1-1	van Bronckhorst	47,465
Dec 12	KILMARNOCK	W 1-0	Wallace	49,781
Dec 19	Hearts	W 3-2	Guivarcíh 2, Kanchelskis	17,134
Dec 26	ST JOHNSTONE	W 1-0	Porrini	49,479
Dec 30	Dundee United	W 2-1	Wilson, Wallace	11,707
Jan 3	CELTIC	D 2-2	Amato, Wallace	50,059
Jan 27	Dundee	W 4-0	Miller 2, Guivarcíh, Johansson	10,043
Jan 30	Aberdeen	W 4-2	Porrini, Wallace, Albertz (pen), Kanchelskis	19,507
Feb 7	Dunfermline	W 3-0	Kanchelskis, Johansson 2	10,360
Feb 20	DUNDEE	W 6-1	Albertz 3 (1 pen), McCann 2, van Bronckhorst	49,462
Feb 28	Kilmarnock	W 5-0	McCann, Wallace 3, Johansson	16,242
Mar 13	MOTHERWELL	W 2-1	Wallace, Johansson	49,483
Mar 20	DUNDEE UNITED	L 0-1		49,164
Apr 4	St Johnstone	L 1-3	Moore	9,742
Apr 14	DUNFERMLINE	W 1-0	van Bronckhorst	46,220
Apr 18	Dundee	D 1-1	Vidmar	11,070
Apr 25	ABERDEEN	W 3-1	Amato (pen), Kanchelskis, Wallace	49,145
May 2	Celtic	W 3-0	McCann 2, Albertz (pen)	59,918
May 9	HEARTS	D 0-0		49,495
May 15	Motherwell	W 5-1	Amato 3 (1 pen), van Bronckhorst, Kanchelskis	11,078
May 23	KILMARNOCK	D 1-1	Amato	48,835

Scottish Cup

Jan 23	STENHOUSEMUIR	(Rd3) W 2-0	Guivarcíh, Wallace	37,759
Feb 14	Hamilton	(Rd4) W 6-0	Johansson 2, Albertz (pen), Vidmar, Kanchelskis, McCann	7,339
Mar 7	FALKIRK	(QF) W 2-1	McCann, Amoruso	39,250
Apr 11	St Johnstone*	(SF) W 4-0	Wallace, van Bronckhorst, Johansson, McCann	20,664
May 29	Celtic#	(F) W 1-0	Wallace	51,746

*Played at Parkhead. #Played at Hampden Park.

Scottish League Cup

Aug 18	ALLOA	(Rd3) W 4-0	Amoruso, B.Ferguson, Albertz 2	37,201
Sep 8	Ayr United	(QF) W 2-0	Amato, Miller	11,198
Oct 25	Airdrie*	(SF) W 5-0	Johansson, I.Ferguson, Wallace 2, Durie	21,171
Nov 29	St Johnstone*	(F) W 2-1	Guivarcíh, Albertz	45,533

*Played at Parkhead.

UEFA Cup

Jul 22	Shelbourne*	(1QR/FL) W 5-3	Albertz 2 (2 pens), Amato 2, van Bronckhorst	6,047
Jul 29	SHELBOURNE	(1QR/SL) W 2-0	Johansson 2	46,906
Aug 11	PAOK SALONIKA	(2QR/FL) W 2-0	Kanchelskis, Wallace	45,000
Aug 25	PAOK Salonika	(2QR/SL) D 0-0		36,000
Sep 15	Beitar Jerusalem	(Rd1/FL) D 1-1	Albertz	14,000
Oct 1	BEITAR JERUSALEM	(Rd1/SL) W 4-2	Gattuso, Porrini, Johansson, Wallace	45,610
Oct 22	Bayer Leverkusen	(Rd2/FL) W 2-1	van Bronckhorst, Johansson	22,000
Nov 5	BAYER LEVERKUSEN	(Rd2/SL) D 1-1	Johansson	50,012
Nov 24	PARMA	(Rd3/FL) D 1-1	Wallace 69	49,514
Dec 8	Parma	(Rd3/SL) L 1-3	Albertz	17,000

*Played at Prenton Park, Tranmere.

League & Cup Appearances

PLAYER	LEAGUE	CUP COMPETITION			TOTAL
		S CUP	SL CUP	UEFA	
Albertz	33 (1)	5	4	8 (2)	50 (3)
Amato	13 (7)	1 (2)	2	(6)	16 (15)
Amoruso	33	4	3	9	49
Charbonnier	11		3	5	19
Durie	1 (4)		0 (2)	4 (2)	5 (8)
Feeney	(1)				(1)
Ferguson B	23	2 (1)	4	10	39 (1)
Ferguson I	4 (9)	0 (1)	0 (3)	5 (4)	9 (17)
Gattuso	3 (2)		1	2 (3)	6 (5)
Graham	(3)			1 (1)	1 (4)
Guivarcíh	11 (3)		3 (1)	1	14 (4)
Hendry	16 (3)	3	3 (1)	4 (1)	26 (5)
Johansson	13 (12)	1 (2)	2	6 (1)	22 (15)
Kanchelskis	29 (1)	4 (1)	2	7	42 (2)
Klos	18	5			23
McCann	15 (4)		5		19 (4)
McInnes	0 (7)		1 (1)		1 (8)
Miller	2 (14)	1 (1)	0 (2)	0 (2)	3 (19)
Moore	8		1 (1)	5	14 (1)
Nicholson	3 (3)				3 (3)
Niemi	7		1	5 (1)	13 (1)
Numan	8 (2)		2 (1)	6	16 (3)
Petric				1 (1)	1 (1)
Porrini	35	5	4	10	54
Reyna	6				6
Riccio	0 (1)				0 (1)
Rozental	0 (3)				0 (3)
Stensaas	1			(1)	1 (1)
Thern	1		1		2
van Bronckh'st	35	4	0 (1)	4	9	52 (1)
Vidmar	26 (2)	5	2	3 (1)	36 (3)
Wallace	34	5	4	8	51
Wilson	7 (5)	1 (4)	1	1 (1)	10 (10)

Goalscorers

PLAYER	LEAGUE	CUP COMPETITION			TOTAL
		S CUP	SL CUP	UEFA	
Wallace	18	3	2	3	26
Albertz	11	1	3	4	19
Johansson	8	3	1	5	17
Kanchelskis	8	1		1	10
van Bronckh'st	7	1		2	10
Amato	6		1	2	9
McCann	5	3			8
Guivarcíh	5	1	1		7
Miller	3		1		4
Amoruso	1		1	1	3
Porrini	2			1	3
Ferguson B	1		1		2
Vidmar	1	1			2
Durie			1		1
Ferguson I			1		1
Gattuso				1	1
Moore	1				1
Wilson	1				1

MANAGER: Dick Advocaat **CAPTAIN:** Lorenzo Amoruso

MAJOR TRANSFERS IN: Giovanni van Bronckh'st from Feyenoord, Arthur Numan from PSV Andrei Kanchelskis from Fiorentina, Rod Wallace from Leeds United

MAJOR TRANSFERS OUT: Brian Laudrup to Chelsea, Joachim Bjorklund to Valencia

---

Final Scottish Premier Division Table

		P	W	D	L	F	A	Pts
1	RANGERS	36	23	8	5	76	31	77
2	CELTIC	36	21	8	7	84	35	71
3	ST JOHNSTONE	36	15	12	9	39	38	57
4	KILMARNOCK	36	14	14	8	47	29	56
5	DUNDEE	36	13	7	16	36	56	46
6	HEARTS	36	11	9	16	44	50	42
7	MOTHERWELL	36	10	11	15	35	54	41
8	ABERDEEN	36	10	7	19	43	71	37
9	DUNDEE UTD	36	8	10	18	37	48	34
10	DUNFERMLINE	36	4	16	16	28	59	28

Season 1999-2000

Scottish Premier League

DATE	OPPONENTS	SCORE	GOALSCORERS	ATTENDANCE
Jul 31	KILMARNOCK	W 2-1	Wallace, Reyna	48,074
Aug 7	Hearts	W 4-0	Reyna 2, Mols, Albertz	17,893
Aug 15	MOTHERWELL	W 4-1	Mols 4	45,264
Aug 21	DUNDEE UNITED	W 4-1	Reyna, van Bronckhorst, Wallace, Vidmar	48,849
Aug 28	Hibernian	W 1-0	Johansson	15,587
Sep 11	ABERDEEN	W 3-0	Mols 2, Albertz (pen)	49,226
Sep 25	ST JOHNSTONE	W 3-1	Albertz 2 (1 pen), Mols	47,475
Oct 2	Dundee	W 3-2	Kanchelskis, Wallace, Amato	10,494
Oct 16	Kilmarnock	D 1-1	van Bronckhorst	15,795
Oct 30	Aberdeen	W 5-1	Johansson 3, Mols, Amato	16,846
Nov 7	CELTIC	W 4-2	Johansson, Albertz (pen), Amoruso, Amato	50,026
Nov 20	HIBERNIAN	W 2-0	Johansson, Albertz	49,544
Nov 28	DUNDEE	L 1-2	Wallace	47,154
Dec 11	KILMARNOCK	W 1-0	Albertz	47,169
Dec 18	Motherwell	W 5-1	Kanchelskis 2, Amoruso, Dodds 2	12,640
Dec 22	HEARTS	W 1-0	Albertz	49,907
Dec 27	Celtic	D 1-1	Dodds	59,619
Jan 22	ABERDEEN	W 5-0	Moore, van Bronckhorst, Numan, Wallace, B.Ferguson	50,023
Feb 2	Dundee United	W 4-0	Vidmar 2, Wallace, McCann	11,241
Feb 6	Hibernian	D 2-2	Wallace, McCann	13,420
Feb 15	St Johnstone	D 1-1	Vidmar	9,608
Feb 27	Dundee	W 7-1	Wallace 3, Vidmar, Albertz, Rozental, Tweed o.g	9,297
Mar 4	ST JOHNSTONE	D 0-0		49,907
Mar 8	Celtic	W 1-0	Wallace	59,220
Mar 18	MOTHERWELL	W 6-2	Wallace 3, Rozental (pen), Albertz, Tugay (pen)	49,622
Mar 26	CELTIC	W 4-0	Albertz 2, Kanchelskis, van Bronckhorst	50,039
Apr 1	Aberdeen	D 1-1	B.Ferguson	16,521
Apr 4	DUNDEE UNITED	W 3-0	Albertz, Dodds, Wallace	45,829
Apr 12	Hearts	W 2-1	Wallace, Dodds	16,314
Apr 15	Dundee United	W 2-0	B.Ferguson, Albertz	11,419
Apr 23	St Johnstone	W 2-0	Dodds 2	10,016
Apr 30	DUNDEE	W 3-0	Dodds, McCann, Rozental	50,032
May 3	HIBERNIAN	W 5-2	B.Ferguson, Dodds, Dennis o.g., Albertz 2 (1 pen)	39,349
May 7	Kilmarnock	W 2-0	Reyna, Albertz	13,284
May 13	HEARTS	W 1-0	Dodds	49,109
May 21	Motherwell	L 0-2		12,310

Scottish Cup

Jan 30	St Johnstone	(Rd3) W 2-0	Numan, van Bronckhorst	9,099
Feb 19	Morton	(Rd4) W 1-0	Moore	8,600
Mar 12	HEARTS	(QF) W 4-1	Ferguson, Numan, Amoruso, Dodds (pen)	31,864
Apr 8	Ayr United*	(SF) W 7-0	Rozental 2, Kanchelskis, Wallace, Dodds 3	38,357
May 27	Aberdeen*	(F) W 4-0	van Bronckhorst, Vidmar, Dodds, Albertz	50,865

*Played at Hampden Park.

Scottish League Cup

Oct 12	DUNFERMLINE	(Rd3) W 1-0	Wallace	30,024
Dec 1	Aberdeen	(QF) L 0-1		12,108

Champions League

Jul 28	Haka	(2QR/FL) W 4-1	Amoruso, Mols 2, Nicholson	3,341
Aug 4	HAKA	(2QR/SL) W 3-0	Wallace, Johansson, Amato	46,443
Aug 11	PARMA	(3QR/FL) W 2-0	Vidmar, Reyna	49,263
Aug 25	Parma	(3QR/SL) L 0-1		28,500
Sep 15	Valencia	(Gp F) L 0-2		54,971
Sep 21	BAYERN MUNICH	(Gp F) D 1-1	Albertz	49,960
Sep 28	PSV Eindhoven	(Gp F) W 1-0	Albertz	30,000
Oct 20	PSV EINDHOVEN	(Gp F) W 4-1	Amoruso, Mols 2, McCann	50,083
Oct 26	VALENCIA	(Gp F) L 1-2	Moore	50,063
Nov 3	Bayern Munich*	(Gp F) L 0-1		54,000

*Rangers failed to qualify from Group F.

UEFA Cup

Nov 25	B.DORTMUND	(Rd 3/FL) W 2-0	Kohler o.g., Wallace	49,268
Dec 7	B.Dortmund	(Rd 3/SL) L 0-2*		30,000

*Borussia Dortmund won 3-1 on penalties.

League & Cup Appearances

PLAYER	LEAGUE	CUP COMPETITION			TOTAL
		S CUP	SL CUP	CL/UEFA	
Adamczuk	5 (5)		1	5	11 (5)
Albertz	30 (5)	4 (1)	1	5 (7)	40 (13)
Amato	4 (4)		1	2 (2)	7 (6)
Amoruso	30	3	2	11	46
Brown	1	1			2
Carson			0 (1)		0 (1)
Charbonnier	7		4		11
Dodds	16 (2)		1 (2)		21
Durie	1 (6)		2	1 (1)	4 (7)
Ferguson B	31	5	1	12	49
Ferguson I	0 (2)		0 (1)		0 (3)
Gibson	0 (1)				0 (1)
Hendry	1 (1)		0 (2)		1 (3)
Hughes	(1)				(1)
Johansson	8 (8)		2	2 (6)	12 (14)
Kanchelskis	25 (3)	4 (1)	2	0 (5)	31 (9)
Klos	24	5	6		35
Malcolm	1 (2)				1 (2)
McCann	12 (18)	1 (3)	1	7 (4)	21 (25)
McInnes	0 (1)		1	2	3 (1)
Mols	9		0 (1) 10		19 (1)
Moore	22	4	1	12	39
Myhre	3	1	2		6
Negri		0 (1)			0 (1)
Nicholson	0 (2)		1	0 (2)	1 (4)
Niemi	1				1
Numan	29 (1)	5	1	7	42 (1)
Penttila	3	0 (1)			3 (1)
Porrini	11 (1)	0	0 (1) 0 (1)	8	19 (3)
Reyna	25 (4)	3 (1)	9		37 (5)
Ross	0 (1)				0 (1)
Rozental	6 (5)	2			8 (5)
Tugay	9 (7)		2 (2)		11 (9)
van Bronckh'st	27	5	1	12	45
Vidmar	21 (6)	3	1	6 (2)	31 (8)
Wallace	25 (3)	5	1	10	41 (3)
Wilson	9	1 (1)	1		11 (1)

Goalscorers

PLAYER	LEAGUE	CUP COMPETITION			TOTAL
		S CUP	SL CUP	CL/UEFA	
Albertz	17	1		2	20
Wallace	16	1	1	2	20
Dodds	10	5			15
Mols	9			4	13
Johansson	6			1	7
Vidmar	5	1		1	7
Reyna	5			1	6
van Bronckh'st	4	2			6
Amoruso	2	1		2	5
Ferguson	4	1			5
Kanchelskis	4	1			5
Rozental	3	2			5
Amato	3			1	4
McCann	3			1	4
Moore	1	1		1	3
Numan	1	2			3
Nicholson				1	1
Tugay	1				1
Opps' o.gs.	2			1	3

Final Scottish Premier Division Table

		P	W	D	L	F	A	PTS
1	RANGERS	36	28	6	2	96	26	90
2	CELTIC	36	21	6	9	90	38	69
3	HEARTS	36	15	9	12	47	40	54
4	MOTHERWELL	36	14	10	12	49	63	52
5	ST JOHNSTONE	36	10	12	14	36	44	42
6	HIBERNIAN	36	10	11	15	49	61	41
7	DUNDEE	36	12	5	19	45	64	41
8	DUNDEE UTD	36	11	6	19	34	57	39
9	KILMARNOCK	36	8	13	15	38	52	37
10	ABERDEEN	36	9	6	21	44	83	33

Season 2000-01

Scottish Premier League

DATE	OPPONENTS	SCORE	GOALSCORERS	ATTENDANCE
Jul 29	ST JOHNSTONE	W 2-1	Dodds 2	48,062
Aug 5	Kilmarnock	W 4-2	Dodds 2 (1 pen), Miller, Tugay	14,680
Aug 13	St Mirren	W 3-1	Albertz 2, Dodds	9,251
Aug 19	DUNFERMLINE	W 4-1	Albertz (pen), Dodds, van Bronckhorst, Wallace	47,452
Aug 27	Celtic	L 2-6	Reyna, Dodds (pen)	59,476
Sep 9	Dundee	D 1-1	McCann	10,439
Sep 17	HEARTS	W 1-0	De Boer	47,496
Sep 23	Motherwell	W 1-0	Mols	11,275
Oct 1	DUNDEE UNITED	W 3-0	Kanchelskis, Albertz, van Bronckhorst	44,324
Oct 14	Hibernian	L 0-1		14,524
Oct 22	St Johnstone	L 1-2	Miller	7,763
Oct 28	KILMARNOCK	L 0-3		49,659
Nov 4	ST MIRREN	W 7-1	Miller 5, Dodds, McCann	48,795
Nov 12	Aberdeen	W 2-1	Miller, Mols	16,798
Nov 18	Dunfermline	D 0-0		10,706
Nov 26	CELTIC	W 5-1	Ferguson, Flo, De Boer, Amoruso, Mols	50,083
Dec 3	Hearts	W 1-0	Albertz (pen)	16,710
Dec 10	MOTHERWELL	W 2-0	Konterman, Ferguson	46,058
Dec 13	ABERDEEN	W 3-1	Mols, Dodds, Albertz	45,285
Dec 17	Dundee United	D 1-1	Reyna	10,750
Dec 23	HIBERNIAN	W 1-0	De Boer	49,983
Dec 26	ST JOHNSTONE	W 3-0	McCann, Ricksen, Flo	46,180
Jan 2	St Mirren	W 3-1	Flo 2, Konterman	8,142
Jan 31	ABERDEEN	W 1-0	Tugay	45,621
Feb 3	DUNFERMLINE	W 2-0	Tugay, Mols	46,302
Feb 11	Celtic	L 0-1		59,496
Feb 24	Dundee	W 1-0	Konterman	9,778
Mar 3	HEARTS	W 2-0	Flo 2	49,003
Mar 14	DUNDEE	L 0-2		45,035
Mar 17	Motherwell	W 2-1	Fernandes, Malcolm	11,208
Mar 31	DUNDEE UNITED	L 0-2		48,382
Apr 8	Hibernian	D 0-0		9,704
Apr 11	Kilmarnock	W 2-0	Flo 2	14,585
Apr 21	Dundee	W 3-0	Wallace, Flo, Albertz	10,687
Apr 29	CELTIC	L 0-3		50,057
May 5	Hearts	W 4-1	Albertz 2, Wallace, Flo	15,315
May 12	KILMARNOCK	W 5-1	De Boer, Wallace 2, Amoruso, Flo	46,577
May 20	HIBERNIAN	W 4-0	Albertz, De Boer 2, Vidmar	47,023

Scottish Cup

Jan 27	BRECHIN CITY	(Rd3) W 2-0	Johnston, Miller	22,309
Feb 18	Ross County	(Rd4) W 3-2	Flo 2, Ferguson	5,972
Mar 11	Dundee United	(QF) L 0-1		11,793

Scottish League Cup

Sep 6	ABERDEEN	(Rd3) W 4-2	van Bronckhorst, Wallace, Dodds, Amoruso	37,026
Oct 31	DUNDEE UNITED	(QF) W 2-0	Miller, Ferguson	30,966
Feb 7	Celtic*	(SF) L 1-3	Albertz (pen)	50,019

*Played at Hampden Park.

Champions League

Jul 26	ZALGIRIS	(2QR/FL) W 4-1	Johnston, Albertz (pen), Dodds 2	45,974
Aug 2	Zalgiris	(2QR/SL) D 0-0		4,000
Aug 9	Herfolge	(3QR/FL) W 3-0	Albertz, Wallace, Amoruso	3,523
Aug 23	HERFOLGE	(3QR/SL) W 3-0	Wallace, Johnston, Kanchelskis	34,141
Sep 12	STURM GRAZ	(Gp F) W 5-0	Mols, De Boer, Albertz, van Bronckhorst, Dodds	49,300
Sep 20	Monaco	(Gp F) W 1-0	van Bronckhorst	11,161
Sep 27	Galatasaray	(Gp F) L 2-3	Kanchelskis, van Bronckhorst	20,954
Oct 17	GALATASARAY	(Gp F) D 0-0		49,603
Oct 25	Sturm Graz	(Gp F) L 0-2		15,400
Nov 7	MONACO*	(Gp F) D 2-2	Miller, Mols	50,220

*Rangers failed to qualify from Group F.

UEFA Cup

Nov 30	KAISERSLAUTERN	(Rd 3/FL) W 1-0	Albertz	47,279
Dec 7	Kaiserslautern	(Rd 3/SL) L 0-3		25,757

MANAGER: Dick Advocaat **CAPTAIN:** Lorenzo Amoruso/Barry Ferguson

TOP SCORER: Jorg Albertz

League & Cup Appearances

PLAYER	LEAGUE	CUP COMPETITION			TOTAL
		S CUP	SL CUP	CL/UEFA	
Adamczuk	1 (1)				1 (2)
Albertz	20 (4)	1	1	8	30 (4)
Amoruso	29	1	2	10	42
Brown	3				3
Carson	1 (1)	0 (1)			1 (2)
Christiansen	3	1	2		6
De Boer	17	1	1	7	26
Dodds	16 (14)	1	2	3 (5)	22 (19)
Ferguson	30	3	3	11	47
Fernandes	0 (4)				0 (4)
Flo	18 (1)	2	1		21 (1)
Gayle	4				4
Hughes	0 (1)				0 (1)
Johansson			1		1
Johnston	9 (4)	2 (1)	0 (2)	4 (3)	15 (10)
Kanchelskis	3 (4)		2 (5)		5 (9)
Kauppila	1 (3)				1 (3)
Klos	32	3	2	10	47
Konterman	36 (1)	3	10		49 (1)
Lovenkrands	1 (7)		0 (1)	1	2 (8)
Malcolm	3 (3)		1 (1)	1	5 (4)
McCann	16 (5)	1	3	2 (8)	22 (13)
Miller	12 (15)	2 (1)	1	3 (2)	18 (18)
Mols	10 (3)	0 (1)	0 (1)	5 (1)	15 (6)
Moore	5	1	1		7
Negri	1		0 (1)		1 (1)
Numan	22	1	3	7	33
Porrini	12	1	1	2 (1)	16 (1)
Reyna	16 (2)	2	1	10	29 (2)
Ricksen	26 (1)	3	2	5	36 (1)
Ross	0 (1)				0 (1)
Tugay	17 (9)	1 (1)	2 (1)	6 (1)	26 (12)
van Bronckh'st	10 (1)		1	7	18 (1)
Vidmar	11 (4)	1	4 (2)		16 (6)
Wallace	14 (1)	0 (1)	1	6 (2)	21 (4)
Wilson	19 (1)	2	3	4 (1)	28 (2)

Goalscorers

PLAYER	LEAGUE	CUP COMPETITION			TOTAL
		S CUP	SL CUP	CL/UEFA	
Albertz	10		1	4	15
Dodds	9		1	3	13
Flo	11	2			13
Miller	8	1	1	1	11
Wallace	5		1	2	8
De Boer	6			1	7
Mols	5			2	7
van Bronckh'st	2		1	3	6
Amoruso	2		1	1	4
Ferguson	2	1	1		4
Johnston		1		2	3
Kanchelskis	1		2		3
Konterman	3				3
McCann	3				3
Tugay	3				3
Reyna	2				2
Fernandes	1				1
Malcolm	1				1
Ricksen	1				1
Vidmar	1				1

Final Scottish Premier Division Table

		P	W	D	L	F	A	Pts
1	CELTIC	38	31	4	3	90	9	97
2	RANGERS	38	26	4	8	76	36	82
3	HIBERNIAN	38	18	12	8	57	35	66
4	KILMARNOCK	38	15	9	14	44	53	54
5	HEARTS	38	14	10	14	56	50	52
6	DUNDEE	38	13	8	17	51	49	47
7	ABERDEEN	38	11	12	15	45	52	45
8	MOTHERWELL	38	12	7	19	42	56	43
9	DUNFERMLINE	38	11	9	18	34	54	42
10	ST JOHNSTONE	38	9	13	16	40	56	40
11	DUNDEE UTD	38	9	8	21	38	63	35
12	ST MIRREN	38	8	6	24	32	72	30

Season 2001-02

Scottish Premier League

DATE	OPPONENTS	SCORE	GOALSCORERS	ATTENDANCE
Jul 28	Aberdeen	W 3-0	Nerlinger, Latapy (pen), Caniggia	18,800
Aug 4	LIVINGSTON	D 0-0		47,805
Aug 11	Dunfermline	W 4-1	Latapy, Flo, Konterman 2	10,902
Aug 18	HIBERNIAN	D 2-2	Hughes, Flo	45,540
Aug 26	DUNDEE	W 2-0	Mols, Ricksen	48,038
Sep 8	Hearts	D 2-2	Latapy, Flo	14,014
Sep 16	MOTHERWELL	W 3-0	Flo, De Boer, Latapy	47,137
Sep 22	Dundee United	W 6-1	Buchan o.g., Flo 3, De Boer, McCann	11,117
Sep 30	CELTIC	L 0-2		50,097
Oct 13	KILMARNOCK	W 3-1	Arveladze, Caniggia, Flo	49,379
Oct 21	St Johnstone	W 2-0	Arveladze, Flo	8,331
Oct 27	Livingston	W 2-0	Reyna 2	10,012
Nov 4	ABERDEEN	W 2-0	Flo 2	49,739
Nov 17	DUNFERMLINE	W 4-0	Arveladze 2, Flo 2	48,554
Nov 25	Celtic	L 1-2	Lovenkrands	59,609
Dec 1	Dundee	D 0-0		11,085
Dec 9	HEARTS	W 3-1	De Boer, Latapy, Arveladze	47,891
Dec 12	HIBERNIAN	D 1-1	Ricksen	46,179
Dec 15	Motherwell	D 2-2	Arveladze, McCann	9,864
Dec 22	DUNDEE UNITED	W 3-2	Arveladze 2, Amoruso	47,315
Dec 26	Hibernian	W 3-0	Moore, Flo, Arveladze (pen)	14,021
Dec 29	ST JOHNSTONE	W 1-0	Mols	48,827
Jan 12	LIVINGSTON	W 3-0	Flo, Caniggia 2	48,044
Jan 19	Aberdeen	W 1-0	Amoruso	17,846
Jan 23	Dunfermline	W 4-2	Vidmar, De Boer 2, Arveladze (pen)	8,795
Jan 30	Kilmarnock	D 2-2	De Boer, Flo	11,589
Feb 2	DUNDEE	W 2-1	Arveladze, Moore	48,861
Feb 9	Hearts	W 2-0	De Boer, McCann	14,128
Feb 16	MOTHERWELL	W 3-0	Latapy, Flo, Ricksen	49,284
Mar 3	Dundee United	W 1-0	Amoruso (pen)	9,386
Mar 6	St Johnstone	W 2-0	Flo, Ricksen	6,382
Mar 10	CELTIC	D 1-1	Numan	49,765
Mar 20	KILMARNOCK	W 5-0	McCann 3, Kanchelskis, Burke	40,768
Apr 7	HEARTS	W 2-0	Dodds 2	47,492
Apr 13	Livingston	L 1-2	Amoruso	10,019
Apr 21	Celtic	D 1-1	Lovenkrands	59,384
Apr 27	ABERDEEN	W 2-0	McCann, Ferguson	48,878
May 12	Dunfermline	D 1-1	Moore	8,716

Scottish Cup

Jan 15	Berwick	(Rd3) D 0-0		4,280
Jan 21	BERWICK	(R) W 3-0	Amoruso, Konterman, Arveladze	17,459
Jan 26	HIBERNIAN	(Rd4) W 4-1	Flo 2, Lovenkrands, Dodds	25,636
Feb 24	Forfar	(QF) W 6-0	Dodds 3, Arveladze 2, Kanchelskis	4,504
Mar 24	Partick Thistle*	(SF) W 3-0	Nerlinger 2, Ferguson	31,969
May 4	Celtic*	(F) W 3-2	Lovenkrands 2, Ferguson	51,138

Scottish League Cup

Oct 9	AIRDRIE	(Rd3) W 3-0	Arveladze 2, Numan	34,067
Nov 28	Ross County	(QF) W 2-1	Arveladze, Reyna	5,972
Feb 5	Celtic*	(SF) W 2-1	Lovenkrands, Konterman	43,457
Mar 17	Ayr United*	(F) W 4-0	Flo, Ferguson (pen), Caniggia 2	50,076

*Played at Hampden Park.

Champions League

Jul 25	Maribor	(2QR/FL) W 3-0	Flo 2 (1 pen), Nerlinger	8,000
Aug 1	MARIBOR	(2QR/SL) W 3-1	Flo, Caniggia 2	50,045
Aug 8	FENERBAHCE	(3QR/FL) D 0-0		49,472
Aug 22	Fenerbahce	(3QR/SL) L 1-2	Ricksen	30,000

UEFA Cup

Sep 27	Anzhi Makhachkala#	(Rd1) W 1-0	Konterman	3,700
Oct 18	DINAMO MOSCOW	(Rd2/FL) W 3-1	Amoruso, Ball, De Boer	45,008
Nov 1	Dinamo Moscow	(Rd2/SL) W 4-1	De Boer, Ferguson, Flo, Lovenkrands	6,000
Nov 22	PARIS SG	(Rd3/FL) D 0-0		49,223
Dec 6	Paris SG	(Rd3/SL) D 0-0*		32,000

*Rangers won 4-3 on penalties.

Feb 21	FEYENOORD	(Rd4/FL) D 1-1	Ferguson (pen)	49,041
Feb 28	Feyenoord	(Rd4/SL) L 2-3	McCann, Ferguson (pen)	45,000

#Played in Warsaw.

League & Cup Appearances

PLAYER	LEAGUE	CUP COMPETITION			TOTAL
		S CUP	SL CUP	CL/UEFA	
Amoruso	27	6	4	9	46
Arveladze	20 (1)		3 (1)	3	26 (2)
Ball	5 (2)		2	1 (1)	8 (3)
Brighton	1				1
Burke	1 (1)				1 (1)
Caniggia	16 (8)	3	4	8 (3)	31 (11)
De Boer	18 (6)	2 (2)	3	7	30 (8)
Dodds	5 (5)	1 (2)	0 (1)	0 (1)	6 (9)
Dowie	0 (1)				0 (1)
Ferguson	19 (1)	5	3	7 (1)	34 (2)
Flo	24 (5)	3	1 (1)	10(1)	38 (7)
Gibson	0 (1)				0 (1)
Hughes	11 (5)	3 (1)	0 (2)	3 (2)	17 (10)
Johnston	1				1
Kanchelskis	8 (4)		2 (1)	1	11 (5)
Klos	36	6	4	11	57
Konterman	26	2		2	11
Latapy	14 (2)	2 (1)	2 (1)	3 (4)	21 (8)
Lovenkrands	9 (9)	2 (2)	3	3 (2)	17 (13)
Malcolm	6 (1)		1		7 (1)
McCann	14 (11)	5	1 (1)	3 (3)	23 (15)
McGregor	2	0 (1)			2 (1)
Miller	0 (3)				0 (3)
Mols	8 (7)	2	0 (2)	0 (4)	10 (13)
Moore	16	2	2	7	27
Nerlinger	7 (1)	1	2		10 (1)
Penttila	0 (1)				0 (1)
Numan	28 (2)	2	3	10	43 (2)
Ricksen	30	4	3	9	46
Ross	19 (2)	3 (1)	1	1 (2)	24 (5)
Vidmar	22 (1)	5	1 (2)	5 (1)	33 (4)
Wilson	6	1	1	3 (1)	11 (1)

Goalscorers

PLAYER	LEAGUE	CUP COMPETITION			TOTAL
		S CUP	SL CUP	CL/UEFA	
Flo	18	2	1	4	25
Arveladze	12	3	3		17
Caniggia	5		2	2	9
De Boer	6			2	8
Ferguson	7		2	3	7
Lovenkrands	2	3	1	1	7
McCann	6			1	7
Amoruso	4	1		1	6
Dodds	2	4			6
Konterman	2	1	1	1	5
Latapy	6				5
Ricksen	4			1	5
Nerlinger	1	2		1	4
Moore	3				3
Kanchelskis	2	1			2
Mols	2				2
Numan	1		1		2
Ball			1		1
Burke	1				1
Hughes	1				1
Vidmar	1				1
Reyna	2		1		3
Opps' o.gs.	1				1

Final Scottish Premier Division Table

		P	W	D	L	F	A	PTS
1	CELTIC	38	33	4	1	94	18	103
2	RANGERS	38	25	10	3	82	27	85
3	LIVINGSTON	38	16	10	12	50	47	58
4	ABERDEEN	38	16	7	15	51	49	55
5	KILMARNOCK	38	13	10	15	44	54	49
6	HEARTS	38	14	6	18	52	57	48
7	DUNDEE UTD	38	12	10	16	38	59	46
8	DUNFERMLINE	38	12	9	17	41	44	45
9	DUNDEE	38	12	8	18	41	55	44
10	HIBERNIAN	38	10	11	17	51	56	41
11	MOTHERWELL	38	11	7	20	49	69	40
12	ST JOHNSTONE	38	5	6	27	24	62	21

Trophy-winning Rangers. Above left: Ian Ferguson and Ally McCoist in 1988 with the Scottish League Cup. Above right: John Greig lifts the Scottish Cup in 1973. Below left: Greig with the European Cup-Winners' Cup in 1972. Below right: Ally McCoist, Mark Hateley and Richard Gough with the league championship trophy in 1992.

Complete Players' Career Records

The list includes every player who has made a recorded competitive first team appearance for Rangers from the club's first Scottish Cup tie in 1874 to the Scottish Cup final of 2002. Key: LG – Scottish League, Scottish Premier League. SC – Scottish Cup. SLC – Scottish League Cup. EU – Champions League, European Cup, European Cup-Winners' Cup, Inter-Cities Fairs/UEFA Cup, European Super Cup. Totals are inclusive of substitute appearances.

Player	Nationality	Year Joined	Year Left	League Apps	Goals
Adamczuk, D	Polish	1999		13	
Aird	Scottish	1888	1888	1	1
Aitken, W	Scottish	1918	1919	21	2
Albertz, J	German	1996	2001	156	58
Alexander, T	Scottish	1970	1971	2	
Allan	Scottish	1904	1905	8	
Allan, J	Scottish	1889	1892	3	1
Allan, S	Scottish	1912	1912	1	
Amato, G	Argentinian	1998	2000	28	9
Amoruso, L	Italian	1997		123	9
Andersen, E	Danish	1995	1997	24	15
Anderson	Scottish	1915	1917	5	1
Anderson, S	Scottish	1959	1960	1	
Angus, G	Scottish	1879	1882		
Archibald, A	Scottish	1917	1934	513	126
Archibald, R	Scottish	1916	1917	12	3
Armour, D	Scottish	1974	1979	3	
Arnison, N	Scottish	1955	1957		
Arnison, W	South African	1946	1947	7	1
Arveladze, S	Georgian	2001		21	11
Austin, A	Scottish	1957	1958	1	
Baillie, D	Scottish	1960	1964	31	
Baird	Scottish	1915	1915	1	
Baird, S	Scottish	1955	1961	121	39
Ball, M	English	2001		7	
Ballantyne	Scottish	1916	1916	1	
Barker, J	Scottish	1892	1896	59	30
Barrie, A	Scottish	1908	1908	11	1
Bartram, J	Danish	1987	1988	11	3
Baxter, J	Scottish	1960	1970	150	19
Beattie, S	Scottish	1985	1987	5	
Beck, T	Icelandic	1964	1966	11	2
Beckett, W	Scottish	1950	1951	1	
Bell, D	Scottish	1985	1987	35	1
Bell, John	Scottish	1895	1896	7	
Bell, Joseph	Scottish	1909	1910	1	
Bell, R	Scottish	1916	1917	15	1
Bennett, A	Scottish	1908	1917	188	51
Bett, J	Scottish	1980	1983	104	21
Bjorklund, J	Swedish	1996	1998	60	
Black, K	Scottish	1981	1984	24	1
Blair, J	Scottish	1916	1919	91	7
Blyth, R	Scottish	1891	1894	10	2
Boli, B	French	1994	1995	28	2
Bollan, G	Scottish	1994	1998	11	
Bolt	Scottish	1939	1939	5	
Bone	Scottish	1916	1916	2	
Bonnyman, P	Scottish	1972	1973		
Bovill	Scottish	1908	1908	2	
Bowie, J	Scottish	1910	1922	299	62
Boyack, S	Scottish	1996	1999	1	
Boyd, D	Scottish	1893	1896	27	8
Boyd, G	Scottish	1975	1976	1	
Boyd, W	Scottish	1951	1952	2	
Brand, Ralph	Scottish	1954	1965	206	127
Brand, Robert	Scottish	1887	1888	2	2
Brander	Scottish	1916	1916	3	
Branscombe	Scottish	1916	1916	7	5
Brighton, T	Scottish	2001		1	
Brodie	Scottish	1902	1903	1	1
Brown, A	Scottish	1910	1914	27	7
Brown, D	Scottish	1917	1919	20	14

SC Apps	Goals	SLC Apps	Goals	European Apps	Goals	Totals Apps	Goals
1				5		19	
						1	1
						21	2
19	5	12	7	42	12	229	82
						2	
						8	
4	2					7	3
1						2	
3		3	1	10	3	44	13
16	3	11	2	39	4	189	18
3	1	2	2	6		35	18
						5	1
						1	
5	7					5	7
67	22					580	148
						12	3
		1				4	
2	2					2	2
1		2	3			10	4
4	3	3	3			28	17
						1	
4		3		2		40	
						1	
16	2	26	6	16	5	179	52
2				2	1	11	1
						1	
7	2					66	32
3						14	1
3						14	3
21		54	2	29	3	254	24
						5	
2	1					14	2
						1	
4		5				44	1
4						11	
						1	
						15	1
13	2					201	53
18	2	24	6	6	1	152	30
8		4		12		84	
3		7	1			34	2
						91	7
2	2					12	4
1		1		1		31	2
1		3				15	
						5	
						2	
1						1	
						2	
22	4					321	66
						1	
4	4					31	12
						1	
						2	
33	29	54	38	24	12	317	206
						2	2
						3	
						7	5
						1	
						1	1
2	1					29	8
						20	14

Player	Nationality	Year Joined	Year Left	League Apps	Goals
Brown, G	Scottish	1929	1941	299	22
Brown, J	Scottish	1912	1912	1	
Brown, John	Scottish	1987	1996	207	14
Brown, M	Scottish	1997	2001	4	
Brown, Robert	Scottish	1910	1915	46	
Brown, R (Bobby)	Scottish	1946	1956	211	
Bruce, A	Scottish	1981	1986	2	
Bruce, D	Scottish	1892	1892	4	5
Buchanan, James	Scottish	1886	1887	6	1
Buchanan, Jock	Scottish	1927	1931	96	3
Burke, C	Scottish	2001		2	1
Burns	Scottish	1895	1896	6	
Burns, H	Scottish	1983	1987	52	4
Butcher, T	English	1986	1991	127	8
Cairns, T	Scottish	1913	1927	407	138
Calder	Scottish	1933	1933	1	
Caldow, E	Scottish	1953	1966	265	17
Caldwell, N	Scottish	1994	1995	1	
Cameron, D	Scottish	1900	1901	9	5
Cameron, J	Scottish	1883	1887		
Campbell	Scottish	1932	1933	2	1
Campbell, D	Scottish	1903	1905	6	1
Campbell, James	Scottish	1875	1878		
Campbell, John	Scottish	1872	1875	4	
Campbell, John	Scottish	1898	1902	53	27
Campbell, P	Scottish	1872	1879		
Campbell, RG	Scottish	1906	1914	194	54
Caniggia, C	Argentinian	2001		24	5
Carson, S	N.Irish	1997	2001	2	
Caskie, J	Scottish	1946	1949	26	3
Chalk, C	Scottish	1904	1904	4	1
Chalmers	Scottish	1905	1905	1	2
Chalmers	Scottish	1924	1927	19	5
Chalmers, W	Scottish	1883	1887	24	
Chapman, G	Scottish	1910	1911	30	4
Charbonnier, L	French	1998	2001	18	
Cherry, R	Scottish	1885	1885	1	
Cheyne, W	Scottish	1933	1938	56	1
Christiansen, J	Danish	2000		3	
Christie, J	Scottish	1881	1884	5	2
Christie, J	Scottish	1961	1962	3	3
Clark, A	Scottish	1982	1985	41	14
Clark, D	Scottish	1892	1893	1	1
Clark, R	Scottish	1980	1982	1	
Cleland, A	Scottish	1994	1998	96	4
Cochrane, A	Scottish	1905	1906	10	
Cohen, A	Israeli	1986	1988	7	
Conlin, G	Scottish	1930	1931	2	
Conn, A	Scottish	1968	1974	93	23
Cook, T	Scottish	1884	1885	4	1
Cooper, D	Scottish	1977	1989	376	49
Cooper, N	Scottish	1988	1991	17	1
Corbett, W	Scottish	1881	1884		
Cowan	Scottish	1939	1939	1	
Cowan, J	Scottish	1894	1895	16	3
Cowan, T	Scottish	1988	1991	12	
Cox, S	Scottish	1946	1955	207	14
Craig	Scottish	1914	1916	42	
Craig, A	N.Irish	1905	1911	102	
Craig, J	Scottish	1905	1906	1	
Craig, T	Scottish	1923	1935	234	32
Crawford, D	Scottish	1894	1902	62	1
Crawford, R	Scottish	1896	1897	7	3
Croal, J	Scottish	1905	1906	3	
Croot	Scottish	1916	1917	9	1
Cullen	Scottish	1891	1891	5	
Cunning, R	Scottish	1954	1955	3	
Cunningham	Scottish	1906	1908	13	3

SC Apps	Goals	SLC Apps	Goals	European Apps	Goals	Totals Apps	Goals
40	1					339	23
						1	
33	4	18		20		278	18
		1				5	
3						49	
33		52				296	
						2	
						4	5
						6	1
19						115	3
						2	1
						6	
1		8		2		63	4
11		21	1	17	2	176	11
34	6					441	144
						1	
39	4	68	1	35	3	407	25
						1	
						9	5
19						19	
						2	1
3						9	1
10	5					10	5
						4	
9	2					62	29
24	15					24	15
17	2					211	56
3		4	2	11	2	42	9
1		1				4	
4		9	2			39	5
						4	1
2						3	2
2	2					21	7
						24	
2						32	4
		3		9		30	
						1	
4						60	1
		1		2		6	
						5	2
		4	3	1	2	8	8
7	2	10	5	4	1	62	22
2	1					3	2
						1	
14	3	10		14		134	7
						10	
		2		3		12	
						2	
13	3	31	11	12	2	149	39
						4	1
49	7	77	18	38	1	540	75
2		1				20	1
6	2					6	2
						1	
1	1					17	4
1		2				15	
40	3	63	3			310	20
						42	
16						118	
						1	
41	6					275	38
15						77	1
						7	3
						3	
						9	1
						5	
		2				5	
						13	3

Player	Nationality	Year Joined	Year Left	League Apps	Goals
Cunningham, A	Scottish	1915	1929	350	162
Dalrymple	Scottish	1905	1906	13	4
Dalziel, G	Scottish	1978	1984	34	9
Davie, J	Scottish	1893	1893	6	
Davies, W	Scottish	1980	1986	13	1
Davis, H	Scottish	1956	1964	168	8
Dawson, A	Scottish	1975	1987	218	6
Dawson, J	Scottish	1929	1945	241	
Deans	Scottish	1932	1932	2	
De Boer, R	Dutch	2000		41	12
Denny, J	Scottish	1970	1979	37	
Dibble, A	English	1997	1997	7	
Dick	Scottish	1893	1893	2	1
Dick	Scottish	1917	1919	2	
Dick	Scottish	1924	1925	1	1
Dickie, J	Scottish	1906	1908	29	3
Dickie, M	Scottish	1896	1904	141	
Dinsmore, H	Scottish	1903	1903	1	
Dixon, A	English	1917	1926	326	6
Dodds, B	Scottish	1999		58	21
Dodds, D	Scottish	1989	1991	17	4
Donaghy	Scottish	1904	1905	7	2
Donaldson, G	Scottish	1972	1974	5	
Donnachie	Scottish	1919	1919	5	
Douglas, W	Scottish	1875	1878		
Dowie, A	Scottish	2001		1	
Drinkell, K	English	1988	1989	36	11
Drinnan, J	Scottish	1878	1882	19	
Drummond, J	Scottish	1892	1904	185	2
Drummond, R	Scottish	1894	1894	1	
Drysdale, J	Scottish	1935	1938	18	5
Dunbar, T	Scottish	1891	1892	11	
Duncan, C	Scottish	1916	1917	25	15
Duncan, G	Scottish	1957	1960	12	5
Duncan, J	Scottish	1882	1886	10	1
Duncan, S	Scottish	1913	1919	101	26
Duncanson, J	Scottish	1946	1951	93	41
Dunlop	Scottish	1899	1900	6	
Dunlop, R	Scottish	1950	1953	3	
Dunlop, W	Scottish	1876	1880		
Durie, G	Scottish	1993	2000	125	43
Durrant, I	Scottish	1984	1998	250	26
Eaglesham, R	Scottish	1887	1888		
Easton, A	Scottish	1904	1905	9	
Elliott, A	Scottish	1955	1956	2	
English, S	N.Irish	1931	1933	60	54
Falco, M	English	1987	1988	14	5
Farrington, T	Scottish	1912	1913	8	
Feeney, L	N.Irish	1998	2001	1	
Ferguson	Scottish	1913	1914	1	
Ferguson, A	Scottish	1967	1969	41	25
Ferguson, B	Scottish	1997		112	8
Ferguson, Derek	Scottish	1982	1990	111	7
Ferguson, Duncan	Scottish	1993	1994	14	2
Ferguson, E	Scottish	1983	1986	14	1
Ferguson, Iain	Scottish	1984	1986	32	6
Ferguson, Ian	Scottish	1987	2000	239	28
Fernandes, F	French			4	1
Fiddes, J	Scottish	1935	1939	60	14
Findlay, J	Scottish	1904	1904	1	
Fitzgerald, D	N.Irish	1997	2000	1	
Findlay, W	Scottish	1947	1954	70	37
Fleck, R	Scottish	1983	1988	85	29
Fleming	Scottish	1891	1891	1	
Fleming	Scottish	1915	1915	4	1
Fleming, J	Scottish	1925	1934	225	176
Flo, T	Norwegian	2000		48	29
Forbes, J	Scottish	1887	1888	2	

Complete Players' Career Records: Cunningham, A – Forbes

SC Apps	Goals	SLC Apps	Goals	European Apps	Goals	Totals Apps	Goals
39	20					389	182
2	4					15	8
8	1	6	1			48	11
1						7	
3		5		2	1	23	2
23		42	3	28	2	261	13
36		39	1	23	1	316	8
30						271	
						2	
5		4		14	3	64	15
3		21		5		66	
						7	
						2	1
						2	
						1	1
6	1					35	4
34						175	
						1	
35	2					361	8
7	9	3	1	9	3	77	34
2		2	1			21	5
2						9	2
		5				10	
						5	
1						1	
						1	
8	5	6	2	4	1	54	19
		19					
38						223	2
						1	
						18	5
6						17	
						25	15
2		1				15	5
						10	1
2						103	26
17	7	30	11			140	59
1						7	
						3	
16	8					16	8
19	9	10	2	25	5	179	59
19	3	40	8	39	8	348	45
3						3	
						9	
						2	
12	10					72	64
		3	3	2	2	19	10
						8	
						1	
						1	
6	10	4	9	6		66	35
20	4	11	3	41	3	184	18
8		11	1	15	1	145	9
		3	4	3	2	23	5
						14	1
1	8	3	4	2		45	11
27	6	31	8	39	4	336	46
						4	1
7						67	14
						1	
						1	
11	7	33	21			114	65
3	8	2	8	3		104	34
						1	
						4	1
42	44					267	220
						48	29
						2	

Player	Nationality	Year Joined	Year Left	League Apps	Goals
Forrest, J	Scottish	1962	1967	105	83
Forsyth, A	Scottish	1978	1981	25	5
Forsyth, T	Scottish	1972	1982	218	2
Frame, J	Scottish	1948	1952	1	
Francis, T	English	1987	1988	18	1
Franks, A	English	1959	1960	3	
Fraser, A	Scottish	1902	1906	45	1
Fraser, C	Scottish	1984	1987	52	6
Fraser, R	Scottish	1887	1891	4	4
Fraser, S	Scottish	1983	1985	9	
Freebairn	Scottish	1892	1893	2	
Fulton	Scottish	1913	1914	14	1
Fyfe, G	Scottish	1969	1976	64	22
Galloway, J	Scottish	1938	1939	4	
Galt, J	Scottish	1906	1914	185	5
Gardiner	Scottish	1894	1895	2	
Gardiner, W	Scottish	1951	1955	25	16
Gascoigne, P	English	1995	1998	74	30
Gattuso, R	Italian	1997	1998	34	3
Gayle, M	Jamaican	2001	2001	4	
Gibb, D	Scottish	1874	1875		
Gibson, A	Scottish	1910	1913	9	5
Gibson, J	Scottish	1996		2	
Gibson, N	Scottish	1894	1904	157	12
Gibson, W	Scottish	1894	1895	17	1
Gilchrist	Scottish	1904	1904	1	
Gilchrist, T	Scottish	1908	1910	21	6
Gillespie, G	Scottish	1876	1883		
Gillick, T	Scottish	1933	1950	104	49
Gilmour	Scottish	1939	1939	3	1
Ginzberg, B	Israeli	1989	1991	4	
Glass	Scottish	1891	1891	1	
Glen	Scottish	1897	1898	6	
Glenn	Scottish	1913	1914	4	
Goodwin, J	Scottish	1910	1914	47	19
Goram, A	Scottish	1991	1998	185	
Gordon, D	English	1991	1993	45	6
Gordon, J	Scottish	1907	1920	315	64
Gossland, J	Scottish	1883	1886	15	8
Goudie, D	Scottish	1898	1901	1	1
Gough, R	Scottish	1987	1998	317	25
Gourlay, A	Scottish	1904	1906	10	
Gow, D	Scottish	1886	1893	27	1
Gow, J	Scottish	1886	1890	3	2
Graham, D	Scottish	1995	1998	3	
Graham, J	Scottish	1899	1902	23	5
Grant, B	Scottish	1959	1960	1	
Gray	Scottish	1917	1917	2	1
Gray, A	Scottish	1988	1989	14	5
Gray, David	Scottish	1946	1947	9	
Gray, Douglas	Scottish	1925	1945	490	2
Gray, John	Scottish	1893	1895	25	13
Gray, Josiah	Scottish	1903	1907	47	
Greig, J	Scottish	1961	1978	498	87
Grierson, D	Scottish	1952	1957	72	42
Guivarc'h, S	French	1998	1999	14	5
Hadden	Scottish	1908	1908	2	
Haddow	Scottish	1928	1928	1	
Haddow, D	Scottish	1891	1895	66	
Hagen, D	Scottish	1989	1994	16	3
Hair	Scottish	1927	1928	2	2
Hamilton	Scottish	1916	1916	1	
Hamilton, A	Scottish	1882	1884		
Hamilton, James	Scottish	1894	1894	2	1
Hamilton, James	Scottish	1925	1928	35	2
Hamilton, Johnny	Scottish	1973	1978	59	5
Hamilton, JR	Scottish	1900	1907	3	1
Hamilton, R	N.Irish	1927	1932	121	

SC Apps	Goals	SLC Apps	Goals	European Apps	Goals	Totals Apps	Goals
10	6	37	50	11	6	163	145
1		8		7		41	5
36	2	50	2	22		326	6
						1	
		2		4		25	
						3	
14						59	1
3	1	12	2	8		75	9
3						7	4
1						10	
						2	
2						16	1
1		20	8	6	1	91	31
						4	
21						206	5
						2	
3	2	3	1			31	19
8	3	7	4	15	2	104	39
4	4			7	2	49	5
						4	
3	1					3	1
						9	5
						2	
35	10					192	22
1						18	1
						1	
6	2					27	8
30						30	
16	5	20	8			140	62
						3	1
3		1				8	
						1	
						6	
						4	
3	1					50	20
26		19		31		261	
7	1	2	1	1		55	8
19	1					334	65
						15	8
1						2	1
37	2	37	3	36	4	427	34
						10	
17	1					44	2
						3	2
		2				5	
6	2					29	7
						1	
						2	1
1		1				16	5
		3				12	
65						555	2
6						31	13
6						53	
72	9	121	17	64	7	755	120
13	6	21	11			106	59
4	1	1	1			19	7
						2	
						1	
16						82	
1		1		2		20	3
						2	2
						1	
8	1					8	1
						2	1
5						40	2
11	2	6	1	1		77	8
2	2					5	3
22						143	

Player	Nationality	Year Joined	Year Left	League Apps	Goals
Hamilton, RC	Scottish	1897	1908	175	157
Hamilton, T	Scottish	1923	1934	243	
Hansen, C	Danish	1921	1924	23	14
Harris	Scottish	1917	1917	1	1
Harrison	Scottish	1937	1939	14	5
Hart	Scottish	1918	1918	6	5
Hart, W	Scottish	1883	1883		
Hartley	Scottish	1903	1903	4	
Hateley, M	English	1990	1997	169	88
Hay, W	Scottish	1935	1935	1	
Hay, William	Scottish	1889	1896	2	
Heggie, C	Scottish	1882	1886	11	2
Hempsey, J	Scottish	1912	1919	147	
Henderson, G	Scottish	1919	1927	170	123
Henderson, GH	Scottish	1902	1905	34	
Henderson, J	Scottish	1889	1892	21	6
Henderson, M	Scottish	1974	1978	33	10
Henderson, W	Scottish	1960	1972	276	36
Hendry, C	Scottish	1998	2000	21	
Hendry, Joe	Scottish	1906	1917	179	6
Hendry, John	Scottish	1889	1890	3	
Heron, B	Scottish	1969	1970	7	
Hill	Scottish	1936	1936	1	
Hill, D	Scottish	1875	1884	26	8
Hislop, D	Scottish	1890	1891	19	10
Hodge	Scottish	1925	1926	2	
Hodge, W	Scottish	1891	1892	25	
Hogg, B	Scottish	1957	1959	2	1
Hogg, W	English	1909	1913	102	43
Hotson, R	Scottish	1887	1889	5	
Houston, D	Scottish	1973	1974	10	
Howden, W	Scottish	1900	1903	1	
Hubbard, J	South African	1949	1959	172	77
Hughes, S	Scottish	1999		18	1
Huistra, P	Dutch	1990	1995	125	22
Hume, R	Scottish	1959	1962	17	3
Hunter, D	Scottish	1973	1975	3	
Hunter, Willie	Scottish	1909	1910	17	19
Hunter, Willie	Scottish	1962	1964	1	
Hurlock, T	English	1990	1991	29	2
Hynd, R	Scottish	1963	1969	31	4
Hyslop, T	Scottish	1896	1900	35	25
Inglis, J	Scottish	1881	1884		
Ireland, R	Scottish	1923	1929	18	
Jackson, C	Scottish	1963	1982	341	23
Jackson, J	Scottish	1896	1909	33	
Jamieson	Scottish	1897	1897	1	
Jamieson, I	Scottish	1921	1925	32	
Jardine, S	Scottish	1965	1982	451	42
Jenkins, G	Scottish	1933	1945	25	
Johansen, K	Danish	1965	1970	158	4
Johansson, J	Finnish	1997	2000	47	14
Johnson, J	Scottish	1947	1952	32	8
Johnston, A	Scottish	2000	2001	14	
Johnston, M	Scottish	1989	1992	76	31
Johnston, W	Scottish	1964	1982	246	91
Johnstone	Scottish	1894	1894	1	
Johnstone, A	Scottish	1919	1924	25	1
Johnstone, D	Scottish	1970	1986	369	132
Kanchelskis, A	Russian	1998	2002	77	14
Kauppila, J	Finnish	2000	2002	4	
Kelso, T	Scottish	1914	1915	22	
Kennedy, A	Scottish	1982	1984	15	3
Kennedy, J	Scottish	1932	1937	61	
Kennedy, S	Scottish	1973	1980	99	
Kerr	Scottish	1898	1989	1	
Kerr, N	Scottish	1890	1893	59	20
Kerr, R	Scottish	1880	1880	1	

SC Apps	Goals	SLC Apps	Goals	European Apps	Goals	Totals Apps	Goals
34	27					209	184
38						281	
						23	14
						1	1
1						15	5
						6	5
5						5	
						4	
17	10	19	11	17	6	222	115
						1	
5						7	
						11	2
3						150	
25	19					195	142
9						43	
7	5					28	11
5	3	6	1	1		77	8
44	5	60	11	46	10	426	62
3		4		7		35	
11	1					190	7
						3	
		2				9	
						1	
						26	8
1						20	10
						2	
6						31	
						2	1
5	2					107	45
						5	
4		3				17	
						1	
19	5	41	23	6	1	238	106
4		2		5		29	1
9	1	15	1	9	2	158	26
3		3				23	3
1						4	
1						18	19
						1	
2	4					35	2
4	1	6	7			48	5
8	6					43	31
16	3					16	3
1						19	
53	8	75	8	36	1	505	40
						33	
						1	
1						33	
64	8	107	25	52	2	674	77
2						27	
21	2	32	2	27	1	238	9
6	3	4	1	17	6	74	24
2	2	2	1			36	11
3	1	2		7	2	26	3
5	1	13	9	6	5	100	46
42	10	65	16	40	8	393	125
						1	
						25	1
57	30	85	39	35	9	546	210
13	3	4		20	3	114	20
						4	
						22	
3	1	2				20	4
3						64	
10		19		3		131	
2	1					3	1
10	8					69	28
						1	

Player	Nationality	Year Joined	Year Left	League Apps	Goals
Kilpatrick, J	Scottish	1922	1925	3	
King, R	Scottish	1961	1962	2	
Kinnear, D	Scottish	1934	1944	106	32
Kirkwood, A	Scottish	1922	1925	9	
Kirkwood, D	Scottish	1924	1927	1	
Kirkwood, David	Scottish	1986	1989	7	
Kitchenbrand, D	South African	1956	1958	29	26
Kivlichan, W	Scottish	1905	1907	20	7
Klos, S	German	1998		110	
Konterman, B	Dutch	2000		63	5
Kuznetsov, O	Ukrainian	1990	1994	34	1
Kyle, A	Scottish	1904	1908	99	47
Lafferty, P	Scottish	1887	1887	2	2
Laird, E	Scottish	1921	1922	2	
Latapy, R	Trinidadian	2001		16	5
Latif, M	Egyptian	1935	1935	1	
Laudrup, B	Danish	1994	1998	117	34
Law	Scottish	1916	1917	4	
Law, G	Scottish	1906	1912	96	1
Law, J	Scottish	1892	1892	5	4
Lawrie, M	Scottish	1884	1887	17	7
Lawson, H	Scottish	1916	1924	47	4
Lennie, W	Scottish	1902	1903	5	2
Liddell, C	Scottish	1951	1955	35	8
Lindsay, Joe	Scottish	1886	1887		
Lindsay, John	Scottish	1946	1952	17	
Lister	Scottish	1915	1916	5	1
Little, A	Scottish	1938	1951	6	
Little, J	Scottish	1950	1961	178	1
Livingston	Scottish	1917	1917	5	3
Livingston, G	Scottish	1907	1909	47	20
Lock, H	English	1909	1920	221	
Lockie, T	Scottish	1929	1930	2	
Logan, J	Scottish	1912	1917	113	8
Logie, W	Scottish	1956	1957	16	
Lovenkrands, P	Danish	2000		26	2
Low, J	Scottish	1919	1921	4	
Low, T	Scottish	1896	1906	24	7
Lockhart	Scottish	1884	1884		
Lyall, K	Scottish	1981	1984	9	1
Lyness, A	Scottish	1938	1939	6	3
Macaulay, A	Scottish	1933	1937	36	7
MacDonald, A	Scottish	1968	1981	336	51
MacDonald, I	Scottish	1969	1973	11	2
MacDonald, J	Scottish	1978	1986	163	44
MacDonald, K	Scottish	1988	1989	3	
MacFarlane, D	Scottish	1984	1989	7	
Mackay, W	Scottish	1975	1985	24	1
Mackie, J	Scottish	1887	1887	1	
Mackie, A	Scottish	1902	1905	51	24
MacKinnon, D	Scottish	1982	1986	102	1
Main, R	Scottish	1929	1939	139	31
Mainds	Scottish	1906	1907	13	1
Maitland, A	Scottish	1881	1883		
Malcolm, R	Scottish	1997		16	1
Malone	Scottish	1925	1926	15	2
Manderson, B	N.Irish	1915	1927	370	5
Marshall, A	Scottish	1876	1880	15	10
Marshall, D	Scottish	1946	1953	14	
Marshall, J	Scottish	1925	1934	200	111
Marshall, R	Scottish	1889	1896	100	4
Mason, C	Scottish	1932	1933	3	
Mason, J	Scottish	1972	1974	16	2
Martin	Scottish	1892	1892	2	
Martin	Scottish	1916	1919	39	5
Martin, J	Scottish	1876	1880		
Martin, N	Scottish	1958	1970	75	
Mathie	Scottish	1895	1895	1	
Mathieson, W	Scottish	1964	1975	174	2

Complete Players' Career Records: Kilpatrick – Mathieson

SC Apps	Goals	SLC Apps	Goals	European Apps	Goals	Totals Apps	Goals
						3	
		1				3	
3						109	32
						9	
						1	
		1		2		10	
3	2	3	1	2	1	37	30
						20	7
19		6		27		162	
5	1	2	1	21	1	91	8
		1				35	1
11	5					110	52
						2	2
						2	
3		3		7		29	5
						1	
13	5	4	3	17	3	151	45
						4	
11						107	1
2	1					7	5
						17	7
						47	4
						5	2
6	2	11	2			52	12
3	2					3	2
1		4				22	
						5	1
						6	
32		55		10		275	1
						5	3
6	3					53	23
17						238	
						2	
5						118	8
		3				19	
4	3	4	1	6	1	40	7
						4	
9	4					33	11
1						1	
		2				12	
2	2					8	5
1						37	7
50	15	79	18	38	10	503	94
1		2				14	2
24	13	34	15	9	5	230	77
						3	
		1				9	
3		7	2	3	1	37	4
						1	
7	2					58	26
7		23	1	9		141	2
19	4					158	35
						13	1
2						2	
3		1				20	1
3						18	2
32						402	5
						15	10
7	9	6	2	9		20	9
25	14					225	125
25						125	4
						3	
1		2				19	2
						2	
						39	5
1						1	
6		14		15		110	
						1	
36		38		28	1	276	3

Player	Nationality	Year Joined	Year Left	League Apps	Goals
Matthew, A	Scottish	1958	1960	28	7
Maxwell, A	Scottish	1992	1995	53	
May, J	Scottish	1904	1910	130	13
McAdam, C	Scottish	1980	1985	65	15
McAllan	Scottish	1896	1896	1	
McAllister	Scottish	1888	1888	1	
McArthur, J	Scottish	1907	1909	9	
McAulay	Scottish	1910	1910	1	
McAulay, R	Scottish	1930	1932	39	
McBain, W	Scottish	1891	1892	3	2
McBeath, W	Scottish	1872	1875		
McCall, I	Scottish	1987	1990	21	2
McCall, S	Scottish	1991	1998	194	15
McCallum, A	Scottish	1970	1971	1	
McCandless, W	N.Irish	1920	1930	202	8
McCann, N	Scottish	1998		95	17
McCartney, J	Scottish	1886	1887	7	
McClelland, J	N.Irish	1981	1985	96	4
McCloy, P	Scottish	1970	1986	351	
McCoist, A	Scottish	1983	1998	418	251
McColl, I	Scottish	1946	1961	360	11
McColl, RS	Scottish	1904	1907	27	13
McCrae	Scottish	1916	1916	3	
McCreadie, A	Scottish	1890	1898	89	10
McCreadie, H	Scottish	1889	1896	78	28
McCulloch, J	Scottish	1918	1918	2	1
McCulloch, W	Scottish	1949	1955	49	9
McDermid, R	Scottish	1917	1922	52	12
McDonald, A	Scottish	1902	1903	14	5
McDonald, J	Scottish	1907	1909	46	10
McDonald, M	Scottish	1922	1924	1	
McDonald, R	Scottish	1928	1938	185	1
McDonald, T	Scottish	1919	1921	5	1
McDougall, I	Scottish	1973	1977	31	3
McDougall, L	Scottish	1901	1902	4	3
McEwan	Scottish	1904	1905	9	
McEwan, A	Scottish	1958	1959	1	
McFarlane	Scottish	1907	1907	1	
McFarlane, A	Scottish	1887	1890		
McFarlane, W	Scottish	1881	1882	5	2
McFie	Scottish	1905	1907	16	3
McGhee	Scottish	1906	1906	1	
McGinty, B	Scottish	1993	1999	3	
McGowan	Scottish	1891	1891	1	1
McGowan, R	Scottish	1929	1932	12	10
McGregor	Scottish	1924	1926	9	
McGregor, A	Scottish	2001		2	
McGregor, J	Scottish	1987	1992	26	
McGregor, W	Scottish	1883	1884	5	1
McHardy, H	Scottish	1883	1886	14	3
McInnes, T	Scottish	1892	1892	4	2
McInnes, D	Scottish	1995	1999	35	1
McIntyre	Scottish	1895	1896	3	
McIntyre, H	Scottish	1877	1882	13	
McIntyre, I	Scottish	1949	1950	2	
McIntyre, James	Scottish	1880	1891	11	
McIntyre, Jim	Scottish	1981	1982	1	
McIntyre, M	Scottish	1880	1880		
McKay, R	Scottish	1925	1926	25	7
McKean, R	Scottish	1974	1978	91	12
McKenna, H	Scottish	1916	1921	40	
McKenzie	Scottish	1909	1910	26	
McKenzie, A	Scottish	1884	1894	6	5
McKenzie, George	Scottish	1954	1955	1	
McKenzie, Gordon	Scottish	1954	1955	9	
McKillop, T	Scottish	1935	1941	73	1
McKinlay	Scottish	1900	1900	2	
McKinnon, R	Scottish	1960	1973	301	2

SC Apps	Goals	SLC Apps	Goals	European Apps	Goals	Totals Apps	Goals
3	2	4	1	2	2	37	12
7		7		2		69	
19	3					149	16
12	8	19	9	3		99	32
						1	
						1	
						9	
						1	
7						46	
3	1					6	3
5						5	
1		1		1		24	2
27		16	3	28	2	265	20
						1	
29	1					231	9
15	3	6		27	2	143	22
						7	
13	1	30	2	14	1	153	8
55		86		43		535	
47	29	62	54	54	21	581	355
59	1	100	2	7		526	14
6	3					33	16
						3	
20	1					109	11
18	9					96	37
						2	1
14	5	5	1			68	15
3	2					55	14
7	3					21	8
2						48	10
						1	
24						209	1
						5	1
2		3		1		37	3
						4	3
3						12	
						1	
						1	
5						5	
						5	2
2	1					18	4
						1	
		1				4	
2						3	1
1						13	10
						9	
						3	
1							
		4		4		34	
						5	1
						14	3
						4	2
3		6	2	9	1	53	4
						3	
						13	
						2	
46	2					57	2
						1	
1						1	
4	1					29	8
8	4	15	1	5		119	17
						40	
2						28	
13	3					19	8
2						3	
						9	
8						81	1
						2	
44		83		45	1	473	3

Player	Nationality	Year Joined	Year Left	League Apps	Goals
McKnight, P	N.Irish	1994	2000	1	
McLaren, A	Scottish	1994	1998	79	5
McLean	Scottish	1909	1910	2	1
McLean, D	Scottish	1918	1919	24	29
McLean, George	Scottish	1959	1962	8	3
McLean, George	Scottish	1962	1967	69	49
McLean, T	Scottish	1971	1982	300	35
McLeod	Scottish	1895	1896	5	
McMillan, D	Scottish	1905	1906	9	1
McMillan, G	Scottish	1926	1930	33	12
McMillan, H	Scottish	1953	1956	5	1
McMillan, I	Scottish	1958	1964	127	36
McMinn, T	Scottish	1984	1987	63	2
McMurray	Scottish	1903	1903	1	
McNee, C	Scottish	1939	1947	14	3
McNeil, M	Scottish	1872	1882	34	9
McNeil, P	Scottish	1872	1876	7	
McNeil, W	Scottish	1872	1878	11	
McPhail, B	Scottish	1927	1940	354	230
McPhee, W	Scottish	1968	1970	1	
McPherson	Scottish	1939	1939	1	
McPherson, A	Scottish	1928	1929	6	2
McPherson, D	Scottish	1981	1995	232	18
McPherson, DM	Scottish	1892	1893	10	1
McPherson, I	Scottish	1947	1948	1	1
McPherson, J	Scottish	1890	1902	176	98
McPherson, N	Scottish	1901	1902	2	
McPherson, W	Scottish	1908	1910	51	24
McQuarrie, C	Scottish	1878	1880	1	1
McQueen, G	Scottish	1917	1921	23	
McSwegan, G	Scottish	1987	1993	18	4
Meikle	Scottish	1887	1889		
Meiklejohn, D	Scottish	1919	1936	490	42
Melrose, H	Scottish	1957	1958		
Menzies	Scottish	1906	1906	1	
Menzies, R	Scottish	1954	1955		
Mikhailichenko, A	Ukrainian	1991	1996	110	20
Millar, James	Scottish	1896	1900	53	30
Millar, Jimmy	Scottish	1954	1967	197	92
Miller	Scottish	1889	1889		
Miller	Scottish	1906	1910	11	1
Miller	Scottish	1919	1919	1	
Miller, Alec	Scottish	1896	1896	2	
Miller, Alex	Scottish	1967	1983	197	17
Miller, Colin	Canadian	1985	1987	2	
Miller, Charlie	Scottish	1993	1999	83	10
Miller, JE	Scottish	1898	1899	5	
Miller, K	Scottish	2000	2001	30	8
Miller, T	Scottish	1895	1896	8	4
Mitchell, Dave	Australian	1983	1985	26	6
Mitchell, Davy	Scottish	1889	1900	133	6
Moles, W	Scottish	1957	1958	3	
Mols, M	Dutch	1999		37	16
Montgomery	Scottish	1894	1895	8	
Montgomery, W	Scottish	1912	1913	7	2
Moore, C	Australian	1993		118	9
Morris, E	Scottish	1973	1979	8	
Morrison, B	Scottish	1956	1958	5	6
Morrow, J	N.Irish	1991	1996	5	
Morton, Alan	Scottish	1920	1933	382	83
Morton, Archie	Scottish	1924	1924	1	
Morton, H	Scottish	1901	1902	2	
Morton, J	Scottish	1921	1921	2	
Morton, P	Scottish	1884	1885	4	3
Moyies	Scottish	1927	1928	3	
Muir, H	Scottish	1913	1916	64	
Muir, J	Scottish	1885	1895	19	2
Muirhead, T	Scottish	1917	1930	291	38

SC Apps	Goals	SLC Apps	Goals	European Apps	Goals	Totals Apps	Goals
		1				2	
8	3	5				95	5
						2	1
						24	29
						8	3
14	8	28	23	6	2	117	82
46	10	74	8	32	4	452	57
						5	
						9	1
5						38	12
		3	1			8	2
23	6	22	6	22	7	194	55
		6	2	6		75	4
						1	
						14	3
						34	9
						7	
						11	
54	31					408	261
		2				3	
						1	
						6	2
24	5	37	2	29	7	322	32
1						11	1
						1	1
42	23					218	121
						2	
9	3					60	27
						1	1
						23	
2	1	3		1		24	5
1						1	
73	4					563	46
1	2					1	2
						1	
1						1	
12	3	6	1	6		134	24
18	9					71	39
35	30	54	28	31	12	317	162
1						1	
						11	1
						1	
						2	
27	1	63	12	19		306	30
1				1		4	
7	3	11	1	17	2	118	16
						5	
3	1	1	1	5	1	39	11
						8	4
3	1	11	3	5	4	45	14
38	2					171	8
		2				5	
3	4	20	6			64	22
						8	
						7	2
15	1	13		34	1	180	11
2		1	1			11	1
2	1	1				8	7
		1				6	
58	22					440	105
						1	
1						3	
						2	
						4	3
						3	
						64	
16						35	2
36	6					327	44

Player	Nationality	Year Joined	Year Left	League Apps	Goals
Munro, I	Scottish	1976	1977	5	
Munro, S	Scottish	1983	1991	179	3
Murdoch	Scottish	1895	1895	1	
Murray	Scottish	1897	1898	3	
Murray, J	Scottish	1930	1932	10	2
Murray, M	Scottish	1955	1963	103	80
Murray, N	Scottish	1989	1997	63	
Murray, T	Scottish	1908	1909	14	11
Myhre, T	Norwegian	1999	1999	3	
Neef, G	German	1968	1973	33	3
Negri, M	Italian	1997	2001	30	32
Neil, R	Scottish	1897	1904	92	24
Neillands, I	Scottish	1951	1952	6	1
Nerlinger, C	German	2001		8	1
Ness, W	Scottish	1882	1883		
Newbigging, A	Scottish	1906	1908	60	6
Nicholl, J	N.Irish	1983	1989	74	
Nicholson, B	Scottish	1995	2000	8	
Nicholson, J	Scottish	1921	1924	30	1
Nicholson, W	Scottish	1929	1935	70	15
Nicol, A	Scottish	1887	1887		
Nicol, J	Scottish	1887	1890		
Niemi, A	Finnish	1997	1999	13	
Nisbet, S	Scottish	1985	1993	90	6
Niven, G	Scottish	1951	1960	221	
Niven, J	Scottish	1885	1885		
Noble, R	Scottish	1908	1909	10	1
Numan, A	Dutch	1998		92	2
O'Hara, A	Scottish	1973	1977	32	7
Ormond, G	Scottish	1911	1914	53	
Orr, R	Scottish	1958	1959	1	
Osborne, J	Scottish	1925	1930	12	1
Oswald, J	Scottish	1895	1899	26	13
Parker, R	Scottish	1910	1916	18	17
Parlane, D	Scottish	1970	1980	202	80
Parlane, J	Scottish	1946	1948	5	3
Paterson, B	Scottish	1958	1962	67	12
Paterson, C	Scottish	1982	1987	83	4
Paterson, J	Scottish	1910	1920	156	38
Paterson, W	Scottish	1916	1916	5	3
Paton, T	Scottish	1904	1904	2	
Paton, W	Scottish	1947	1957	110	40
Paul, B	Scottish	1966	1967	1	
Peacock, A	Scottish	1884	1888		
Penman, A	Scottish	1967	1973	101	36
Penman, W	Scottish	1960	1961	3	
Penttila, T	Finnish	1999	2002	4	
Persson, O	Swedish	1967	1970	72	22
Petric, G	Yugoslav	1995	1998	66	3
Phillip	Scottish	1916	1917	1	
Phillips, G	Scottish	1874	1876	6	1
Phillips, J	English	1986	1989	25	
Porrini, S	Italian	1997	2001	85	6
Pray	Scottish	1894	1896	3	1
Prentice, J	Scottish	1950	1956	96	18
Pressley, S	Scottish	1991	1995	34	1
Pringle, W	Scottish	1880	1888	33	9
Provan, D	Scottish	1958	1970	170	9
Pryde, W	Scottish	1953	1955	11	
Prytz, R	Swedish	1982	1985	78	12
Purdon, J	Scottish	1924	1930	6	
Pursell, P	Scottish	1914	1919	128	1
Queen, J	Scottish	1955	1958	2	
Rae, W	Scottish	1946	1957	130	6
Ralston	Scottish	1889	1889	1	
Ramage	Scottish	1909	1910	6	2
Ramsay, G	Scottish	1912	1912	3	
Ramsay, R	Scottish	1882	1882	2	

SC Apps	Goals	SLC Apps	Goals	European Apps	Goals	Totals Apps	Goals
		6	1			11	1
13		22		19		233	3
						1	
						3	
1	1					11	3
16	19	27	19	8	3	154	121
5	2	4		9		81	2
1						15	11
		1		2		6	
		6		6		48	
5	1	2		6	3	43	36
17	4					109	28
1						7	1
1	2			2	1	11	4
1						1	
						66	
7		14		11		106	
		1		2	1	11	1
						30	1
5	3					75	18
1						1	
4						4	
		1		8		22	
8	1	8	1	12	1	118	9
32		59		15		327	
1						1	
						10	1
8	2	10	1	30		140	5
3		6	1	4	2	45	10
4						57	
						1	
1						13	1
7	4					33	17
2	2					20	19
25	8	51	21	22	2	300	111
2						7	3
19		18				116	
8	26	5	13	3		130	12
12	3					168	41
						5	3
						2	
24	9	30	19			164	68
						1	
13	4					13	4
12	4	19	7	18	2	150	49
						3	
						5	
1							
10	3	14	4	17	2	113	31
8	9	15	1			98	4
						1	
						6	1
		4		4		33	
11	8			26	1	130	7
						4	
16	8	30	11			142	37
3		3		4		44	1
						33	9
20	1	50	1	22		262	11
2						13	
11	1	19	5	10	2	118	20
						6	
						128	1
						2	
16		33	1			179	7
						1	
						6	2
						3	
						2	

Player	Nationality	Year Joined	Year Left	League Apps	Goals
Rankine	Scottish	1905	1906	15	3
Rankine, J	Scottish	1874	1874		
Redford, I	Scottish	1980	1986	172	23
Reid, A	Scottish	1964	1968	3	2
Reid, B	Scottish	1991	1996	5	
Reid, D	Scottish	1889	1891	17	
Reid, J	Scottish	1936	1939	11	3
Reid, R	Scottish	1893	1893	1	
Reid, T	Scottish	1920	1925	29	
Reid, W	Scottish	1909	1920	217	188
Rennie, H	Scottish	1908	1910	33	
Reyna, C	American	1999	2001	63	9
Riccio, L	Italian	1998	1999	1	
Richmond, A	Scottish	1910	1912	32	
Ricketts, S	Scottish	1875	1885	12	1
Ricksen, F	Dutch	2000		57	5
Riddell, J	Scottish	1912	1913	1	
Rideout, P	English	1991	1993	9	1
Ritchie, A	Scottish	1919	1920	21	
Ritchie, B	Scottish	1955	1967	207	
Robb, W	Scottish	1920	1926	227	
Roberts, G	English	1986	1988	55	3
Roberts, S	Scottish	1934	1935	8	1
Robertson, C	Scottish	1977	1980	15	2
Robertson, David	Scottish	1991	1997	184	15
Robertson, Douglas	Scottish	1981	1984	6	
Robertson, Jacky	Scottish	1899	1905	102	18
Robertson, John	Scottish	1912	1913	14	
Robertson, S	Scottish	1987	1994	26	1
Robertson, T	Scottish	1957	1958		
Robin, J	Scottish	1889	1890		
Rodger, J	Scottish	1953	1955	3	
Ross, M	Scottish	1997		23	
Ross, R	Scottish	1937	1938	8	
Rozental, S	Chilean	1997	2001	17	3
Ruddiman, T	Scottish	1905	1906	7	3
Russell	Scottish	1895	1895	2	
Russell, R	Scottish	1977	1987	250	31
Russell, T	Scottish	1933	1934	8	
Rutherford	Scottish	1917	1917	1	1
Rutherford, E	Scottish	1946	1952	95	19
Salenko, O	Russian	1995	1996	16	7
Scott	Scottish	1914	1914	3	
Scott, Alex	Scottish	1954	1963	216	67
Scott, Ally	Scottish	1973	1976	35	9
Scott, C	Scottish	1992	1996	13	
Scott, R	Scottish	1891	1898	22	2
Semple, W	Scottish	1967	1972	8	2
Setterington, D	Scottish	1965	1970	13	4
Sharp, A	Scottish	1898	1901	9	6
Sharp, J	Scottish	1898	1898	1	1
Sharp, James	Scottish	1908	1909	19	
Sharp, R	Scottish	1974	1975		
Shaw	Scottish	1926	1927	36	2
Shaw, H	Scottish	1905	1906	6	3
Shaw, Jock	Scottish	1938	1953	173	1
Shaw, John	Scottish	1946	1947		
Shearer, R	Scottish	1955	1965	268	2
Shields, G	Scottish	1995	1997	7	
Simpson, Billy	N.Irish	1950	1959	172	113
Simpson, Bobby	Scottish	1950	1951	2	2
Simpson, J	Scottish	1927	1940	289	5
Sinclair, T	Scottish	1904	1907	47	
Singleton, T	Scottish	1918	1918	2	
Sloan	Scottish	1888	1888	2	2
Smith	Scottish	1885	1885		
Smith, Alec	Scottish	1894	1915	407	128
Smith, Alex	Scottish	1966	1969	41	20

SC Apps	Goals	SLC Apps	Goals	European Apps	Goals	Totals Apps	Goals
						15	3
2						2	
22	5	40	11	13	3	247	42
						3	2
		1				6	
5						22	
5	2					16	5
						1	
2						31	
13	7					230	195
7						40	
6	2			25	1	96	10
						1	
2						34	
						12	1
7	5			14	1	83	6
						1	
2	1					12	1
5						26	
37		66		30		340	
24						251	
4		5		5		69	3
3						11	1
2	2	1	2			21	3
26	3	19	1	22		251	19
2						8	
28	7					130	25
						14	
1		1		2		30	1
1						1	
4	1					4	1
						3	
4		1		3		31	
						8	
5	3					22	6
						7	3
						2	
39	8	55	6	26	1	370	46
1						9	
						1	1
17	4	28	5			140	28
		2	1	2		20	8
						3	
25	5	62	24	28	12	331	108
4	2	15	9			54	20
						13	
3						25	2
		1				9	2
				1	1	14	5
1						10	6
						1	1
						19	
1						1	
5						41	2
						6	3
27		42				242	1
1						1	
37		72	2	30		407	4
2		2				11	
23	14	38	34	6	2	239	163
						2	2
42	1					331	6
9						56	
						2	
						2	2
1						1	
74	24					481	152
2		14	5	11	1	68	26

Player	Nationality	Year Joined	Year Left	League Apps	Goals
Smith, D	Scottish	1966	1974	195	8
Smith, G	Scottish	1977	1983	100	35
Smith, J	Scottish	1908	1909	7	5
Smith, James	Scottish	1919	1922	17	1
Smith, Jamie	Scottish	1926	1927	2	
Smith, Jimmy	Scottish	1928	1946	234	225
Smith, JR	Scottish	1922	1922	3	2
Smith, N	Scottish	1893	1905	168	3
Smith, W	Scottish	1956	1958	2	
Sneddon	Scottish	1916	1916	5	1
Snelders, T	Dutch	1996	1999	13	
Sorensen, E	Danish	1967	1970	30	
Sorensen, J	Danish	1965	1966	12	3
Souness, G	Scottish	1986	1991	50	3
Soutar, T	Scottish	1936	1937	10	
Sowerby	Scottish	1938	1938	3	1
Spackman, N	English	1989	1993	100	1
Speedie, F	Scottish	1900	1906	98	38
Speirs, J	Scottish	1905	1908	53	24
Spencer, J	Scottish	1986	1993	13	2
Stanners, D	Scottish	1951	1956	20	
Stark, J	Scottish	1900	1910	167	12
Stead, A	Scottish	1946	1947	3	
Steel	Scottish	1905	1908	2	
Steel, A	Scottish	1878	1881		
Steel, J	Scottish	1891	1894	19	8
Steele, J	Scottish	1976	1977	5	
Stein, C	Scottish	1968	1977	128	64
Stensaas, S	Norwegian	1997	2000	21	1
Sterland, M	English	1989	1989	9	3
Steven	Scottish	1907	1908	9	1
Steven, T	English	1989	1997	136	16
Stevens, Gary	English	1988	1994	187	8
Stevens, Gregor	Scottish	1979	1984	64	1
Stevenson, A	N.Irish	1932	1933	12	7
Stevenson, W	Scottish	1958	1962	73	1
Stewart	Scottish	1895	1896	7	2
Stewart, A	Scottish	1879	1880	2	
Stewart, James	English	1913	1914	19	10
Stewart, Jim	Scottish	1980	1984	56	
Strickland, D	Scottish	1977	1979	1	
Struthers, W	Scottish	1878	1881	15	7
Symon, S	Scottish	1938	1947	37	3
Tait	Scottish	1891	1891	6	
Taylor	Scottish	1916	1916	1	
Taylor, D	Scottish	1906	1911	28	
Telfer, W	Scottish	1957	1960	70	
Thern, J	Swedish	1997	1999	23	5
Thomson	Scottish	1914	1915	3	
Thomson, A	Scottish	1955	1956	1	
Thomson, B	Scottish	1994	1996	6	
Thomson, S	Scottish	1884	1884	1	
Thomson, T	Scottish	1881	1881	1	
Thornton, W	Scottish	1937	1954	224	144
Traill, D	Scottish	1963	1966	4	
Tugay, K	Turkish	2000	2001	42	4
Turnbull	Scottish	1904	1904	1	1
Turnbull, J	Scottish	1935	1939	25	7
Turnbull, P	Scottish	1896	1898	15	13
Turnbull, R	Scottish	1892	1892	3	1
Turner	Scottish	1898	1898	1	
Tutty, J	Scottish	1900	1900	1	
Urquhart, B	Scottish	1978	1980	14	6
Valentine, J	Scottish	1956	1958	2	
Vallance, A	Scottish	1877	1886	24	
Vallance, T	Scottish	1874	1884	37	
van Bronckhorst, G	Dutch	1998	2001	73	13
van Vossen, P	Dutch	1995	1998	23	4

Complete Players' Career Records: Smith, D – van Vossen

SC Apps	Goals	SLC Apps	Goals	European Apps	Goals	Totals Apps	Goals
30		42	2	36	3	303	13
18	1	23	12	16	3	157	51
						7	5
						17	1
						2	
25	24					259	249
						3	2
37	2					205	5
						2	
						5	1
		2		3		18	
5		6		6		47	
4						16	3
5		9	2	9		73	5
						10	
						3	1
9	1	10	1	5		124	3
23	12					121	50
9	5					62	29
		2		2	1	17	3
1		2				23	
36	2					203	14
		1		1		4	1
						2	
14	3					14	3
5	5					24	9
						5	
20	9	33	14	25	10	206	97
2		3	1	4		27	2
4						13	3
						9	1
15	3	17	6	16		184	25
22	1	22		15		246	9
11	2	14	1	3		92	4
						12	7
12		9		9		103	1
4	1					11	3
						2	
2	3					21	13
9		21		6		92	
		1				2	
						15	7
3		2				42	3
						6	
						1	
						28	
9		12		6		97	
3				5		31	5
						3	
						1	
		1				7	
						1	
						1	
34	21	50	29			308	194
1						5	
6	3			7		58	4
						1	1
9	1					34	8
1						16	13
						3	1
						1	
						1	
3	1	5		4		26	7
		6		1		9	
						24	
						37	
10	3	6	1	28	5	117	22
3	1	5	4	8	1	39	10

Player	Nationality	Year Joined	Year Left	League Apps	Goals
Venters, A	Scottish	1933	1946	180	93
Vidmar, T	Australian	1997	2002	105	8
Vinnicombe, C	English	1989	1994	24	3
Waddell, G	Scottish	1909	1913	21	
Waddell, W	Scottish	1938	1955	201	39
Walker	Scottish	1884	1884		
Walker, Jimmy	Scottish	1956	1957	2	
Walker, John(1)	Scottish	1902	1905	50	23
Walker, John(2)	Scottish	1905	1906	14	
Walker, N	Scottish	1983	1989	75	
Walker, W	Scottish	1902	1903	2	
Wallace	Scottish	1902	1903	1	
Wallace, D	Scottish	1935	1935	1	
Wallace, R	English	1998	2001	77	39
Walls, J	Scottish	1918	1924	98	4
Walmsley, W	Scottish	1948	1949	1	
Walters, M	English	1987	1991	106	32
Warner, J	Scottish	1879	1881		
Watkins, C	Scottish	1946	1948	9	1
Watson, B	Scottish	1964	1970	52	4
Watson, Craig	Scottish	1962	1966	14	4
Watson, J	Scottish	1874	1884	19	13
Watson, JG	Scottish	1903	1904	13	
Watson, Kenny(1)	Scottish	1969	1971	4	
Watson, Kenny(2)	Scottish	1975	1981	62	5
Watson, R	Scottish	1970	1973		
Watson, S	English	1992	1994	3	
Watt, F	Scottish	1892	1892	2	
Watt, J	Scottish	1876	1878	10	
Weir	Scottish	1926	1927	2	
Weir, C	Scottish	1881	1884	1	1
West, C	English	1986	1987	10	2
White, J	Scottish	1887	1891	2	2
White, W	Scottish	1969	1970	1	
Wilkie	Scottish	1889	1890		
Wilkie, J	Scottish	1898	1902	28	11
Wilkins, R	English	1987	1989	70	2
Williamson, Billy	Scottish	1946	1951	43	24
Williamson, Bobby	Scottish	1983	1987	41	12
Willoughby, A	Scottish	1962	1969	75	39
Wilson	Scottish	1895	1895	3	
Wilson, D	Scottish	1956	1967	227	98
Wilson, S	Scottish	1996	2002	48	1
Wilson, W	Scottish	1891	1891	1	
Winning, A	Scottish	1935	1938	42	1
Wishart, F	Scottish	1993	1995	9	
Wood, W	Scottish	1963	1967	35	4
Woodburn, W	Scottish	1938	1954	220	2
Woods, C	English	1986	1991	173	
Woods, J	Scottish	1954	1955	1	
Woods, N	English	1986	1988	3	
Wright, S	Scottish	1995	1998	7	
Wylie, T	Scottish	1888	1890	4	
Young	Scottish	1918	1918	4	
Young, A	Scottish	1882	1884		
Young, G	Scottish	1901	1902	1	
Young, George	Scottish	1978	1980	2	
Young, GL	Scottish	1946	1957	293	22
Young, Q	Scottish	1972	1976	82	28
Young, R	Scottish	1881	1885	13	
Yuil, J	Scottish	1874	1875	6	
Yuill	Scottish	1928	1928	3	
Yuille, J	Scottish	1896	1899	2	
Yuille, W	Scottish	1908	1911	14	5

SC Apps	Goals	SLC Apps	Goals	European Apps	Goals	Totals Apps	Goals
21	9					201	102
15	2	8		28	1	156	11
		1				28	
						21	
32	4	68	15			301	58
2						2	
						2	
12	9					62	32
						14	
8		9		3		95	
						2	
						1	
						1	
11	4	6	4	26	7	120	54
8						106	4
						1	
14	6	13	12	10	2	143	52
1						1	
3						13	
11	2	14	1	6		83	7
1	4			1		20	4
						19	13
5						18	
						4	
10	1	13		9		94	6
1						1	
						3	
2	1					4	1
						10	
						2	
						1	1
1		2	1	2		15	3
2						4	2
						1	
1						1	
8	6					36	17
9		10	1	7		96	3
9	7	17	8			69	39
4	2	5	6	2		52	20
4	1	11	6	5	1	95	47
						3	
38	21	71	28	37	10	373	157
10	6			14		78	1
						1	
4						46	1
		4	1			14	
2	6			4		47	4
38	71					329	2
15		21		21		230	
						1	
						3	
		5		7		19	
7	5					11	5
						4	
2						2	
						1	
						2	
50	5	83	4	2		428	31
7	2	19	7	8	1	116	38
						13	
						6	
2						5	
						2	
						14	5

OTHER TITLES IN THE SERIES

The Essential History of...

Aston Villa	Adam Ward/Jeremy Griffin	*0 7553 1140 X*
Blackburn Rovers	Mike Jackman	*0 7553 1022 5*
Celtic	Graham McColl/George Sheridan	*0 7553 1141 8*
Charlton Athletic	Paul Clayton	*0 7553 1020 9*
England	Andrew Mourant/Jack Rollin	*0 7553 1142 6*
Ipswich Town	Paul Voller/Mel Henderson	*0 7553 1021 7*
Leeds United	Andrew Mourant	*0 7553 1170 1**
Leicester City	Tony Matthews	*0 7553 1023 3*
Manchester City	Ian Penney	*0 7553 1168 X**
Middlesbrough	Richard Jones	*0 7553 1143 4*
Nottingham Forest	Bob Bickerton	*0 7553 1144 2*
Rangers	Stephen Halliday	*0 7553 1145 0*
Tottenham Hotspur	Bob Goodwin	*0 7553 1019 5*
West Ham United	Kirk Blows/Tony Hogg	*0 7553 1169 8**

*Trade paperback editions

Please contact your local WHSmith store for details about ordering any of these titles